JA

MW01122702

FOR
COMPUTER
INFORMATION
SYSTEMS

Andrew C. Staugaard, Jr.

College of the Ozarks

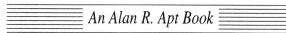

An Alan R. Apt Book

PRENTICE HALL, Upper Saddle River, NJ 07458

Library of Congress Cataloging-in-Publication Data

Staugaard, Andrew C.
　　Java for computer information systems / Andrew C. Staugaard, Jr.
　　p.　　cm.
　　"An Alan R. Apt book."
　　ISBN: 0-13-010806-5
　　1. Java (Computer program language) 2. Object-oriented programming (Computer science)
3. Management information systems.
I. Title.
　　Q.A76.J38S79 1999
　　005.13'3--dc21　　　　　　　　　　98-56034
　　　　　　　　　　　　　　　　　　CIP

Publisher: *ALAN APT*
Acquisitions editor: *LAURA STEELE*
Production editor: *CAROLE SURACI*
Editor-in-chief: *MARCIA HORTON*
Managing editor: *EILEEN CLARK*
Assistant vice president of production and manufacturing: *DAVID W. RICCARDI*
Cover designer: *BRUCE KENSELAAR*
Copy editor: *MARTHA WILLIAMS*
Manufacturing buyer: *PAT BROWN*
Editorial Assistant: *KATE KAIBNI*

Printed in the United States of America

10 9 8 7 6 5 4

ISBN: 0-13-010806-5

Prentice-Hall International (UK) Limited, *London*
Prentice-Hall of Australia Pty. Limited, *Sydney*
Prentice-Hall Canada Inc., *Toronto*
Prentice-Hall Hispanoamericana, S.A., *Mexico*
Prentice-Hall of India Private Limited, *New Delhi*
Prentice-Hall of Japan, Inc., *Tokyo*
Simon & Schuster Asia Pte. Ltd., *Singapore*
Editora Prentice-Hall do Brasil, Ltda., *Rio de Janeiro*

PREFACE

In recent years, Java has become a premier programming language because of its portability, making it completely platform independent. Java application programs support large systems and commercial "shrink-wrap" software development, while Java applet programs support Internet programming. This book has been written to provide an introduction to programming using the Java language. It is no harder learning how to program using Java than it is using a traditional language such as BASIC, Pascal, or C++. In fact, because of the object orientation and built-in graphics ability of Java, you can become a productive programmer in much less time than you can using these older languages. The text starts from the beginning, assuming no previous knowledge of any other programming language. The text is appropriate for any introductory programming course using the Java language as well as experienced programmers wanting an introduction to Java.

Approach

The text emphasizes problem solving techniques using the Java language. In fact, problem solving is the essential theme throughout the text. The student begins mastering the art of problem solving in Chapter 2, using problem abstraction and stepwise refinement via the *programmer's algorithm.* Emphasis is first placed on the "nuts and bolts" of problem solving and programming, building gradually into the object-oriented programming paradigm. This approach gradually prepares the student for in-depth coverage of classes and objects later in the text, while building essential programming skills. Furthermore, beginning with Chapter 1, a series of *GUI10X* and *Applet10X* experiment modules run in parallel with the text chapters to hold student interest and prepare them for in-depth coverage of event-driven, graphics programming discussed in later chapters. The text is highly readable and student oriented, with a teachable pedagogy and excellent features. The text provides sufficient material for a fast-paced one-semester course or slower paced two-semester course sequence.

Features

- Highly readable and student oriented.
- Prepared especially for CIS and MIS students but will also satisfy the requirements of an introductory programming course for CS students.
- Thoroughly instructor and student tested.
- Totally portable, platform independent.
- Introduces object-oriented programming *after* students have mastered the basics.
- Excellent reviews from instructors of both CS and CIS.
- Presentation and coverage of Java, compliant with version 1.2.
- Covers both Java applications and applets, with emphasis on CIS applications.
- A series of *GUI10X* and *Applet10X* experiment modules that run in parallel with the text chapters to hold student interest and prepare them for in-depth coverage of event-driven graphics programming discussed in later chapters.
- Early introduction to problem solving in Chapter 2 and used as a theme throughout the text with 20 *Problem Solving in Action* case studies.
- A gentle introduction to classes and objects, beginning in Chapter 3. In-depth coverage of Java classes and objects in Chapter 9.
- Realistic, real-world business programming examples and case studies throughout.
- Entire chapter on Graphical User Interfaces, GUIs.
- The *Programmer's Algorithm*: A step-by-step process used to get students started on the right programming tract by considering problem definition, solution planning, and good documentation. Problem solving using problem abstraction and stepwise refinement, prior to coding, is stressed throughout the text. All *Problem Solving in Action* case studies follow these proven software engineering techniques.
- Early introduction to Java methods in Chapter 2.
- Discussion of a class at both the abstract and implementation levels provides the student with the bigger software design picture as well as the coding details.
- Comprehensive development of the stack and queue ADTs using Java classes to ensure encapsulation and information hiding.

- Classes and ADTs viewed as black boxes, thus illustrating the importance of the method interfaces over the implementation details at the software design level.
- Over 70 tip and note boxes for students throughout, including
  Programming Tips
  Programming Notes
  Style Tips
  Debugging Tips
  Debugging Results
  Caution Boxes
- Over 300 section-by-section quick-check exercises for students to check their progress with all answers in an appendix.
- Over 50 examples that pose problems and then give solutions immediately.
- Over 200 chapter questions.
- Over 150 chapter programming problems with solutions in an instructor's manual and accompanying disk.
- Important terms and concepts are magnified and boxed throughout the text.
- Entire chapter on class inheritance, including a real-world *Problem Solving in Action* case study for using inheritance via a banking example.
- All Java syntax formatting is shown throughout within shaded boxes
- Comprehensive glossary of general computer as well as object-oriented programming and graphics terms.
- Comprehensive index.

To the Instructor

This text has been written to teach problem solving using the Java language at the freshman level in a first programming course. In today's market, it is imperative that students know both object-oriented programming techniques and the Java language. In this text, students will understand the roles of, and relationship between, classes and objects early-on, gradually building into in-depth coverage after they have mastered the language basics.

Some will say that you can't teach a first course in programming using Java, because the language is too complicated. I disagree. I have used Java to teach fundamental structuring and object-oriented concepts and have found that beginning students do not have any more difficulty using Java than BASIC, C++, or Pascal with the approach employed in this text. In fact, they are more enthusiastic about programming and have more fun learning Java because of its graphics and GUI capabilities, as well as the fact that they see Java plastered all over the Internet and news media.

The text can be taught in one or two terms, depending on the ability of the students. In a two term sequence, I would suggest coverage through the topic of methods (Chapters 1–8). Then, begin the second term with classes and objects, in-depth, and finish out the book (Chapters 9–14).

The text begins with a traditional review of hardware and software. This can be covered quickly, especially when students have already been exposed to these topics. Chapter 2 covers problem solving using problem abstraction and stepwise refinement. These concepts are presented in detail here and used as a theme throughout the text. The chapter discusses problem solving using what I call the *Programmer's Algorithm* and should be covered thoroughly. The programmer's algorithm is a step-by-step process that I have used to get students started on the right programming track by considering problem definition, step-by-step solution planning, and good documentation. I have employed a pseudocode algorithmic language for problem solution that is generic, simple, and allows for easy translation to the coded Java program. In addition, Chapter 2 introduces students to Java methods as a way of implementing their problem solutions.

Chapter 3 introduces the concepts of data abstraction and ADTs. Traditional data types are covered here as well as how to define constants, variables, and objects. Here is where we begin planting the seeds for object-oriented programming before it is covered in depth in Chapter 9. I suggest that you emphasize the concepts of classes, objects, and ADTs here to get students accustomed to object-oriented concepts.

In Chapters 4–7, students learn about program I/O, decision making, and iteration. These chapters provide the "nuts and bolts" required to write workable Java programs. The sequence, decision, and iteration control structures available in Java are covered thoroughly, emphasizing program logic and the required Java syntax. The common pitfalls of program logic design are pointed out throughout this material via program debugging tips and programming notes boxes. Again, I have integrated object-oriented techniques within these traditional structured programming topics, especially in Chapter 4 when using classes and objects for I/O. I have provided a Java package called *keyboardInput* on the accompanying CD and used its *KeyboardInput* class to perform program I/O throughout the text. Since Java treats all I/O as string I/O, you must develop your own classes and methods to provide for simple numeric and character I/O. This is much too complex for the beginning student and is the reason for my *keyboardInput* package. Later in the text, I "up-wrap" this package to expose its internal workings.

After Chapter 7, your students will have a solid knowledge of the important role of methods for program structuring. Since Chapter 2, they have been designing programs using functional decomposition and have observed the role of methods relative to object behavior. In Chapter 8, methods are covered in depth. I have incorporated easy to follow guidelines for building method interfaces relative to the topics of return values and parameter passing. It is critical that students understand this material in order to become successful Java programmers and understand the object-oriented concepts presented in later chapters.

At this point, the student is prepared to learn about classes and objects in depth. Again, there should be no problem here, because I have integrated these topics into the course since Chapter 3. In-depth coverage of classes and objects is provided in Chapter 9 and a solid introduction to class inheritance is provided in Chapter 10. In Chapter 9, students learn how to create their own classes and objects, using them in object-oriented programs. Chapter 10 expands on the material in Chapter 9 by discussing inheritance. Many texts avoid the topic of inheritance. However, inheritance is one of the cornerstones of object-oriented programming and is relatively easy to cover at this point. Chapter 10 provides the student with solid understanding of inheritance through a comprehensive banking example. The chapter closes with a discussion of polymorphism and dynamic binding.

Chapter 11 is devoted entirely to designing graphical user interfaces, or GUIs. By this time, the student has experimented extensively with GUIs via the *GUI10X* modules attached to previous chapters. The material in Chapter 11 simply fills in the details and solidifies the students knowledge of GUIs and how to create them. A comprehensive GUI design problem is provided in a *Problem Solving in Action* case study at the end of the chapter. In addition, an *Applet10X* module is attached to this chapter to teach the student how to use the Java *Graphics* class to create graphical images for both Java applet and application programs to augment their GUI designs.

File manipulation is discussed in depth in Chapter 12. Here, the student learns how to read and write sequential disk files using Java classes. The topic of files in Java provides a great opportunity to show how Java employs inheritance to create reusable code. Here, the student learns how to employ inheritance through the Java file stream class hierarchy to implement files.

Students get their first exposure to data structures in Chapter 13, which covers one-dimensional arrays. I feel it is important that students have a solid knowledge of arrays and their manipulation. As result, this chapter covers traditional arrays and not some array class built by the author to hide the details and pitfalls associated with arrays. I have also used this topic to present several classic searching and sorting algorithms which are essential at this level. This chapter can be covered earlier, prior to classes and objects, if desired without loss of continuity.

Chapter 14 provides an introduction to recursion and ADTs. Recursion is introduced via a simple compound interest example, followed by an in-depth discussion of how recursion works and when it should be applied. A comprehensive *Problem Solving in Action* case study is provided on recursive binary search. Next, the classic stack and queue ADTs are covered thoroughly. In this chapter, ADTs are covered at two levels: the purely abstract level using the black box interface approach, and at the implementation level using Java classes. Here is where the student really appreciates object-oriented programming, because the stack and queue ADTs are naturally implemented using Java classes.

Finally, beginning with Chapter 1, a series of *GUI10X* and *Applet10X* experiment modules run in parallel with the text chapters to hold student interest and prepare them for in-depth study of event-driven graphics programming discussed in later chapters. Encourage your students to go through these modules and just have some fun. They are designed to hold their interest as well as plant some important seeds which will be cultured later on in the text. Give them plenty of computer time and encourage them to try different things. If they ask "What happens if I do this or that?" tell them to "try it." This is how they will really learn!

The following supplements are available to support this text:

- *GUI10X*, *Applet10X*, and *Problem Solving in Action* source code included on the accompanying CD.

- JBuilder University edition from Inprise (formally Borland) included on the accompanying CD.

- A solutions manual that provides solutions to all the chapter questions and problems.

- An instructor's disk that provides source code to all the chapter programming problems.

- A companion Web site at www.prenhall.com that provides materials for instructors, such as transparency masters, as well as students, such as an on-line study guide.

To the Student

The market demands that computing professionals know the latest programming and software engineering techniques to solve today's complex problems. This book has been written to do just that. The book has been written to provide you with an introduction to problem solving using object-oriented programming techniques and the Java language. The text emphasizes problem solution through the use of problem abstraction and stepwise refinement throughout. By the end of the text you will have the knowledge required to solve complicated problems using this methodical approach that today's computer solutions require. In addition, you will learn about *object-oriented programming (OOP)*, *graphical user interfaces*, or *GUIs*, *graphics programming*, and *abstract data types (ADTs)*.

Make sure that you go through all the examples and *Problem Solving in Action* case studies. These have been written in short, understandable modules that stress the fundamental concepts being discussed. These problems are integrated into the text at key points in an effort to tie things together and present a methodical design approach to problem solving using the Java language.

Finally, above all, get your hands dirty early and often! Just have some fun programming. Don't be afraid to try different things. A series of *GUI10X* and *Applet10X* modules have been provided beginning in Chapter 1 to let you do just that. All the code for these modules is included on the accompanying CD or can be downloaded from www.prenhall.com. Have fun experimenting with these modules. Become an *active learner*. You cannot become a competent programmer by just reading this book and listening to your instructor's lectures. You must get your hands dirty at the machine. Get started early by sitting down at a computer, getting acquainted with your Java compiler, running the *GUI10X* and *Applet10X* experiment modules as you go through this text, and writing *your own* Java programs. This is how you will really learn how to program in Java.

To the Professional

The Java programming language has taken the commercial software development industry by storm. Most of today's Internet software is being developed using Java because of its portability. Whether you are an experienced programmer or a novice, you will find that this book provides the "nuts and bolts" required to get you writing Java programs quickly. In fact, this book is all that you will need to begin learning the Java language. The text provides comprehensive coverage of both Java applications and applets, with an emphasis on business application programs using graphical user interfaces, GUIs.

Acknowledgments

Contributions to this text have come from many circles. From the academic world I would like to thank Jeff Bauer of Florida State University, Alan Eliason of Williamette University, Michael Godfrey of Cornell University, Jim Roberts of Carnegie-Mellon University, and m.c. schraefel of the University of Victoria. They were a great bunch of reviewers and have made many valuable suggestions for the text.

From the student world, I would like to thank my own students who, over that past two years, have inspired the creation of this text and have made many valuable suggestions. In particular I would like to thank Erik Shuttleworth who developed the *keyboardInput* package.

From the publishing world of Prentice Hall, I would like to thank my publisher Alan Apt, who has created one of the best series of computer textbooks in the business and surely has a hit with this one. I also thank my editor Laura Steele for her guidance during the preparation of the text.

Please direct all correspondence to my E-mail address **staug@cofo.edu**. I strongly encourage any comments or suggestions that you might have, pro or con.

Enjoy!

Andrew C. Staugaard, Jr.

CONTENTS

CHAPTER 3: DATA: TYPES, CLASSES, AND OBJECTS

CHAPTER 7: LOOPING OPERATIONS: ITERATION

CHAPTER 8: METHODS IN-DEPTH

CHAPTER 9: CLASSES AND OBJECTS IN-DEPTH

CHAPTER 10: CLASS INHERITANCE

APPLET 101: APPLETS

CHAPTER 11: GRAPHICAL USER INTERFACES: GUIs

APPLET 102: GRAPHICS I

CHAPTER 12: FILE I/O AND EXCEPTION HANDLING

CHAPTER 13: ONE-DIMENSIONAL ARRAYS

CHAPTER 14: INTRODUCTION TO RECURSION, DATA STRUCTURES, AND ADTs

APPENDIX A: QUICK-CHECK SOLUTIONS

1
GETTING ACQUAINTED WITH COMPUTERS, PROGRAMS, AND JAVA

OBJECTIVES

When you are finished with this chapter, you should have a good understanding of the following:

- The hardware components of typical computer system, including CPU, RAM, ROM, secondary storage, and I/O.
- Different levels of software, including machine, assembly, and high-level software.
- The use of a compiler and an interpreter in translating and running Java programs.
- How Java uses byte codes to achieve portability.
- Why Java has become such a popular language.
- A short history of the Java language.
- The difference between a Java application and a Java applet.

INTRODUCTION

In this first chapter, you will begin your learning journey in the important topic of programming, using the Java programming language. This chapter has been written to provide you with an introduction to computers, computer programs, and Java in general. You will first review the hardware that makes up a typical computer system. Then, you will learn about the relationship between the computer system and the computer programs that operate the system.

The three major steps required to create a working Java program are *edit*, *compile*, and *run*. In this chapter, you will get your hands dirty early by performing these steps to create your first Java program.

1-1 THE HARDWARE

You undoubtedly have seen some of the hardware components of a computer. These are the physical devices that you can see and touch, such as those shown in Figure 1-1a. This typical PC system obviously has a keyboard for user input, a display monitor for output, and magnetic disk drives for program and data storage. Two very important parts of the system that cannot be seen, because they are inside the console, are the *central processing unit* and its *primary memory*.

The block diagram in Figure 1-1b shows all of the major hardware sections of the system. From this figure, you see that the system can be divided into five functional parts: the central processing unit (CPU), primary memory, secondary memory, input, and output.

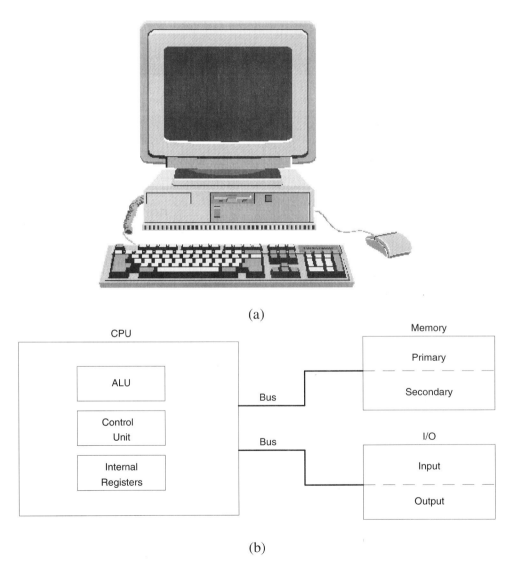

(a)

(b)

Figure 1-1 (a) A typical PC system and (b) its hardware structure, or architecture.

The Central Processing Unit (CPU)

The central processing unit (CPU) is the brain and nerve center of the entire system. This is where all of the calculations and decisions are made. In a PC system, the entire CPU is contained within a single integrated circuit (IC) chip called a ***microprocessor***.

A ***microprocessor*** is a single integrated-circuit (IC) chip that contains the entire central processing unit (CPU).

In fact, a microprocessor is what distinguishes a PC from a minicomputer or mainframe computer. In minicomputers and mainframe computers, several ICs make up the CPU, not just one as in a PC. A typical microprocessor IC is pictured in Figure 1-2. There are three functional parts within the CPU. They are the ***arithmetic and logic unit (ALU)***, the ***control unit***, and the ***internal registers***, as shown in Figure 1-3.

Figure 1-2   A microprocessor chip is the CPU of a PC system.

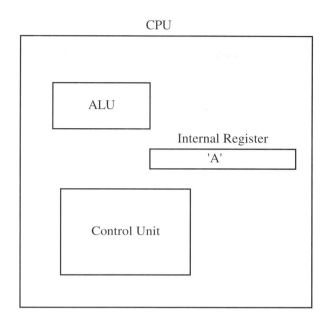

Figure 1-3 The CPU consists of an ALU, control unit, and internal registers.

The Arithmetic and Logic Unit (ALU)

As its name implies, the arithmetic and logic unit performs all of the arithmetic and logic operations within the CPU. The arithmetic operations performed by the ALU include addition, subtraction, multiplication, and division. These four arithmetic operations can be combined to perform just about any mathematical calculation, from simple arithmetic to calculus.

Logic operations performed by the ALU are *comparison* operations that are used to *compare* numbers and characters. The three logic comparison operations are equal (==), less than (<), and greater than (>). Notice that two equals symbols (==) are used to denote the equals operation. From now on, we will use this to denote an equals operation. More about this later. These three operations can be combined to form the three additional logic operations of not equal (!=), less than or equal (<=), and greater than or equal (>=).

Take a look at Table 1-1. It summarizes the arithmetic and logic operations performed by the ALU. The symbols listed in the table are those that you will use later to perform arithmetic and logic operations when writing Java programs.

TABLE 1-1 A SUMMARY OF ARITHMETIC
AND LOGIC OPERATIONS PERFORMED
BY THE ALU AREA OF THE CPU

Arithmetic Operation	Java Symbol
Addition	+
Subtraction	−
Multiplication	*
Division	/

Logic Operation	Java Symbol
Equal to	==
Not equal to	!=
Less than	<
Less than or equal to	<=
Greater than	>
Greater than or equal to	>=

The Control Unit

The control unit area of the CPU directs and coordinates the activities of the entire system. This area interprets program instructions and generates electrical signals to the other parts of the system in order to execute those instructions. The control unit communicates with other sections of the CPU via internal signal paths called **buses**. The control unit often is likened to a traffic cop or orchestra leader, because it directs the activity of the entire system.

Internal Registers

The internal register area of the CPU contains temporary storage areas for program instructions and data. In other words, these registers temporarily hold information while it is being processed by the CPU. In Figure 1-3, the internal register shown is holding the character 'A' in preparation for processing this character or as a result of some previous processing step. (Actually, the character 'A' is represented within the register by a series of bits rather than the character symbol). Be aware that a CPU contains several internal registers, even though only one is shown in Figure 1-3.

Primary Memory

Primary memory often is called main working memory. The reason for this is that ***primary***, or ***main***, ***memory*** is used to store programs and data while they are being "worked," or executed, by the CPU. As Figure 1-4 shows, there are two types of primary memory: ***random access memory (RAM)*** and ***read-only memory (ROM)***.

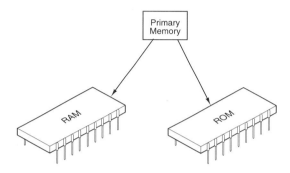

Figure 1-4   Primary memory consists of RAM and ROM.

Random-Access Memory (RAM)

Random-access memory is memory for you, the user, along with the programs and data that you are using at any given time. When you enter a program or data into the system, it goes into RAM. This is why the amount of RAM often is quoted when you buy a computer system. You most likely have heard the terms 640 kilobytes (640K), 16 megabyte (16M), 32 megabyte (32M), and so on, when describing a PC system. This is the amount of RAM, or user memory, that the system contains. Here, the letter K stands for the value 1024 (approximately one thousand), and M for the value K^2, or 1024×1024 (approximately one million). Thus, a 32M system has $32 \times 1024 \times 1024 = 33,554,432$ bytes of RAM. The more bytes of RAM a system has, the more room there is for your programs and data. As a result, larger and more complex programs require larger amounts of RAM.

By definition, RAM is ***read/write memory***. This means that information can be written into, or stored, into RAM and read from, or retrieved, from it. When writing new information into a given area of RAM, any previous information in that area is destroyed. Fortunately, you don't have to worry about this when entering programs, because the system makes sure that the new program information is not written over any important old information.

Once information has been written into RAM, it can be read, or retrieved, by the CPU during program execution. A read operation is nondestructive. Thus, when data are read from RAM, the RAM contents are not destroyed and remain unchanged. Think of a read operation as a "copy" operation.

One final point about RAM: It is **volatile**. This means that any information stored in RAM is erased when power is removed from the system. As a result, any programs that you have entered in main working memory (RAM) will be lost when you turn off the system. You must always remember to save your programs on a secondary memory device, such as a disk, before turning off the system power.

Also, be aware that RAM can be placed in other parts of the system, such as a printer. This allows the CPU to send large amounts of data to be printed to the printer and stored there without clogging up the system RAM.

> You have probably heard the terms **cache memory**, or simply **cache**, and **virtual memory**. These are different than RAM but serve a similar purpose. Cache is high-speed RAM that is usually contained within the same chip as the CPU. Instructions waiting to be processed are fetched from primary memory and placed in the cache so that they are ready for execution when the CPU needs them. Virtual memory is hard-disk memory that is being used by the CPU as RAM when no more actual RAM is available.. The term "virtual" means "illusion." Thus, when the CPU needs more memory space, it borrows hard-disk memory to create the illusion that it is reading/writing RAM. In this case, the apparent size of the system RAM is unbounded. However, system performance is seriously degraded, since it takes much longer to access an electromechanical disk drive than it does actual semiconductor RAM.

Read-Only Memory (ROM)

Read-only memory often is called **system memory** because it stores system-related programs and data. These system programs and data take care of tasks such as reset, cursor control, binary conversions, input/output (I/O), and so on. All of these system programs are part of a larger operating system program that is permanently stored in ROM or on a disk. In IBM PC and compatible systems, the system software stored in ROM is called **BIOS**. The operating system, **DOS** or **Windows**, is stored on disk and works with BIOS to perform **transparent** system operations. The term transparent means that the user is not aware of the underlying system operations being performed.

As its name implies, read-only memory can only be read from and not written into. Consequently, information stored in ROM is permanent and cannot be changed. Because the information is permanent, ROM must be **nonvolatile**. This means that any information stored in ROM is not lost when power is removed from the system. Due to this feature, ROM programs often are called **firmware**.

Secondary Memory

Secondary memory, sometimes called **bulk** or **mass storage**, is used to hold programs and data on a semipermanent basis. The most common type of secondary memory used in PC systems are magnetic disks, shown in Figure 1-5.

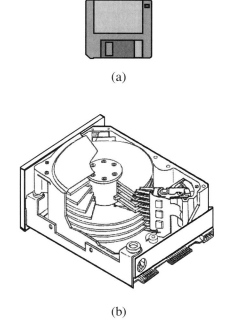

(a)

(b)

Figure 1-5   The common (a) 3½-inch disk, and (c) hard disk.

A floppy disk, like that shown in Figure 1-5a, gets its name because the actual disk is flexible, rather than rigid, or hard. The disk is coated with a magnetic material and enclosed within a 3½-inch hard plastic cover. When inserted into a disk drive, the disk is spun on the drive at about 300 rpm. A read/write recording head within the drive reads and writes information on the disk through the access slot, or window, in the disk jacket. Virtually all systems today include a built-in hard disk drive like the one shown in Figure 1-5b. In fact, a hard drive system is a must when working with professional-level integrated program development software such as you find with most Java compilers.

When writing programs, you will first enter the program code into the system primary memory, or RAM. When *saving* Java programs, you must create a work file name for the program. This work file name creates an area, or file, on the disk where your program will be saved. As you enter and work with your program in RAM, you will periodically save the program on the disk so that it is permanently stored. When you save the program, the system simply copies the program from RAM and saves it on the disk under the work file name that you created. This process is illustrated in Figure 1-6a.

Saving a program on disk allows you to retrieve it later. To read a program from disk, you simply *load* the work file name assigned to the program. This tells the system to read the work file and transfer it into primary memory (RAM), as illustrated in Figure 1-6b. Once it is in working memory, the program can be compiled, executed (run), or changed (edited). Of course, if any changes are made, the program must be saved on disk again so that the changes are also made on the disk. By the way, all Java program files must have a file extension of *.java*

Input

Input is what goes into the system. Input devices are hardware devices that provide a means of entering programs and data into the system. The major input devices for a PC system such as the one pictured back in Figure 1-1a are the keyboard and mouse. The computer keyboard contains all of the characters that you will need to write a program. In addition, there are also special control functions and special control keys that provide for system operations such as cursor movement.

The disk drive is another form of input device, because it also provides a means of loading programs and data into the system. There are many other types of input devices used with computer systems, such as modems, network cards, and so on. However, the keyboard, mouse, and disk drive are the primary input devices that you will be using when learning how to write Java programs.

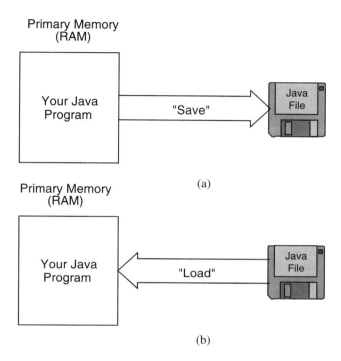

Figure 1-6   (a) Saving a program on disk, and (b) loading a program from disk.

Output

Output is what comes out of the system. Output devices are hardware devices that provide a means of getting data out of the system. The four major output devices with which you will be concerned are the display monitor, printer, disk drive, and modem. The display monitor is just the screen in front of you. It allows you to observe programs and data that are stored in primary memory (RAM).

A printer provides you with a hard copy of your programs and data. During a printing operation, the system actually copies information from primary or secondary memory to the printer. Thus, any information to be printed must be stored in primary or secondary memory.

A disk drive is also an output device, because information stored in primary memory can be written to the disk. You could say that a disk drive is an input/output (I/O) device, because it provides a means of getting information both in and out of the system.

Finally, a modem lets you communicate over the telephone or cable networks with other computers.

The Fetch/Execute Cycle

The fetch/execute cycle is what takes place when you ***run*** a program. To run a program, you must first enter it into primary memory via the keyboard or load it from disk. Once in primary memory, the program must be ***compiled***. The compiling process is performed by a Java compiler. The compiler converts the Java instructions into binary byte codes that can be executed by a Java interpreter. The Java interpreter generates executable machine code that can be run by a particular CPU. Your program cannot be run, or executed, until it is free of errors and completely compiled. The compiler checks the program for errors and generates error messages and warnings to you via the display monitor. The compiling and interpreting processes associated with Java will be discussed in more detail in the next section.

Once a Java program has been translated into machine code, the machine instructions are ***fetched*** from primary memory or cache and ***executed***, or ***run***, one at a time as shown in Figure 1-7.

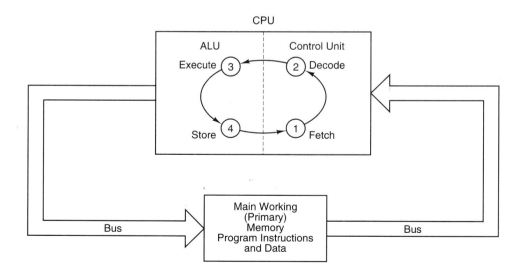

Figure 1-7   The fetch/execute cycle between the CPU and main working memory.

Observe the *fetch/execute* cycle within the CPU. The control unit first fetches a given program instruction from primary memory or cache. The instruction is then decoded, or translated, to determine what is to be done. Next, the control unit makes available any data required for the operation and directs the ALU to perform the operation. The ALU executes the operation, and the control unit stores the operation results in an internal register or primary memory. The resulting data are temporarily stored in an internal register or primary memory until they are used for another operation or sent to an output device such as a disk or printer. In summary, you can see from Figure 1-7 that the four basic fetch/execute cycle operations are *fetch*, *decode*, *execute*, and *store*. That's it in a nutshell!

Quick Check

1. List the three major areas of a PC's architecture.

2. A CPU contained within a single integrated circuit is called a(n) _____.

3. List at least three arithmetic and three logic operations performed by the ALU area of a CPU.

4. List three things that are found in a CPU.

5. A 16M system has _____ bytes of RAM.

6. Programs stored in ROM are often called _____.

7. Explain what takes place between the CPU and memory when you run a program.

1-2 SOFTWARE

If computer hardware can be likened to an automobile, computer software can be likened to the driver of the automobile. Without the driver, nothing happens. In other words, the computer hardware by itself can do nothing. The hardware system requires software that provides step-by-step instructions to tell the system what to do. A set of software instructions that tells the computer what to do is called a *computer program*. To communicate instructions to the computer,

computer programs are written in different languages. In general, computer languages can be grouped into three major categories: *machine language*, *assembly language*, and *high-level language*.

> A *computer program* is a set of software instructions that tells the computer what to do.

Machine Language

All of the hardware components in a computer system, including the CPU, operate on a language made up of binary 1's and 0's. A CPU does not understand any other language. When a computer is designed, the CPU is designed to interpret a given set of instructions, called its *instruction set*. Each instruction within the instruction set has a unique binary code that can be translated directly by the CPU. This binary code is called *machine code*, and the set of all machine-coded instructions is called the *machine language*.

A typical machine-language program is provided in Figure 1-8a. To write such a program, you must determine the operation to be performed, and then translate the operation into the required binary machine code from a list of instruction set machine codes provided by the CPU manufacturer. As you might imagine, this is an extremely inefficient process. It is time-consuming, tedious, and subject to a tremendous amount of error. In addition, simple operations, such as multiplication and division, often require several lines of machine code. For these reasons, machine-language programming is rarely used. However, remember that high-level language programs are always translated to machine language to enable the CPU to perform the fetch/execute cycle.

Assembly Language

Assembly language is a step up from machine language. Rather than using 1's and 0's, assembly language employs alphabetic abbreviations called *mnemonics* that are easily remembered by you, the programmer. For instance, the mnemonic for addition is ADD, the mnemonic for move is MOV, and so forth. A typical assembly-language program is listed in Figure 1-8b.

The assembly-language mnemonics provide us with an easier means of writing and interpreting programs. Although assembly-language programs are more easily understood by us humans, they cannot be directly understood by the CPU. As a result, assembly-language programs must be translated into machine code. This is the job of another program, called an ***assembler***. The assembler program translates assembly-language programs into binary machine code that can be decoded by the CPU.

Although programming in assembly language is easier than machine-language programming, it is not the most efficient means of programming. Assembly-language programming is also tedious and prone to error, because there is usually a one-to-one relationship between the mnemonics and corresponding machine code. The solution to these inherent problems of assembly-language programming is found in high-level languages.

This does not mean that assembly language is not useful. Because of its one-to-one relationship with machine language, assembly-language programs are very efficient relative to execution speed and memory utilization. In fact, many high-level-language programs include assembly-language routines, especially for those tasks requiring high-speed software performance.

01001100	mov bx, offset value	x = 2;
11101001	mov ax, [bx]	if (x<=y)
10101010	add ax, 5	x = x + 1;
10001110	add bx, 2	else
00001111	add ax, [bx]	x = x − 1;
(a)	(b)	(c)

Figure 1-8 (a) Machine language, (b) assembly language, and (c) high-level language.

Operating Systems

An ***operating system***, or ***OS***, is the "glue" that binds the hardware to the application software. Actually, an operating system is a collection of software programs dedicated to managing the resources of the system. These resources include memory management, file management, I/O management, monitoring system activity, system security, and system performance, just to mention a few.

In the early days, operating systems, such as DOS and UNIX, were text-based. Today, however, most operating systems like Windows 98 and the Macintosh operating systems are GUI-based. The acronym "GUI" stands for "graphical user interface," implying a windows-based user interface.

Until not too long ago, assembly language was used to develop operating systems, due to its execution efficiency and its ability to access system components directly. Then, in the 1970s, Bell Telephone Laboratories developed a high-level language called C to write the UNIX operating system. The C language is sometimes referred to as a "mid-level" language since it contains many of the high-level commands of a high-level language, but also many of the "bit-level" commands of an assembly language.

High-Level Language

A high-level language consists of instructions, or statements, that are similar to English and common mathematical notation. A typical series of high-level statements is shown in Figure 1-8c. High-level-language statements are very powerful. A typical high-level-language statement is equivalent to many machine-code instructions.

High-level languages were developed in the early 1950s to take some of the work out of programming. When programming in a high-level language, you do not have to concern yourself with the specific instruction set of the CPU. Rather, you can concentrate on solving the problem at hand. Once you learn a given high-level language, you can program any computer that runs that language.

You must be aware that even when programming in a high-level language, the system must still translate your instructions into machine code that can be understood by the CPU. There are two types of system programs that can be employed for this purpose: a **compiler** and an **interpreter**. A compiler is a program that accepts a high-level–language program and translates the entire program into machine code all at one time, before it is executed by the CPU. On the other hand, an interpreter translates and executes one high-level statement at a time. Once a given statement has been executed, the interpreter then translates and executes the next statement, and so on, until the entire program has been executed. Java employs both a compiler and an interpreter as shown in Figure 1-9. Here's how it works. Initially, you will type your program into a computer using an **editor** and save it in a file that must have a *.java* extension. The program that you enter is referred to as a **source code** program. After saving your program, you must invoke the Java compiler to translate your Java source code into Java **byte code**.

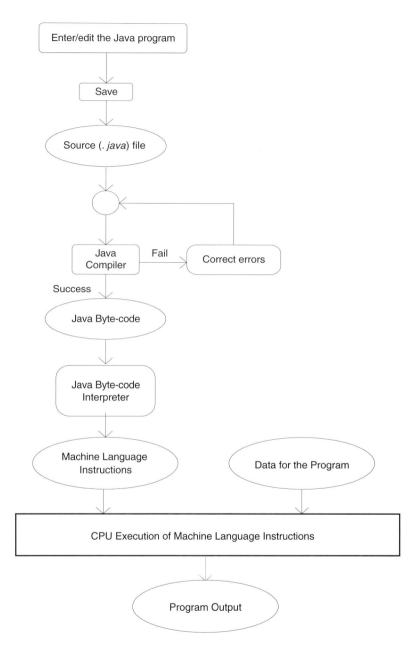

Figure 1-9 The Java compiler and byte-code interpreter translate source code into machine code that can be executed by the CPU.

> A *source code program* is the one that you write in the Java language and, when saved on disk, must always have a file extension of *.java*.

As the program is being translated, the Java compiler checks for errors. After the program is compiled, the compiler displays a list of error messages and warnings. You must correct all the errors and recompile until you get a successful compilation. You may, however, encounter other errors later on when you actually run the program. The byte-code program generated by the compiler is a low-level program, similar to machine language. However, the Java byte code is not associated with any specific CPU. In other words, Java byte code is a generic code that can be executed by any computer that has a Java interpreter. This is what allows Java to be totally portable across many different operating system platforms. The Java interpreter translates the Java byte code into machine language instructions specific to the CPU of a given computer. Since the translation is being performed by an interpreter, a given instruction is translated and executed before the next instruction is translated and executed, and so on.

> Java *byte code* is generated by the Java compiler. The resulting byte code is a low-level program similar to machine language, but generic and not specific to any particular CPU. Any given computer will have its own Java interpreter which translates the generic byte code into machine language for that CPU. This allows Java to be portable across many different computer platforms. For example, an Internet browser that is "Java compliant" includes the Java byte-code interpreter.

Why Java?

As you are probably aware, there are several popular high-level languages, including COBOL, Pascal, FORTRAN, BASIC, LISP, Ada, and C/C++, among others. Each has been developed with a particular application in mind. For instance, COBOL, which stands for COmmon Business Oriented Language, was developed for business programming. FORTRAN, which means FORmula TRANslator, was developed for scientific programming. LISP was developed for artificial-intelligence programming, and Pascal was developed primarily for education to teach the principles of software design. The C language is a structured language that allows complex problems to be solved using a modular, top/down, approach. The C++ language contains the C language for structured programming, but in addition extends the C language to provide for ***object-oriented programming (OOP)***. Object-oriented programming allows complex problems to be solved using a more natural object approach, similar to the way in which we humans tend to look at the real world. It allows complex programs to be developed using simpler constructs called ***objects*** that can communicate by exchanging messages. More about this later. Thus, C++ is a hybrid language, allowing for both structured and object-oriented programming.

The Java language evolved from the C++ language. In fact, much of the Java language syntax is identical to C++. However, Java is strictly an object-oriented language. Java is taking the software development industry by storm as both a commercial application language and an Internet language. The main reason is that Java is totally portable across any system platform due to its compiler/interpreter method of translation discussed earlier. This is why you can link to a given Internet site and run the same Java program through your browser whether you are using a PC or a Mac computer platform. Your Internet browser contains a Java interpreter that translates the generic byte codes into the machine language of that computer.

> ***Portability*** is that feature of a language that allows programs written for one type of computer to be used on another type of computer with few or no changes to the program source code. Java is totally portable, meaning that programs written and compiled on one computer can run on any other computer that has a Java interpreter.

A Little Java History

Java was developed by Sun Microsystems, Inc. The first version of Java was intended to be a programming language to program microprocessors for dedicated applications such as VCRs and TVs. James Gosling and his team at Sun realized that such applications were controlled by a variety of incompatible microprocessors. As a result, the language that they were developing needed to work on many different processors. This is where they developed the idea of using generic byte codes that could be translated into any specific machine language using an interpreter. When the World Wide Web became popular around 1994, Gosling and his team thought that, due to its portability, Java would be an ideal language for Internet browsers. In 1995, Sun developed the HotJava Web browser. Then, also in 1995, Netscape announced that their Web browser would be Java compliant. Since then, almost all the Web browser companies have followed Netscape's lead and made their browser's Java compliant. As a result, Java programs have become a standard across the ever-growing and popular Web.

As you might suspect, the name "Java" has its roots in coffee. At first, the language was called "Oak," supposedly named after an oak tree outside one of the office windows at Sun. As the story goes, the developers were agonizing over a better name for the language when they decided to go out for coffee. The rest is history.

Java Applications, Applets, and the World Wide Web

Using Java, you can write two different kinds of programs: ***applications*** or ***applets***. Java application programs are designed to be run on your computer just like any other computer program written in any other language. Java applets are designed only to be run over the Internet using a Web browser. When you link to a Web site with your browser, the Web site transfers Java byte code over the Internet to your browser. Your browser then translates and executes those byte codes to produce the dynamic things, such as animation and moving messages, that you view on your browser. By the way, the word "applet" has nothing to do with apples, it simply denotes a "little application," just as the term piglet denotes a little pig. In this text, we will deal primarily with Java applications. Once you know how to program Java applications, it is easy to learn how to do Java applets.

Quick Check

1. What is the major difference between Java and C++?

2. List the steps that must be performed to translate a Java source code program to an executable program.

3. What are byte codes?

4. What makes Java an extremely portable language?

5. What is the difference between a Java application and a Java applet?

6. What is the difference between a compiler and an interpreter?

7. What are the three levels of language used by computers?

8. Your Java program code is referred to in general as _____ code.

9. What is the purpose of an operating system.

CHAPTER SUMMARY

Any computer system can be divided into two major components: hardware and software. Hardware consists of the physical devices that make up the machine, and software consists of the instructions that tell the hardware what to do.

There are five functional parts that make up the system hardware: the CPU, primary memory, secondary memory, input, and output. The CPU directs and coordinates the activity of the entire system as instructed by the software. Primary memory consists of user memory (RAM) and system memory (ROM). Secondary memory is usually magnetic and is used to store programs and data on a semipermanent basis. Input is what goes into the system via hardware input devices, such as a keyboard. Output is what comes out of the system via hardware output devices, such as a display monitor or printer.

There are three major levels of software: machine language, assembly language, and high-level language. Machine language is the lowest level, because it consists of binary 1's and 0's that can only be easily understood by the CPU. Assembly language consists of alphabetic instruction abbreviations that are easily understood by the programmer but must be translated into machine code for the CPU by a system program called an assembler. High-level languages consist of Englishlike statements that simplify the task of programming. However, to be understood by the CPU, high-level-language programs must still be translated to machine code using a compiler/interpreter. A byte code program is generated by the Java compiler. This is a low-level program, similar to machine language. However, the Java byte code is not associated with any specific CPU. In other words, Java byte code is a generic code that can be executed by any computer that has a Java interpreter. This is what allows Java to be totally portable across many different operating system platforms. The Java interpreter translates the Java byte code into machine-language instructions specific to the CPU of a given computer. Since the translation is being performed by an interpreter, a given instruction is translated and executed before the next instruction is translated and executed, and so on.

Java was developed at Sun Microsystems, Inc. by James Gosling and his team to be portable over a variety of incompatible microprocessors. When the World Wide Web became popular around 1994, Gosling and his team thought that, due to its portability, Java would be an ideal language for Internet browsers. In 1995, Sun developed that HotJava Web browser. Then, also in 1995, Netscape announced that their Web browser would be Java compliant. Since then, almost all the Web browser companies have followed Netscape's lead and made their browser's Java compliant. As a result, Java programs have become a standard across the ever-growing and popular Web.

Using Java, you can write two different kinds of programs: applications or applets. Java application programs are designed to be run on your computer just like any other computer program written in any other language. Java applets are designed only to be run over the Internet using a Web browser.

QUESTIONS AND PROBLEMS

Questions

1. Name the three operational regions of a CPU and explain their function.

2. Explain the term *volatile* as it relates to computer memory.

3. Another name for software located in read-only memory (ROM) is _____.

4. A floppy disk is a form of _____ memory.

5. Name the three levels of software and describe the general characteristics of each.

6. List at least four functions of an operating system.

7. Explain the operational difference between a compiler and an interpreter.

8. A Java compiler translates a source program into a(n) _____ program.

9. True or false: Java employs both a compiler and an interpreter to produce an executable program.

10. Explain how Java is portable across all computer platforms.

11. What is the difference between a Java application and a Java applet?

12. The Java language was developed by _____ and his team at _____.

13. Object-oriented programming allows complex programs to be developed using simpler programming constructs called _____.

14. The Java language evolved from the _____ language.

15. What is a Java byte code?

Problems

1. The following is a typical Java application program. Enter, compile, and run the program using your Java development environment.

```
1    /*
2       PROBLEM 1_1
3       YOUR FIRST LOOK AT A JAVA APPLICATION PROGRAM
4    */
5    public class Problem1_1
6    { // BEGIN Problem1_1
7       public static void main(String args[])
8       { // BEGIN main()
9          System.out.println( "Hello World!\nWhat a beautiful day!" );
10      } // END main()
11   } // END Problem1_1
```

2. What do you suppose the /∗ and ∗/ symbols accomplish in lines 1 and 4 of the program in problem 1?

3. What do you suppose is the purpose of the forward double slash, //, symbols in the program in problem 1?

4. What do you suppose is the purpose of the statement in line 9 of the program?

5. Run the program in problem 1 again. Observe the output generated on the display. Now, look closely at the statement in line 9 of the program. What is the purpose of the \n character in this statement?

GUI 101: GRAPHICAL USER INTERFACES

PURPOSE

- *To become familiar with loading and executing a Java program.*
- *To demonstrate a typical graphical user interface, or GUI.*
- *To identify the various components that are used to build a GUI.*
- *To observe the behavior of GUI components.*

Introduction

A **graphical user interface**, or **GUI**, is a window-based program whereby input and output are handled via **graphical components**. Components include menus, buttons, checkboxes, text fields, and radio buttons, just to mention a few. Windowed programs are event-driven programs, whereby the flow of the program logic is dictated by events. These events usually are the result of a mouse action, such a clicking or movement, or a keyboard stroke.

Beginning in this chapter and continuing through succeeding chapters, you will be acquainted with the topic of graphical user interfaces, or GUIs, through a series of hands-on "*GUI 10X*" modules. These modules will familiarize you with the components and related Java code that are required to build a GUI. The prewritten Java programs that you will use are located on the CD that accompanies this book. If you do not have a CD drive as part of your system, the files are also available for download from the Prentice Hall Web site (www.prenhall.com). You will be asked to load a given program, execute the program, and exercise the GUI. In some cases you will be asked to modify the program code and observe the effect on the GUI and its components. Don't worry about how to design your own GUIs yet—this will be covered in detail in a later chapter. For now, it is only important that you get aquainted with GUIs in general along with some GUI terminology and behavior.

Procedure

1. Later on you will develop the GUI shown in Figures 1 or 2 for a student database program, but right now you will just have some fun running and experimenting with the GUI programs that we provide. The GUI in Figure 1 is what you would see in a Windows environment, while the one in Figure 2 is a Mac GUI. However, the same Java program produced both GUIs! This is one of the reasons that Java is so popular, because it is totally ***portable*** across all platforms. The program that produced the GUI in Figures 1 and 2 is included on your CD as the file *GUI101.java*. Load, run, and exercise this program via your Java development environment. If you do not have a CD drive as part of your system, the file is also available for download from the Prentice Hall Web site at www.prenhall.com.

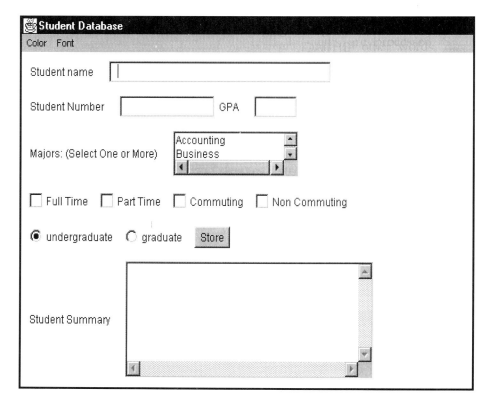

Figure 1 The student database GUI generated by the *GUI101.java* program in a Windows environment.

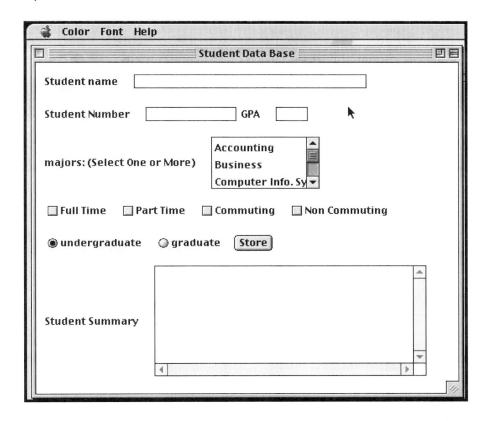

Figure 2 The student database GUI generated by the *GUI101.java* program in a Mac environment.

Procedure(continued)

2. Resize the window by grabbing and moving the window borders.
3. Fill in your student name, student number, and GPA.
4. Select one or more majors from the list of majors.
5. Check any student status items that apply: full-time, part-time, commuting, or non-commuting.
6. The GUI is already set for an undergraduate student; click the graduate student button if it applies. Notice that clicking the *Graduate* button on turns the *Undergraduate* button off, and visa versa.
7. Click the *Store* button and notice that the student information you entered now appears in the *Student Summary* area. To see all the information you will have to use the scrollbars around the *Student Summary* area.

8. Click on the *Color* menu and select a color. Notice that the *Student Summary* area changes its background color to the color you selected.
9. Click on the *Font* menu and select the *Font Name* submenu. Select a font from this menu and notice that the text in the *Student Summary* area changes to the selected font.
10. Click on the *Font* menu and select the *Font Style* submenu. Select a style from this menu and notice that the text in the *Student Summary* area changes to the selected font style, while keeping the same type of font.
11. Change the student information and click the *Store* button again. Notice that the *Student Summary* area reflects any changes you made.
12. Check both the full-time and part-time student status and click the *Store* button. Notice that an error message appears in the *Student Summary Area*, since you cannot be a full-time and a part-time student at the same time.
13. See if you can identify the following components of the GUI:

*   Title bar
*   Scrollbars
*   Close button
*   Menu bar
*   Menu
*   Submenu
*   Labels
*   Button
*   Text field
*   Text area
*   Checkboxes
*   Radio buttons

Discussion

The GUI that you just exercised contains most of the components required for any GUI. First, you observed a standard window that contained a title bar with title and window borders just like any other window. The window could be maximized, minimized, resized, and closed. These features are common to all windows and any GUI we create will "inherit" these basic features. This is the beauty of object-oriented programming. You *inherit* things, like standard window features, from other things that have already been developed. You do not have to reinvent the wheel each time you want to create a new GUI. In Java application programs, windows are created by a Java *container* called a *frame*. A frame is the basis for a GUI in all Java application programs and is used as a container to hold the GUI components.

The areas where you type in information are called *text fields*. There is a *label* designation, or name, for each text field such as *Student Name*. When you selected one or more majors, you were selecting from a *list box*. When you checked student status, you were using *checkboxes*. When you selected undergraduate or graduate, you were using *radio buttons*. The *Store* button is a Java component called a *button*. When you selected a color and font, you were using a *menu* component. Finally, all the student information was displayed in a *text area*. All these things are components of a GUI.

In the *GUI 10X* modules that follow you will deal with each of these components independently and learn more about them. Then, in a later chapter, you will learn all the coding details of how to design your own GUIs using these components. Be patient, just read on and have some fun on the way playing with our GUI modules.

2

PROBLEM SOLVING, ABSTRACTION, AND STEPWISE REFINEMENT

OBJECTIVES

When you are finished with this chapter, you should have a good understanding of the following:

- How to define a problem in terms of input, output, and processing.
- How to plan a problem solution using algorithms.
- The attributes required for a good computer algorithm.
- The role of pseudocode in problem solution planning.
- The use of a problem solving diagram.
- The concept of problem abstraction.
- The concepts of stepwise refinement and modular programming.
- The steps required to test and debug a program.
- Different types of programming errors, including syntax errors, type errors, logic errors, and run-time errors.
- What good program documentation must include.
- The importance of comments within a program.

INTRODUCTION

Programming reduces to the art and science of problem solving. To be a good programmer, you must be a good problem solver. To be a good problem solver, you must attack a problem in a methodical way, from initial problem inspection and definition to final solution, testing, and documentation. In the beginning, when confronted with a programming problem, you will be tempted to get to the computer and start coding as soon as you get an idea of how to solve it. However, you *must* resist this temptation. Such an approach might work for simple problems but will *not* work when you are confronted with the complex problems found in today's real world. A good carpenter might attempt to build a dog house without a plan but would never attempt to build your "dream house" without a good set of blueprints.

In this chapter, you will learn about a systematic method that will make you a good problem solver, and therefore a good programmer—we call it the ***programmer's algorithm***. In particular, you will study the steps required to solve just about any programming problem. You will be introduced to the concept of ***abstraction***, which allows problems to be viewed in general terms without agonizing over the implementation details required by a computer language. From an initial abstract solution, you will refine the solution step by step until it reaches a level that can be coded directly into a Java program. Make sure you understand this material and work the related problems at the end of the chapter. As you become more experienced in programming, you will find that the "secret" to successful programming is good planning through abstract analysis and stepwise refinement, which results in workable software designs. Such designs are supported by languages like Java. In the chapters that follow, you will build on this knowledge to create workable Java programs.

2-1 THE PROGRAMMER'S ALGORITHM

Before we look at the programmer's algorithm, it might be helpful to define what is meant by an algorithm. In technical terms, it is as follows:

> An *algorithm* is a series of step-by-step instructions that produces a solution to a problem.

Algorithms are not unique to the computer industry. Any set of instructions, such as those you might find in a recipe or a kit assembly guide, can be considered an algorithm. The programmer's algorithm is a recipe for you, the programmer, to follow when developing programs. The algorithm is as follows:

THE PROGRAMMER'S ALGORITHM

- Define the problem.
- Plan the problem solution.
- Code the program.
- Test and debug the program.
- Document the program.

Defining the Problem

You might suggest that defining the problem is an obvious step in solving any problem. However, it often is the most overlooked step, especially in computer programming. The lack of good problem definition often results in "spinning your wheels," especially in more complex computer programming applications.

Think of a typical computer programming problem, such as controlling the inventory of a large department store. What must be considered as part of the problem definition? The first consideration probably is what you want to get out of the system. Will the output information consist of printed inventory reports or, in addition, will the system automatically generate product orders based on sales? Must any information generated by a customer transaction be saved permanently on disk, or can it be discarded? What type of data is the output information to consist of? Is it numerical data, character data, or both? How must the output data be formatted? All of these questions must be answered in order to define the output requirements.

Careful consideration of the output requirements usually leads to deciding what must be put into the system in order to obtain the desired system output. For instance, in our department store inventory example, a desired output would be most likely a summary of customer transactions. How are these transactions to be entered into the system? Are the data to be obtained from a keyboard, or is product information to be entered automatically via an optical character recognition (OCR) system that reads the bar code on the product price tags? Does the input consist of all numerical data, character data, or a combination of both? What is the format of the data?

The next consideration is processing. Will most of the customer processing be done at the cash register terminal, or will it be handled by a central store computer? What about credit card verification and inventory records? Will this processing be done by a local PC, a minicomputer located within the store, or a central mainframe computer located in a different part of the country? What kind of programs will be written to do the processing, and who will write them? What sort of calculations and decisions must be made on the data within individual programs to achieve the desired output?

All of these questions must be answered when defining any computer programming problem. In summary, you could say that problem definition must consider the application requirements of output, input, and processing. The department store inventory problem clearly requires precise definition. However, even with small application programs, you must still consider the type of output, input, and processing that the problem requires.

The reason this inventory problem lends itself to computer solution is that it deals with input, processing, and output, thus lending itself to an algorithmic approach to problem solving. Many real-world problems, such as long-range weather forecasting, do not lend themselves to this approach. So, when trying to define a problem you must first decide if it is a candidate for computer solution. To do this, you must ask yourself whether it lends itself to input and processing that input to producing useful output information. Once a problem is identified as a candidate for computer solution, then you need to define the problem in terms of specific input, processing, and output.

When defining a problem, look for the nouns and verbs within a problem statement. The nouns often suggest input and output information, and the verbs suggest processing steps. The application will always dictate the problem definition. We will discuss problem definition further, as we begin to develop computer programs to solve real problems.

PROBLEM SOLVING TIP

Look for the nouns and verbs within a problem statement; they often provide clues to the required output, input, and processing. The nouns suggest output and input, and the verbs suggest processing steps.

Planning the Solution

The planning stage associated with any problem is probably the most important part of the solution, and computer programming is no exception. Imagine trying to build a house without a good set of blueprints. The results could be catastrophic! The same is true of trying to develop computer software without a good plan. When developing computer software, the planning stage is implemented using a collection of algorithms. As you already know, an algorithm is a series of step-by-step instructions that produce results to solve problems. When planning computer programs, algorithms are used to outline the solution steps using Englishlike statements, called *pseudocode*, that require less precision than a formal programming language. A good pseudocode algorithm should be independent of, but easily translated into, *any* formal procedural programming language.

Pseudocode is an informal set of Englishlike statements that are generally accepted within the computer industry to denote common computer programming operations. Pseudocode statements are used to describe the steps in a computer algorithm.

Coding the Program

Coding the program should be one of the simplest tasks in the whole programming process, provided you have done a good job of defining the problem and planning its solution. Coding involves the actual writing of the program in a formal programming language. The computer language you use will be determined by the nature of the problem, the programming languages available to you, and the limits of the computer system. Once a language is chosen, the program is written, or coded, by translating your algorithm steps into the formal language code.

You should be cautioned, however, that coding is really a mechanical process and should be considered secondary to algorithm development. In the future, computers will generate their own program code from well-constructed algorithms. Research in the field of artificial intelligence has resulted in "code-generation" software. The thing to keep in mind is that computers might someday generate their own programming code from algorithms, but it takes the creativity and common sense of a human being to plan the solution and develop the algorithm.

Debugging the Program

You will soon find out that it is a rare and joyous occasion when a coded program actually "runs" the first time without any errors. Of course, good problem definition and planning will avoid many program mistakes, or "bugs." However, there always are a few bugs that manage to go undetected, regardless of how much planning you do. Getting rid of the program bugs (*debugging*) often is the most time-consuming job in the whole programming process. Industrial statistics show that often over 50 percent of a programmer's time is often spent on program debugging.

There is no absolute correct procedure for debugging a program, but a systematic approach can help make the process easier. The basic steps of debugging are as follows:

- Realizing that you have an error.
- Locating and determining the cause of the error.
- Fixing the error.

First of all, you have to realize that you have an error. Sometimes, this is obvious when your computer freezes up or crashes. At other times, the program might work fine until certain unexpected information is entered by someone using the program. The most subtle errors occur when the program is running fine and the results look correct, but when you examine the results closely, they are not quite right.

The next step in the debugging process is locating and determining the cause of the errors—sometimes the most difficult part of debugging. This is where a good programming tool, called a ***debugger***, comes into play.

Fixing the error is the final step in debugging. Your knowledge of the Java language, this book, Java on-line help, a Java debugger, and your Java reference manuals are all valuable tools in fixing the error and removing the "bug" from your program.

When programming in Java, there are four things that you can do to test and debug your program: ***desk-check*** the program, ***compile*** the program, ***run*** the program, and ***debug*** the program.

Desk-Checking the Program

Desk-checking a program is similar to proofreading a letter or manuscript. The idea is to trace through the program mentally to make sure that the program logic is workable. You must consider various input possibilities and write down any results generated during program execution. In particular, try to determine what the program will do with unusual data by considering input possibilities that "shouldn't" happen. Always keep Murphy's law in mind when desk-checking a program: If a given condition can't or shouldn't happen, it will!

For example, suppose a program requires the user to enter a value whose square root must be found. Of course, the user "shouldn't" enter a negative value, because the square root of a negative number is imaginary. However, what will the program do if he or she does? Another input possibility that should always be considered is an input of zero, especially when used as part of an arithmetic operation, such as division.

When you first begin programming, you will be tempted to skip the desk-checking phase, because you can't wait to run the program once it is written. However, as you gain experience, you soon will realize the time-saving value of desk-checking.

Compiling the Program

At this point, you are ready to enter the program into the computer system. Once entered, the program must be compiled, or translated, into machine code. Fortunately, the compiler is designed to check for certain program errors. These usually are *syntax* errors that you have made when coding the program. A syntax error is any violation of the rules of the programming language, such as using a period instead of a semicolon. There might also be type errors. A *type error* occurs when you attempt to mix different types of data, such as numeric and character data. It is like trying to add apples to oranges.

> A *syntax error* is any violation of the rules of the programming language, and a *type error* occurs when you attempt to mix different types of data.

During the compiling process, many Java compilers will generate error and warning messages as well as position the display monitor cursor to the point in the program where the error was detected. The program will not compile beyond the point of the error until it is corrected. Once an error is corrected, you must attempt to compile the program again. If other errors are detected, you must correct them, recompile the program, and so on, until the entire program is successfully compiled.

Running the Program

Once the program has been compiled, you must execute, or run, it. However, just because the program has been compiled successfully doesn't mean that it will run successfully under all possible conditions. Common bugs that occur at this stage include *logic errors* and *run-time* errors. These are the most difficult kinds of errors to detect. A logic error will occur when a loop tells the computer to repeat an operation but does not tell it when to stop repeating. This is called an *infinite loop*. Such a bug will not cause an error message to be generated, because the computer is simply doing what it was told to do. The program execution must be stopped and debugged before it can run successfully.

> A *logic error* occurs when the compiler does what you tell it to do but is not doing what you meant it to do. A *run-time* error occurs when the program attempts to perform an illegal operation as defined by the laws of mathematics or the particular compiler in use.

A run-time error occurs when the program attempts to perform an illegal operation, as defined by the laws of mathematics or the particular compiler in use. Two common mathematical run-time errors are division by zero and attempting to take the square root of a negative number. A common error imposed by the compiler is an integer value out of range. Java limits byte-sized integers to a range of −128 to +127. Unpredictable results can occur if a byte value exceeds this range.

Sometimes, the program is automatically aborted and an error message is displayed when a run-time error occurs. Other times, the program seems to execute properly but generates incorrect results, commonly called *garbage*. Again, you should consult your compiler reference manual to determine the exact nature of the problem. The error must be located and corrected before another attempt is made to run the program.

Using a Debugger

One of the most important programming tools that you can have is a debugger. A debugger provides a microscopic view of what is going on in your program. Many Java compilers include a built-in, or *integrated*, debugger that allows you to single-step program statements and view the execution results in the CPU and memory.

DEBUGGING TIP

A word from experience: Always go about debugging your programs in a systematic, commonsense manner. Don't be tempted to change something just because you "hope" it will work and don't know what else to do. Use your resources to isolate and correct the problem. Such resources include your algorithm, a program listing, your integrated Java debugger, your reference manuals, this textbook, and your instructor, just to mention a few. Logic and run-time errors usually are the result of a serious flaw in your program. They will not go away and cannot be corrected by blindly making changes to your program. One good way to locate errors is to have your program print out preliminary results as well as messages that tell when a particular part of the program is running.

Documentation

This documentation step in the programmer's algorithm often is overlooked, but it probably is one of the more important steps, especially in commercial programming. Documentation is easy if you have done a good job of defining the problem, planning the solution, coding, testing, and debugging the program. The final program documentation is simply the recorded result of these programming steps. At a minimum, good documentation should include the following:

- A narrative description of the problem definition, which includes the type of input, output, and processing employed by the program.
- A set of algorithms.
- A program listing that includes a clear commenting scheme. Commenting within the program is an important part of the overall documentation process. Each program should include comments at the beginning to explain what it does, any special algorithms that are employed, and a summary of the problem definition. In addition, the name of the programmer and the date the program was written and last modified should be included.
- Samples of input and output data.
- Testing and debugging results.
- User instructions.

The documentation must be neat and well organized. It must be easily understood by you as well as any other person who might have a need to use or modify your program in the future. What good is an ingenious program if no one can determine what it does, how to use it, or how to maintain it?

One final point: Documentation should always be an ongoing process. Whenever you work with the program or modify it, make sure the documentation is updated to reflect your experiences and modifications. Someday you might have to maintain a program written by yourself or somebody else. Without good documentation, program maintenance becomes a nightmare. Just look at what has happened with the Y2K (Year 2000) problem. This is a classic example of a problem caused by large-scale software systems created without good documentation. Even after the year 2000 this bug will be a major concern.

 Quick Check

1. Englishlike statements that require less precision than a formal programming language are called _____.

2. What questions must be answered when defining a computer programming problem?

3.   What can be done to test and debug a program?

4.   Why is commenting important within a program?

5.   What is a syntax error?

6.   What is a logic error?

2-2 PROBLEM SOLVING USING ALGORITHMS

In the previous section, you learned that an algorithm is a sequence of step-by-step instructions that solves a problem.

For instance, consider the following series of instructions:

> Apply to wet hair.
> Gently massage lather through hair.
> Rinse, keeping lather out of eyes.
> Repeat.

Look familiar? Of course, this is a series of instructions that might be found on the back of a shampoo bottle. But does it fit the technical definition of an algorithm? In other words, does it produce a result? You might say "yes," but look closer. The algorithm requires that you keep repeating the procedure an infinite number of times, so theoretically you would never stop shampooing your hair! A good computer algorithm must terminate in a finite amount of time. The repeat instruction could be altered easily to make the shampooing algorithm technically correct:

> Repeat until hair is clean.

Now the shampooing process can be terminated. Of course, you must be the one to decide when your hair is clean.

The foregoing shampoo analogy might seem a bit trivial. You probably are thinking that any intelligent person would not keep on repeating the shampooing process an infinite number of times, right? This obviously is the case when we humans are executing the algorithm, because we have some commonsense judgment. But what about a computer; does it have commonsense judgement? Most computers do exactly what they are told to do via the computer program. As a result, a computer would repeat the original shampooing algorithm over and over an infinite number of times. This is why the algorithms that you write for computer programs must be precise.

Now, let's develop an algorithm for a process that is common to all of us—mailing a letter. Think of the steps that are involved in this simple process. You must first address an envelope, fold the letter, insert the letter in the envelope, and seal the envelope. Next, you need a stamp. If you don't have a stamp, you have to buy one. Once a stamp is obtained, you must place it on the envelope and mail the letter. The following algorithm summarizes the steps in this process:

> Obtain an envelope.
> Address the envelope.
> Fold the letter.
> Insert the letter in the envelope.
> Seal the envelope.
> If you don't have a stamp, then buy one.
> Place the stamp on the envelope.
> Mail the letter.

Does this sequence of instructions fit our definition of a good algorithm? In other words, does the sequence of instructions produce a result in a finite amount of time? Yes, assuming that each operation can be understood and carried out by the person mailing the letter. This brings up two additional characteristics of good algorithms: Each operation within the algorithm must be **well defined** and **effective**. By well defined, we mean that each of the steps must be clearly understood by people in the computer industry. By effective, we mean that some method must exist in order to carry out the operation. In other words, the person mailing the letter must be able to perform each of the algorithm steps. In the case of a computer program algorithm, the compiler must have the means of executing each operation in the algorithm.

In summary, a good computer algorithm must possess the following three attributes:

1. Employ well defined instructions that are generally understood by people in the computer industry.

2. Employ instructions that can be carried out effectively by the compiler executing the algorithm.

3. Produce a solution to the problem in a finite amount of time.

In order to write computer program algorithms, we need to establish a set of well defined, effective operations. The set of pseudocode operations listed in Table 2-1 will make up our algorithmic language. We will use these operations from now on, whenever we write computer algorithms.

Notice that the operations in Table 2-1 are grouped into three major categories: *sequence*, *decision*, and *iteration*. These categories are called *control structures*. The sequence control structure includes those operations that produce a single action or result. Only a partial list of sequence operations is provided here. This list will be expanded, as additional operations are needed. As its name implies, the decision control structure includes the operations that allow the computer to make decisions. Finally, the iteration control structure includes those operations that are used for looping, or repeating, operations within the algorithm. Many of the operations listed in Table 2-1 are self-explanatory. Those that are not will be discussed in detail as we begin to develop more complex algorithms.

TABLE 2-1 PSEUDOCODE OPERATIONS USED IN THIS TEXT

Sequence	**Decision**	**Iteration**
Add (+)	If/Then	While
Calculate	If/Else	Do/While
Decrement	Switch/Case	For
Divide (/)		
Increment		
rint		
Read		
Set or assign (=)		
Square		
Subtract (−)		
Write		

Quick Check

1. Why is it important to develop a set of algorithms prior to coding a program?

2. What are the three major control structure categories of pseudocode operations?

3. List three decision operations.

4. List three iteration operations.

2-3 PROBLEM ABSTRACTION AND STEPWISE REFINEMENT

At this time, we need to introduce a very important concept in programming—
abstraction. Abstraction allows us to view a problem in general terms, without worrying about the details. As a result, abstraction provides for generalization in problem solving.

> ***Abstraction*** provides for generalization in problem solving by allowing you to view a problem in general terms, without worrying about the details of the problem solution.

You might have heard the old saying, "You can't see the forest for the trees." This means that it is very easy to get lost within the trees of the forest without seeing the big picture of the entire forest. This saying also applies to problem solving and programming. When starting out to solve a program, you need to get the "big picture" first. Once you have the big picture of the problem solution, the "forest," you can gradually *refine* the solution by providing more detail until you have a solution, the "trees," that is easily coded in a computer language. The process of gradually adding more detail to a general problem solution is called ***stepwise refinement***.

> ***Stepwise refinement*** is the process of gradually adding detail to a general problem solution until it can be easily coded in a computer language.

As an example, consider the problem of designing your own "dream house." Would you begin by drafting the detailed plans of the house? Not likely, because you would most likely get lost in detail. A better approach would be to first make an artist's general-perspective rendition of the house; then make a general floor plan diagram, and finally make detailed drawings of the house construction that could be followed by the builders.

The concepts of problem abstraction and stepwise refinement allow you to *divide and conquer* the problem and solve it from the *top down*. This strategy has been proven to conquer all types of problems, especially programming problems. In programming, we generate a general problem solution, or algorithm, and gradually refine it, producing more detailed algorithms, until we get to a level that can be easily coded using a programming language.

In summary, when attacking a problem, always start with the big picture and begin with a very general, or *abstract*, model of the solution. This allows you to concentrate on the problem at hand without getting lost in the "trees" by worrying about the implementation details of a particular programming language. You then gradually refine the solution until you reach a level that can be easily coded using a programming language, like Java. The *Problem Solving in Action* examples that follow illustrate this process.

Quick Check

1. Explain why abstraction is important when solving problems.

2. Explain the process of stepwise refinement.

3. How do you know when you have reached a codeable level of an algorithm when using stepwise refinement?

PROBLEM SOLVING IN ACTION: SALES TAX

Problem

Develop a set of algorithms to calculate the amount of sales tax and the total cost of a sales item, including tax. Assume the sales tax rate is 7 percent and the user will enter the cost of the sales item.

Defining the Problem

When defining the problem, you must consider three things: *output, input*, and *processing* as related to the problem statement. Look for the nouns and verbs within the problem statement, as they often provide clues to the required output, input, and processing. The nouns suggest output and input, and the verbs suggest processing steps. The nouns relating to output and input are *sales tax*, *total cost*, and *cost*. The total cost is the required output, and the sales tax and item cost are needed as input to calculate the total cost of the item. However, the sales tax rate is given (7 percent), so the only data required for the algorithm are the item cost.

The verb *calculate* requires us to process two things: the amount of sales tax, and the total cost of the item, including sales tax. Therefore, the processing must calculate the amount of sales tax and add this value to the item cost to obtain the total cost of the item. In summary, the problem definition in terms of output, input, and processing is as follows:

Output: The total cost of the sales item, including sales tax to be displayed on the system monitor.

Input: The cost of the sales item to be entered by the user on the system keyboard.

Processing: $tax = 0.07 \times cost$
$totalCost = cost + tax$

Notice that we have indicated *where* the output is going (the system monitor), and *where* the input is coming from (the user). Where the output is going and the input is coming from should always be indicated for each item in the problem definition.

Planning the Solution

Now that the problem has been defined in terms of output, input, and processing, it is time to plan the solution by developing the required algorithms. Using the foregoing problem definition, we are now ready to write the initial algorithm. We will call this initial algorithm *main( )*. (*Note:* The parentheses after the algorithm name will be used from now on to indicate an algorithm, or method, to perform some given task.) Here is the required initial algorithm, *main( )*:

Initial Algorithm

    main( )
    BEGIN
       Read the cost of the sales item from the user.
       Calculate the sales tax and total cost of the sales item.
       Write the total cost of the sales item, including sales tax on the system monitor.
    END.

Notice that, at this level, you are not concerned with how to perform the foregoing operations in a computer language. You are only concerned about the major program operations, without agonizing over the language implementation details. This is problem abstraction!

We have divided the problem into three major tasks relating to input, processing, and output derived from our problem definition. The next step is to refine repeatedly the initial algorithm until we obtain one or more algorithms that can be coded directly in a computer language. This is a relatively simple problem, so we can employ the pseudocode operations listed in Table 2-1 at this first level of refinement. Three major operations are identified by the preceding algorithm: reading data from the user, calculating the tax and total cost, and displaying the results to the user. As a result, we will create three additional algorithms that implement these operations. First, reading the data from the user. We will call this algorithm *readData( )* as follows:

First Level of Refinement

    readData( )
    BEGIN
       Write a program description message to the user.

> Write a user prompt to enter the cost of the item (*cost*).
> Read (*cost*).
END.

In Table 2-1, you will find two sequence operations called **Read** and **Write**. The *Read* operation is an input operation. We will assume that this operation will obtain data entered via the system keyboard. The *Write* operation is an output operation. We will assume that this operation causes information to be displayed on the system monitor. The *readData()* algorithm uses the *Write* operation to display a **prompt** to the user and a corresponding *Read* operation to obtain the user input and assign it to the respective variable.

STYLE TIP

The *readData()* algorithm illustrates some operations that result in good programming style. Notice that the first *Write* operation is to write a program description message to the person running the program—the user. It is good practice always to include such a message so that the user understands what the program will do. In addition, the second *Write* operation will display a message to tell the user to "Enter the cost of the item (*cost*)." Without such a prompt, the user will not know what to do. You must write a user prompt message anytime the user must enter data via the keyboard. Such a message should tell the user what is to be entered and in what format the information is to be entered. (More about this later.)

The next task is to develop an algorithm to calculate the cost of the sales item, including tax. We will call this algorithm *calculateCost()* and employ the required pseudocode operations from Table 2-1, as follows:

> *calculateCost()*
> BEGIN
>   Set *tax* to (0.07 × *cost*).
>   Set *totalCost* to (*cost* + *tax*).
> END.

Finally, we need an algorithm to display the results. We will call this algorithm *displayResults()*. All we need here is a *Write* operation as follows:

displayResults( )
BEGIN
   Write (*totalCost*).
END.

That's all there is to it. The illustration in Figure 2-1 is called a ***problem solution diagram***, because it shows the overall structure of our problem solution. The problem solution diagram shows how the problem has been divided into a series of subproblems, whose collective solution will solve the initial problem. By using the above algorithms and problem solution diagram, this problem can be coded easily in any language, such as Java.

When you begin coding in Java, you will translate the preceding algorithms directly into Java code. Each of the algorithms will be coded as a Java ***method***. Methods in Java are subprograms designed to perform specific tasks, such as those performed by each of our algorithms. Thus, we will code a method called *readData( )* to get the data from the user, another method called *calculateCost( )* to calculate the total cost of the sales item, and a third method called *displayResults( )* to display the final results to the user. In addition, we will code a method called *main( )* to sequentially ***call*** these methods as needed to produce the desired result.

A ***method*** in Java is a subprogram designed to perform specific tasks, such as those performed by an algorithm. In other programming languages, methods might be referred to as *procedures*, *functions*, or *subroutines*.

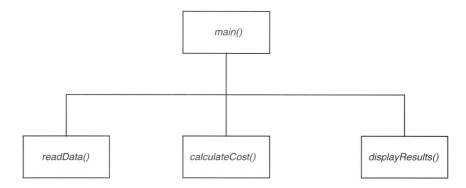

Figure 2-1 A problem solution diagram for the sales tax problem shows the abstract analysis and stepwise refinement required for solving complex problems.

PROBLEM SOLVING IN ACTION: CREDIT CARD INTEREST

Problem

The interest charged on a credit card account depends on the remaining balance according to the following criteria: Interest charged is 18 percent up to $500 and 15 percent for any amount over $500. Develop the algorithms required to find the total amount of interest due on any given account balance.

Let's begin by defining the problem in terms of output, input, and processing.

Defining the Problem

Output: According to the problem statement, the obvious output must be the total amount of interest due. We will display this information on the system monitor.

Input: We will assume that the user will enter the account balance via the system keyboard.

Processing: Here is an application in which a decision-making operation must be included in the algorithm. There are two possibilities as follows:

1. *If* the balance is less than or equal to $500, *then* the interest is 18 percent of the balance, or

$$interest = 0.18 \times balance$$

2. *If* the balance is over $500, *then* the interest is 18 percent of the first $500 plus 15 percent of any amount over $500. In the form of an equation,

$$interest = (0.18 \times 500) + [0.15 \times (balance - 500)]$$

Notice the use of the two *if/then* statements in these two possibilities.

Planning the Solution

Our problem solution begins with the initial algorithm we have been calling *main()*. Again, this algorithm will simply reflect the problem definition as follows:

Initial Algorithm

main( )
BEGIN
    Read the account balance from the user.
    Calculate the interest on the account balance.
    Write the calculated interest on the system monitor.
END.

Due to the simplicity of the problem, only one level of refinement is needed, as follows:

First Level of Refinement

readData( )
BEGIN
    Write a program description message to the user.
    Write a user prompt to enter the account balance (*balance*).
    Read (*balance*).
END.

calculateInterest( )
BEGIN
    If *balance* <= 500 Then
        Set *interest* to $(0.18 \times balance)$.
    If *balance* > 500 Then
        Set *interest* to $(0.18 \times 500) + [0.15 \times (balance - 500)]$.
END.

displayResults( )
BEGIN
    Write(*interest*).
END.

As you can see, the two decision-making operations stated in the problem definition have been incorporated into our *calculateInterest( )* algorithm. Notice the use of indentation to show which calculation goes with which *if/then* operation. The use of indentation is an important part of pseudocode, because it shows the algorithm structure at a glance.

How might you replace the two *if/then* operations in this algorithm with a single *if/else* operation? Think about it, as it will be left as a problem at the end of the chapter!

PROBLEM SOLVING IN ACTION: PYTHAGOREAN THEOREM

Problem

Develop a set of algorithms to find the hypotenuse of a right triangle, given its two right angle sides, using the Pythagorean theorem depicted in Figure 2-2. Construct the final algorithms using the pseudocode instructions listed in Table 2-1.

$$H^2 = A^2 + B^2$$

Figure 2-2   Solving the hypotenuse of a right triangle using the Pythagorean theorem.

Defining the Problem

When defining the problem, you must consider three things: *output, input*, and *processing* as related to the problem statement. Let's label the two sides *a* and *b*, and the hypotenuse *h*. The problem requires us to find the hypotenuse (*h*), given the two sides (*a* and *b*). So the output must be the hypotenuse (*h*). We will display the hypotenuse value on the system monitor. In order to obtain this output, the two sides (*a* and *b*) must be received by the program. Let's assume that the user must enter these values via the system keyboard.

The Pythagorean theorem states that the hypotenuse squared is equal to the sum of the squares of the two sides. In symbols,

$$h^2 = a^2 + b^2$$

This equation represents the processing that must be performed by the computer. In summary, the problem definition is as follows:

Output: The hypotenuse (*h*) of a right triangle displayed on the system monitor.

Input: The two sides (*a* and *b*) of a right triangle to be entered by the user via the system keyboard.

Processing: Employ the Pythagorean theorem: $h^2 = a^2 + b^2$.

Now that the problem has been defined in terms of output, input, and processing, it is time to plan the solution by developing the required algorithms.

Planning the Solution

We will begin with an abstract model of the problem. This will be our initial algorithm, which we refer to as *main()*. At this level, we are only concerned about addressing the major operations required to solve the problem. These are derived directly from the problem definition. As a result, our initial algorithm is as follows:

Initial Algorithm

main()
BEGIN
    Read the two sides (*a* and *b*) of a right triangle from the user.
    Calculate the hypotenuse (*h*) of the triangle using the Pythagorean theorem.
    Write the results on the system monitor.
END.

The next step is to refine repeatedly the initial algorithm until we obtain one or more algorithms that can be coded directly in a computer language. This is a relatively simple problem, so we can employ the pseudocode operations listed in Table 2-1 at this first level of refinement. Three major operations are identified by the preceding algorithm: reading data from the user, calculating the hypotenuse, and displaying the results to the user. As a result, we will create three additional algorithms that implement these operations. First, reading the data from the user. We will call this algorithm *readData()*.

First Level of Refinement

readData( )
BEGIN
   Write a program description message to the user.
   Write a user prompt message to enter the first side of the triangle (*a*).
   Read (*a*).
   Write a user prompt message to enter the second side of the triangle (*b*).
   Read (*b*).
END.

The next task is to develop an algorithm to calculate the hypotenuse of the triangle. We will call this algorithm *calculateHypot( )* and employ the required pseudocode operations from Table 2-1, as follows:

calculateHypot( )
BEGIN
   Square(*a*).
   Square(*b*).
   Assign ($a^2 + b^2$) to h^2.
   Assign square root of h^2 to *h*.
END.

The operations in this algorithm should be self-explanatory. Notice how the *Assign* operation works. For example, the statement *Assign square root of h^2 to h* sets the variable *h* to the value obtained from taking the square root of h^2. We could also express this operation as *Set h to square root of h^2*. The *Assign* and *Set* operations are equivalent; however, the verb objects within the respective phrases are reversed. You should be familiar with either terminology.

The final task is to develop an algorithm to display the results. We will call this algorithm *displayResults( )*. All we need here is a *Write* operation as follows:

displayResults( )
BEGIN
   Write(H).
END.

CHAPTER SUMMARY

The five major steps that must be performed when developing software are (1) define the problem, (2) plan the problem solution, (3) code the program, (4) debug the program, and (5) document the program. When defining the problem, you must consider the output, input, and processing requirements of the application. Planning the problem solution requires that you specify the problem solution steps via an algorithm. An algorithm is a series of step-by-step instructions that provides a solution to the problem in a finite amount of time.

Abstraction and stepwise refinement are powerful tools for problem solving. Abstraction allows you to view the problem in general terms, without agonizing over the implementation details of a computer language. Stepwise refinement is applied to an initial abstract problem solution to develop gradually a set of related algorithms that can be directly coded using a computer language, such as Java.

Once a codeable algorithm is developed, it must be coded into some formal language that the computer system can understand. The language used in this text is Java. Once coded, the program must be tested and debugged through desk-checking, compiling, and execution. Finally, the entire programming process, from problem definition to testing and debugging, must be documented so that it can be easily understood by you or anyone else working with it.

Your Java debugger is one of the best tools that you can use to deal with bugs that creep into your programs. It allows you to do source-level debugging and helps with the two hardest parts of debugging: finding the error and finding the cause of the error. It does this by allowing you to trace into your programs and their methods one step at a time. This slows down the program execution so that you can examine the contents of the individual data elements and program output at any given point in the program.

QUESTIONS AND PROBLEMS

Questions

1. Define an algorithm.
2. List the five steps of the programmer's algorithm.
3. What three things must be considered during the problem-definition phase of programming?

4. What tools are employed for planning the solutions to a programming problem?

5. Explain how problem abstraction aids in solving problems.

6. Explain the process of stepwise refinement.

7. The writing of a program is called _____.

8. State three things that you can do to test and debug your programs.

9. List the minimum items required for good documentation.

10. What three characteristics must a good computer algorithm possess?

11. The three major control structures of a programming language are _____, _____, and _____.

12. Explain why a single *if/then* operation in the credit card interest problem won't work. If you know the balance is not less than or equal to $500, the balance must be greater than $500, right? So, why can't the second *if/then* operation be deleted?

Problems

Least Difficult

1. Develop a set of algorithms to compute the sum, difference, product, and quotient of any two integers entered by the user.

2. Revise the solution you obtained in problem 1 to protect it from a divide-by-zero run-time error.

More Difficult

3. Develop a set of algorithms to read in an employee's total weekly hours worked and rate of pay. Determine the gross weekly pay using "time-and-a-half" for anything over 40 hours.

4. Revise the solution generated in the credit card problem to employ a single *if/else* operation in place of the two *if/then* operations. As you will see later, an *if/else* operation does one thing "if" a condition is true, "else" is does something different if the same condition is false.

5. A dimension on a part drawing indicates that the length of the part is 3.00 ± 0.25 inches. This means that the minimum acceptable length of the part is 3.0 − 0.25 = 2.75 inches and the maximum acceptable length of the part is 3.00 + 0.25 = 3.25 inches. Develop a set of algorithms that will display "ACCEPTABLE" if the part is within tolerance and "UNACCEPTABLE" if the part is out of tolerance. Also, show your problem definition in terms of output, input, and processing.

6. Develop a problem definition and set of algorithms to process a standard bank account. Assume that the user must enter the beginning bank account balance as well as any deposits or withdrawals on the account. The banking transactions that must be implemented are adding any deposits to the balance and subtracting any withdrawals from the balance. Of course, the program should display the account status, including the old balance, amount of deposits, amount of withdrawals, and the new balance.

7. Develop a problem solution diagram for the banking problem in problem 6.

8. Develop a problem definition and set of algorithms to process a business inventory. Assume that the user must enter five inventory items for a local bait and tackle store. Each entry is to consist of the item name, quantity on hand, and item price. The program should calculate the expected profit on each item and total profit for all items, assuming a profit margin of 20%. The program should then display the expected profit on each item and total expected profit of all items.

GUI 102: FRAMES

PURPOSE

- *To become familiar with Java frames.*
- *To demonstrate that frames have all the generic window features, except the closing feature.*
- *To show how to set the title of a frame/window.*
- *To show how to set the initial size of a frame/window.*
- *To demonstrate multiple frames.*

Introduction

The *frame* is the basis for a GUI in all Java application programs. Frames are used as containers to hold GUI components. When you build a GUI in a Java application program, you will first create a frame, then add the desired components to the frame. In this module, you will load and execute a Java program that produces a frame. You will modify the code and observe the effect on the window generated by the frame.

Procedure

1. Load and execute the *GUI102_1.java* program contained on the CD that accompanies this book or download it from www.prenhall.com. You should observe the window shown in Figure 1 if you are in a Windows environment or Figure 2 if you are in a Mac environment.

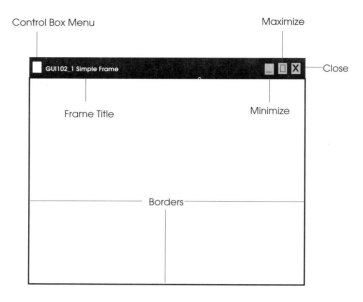

Figure 1 The simple frame generated by the *GUI102_1.java* program in a Windows environment.

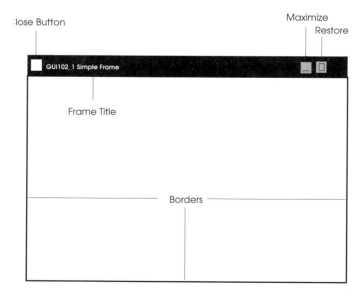

Figure 2 The simple frame generated by the *GUI102_1.java* program in a Mac environment.

2. Resize the window to different sizes by grabbing and moving the window borders.

3. If you are in a Windows environment, minimize the window by clicking the *Minimize* button in the upper-right-hand corner of the window. Restore the window by switching to the *GUI102_1.java* task (Alt-Tab).

4. Try to close the window by clicking the *Close* button in the upper-right-hand corner of the window (Windows), or upper-left-hand corner of the window (Mac). What? You can't close the window? That's right, this program does not include the code necessary to close the window and terminate the task.

5. Load and execute the *GUI102_2.java* program. You should see the same window as before except for the window title.

6. Now try to close the window by clicking the *Close* button. You should find the window closes fine and the program task ends.

Here is the Java code that produced the frame window with the closing feature:

```
1    import java.awt.*;          //FOR FRAME CLASS
2    import java.awt.event.*;    //FOR EVENT HANDLING

3    //INHERITS AND CUSTOMIZES FRAME CLASS TO ADD DESIRED
     //FEATURES
4    class FrameWithClose extends Frame implements WindowListener
5    {
6      //CONSTRUCTOR
7      public FrameWithClose(String title)
8      {
9        super(title);
10       addWindowListener(this);
11     }//END FrameWithClose()

12     //WindowListener METHODS
13     public void windowClosing(WindowEvent e)
14     {
15       System.exit(0);
16     }//END windowClosing()

17   public void windowClosed(WindowEvent e)
18   {
19   }
```

```
20   public void windowDeiconified(WindowEvent e)
21   {
22   }
23   public void windowIconified(WindowEvent e)
24   {
25   }
26   public void windowActivated(WindowEvent e)
27   {
28   }
29   public void windowDeactivated(WindowEvent e)
30   {
31   }
32   public void windowOpened(WindowEvent e)
33   {
34   }
35   }//END FrameWithClose

36   //CLASS TO TEST FrameWithClose CLASS
37   public class GUI102_2
38   {
39     public static void main(String[] args)
40     {
41       //DEFINE FRAME OBJECT
42       FrameWithClose window = new FrameWithClose("GUI102_2 Frame With
                                                                    Close");
43
44       //SET FRAME SIZE
45       window.setSize(500,300);
46
47       //MAKE FRAME VISIBLE
48       window.setVisible(true);
49
50     }//END main()
51   }//END GUI102_2
```

7. Wow, what a program! Don't be overwhelmed and worry about all the coding
    details now. You will learn them in time. We will just focus on a few
    statements that are pertinent to our window frame. Change the "GUI102_1
    Frame With Close" phrase in line 42 to "This Is My First Frame." Do not
    change anything else in this line. Run the program again and notice that the
    title in the window title bar has changed.

8. Close the window and change the statement in line 45 to:

    window.setSize(100,200);

    Notice that there is a dot (period) between the words *window* and *setSize* and a semicolon ends the statement. Run the program again and notice that the window is now smaller, but can still be resized, minimized, maximized, or closed.

9. Try different values in line 45. You should find the first value controls the width of the frame and the second value controls the frame height. Of course, if you exceed the size of your monitor screen, the frame is maximized.

10. Add the following statement on line 43:

    FrameWithClose win = new FrameWithClose("My Frame With Close");

11. Add the following statement on line 46:

    win.setSize(500,300);

12. Add the following statement on line 49:

    win.setVisible(true);

13. Run the program again and observe that two windows are produced. Notice that you can switch back and forth between these multiple frames.

Discussion

The two programs that you just ran create a Java frame which, when executed, each creates a window. A Java frame is created from the standard *Frame* class available in the ***Java Abstract Windowing Toolkit***, or ***AWT***. This toolkit is found in the *java.awt* package and is why we "imported" this package in line 1, at the beginning of the program. Packages contain Java classes. The *java.awt* package contains all the components necessary to build a GUI.

In the first program, the window closing feature is not operable because a frame by itself is not able to handle this ***event***. The second program imports the *java.awt.event* package in line 2 and adds additional code to handle the window closing event when it occurs.

When you changed line 42, you found that you changed the window title in the title bar. The window title will reflect whatever ***string*** is placed within the parentheses of line 42. A string is simply a collection of characters and recognized by Java by enclosing them within double quotation marks.

When you changed line 45, you changed the initial size of the frame. Of course, the frame could still be resized after it appeared. The first value, called an **argument**, is the initial frame width, in **pixels** (picture elements), while the second argument is the initial frame height, in pixels.

In steps 10-12 you created a new frame **object** called *win*, set the size of the *win* frame, and made the *win* frame visible, respectively. This added a second frame to the program, thus creating multiple windows, or frames, when the program was executed.

DATA: TYPES, CLASSES, AND OBJECTS

OBJECTIVES

When you are finished with this chapter, you should have a good understanding of the following:

- The concepts of data abstraction and abstract data types (ADTs).
- The concept of class behavior.
- The relationship between a class and its objects.
- Methods and their use in Java programs.
- The primitive data types in Java.
- The Java **String** class.
- How to create constants and variables in a Java program.
- How to create string objects in a Java program.
- Numeric overflow errors.
- Fixed decimal versus exponential format of floating-point numbers.
- How to display information using the Java *println()* method.
- How to call methods using objects in Java.
- Where and when to use comments in a program.
- The structure of a Java application program.
- How to create a Java program from a set of algorithms.

INTRODUCTION

You are now ready to begin learning the building blocks of the Java language. The Java language is what is called an *object-oriented language*. Object-oriented programming, OOP, is built around *classes* and *objects* that model real-world entities in a more natural way than do procedural languages, such as BASIC and COBOL. By natural we mean that object-oriented programming allows you to construct programs the way we humans tend to think about things. For example, we tend to classify real-world entities such as vehicles, airplanes, ATM machines, and so on. We learn about such things by studying their *characteristics* and *behavior*. Take a class of vehicles, for example. All vehicles have certain characteristics, or *attributes*, such as engines, wheels, transmissions, and so on. Furthermore, all vehicles exhibit *behavior*, like acceleration, deceleration (braking), and turning. In other words, we have a general abstract impression of a vehicle through its attributes and behavior. This abstract model of a vehicle hides all the "nuts and bolts" that are contained in the vehicle. As a result, we think of the vehicle in terms of its attributes and behavior rather than its nuts and bolts, although without the nuts and bolts, a real-world vehicle could not exist. How do objects relate to classes? Well, your car is an example, or instance, of the vehicle class. It possesses all the attributes and behavior of any vehicle but is a specific example of a vehicle. Likewise, in object-oriented programming, we create an abstract class that describes the general attributes and behavior of a programming entity, then create objects of the class that will be actually manipulated within the program, just as your car is the thing that you actually drive, not your general abstract notion of a vehicle. You will begin learning about classes and objects in this chapter.

You will get your first exposure to the structure of Java in this chapter as you learn about the various types of data contained in the Java language. Data are any information that must be processed by the Java program. However, before Java can process any information, it must know what type of data it is dealing with. As a result, any information processed by Java must be categorized into one of the legal *data types* defined for Java.

The *primitive data types* that you will learn about in this chapter are the *integer*, *floating-point*, *character*, and *Boolean* data types. It is important that you understand this idea of data classification, because it is one of the most important concepts in any language. Once you learn the general characteristics and behavior of each data type, you will learn how to create constants and variables for use in a Java program.

In addition to the primitive data types employed by Java, this chapter will introduce you to the programmer-defined data type called a ***class***. Here, the term programmer-defined refers to classes that you, the programmer, will define. The class construct is particularly important for you to learn, because it allows you to create your own classes for developing object-oriented programs.

Finally, you will be introduced to the overall structure of a Java program in general.

At the end of this chapter, you will be asked to write, enter, and execute your first Java programs. If you have not already done so, it's probably a good idea for you to familiarize yourself with the operation of your system at this time. You should know how to load the Java compiler, enter and edit programs, compile programs, debug programs, and run programs.

3-1 THE IDEA OF DATA ABSTRACTION AND CLASSES

Just as Java programs are object-oriented, so are the data that the programs operate upon. You might be thinking: "Data are data, what's all this fuss about data?" First, you must think of data as any information that the computer might perform operations on or manipulate. So, let's define a ***data object*** to be any item of information that is manipulated or operated on by the computer. Many different types of data objects exist during the execution of a program. Some of these data objects will be programmer-defined while others will be system-defined.

Now, think about the types of information, or data objects, that a computer manipulates. Of course, a computer manipulates numbers, or ***numeric data***. One of the primary uses of a computer is to perform calculations on numeric data, right? But what about ***character*** data? Isn't the computer operating with character data when it prints out your name? Thus, numeric data and character data comprise two different ***classes*** of data. What makes them different? Well, numeric data consist of numbers, whereas character data consist of alphanumeric symbols. In addition, the operations defined for these two classes of data will be different.

A ***class*** describes the data attributes and behavior of its objects.

Now, what's all this class stuff? Well, we say that a ***class*** describes the data characteristics, or attributes, as well as legal operations, or behavior, of its objects. Remember the vehicle analogy cited in the chapter introduction. The notion of a vehicle describes things such as engines and transmissions (the attributes), as well as acceleration and deceleration (the behavior), for any actual vehicle objects such as your own car. Well, we can look at data in the same natural way. Take the integers as an example of a data class. The attributes, or characteristics, of integers is that they include all the whole number data values between minus infinity and plus infinity. Furthermore, there is a set of operations specifically defined for the integers. These operations include addition, subtraction, multiplication, and division, among others, and define the behavior of the integers. Thus, the set of whole numbers from minus infinity to plus infinity, along with their related operations, form a class. Any object created for this integer class, such as an integer variable, can only be a whole number value and only be used in an operation specifically defined for integers just as any actual vehicle objects looks and behaves like a vehicle. In fact, we say that the integer class forms an ***abstract data type***, or **ADT**, as shown in Figure 3-1.

An ***abstract data type (ADT)*** is a class that describes the data attributes and behavior of its objects.

You were introduced to the idea of abstraction in the last chapter. You found that abstraction, as applied to problem solving, allowed you to concentrate on the problem solution, without worrying about the implementation details. The same is true with ADTs. Abstract data types allow you to work with data objects without concern for how the data objects are stored inside the computer or how the data operations are performed inside the computer. This is referred to as ***data abstraction***. Let's take the addition operation as an example. Integer addition, by definition, dictates that you must supply two integer arguments to be added, and it will return the integer sum of the two. Do you care about the details of how the computer implements addition or how the computer represents integers in memory? Of course not! All you care about is what information needs to be supplied to the addition operation to perform its job and what information is returned by the operation. In other words, all you care about is *what* must be supplied to the addition operation and *how* the operation will respond. This is called ***behavior***—how the ADT, or class, will act and react for a given operation.

> The term ***behavior***, as associated with classes and ADTs, has to do with how the ADT, or class, will act and react for a given operation.

You will learn more about ADTs and behavior later in the text. For now, it is only important that you understand the concept as applied to Java ADTs.

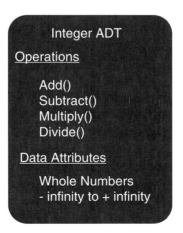

Figure 3-1 The integers can be considered an abstract data type, or class of data, where the arithmetic operations on the integers define the behavior of any objects defined for the integer class.

The Java language supports several different classes, or types, of data as shown in Figure 3-2.

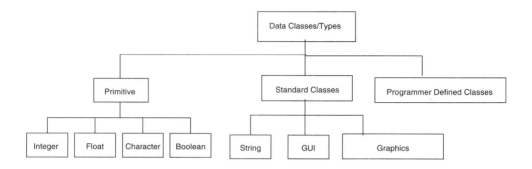

Figure 3-2 Data class/type hierarchy in the Java language.

The primitive data types are those that are simple and are predefined to, or "built into," the Java language. These consist of integer numbers and floating-point (real, decimal) numbers, as well as character data. You will learn about these primitive data types shortly.

The standard class category consists of classes that are also predefined by the Java language. These include the string, GUI, and graphics classes, among others. We say that these classes are complex data classes, in the sense that they are made up of the other simpler primitive data types. As an example, your name is simply a collection of simple characters that are combined to form a *string*. Other classes in this category include graphical component classes such as *polygon*, *rectangle*, *button*, *menu*, and *checkbox*, just to mention a few. These standard classes allow you to create graphical images and windowed programs and are part of Java's *Abstract Windowing Toolkit (AWT)* package of classes. In fact, Java includes literally hundreds of built-in classes that allow you to do everything from taking the square root of a number to generating graphics and windows. You will learn about many of these as you go through this book.

The programmer-defined *class* category provides the foundation for object-oriented programming (OOP) in Java. You now know that the Java language includes *standard* classes. Well, the Java *class* construct allows you, the programmer, to create your own data classes. For example, suppose that you have been hired to write an application program to control an ATM machine. The ATM machine is required to handle various types of data with specific operations defined for those data, such as deposit and withdrawal. Doesn't this sound like an ideal application for a class, because a class is a collection of data along with a set of operations defined for those data? Obviously, there is no standard ATM machine class built into the Java language. However, the Java class construct allows you to build your own ATM class, which will define all the data attributes and behavior associated with an ATM machine.

   A Java class is usually composed of primitive data types. In addition, classes include ***methods*** that operate on the class data. These methods define the behavior of the class. Thus, the Java class is ideal for implementing ADTs, because it can be used to define the data attributes of the ADT as well as the behavior of the ADT.

> A ***method*** in Java is a subprogram that returns a value or performs some specific task related to an algorithm, such as I/O.

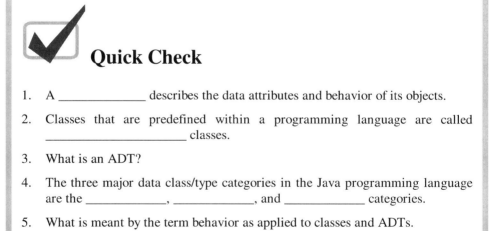

Quick Check

1. A _____ describes the data attributes and behavior of its objects.

2. Classes that are predefined within a programming language are called _____ classes.

3. What is an ADT?

4. The three major data class/type categories in the Java programming language are the _____, _____, and _____ categories.

5. What is meant by the term behavior as applied to classes and ADTs.

6. What is a method?

7. Why is the Java class ideal for implementing your own ADTs?

3-2 THE PRIMITIVE DATA TYPES IN JAVA

Recall that primitive data types are built into the Java language. This built-in feature simply means that the Java compiler recognizes any legal data values contained in a primitive type. There are four primitive types of data that we need to discuss: *integer*, *floating-point*, *character* and *Boolean*.

The Integer Types

As you know, integers are the whole numbers. They may be positive, negative, or 0. In a math course, you most likely learned that there are no theoretical limits to the integers. They can range from minus infinity ($-\infty$) to plus infinity ($+\infty$). However, there are practical limits in the real world of computers. In Java, the largest and smallest possible integer values depend on the particular type of integer that is being used. So, you're thinking that integers are integers; how can there be different types of integers? Well, the Java language defines four separate integer types that define four separate ranges for integer objects. They are **byte**, **short**, **int**, and **long**. As you can see from Table 3-1, each integer type defines a legal range of integer values.

TABLE 3-1 JAVA INTEGER TYPES AND CORRESPONDING RANGES

Integer Type	Range	Bytes
byte	−128 to +127	1
short	−32768 to +32767	2
int	−2147483648 to +2147483647	4
long	−9223372036854775808 to +9223372036854775807	8

You might be wondering why there are different types of integers. Why not just define one type that will provide enough range for most applications? For instance, why not use the **long** type all the time, because it provides the largest range of values? Well, each of the preceding integer types employs a predefined number of memory bytes to represent an integer value. For example, **int** requires 4 bytes of memory to represent a value, and **long** requires twice as many, or 8 bytes, to represent a value. Thus, it takes twice as much memory space to represent **long** integers as it does **int** integers. In addition, it would take twice as long to fetch a **long** as an **int**, using a 16-bit CPU. So, the idea is to use the type of integer that has enough range to satisfy a given application. For most applications, **int** will do the job and provide for efficient execution and memory utilization. In this text, we will always use **int**, unless we know we need a **long** to store a very big integer. The **byte** and **short** integer types are more for advanced programmers who will know best when to use them.

Example 3-1

Which of the following are *not* legal **short** integer values according to Table 3-1?

a. +35
b. 35
c. −247
d. 0
e. 3.14
f. 32,767
g. 32768

Solution

The values in a, b, c, and d are all legal **short** values in Java, because they are all whole numbers within the defined range of **short**. Notice that +35 and 35 are both legal representations of the integer value 35.

The values in e, f, and g are not legal **short** values in Java. The value 3.14 is not an integer because it is not a whole number. The value 32,767 is an integer within the predefined range but is not legal in Java, because it contains a comma. Commas are not allowed as part of numeric values in Java. Finally, the value 32768 is not a legal **short** value in Java, because it is outside the predefined **short** range.

DEBUGGING TIP

You must be especially aware of the integer range limits imposed by Java when performing integer calculations within your Java programs. For example, multiplying two integers could easily produce an integer result beyond this range, resulting in an incorrect result. This is called an *overflow* condition. Depending on where it occurs, an overflow condition might or might not generate an error message during program compiling or execution. Even if no overflow error message is generated, the operation will always produce an incorrect result.

Example 3-2

Which of the following **short** operations will generate an overflow condition in Java? (Use Table 3-1 to determine the legal **short** range, and assume that the * symbol means multiplication and the / symbol means division.)

a. 32 * 1000
b. 100 * 1000
c. (100 * 1000)/5

Solution

a. 32 * 1000 = 32000, which is within the predefined **short** range. No overflow condition exists.
b. 100 * 1000 = 100000, which is outside the predefined **short** range. The overflow condition will result in an incorrect integer result.
c. (100 * 1000)/5 = 100000/5 = 20000. Although the final result is within the predefined **short** range, an overflow condition will occur, thereby generating an incorrect result. Why? Because the multiplication operation in the numerator results in a value outside the **short** range.

One final point: You probably have noticed that the word **short**, for example, is set in bold type. Such a word in Java is called a *keyword*. Keywords have a specific meaning to the Java compiler and are used to perform a specific task. You cannot use a keyword for anything other than the specific operation for which it is defined. Java contains about 60 keywords, including **short**. You will learn about other keywords in subsequent chapters. In any event, from now on all keywords will be printed in bold type so that you can easily recognize them.

The Floating-Point Types

Floating-point data values include all of the whole number integers as well as any value between two whole numbers that must be represented using a decimal point. Examples include the following:

$$-2.56$$
$$1.414$$
$$-3.0$$

All of the foregoing values have been written using *fixed decimal-point* notation. Fixed decimal-point notation requires a sign, followed by an unsigned integer, followed by a decimal point, followed by another unsigned integer. This format is as follows:

FIXED DECIMAL FORMAT FOR A FLOATING-POINT VALUE

(+ or − sign)(integer).(integer)

Another way to represent a very large or a very small floating-point value is with scientific notation, called *exponential format*. With this notation, the floating-point value is written as a decimal-point value multiplied by a power of 10. The general format is as follows:

EXPONENTIAL FORMAT FOR A FLOATING-POINT VALUE

(+ or − sign)(decimal-point value)e(integer exponent value)

In both the foregoing formats, the leading + sign is optional if the value is positive. Examples of floating-point values using exponential format include

$$1.32e3$$
$$0.45e{-}6$$
$$-35.02e{-}4$$

Here, the letter *e* means "times 10 to the power of." The letter *e* is used because there is no provision on a standard computer keyboard to type above a line to show exponential values. Again, the + sign is optional for both the decimal-point value and the exponential value when they are positive.

Example 3-3

Convert the following exponential values to fixed decimal values.

a. 1.32e3
b. 0.45e−6
c. −35.02e−4
d. −1.333e7

Solution

a. $1.32e3 = 1.32 \times 10^3 = 1320.0$
b. $0.45e{-}6 = 0.45 \times 10^{-6} = 0.00000045$
c. $-35.02e{-}4 = -35.02 \times 10^{-4} = -0.003502$
d. $-1.333e7 = -1.333 \times 10^7 = -13330000.0$

You might be wondering if there is any practical limit to the range of floating-point values that can be used in Java. As with integers, Java defines different types of floating-point data that dictate different legal value ranges. The floating-point types defined by Java are summarized in Table 3-2.

TABLE 3-2 FLOATING-POINT TYPES AND CORRESPONDING RANGES IN JAVA

Float type	Range	Bytes
float	Roughly $\pm3.40282347 \times 10^{38}$ (7 significant digits)	4
double	Roughly $\pm1.79769313 \times 10^{+308}$ (15 significant digits)	8

The greater the value range, the greater precision you will get when using floating-point values. However, as you can see from Table 3-2, it costs you more memory space to achieve greater precision when using a floating-point type. Again, the application will dictate the required precision, which, in turn, dictates which floating-point type to use. For most applications, we will use **double** to assure the proper precision.

Example 3-4

In data communications, you often see quantities expressed using the prefixes in Table 3-3.

TABLE 3-3 COMMON PREFIXES USED IN DATA COMMUNICATIONS

Prefix	Symbol	Meaning
pico	p	10^{-12}
nano	n	10^{-9}
micro	μ	10^{-6}
milli	m	10^{-3}
kilo	k	10^{3}
mega	M	10^{6}
giga	G	10^{9}

Given the following quantities

220 picoseconds (ps)
1 kilohertz (kHz)
10 megahertz (MHz)
1.25 milliseconds (ms)
25.3 microseconds (μs)
300 nanoseconds (ns)

a. Express each of the listed quantities in exponential form.
b. Express each of the listed quantities in fixed decimal form.

Solution

a. To express in exponential form, you simply convert the prefix to its respective power of 10 using Table 3-3. Then, use exponential notation to write the value, like this:

220 ps = 220e−12 second
1 kHz = 1e3 hertz
10 MHz = 10e6 hertz
1.25 ms = 1.25e−3 second
25.3 μs = 25.3e−6 second
300 ns = 300e−9 second

b. To express each in its fixed decimal form, simply move the decimal point according to the exponent value.

220 ps = 220e−12 second = 0.000000000220 second
1 kHz = 1e3 hertz = 1000.0 hertz
10 MHz = 10e6 hertz = 10000000.0 hertz
1.25 ms = 1.25e−3 second = 0.00125 second
25.3 μs = 25.3e−6 second = 0.0000253 second
300 ns = 300e−9 second = 0.000000300 second

Example 3-5

Java includes several ***standard methods*** that you can call upon to perform specific operations.

A ***standard method*** is a predefined operation that the Java compiler will recognize and evaluate to return a result.

One such method is the *sqrt()* method. The *sqrt()* method is part of the built-in *Math* class in Java and is used to find the square root of a floating-point number. As an example, execution of *Math.sqrt(2)* will return the value 1.414. Notice that the *Math* class *calls* the *sqrt()* method using the dot, •, operator. Now, given the standard *sqrt()* method, determine the result of the following operations:

a. Math.sqrt(3.5)
b. Math.sqrt(–25)
c. Math.sqrt(4e–20)

Solution

a. Math.sqrt(3.5) = 1.87
b. Math.sqrt(–25) is imaginary and will generate a run-time error when encountered during a program execution.
c. Math.sqrt(4e–20) = 2e–10

The Character Type

All of the symbols on your computer keyboard are characters. This includes all the upper- and lowercase alphabetic characters as well as the punctuation, numbers, control keys, and special symbols. Java employs the *Unicode* character code to represent characters inside the computer. Some of the more common codes are given in Table 3-4. As you can see from the table, each character has a unique numeric representation code because, in order for the CPU to work with character data, the individual characters must be converted to a numeric (actually, binary) code. When you press a character on the keyboard, the CPU "sees" the binary representation of that character, not the character itself. Table 3-4 provides decimal equivalents of the Unicode characters. The developers of Java decided to go with the Unicode character code because it is an international standard and is used to represent characters of many different languages. Unicode is a 2-byte code where the first 128 values of code represent the common ASCII character codes used in the U.S.A, Canada, and the U.K.

TABLE 3-4 UNICODE/ASCII CHARACTER CODE TABLE

Dec	Char	Dec	Char	Dec	Char	Dec	Char
0	^@ NUL	32	SPC	64	@	96	
1	^A SOH	33	!	65	A	97	a
2	^B STX	34	"	66	B	98	b
3	^C ETX	35	#	67	C	99	c
4	^D EOT	36	$	68	D	100	d
5	^E ENQ	37	%	69	E	101	e
6	^F ACK	38	&	70	F	102	f
7	^G BEL	39	'	71	G	103	g
8	^H BS	40	(	72	H	104	h
9	^I HT	41	)	73	I	105	i
10	^J LF	42	*	74	J	106	j
11	^K VT	43	+	75	K	107	k
12	^L FF	44	,	76	L	108	l
13	^M CR	45	-	77	M	109	m
14	^N SO	46	.	78	N	110	n
15	^O SI	47	/	79	O	111	o
16	^P DLE	48	0	80	P	112	p
17	^Q DC1	49	1	81	Q	113	q
18	^R DC2	50	2	82	R	114	r
19	^S DC3	51	3	83	S	115	s
20	^T DC4	52	4	84	T	116	t
21	^U NAK	53	5	85	U	117	u
22	^V SYN	54	6	86	V	118	v
23	^W ETB	55	7	87	W	119	w
24	^X CAN	56	8	88	X	120	x
25	^Y EM	57	9	89	Y	121	y
26	^Z SUB	58	:	90	Z	122	z
27	^[ESC	59	;	91	[	123	{
28	^\ FS	60	<	92	\	124	|
29	^] GS	61	=	93	]	125	}
30	^^ RS	62	>	94	^	126	~
31	^-- US	63	?	95	--	127	DEL

Example 3-6

Using Table 3-4, look up the decimal code for each of the following characters.

a. 'A'
b. 'Z'
c. 'a'
d. 'z'
e. '#'

Solution

Using Table 3-4, you get the following:

a. 'A' = 65
b. 'Z' = 90
c. 'a' = 97
d. 'z' = 122
e. '#' = 35

The foregoing example points out several characteristics of character data. First, each character has a unique numeric representation inside the computer. Because each character has a unique numeric representation, the characters are ordered, or scalar. For instance, 'A' < 'Z', because the numeric representation for 'A' (65) is less than the numeric representation for 'Z' (90). Likewise, '#' < 'a' < 'z', because 35 < 97 < 122. In general the uppercase characters have a lower order than the lowercase characters. Next, notice that whenever a character is specified, it is always enclosed in single quotes like this: 'a'. This is a requirement of the Java language.

Characters are stored in the machine as integer values, so you can perform arithmetic operations on character data. For instance, you can add 1 to the character 'A' and get the character 'B'. This is an example of the flexibility built into the Java language; however, *with this flexibility comes responsibility*. You must be able to predict the results you will get. Other languages, like Pascal, will not allow you to perform arithmetic operations on characters.

CAUTION

Java will allow you to perform arithmetic operations on character data; however, be careful because the results can sometimes be difficult to predict. What do you get when you add the character 'A' to the character 'B' or when you multiply these two characters?

The Boolean Type

Boolean data, consisting solely of the values **true** and **false**, is the simplest type of data that can be employed in a program. Boolean data play an important role in a program's ability to make decisions, because all program decisions are Boolean decisions, based on whether a given condition is true or false. You will learn this later when we discuss program decision making and iteration.

Java specifies a Boolean data type called **boolean**. This type contains two elements, **true** and **false**. The **boolean** type is a scalar type, meaning that the elements within the type are ordered. By definition, **false** is defined to be less than **true**. The words **boolean**, **true**, and **false** are keywords and, therefore, cannot be used for any other purpose in a program.

 Quick Check

1. What is the approximate range of values that can be provided via the standard **int** class?

2. What type of error occurs when, as a result of a calculation, a value exceeds its predefined range?

3. The two ways that floating-point values can be represented in a Java program are using either _____ or _____ format.

4. Which is larger, the character 'a' or the character 'z'?

5. Which is larger, the character 'a' or the character 'A'?

6. How many bytes of storage are required by the string "The United States of America"?

7. The primitive data type that contains only two elements, **true** and **false**, is the _____ data type.

3-3 CONSTANTS, VARIABLES, AND STRING OBJECTS

From mathematics, you know that a constant is a value that never changes, thereby remaining a fixed value. A common example is the constant *pi* (π). Here, the Greek symbol π is used to represent a floating-point value of approximately 3.14159. This value of π never changes, thus remaining constant regardless of where and how it might be used in a calculation.

On the other hand, a variable is something that can take on different values. In mathematics, the symbols x and y are often used to denote variables. Using the equation $y = 3x + 2$, you can substitute different values of x to generate different values of y. Thus, the values of x and y in the equation are variable.

The values of variables are stored in main working memory of a computer for later use within a program. Each variable has a symbolic name, or ***identifier***, that locates its value in memory. This idea is illustrated in Figure 3-3. The memory contents located by the identifiers *age*, *studentID*, and *gpa* might change during the execution of the program. As a result, these symbols are called variables.

All constants and variables to be used in a Java program must be defined prior to their use in the program. The reason that we must define constants and variables in a language is twofold. First, the compiler must know the value of a constant before it is used and must reserve memory locations to store variables. Second, the compiler must know the data type of the constants and variables so that it knows their attributes and behavior. Now, let's see how constants and variables are defined in Java.

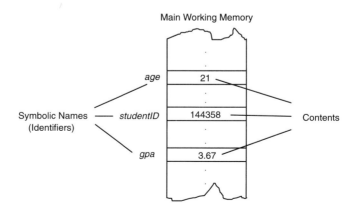

Figure 3-3   Each variable has a symbolic name, or identifier, that locates its value in memory.

Defining Constants

To define a constant, you must use the keywords **static** and **final**, like this:

CONSTANT DEFINITION FORMAT

static final *data type constant identifier* **=** *constant value*;

First, a word about how syntax will be formatted in this text. Words or symbols that must appear as part of the syntax will be shown outright in bold, such as the words **static** and **final** and the symbol **=** in the foregoing format box. Those things that you must decide as a programmer will be shown in italic type such as the data type, constant identifier, and constant value in the foregoing format box.

Now, let's look at the syntax required to define a constant. The definition begins with the keywords **static** and **final**. The keyword **static** makes the constant a class item. This means that a constant can only be defined at the class level and not inside a method, even *main()*. More about this later. The keyword **final** is used to signify that the value of the constant can never change within the course of the program execution. Next, you must specify the primitive data type of the constant, followed by a constant identifier. The identifier is the name of the constant that will be replaced by the constant value during compile time. To identify constants easily within your program, we suggest that your constant identifiers always be in all capital letters. This way, it makes it much more clear that no statement should attempt to alter the constant value. An equals sign (=) is used to separate the constant identifier from its defined value. Finally, each constant definition must end with a semicolon.

Example 3-7

Suppose you wish to use the price of 33 cents for a first-class postage stamp in your Java program. In addition, your program must calculate the sales tax required for a given sales item based on a sales tax rate of 7 percent. Define appropriate constants to represent the price of a stamp and the sales tax rate.

Solution

By using the format given before, the postage price and sales tax rate are defined as follows:

```
static final double POSTAGE = 0.33;
static final double TAX_RATE = 0.07;
```

With these definitions, you would simply use the words *POSTAGE* and *TAX_RATE* when performing calculations within the program. For instance, to find the total price of a sales item, you would write the expression

totalPrice = price + (price * TAX_RATE);

When the program is compiled, the compiler simply substitutes the constant value 0.07 for the *TAX_RATE* identifier. What about the identifiers *price* and *totalPrice* in this expression? Are these constants or variables? You're right—they are both variables, because their values will change, depending on the price of the item. What data type must *price* and *totalPrice* be? In other words, what type of data is required for this application: integer, floating-point, or character? Right again—floating-point, because you must provide for decimal quantities to allow for dollars and cents. Thus, *price* and *totalPrice* must be defined as a floating-point variables. You will find out how to do this shortly.

STYLE TIP

Always code your constant identifiers in all caps so that they are easily identified as constants within your program. Always code variable identifiers in lowercase. For a multiword variable identifier, the first letter of the first word should be lowercase, then the first letter of each succeeding word should be uppercase. For example, the two foregoing variable identifiers were *totalPrice* and *price*. This is the standard Java convention for variable identifiers.

Notice also in Example 3-7 that the constant identifier *TAX_RATE* is made up of two words, *TAX* and *RATE*. The Java compiler will not allow you to separate multiword identifiers using spaces. Thus, we have chosen to separate the two words with the underscore symbol (_). Also, notice that the variable identifier *totalPrice* is made up of two words. Here, the two words are run together with the first letter of the second word capitalized. These two techniques will be used throughout the text when using multiword identifiers:

1. Uppercase for constant identifiers, separating words within a multiword identifier with the underscore, _, symbol.
2. Lowercase for variable identifiers, capitalizing the first letter of each word in a multiword identifier, except for the first word.

Here are some other rules that govern the use of identifiers in the Java language:

- The first 32 characters of an identifier are significant.
- Identifiers can contain the letters *a* to *z*, *A* to *Z*, the digits *0* to *9*, and the underscore, _, symbol.
- No spaces or punctuation, except the underscore, _, symbol, are allowed.
- Identifiers in Java are *case-sensitive*. Thus, the identifiers *Tax* and *tax* are seen as two different identifiers by the compiler.

You are probably wondering why we should define constants using identifiers. Why not just insert the constant value into the expression whenever it is needed, like this:

totalPrice = price + (price * 0.07);

Have you ever known postage or sales tax rates to change? Of course you have! You might say that these types of "constants" are not constant forever. So, when using constants such as these, which might be subject to change in the future, it is much easier to define them in one single place. Then if they need to be changed, you only have to make a single change in your program. Otherwise, a change must be made in each place that you use the constant within the program.

Defining Variables

Before you can use a variable in a Java program, it must be defined. When you define a variable, the compiler reserves a location inside the computer memory for the variable value. When you define a variable, you are telling Java what type of data you will be storing for the variable. To define a variable, you must specify its data type, its name, and an optional initializing value. Here's the format:

VARIABLE DEFINITION FORMAT

data type   variable object identifier = optional initializing value;

The foregoing format requires that the variable data type be listed first, followed by the variable identifier, or name. The first word in a variable name should begin with a lowercase letter, with all subsequent words beginning with an uppercase letter. You can terminate the definition at this point with a semicolon, or you can add an optional equals symbol, =, followed by an initializing value, and then the semicolon to terminate the definition.

PROGRAMMING NOTE

It is always good practice to initialize variables when they are defined. When a variable is not initialized, you will often get a compiler error in Java. Generally, numeric variables will be initialized to the value 0 or 1, and character variables will be initialized with a blank.

Example 3-8

Suppose you were asked to write a Java program to calculate the part-time hourly pay for an employee, given his/her rate of hourly pay and hours worked over the given time period. Define the necessary variables that will be used in the program for the calculation.

Solution

To solve this problem, you simply multiply the hourly rate by the number of hours worked like this:

$$P = R \times H$$

where

P is the pay, in dollars and cents.
R is the hourly rate of pay, in dollars and cents.
H is the number of hours worked.

Here, the variable identifiers are given to be P, R, and H. Now, the question is: What data type must these variables belong to? You know that P, R, and H will be used to represent numeric data, so your decision as to their type reduces to integer or floating-point. If you define P, R, and H as integers, you will be limited to using whole number values for these variables within your program; however, this might create a problem because pay, rate of pay, and hourly values often are decimal values. So, let's define them as double floating-point variables, like this:

```
double P = 0.0;     // GROSS PAY
double R = 0.0;     // HOURLY RATE OF PAY
double H = 0.0;     // NUMBER OF HOURS WORKED
```

Notice that each variable is defined as a double floating-point variable and initialized to the value 0.0. Of course, because these are variables, their values will change during the execution of the program. Notice also that each variable is commented to indicate its purpose within the program.

STYLE TIP

Java allows identifiers, or names, to be any length, where the first 32 characters are significant. Thus, your programs will become much more readable and self-documenting if you use words, rather than letters and symbols, to represent constants and variables. For instance, the variable definition in Example 3-8 would be much more readable to a user if you were to define pay, rate of pay, and hours worked like this:

```
double grossPay = 0.0;      // GROSS PAY
double hourlyRate = 0.0;    // HOURLY RATE OF PAY
double hoursWorked = 0.0;   // NUMBER OF HOURS WORKED
```

By using this definition, the actual words (*grossPay*, *hourlyRate*, and *hoursWorked*) would be used within your program when calculating payroll. So, the statement required to calculate the gross pay would appear in your program as follows:

```
grossPay = hourlyRate * hoursWorked;
```

Notice the use of the equals symbol, =, in this statement. This is the way that you must *assign* quantities in Java. Also, notice the use of the star symbol, *, for multiplication.

A word of caution: When using names as variable identifiers, you cannot use any punctuation within the name. For instance, the variable identifier *total(Sales)* to represent total sales is an illegal identifier in Java because of the parentheses. Two legal identifiers would be *totalSales* or *total_Sales*. In the first case, the two words are connected, with the first letter of the second word capitalized. In the second case, the underscore symbol, _, is used to separate the two words instead of a space. This symbol is okay to use within Java identifiers. You will see both of these techniques employed for identifiers throughout the remainder of this text.

Example 3-9

You must write a program to calculate the sales tax of a sales item using a sales tax rate of 7 percent. Define the appropriate constants and variables.

Solution

First, you must decide what identifiers to use. Always use word identifiers that best describe the related constant or variable. Let's use the word *salesTax* to identify the resulting calculation, the word *price* to identify the cost of the item, and the word *TAX_RATE* to identify the sales tax rate. So, using these identifiers, the sales tax calculation would be

salesTax = price * TAX_RATE;

Now, the question is: Which of these are variables and which are constants? Obviously, *salesTax* and *price* are variables, because they will change depending on the cost of the item. However, the *TAX_RATE* will be a constant, regardless of the cost of the item. So, we will define *salesTax* and *price* as variables and *TAX_RATE* as a constant, like this:

static final double TAX_RATE = 0.07; // CURRENT SALES TAX RATE
double price = 0.0;   // PRICE OF AN ITEM
double salesTax = 0.0;   // SALES TAX OF AN ITEM

Notice that both the variables are defined as double floating-point, because both will be decimal values. Suppose that you were to define the tax rate as a variable rather than a constant and initialize it to the value 0.07, like this:

double taxRate = 0.07;

There is no problem with this definition. The compiler will reserve storage for the variable *taxRate* and place the initial value of 0.07 at this storage location. However, the value of *taxRate* could be changed by the program, whereas it could not be changed if defined as a constant. Would this be desirable? Probably not, since the sales tax rate would not likely change during the course of the program execution.

Once a constant or a variable is defined, you can write its value to the screen like this:

System.out.println(salesTax);

As you will discover in Chapter 4, *println()* is a standard method used by Java to display information to the screen. Here, *System.out* is an object and *println()* is a method defined for this object. It might seem awkward spelling an object name with a dot in the middle of it as in *System.out*. However, this is just the required Java syntax and it will take on more meaning later, when we discuss classes and objects in more detail.

We say that the *System.out* object calls its *println()* method using the dot, •, operator like this: *System.out.println()*. The items to be displayed are placed between the parentheses of the *println()* method.

> The *println()* method is used by Java to display information on your system monitor. The *println()* method is called by the *System.out* object using the dot, •, operator like this: *System.out.println();*

Example 3-10

Choose an appropriate name and define a variable that could be used to represent the days of the week. Assume that the days of the week are represented by the first letter of each day.

Solution

Let's pick a meaningful variable identifier, such as *daysOfWeek*. Now, because the days of the week will be represented by the first letter of each day, the variable must be of the character data type. When defining character variables, you must use the keyword **char** in the variable definition, as follows:

```
char daysOfWeek = ' ';  // SINGLE CHARACTER FOR ANY DAY OF THE WEEK
                        //INITIALIZED WITH A BLANK
```

Notice that the character variable is initialized with a blank character. To code a blank character, simply type a single quote, a space, then another single quote.

Do you see any problems with the definition in Example 3-10? There are no syntax errors, and it is perfectly legal as far as Java is concerned. But are there any problems associated with the usage of this variable? A character variable is limited to representing a *single* character at a given time. This is why each day of the week must be represented by a single letter. However, using the first letter of each day creates a problem. Does an 'S' represent Saturday or Sunday? Likewise, does a 'T' mean Tuesday or Thursday? The solution to this dilemma is found in the use of strings, the topic of the next section.

Boolean Variables

Variables can be defined for the **boolean** type just as you define any other variable—by listing its data type followed by the variable identifier. Here's an example that illustrates this idea.

Example 3-11

Define a **boolean** variable called *decision* for use in a decision-making operation. Initialize the variable with a **boolean** value of **false**.

Solution

Boolean variables are often used in a program for decision-making operations. A **boolean** variable, called *decision*, can be defined for such a purpose as follows:

```
boolean decision = false;
```

With this definition, the variable *decision* can be used in a program, taking on the values of **true** or **false** as required by the program logic.

String Objects

A string is simply a collection of characters. Examples of strings include your name, address, and phone number, as well as the sentence you are now reading.

Strings in Java are always enclosed in double quotes, like this: "Java". Recall that individual characters are enclosed in single quotes. Thus, 'J' denotes an individual character, whereas "J" denotes a string of one character.

A string is not a primitive data type in Java because, by definition, a string is a complex data type formed by combining simpler data types, namely characters. Also, there are special operations, or methods, defined for the specific purpose of manipulating strings. Doesn't this sound like a class (data combined with operations defined for that data)? For this reason, Java provides a **String** class that defines what a string should be (a collection of characters) as well as operations, or methods that can be used on a string.

PROGRAMMING TIP

Double quotes around a number, such as "1234", indicate a string of characters and *not* numeric data. In fact, the string "1234" requires 8 bytes of storage, whereas the **int** 1234 requires only 4 bytes of storage. In addition, arithmetic operations cannot be performed on the string "1234". For these reasons, numeric data should be represented using a numeric type and not the string class.

Recall that a class describes the attributes (characteristics) and behavior (operations) for its objects. In other words, a class is a blueprint for any objects of the class. You *do not* manipulate a class within your program. Instead, you define an object of a given class, then manipulate the object within your program, just as you define a variable of a primitive data type and manipulate the variable within your program.

To define an object of a predefined class, you simply list the class name, followed by a space, then the object name like this:

OBJECT DEFINITION FORMAT

class name   object name;

To define a string object, we use the class name **String**, followed by an appropriate string name, or identifier. For example, suppose you need to create three string objects, one for your name, one for your address, and one for your phone number. Here is how these objects could be created:

```
String name = "Andrew C. Staugaard, Jr. ";        // MY NAME
String address = "999 Code Road, Java City, USA ";  // MY ADDRESS
String phoneNumber = "(012)345-6789 ";              // MY PHONE NUMBER
```

These definitions tell Java that *name*, *address*, and *phoneNumber* are objects of the **String** class. In addition, each object is initialized with a string value. Could the string values of these objects be changed? Of course they could, because each object is a variable object. Notice also that the string values are enclosed within double quotation marks and a comment is placed after each object definition. Get used to commenting the purpose of all of your variables and objects, because it's just a good habit to get into.

Once a string object is defined, you can display its value using the *println()* method like this:

```
System.out.println(name);
System.out.println(address);
System.out.println(phoneNumber);
```

We can even use the *println()* method, along with the + operator to display two strings together like this:

System.out.println("My name: " + name);

This statement displays the fixed string, "My name: ", followed by the string stored in the object *name*. Notice that the fixed string is surrounded with double quotation marks while the string object is not. The + operator tells Java to display the first string, "My name: ", followed by the second string, *name*. Also, notice that there is a space or two after the colon and before the ending quotation marks in "My name: ". The purpose of the spacing is to separate the colon from the actual name stored in memory. Thus the display will show the following:

My name: Andrew C. Staugaard, Jr.

> The + operator is used in the *println()* method to concatenate the display items together. The term *concatenate* means to join together.

Example 3-12

Using the character variable definition back in Example 3-11 presents a usage problem when representing the days of the week, because a character variable can only represent a single character at a time. Solve this problem by using a string object definition.

Solution

A string object can be used to represent any number of consecutive characters. So why not define *daysOfWeek* as a string object, like this:

String daysOfWeek = " ";   //DAYS OF THE WEEK INITIALIZED WITH BLANKS

With this definition, the object *daysOfWeek* can be used to represent the entire day of the week word ("Sunday", "Monday", "Tuesday", etc.). Notice that the string object is initialized with an empty string using empty double quotation marks. It is always good practice to initialize variables and objects when they are defined. Of course, during the execution of the program, an actual string value can be stored in *daysOfWeek* using an *assignment* statement, like this:

daysOfWeek = "Friday";

The assignment stores the string *"Friday"* in memory for the value of the *daysOfWeek* string object. Now, what will the following statement do?

```
System.out.println("The current day of the week is " + daysOfWeek);
```

You're right, this statement will display the following on the system monitor:

```
The current day of the week is Friday
```

String Methods

Since **String** is a class, it includes operations, or methods, that are specifically written to manipulate string data. As a result, any object of the **String** class can call upon one of these methods to manipulate or provide information about its string. Some of the methods available in the **String** class are summarized in Table 3-5.

As you have seen before, a method is called by its object by placing a dot between the object name and the method. For example, suppose that you wish to display the length of a string in your program. Here is a code segment that will accomplish this task:

```
String employee = "John Doe";
System.out.println(employee.length());
```

Notice that the *System.out* object is calling the *println()* method via the dot operator and our *employee* string object is calling the *length()* method via the dot operator. This code would simply cause the length of the *employee* string, 8, to be displayed on the system monitor.

Example 3-13

Write a Java code segment that will display each of the *name*, *address*, and *phoneNumber* strings defined earlier, in all uppercase characters.

Solution

To convert each string to uppercase, each string object must call the *toUpperCase()* method from Table 3-5. This can be done within the *println()* method like this:

```
System.out.println(name.toUpperCase());
System.out.println(address.toUpperCase());
System.out.println(phoneNumber.toUpperCase());
```

The resulting display is:

ANDREW C. STAUGAARD, JR.
999 CODE ROAD, JAVA CITY, USA
(012)345-6789

TABLE 3-5 SOME STANDARD STRING METHODS

Method	Description	Use of
compareTo(s2)	Returns 0 if the calling string object equals *s2*, else returns a negative value if the calling string object is less than *s2* and a positive value if the calling string object is greater than *s2*.	String s1 = "Hello World"; String s2 = "hello world"; s1.compareTo(s2) returns a negative value
equals(s2)	Returns **true** if the calling string object equals *s2*, else returns **false**.	String s1 = "Hello World"; String s2 = "hello world"; s1.equals(s2) returns **false**
equalsIgnoreCase(s2)	Returns **true** if the calling string object equals *s2*, else returns **false**. Ignores case.	String s1 = "Hello World"; String s2 = "hello world"; s1.equalsIgnoreCase(s2) returns **true**
length()	Returns the length of the calling string object.	String s = "Hello World"; s.length() returns 11
toLowerCase()	Returns calling string object with all characters converted to lowercase.	String s = "Hello World"; s.toLowerCase() returns "hello world"
toUpperCase()	Returns calling string object with all characters converted to uppercase.	String s = "Hello World"; s.toUpperCase() returns "HELLO WORLD"
trim()	Returns calling string object with leading and trailing whitespace removed.	String s = " Hello World "; s.trim() returns "Hello World"

DEBUGGING TIP

Remember that Java is case-sensitive. Thus, using *ToUpperCase()* in place of *toUpperCase()* in the above code will cause a compile-time error.

You will have many occasions to manipulate strings within your Java programs using the string methods shown in Table 3-5. For now, just review each method in the table so that you get an idea of what can be done with strings. We will demonstrate the use of many of these methods as the need arises throughout the remainder of the text.

 Quick Check

1. What are two reasons for defining constants and variables in a Java program?

2. Define a constant called *PERIOD* that will insert a period wherever it is referenced in a program.

3. Define a constant object called *BOOK* that will insert the string "Java: For CIS" wherever it appears in a program.

4. Define a variable called *age* that will store the age of an employee.

5. Define a string object called *course* that will be initialized to a string value of "Accounting".

6. Write a statement to display the string stored in the object in question 5.

3-4 THE STRUCTURE OF A JAVA PROGRAM

You now have some of the basic ingredients to begin writing Java programs. You will be doing this shortly. However, before we leave this chapter, let's put things into some perspective and take an initial look at the overall structure of a Java program.

Recall that the Java language is a language based on classes. This idea is evident from the overall appearance of a Java application program. Look at Figure 3-4. Observe that any Java program consists of two sections: an ***import*** section and a ***class*** section.

```
//  ********************************************************************
//  A GENERAL COMMENT ABOUT THE PURPOSE OF THE
//  PROGRAM SHOULD GO HERE
//  ********************************************************************
//  IMPORT SECTION
        import  package1;
        import  package2;

//  CLASS SECTION
        public class <class name>
      {  // BEGIN CLASS BLOCK

        ┌─────────────────────────────────────┐
        │  CONSTANT DEFINITIONS GO HERE        │
        └─────────────────────────────────────┘
            public static void main(String[]args)
          {  // BEGIN MAIN METHOD BLOCK

            ┌─────────────────────────────────────────────────────┐
            │       VARIABLE DEFINITIONS GO HERE                   │
            └─────────────────────────────────────────────────────┘

            ┌─────────────────────────────────────────────────────┐
            │   STATEMENT SECTION OF PROGRAM GOES HERE             │
            │                                                     │
            └─────────────────────────────────────────────────────┘

          }  // END MAIN METHOD BLOCK
      }  // END CLASS BLOCK
```

Figure 3-4   The general structure of a Java program.

Notice at the top of the figure there is a general comment about the purpose of the program. As you have already seen, comments in Java are inserted into a program using a double *forward* slash (//). The double forward slash tells the compiler to ignore the rest of that particular line. Thus, a comment on any given line must begin with the double forward slash. The double forward slash can appear anyplace on a given line but anything after // on a given line is ignored by the compiler. We will be making extensive use of comments within programs in this text to *self-document* the Java code. We suggest that you do the same in your programs. Comments within your programs make them much easier to read and maintain.

The Import Section

The Java language contains many standard classes that are grouped into *packages*. A package is a set of related classes. The set of all packages forms the Java class library, sometimes called the *Java applications programming interface*, or *Java API*. To use any of the API classes, you must load them into your program using the **import** statement. For instance, later on you will be using the *Graphics* class in the *AWT* (*Abstract Windowing Toolkit*) package. The *Graphics* class will let you add some powerful graphics to your program. However, to use the *Graphics* class, it must be loaded into your program using the **import** statement like this:

```
import java.awt.Graphics;
```

This statement tells Java to load the *Graphics* class of the *awt* (*abstract windowing toolkit*) package and compile it as part of your program. What do you suppose this statement does?

```
import java.awt.*;
```

You're right if you thought to import all classes of the Java *awt* package. Here, the * is a wildcard character to mean "all" classes.

A ***package*** is a set of related classes.

What makes Java a great language is the large number of prewritten classes available in the Java API. Why develop your own class if there is already one included in the API? Using the Java API means that programmers can reuse the code already developed, rather than "reinventing the wheel" to develop their own code.

The Class Section

The class section of the program is where access to all the executable Java code resides. As you are already aware, a Java program is simply a collection of classes which interact with each other via class methods.

In Figure 3-5, there are only a single class and a single method. As you begin to build more complex programs, your programs will contain many classes and many different methods. For now, we will keep things simple.

The program class name should be something that is related to the application for which the program was written. For example, the following code might be used to declare a class for a payroll program:

```
public class Payroll
```

The keyword **public** means that this class is accessible to the entire program and the keyword **class** means that that *Payroll* is being declared as a class. The name of the class will be determined by the specific application for which the class is developed, in this case a payroll application. However, once a class name is determined, the program must be saved using this class name as the file name with a *.java* extension. From Figure 3-4 you see that a left curly brace, {, must follow the first line of the class declaration, prior to any other statements. This brace defines the beginning of the class block. At the bottom of Figure 3-5, you see a right curly brace, }. This brace is used to indicate the end of the class block. You must always use a set of curly braces, { }, to "frame" a block of code in Java.

> A Java application program must have the same name as the main class name plus a *.java* extension. Thus, if your program class name is *Sample*, the program must be saved with a file name of *Sample.java*. Class names always begin with a capital letter in Java.

Once the program class is declared, you will define any constants used by the program. An example of a constant definition that might go here is:

    static final double TAX_RATE = 0.07;

The keyword **static** makes the constant a class item. This means that a constant can only be defined at the class level and not inside a method, even *main()*. Thus, all constants will be defined immediately after the opening brace of a class. This makes them global, or accessible, to all methods within the class.

Method *main()*

Java applications always begin execution with a method called *main()*. The *main()* method must be declared inside the program class and the first line of this method must be:

public static void main(String args[])

The *main()* method identifier is preceded by the keywords **public**, **static**, and **void**. The reason for this will become apparent later on, so don't worry about it now. Again, you see a set of beginning/ending curly braces to frame the *main()* method block. Notice that the ending braces are commented at the bottom of the figure to indicate which brace ends method *main()* and which brace ends the class. It is always good practice to comment closing braces.

The statement section of *main( )* is the main executable body of the application program. The program instructions, or statements, go here. Each statement must be terminated with a semicolon. Even though a variable or object can be defined anywhere in a Java program prior to its use, we will usually define our program variables and objects at the beginning of *main( )* for clarity. This is just good style, since it acts as a table of contents of variables and objects used in the program.

Example 3-14

Using the program structure shown in Figure 3-5 and the definitions in Example 3-9, write a program that will calculate the sales tax of a sales item.

Solution

In Example 3-9, we used the following statement to calculate the sales tax:

salesTax = price * TAX_RATE;

where *salesTax* and *price* were defined as floating-point variables and *TAX_RATE* was defined as a constant with a value of 0.07.

Putting this information into the required Java program structure shown in Figure 3-5, you get the following:

```
//*****************************************************************
//
//THIS PROGRAM WILL CALCULATE THE SALES TAX  OF A SALES ITEM
//
//*****************************************************************

public class SalesTax
{ // BEGIN SalesTax CLASS

    //DEFINE CONSTANTS
    static final double TAX_RATE = 0.07;      // CURRENT SALES TAX RATE

    public static void main(String args[])
    { // BEGIN main() METHOD

        //DEFINE VARIABLES
        double price = 0.0;                    // PRICE OF AN ITEM
        double salesTax = 0.0;                 // SALES TAX OF AN ITEM

        //CALCULATE SALES TAX
        price = 1.95;                          // ASSIGN $1.95 TO Price
        salesTax = price * TAX_RATE;           // CALCULATE TAX
```

```
    //DISPLAY SALES TAX
    System.out.println("The sales tax is: " + salesTax);
  } //END main() METHOD
} // END SalesTax CLASS
```

This program will calculate the sales tax of an item, given the item price of $1.95. The program is very readable, and everything used within the program is clearly defined. We decided to name this class *SalesTax*. Very appropriate don't you think? Prior to *main()*, the *TAX_RATE* constant is defined to be 0.07. Method *main()* begins by defining the variables that are to be used within the main block. A value is assigned to *price*, followed by the calculation of the sales tax amount. Once the calculation is performed, the resulting sales tax value (*salesTax*) is displayed on the monitor using the *println()* method.

Note that the program statements are indented about two or three spaces within the *main()* method block. Such indentation is permissible, because Java ignores spaces. In addition, the indentation clearly shows that the statements are part of the method block *main()*. Indentation is used to "set off" a block of code so that it is not confused with other blocks of code. We will make extensive use of indentation within our Java programs to make them easier to read and understand. Also, notice the use of commenting within the program. You always want to make liberal use of meaningful comments in order to self-document the program.

That's all there is to it! We have just written our first Java program!

DEBUGGING TIP

Program comments in Java are inserted using double forward slashes, //. When the Java compiler encounters double forward slashes, it ignores the remainder of the line in which the slashes appear. Here's an example:

// THIS LINE IS A COMMENT AND IGNORED BY THE JAVA COMPILER

When commenting a large area, you can use a /* to begin the commented area and a */ to end the commented area like this:

```
/**************************************************************************
THIS  IS  ANOTHER  WAY  TO  COMMENT  IN  JAVA,  PARTICULARY
WHEN LARGE AREAS MUST BE COMMENTED.
**************************************************************************/
```

Notice how we have used asterisks to "frame" the comment and make it standout to anyone reading the program. Also, in this text, program comments will appear in all caps so that they can be readily distinguished from the program code.

Program comments are an important part of the program documentation and should be used liberally. At a minimum, the program should include the following comments:

- The beginning of the program should be commented with the programmer's name, date the program was written, date the program was last revised, and the name of the person doing the revision. In other words, a brief ongoing maintenance log should be commented at the beginning of the program.

- The comments at the beginning of the program should explain the purpose of the program, which includes the problem definition and program algorithms. This provides an overall perspective by which anyone, including you, the programmer, can begin debugging or maintaining the program.

- Constants and variables should be commented as to their purpose.

- Major sections of the program should be commented to explain the overall purpose of the respective section.

- Individual program lines should be commented when the purpose of the code is not obvious relative to the application.

- All major subprograms (methods in Java) should be commented just like the *main()* program method.

- The end of each program block (right curly brace) should be commented to indicate what the brace is ending.

Remember, someone (including you) might have to debug or maintain the program in the future. A good commenting scheme makes these tasks a much more efficient and pleasant process.

Quick Check

1. Any Java program consists of two sections, called the _____ and _____ sections.

2. Write an ***import*** statement to load all classes in a package called *myPackage* into a program.

3. A subprogram that returns a single value, a set of values, or performs some specific task in Java is called a _____.

4. Where should global constants be defined in a Java application program?

5. Where should variables and objects be defined in a Java application program?

6. Suppose a Java application declares a class called *Inventory* and this is the class in which *main()* resides. What must the source file be named for this program?

7. Comments are inserted into a Java program using
   a. left and right curly braces like this {COMMENT}.
   b. a semicolon like this ;COMMENT.
   c. a star like this *COMMENT.
   d. double forward slashes like this //COMMENT.
   e. double backward slashes like this \\COMMENT.

8. State at least four places where your program should include comments.

PROBLEM SOLVING IN ACTION: BANK ACCOUNT PROCESSING

Problem

Your local bank has contracted you to design a Java application program that will process savings account data for a given month. Assume that the savings account accrues interest at a rate of 12% per year and that the user must enter the current account balance, amount of deposits, and amount of withdrawals. Develop a problem definition, set of algorithms, and Java program to solve this problem.

Defining the Problem

Output: The program must display a report showing the account transactions and balance for a given savings account in a given month.

Input: To process a savings account, you need to know the initial balance, amount of deposits, amount of withdrawals, and interest rate. We will assume that these values will be entered by the program user, with the exception of the interest rate, which will be coded as a constant.

Processing: The program must process deposits and withdrawals and calculate interest to determine the monthly balance.

We will divide the problem into individual subproblems to solve the overall banking problem. Now, try to identify the separate tasks that must be performed to solve the problem. First, the user must enter the required transaction data, which will include the previous month's balance, current month's deposits, and current month's withdrawals. Once the transaction data are entered, the program must add the deposits to the account balance, subtract the withdrawals from the account balance, calculate the interest, and generate the required report. As a result, we can identify five program tasks as follows:

- Obtain the transaction data entered by the program user.
- Add the deposits to the account balance.
- Subtract the withdrawals from the account balance.
- Calculate the account interest.
- Generate the monthly account report.

The problem solving diagram in Figure 3-5 shows the structure required for the program.

Planning the Solution

Now we will employ stepwise refinement to develop the required set of algorithms. The initial algorithm level, *main()*, will reflect the problem definition and call the individual subprogram, or method, modules as follows:

Initial Algorithm

> *main( )*
> BEGIN
>   Call the method to obtain the transaction data from user.
>   Call the method to add the account deposits.
>   Call the method to subtract the account withdrawals.
>   Call the method to calculate the account interest.
>   Call the method to generate the account report.
> END.

The first level of refinement requires that we show a detailed algorithm for each subprogram module, or method. They are as follows:

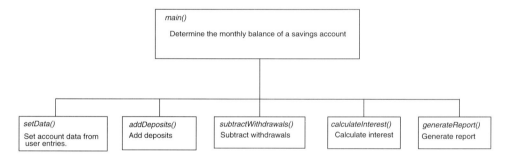

Figure 3-5   A problem solving diagram for the banking problem.

First Level of Refinement

> *setData( )*
> BEGIN
>   Write a prompt to enter the current account balance.
>   Read(*balance*).
>   Write a prompt to enter the monthly deposits.
>   Read(*deposits*).
>   Write a prompt to enter the monthly withdrawals.
>   Read(*withdrawals*).
> END.

addDeposits( )
BEGIN
   Calculate *balance = balance + deposits.*
END.

subtractWithdrawals( )
BEGIN
   Calculate *balance = balance − withdrawals.*
END.

addInterest( )
BEGIN
   Calculate *balance = balance + (balance ∗ interest).*
END.

generateReport( )
BEGIN
   Write(*balance*).
   Write(*deposits*).
   Write(*withdrawals*).
END.

Coding the Program

Here is how the foregoing algorithms are translated into Java application code:

```
/*********************************************************************************
ACTION 3-1 (ACTION03_01.JAVA)
THIS PROGRAM WILL PROCESS A BANKING ACCOUNT


*********************************************************************************/
import keyboardInput.*;      //FOR readDouble()

public class Action03_01
{
  //DECLARE INTEREST CONSTANT
  static final double INTEREST = 0.01;     //MONTHLY INTEREST RATE
                                           //IN DECIMAL FORM
```

```
public static void main(String args[])
{
    //DEFINE VARIABLES
    double balance = 0.0;            //ACCOUNT BALANCE
    double deposits = 0.0;          //MONTHLY DEPOSITS
    double withdrawals = 0.0;       //MONTHLY WITHDRAWALS
    char pause = ' ';               //PAUSE VARIABLE

    //CREATE INPUT OBJECT
    Keyboard in = new Keyboard();

    // DISPLAY PROGRAM DESCRIPTION MESSAGE
    System.out.println("\nThis program will generate a banking account report\n"
                + "based on information entered by the user.\n");

    //setData ():  SET ACCOUNT DATA TO USER ENTRIES
    System.out.print("Enter the current balance of the account: $");
    balance = in.readDouble();
    System.out.print("Enter the deposits this month:  $");
    deposits = in.readDouble();
    System.out.print("Enter the withdrawals this month:  $");
    withdrawals = in.readDouble();

    //addDeposits():  ADD THE MONTHLY DEPOSITS
    balance = balance + deposits;

    //subtractWithdrawals():  SUBTRACT THE MONTHLY WITHDRAWALS
    balance = balance - withdrawals;

    //addInterest():  ADD MONTHLY INTEREST
    balance = balance + (balance * INTEREST);

    //generateReport():  DISPLAY THE MONTHLY ACCOUNT REPORT
    System.out.println("\n\nThe account balance is currently:  $" + balance);
    System.out.println("Deposits were  $" + deposits);
    System.out.println("Withdrawals were  $" + withdrawals);

    //FREEZE DISPLAY
    System.out.println("\nPress ENTER to continue.");
    pause = in.readChar();
} //END main()
} //END Action03_01 CLASS
```

At this point, the code might look a little overwhelming. However, don't agonize over the coding details; just observe the things that relate to what we discussed in this chapter. Notice the overall structure of the program. A general program comment is at the top of the program, followed by an **import** statement, followed by the *Action03_01* class declaration and method *main()*. The **import** statement loads the *keyboardInput* package into the program. This package has been specifically designed for this text to allow convenient keyboard entry of numeric data. Keyboard input is discussed in detail in the next chapter, so we will defer discussion of the *keyboardInput* package until that time.

The program starts off by declaring our program class called *Action03_01*. Since the class name is *Action03_01*, the program file name must be *Action03_01.java*. Next, *INTEREST* is defined as a constant with the value 0.10. Method *main()* follows the constant definition. The code in *main()* simply implements the algorithms developed in our problem solution. However, we must define any variables used in the program before we can code our program logic. The required variables are *balance*, *deposits*, and *withdrawals*, which have been defined as **double** floating-point variables. Notice that each constant and variable definition is appropriately commented.

Now we can begin our program logic. All we have to do here is to translate our pseudocode to Java code. The first segment of code implements our *setData()* method. You do not know how to code your own methods yet, so we will just implement our methods in a straight line as part of *main()*. Later on, you will learn how to code these algorithms as individual methods. The implementation of *setData()* prompts the user for the required data and reads them from the keyboard. The *print()* method is used for prompting and the *readDouble()* method is used to read the user input. The *readDouble()* method is provided in the *keyboardInput* package. This package and all of its methods will be discussed in the next chapter. For now, just observe that we have defined an object called *in* of the *Keyboard* class at the beginning of the program, after the program variables have been defined. Then we use our *in* object to call the *readDouble()* method when it is needed to read a user entry from the keyboard.

Next, our *addDeposits()* method is coded, followed by the *subtractWithdrawals()* method, followed by the *addInterest()* method. The coding of these methods should be straightforward. Finally, a series of *println()* statements are used to implement our *generateReport()* method.

Notice the extensive use of comments. The purpose of the program is commented, as well as the purpose of each method. Furthermore, a comment is placed with each constant and variable definition to specify its purpose in the program. The comments are easily identified from the executable code, because they are coded in uppercase characters.

We have used a *flat* implementation for this program. The term *flat* comes from the idea that we will flatten the hierarchical structure of the program by coding all the program steps as one long *in-line* sequence of statements as part of method *main()*. This type of implementation is adequate for simple problems such as this. The program code is clear and easy to understand, given the appropriate program comments. For the next few chapters, we will employ flat implementations. Then, as the problems get more complex, we will need to implement the program modules as Java methods and replace the in-line program statements with calls to those methods. However, before you can do this, you need to learn the basic implementation details of the Java language. The next few chapters are devoted to this purpose.

CHAPTER SUMMARY

Data abstraction allows us to work with a class without agonizing over the internal implementation details of the class; this gives rise to the term abstract data type, or ADT. The term behavior has to do with how an ADT, or class, will act and react for a given operation. As a result, all classes (ADTs) exhibit a given behavior, which is determined by the operations defined for the ADT.

Java is a typed language. This means that all of the data processed by a Java program must be part of a given data type or class that is defined within the program. There are three major data type/class categories: primitive, standard classes, and programmer-defined classes.

Primitive data types consist of the standard types built into the Java language. These include the integer, floating-point, character, and Boolean data types. The integer types in Java include **byte**, **short**, **int**, and **long**, each of which defines a given range of integers.

The floating-point data type consists of decimal values that can be represented in either fixed decimal or exponential form. Floating-point constants and variables can be defined as **float** or **double**, each of which defines a given precision of floating-point values.

Character data include all of the symbols on your computer keyboard. Characters are ordered, because they are represented internally using a numeric code (Unicode).

The Boolean data type, **boolean**, consists of only two data elements, **true** and **false**. Boolean values are used in programs to make decisions.

A string is a collection of characters. There is a standard **String** class built into the Java language that allows you to create string objects and manipulate string data using predefined string methods.

All constants and variables used in a Java program must be defined prior to their use in the program. Constants are defined using the keywords **static** and **final**. The constant identifier is set equal to its constant value. Variables are defined by listing the variable data type followed by the variable identifier. An optional initializing value should always be included in the definition.

String objects are defined as objects of the **String** class. The keyword **String** is listed first, followed by an appropriate object identifier. Like primitive variables, string objects should always be initialized when they are defined. Empty strings can be initialized with double quotation marks.

Java programs consist of two sections: the import section and the class section. The import section contains **import** statements that load predefined, or standard, Java packages into your source program. A Java package is a collection of related classes.

A Java program is one big class. As a result, the class section of the program is where access to all the executable Java code resides. Each Java application program will contain a central class whose name must be the same as the program file name. The central program class begins with an opening left curly brace which is followed by any constant definitions. A right curly brace closes the central program class at the end of the program. For now, our programs will consist of a single method called *main()*. The main method block of the program begins with a left curly brace and is closed with a right curly brace. Any primitive data type variables or string objects are defined at the beginning of *main()*, followed by the coded program logic.

QUESTIONS AND PROBLEMS

Questions

1. What is an abstract data type, or ADT?

2. Give an example of an ADT.

3. What is meant by the term *behavior*, as related to classes and ADTs?

4. Why is the Java class ideal for implementing ADTs?

5. Name the four standard primitive types defined in Java.

6. Which of the following are *not* legal integer values in Java? Explain why they are not valid. Assume the **short** data type.

    a. −32.0
    b. +256
    c. 256
    d. 3,240
    e. 32000
    f. 40000

7. What is an overflow condition, and when will it generate incorrect results in Java?

8. Which of the following are not legal floating-point values in Java? Explain why they are not valid. Assume the **float** data type.

    a. 35.7
    b. −35.7
    c. 0.456
    d. 1.25e−9
    e. −2.5−e3
    f. −0.375e−3
    g. 25

9. Convert the following decimal numbers to exponential notation.

    a. −0.0000123
    b. 57892345.45
    c. 1.00004536
    d. +012.345

10. Convert the following exponential values to fixed decimal notation.

    a. 3.45e−7
    b. −2.25e−5
    c. 2.22e6
    d. −3.45e4

11. Three values in a data communications problem are 15.3 kHz, 2.2 MHz, and 10 ps.

    a. Express each as a floating-point value in fixed decimal form.
    b. Express each as a floating-point value in exponential form.
    c. Express each as an integer value.

12. The following current and voltage values are measured in a circuit: 1 milliampere, 32 millivolts, 100 microvolts, and 125 nanoamperes.

    a. Express each current and voltage value in fixed decimal form.
    b. Express each current and voltage value in exponential form.

13. What is the data type or class of each of the following?
    a. 250
    b. −250.0
    c. −16
    d. −3.5e−4
    e. 'x'
    f. '$'
    g. "2"
    h. "175"
    i. "1.25e−3"

14. List at least three places where comments should occur in your Java program.

15. State the difference between a character and a string.

16. Choose appropriate identifiers and define constants to represent each of the following.
    a. A maximum value of 100.
    b. Your name.
    c. Your student number.
    d. Your age.
    e. A period.
    f. Your birth date.
    g. Your school.

17. Define a series of constants that would represent the months of the year.

18. Choose appropriate identifiers and define variables or objects for each of the following.
    a. Grade point average (GPA).
    b. Grade for a course.
    c. Gross pay on a paycheck.
    d. Student name.

19. Suppose that *Name* is a string object. Explain what happens as the result of executing the following:

    ```
    System.out.println(Name.length());
    ```

20. What will be displayed by each of the following *println()* statements:
    a. String s = "JAVA";
       ```
       System.out.println(s.toLowerCase());
       ```
    b. String s = "JAVA";
       ```
       System.out.println(s.length());
       ```

Problems

Least Difficult

1. The = symbol is used in Java to denote an assignment operation. For now, you can think of it as an equals operation but you will find out later that it actually has a different meaning than just equals. Given the following,

```
//PROBLEM 3-1

public class Problem3_1
{
  //DEFINE CONSTANT
  static final double VALUE = 2.5;

  public static void main(String args[])
  {
    //DEFINE VARIABLES
    int x = 0;
    int y = 0;
    double a = 0.0;
    double b = 0.0;
  }//END main()
}//END CLASS
```
    determine the results of each of the following program segments:

    a. x = 25;
        b = Math.sqrt(x);
    b. y = 5;
        a = Math.sqrt(Math.sqrt(y));
    c. x = 1;
        x = x + 1;
        y = Math.sqrt(x);
    d. x = 2;
        y = x + x;
        a = (y + 1) * VALUE;
    e. x = 2;
        y = x + x;
        a = y + 1 * VALUE;

More Difficult

2. The *println()* method is used in Java to display a value on the system monitor. The format for this operation is

    System.out.println(*items to be displayed*);

Notice that the *println()* method is called by the *System.out* object using the dot operator. Thus, to display the value of the variable *x* in a program, use the following statement:

```
System.out.println(x);
```

Code the program given in problem 1, including the program segments given in part a through part e of the problem. Add a *println()* statement to each of these segments to display the resulting variable value. Compile and run the program. Verify that the output generated by the program is correct according to the respective program calculations.

3. Design and code a Java program that will find the sum of three test score values and display the sum on the system monitor. Call the variables *score1*, *score2*, and *score3*, and assume that they have initial values of 95.3, 78.5, and 85.2, respectively. Use the program structure given in Figure 3-4. Compile and run your program using your Java compiler.

4. Expand the program you wrote in problem 3 to calculate and display the average of the three scores. (*Note:* The / symbol is used for division in Java.) Compile and run your program.

5. Design and code a Java program that will generate a weekly payroll report for Bill Gates. Assume that Bill worked 22.5 hours this week at a rate of $1,000,000 per hour. Also, assume that Bill's payroll deductions were 35% of his gross pay. The report should show the employee name, number of hours worked, hourly rate, gross pay, payroll deduction amount, and net pay.

6. Use your Java compiler to find and correct the syntax errors in the following program:

```
public class Problem3_6
{
    //DEFINE CONSTANT
    final double INTEREST_RATE = 10.0;    //ANNUAL INTEREST RATE

    public void main(String args[]
    {
        //DEFINE VARIABLES
        double principle = 1000.0;        //PRINCIPLE LOAN VALUE
        term = 2;                         //TERM OF LOAN IN YEARS
        Doble TotalAmount                 //TOTAL AMOUNT OF LOAN

        / GENERATE PROGRAM DESCRIPTION MESSAGE
        System.out.println( "This program will calculate a total loan amount "
                        + "given a  principle of  $1000, a term of 2 yrs. "
                        + " and an interest rate of  10 percent.”
```

```
//CALCULATE TOTAL LOAN AMOUNT
totalAmount = principle + ((principle * interestRate) * term)

//DISPLAY RESULTS
System.out.prinln( "Given a principle amount of  $" +  principle
                  + " a term of " + term " years "
                  + " and an interest rate of " + interestRate "%"
                  + " the total amount of the load is $" + totalAmount);
    } //END main()
```

7. Enter, compile, and run the following program. Does the output generated by the program make sense, especially if you were the customer? Of course not! There is a logic error in the program. Use your Java debugger to locate and correct the logic error. (*Hint:* Watch the variable *tax* as you single-step the program with you debugger.)

```
public class Problem3_7
{
    //DEFINE CONSTANTS
    static final double RATE = 7.0;     // INTEREST IN PERCENT FORM

    public static void main(String args[])
    {
        //DEFINE VARIABLES
        double cost = 0.0;              //COST OF ITEM
        double tax = 0.0;              //SALES TAX
        double totalCost = 0.0;        //TOTAL COST OF ITEM

        //DISPLAY PROGRAM DESCRIPTION MESSAGE
        System.out.println("This program will calculate total cost of a sales item.");

        //ASSIGN COST VALUE
        cost = 10.95;

        //CALCULATE TAX
        tax = RATE * cost;

        //CALCULATE TOTAL COST
        totalCost = cost + tax;

        //DISPLAY RESULT
        System.out.println( "The total cost of the sales item is:  $" + totalCost);
    } //END main()
} //END Problem3_7
```

GUI 103: BUTTONS AND LAYOUT MANAGERS

PURPOSE

- *To become familiar with the GUI button component.*
- *To show how buttons are added to a frame container.*
- *To demonstrate the purpose of a listener.*
- *To experiment with frame background and foreground color.*
- *To become familiar with a frame layout manager.*
- *To demonstrate the flow layout manager.*
- *To show how component alignment and gapping can be set within a frame.*

Introduction

The **button** is one of the most common components found in GUI. Buttons are often used to execute an event, such as a calculation or store event. In this module, you will load and execute a Java program that produces a frame with a single button. Then, you will load a program that produces a frame with several buttons. You will modify the code and observe the effect on the windows generated by the program.

Procedure

1. The *GUI102_2.java* program from the *GUI102* module should have created a class file named *FrameWithClose.class*. Your Java compiler should have placed this file in a class directory. Make sure the file is present and, if not, copy it from the CD that a accompanies this book, or download it from www.prenhall.com. Load and execute the *GUI103_1.java* program contained on the CD that accompanies this book, or download it from www.prenhall.com.. You should observe the window shown in Figure 1. This is a window generated by Windows®. If you are in a Mac environment, you will see a similar window.

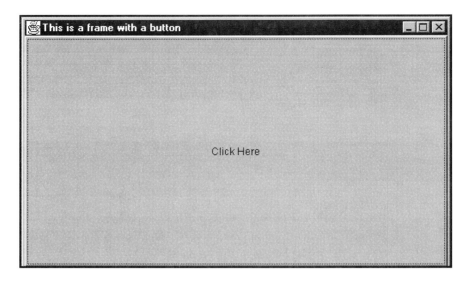

Figure 1 A frame with a single button and no layout manager.

2. Here, you see one BIG button. Click the button and observe the results. You should hear your computer beep each time the button is clicked.

3. Here is the Java code that produced the window you see in Figure 1.

```
1   import java.awt.*;              //FOR FRAME CLASS
2   import java.awt.event.*;        //FOR EVENT HANDLING
3
4   //A FRAME CLASS WITH A SINGLE BUTTON
5   class FrameWithButton extends FrameWithClose implements ActionListener
6   {
7     //CONSTRUCTOR
8     public FrameWithButton(String title)
9     {
10    //CALL SUPERCLASS CONSTRUCTOR
11      super(title);
12
13    //SET WINDOW BACKGROUND COLOR
14      setBackground(Color.cyan);
15
16    //SET COMPONENT FOREGROUND COLOR
17      setForeground(Color.red);
18
```

```
19
20
21     //DEFINE BUTTON OBJECT
22     Button beepButton = new Button("Click Here");
23
24     //ADD BUTTON TO FRAME
25     add(beepButton);
26
27     //ADD EVENT LISTENER THIS BUTTON
28     beepButton.addActionListener(this);
29   }//END FrameWithButton()
30
31    //ActionListener METHOD
32    public void actionPerformed(ActionEvent e)
33    {
34     final char SOUND = 7;                    //DECLARE SOUND CONSTANT
35     //DID BUTTON CAUSE EVENT?
36     if (e.getSource() instanceof Button)
37     //IF SO, BEEP
38       System.out.println(SOUND);
39    }//END actionPerformed
40   }//END FrameWithButton
41
42   //APPLICATION CLASS TO TEST FrameWithButton
43   public class GUI103_1
44   {
45    public static void main(String[] args)
46    {
47     //DEFINE FRAME OBJECT
48     FrameWithButton window = new FrameWithButton("This is a frame
49                                              with a button");
50
51     //SET FRAME SIZE
52     window.setSize(500,300);
53
54     //MAKE FRAME VISIBLE
55     window.setVisible(true);
56    }//END main()
57   }//END GUI103_1
```

4. Again, don't be overwhelmed and worry about all the coding details now. You
    will learn how to do all of this later. We will just focus on a few statements
    that are pertinent to our frame. Change the color in line 14 from "cyan" to

"pink." Execute the program again and observe that nothing has changed because this statement sets the background color of the frame. Again, our giant button is covering the entire frame. As a result, there is no background visible.

5.   Change the color in line 17 from "red" to "blue." Execute the program again and observe the color of the button label has changed to blue. This is the foreground color of the frame.

6.   Add the following statement on line 19 of the program:

setLayout(new FlowLayout());

7.   Execute the program again. You should observe a window similar to the one shown in Figure 2. Now, this is much better. We now have a window with a single manageable button. The window background color should be pink and the button foreground color should be blue.

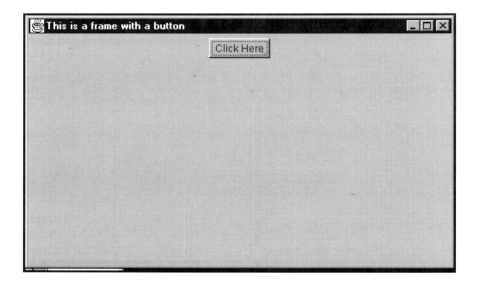

Figure 2 A frame with a single button using the flow layout manager.

Discussion

First, look at line 5 in the program. This line tells Java that this class name is *FrameWithButton*, which **extends** a class called *FrameWithClose*. The

FrameWithClose class is the class you used in the *GUI102* module to produce a window with a closing feature. The *FrameWithButton* class in this module **inherits** the *FrameWithClose* class from the previous module so that we do not have to rewrite the code to produce a window with a closing feature. Why rewrite this code if it is already available? The concept of **inheritance** is one of the cornerstones of object-oriented programming. Inheritance allows the reuse of code that has already been developed, just as we reused the *FrameWithClose* class code here by inheriting, or extending, it into our *FrameWithButton* class code. The *GUI102_2.java* program contains the *FrameWithClose* class needed for this program. When you executed the *GUI102_2* program in the last module, your Java compiler should have compiled the *FrameWithButton* class and placed it in a class directory so that it is available to other classes using the inheritance property.

Now, back to the window in Figure 2. The background color of a frame is the color visible behind any components on the frame. The foreground color of a frame is the color of any labeling on a GUI component. In steps 4 and 5 you changed both the frame background and foreground colors. There are 13 different colors available in Java as follows:

- black
- blue
- cyan
- darkGray
- gray
- green
- lightGray
- magenta
- orange
- pink
- red
- white
- yellow

Try experimenting with these different colors in lines 14 and 17 of the program.

The first button you generated was so big that it covered the entire frame. The reason this happened is because the frame did not use a **layout manager**. A layout manager lays out the components within a frame so that they are manageable. In step 6, you set the frame layout to the *FlowLayout* manager. This layout manager places components on the frame, from left-to-right, center justified. This is why you observed a single button in the middle of the frame, just below the title bar.

Procedure (continued)

8. Load and execute the *GUI103_2.java* program contained on the CD that accompanies this book, or download it from www.prenhall.com. You should observe the window shown in Figure 3. Here you see five buttons centered across the top of the frame.

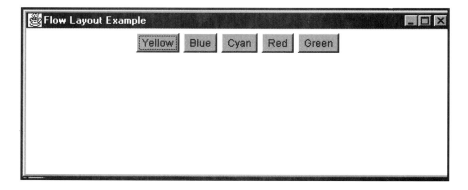

Figure 3 A frame with five buttons using the flow layout manager.

9. Click on the buttons and notice that the frame background color changes to the color indicated by the button label. Here is the program that generated the five-button frame:

```
1   import java.awt.*;              //FOR FRAME CLASS
2   import java.awt.event.*;        //FOR EVENT HANDLING
3
4   //A FRAME CLASS WITH FIVE BUTTONS
5   class FrameWithButton extends FrameWithClose implements ActionListener
6   {
7     //CONSTRUCTOR
8     public FrameWithButtons(String title)
9     {
```

```
10    //CALL SUPERCLASS CONSTRUCTOR
11    super(title);
12
13    //SET LAYOUT TO FLOW LAYOUT
14    setLayout(new FlowLayout());
15
16     //DEFINE BUTTON OBJECTS
17    Button yellowButton = new Button("Yellow");
18    Button blueButton = new Button("Blue");
19    Button cyanButton = new Button("Cyan");
20    Button redButton = new Button("Red");
21    Button greenButton = new Button("Green");
22
23    //ADD BUTTONS TO FRAME
24    add(yellowButton);
25    add(blueButton);
26    add(cyanButton);
27    add(redButton);
28    add(greenButton);
29
30    //ACTIVATE EVENT LISTENERS FOR BUTTONS
31    yellowButton.addActionListener(this);
32    blueButton.addActionListener(this);
33    cyanButton.addActionListener(this);
34    redButton.addActionListener(this);
35    greenButton.addActionListener(this);
36  }//END FrameWithButtons()
37
38 //PROCESS EVENT
39  public void actionPerformed(ActionEvent e)
40  {
41    //GET LABEL OF EVENT OBJECT
42    String buttonLabel = e.getActionCommand();
43
44    //DID A BUTTON CAUSE EVENT?
45    if (e.getSource() instanceof Button)
46     //IF SO, WHICH BUTTON?
47     if (buttonLabel.equals("Yellow"))
48     {
49       setBackground(Color.yellow);
50       repaint();
51     }//END IF "Yellow"
52
```

```
53      if (buttonLabel.equals("Blue"))
54      {
55        setBackground(Color.blue);
56        repaint();
57      }//END IF "Blue"
58      if (buttonLabel.equals("Cyan"))
59      {
60        setBackground(Color.cyan);
61        repaint();
62      }//END IF "Cyan"
63      if (buttonLabel.equals("Red"))
64      {
65        setBackground(Color.red);
66        repaint();
67      }//END IF "Red"
68      if (buttonLabel.equals("Green"))
69      {
70        setBackground(Color.green);
71        repaint();
72      }//END IF "Green"
73    }//END actionPerformed()
74  }//END FrameWithButtons
75
76 //APPLICATION CLASS TO TEST FrameWithButton
77 public class GUI103_2
78 {
79   public static void main(String[] args)
80   {
81     //DEFINE FRAME OBJECT
82     FrameWithButtons window = new FrameWithButtons("Flow Layout Example");
83
84     //SET FRAME SIZE
85     window.setSize(500,200);
86
87     //MAKE FRAME VISIBLE
88     window.setVisible(true);
89   }//END main()
90 }//END GUI103_2
```

10. Change line 14 to the following:

    setLayout(new FlowLayout(FlowLayout.LEFT));

Notice that there is a dot between the words FlowLayout and LEFT in the above statement. Execute the program and notice that the buttons are left-justified within the window.

11. Change line 14 to the following:

setLayout(new FlowLayout(FlowLayout.RIGHT));

Execute the program and notice that the buttons are right-justified within the window.

12. Change line 14 to the following:

setLayout(new FlowLayout(FlowLayout.CENTER));

Execute the program and notice that the buttons are center-justified within the window.

13. Change line 14 to the following:

setLayout(new FlowLayout(FlowLayout.CENTER,10,50));

Execute the program and notice that the buttons are center-justified but placed farther down within window.

14. Change line 14 to the following:

setLayout(new FlowLayout(FlowLayout.CENTER,50,50));

Execute the program and notice that the buttons are center-justified toward the top of the window but with more of a gap between them.

Discussion

The *GUI103_2.java* program contains a *FrameWithButtons* class that creates a frame with five buttons using the *FlowLayout* manager. Notice that the *FlowLayout* manager centered the buttons, from left to right, in the order in which they were *added* to the frame in lines 24 through 28 of the program. The frame background defaulted to white and the frame foreground (button labels) defaulted to black. When a given button was clicked the button generated an *event* which was "handled" by the program to change the frame background color. Again, this program inherits the *FrameWithClose* class so that we do not have to code the window closing feature again in this class.

When you changed the statement in line 14, you changed the way in which the *FlowLayout* manager was set. You found that you could direct the layout manager to left-justify, right-justify, or center-justify the buttons within the window. This is referred to as ***component alignment*** in Java. The default alignment is center. Then, you changed line 14 to add two integer values toward the end of the statement. The first value controls the horizontal gapping of the components within the frame, while the second value controls the vertical gapping of components within the frame. When the statement included the values 10,50 the buttons were relatively close together, due to a horizontal gapping value of 10 but displaced farther down the window, due to a vertical gapping value of 50. When the statement included the values 50,50 the buttons were gapped farther apart horizontally, by changing the horizontal gapping value from 10 to 50.

Procedure (continued)

15. Comment line 28 by placing two forward slashes, //, at the begiining of the line. Execute the program and notice that the green button does not appear on the frame. (Why?)
16. Comment line 31 by placing two forward slashes, //, at the begiining of the line. Execute the program and click the yellow button. Notice that nothing happens. (Why?)

Discussion

When you commented line 28, you commented the statement that added the *Green* button to the frame. A component must be added to a frame using the *add()* method or else it will not appear on the resulting window.

When you commented line 31, you commented the statement that added an *ActionListener* for the *Yellow* button. A component must be *registered* as a **listener** if the GUI is to respond to an event generated by the component. A button component must be registered as a listener using the *addActionListener()* method. When you commented line 31, you commented out the line that registered the *Yellow* button as a listener. As a result, the GUI did not respond to the clicking event.

4
GETTING STUFF IN AND OUT

```
OBJECTIVES
```

When you are finished with this chapter, you should have a good understanding of
the following:

- The use of *print()* and *println()* to display both fixed and variable
  information.
- The use of a layout chart to generate well-formatted output to the display.
- The Java escape sequences used to format output.
- The purpose of an exception handler routine.
- The use of the *keyboardInput* package of classes for keyboard input.
- How to create objects to read keyboard entries.
- How to use the *readInt()*, *readDouble()*, *readChar()*, and *readString()*
  methods to read all kinds of keyboard entries.
- How to design and implement user-friendly programs.

INTRODUCTION

In Chapters 2 and 3, you learned the general concepts of problem solving, data
abstraction, and Java program design. In this chapter, you will begin learning the
implementation details of the Java language. In particular, you will learn how to
get information into and out of your system via Java objects and methods. Getting
data into the system is called **reading**, and generating data from the system is
called **writing**. You will discover how to write information to your display
monitor. Then, you will learn how to read information from your keyboard. In a
later chapter, you will learn how to read and write disk files, since this requires
more knowledge about classes and objects.

Armed with the knowledge gained from this chapter, you will be ready to
write some *interactive* Java programs. By interactive, we mean programs that will
interact with the user—writing user prompts and reading user input data. Make
sure that you do the programming problems at the end of the chapter. You *must*
get your hands dirty with some actual programming experience to learn how to
program in Java.

4-1 GETTING STUFF OUT

When executing your Java programs, you usually will want to generate information to one of three hardware devices: a monitor, a printer, or a disk file. In fact, there will be occasions when you will need to generate information to all three of these devices during the execution of a program.

As you already know, you can write information to a display monitor using the *println()* (pronounced "print line") method.

Using *println()*

You are already familiar with the *println()* method, so let's just review its operation by looking at a few examples. Probably the simplest use of the *println()* method is to write fixed, or constant, information. There are two types of fixed information that can be written: numeric and character.

Getting Out Fixed Numeric Information

When you want to write fixed numeric information, you simply insert the numeric values as arguments into the *println()* method. Of course, the *println()* method must be called by the *System.out* object. Thus, the statement

System.out.println(250);

generates an output of

250

The statement

System.out.println(–365);

generates an output of

–365

The statement

System.out.println(2.75);

generates an output of

2.75

Getting Out Fixed Character Information

To write character information, you must enclose the output information in quotes—single quotes for single characters and double quotes for strings. Consequently, the statement

System.out.println('A');

generates an output of

A

The statement

System.out.println("This text is great!");

produces an output of

This text is great!

The statement

System.out.println("My GPA is: " + 3.95 + " Wow!");

produces an output of

My GPA is 3.95 Wow!

Notice the use of the concatenation operator, +, to concatenate, or put together, the output items. The first output item is the string "My GPA is: ". The second item is the numeric value 3.95 which is concatenated to the first item using the + concatenation operator. Finally, the third item, "Wow!" is concatenated to the second item using the + concatenation operator. In summary, to display several items using a single *println()* statement, simply separate them as arguments within the *println()* method using the + concatenation operator.

Example 4-1

Construct *println()* statements to generate the following outputs:

a. 3.14
b. 1 2 3 4

Solution:

a.   System.out.println(3.14);

    b. System.out.println("1 2 3 4");

To get spacing in the output, use blank characters between the output values. Remember that blanks are also characters. As a result, the preceding statement generates blanks, or spaces, where they are inserted within the output string.

Getting Out Variable Information

The next thing you must learn is how to write variable information. Again, this is a simple chore using the *println()* method: You simply insert the variable identifiers as arguments into the *println()* method. For instance, if your program has declared *sales*, *cost*, and *profit* as variables, you would write their respective values by inserting them as arguments into the *println()* method, like this:

```
System.out.println(sales);
System.out.println(cost);
System.out.println(profit);
```

The foregoing statements would write the values stored in memory for *sales*, *cost*, and *profit*, in that order on separate lines.

Example 4-2

Suppose your sales of widgets last month amounted to $5,346.75 but your cost for the widgets was $3,045.50. Write a program to calculate and display your profit.

Solution

Of course, you probably would not go to all the trouble of writing a Java program for such a simple chore. However, let's do it just to get some practice. Suppose we define three variables to represent the sale of widgets last month, the cost of the widgets, and the profit we made on selling the widgets. We will initialize the given sales and cost values and subtract the two to determine the profit we made. The resulting profit will then be displayed using the *println()* method. Here's the program:

```
//THIS PROGRAM CALCULATES AND DISPLAYS PROFIT FOR MONTHLY
//SALES

public class Profit
{
    public static void main(String args[])
    {
        //DEFINE AND INITIALIZE VARIABLES
        double sales = 5346.75;          //SALES LAST MONTH
```

```
        double cost = 3045.50;        //COST OF SALES LAST MONTH
        double profit = 0.0;          //PROFIT MADE LAST MONTH

        //CALCULATE PROFIT
        profit = sales - cost;  //SUBTRACT COST FROM SALES TO GET PROFIT

        //DISPLAY PROFIT
        System.out.println(profit);
    } //END main()
  } //END Profit
```

The output produced by the program is

2301.25

STYLE TIP

The output generated in Example 4-2 is simply the number 2301.25. What a bore! You need to "dress up" your program outputs so that the user of the program understands what's going on. First, you should always use a *println()* statement at the beginning of your program that tells the user what the program is going to do. This is called a ***program description message***. A program description message does two things:

1. It tells the user (the person running the program) what the program will do.
2. It provides documentation within the program listing as to what the program will do. As a result, the program listing becomes self-documenting.

A program description message for the program in Example 4-2 might be coded something like this:

```
System.out.println("This program will calculate monthly profit,\n"
                 + "given sales and cost of  values. ");
```

This one *println()* statement will generate the following output:

```
This program will calculate monthly profit,
given sales and cost of sales values.
```

Observe that one *println()* statement is used to write two lines of character information. The trick is to divide the output sentence into two strings on two separate lines. Notice that each string item must be enclosed within double quotes.

Also, notice the symbol '\n' (a backslash followed by the character *n*) at the end of the first line. The '\n' symbol is treated like a single character and is called an *escape sequence*. When inserted into the output stream, a carriage return/line feed (CRLF) is generated wherever it appears. Thus, in the foregoing *println()* statement, the first string item is written on one line, a CRLF is generated to move the cursor to the beginning of the next line, and the second string item is written. Figure 4-1 illustrates how the '\n' escape sequence controls the location of the cursor when used in the *println()* statement.

Figure 4-1 Using the '\n' escape sequence forces the cursor to the beginning of the next line.

Now, good style would dictate that output information should be descriptive. In other words, the output information should be self-documenting and easily understood by the user. In Example 4-2, the profit output statement could be modified, like this:

```
System.out.println("Given a monthly sales value of $" + sales + "\n"
                  + "and a  total cost value of $" +  cost + ", the \n"
                  + "resulting profit is $"  + profit);
```

This one *println( )* statement will generate the following output:

```
Given a monthly sales value of $5346.75
and a total cost of $3045.50, the
resulting profit is $2301.25.
```

Let's analyze this output. First, observe that a '\n' escape sequence has been placed at the end of the first two lines in the *println( )* statement. This generates a CRLF after each of these two lines, thereby creating three separate lines on the screen. Notice that the '\n' escape sequence is concatenated as a string of one character at the end of the first line but included as part of a string at the end of the second line. You can treat '\n' as a single character, just as you would any other character. However, it must appear as a string of one character or as part of another string within double quotations marks when using the string concatenation operator, +.

Next, look at the output lines themselves. See how an output sentence is constructed using separate string items. The sentence is formed by separate character strings enclosed within double quotation marks. The monthly sales, cost of sales, and profit values are inserted into the output, between the string items, by concatenating the variables (*sales*, *cost*, and *profit*) when they are needed as part of the output. Notice that the character strings and variable items are concatenated to each other using the + operator. It is important that you see that the quotation marks are around the string information and *not* around the variables.

Of course, the same thing could be accomplished with three separate *println( )* statements, like this:

```
System.out.println("Given a monthly sales value of $" + sales);
System.out.println("and a  total cost value of $" +  cost  + ", the");
System.out.println("resulting profit is $" + profit);
```

Example 4-3

Insert the *println()* statements given in the previous style tip into the program developed in Example 4-2 to form a complete program.

Solution

```
public class Profit
{
    public static void main(String args[])
    {
        //DEFINE AND INITIALIZE VARIABLES
        double sales = 5346.75;      //SALES LAST MONTH
        double cost = 3045.50;       //COST OF SALES LAST MONTH
        double profit = 0.0;         //PROFIT MADE LAST MONTH

        System.out.println("This program will calculate monthly profit,\n"
                    + "given sales and cost of  values.");

        //CALCULATE PROFIT
        profit = sales - cost;  //SUTRACT COST FROM SALES TO GET PROFIT

        //DISPLAY PROFIT
        System.out.println("Given a monthly sales value of $" + sales);
        System.out.println("and a  total cost value of $" +  cost  + ", the");
        System.out.println("resulting profit is $" + profit);
    } //END main()
} //END Profit
```

As you can see from Example 4-3, the general idea of using the *println()* statement is simple: You place the *println()* statement in your program whenever you want to display information on your system monitor.

Up to this point, you have seen the use of the '\n' escape sequence (CRLF) to control cursor positioning. There are other escape sequences that you might need to use from time to time, some of which are listed in Table 4-1.

To use any of these escape sequences, simply include them as part of a string or concatenate them as single characters (using double quotes) into the output via the + operator. The purpose of each should be obvious from the action described in the table.

DEBUGGING TIP

The + concatenation operator requires that single characters be concatenated as a string of one character using double quotation marks, *not single quotation marks.*

TABLE 4-1 ESCAPE SEQUENCES DEFINED FOR JAVA

Sequence	Action
\b	Backspace
\f	Formfeed
\n	CRLF, carriage return/line feed
\r	CR, carriage return
\t	Horizontal tab
\\	Backslash
\'	Single quote
\"	Double quote

Using *print()*

There is another method, called *print()*, that you can use with *System.out* to display information. The only difference between *print()* and *println()* is that *print()* keeps the cursor on the same output line, while *println()* forces the cursor to the *next* line after the items are displayed. Thus, the statements

```
System.out.print("Hello");
System.out.println("World");
System.out.print("Goodbye");
System.out.println("World");
```

will produce an output of

```
Hello World
Goodbye World
```

See how the *print()* method leaves the cursor on the existing line, while the *println()* method forces the cursor to the next line. Note: The cursor would be left on a new line by the last *println()* statement. Thus, any subsequent output would begin on a new line.

Formatting the Output

By formatting an output, we mean structuring it to meet a given application. Java allows output formatting using special commands within the output statements. These commands are referred to as ***escape sequences***. You have already seen the use of the '\n' escape sequence but there are others from Table 4-1 that we need to discuss. However, before discussing the details, let's learn how the computer "sees" a display screen.

Many PCs divide a page of output into 25 rows and 80 columns as shown by the text screen layout chart in Figure 4-2. Layout charts are used to lay out, or format, your output. A layout chart allows you to align output information so that the following happens:

- Proper margins are provided for header information.
- Numeric and character data are properly aligned under column headings and evenly spaced across the page.
- The output looks professional.

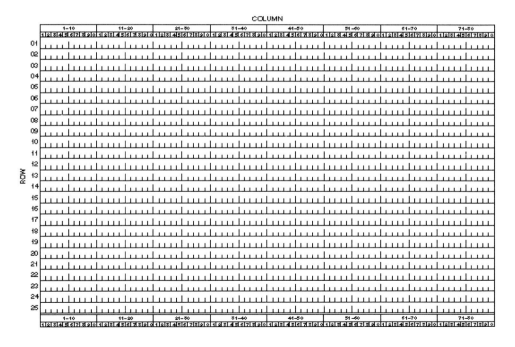

Figure 4-2 A typical text screen layout chart.

The first thing to do when using a layout chart is to fill in the chart with the information to be written. For instance, suppose you must create three columns of output: the first for a person's name, the second for the person's address, and the third for a person's phone number. Each column will be titled with an underscored column heading in all caps. You should begin by laying out the output information on the forgoing layout chart. As you do this, suppose you decide the following:

- You will locate the three headings in row 4.
- The NAME heading will begin in column 10, two tabs from the left edge of the screen.
- The ADDRESS heading will begin in column 30, three tabs from the NAME heading.
- The PHONE heading will begin in column 50, three tabs from the ADDRESS heading.
- Row 5 will contain dashes for underscoring the column headings.

Using this information, let's write a program that will display the headings just as they would appear on a layout chart. Here it is:

```
public class Layout
{
    public static void main(String args[])
    {
      System.out.print("\n\n\n");
      System.out.println("\t\tNAME\t\t\tADDRESS\t\t\tPHONE");
      System.out.println("\t\t----\t\t\t-------\t\t\t-----");
    } //END main()
  } //END Layout
```

The first thing to be displayed is a string of three CRLF escape sequences via a *print()* method. These three escape sequences generate the three blank lines in rows 1, 2, and 3, respectively, leaving the cursor at the beginning of row 4. Now, the first heading, "NAME", is to be two tabs from the left edge of the screen. Thus, the string in the first *println()* statement begins with two '\t' escape sequence characters, followed by the heading, "NAME". Next, the "ADDRESS" heading must be three tabs from the "NAME" heading. As a result, three '\t' escape sequence characters are inserted after "NAME" and prior to "ADDRESS" in the *println()* string. Finally, the "PHONE" heading is located three tabs from the "ADDRESS" heading. Get the idea? You might have trouble aligning the output information precisely with output columns using tabs. To "fine-tune" the alignment, you can insert blanks within the output heading strings. Thus, for proper alignment per a layout chart, the output information is often formatted using a combination of tabs and blanks.

The same basic idea is then repeated within the next *println()* statement to produce row 5. This statement generates the dashes that provide underscoring for the headings.

The layout chart shown in Figure 4-2 is available on the CD that accompanies this book, or you can download it from the Prentice Hall Web site at www.prenhall.com. There are two files containing the chart: an *HTML* file called *LayoutChart.html* whereby you can view and print the chart via your Web browser, and a Word 97® file called *LayoutChart.doc* whereby you can view and print the chart via Word 97®. The Word 97® chart is easier to use, because it is in landscaped format.

Unfortunately, the current version of Java does not have many features to produce professional-looking, formatted output, as do languages such as C/C++, COBOL, and BASIC. About all you can do at this time is to use the escape sequence characters and spacing as we have done in the foregoing example. However, Java does have some very powerful classes and associated methods to produce formatted windowed output, as you have already seen in the GUI modules and will learn later on in this text.

 Quick Check

1. Write a *println()* statement to display your name as a fixed string of information.

2. Write a *println()* statement to display your name when it is stored in a string variable called *name*.

3. The escape sequence that must be used to generate a CRLF is the _____.

4. The escape sequence that must be used to generate a tab is the _____.

5. Explain the difference between using the *print()* and *println()* methods.

4-2 GETTING STUFF IN

Getting information into a program for processing is called *reading*. In most present-day systems, information is read from one of two sources: from a keyboard or from a disk file. In this section, you will learn how to read information that is being entered via a keyboard by the system user.

Unfortunately, Java does not include any simple methods for reading keyboard data, especially numeric data. There is a *System.in* object in Java, which is similar to the *System.out* object that you have been using to call the *print()* and *println()* methods. However, *System.in* can only read one character at a time. In fact, all input from the keyboard to a Java program is considered as string input. Thus, to read numerical data, you must convert the ASCII string digit characters to their numerical value. In addition, an **exception hander** must be written to trap any errors that might occur during the conversion process. Exception handling is an advanced topic in Java and is covered later in this text. To make things simple for now we have developed a Java package, called *keyboardInput*, that includes all the classes and methods that you will need to read keyboard data.

> An **exception handler** is a Java program segment that is used to *catch* and handle errors as they occur during the execution of a Java program.

The *keyboardInput* package includes a *Keyboard* class which defines four easy-to-use methods for reading keyboard data as shown in Table 4-2 .

TABLE 4-2 KEYBOARD INPUT METHODS USED IN THIS TEXT

Method	Description
readInt()	Returns the integer value entered by the user.
readDouble()	Returns the double-float value entered by the user.
readChar()	Returns a single character value entered by the user.
readString()	Returns the string entered by the user.

To use any of these methods, you must first import the *keyboardInput* package into your program like this:

```
import keyboardInput.*;          //FOR KEYBOARD INPUT METHODS
```

Remember, the *keyboardInput* package is not a standard part of the Java language. It has been created specifically for this text and is available on the accompanying CD as well as the Prentice Hall Web site at www.prenhall.com. You will need to copy the *Keyboard.class* and *KeyboardReadException.class* files into a folder called *keyboardInput* within your Java system directory before importing the *keyboardInput* package into your Java programs.

Once the *keyboardInput* package has been imported into your program, you must create an input object for the *Keyboard* class, then use this object to call the desired input method. Creating an object for a *user-defined* class is a two-step process. First, you must declare an object identifier of the user-defined class. To declare an object you first list the class, followed by the object identifier. Second, you must allocate memory for the object using the **new** operator. For example, suppose we decide to name our input object *in*. Then, the appropriate definition would be:

    Keyboard in;   //DECLARE OBJECT NAME
    in = **new** Keyboard();   //ALLOCATE OBJECT MEMORY

These two lines can be replaced with a single line like this:

    Keyboard in = **new** Keyboard(); //CREATE in OBJECT OF Keyboard CLASS

CREATING A USER-DEFINED OBJECT

class   object identifier;
*object identifier = **new** class();*

         OR

*class object identifier = **new** class();*

DECLARATIONS VERSUS DEFINITIONS

The words *define* and *declare* are often used interchangeably in connection with programming languages. Actually, a declaration specifies the name and attributes of an object but does not reserve storage. On the other hand, a definition is a declaration that also reserves storage. Variables and string objects are *defined* in Java, meaning that an identifier is specified and memory is reserved to store the variable or string object values by the Java compiler. On the other hand, user-defined objects must first be *declared* which only specifies an object identifier and the class name of the object. Then, memory must be allocated using the **new** operator.

Reading Numeric Data: *readInt()* and *readDouble()*

To read numeric data, you will use *readInt()* to read integer values or *readDouble()* to read floating-point, or decimal, values. First, notice that each of the input methods in Table 4-2 *returns* the value entered by the user. As a result, a variable must be defined to receive the returned value from the method. In other words, the value returned by the method must have a place to go. So, to read an integer from the keyboard you must define an integer variable, then call the *readInt()* method like this:

```
int value = 0;
value = in.readInt();
```

Notice that the variable *value* has been defined as an *int* and initialized to zero. Then, our *in* object is used to call the *readInt()* method via the dot operator. The *readInt()* method will halt execution of the program until the user enters a value and presses the **ENTER** key. Once the **ENTER** key is pressed, the *readInt()* method returns the entered value. The returned value is assigned to the variable *value* using the assignment, =, operator.

Suppose, for example, that you have defined three integer variables called *score1*, *score2*, and *score3*. After importing the *keyboardInput* package and creating an input object, such as *in*, you insert three *readInt()* statements into your program, like this:

```
score1 = in.readInt();    //READ score1
score2 = in.readInt();    //READ score2
score3 = in.readInt();    //READ score3
```

When Java encounters the foregoing statements in your program, it halts execution until the user enters the required data. Now suppose the user enters the following via the system keyboard:

74 ↵
92 ↵
88 ↵

What do you suppose happens? You're right—the value 74 is assigned to *score1*, the value 92 is assigned to *score2*, and the value 88 to *score3*. One other point: You should always generate a **prompt** to the screen using a *print()* or *println()* statement prior to reading *each* variable, like this:

```
System.out.print("Enter an integer value for score 1: ");    //PROMPT FOR score1
score1 = in.readInt();                                        //READ score1
System.out.print("Enter an integer value for score 2: ");    //PROMPT FOR score2
score2 = in.readInt();                                        //READ score2
System.out.print("Enter an integer value for score 3: ");    //PROMPT FOR score3
score3 = in.readInt();                                        //READ score3
```

The two cardinal rules that apply when reading any data are as follows:

1. Any variable used in a read statement must be defined prior to its use in the statement.
2. The type of data entered for a given variable should match the data type defined for that variable.

By now, the first rule should be obvious. You cannot use a variable in a Java program unless it has been previously defined in your program. The second rule needs to be explored a bit further. Look at an entire program that reads numerical data:

```
import keyboardInput.*;           //FOR readInt() and readDouble()

public class NumberInput
{
  public static void main(String[] args)
  {
    //DEFINE INPUT VARIABLES
    int score1 = 0;
    double score2 = 0.0;
```

```
    //CREATE KEYBOARD OBJECT
    Keyboard in = new Keyboard();

    //PROMPT AND READ USER DATA
    System.out.print("Enter a test score: ");        //PROMPT FOR score1
    score1 = in.readInt();                            //READ score1
    System.out.print("Enter another test score: ");   //PROMPT FOR score2
    score2 = in.readDouble();                         //READ score2
  }//END main()
}//END NumberInput
```

First, notice the *keyboardInput* package is imported at the beginning of the program, before the program class heading. Next, you see two variables defined, one an *int* and the other a *double*. These variables will store the values returned by the keyboard read methods. Then, an object called *in* is created for the *Keyboard* class contained in the *keyboardInput* package. Now the program is ready to read information from the keyboard.

After a prompt, the *readInt()* method is called to read an integer, then another prompt is generated and the *readDouble()* method is called to read a floating-point value. Now, suppose the user enters the following data when the read statements are encountered:

Enter a test score: **98.5**↵
Enter another test score: **78**↵

What happens? Notice that the program defines *score1* as an integer and *score2* as a floating-point variable. However, the user has entered a decimal value for *score1* and an integer value for *score2*. Thus, Java attempts to assign a decimal value (98.5) to an integer variable (*score1*). This is called a **type mismatch** and will result in an error in many strongly typed languages, like Pascal. However, our *readInt()* method actually assigns the integer portion of the first value to *score1* and discards the decimal portion of the value. Thus, *score1* takes on the value 98. Then, the *readDouble()* method reads the second value, 78. Although the value 78 is an integer, the Java compiler converts it to the floating-point value of 78.0. This is okay, since the integers are a subset of the real, or floating-point, numbers. This example shows why you should define a variable so that it is the same data type as the data that are expected to be entered for that variable. In addition, the prompt should clearly state the type of data the user must enter. In this case, the first prompt should have directed the user to enter an integer, or whole number, value and the second prompt should have directed the user to enter a decimal value. Otherwise, you are likely to obtain invalid data. Such a bug is often very difficult to track down.

DEBUGGING TIP

When you initially code a program, it is usually wise to echo an input value to the display. This assures you that the program has performed the read operation and made the correct variable assignment. To echo an input value to the display, you simply insert a *println()* statement after the read statement. Within the *println()* statement, you list the same variable that is listed within the read statement. For instance, to echo the test scores in the foregoing program, you would add echoing *println()* statements, like this:

```
//THIS PROGRAM DEMONSTRATES HOW TO ECHO
//INPUT VARIABLES DURING PROGRAM DEVELOPMENT

import keyboardInput.*;          //FOR readInt() and readDouble()

public class InputTest
{
  public static void main(String[] args)
  {
    //DEFINE INPUT VARIABLES
    int score1 = 0;
    double score2 = 0.0;

    //CREATE KEYBOARD OBJECT
    Keyboard in = new Keyboard();

    //PROMPT AND READ USER DATA
    System.out.print("Enter an integer test score: ");    //PROMPT FOR score1
    score1 = in.readInt();                                 //READ score1
    System.out.println(score1);                            //ECHO score1
    System.out.print("Enter a decimal test score: ");     //PROMPT FOR score2
    score2 = in.readDouble();                              //READ score2
    System.out.println(score2);                            //ECHO score2
  }//END main()
}//END InputTest
```

Once the program has been debugged and is completely operational, you can comment-out or remove the echoing *println()* statements.

Reading Single-Character Data: *readChar()*

Reading numeric data is straightforward, as long as you adhere to the two rules for reading data. However, there are several things that you will want to keep in mind when reading character data using the *readChar()* method.

1. Only one character is read at a time.
2. **Whitespace** (blanks, tabs, new lines, carriage returns, etc.) characters are read just like nonwhitespace characters.
3. Numeric values can be read as characters but each digit is read as a separate character.

Let's look at a simple program that illustrates most of these concepts. Consider the following:

```java
//THIS PROGRAM DEMONSTRATES HOW TO READ SINGLE CHARACTERS

import keyboardInput.*;          //FOR readChar()

public class CharacterInput
{
  public static void main(String[] args)
  {
  //DEFINE CHARACTER VARIABLES AND INITIALIZE WITH BLANKS
  char grade1 = ' ';
  char grade2 = ' ';
  char grade3 = ' ';

  //CREATE KEYBOARD OBJECT
  Keyboard in = new Keyboard();

  //READ/WRITE USER DATA
  System.out.print("Enter a test grade: ");
  grade1 = in.readChar();
  System.out.println("The test grade you entered was: " + grade1);
  System.out.print("Enter a test grade: ");
  grade2 = in.readChar();
  System.out.println("The test grade you entered was: " + grade2);
  System.out.print("Enter a test grade: ");
  grade3 = in.readChar();
  System.out.println("The test grade you entered was: " + grade3);
  }//END main()
}//END CharacterInput
```

The foregoing program defines three variables (*grade1*, *grade2*, *grade3*) as character variables, which are initialized with blanks. The program then prompts for and reads the three character variables from the system keyboard using the *readChar()* method. Each variable value is echoed to the display after it is read. Now, let's see what the program will do for several input cases.

Case 1:

Enter a test grade: **A**↵
The test grade you entered was A
Enter a test grade: **B**↵
The test grade you entered was B
Enter a test grade: **C**↵
The test grade you entered was C

You see the output that you would expect. The *readChar()* method returns a single input character to the respective character variable listed in the read statement.

Case 2:

Enter a test grade: **ABC**↵
The test grade you entered was A
Enter a test grade: **D**↵
The test grade you entered was D
Enter a test grade: **F**↵
The test grade you entered was F

Here, the user has first entered the input characters 'A', 'B', and 'C', on a single line. However, the output echo shows that only the first character was read. This shows that the *readChar()* method returns the character 'A' to *grade1* and discards the remaining characters on that line. The user then enters the 'D' and 'F' on separate lines and the corresponding echoes show the correct assignments to *grade2* and *grade3*.

Case 3:

Enter a test grade: **A**↵
The test grade you entered was A
Enter a test grade: **'blank'**↵
The test grade you entered was ' blank'
Enter a test grade: **B**↵
The test grade you entered was B

Notice here that a blank, or space, was entered for *grade2*. The corresponding echo shows that the *readChar()* method read the blank whitespace and assigned it to *grade2* just as if it were a nonwhitespace character.

Case 4:

Enter a test grade: **75.**↵
The test grade you entered was 7
Enter a test grade: **92.**↵
The test grade you entered was 9
Enter a test grade: **88.**↵
The test grade you entered was 8

In this case, the user has typed in three numeric test grades rather than letter grades. However, because the variables are defined as character data, the *readChar()* method treats the digits as characters during the read operation. Each digit within a number is seen as a separate character. Thus, the character '7' is assigned to *grade1*, the character '9' is assigned to *grade2*, and the character '8' is assigned to *grade3*. The remaining characters on each line are ignored. The lesson to be learned here is to always use numeric variables (integer or floating-point) to read numeric data. As you can see, data can easily be corrupted when using character variables to read numeric data.

Example 4-4

There will be times when you want to "freeze" the display for the user until he or she takes some action, such as pressing the **ENTER** key. This can be accomplished by inserting a call to the *readChar()* method into your program, along with an appropriate prompt, at the point you want to freeze the display. Write the Java code required to accomplish this task.

Solution

```
System.out.print("HELLO THERE! Press the ENTER key to continue");
pause = in.readChar();
System.out.println("GOOD LOOKING!");
```

With this code, the message "HELLO THERE! Press the ENTER key to continue" is displayed, and program execution is halted by the *readChar()* method until the user presses the **ENTER** key. The *readChar()* method reads the CRLF produced by the **ENTER** key, and program execution continues, displaying the message "GOOD LOOKING!". The variable *pause* is assigned the CRLF ('\n') character.

As you can see, reading only one character at a time imposes a severe limitation on entering character data. A separate variable is required for each individual character to be read. Because most real-world character information appears in the form of strings, we need a way to read string data.

Reading String Data: *readString()*

You will use the *readString()* method to read string data. Let's see what happens when we use it in the following program:

```
//THIS PROGRAM DEMONSTRATES HOW TO READ A STRING

import keyboardInput.*;      //FOR readString()

public class StringInput
{
  public static void main(String[] args)
  {
  //DEFINE INPUT STRING OBJECT AND INITIALIZE WITH BLANKS
  String name = " ";

  //CREATE KEYBOARD OBJECT
  Keyboard in = new Keyboard();

  //READ/WRITE USER DATA
  System.out.print("Enter your name: ");
  name = in.readString();
  System.out.println("The name you entered was: " + name);
  }//END main()
}//END StringInput
```

Reading a string entry is straightforward. You simply define a string object to receive the user entry, prompt the user, and call the *readString()* method with your keyboard object. The string returned by the *readString()* method must be assigned to your string object. The following user dialog shows the results:

Enter your name: **Andrew C. Staugaard, Jr.**⏎
The name you entered was Andrew C. Staugaard, Jr.

Example 4-5

Write a program that will read and write the user's name and address.

Solution

Obviously, the data to be entered will be string data. So, you must define several string objects to accommodate the input strings. How must the input information be partitioned? Should you declare one object for the user's name and another for his/her address? But, what if our program needs to access just the user's zip code? It might make more sense to break up the address into several objects that could be individually accessed. So, let's define one object to store the user's name and then define five additional objects to store the user's street, city, address, state, and zip code, respectively. Then we will insert individual *readString()* and *println()* statements to read and write the required information. Here's the program:

```
//THIS PROGRAM WILL READ AND WRITE THE USER'S
//NAME, ADDRESS, AND PHONE NUMBER

import keyboardInput.*;     //FOR readString()
public class AddressInput
{
  public static void main(String[] args)
  {
   //DEFINE STRING OBJECTS AND INITIALIZE WITH BLANKS
   String name = " ";          //USER NAME
   String street = " ";        //USER STREET
   String city = " ";          //USER CITY
   String state = " ";         //USER STATE ABBREVIATION
   String zip = " ";           //USER ZIP
   String phone = " ";         //USER PHONE

   //CREATE KEYBOARD OBJECT
   Keyboard in = new Keyboard();

   //PROMPT USER AND READ ADDRESS STRINGS
   System.out.print("Enter your name: ");
   name = in.readString();
   System.out.print("Enter your street address: ");
   street = in.readString();
   System.out.print("Enter your city: ");
   city = in.readString();
   System.out.print("Enter your state: ");
   state = in.readString();
   System.out.print("Enter your zip code: ");
   zip = in.readString();
   System.out.print("Enter your phone number in (xxx)xxx-xxxx format: ");
   phone = in.readString();
```

```
                    //DISPLAY NAME AND ADDRESS STRINGS
                    System.out.println(name);
                    System.out.println(street);
                    System.out.println(city);
                    System.out.println(state);
                    System.out.println(zip);
                    System.out.println(phone);
               }//END main()
          }//END AddressInput
```

Once the string objects are properly defined, the program reads each string with a separate *readString()* statement and then writes each string with a separate *println()* statement.

Here is what will happen when the program is executed:

User types in:

Enter your name: **Andrew C. Staugaard, Jr.**↵
Enter your street address: **Route 999.**↵
Enter your city: **Java City**↵
Enter your state: **MO**↵
Enter your zip code: **12345**↵
Enter your phone number in (xxx)xxx-xxxx format: **(000)123-4567**↵

System displays:

Andrew C. Staugaard, Jr.
Route 999
Java City
MO
12345
(000)123-4567

 Quick Check

1. Write a statement to create a keyboard input object called *myInput*.

2. What is the purpose of the **new** operator in an object definition?

3. What is the difference between a declaration and a definition?

4. Write the code required to prompt and read an integer value from the user. Make sure you define the appropriate variables and objects.

5. Write the code required to prompt and read a single character from the user. Make sure you define the appropriate variables and objects.

6. Provide some examples of whitespace.

7. Write a statement that will freeze the display until the user presses the **ENTER** key. Make sure you define the appropriate variables and objects.

8. True or false: The *readChar()* method does not read whitespace.

9. What is an exception?

10. Write the code required to prompt and read a string from the user. Make sure you define the appropriate variables and objects.

11. Why is it important to echo user input to the display when developing a program?

PROBLEM SOLVING IN ACTION: USER-FRIENDLY PROGRAMS

Problem

As an overall program summary to the material presented in this chapter, let's write a user-friendly program that will calculate the monthly payment for an installment loan from different values of principle, interest rate, and term entered by the user. We will format a four-column table for principle, interest rate, term, and payment and underscore each column heading. Thus, the final program output will be a table showing the loan principle, interest rate, term, and monthly payment. In addition, we will display the program user's name and the date the program was run.

    Let's first define the problem in terms of output, input, and processing as follows.

Defining the Problem

Output: The final program output must be a table showing the calculated monthly loan payment along with the loan principle, interest rate, and term used in the calculation. The user's name and date the program was run will be displayed above the table. In addition, user prompts should be provided on the monitor to direct the user to enter the required values.

Input: The input must be the user's name, date the program was run, and values for the loan principle, interest rate, and term.

Processing: $payment = principle * rate/(1-(1+rate)^{-term})$

where: *principle* is the amount of the loan.
rate is a monthly interest rate in decimal form.
term is the number of months of the loan.

PROGRAMMING TIP

You must always strive to make your programs as user friendly as possible. By a user-friendly program, we mean a program that is easy to use and does not confuse the user. Such a program should always include the following (at a minimum):

1. A program description message that tells the user what the program is going to do.
2. Prompting messages prior to any read operations. These user prompts must tell the user what information to enter and how to enter it in clear, unconfusing terms.
3. Output information that is well formatted and whose meaning is easily understood by the user.

Planning the Solution

The next step is to construct a set of algorithms from the problem definition. Now, try to identify the separate tasks that must be performed to solve the problem. First, the program must obtain the required data from the user. Once the data are entered, the program must calculate the payment. Finally, the program must display the results. Thus, we can identify three program tasks, or methods, as follows:

- Obtain the user's name, date of program run, loan principle, interest rate, and term from the user.
- Calculate the monthly payment using the equation
  $payment = principle * rate/(1-(1+rate)^{-term})$
- Display the user's name, date the program was run, and table of results.

The problem solving diagram in Figure 4-3 shows the structure required for the program.

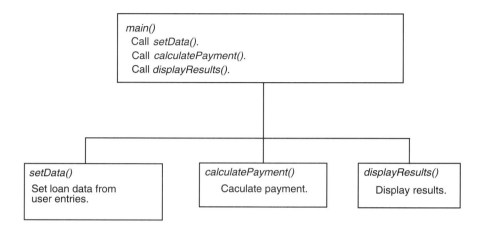

Figure 4-3   A problem solving diagram for loan problem.

Because we are using the modular technique to design the program, we must employ stepwise refinement to develop the algorithms. The initial algorithm level, *main()*, will simply reflect the problem definition and call the individual subprogram methods, as follows:

Initial Algorithm

> *main()*
> BEGIN
>   Call method to obtain the input data from the user.
>   Call method to calculate the loan payment.
>   Call method to display the results.
> END.

The first level of refinement requires that we show a detailed algorithm for each subprogram module, or method. They are as follows:

First Level of Refinement

> *setData()*
> BEGIN
>   Write a user prompt to enter the user's name.

Read(*name*).
Write a user prompt to enter the date.
Read(*date*).
Write a user prompt to enter the loan principle, or amount.
Read(*principle*).
Write a user prompt to enter the annual interest rate of the loan.
Read (*rate*).
Write a user prompt to enter the term of the loan, in months.
Read (*term*).
END.

calculatePayment( )
BEGIN
Calculate *decRate = rate/12/100.*
Calculate *payment = principle * decRate/(1-(1+decRate)$^{-term}$).*
END.

displayResults( )
BEGIN
Display user's name and date of program run.
Display table headings for principle, rate, term, and payment.
Display the principle, rate, term, and payment values under the respective headings.
END.

Notice that *rate* is converted to a monthly value in decimal form. Why? Because the user entry is an annual value in percentage form; however, the payment calculation formula requires a monthly value in decimal form.

Coding the Program

Here is how the foregoing algorithms are translated into Java code using a flat implementation:

```
/*ACTION 4-1 (ACTION04_01.JAVA)
OUTPUT:     A TABLE MENU SHOWS THE LOAN AMOUNT, INTEREST,
            TERM, AND MONTHLY PAYMENT.
            USER PROMPTS AS NECESSARY.
```

```
    INPUT:          LOAN AMOUNT, INTEREST RATE, AND TERM.

    PROCESSING: PAYMENT = PRINCIPLE * RATE/(1-(1+RATE)^ –TERM)
                    WHERE: PRINCIPLE IS THE AMOUNT OF THE LOAN.
                    RATE IS A MONTHLY INTEREST RATE IN DECIMAL FORM.
                    TERM IS THE NUMBER OF MONTHS OF THE LOAN.
    */

    import keyboardInput.*;          //FOR readString(), readDouble(), readInt()

    public class Action04_01
    {
      public static void main(String[] args)
      {
      //DEFINE AND INITIALIZE OBJECTS AND VARIABLES
      String name = " ";          //CUSTOMER NAME
      String date = " ";          //DATE OF REPORT
      double principle = 0.0;     //LOAN PRINCIPLE
      int term = 0;               //TERM OF LOAN IN MONTHS
      double rate = 0.0;          //ANNUAL INTEREST IN PERCENT FORM
      double payment = 0.0;       //MONTHLY PAYMENT
      double decRate = 0.0;       //MONTHLY INTEREST IN DECIMAL FORM
      char pause = ' ';           //TO FREEZE DISPLAY

      //CREATE KEYBOARD OBJECT
      Keyboard in = new Keyboard();

      //DISPLAY PROGRAM DESCRIPTION MESSAGE
      System.out.println("This program will calculate a monthly loan interest\n"
                    + "payment, total loan interest, or total loan amount.");

      //setData () METHOD:  SET VARIABLES TO DATA ENTERED BY USER
      System.out.print("\n\nPlease enter your name: ");
      name = in.readString();
      System.out.print("Enter the date in XX/XX/XX format: ");
      date = in.readString();
      System.out.print("\nEnter the amount of the loan: ");
      principle = in.readDouble();
      System.out.print("\nEnter the duration of the loan in months: ");
      term = in.readInt();
      System.out.print("\nEnter the annual interest rate in percent: ");
      rate = in.readDouble();
```

```
//calculatePayment() METHOD
decRate = rate/12/100;
payment = principle * decRate/(1-Math.pow((1+decRate),-term));

//displayResults() METHOD
System.out.println("\n\n");
System.out.println(name);
System.out.println(date);
System.out.println("\n\n"
                    + "LOAN AMOUNT"
                    + "\tINTEREST RATE"
                    + "\t\tTERM"
                    + "\t\tPAYMENT\n"
                    + "-----------"
                    + "\t-------------"
                    + "\t\t----"
                    + "\t\t-------\n");
System.out.println("$" + principle
                    + "\t\t" + rate + "%"
                    + "\t\t\t" + term + " Months"
                    + "\t$" + payment);

//FREEZE DISPLAY
System.out.println("\n\nPress ENTER to continue.");
pause = in.readChar();
} //END main()
} //END Action04_01 CLASS
```

Here is a sample of what the user would see when executing the program.

This program will calculate a monthly loan interest payment
based on user entries of loan amount, interest rate, and term.

Please enter your name: **Andrew C. Staugaard, Jr.** ↵
Enter the date in XX/XX/XX format: **05/25/99**↵

Enter the amount of the loan: $**1000.00**↵
Enter the duration of the loan in months: **12**↵
Enter the annual interest rate in percent: **12**↵

Name: Andrew C. Staugaard, Jr.
Date: 05/25/99

LOAN AMOUNT	INTEREST RATE	TERM	PAYMENT
---------------------	------------------------	---------	---------------
$1000	12.0%	12 Months	$88.85

Press ENTER to continue

Compare the program code to the corresponding output seen by the user. Make an effort to look at each of the coding details. You should pay particular attention to the following:

- The **import** statement at the beginning of the program required to use the keyboard input methods.
- The creation of the *in* object of the *Keyboard* class.
- The way in which the prompts are generated using *print()* rather than *println()* statements so that the user's entry appears on the same line as the prompt.
- The use of the *in* object to call the required keyboard method.
- The assignment of the keyboard entry to a variable.
- The conversion of the annual percentage rate entered by the user to a monthly decimal rate required by the payment formula.
- The payment calculation which uses a standard *Math* object to call the standard *pow()* method to raise *(1+decRate)* to the *–term* power. More about this in the next chapter.
- The output table formatting using the '\n' and '\t' escape sequence characters. (*Note:* It is often a job of trial and error to fine-tune the output to get what you want.)
- The strategic placement of the % and $ symbols when required for clarity.
- The use of the *readChar()* method to freeze the display until the ENTER key is pressed.

You now should have no trouble understanding this program with the material presented in this chapter. Now, make a serious effort to complete all of the questions and problems that follow. It is time to get your hands dirty and program your system to apply the program exercises that follow. This is where you will really begin learning how to program in Java.

CHAPTER SUMMARY

Getting information into your system is called *reading*, and getting information out of your system is called *writing*. The methods used for reading are in the *Keyboard* class, found in the *keyboardInput* package especially developed for this textbook. The methods used for writing are the standard *print()* and *println()* methods contained in the Java language.

A *print()* or *println()* method must be called with the standard *System.out* object using the dot operator. The items to be displayed must be listed as arguments within the method and concatenated using the + operator. The *print()* or *println()* methods can be used to write either fixed or variable information. Fixed numeric information is written by simply listing the numeric values as arguments within the *print()* or *println()* method. When writing fixed character information or strings, the information to be written must be enclosed double quotation marks. When writing variable information, the variable identifier must be listed as an argument within the *print()* or *println()* method. To format an output, you must often include an escaped sequence character within the argument listing. As an example, the '\n' CRLF escape sequence must be included to move the cursor to the next line on the display. The '\t' tab escape sequence must be used to generate a tab to the display. In addition, you should always use a layout chart to lay out your output prior to coding. Tools such as layout charts save valuable time at the keyboard.

Java does not include any convenient methods for reading keyboard data. Therefore, we have developed a custom package, called *keyboardInput*, to read the keyboard. The *keyboardInput* package contains a *Keyboard* class and a *KeyboardReadException* class. The *Keyboard* class contains the *readInt()*, *readDouble()*, *readChar()*, and *readString()* methods for reading any type of keyboard data. The *KeyboardReadExeception* class contains code to protect the user from entering invalid keyboard data. To use any of the *Keyboard* class methods you must:

- Import the *keyboardInput* package at the beginning of your program.
- Create an input object for the *Keyboard* class using the **new** operator.
- Define variables to receive the data returned by the keyboard methods. The data type of a given variable must be the same as that returned by a given method.
- Call the required keyboard method using your input object and the dot operator as part of an assignment statement which assigns the value returned by the method to the input variable.

User-friendly programs require interaction between the program and the user. At a minimum, a user-friendly program must do the following:
- Write a program description message to the user.
- Prompt the user prior to any read operations.
- Generate well-formatted outputs whose meanings are easily understood by the user.

QUESTIONS AND PROBLEMS

Questions

1. Indicate the output for each of the following:
   a. System.out.println();
   b. System.out.println("HELLO\tWORLD");
   c. System.out.println("1\t2\t3\t4");
   d. System.out.println("\t\t\t\tMy test score is: 97.6");
   e. System.out.println("\n\t\tTEST SCORE\t\t97.5");
   f. System.out.println("\n\t\tTEST SCORE\n\t\t97.5");
   g. System.out.print("\t\tTEST SCORE\n\t\t97.5");

2. Suppose that you define a constant as follows:
   static final char SPACE = ' ';
   What will the following statement do?
   System.out.println("HELLO" + SPACE + "WORLD");

3. What is the difference between the output produced by the following two statements?
   System.out.println("\n#\n#\n#");
   System.out.println("###");

4. Create an object called *input* for the *Keyboard* class.

5. Consider the following program segment:
   char char1 = ' ';
   char char2 = ' ';
   Keyboard input = new Keyboard();
   char1 = input.readChar();
   char2 = input.readChar();
   System.out.println("The value of char1 is: "+ char1);
   System.out.println("The value of char2 is: "+ char2);
   What will be displayed for each of the following user entries?
   a. **A⏎**
      B⏎

b. **AB.⌐**
   C⌐
c. **3.14⌐**
   'blank'⌐

6. What package must be imported in order to use the *readChar()* method in question 5?

7. What method must be used to obtain string data?

8. Define the appropriate variables and objects and write statements to read and then display your school name.

9. What is the relationship between *keyboardInput, Keyboard*, and *readInt()*?

10. True or false: The *Keyboard* class is a standard class in the Java language.

11. List and explain at least four commonly used escape sequences.

12. Write the statements required to display the following table headings, approximately one tab apart.

EMPLOYEE NAME   EMPLOYEE NUMBER   ANNUAL SALARY
------------------------   ----------------------------   ------------------------

13. The Java operator used to concatenate items within a *print()* or *println()* method is the _____ operator.

14. Explain the difference between the *print()* and *println()* methods.

15. Write the code necessary to freeze the display until the user presses the **ENTER** key. Make sure to define the appropriate variables and objects.

16. List several examples of whitespace characters.

17. True or false: The *readChar()* method ignores whitespace.

18. State the difference between a declaration and a definition.

19. What is an exception handler and what class in the *keyboardInput* package provides for exception handling.

Problems

Least Difficult

1. Write a program to display your first name in the middle of the screen.

2. Write a program to display your first name in the upper-left-hand corner of the screen using characters that are six lines high.

3. Write a program that will display a rectangle whose center is located in the middle of the screen. Construct the rectangle 8 lines high and 20 columns wide using X's.

4. Write a program that will display the following in the middle of the screen:

STUDENT	SEMESTER AVERAGE
1	84.5
2	67.2
3	77.4
4	86.8
5	94.7

More Difficult

In the problems that follow, you will need to employ several arithmetic operations. In Java, a plus symbol (+) is used for addition, a minus symbol (−) is used for subtraction, a star symbol (∗) is used for multiplication, and a slash symbol (/) is used for division.

5. Write a program to calculate simple interest on a $2000 loan for 2 years at a rate of 12.5 percent. Format your output appropriately, showing the amount of the loan, time period, interest rate, and interest amount.

6. Write a program that will prompt the user to enter any four-letter word one character at a time. Then display the word backwards. (Keep it clean!)

7. Electrical power in a direct-current (dc) circuit is declared as the product of voltage and current. In symbols, *power = voltage × current*. Write a program to calculate dc power from a voltage value of 12 volts and a current value of 0.00125 ampere. Generate a tabular display of input and output values in decimal form.

8. Write a user-friendly program that will calculate power from voltage and current values entered by the user. Generate a tabular display of input and output values in decimal form.

9. The rumor mill at the Java∗Mart supercenter is saying that employees are about to get a 5.5% raise. Write a user-friendly program for the employees that will allow them to determine their new annual as well as monthly gross salary if the rumor is true. Assume that the user will enter his/her current monthly salary.

Most Difficult

10. Write a user-friendly program that will calculate the weekly gross pay amount for an employee from user entries of the employee's rate of pay and number of hours worked. Assume the employee is part-time and, therefore, works less than 40 hours per week. Generate a display showing the employee's name, rate of pay, hours worked, and gross pay. Provide the appropriate display headings.

11. Write a user-friendly program to calculate the circumference and area of a circle from a user's entry of its radius. Generate a tabular display showing the circle's radius, circumference, and area. (*Note:* Circumference of a circle = *2 × pi × r*. Area of a circle = *pi × r²*.)

12. Write a user-friendly program that will allow a student to calculate his/her test average from four test scores. Generate a display of the student's name, course name, individual test scores, and test average.

13. The "4 Squares" bowling team has four bowlers. On a given bowling night, each team member bowls three games. Write a program that will read the date, each bowler's name, and the individual game scores for each bowler. Using the input information, display a bowling report. The report should show the date at the top of the screen, and then a table showing each bowler's scores, total, and integer average.

14. Write a user-friendly program to act as an electronic cash register. The program must display a receipt showing four sales items, their price, a subtotal of the four sales items, the sales tax at a rate of 7%, the total amount due, the amount tendered, and the amount of change returned.

Example Output:

Fish Hooks	1.29
Sinkers	.98
Line	7.45
Worms	2.00
Sub Total	11.72
sales tax	.82
Total	12.54
Amount Tendered	20.00
Change	7.46

GUI 104: LABELS AND TEXT FIELDS

PURPOSE

- *To become familiar with the GUI label and text field components.*
- *To demonstrate how to set the length of a text field.*
- *To show how to initialize a text field with text.*
- *To demonstrate the order in which components are added to a frame.*

Introduction

The *label* is a GUI component that is normally used to label other components within a window. A *text field* is a GUI component that displays a single line of text, or allows the user to enter a single line of text. In this module, you will load and execute a Java program that produces a frame with labels and text fields. You will modify the code and observe the effect on the window generated by the program.

Procedure

1. Load and execute the *GUI104_1.java* program contained on the CD that accompanies this book, or download it from www.prenhall.com. You should see a window similar to the one shown in Figure 1. Here, you see three text fields. The first text field contains the text "This is a text field", while the second and third text fields do not contain any text. Press the *Tab* key on the keyboard and notice that the window cursor will move from one text field to the next each time you press *Tab*. Place the cursor in the first text field and edit the text in the field. This text field is called an editable text field, since you can edit the text within it. Move the cursor to the other two text fields and enter some text into these fields. Notice that these are also editable text fields. All text fields are editable in Java, even if they are preinitialized with text by the program.

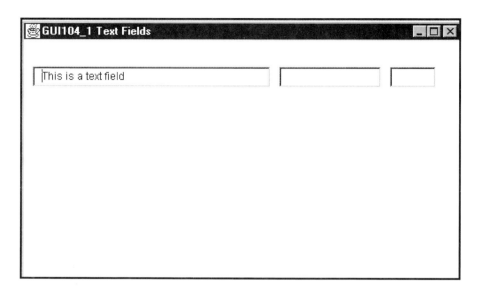

Figure 1 A frame with three text fields

2. Here is the Java code that produced the frame in Figure 1:

```
1    import java.awt.*;              //FOR GUI COMPONENTS

2    class TextFields extends FrameWithClose
3    {
4      //DEFINE TEXT FIELD OBJECTS AS PRIVATE CLASS DATA
5      private TextField nameField = new TextField("This is a text field",35);
6      private TextField numberField = new TextField(13);
7      private TextField gpaField = new TextField(4);

8      //CONSTRUCTOR
9      public TextFields (String title)
10     {
11     //CALL SUPERCLASS CONSTRUCTOR
12     super(title);

13     //SET FRAME LAYOUT MANAGER
14     setLayout(new FlowLayout(FlowLayout.LEFT,10,30));

15     //ADD TEXT FIELDS TO FRAME
16     add(nameField);
```

```
17    add(numberField);
18    add(gpaField);
19  }//END TextFields()
20 }//END TextFields

21 //APPLICATION CLASS TO TEST TextFields CLASS
22 public class GUI104_1
23 {
24    public static void main(String[] args)
25    {
26        //DEFINE FRAME OBJECT
27        TextFields window = new TextFields("GUI104_1 Text Fields");

28        //SET FRAME SIZE
29        window.setSize(500,300);

30        //MAKE FRAME VISIBLE
31        window.setVisible(true);
32   }//END main()
33 }//END GUI104_1
```

3. Change the text within the quotation marks in line 5 to something different. Execute the program again and notice that the first text field is initialized with the new text.

4. Change the values at the end of lines 5, 6, and 7 to different values and execute the program again. Notice that the length of each text field changes in proportion to the value entered. Also, notice that, depending on the size of the value, the text fields are layed out differently across the window.

Discussion

The foregoing program produced three text field components within the frame. A text field is a single editable line of text. When a text field is created, its length in columns across the screen must be set to the anticipated length of text to be entered by the user. In addition, the field can be optionally initialized with a text string. Unlike a button, a text field does not have a built-in label associated with it. In order to label a text field, you must add a *label* component to the frame adjacent to the text field. Guess what we are going to do next?

Procedure (continued)

5.   You guessed it! Load and execute the *GUI104_2.java* program contained on the CD that accompanies this book, or download it from www.prenhall.com. The window generated by this program should look similar to the one in Figure 2. Now, that looks a little better. Each text field has an associated label to indicate its purpose.

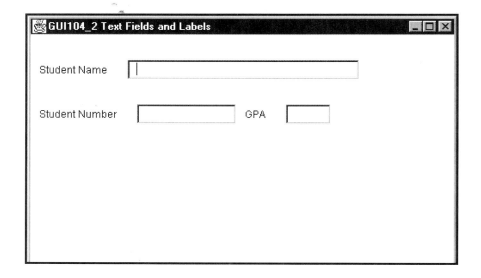

Figure 2 A frame with text fields and associated labels.

Here is the code that generated this window:

```
1    import java.awt.*;              //FOR GUI COMPONENTS
2
3    class TextFieldsAndLabels extends FrameWithClose
4    {
5      //DEFINE TEXT FIELD OBJECTS AS PRIVATE CLASS DATA
6      private TextField nameField = new TextField(35);
7      private TextField numberField = new TextField(13);
8      private TextField gpaField = new TextField(4);
9
10     //CONSTRUCTOR
11     public TextFieldsAndLabels (String title)
12     {
```

```
13   //CALL SUPERCLASS CONSTRUCTOR
14   super(title);
15
16   //SET FRAME LAYOUT MANAGER
17   setLayout(new FlowLayout(FlowLayout.LEFT,10,30));
18
19   //DEFINE LABEL OBJECTS
20   Label nameLabel = new Label("Student Name");
21   Label numberLabel = new Label("Student Number");
22   Label gpaLabel = new Label("GPA");
23
24   //ADD COMPONENTS TO FRAME
25   add(nameLabel);
26   add(nameField);
27   add(numberLabel);
28   add(numberField);
29   add(gpaLabel);
30   add(gpaField);
31
32  }//END TextFieldsAndLabels()
33 }//END TextFieldsAndLabels
34
35 //APPLICATION CLASS TO TEST TextFieldsAndLabels CLASS
36 public class GUI104_2
37 {
38   public static void main(String[] args)
39   {
40     //DEFINE FRAME OBJECT
41     TextFieldsAndLabels window = new TextFieldsAndLabels("GUI104_2
                                      Text Fields and Labels");
42
43     //SET FRAME SIZE
44     window.setSize(500,300);
45
46     //MAKE FRAME VISIBLE
47     window.setVisible(true);
48   }//END main()
49 }//END GUI104_2
```

6. The three label objects are created in lines 20, 21, and 22 of the program. Notice that the text which forms the *label* is provided in each case. Change the

text and execute the program again. You should find that the label text has changed accordingly.

7. Notice how the text fields and labels are added to the frame in lines 25 through 30. A label is added, then its associated text field, then another label, followed by its text field, and so on. Remember that components are placed into a frame in the order in which they are added within the program. Change the order, execute the program, and observe the results.

Discussion

When label objects are created, the label text must be provided within the object definition; otherwise there is no visible label. When components are added to a frame, they will appear in the order in which they are added. This program employs the *FlowLayout* manager. As a result, GUI components are placed within the frame, from left to right, as they are added to the frame class.

Now that we have a place that a user can enter text, wouldn't it be great to read the text entries in order to process the text information? This will be demonstrated in the next GUI module.

5
NUTS AND BOLTS: STANDARD STUFF IN JAVA

OBJECTIVES

When you are finished with this chapter, you should have a good understanding of the following:

- The standard arithmetic operations in Java.
- The order of precedence used for arithmetic operations in Java.
- The standard mathematical methods provided by the *Math* class in Java.
- How to call the *Math* class methods and constants.
- The increment/decrement operations in Java.
- Preincrement/predecrement versus postincrement/postdecrement when used within arithmetic expressions.
- Simple and compound assignment operations in Java.
- The use of trig methods in Java.

INTRODUCTION

In order for your programs to perform meaningful tasks, you must be familiar with several standard, or built-in, operations available to you in Java. The simplest of these are the arithmetic operations. By definition, an arithmetic operation generates a numeric result. Such operations are the topic of the first section of this chapter. Pay particular attention to the division (/), modulus (%), and increment/decrement (++, −−) operations. Java also has a standard *Math* class that includes several commonly used mathematical methods. These methods simplify the chore of programming, because they can simply be called via the built-in *Math* class. Several of these methods will be discussed in this chapter.

The second section deals with the Java assignment operators. Assignment operators assign a value to a variable in memory. There are compound assignment operators in Java that allow you to combine an arithmetic operation with the assignment operation.

The chapter closes with two *Problem Solving in Action* case studies. Make sure you go through these problems in detail, since each focuses on a how to use the operations discussed in this chapter.

5-1 ARITHMETIC OPERATIONS

You are now ready to begin learning how to write simple straight-line programs in Java. By a straight-line program, we mean a program that does not alter its flow; it simply executes a series of statements in a straight line, from beginning to end. In order for your programs to perform meaningful tasks, you must be familiar with several standard, or built-in, operations available to you in Java. The simplest of these are the standard arithmetic operations. By definition, an arithmetic operation generates a numeric result.

Arithmetic operations in Java include the common add, subtract, multiply, and divide operations, as well as increment/decrement operations. The basic add, subtract, multiply, and divide operations can be performed on any numeric data type. Recall that the standard numeric data types in Java are the integers and floats. In addition, you can perform arithmetic operations on character data in Java, because characters are represented as integers (Unicode) within the computer.

Table 5-1 lists the five basic arithmetic operations and the Java symbols used to represent those operations. The addition (+), subtraction (−), and multiplication (∗) operators are straightforward and do not need any further explanation. However, you might note that an asterisk (∗) is used for multiplication rather than a times symbol (×) so that the computer does not get multiplication confused with the character 'x'.

TABLE 5-1 ARITHMETIC OPERATORS DEFINED IN JAVA

Operation	Symbol
Add	+
Subtract	−
Multiply	∗
Division	/
Remainder (modulus)	%

The division operator needs some special attention. This operator will generate a result that is the same data type of the operands used in the operation. Thus, if you divide two integers, you will get an integer result. If you *divide one or more* decimal floating-point values, you get a decimal result. Thus, 10 / 3 = 3 and 10.0 / 3 = 3.333333. Here, the former is integer division and generates an integer result. The latter is floating-point division and generates a floating-point result.

Finally, the modulus operator (%) simply generates the remainder that occurs when you divide two integer values. For example, the result of 5 % 3 is 2, 5 % 4 is 1, and 5 % 5 is 0.

PROGRAMMING NOTE

The modulus operator (%) is only defined for integers. So, what happens if you use a floating-point value with modulus? Well, nothing critical. You will *not* get a compile or run-time error. Java will simply use the integer portion of the floating-point value to generate a result. Thus, the statement

System.out.println(6.0 % 3.6);

produces a totally unpredictable value of 2.4. The lesson to be learned here is *never* use the modulus operator with floating-point values, since the results can be unpredictable.

Let's look at a couple of examples that illustrate these operations. Example 5-1 shows several arithmetic operations on integers, and Example 5-2 deals with arithmetic operations on floating-point values.

Example 5-1

What value will be returned as the result of each of the following operations?

a. 3 * (−5)
b. 4 * 5 − 10
c. 10 / 3
d. 9 % 3
e. −21 / (−2)
f. −21 % (−2)
g. 4 * 5 / 2 + 5 % 2

Solution

a. 3 * (−5) returns the value −15.

b. 4 * 5 − 10 returns the value 10. Note that the multiplication operation is performed before the subtraction operation.

c. 10 / 3 returns the value 3, because this is integer division.

d. 9 % 3 returns the value 0, because there is no remainder.

e. −21 / (−2) returns the integer quotient, 10.

f. −21 % (−2) returns the remainder, −1.

g. 4 * 5 / 2 + 5 % 2 = (4 * 5) / 2 + (5 % 2) = 20 / 2 + (5 % 2) = 10 + 1 = 11. Notice that the multiplication, *, division, /, and remainder, %, operators are performed first, from left to right. The addition operation is performed last.

Aside from showing how the individual operators work, the foregoing example illustrates the priority, or ordering, of the operators. When more than one operation is performed in an expression, you must know the order in which they will be performed to determine the result. Java performs operations in the following order:

- All operators within parentheses are performed first.

- If there are nested parentheses (parentheses within parentheses) the inner-most operators are performed first, from the inside out.

- The *, /, and % operators are performed next, from left to right within the expression.

- The + and − operators are performed last, from left to right within the expression.

This order of precedence is summarized in Table 5-2.

TABLE 5-2 ORDER OF PRECEDENCE FOR JAVA ARITHMETIC OPERATORS

Operator(s)	Operation	Precedence
( )	Parentheses	Evaluated first, inside-out if nested, or left-to-right if same level.
*, /, or %	Multiply Divide Modulus	Evaluated second, left-to-right.
+, −	Add Subtract	Evaluated last, left-to-right.

When performing several floating-point operations within an arithmetic expression, division and multiplication have the same priority. Thus, operators within parentheses are performed first, followed by multiplication and division, followed by addition and subtraction.

DEBUGGING TIP

Beginning programmers, and even experienced programmers for that matter, often forget that the Java division operator only produces a floating-point result if one or both of the operands are floating-point. For example, consider the problem of converting degrees Fahrenheit to degrees Celsius. The equation you all learned in high school for this is $C = 5/9 \times (F - 32)$, where F is degrees Fahrenheit and C is degrees Celsius. Now, suppose you were to code this equation as you see it, as follows:

C = 5/9 ∗ (F − 32);

What do you suppose would happen? You're right, the resulting value for C would always be 0, regardless of the value of F. How could this be corrected? Yes, by coding either the numerator or denominator of the fractional constant as a floating-point value, like this:

C = 5.0/9 ∗ (F − 32);

Example 5-2

Evaluate each of the following expressions:

a. 4.6 − 2.0 + 3.2
b. 4.6 − 2.0 ∗ 3.2
c. 4.6 − 2.0 / 2 ∗ 3.2
d. −3.0 ∗ ((4.3 + 2.5) ∗ 2.0) − 1.0
e. −21.0 / −2
f. −21.0 % −2
g. 10.0 / 3
h. ((4 ∗ 12) / (4 + 12))
i. 4 ∗ 12 / 4 + 12

Solution

a. $4.6 - 2.0 + 3.2 = (4.6 - 2.0) + 3.2 = 2.6 + 3.2 = 5.8$
b. $4.6 - 2.0 * 3.2 = 4.6 - (2.0 * 3.2) = 4.6 - 6.4 = -1.8$
c. $4.6 - 2.0 / 2 * 3.2 = 4.6 - ((2.0 / 2) * 3.2) = 4.6 - (1.0 * 3.2) = 4.6 - 3.2 = 1.4$
d. $-3.0 * ((4.3 + 2.5) * 2.0) - 1.0 = -3.0 * (6.8 * 2.0) - 1.0 = -3.0 * 13.6 - 1.0 = -40.8 - 1.0 = -41.8$
e. $-21.0 / -2 = 10.5$
f. $-21.0 \% -2 = -1$
g. $10.0 / 3 = 3.333333$
h. $((4 * 12) / (4 + 12)) = 48 / 16 = 3$
i. $4 * 12 / 4 + 12 = 48 / 4 + 12 = 12 + 12 = 24$

DEBUGGING TIP

When using parentheses within an arithmetic expression, the number of left parentheses must equal the number of right parentheses. When coding your programs, always count each to make sure that this equality holds.

Notice that we have used parentheses in the solutions for the preceding examples to indicate the order of the operations. As you can see, the parentheses clarify the expression. For this reason, we suggest that you always use parentheses when writing arithmetic expressions. This way, you will always be sure of the order in which the compiler will execute the operators within the expression. Keep in mind, however, that the compiler will always perform the operators within parentheses from inside out, as shown in part d of Example 5-2. In particular, notice how the evaluation of part h of Example 5-2 differs from part i. The parentheses in part h force Java to perform the division operation last, after the addition operation. In part i, the division operation is performed prior to the addition operation, generating a completely different result. This is why you should always use parentheses when writing expressions. It is better to be safe then sorry!

Built-in Arithmetic Methods

To perform more advance mathematical operations, you can use any of the built-in methods contained in the Java *Math* class. Some of these standard mathematical methods are listed in Table 5-3. Most of these operations should be familiar to you from your background in mathematics. When using any of these methods in Java, you must make sure that the argument is the correct data type as specified by the method definition. In addition, any variable to which the method is assigned must be defined as the same data type returned by the method.

The methods in Table 5-3 must be called using the predefined *Math* class name. For example, to call the *sqrt( )* method, you must use the code *Math.sqrt(x)*.

TABLE 5-3 SOME STANDARD MATHEMATICAL METHODS AVAILABLE IN JAVA

Method Name	Operation
abs(x)	Returns the absolute value of *x*.
acos(x)	Returns the arc cosine of *x* (radians).
asin(x)	Returns the arc sine of *x* (radians).
atan(x)	Returns the arc tangent of *x* (radians).
ceil(x)	Rounds *x* up to the next highest integer.
cos(x)	Returns the cosine of *x* (radians).
exp(x)	Returns e^x.
floor(x)	Rounds down to the next lowest integer.
log(x)	Returns the natural log of *x*.
min(x,y)	Returns the smallest of *x* and *y*.
max(x,y)	Returns the largest of *x* and *y*.
pow(x,y)	Returns *x* raised to the power of *y*.
random( )	Generates a random number between 0 and 1.
round(x)	Rounds *x* to the nearest integer value.
sin(x)	Returns the sine of *x* (radians).
sqrt(x)	Returns the square root of *x*.
tan(x)	Returns the tangent of *x* (radians).
E	Value of *e* (2.718281828459045)
PI	Value of π (3.141592653589793)

Use the predefined *Math* class name to call a method in the *Math* class with the dot operator.

Thus, the statement

System.out.println(Math.sqrt(9));

displays the value

3.0

You can raise any value to the power of any other value using the *pow()* method. As a result, the statement

System.out.println(Math.pow(2,3));

displays the value

8.0

Notice that the *Math* class also includes the standard trig operations. However, be careful when using these, because they evaluate radians, not degrees. For example, the statement

System.out.println(Math.sin(90*Math.PI/180));

displays the value

1.0

Let's take a closer look at this last statement. First, you see that the *sin()* method is being called. The intent here is to display the sine of 90 degrees. However, notice from Table 5-3 that the *sin()* method requires radians, rather than degrees, as its argument. To convert degrees to radians, you must multiply the degrees by $\pi/180$. The *Math* class includes a constant called *PI* that can be called upon for this operation. Thus, we multiply 90 by *Math.PI/180* to convert 90 degrees to radians as required by the *sin()* method.

Make sure to check your Java compiler on-line help for more methods available in the *Math* class as well as other standard class methods available in Java.

The standard trig methods in the Java *Math* class evaluate radians, not degrees. Multiply degrees by π/180 within the trig method argument to convert degrees to radians.

Increment and Decrement Operators

There are many times in a program when you will need to increment (add 1) or decrement (subtract 1) a variable. The increment and decrement operators shown in Table 5-4 are provided for this purpose.

TABLE 5-4 INCREMENT AND DECREMENT OPERATORS

Operation	Symbol
Increment	++
Decrement	−−

Increment/decrement can be applied to both integer and floating-point variables, as well as character variables. An increment operation adds 1 to the value of a variable. Thus, $++x$ or $x++$ is equivalent to the statement $x = x + 1$. Conversely, a decrement operation subtracts 1 from the value of a variable. As a result, $--x$ or $x--$ is equivalent to the statement $x = x - 1$. As you can see, you can *pre*increment/*pre*decrement a variable, or *post*increment/*post*decrement a variable.

Here's a short example to illustrate increment/decrement:

Example 5-3

Determine the output generated by the following program:

```
int x = 5;
int y = 10;
System.out.println("x = " + ++x);
System.out.println("x = " + −−x);
System.out.println("y = " + (y = ++x − 2));
x = 5;
System.out.println("y = " + (y = x++ − 2));
System.out.println("x = " + x);
```

```
x = 0;
System.out.println("y = " +  (y = x-- - 2));
System.out.println("x = " +  x);
```

Solution

Here is the output that you will see on the monitor:

```
x = 6
x = 5
y = 4
y = 3
x = 6
y = -2
x = -1
```

Notice that the variable x is initialized with the value 5 at the start of the program. The first *println()* statement simply increments x to the value 6. The second *println()* statement then decrements x back to the value 5. Next, the third *println()* statement **preincrements** the value of x and then subtracts 2 from its value. We say that x is preincremented because the increment symbol appears before x and the increment operation is performed *before* x is used in the expression. Thus, the expression reduces to $y = x + 1 - 2 = 5 + 1 - 2 = 4$. Observe that the arithmetic operations are performed first, and then the result is assigned to y via the assignment operator. Thus, the value displayed by the *println()* statement is the value of y, or 4.

Finally, the fourth *println()* statement involves a *postincrement* operation on x. A postincrement operation is indicated by the increment symbol following x. So, what's the difference between a preincrement and a postincrement operation? Well, a preincrement operation increments the variable *before any expression involving the variable is evaluated*. On the other hand, a postincrement operation increments the variable *after any expression involving the variable is evaluated*. Now, looking at the fourth *println()* statement in the program, you find that x starts out with the value 5. Thus, the expression reduces to $y = x - 2 = 5 - 2 = 3$. *After* the expression is evaluated, x is incremented to the value 6, as shown by the next *println()* statement. Finally, the last two *println()* statements show the result of a postdecrement operation. Here, x is assigned the value 0 to be used in the expression. Thus, $y = 0 - 2 = -2$. *After* the expression is evaluated, the value of x is decremented to -1, as shown by the last output value.

From Example 5-3, you see that a variable can be preincremented or postincremented. Likewise, a variable can be predecremented or postdecremented. If a variable is preincremented or predecremented within an expression, the variable is incremented/decremented *before* the expression is evaluated. On the other hand, if a variable is postincremented or postdecremented within an expression, the variable is incremented/decremented *after* the expression is evaluated.

DEBUGGING TIP

There is often confusion about pre- versus postincrement/postdecrement. Just remember that it doesn't matter *unless* the increment/decrement operation is part of an expression. Within an expression a preincrement/predecrement is executed *before* the expression is evaluated, while a postincrement/postdecrement is executed *after* the expression is evaluated. For example, suppose we define two integer variables called *number* and *value*. Then the statements

++value; and value++;

will produce the same value for *value*. However, the statements

number = (10 − ++value); and number = (10 − value++);

will produce two different values for *number*. Of course, the value of *value* would be incremented by 1 after executing any of the foregoing statements. To avoid potential problems, we suggest that you *do not* use ++ or −− within expressions, even within *println()* statements. Use the more readable and predictable longer form of adding or subtracting 1 from a variable. Only use ++ or −− when a variable is being incremented/decremented as a statement by itself.

Quick Check

1. List the order in which Java performs arithmetic operations. Be sure to mention how parentheses are handled.

2. What can be said about *x* if *x* % 2 returns the value 0?

3. What can be said about *y* if *y* % 17 returns the value 0?

4. What is returned by the expression 1 / 2 % 5?

5. What is returned by the expression $(2 - ++x)$, assuming that x has the value 1 before the expression is evaluated?

6. What is returned by the expression $(2 - x++)$, assuming that x has the value 1 before the expression is evaluated?

7. Write a statement using the decrement operator that is equivalent to the statement $x = x - 1$.

8. True or false: The division operator will produce an integer result when either of the operands is an integer.

9. What is the difference between using the preincrement operator versus the postincrement operator on a variable, especially when the variable is used as part of a compound expression?

10. What is the result of 10 / 100?

11. Write a statement to display a random number between 0 and 100.

12. Write a statement that will display the tangent of 45 degrees.

13. Write a statement that will return the value of π.

14. Explain how you can get an on-line description of a standard method using your compiler.

5-2 ASSIGNMENT OPERATIONS

An assignment operation stores a value in memory. The value is stored at a location in memory that is accessed by the variable on the left-hand side of the assignment operator. As a result, a Java assignment operator *assigns* the value on the right side of the operator to the variable appearing on the left side of the operator. Another way to say this is that the variable on the left side of the operator is *set* to the value on the right side of the operator. The Java assignment operators are listed in Table 5-5.

First, let's say a word about the simple assignment operator, =. Although an equals symbol is used for this operator, you cannot think of it as equals. Here's why: Consider the statement $x = x + 1$. If you put this expression in an algebra exam, your professor would mark it wrong, because x cannot be equal to itself plus 1, right? However, in Java, this expression means to add 1 to x, and then assign the resulting value back to x. In other words, set x to the value $x + 1$. This is a perfectly legitimate operation. As you will soon find out, equals is a Boolean operator and uses two equals symbols, ==, in Java.

TABLE 5-5 ASSIGNMENT OPERATORS USED IN JAVA

Operation	Symbol	Example	Equivalent to
Simple assignment	=	Count = 1	Count = 1
Addition/assignment	+=	Count += 1	Count = Count + 1
Subtraction/assignment	−=	Count −= 1	Count = Count − 1
Multiplication/assignment	*=	Count *= 2	Count = Count * 2
Division/assignment	/=	Count /= 2	Count = Count / 2
Remainder/assignment (integers only)	%=	Count %= 2	Count = Count % 2

The compound assignment operators shown in Table 5-5 simply combine the assignment operator with an arithmetic operator. Suppose that we define x and y as integers; then the following holds:

x += y is equivalent to $x = x + y$

x −= y is equivalent to $x = x - y$

x *= y is equivalent to $x = x * y$

x /= y is equivalent to $x = x / y$

x %= y is equivalent to $x = x \% y$

As you can see, both the increment/decrement operators and the compound assignment operators provide a shorthand notation for writing arithmetic expressions. This shorthand notation takes a bit getting used to. These are simply syntactic shortcuts which you don't have to use. In fact, many instructors prefer the regular notation because it is more readable and less cryptic than the shorthand notation. Ask your instructors which notation they prefer.

 Quick Check

1. Write a statement using the compound addition assignment operator that is equivalent to the statement $x = x + 5$.

2. Write a statement using the compound division assignment operator that is equivalent to the statement $x = x / 10$.

3. Write a statement using the compound division assignment operator that is equivalent to the statement $x = 10 / x$.

4. Why does the statement $x = x + 5$ make sense in Java, but not in your math class?

PROBLEM SOLVING IN ACTION: INVENTORY CONTROL

Problem

Following is a partial inventory listing of items in the sporting goods department of the Java∗Mart supercenter:

Item	Beginning Quantity	Units Sold This Month
Fishing line	132 spools	24 spools
Fish hooks	97 packages	45 packages
Sinkers	123 packages	37 packages
Fish nets	12 ea.	5 ea.

Write a program that will display a monthly report showing the item name, beginning quantity, units sold this month, ending quantity, and percent of quantity sold. The problem solution begins with the problem definition phase.

Defining the Problem

Output: The program must generate a monthly report of the item name, beginning quantity, units sold this month, ending quantity, and percent of quantity sold. Now is a good time to develop the output format. Suppose we use a tabular format, like this:

MONTH:

ITEM BEGIN QTY UNITS SOLD ENDING QTY % SOLD

Input: The sporting goods manager must enter the month of the report and inventory data shown in the above table. Therefore, the program must be very user friendly.

Processing: The program must use the input information to calculate two things: the ending quantity and the percent sold. The ending quantity is found by simply subtracting the units sold from the beginning quantity, like this:

$$ending \ qty \ = \ begin \ qty \ - \ units \ sold$$

The percent sold is found by dividing the units sold by the beginning quantity and multiplying by 100%, like this:

$$\% \ sold \ = \ (units \ sold \ / \ begin \ qty) \ \times \ 100\%$$

Planning the Solution

We must now construct a set of algorithms from the problem definition. Using a modular program design, we will divide the problem into individual subproblems to solve the overall problem. There are three major tasks that follow directly from the problem definition:

- Obtain the inventory data for a given item from the user.
- Calculate the ending quantity and percent sold for the given item.
- Display the item report.

Because we do not yet have a way of telling Java to automatically repeat a task, the last three tasks must be repeated for each item in the inventory. The diagram in Figure 5-1 shows the block structure required for the program.

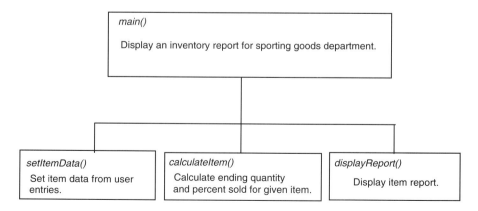

Figure 5-1   A problem solving diagram for the inventory problem.

The initial algorithm level, *main( )*, will reflect the foregoing analysis and call the individual method modules.

Initial Algorithm

> *main( )*
> BEGIN
>   Call method to obtain the inventory data for a given item from the user.
>   Call method to calculate the ending quantity and percent sold.
>   Repeat last two calls for each inventory item.
>   Call method to display the item report.
> END.

In developing the algorithm, you would quickly realize that the processing is the same for each sales item. As a result, we have used a single *repeat* rather than actually repeating the algorithm statements three more times. This has been done to make the algorithm more efficient.

The first level of refinement requires that we show a detailed algorithm for each task, or method, that we have identified. They are as follows:

First Level of Refinement

> *setItemData( )*
> BEGIN
>   Write a user prompt to enter the item name.
>   Read (*item*).
>   Write a user prompt to enter the beginning quantity.
>   Read (*begin qty*).
>   Write a user prompt to enter the number of units sold.
>   Read (*units sold*).
> END.

> *calculateItem( )*
> BEGIN
>   Calculate *ending qty = begin qty − units sold*.
>   Calculate *% sold = (units sold / begin qty) × 100 %*.
> END.

displayReport( )
BEGIN
   Display *item*, *begin qty*, *units sold*, *ending qty*, and *% sold* for each item.
END.

Given our problem definition, the foregoing collection of algorithms is straightforward. The sporting goods manager must enter the month for the inventory report. The three methods must then be executed for each of the items in the inventory. The *setItemData( )* method prompts and reads the item information from the user and assigns it to the item variables. The *calculateItem( )* method will make the required calculations. Finally, the *displayReport( )* method will display the item report.

Now the job is to code these algorithms in Java. With your present knowledge of Java, coding most of these algorithms should not present a problem. But what about the repeat statement at the end of the *main( )* method algorithm? Well, notice that this statement requires that you go back and repeat many of the previous statements over and over until all the items are processed. Such a repeating operation is called an **iteration**, or **looping**, operation. To date, you do not have the Java tools to perform such an operation. So, we will have to repeat all of the processing steps for each of the sales items in the inventory. In Chapter 7 you will learn how to perform iterative operations in Java, thus making the code much more efficient.

Here's the flat implementation of the foregoing algorithms:

Coding the Program

```
/*ACTION 5-1 (ACTION05_01.JAVA)

OUTPUT:      A MONTHLY REPORT OF THE
             ITEM NAME, BEGINNING QUANTITY,
             UNITS SOLD THIS MONTH, ENDING
             QUANTITY, AND PERCENT OF QUANTITY SOLD

INPUT:       MONTH OF REPORT, ITEM NAME, BEGIN QTY.
             UNITS SOLD THIS MONTH

PROCESSING: THE PROGRAM MUST CALCULATE TWO THINGS:
             ENDING QUANTITY AND THE PERCENT SOLD

*/
```

```java
import keyboardInput.*;          //FOR readDouble(), readChar()

public class Action05_01
{
  public static void main(String[] args) throws Exception
  {
  //DEFINE AND INITIALIZE MONTH OBJECT AND PAUSE VARIABLE
  String month = "";            //MONTH OF REPORT
  char pause = ' ';             //PAUSE VARIABLE

  //DEFINE AND INITIALIZE ITEM 1 OBJECTS AND VARIABLES
  String item1 = " ";           //SALES ITEM NAME
  double beginQty1 = 10.0;      //BEGINNING QUANTITY
  double unitsSold1 = 5.0;      //NUMBER OF UNITS SOLD
  double endQty1 = 0;           //ENDING QUANTITY
  double percentSold1 = 0.0;    //PERCENT OF SALES

  //DEFINE AND INITIALIZE ITEM 2 OBJECTS AND VARIABLES
  String item2 = " ";           //SALES ITEM NAME
  double beginQty2 = 0.0;       //BEGINNING QUANTITY
  double unitsSold2 = 0.0;      //NUMBER OF UNITS SOLD
  double endQty2 = 0;           //ENDING QUANTITY
  double percentSold2 = 0.0;    //PERCENT OF SALES

  //DEFINE AND INITIALIZE ITEM 3 OBJECTS AND VARIABLES
  String item3 = " ";           //SALES ITEM NAME
  double beginQty3 = 0.0;       //BEGINNING QUANTITY
  double unitsSold3 = 0.0;      //NUMBER OF UNITS SOLD
  double endQty3 = 0;           //ENDING QUANTITY
  double percentSold3 = 0.0;    //PERCENT OF SALES

  //DEFINE AND INITIALIZE ITEM 4 OBJECTS AND VARIABLES
  String item4 = " ";           //SALES ITEM NAME
  double beginQty4 = 0.0;       //BEGINNING QUANTITY
  double unitsSold4 = 0.0;      //NUMBER OF UNITS SOLD
  double endQty4 = 0;           //ENDING QUANTITY
  double percentSold4 = 0.0;    //PERCENT OF SALES

  //CREATE KEYOARD OBJECT
  Keyboard in = new Keyboard();
```

```
//DISPLAY PROGRAM DESCRIPTION MESSAGE
System.out.println("\n\nDear Sporting Goods Manager\n"
                    + "You will be asked to enter four sales items, one at\n"
                    + "a time.  With each item you will be asked to enter\n"
                    + "the item name, the beginning quantity, and the quantity\n"
                    + "sold this month. The computer will then print a monthly\n"
                    + "inventory report for the sales items.");

//SET MONTH FROM USER ENTRY
System.out.print("\nPlease enter the month in of this report: ");
month = in.readString();

//SET ITEM 1 DATA FROM USER ENTRY
System.out.print("\nPlease enter the item name: ");
item1 = in.readString();
System.out.print("Please enter the beginning quantity of " + item1 + ": ");
beginQty1 = in.readDouble();
System.out.print("Please enter the quantity of " + item1 + " sold in "
                    + month + ": ");
unitsSold1 = in.readDouble();

//CALCULATE ENDING QUANTITY AND PERCENT SOLD FOR ITEM 2
endQty1 = beginQty1 - unitsSold1;
percentSold1 = (unitsSold1 / beginQty1) * 100;

//SET ITEM 2 DATA FROM USER ENTRY
System.out.print("\nPlease enter the item name: ");
item2 = in.readString();
System.out.print("Please enter the beginning quantity of " + item2 + ": ");
beginQty2 = in.readDouble();
System.out.print("Please enter the quantity of " + item2 + " sold in "
                    + month + ": ");
unitsSold2 = in.readDouble();

//CALCULATE ENDING QUANTITY AND PERCENT SOLD FOR ITEM 2
endQty2 = beginQty2 - unitsSold2;
percentSold2 = (unitsSold2 / beginQty2) * 100;

//SET ITEM 3 DATA FROM USER ENTRY
System.out.print("\nPlease enter the item name: ");
item3 = in.readString();
System.out.print("Please enter the beginning quantity of " + item3 + ": ");
beginQty3 = in.readDouble();
```

```
System.out.print("Please enter the quantity of " + item3 + " sold in "
                 + month + ": ");
unitsSold3 = in.readDouble();

//CALCULATE ENDING QUANTITY AND PERCENT SOLD FOR ITEM 3
endQty3 = beginQty3 - unitsSold3;
percentSold3 = (unitsSold3 / beginQty3) * 100;

//SET ITEM 4 DATA FROM USER ENTRY
System.out.print("\nPlease enter the item name: ");
item4 = in.readString();
System.out.print("Please enter the beginning quantity of " + item4 + ": ");
beginQty4 = in.readDouble();
System.out.print("Please enter the quantity of " + item4 + " sold in "
                 + month + ": ");
unitsSold4 = in.readDouble();

//CALCULATE ENDING QUANTITY AND PERCENT SOLD FOR ITEM 4
endQty4 = beginQty4 - unitsSold4;
percentSold4 = (unitsSold4 / beginQty4) * 100;

//PRINT REPORT HEADER INFORMATION
System.out.println("\n\nMONTH:  " +  month);
System.out.println("\n\n\nITEM\tBEGIN QTY\tUNITS SOLD\tENDING QTY"
                 + "\t% SOLD");
System.out.println("----\t---------\t----------\t----------\t------");

//DISPLAY ITEM REPORT
System.out.println(item1 + "\t" + beginQty1 + "\t\t" + unitsSold1
                 + "\t\t" + endQty1 + "\t\t" + percentSold1);
System.out.println(item2 + "\t" + beginQty2 + "\t\t" + unitsSold2
                 + "\t\t" + endQty2 + "\t\t" + percentSold2);
System.out.println(item3 + "\t" + beginQty3 + "\t\t" + unitsSold3
                 + "\t\t" + endQty3 + "\t\t" + percentSold3);
System.out.println(item4 + "\t" + beginQty4 + "\t\t" + unitsSold4
                 + "\t\t" + endQty4 + "\t\t" + percentSold4);

//FREEZE DISPLAY UNTIL USER PRESSES ENTER
System.out.println("Press ENTER to continue");
pause = in.readChar();
} //END main()
} //END Action05_01 CLASS
```

Using the sales data provided, this program will print the following inventory report:

MONTH: May

ITEM	BEGIN QTY	UNITS SOLD	ENDING QTY	%SOLD
Fishing Line	132	24	108	18.18
Fish Hooks	97	45	52	46.39
Sinkers	123	37	86	30.08
Fish Nets	12	5	7	41.67

Again, notice how a whole block of Java code is repeated four times to process the four sales items. Wouldn't it be nice to simply code the processing steps once and then tell the computer to repeat these steps the required number of times? Such a repeating operation would make our coding much more efficient, wouldn't it?

You should be able to understand the above Java code, given the material presented up to this point in the text. However, there are a couple of small, but important, points that need some discussion. First, notice that there is a separate set of variables for each sales item. Would it be possible to use just one set of variables for all the sales items? Well, that depends on the problem definition. The problem definition requires that the output report be in *tabular form*. If we were to use just one set of variables, the report for a given item would have to be displayed before the same set of variables could be used for the next item. But then the prompts required to get the next item data would appear on the display before its report could be displayed. In other words, we could not generate a concise table of results using just one set of variables. We must use a separate set of variables for each item to store all the item results before generating the table. Second, look at the *percentSold* calculation in the program. Notice that it is obtained by dividing the *unitsSold* by the *beginQty* and multiplying by 100. Now, you see that in the definition section at the top of the program that both *unitsSold* and *beginQty* are defined as double floating-point values. Well, why couldn't they be defined as integers, because both will always be whole number values, right? The reason that you can't define them as integers is that if you divide two integers using the / operator, you will get an integer result. Thus, if the units sold were 10 and the beginning quantity were 100, the *integer* quotient would be 10 / 100 = 0. As a result, the *percentSold* would be 0, which is obviously incorrect. So, the solution is to define *unitsSold* and *beginQty* as floating-point values. Then dividing the two will yield a floating-point result. Using the preceding values, you would get 10 / 100 = 0.1, resulting in a correct value of 10% sold.

PROBLEM SOLVING IN ACTION: DATA COMMUNICATIONS

Problem

In the field of data communications, binary digital computer data are converted to analog sine wave data for transmission over long distances via the telephone network. Hardware devices that perform this operation are called ***modems***. As you know digital data is composed of binary 1's and 0's. On the other hand, analog data is composed of sine waves. Thus a modem converts binary 1's and 0's to a series of sine waves for communication over the telephone system. Since binary data are represented using sine waves, the study of data communications often requires the analysis of a sine wave. One such analysis is to find the amplitude, in volts, of a sine wave at any given point in time. This is called the ***instantaneous value*** of the sine wave and is found using the equation

$$v = V_{peak} \sin(2\pi ft)$$

where

v is the instantaneous voltage at any point in time t on the waveform, in volts.

V_{peak} is the peak amplitude of the waveform, in volts.

π is the constant 3.14159.

f is the frequency of the waveform, in hertz.

t is the time, in seconds, for v.

Write a program to find the instantaneous voltage value of the sine wave in Figure 5-2. Have the user enter the peak voltage in volts, the frequency in kilohertz, and the time in milliseconds.

Defining the Problem

Output: The program must display the instantaneous voltage value, v, resulting from the previous equation.

Input: The user must enter the following information:
- The peak amplitude of the waveform, V_{peak}, in volts.
- The frequency of the waveform, f, in kilohertz.
- The point in time, t, in milliseconds for which the instantaneous voltage must be calculated.

Processing:　　　The program must calculate the instantaneous voltage value using the equation $v = V_{peak} \sin(2\pi ft)$

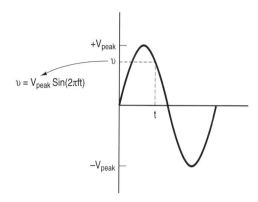

Figure 5-2　A sine wave for the data communications problem.

Planning the Solution

Using the modular approach to solving this problem, we will divide the problem into three subproblems that reflect the problem definition. The three major tasks that follow directly from the problem definition are

- Obtain the user entries for V_{peak}, f, and t.
- Calculate the instantaneous voltage.
- Display the instantaneous voltage value, v, resulting from the calculation.

Here are the respective algorithms:

Initial Algorithm

main()
BEGIN
　　Call method to obtain the user entries for V_{peak}, f, and t.
　　Call method to calculate the instantaneous voltage.
　　Call method to display the instantaneous voltage value, v.
END.

First Level of Refinement

> *setData( )*
> BEGIN
> > Write a user prompt to enter the peak amplitude of the waveform, V_{peak}, in volts.
> > Read (V_{peak}).
> > Write a user prompt to enter the frequency of the waveform, f, in kilohertz.
> > Read (f).
> > Write a user prompt to enter the time, t, in milliseconds.
> > Read (t).
> END.

> *calculateVoltage( )*
> BEGIN
> > Calculate $v = V_{peak} \sin(2\pi ft)$.
> END.

> *displayVoltage( )*
> BEGIN
> > Write the instantaneous voltage value, v.
> END.

Coding the Program

The flat implementation of the above set of algorithms follows:

/*ACTION 5-2 (ACT05_02.CPP)

```
OUTPUT:      THE PROGRAM MUST DISPLAY
             THE INSTANTANEOUS VOLTAGE VALUE, V,
             OF A SINE WAVE.

INPUT:       THE USER MUST ENTER THE FOLLOWING:
             PEAK AMPLITUDE OF THE WAVEFORM IN VOLTS.
             FREQUENCY OF THE WAVEFORM IN KILOHERTZ.
             TIME IN MILLISECONDS
```

```
PROCESSING: THE PROGRAM MUST CALCULATE THE
             INSTANTANEOUS VOLTAGE VALUE USING THE EQUATION
             Voltage = sin(2*PI*f*t)

*/


import keyboardInput.*;  //FOR readDouble() AND readChar()

public class Action05_02
{
   public static void main(String[] args) throws Exception
   {
   //DEFINE AND INITIALIZE VARIABLES
   double vPeak = 0.0;        //PEAK VOLTAGE IN VOLTS
   double frequency = 0.0;    //FREQUENCY IN KILOHERTZ
   double time = 0.0;         //TIME IN MILLISECONDS
   double volts = 0.0;        //INSTANTANEOUS VOLTAGE IN VOLTS
   char pause = ' ';          //PAUSE VARIABLE

   //CREATE KEYBOARD OBJECT
   Keyboard in = new Keyboard();

   //DISPLAY PROGRAM DESCRIPTION MESSAGE
   System.out.println("\n\nThis program will display the instantaneous voltage\n"
              + "value of an AC signal.  You must enter the following\n"
              + "three quantities: "
              + "\n\tPeak voltage of the signal\n"
              + "\tFrequency of the signal\n"
              + "\tThe point in time for which the voltage\n"
              + "\tmust be calculated.\n\n");

   //SET DATA VARIABLES FROM USER ENTRY
   System.out.print("Enter the peak signal voltage in volts:  V_Peak = ");
   vPeak = in.readDouble();
   System.out.print("Enter the signal frequency in kilohertz:  Frequency = ");
   frequency = in.readDouble();
   System.out.print("Enter the time in milliseconds:  Time = ");
   time = in.readDouble();

   //CALCULATE INSTANTANEOUS VOLTAGE VALUE
   volts = vPeak * Math.sin(2 * Math.PI * frequency * time);
```

```
//DISPLAY INSTANTANEOUS VOLTAGE VALUE
System.out.println("\nThe instantaneous voltage at " + time
                + " milliseconds is " + volts + " volts.");

//FREEZE DISPLAY
System.out.println("\nPress ENTER to continue.");
pause = in.readChar();

} //END main()
} //END Action05_02 CLASS
```

It's probably a good idea to take a closer look at some of the features of this program. Here is what you will see on the display after the program has been run:

```
This program will display the instantaneous voltage
value of a sine wave. You must enter the following
three quantities:

        Peak voltage of the signal.
        Frequency of the signal.
        The point in time, t, for which the voltage
        must be calculated.

Enter the peak signal voltage in volts:  V_Peak = 10↵
Enter the signal frequency in kilohertz:  Frequency = 1↵
Enter the time in milliseconds:  Time = .125↵

The instantaneous voltage at 0.1250 milliseconds is
7.0710678 volts.
```

As you can see, the program description message describes the purpose of the program. In addition, it tells the user what values must be entered and identifies the variables to be used for the entered values. Another observation from the above program output is that the user must enter the waveform frequency in kilohertz and the time in milliseconds. These are typical units found in data communications. Notice that the user prompts indicate this entry requirement.

The calculation of the output voltage, *volts*, is performed with the following program statement:

```
volts = vPeak * Math.sin(2 * Math.PI * frequency * time);
```

Notice that the standard *Math* class is used to call the *sin()* method and return the value of *PI* required for the equation. The equation does not have to be altered to accommodate frequency in kilohertz and time in milliseconds, because the product of these two units cancel each other out (10^{+3} cancels 10^{-3}). One final point: The *sin()* method in Java is defined to evaluate angles in *radians*. Fortunately, the quantity (2 * *PI* * *f* * *t*) produces radians and not degrees. This is why there is no conversion factor within the equation. If the value to be evaluated by the *sin()* method is in degrees, it must be converted to radians to obtain a correct result.

CHAPTER SUMMARY

Arithmetic operations in Java include the common add, subtract, multiply, and divide operations that can be performed on any numeric data type. Addition, subtraction, multiplication, and division are basically the same for both the integer and floating-point data types. However, when you divide two integers, you will get an integer result. If you need a floating-point result, at least one of the operands must be defined as a floating-point value. The modulus, or remainder, (%) operator is defined for integers only and will generate unpredictable results if used with floating-point values.

There are increment/decrement operators defined in Java. The increment operator, ++, adds one to a variable, and the decrement operator, −−, subtracts one from a variable. You can preincrement/predecrement a variable or postincrement/postdecrement a variable. There's a big difference when the increment/decrement is used as part of an expression to be evaluated by Java. A preincrement/predecrement operation on a variable is performed *before* the expression is evaluated, and a postincrement/postdecrement operation is performed on the variable *after* the expression is evaluated.

The simple assignment operator in Java is the = operator. A value on the right side of the = operator is assigned to a variable on the left side of the operator. There are compound assignment operators, such as +=, *=, and so on, that combine an arithmetic operation with the assignment operation. These operators are used as a form of shorthand notation within a Java program.

Finally, the Java includes several standard methods that can be used to perform common tasks. There are mathematical methods, conversion methods, and string methods, just to mention a few categories.

QUESTIONS AND PROBLEMS

Questions

1. What value will be returned for each of the following integer operations:
   a. 4 – 2 * 3
   b. –35 / 6
   c. –35 % 6
   d. –25 * 14 % 7 * –25 / –5
   e. –5 * 3 + 9 – 2 * 7
   f. (–13 / 2) % 6

2. Evaluate each of the following expressions:
   a. 0.5 + 3.75 / 0.25 * 2
   b. 2.5 – (1.2 + (4.0 – 3.0) * 2.0) + 1.0
   c. 6.0e–4 * 3.0e+3
   d. 6.0e–4 / 3.0e+3

3. Evaluate each of the following expressions:
   a. 5.0 – (6.0 / 3)
   b. 200 * 200
   c. 5 – 6 / 3
   d. (5 – 6) / 3
   e. 1 + 25 % 5
   f. –33000 + 2000

4. Determine what will be displayed by each *println()* method:
   a. int i = 0;
      int j = 10;
      System.out.println(++i + j++);
   b. float k = 2.5;
      System.out.println(k–– * 2);
   c. char Character = 'a';
      System.out.println(++Character);
   d. int x = 1;
      int y = –1;
      int z = 25;
      System.out.println(++x + ++y – ––z);

5. Determine the output generated by the following:
   a. System.out.println((2 % 5) / (5 % 2));
   b. System.out.println(3 * 6 / 3 + 6);
   c. System.out.println((3 * 6) / (3 + 6));

6. Explain how to get information on how to use a standard method available in your compiler.

7. Determine the value returned by the following methods. Use your compiler reference manual or on-line help feature to make sure that you understand how the method operates.
    a. Math.abs(−5)
    b. Math.sin(1.57)
    c. Math.log(2.73)
    d. Math.pow(2,5)
    e. Math.cos(0)
    f. Math.random() ∗ 10

Problems

Least Difficult

1. Write a program that will allow a user to convert a temperature in degrees Fahrenheit to degrees Centigrade using the following relationship:

$$C = 5 / 9 \times (F - 32)$$

2. Write a program that will allow a user to convert a measurement in inches to centimeters.

3. Write a simple test program that will demonstrate what happens when you use an illegal argument within a method. For example, what happens when you use a character argument in an mathematical method?

4. Write a program to solve the following equation for *x*:

$$3x - 5y + 2 = 35$$

    Assume that values for *y* will be entered by the user.

More Difficult

5. Here is the inventory and price list of the Health and Beauty Aids department in Ma and Pa's General Store.

Item	Price
Grandma's Lye Soap	0.49
Bag Bahm	1.29
Chicken Soup	0.29
Liniment	2.35
Baking Soda	0.63

    Ma and Pa want to run a "big" sale and reduce all Health and Beauty Aid items by 5 percent. Write Ma and Pa a program that will print a listing of all the Health and Beauty Aid items showing the regular and sale price. Assume that Ma or Pa will enter the preceding price list.

6. Revise the program in problem 5 to allow Ma or Pa to enter any percentage sales discount.

Most Difficult

7. Workers at the Java∗Mart supercenter just received a 5.5% pay increase retroactive for seven months. Write a program that accepts the employee name, employee number, and current annual salary. The program must then display the employee's name, number, amount of retroactive pay due, the new annual salary and new monthly salary in a tabular format.

8. Ma and Pa were so elated with the programs you have written so far that they want to expand their computer operations to the payroll department. Write Ma and Pa a payroll program that will calculate Herb's (their only employee) net pay given the following information:

> Employee's name
> Number of weekly hours worked
> Hourly rate of pay
> FICA (7.15%)
> Federal withholding (28%)
> State withholding (10%)

Assume that Ma or Pa will only be required to enter the first three items when running the program. Generate a report using the following format:

Employee Name: XXXXXXXXXXXXXXXXXXXXXXX

Rate of Pay:	$XXX.XX
Hours Worked:	XX.XX
Gross Pay:	$XXXX.XX
Deductions:	
FICA:	$XXX.XX
Fed. Withholding:	XXX.XX
State Withholding:	XXX.XX
	————
Total Deductions:	$XXX.XX
Net Pay:	$XXXX.XX

9. The diagram in Figure 5-3 illustrates how triangulation is used to find the distance to an object. Here's the idea: Two triangulating devices are positioned a certain distance apart, and both devices get a "fix" on an object as shown in the figure. The two triangulating devices and the object form a triangle whose one leg, *d*, and two angles θ*1* and θ*2* are known. The third angle is easily found by subtracting the two known angles from 180 degrees. The distance from each triangulating device to the object is then found using the Law of Sines, which states

$$r_1 / \sin\theta_1 = r_2 / \sin\theta_2 = d / \sin[180 - (\theta_1 + \theta_2)]$$

Write a program to find the distance that the object is from each triangulation device. Assume that the user will enter the distance (*d*) between the devices and the two angles (θ_1 and θ_2) that the object makes with the triangulating devices.

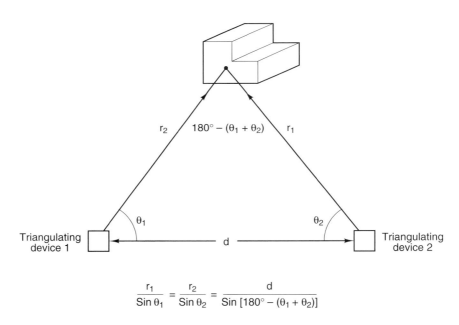

$$\frac{r_1}{\text{Sin } \theta_1} = \frac{r_2}{\text{Sin } \theta_2} = \frac{d}{\text{Sin } [180° - (\theta_1 + \theta_2)]}$$

Figure 5-3   A triangulation diagram for problem 9.

GUI 105: TEXT AREAS

PURPOSE

- *To become familiar with the GUI text area component.*
- *To demonstrate how to set the size of a text area.*
- *To show how to make a text area noneditable by the user.*
- *To experiment with text field events.*
- *To experiment with button events.*

Introduction

A ***text area*** is a GUI component that displays multiple lines of text. It can be set to allow user editing, or placed in a read-only mode such that it cannot be edited. In this module, you will first load and execute a Java program that produces a frame with a single editable text area. Then you will load and execute a program that produces a frame with text fields and a text area. Information entered into the text fields will generate events to display that information in the text area. Finally, you will load and execute a program that produces a frame with text fields, a button, and a text area. Information entered into the text fields will be displayed in the text area when an event is generated by clicking the button. In all programs, you will modify the program code and observe the effect on the GUI generated by the program.

Procedure

1. Load and execute the *GUI105_1.java* program contained on the CD that accompanies this book, or download it from www.prenhall.com. You should see a window similar to the one shown in Figure 1. The window contains a single rectangular text area. Notice that the text area includes both horizontal and vertical scrollbars which are inactive at this point.

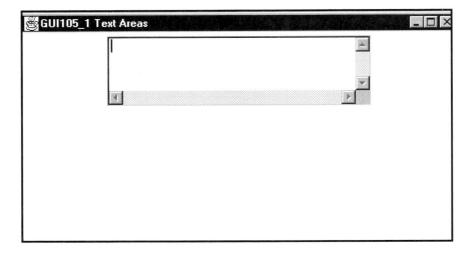

Figure 1 A frame with a text area.

2. Begin typing a information into the area and notice that, when you come to the right edge of the area, the horizontal scrollbar becomes active and begins moving to follow the text, until you press the **ENTER** key. Type several separate lines of text into the area. When you approach the bottom of the area, the vertical scrollbar becomes active and will begin moving to follow the text.

3. Once you have filled-up the text area, use the scrollbars to scroll through the text that you typed.

4. Edit the text area using any editing method you want, such as backspacing, marking and deleting, marking and moving text, copy and paste, and so on. You should find that the text area is totally editable using all common editing techniques.

Here is the Java code that produced the window in Figure 1:

```
1    import java.awt.*;            //FOR GUI COMPONENTS
2    import java.awt.event.*;      //FOR EVENT HANDLING
3
4    class TextAreas1 extends FrameWithClose
5    {
6      //DEFINE TEXT AREA
7      private TextArea studentArea = new TextArea(4,40);
8
```

```
9    //CONSTRUCTOR
10   public TextAreas1 (String title)
11   {
12    //CALL SUPERCLASS CONSTRUCTOR
13    super(title);
14
15    //SET FRAME LAYOUT MANAGER
16    setLayout(new FlowLayout());
17
18    //ADD TEXT AREA COMPONENT TO FRAME
19    add(studentArea);
20   }//END TextAreas1()
21  }//END TextAreas1
22
23 //APPLICATION CLASS TO TEST TextAreas1 CLASS
24 public class GUI105_1
25 {
26   public static void main(String[] args)
27   {
28    //DEFINE FRAME OBJECT
29    TextAreas1 window = new TextAreas1("GUI105_1 Text Areas");
30
31    //SET FRAME SIZE
32    window.setSize(500,300);
33
34    //MAKE FRAME VISIBLE
35    window.setVisible(true);
36   }//END main()
37  }//END GUI105_1
```

5. Our text area object, called *studentArea*, is defined in line 7 of the program. Notice that there are two values within parentheses at the end of the statement in line 7. These two values define the number of rows and number of columns, respectively, of the text area. Change these values to define a different size text area. Execute the program and observe the resulting text area.

6. Add the following statement in line 17 of the program:

    studentArea.setEditable(false);

7. Execute the program and try to type some text in the text area. You should find that the text area is now noneditable.

Discussion

The *GUI105_1.java* program adds a single text area to a frame and displays the frame as a window. By default, a text area is editable by the user and includes both horizontal and vertical scrollbars which become active when the area is filled horizontally and vertically, respectively. You should have found that the text area is totally editable, using any of the common window editing techniques with which you are familiar.

You must define the size of a text area when its object is created in a program. In line 7 of the program, the text area object size was set to 4 rows by 40 columns. When you changed these values in step 5, you observed a different size text area in the resulting window.

In step 6, you added a line to the program which called the *setEditable()* method to make the text area noneditable. An argument of **false** in this method makes the text area noneditable, while an argument of **true** makes it editable. Of course, a text area is born editable by default.

Procedure (continued)

8. Load and execute the *GUI105_2.java* program contained on the CD that accompanies this book, or download it from www.prenhall.com.

9. Here you see that we have added the text fields and labels from the *GUI104* module to the window. Type your name in the student name field and press the **ENTER** key when you are done. Notice that your name appears in the text area as the student name. Enter your student number and GPA in the same manner and notice that as soon as you press the **ENTER** key, the information appears in the text area.

10. Go back and edit any of the text field information, pressing the **ENTER** key after your editing of a given field is complete. You should observe that the new information appears in the text area.

Discussion

Text areas are often used to display information entered by the user for verification purposes. In this program, you entered information into a text field, then pressed the **ENTER** key. What do you suppose caused the event that generated the information in the text area? You're right if you thought the **ENTER** key. The **ENTER** key can be used to generate a text field event. Here is the *GUI105_2.java* code.

```
1    import java.awt.*;          //FOR GUI COMPONENTS
2    import java.awt.event.*;    //FOR EVENT HANDLING
3
4    class TextAreas2 extends FrameWithClose implements ActionListener
5    {
6      //DEFINE TEXT FIELD OBJECTS AS PRIVATE CLASS DATA
7      private TextField nameField = new TextField(35);
8      private TextField numberField = new TextField(13);
9      private TextField gpaField = new TextField(4);
10     private TextArea studentArea = new TextArea(4,40);
11
12     //CONSTRUCTOR
13     public TextAreas2 (String title)
14     {
15     //CALL SUPERCLASS CONSTRUCTOR
16     super(title);
17
18     //SET FRAME LAYOUT MANAGER
19     setLayout(new FlowLayout(FlowLayout.LEFT,10,30));
20
21     //DEFINE LABEL OBJECTS
22     Label nameLabel = new Label("Student Name");
23     Label numberLabel = new Label("Student Number");
24     Label gpaLabel = new Label("GPA");
25     Label summaryLabel = new Label("Student Summary");
26
27     //ADD COMPONENTS TO FRAME
28     add(nameLabel);
29     add(nameField);
30     add(numberLabel);
31     add(numberField);
32     add(gpaLabel);
33     add(gpaField);
34     add(summaryLabel);
35     add(studentArea);
36
37     //REGISTER TEXT FIELD LISTENERS
38     nameField.addActionListener(this);
39     numberField.addActionListener(this);
40     gpaField.addActionListener(this);
41     }//END TextAreas2()
42
```

```
43   //PROCESS TEXT FIELD EVENT
44   public void actionPerformed(ActionEvent e)
45   {
46     //DID A TEXT FIELD CAUSE EVENT?
47     if (e.getSource() instanceof TextField)
48     {
49       //DISPLAY IN TEXT FIELD DATA IN TEXT AREA
50       if (e.getSource() == nameField)
51         studentArea.append("\nStudent Name: " + nameField.getText());
52       if (e.getSource() == numberField)
53         studentArea.append("\nStudent Number: "
54                                      + numberField.getText());
55       if (e.getSource() == gpaField)
56         studentArea.append("\nGPA: " + gpaField.getText());
57     }//END IF
58   }//END actionPerformed()
59 }//END TextAreas2
60
61 //APPLICATION CLASS TO TEST TextAreas2 CLASS
62 public class GUI105_2
63 {
64   public static void main(String[] args)
65   {
66     //DEFINE FRAME OBJECT
67     TextAreas2 window = new TextAreas2("GUI105_2 Text Areas");
68
69     //SET FRAME SIZE
70     window.setSize(450,300);
71
72     //MAKE FRAME VISIBLE
73     window.setVisible(true);
74   }//END main()
75 }//END GUI105_2
```

Notice that in lines 38-40, each text field object is *registered* as a listener for an event. A component object must always be registered as a listener if an event is to be processed for that object. If you comment out any of these lines the program will not respond to a text entry for the respective field.

Next, look at lines 44-57. This code forms the *actionPerformed()* method, which is required to process a text field event. You see that the method consists of a series of **if** statement that determine which text field generated the event. When a given text field event is recognized, its information is appended to the *studentArea* text area object using the standard *append( )* method.

Procedure (continued)

11. Load and execute the *GUI105_3.java* program contained on the CD that accompanies this book, or download it from www.prenhall.com.

12. Notice that we have added a *Store* button to this window. Enter your student name, number, and GPA. Notice that pressing the **ENTER** key has no effect on the text fields or the text area.

13. Press the *Store* button and you should see that the text field data appears in the text area.

Discussion

The program is now responding to a button event and not a text field event. Here is the code that produced the window:

```
1    import java.awt.*;           //FOR GUI COMPONENTS
2    import java.awt.event.*;     //FOR EVENT HANDLING
3
4    class TextAreas3 extends FrameWithClose implements ActionListener
5    {
6      //DEFINE TEXT FIELD OBJECTS AS PRIVATE CLASS DATA
7      private TextField nameField = new TextField(35);
8      private TextField numberField = new TextField(13);
9      private TextField gpaField = new TextField(4);
10     private TextArea studentArea = new TextArea(4,40);
11
12     //CONSTRUCTOR
13     public TextAreas3 (String title)
14     {
15     //CALL SUPERCLASS CONSTRUCTOR
16     super(title);
17
18     //SET FRAME LAYOUT MANAGER
19     setLayout(new FlowLayout(FlowLayout.LEFT,10,30));
20
21     //DEFINE LABEL OBJECTS
22     Label nameLabel = new Label("Student Name");
```

```
23    Label numberLabel = new Label("Student Number");
24    Label gpaLabel = new Label("GPA");
25    Label summaryLabel = new Label("Student Summary");
26
27    //DEFINE BUTTON OBJECT
28    Button StoreButton = new Button("Store");
29
30    //ADD COMPONENTS TO FRAME
31    add(nameLabel);
32    add(nameField);
33    add(numberLabel);
34    add(numberField);
35    add(gpaLabel);
36    add(gpaField);
37    add(StoreButton);
38    add(summaryLabel);
39    add(studentArea);
40
41    //REGISTER BUTTON LISTENER
42    StoreButton.addActionListener(this);
43   }//END TextAreas3()
44
45    //PROCESS BUTTON EVENT
46    public void actionPerformed(ActionEvent e)
47    {
48      //DID A BUTTON CAUSE EVENT?
49      if (e.getSource() instanceof Button)
50      {
51        //DISPLAY IN TEXT FIELD DATA IN TEXT AREA
52        studentArea.append("\nStudent Name: " + nameField.getText());
53        studentArea.append("\nStudent Number: "
54                            + numberField.getText());
55        studentArea.append("\nGPA: " + gpaField.getText());
56      }//END IF
57    }//END actionPerformed()
58   }//END TextAreas3
59
60   //APPLICATION CLASS TO TEST TextAreas3 CLASS
61   public class GUI105_3
62   {
63     public static void main(String[] args)
64     {
```

```
65      //DEFINE FRAME OBJECT
66      TextAreas3 window = new TextAreas3("GUI105_3 Text Areas");
67
68      //SET FRAME SIZE
69      window.setSize(500,300);
70
71      //MAKE FRAME VISIBLE
72      window.setVisible(true);
73    }//END main()
74  }//END GUI105_3
```

Look at line 42 and you see that the *storeButton* object is registered as a listener and not the text field objects. Also, the **if** statements in the *actionPerformed( )* method of the previous program are gone, because the program does not need to decide which text field caused an event. It simply detects the button event and appends all the text field information to the text area when the button is clicked.

DECISIONS, DECISIONS, DECISIONS

OBJECTIVES

When you are finished with this chapter, you should have a good understanding of the following:

- The common Boolean relational operators and logical operators used in Java.
- The Java decision control structures of **if**, **if/else**, and **switch**.
- How to read and write Boolean data.
- How to compare strings.
- How to write menu-driven programs.
- Nested **if** and **if/else** structures.
- How to test for invalid user entries in a program.
- When to use the **break** and **default** options in a **switch** statement.
- How methods are used to pass data within a program.

INTRODUCTION

At the basic level of any programming language there are three fundamental patterns called *control structures*. A control structure is simply a pattern for controlling the flow of a program module. The three fundamental control structures of a programming language are *sequence*, *decision* (sometimes called *selection*), and *iteration*. The sequence control structure is illustrated in Figure 6-1. As you can see, there is nothing fancy about this control structure, because program statements are executed sequentially, one after another, in a straight-line fashion. This is called *straight-line programming* and is what you have been doing in Java up to this point.

A *control structure* is a pattern for controlling the flow of a program module. The three fundamental control structures of any programming language are *sequence*, *decision*, and *iteration*.

Figure 6-1   The sequence control structure is a series of sequential step-by-step statements.

The second two control structures, decision and iteration, allow the flow of the program to be altered, depending on one or more conditions. The decision control structure is a decision-making control structure. It is implemented in Java using the **if**, **if/else**, and **switch** statements. These are the topics of this chapter. The iteration control structure is a repetition control structure. It is implemented in Java using the **while**, **do/while**, and **for** statements. These operations are discussed in the next chapter. Both the decision and iteration control structures force the computer to make decisions based on the result of a Boolean operation. So, lets first explore the Boolean operations available in Java.

6-1 BOOLEAN OPERATIONS

The real intelligence of a computer comes from its ability to make decisions. All computer decisions, no matter how complex, reduce to Boolean decisions because of the digital nature of the CPU. A Boolean decision is one that is based on a Boolean result of true or false. That's pretty simple, right? Remember, no matter how complex or sophisticated a digital computer system seems to be, it is only making simple Boolean decisions: on/off, 1/0, true/false. Decisions in a computer program are made by testing one condition against another, such as *if $x < y$*. Here, the condition of x is tested against the condition of y. If x is in fact less than y, the test result is true. However, if the value of x is greater than or equal to the value of y, the test is false. Thus, the result of such a test will be a Boolean result of true or false. To test conditions within a program, you will use a Boolean operator. Boolean operators in Java can be categorized as either *relational* or *logical* operators.

Relational Operators

Relational operators allow two quantities to be compared. The six common relational operators available in Java are listed in Table 6-1. The relational operators in Table 6-1 can be used to compare any two variables or expressions. In general, you should only compare data of the same data type. This means that integers should be compared to integers, floating-point to floating-point, and characters to characters. The one exception to this rule is that floating-point values can be compared to integers, because integers are reals. In all cases, the operation generates a Boolean result of true or false. Let's look at some examples.

TABLE 6-1 THE SIX RELATIONAL OPERATORS USED IN JAVA

Mathematical Symbol	Java Operator	Meaning
=	==	Equal to
≠	!=	Not equal to
<	<	Less than
≤	<=	Less than or equal to
>	>	Greater than
≥	>=	Greater than or equal to

Example 6-1

Evaluate the following relational operations:

a. 5 == 5
b. 0.025 >= 0.333
c. 3 != 3
d. −45.2 < −3
e. 'A' < 'Z'
f. $x = 25$, $y = −10$
    $x <= y$

Solution

a. True , because 5 equals 5.
b. False, because 0.025 is not greater than or equal to 0.333.
c. False, because 3 equals 3.
d. True, because −45.2 is less than −3.
e. True, because Java is actually comparing the Unicode value of 'A' to the Unicode value of 'Z'.
f. False, because the value assigned to x (25) is not less than or equal to the value assigned to y (−10).

Relational operators can also be combined with arithmetic operators, like this:

$$5 + 3 < 4$$

Now the question is: How does the computer evaluate this expression? Does it perform the addition operation or the relational operation first? If it performs the addition operation first, the result is false. However, if it performs the relational operation first, 3 is less than 4 and the result is true. As you might suspect, the addition operation is performed first, and then the relational operation.

Consequently, the result is false, because 8 is not less than 4. Remember, when relational operators are combined with arithmetic operators within an expression, the *relational operators are always performed last*.

Example 6-2

Both arithmetic and relational operators can be part of an output statement to evaluate an expression. Determine the output generated by the following program segment:

```
System.out.println(3 + 4);
System.out.println('J' > 'K');
System.out.println(3 * 10 % 3 - 2 > 20 / 6 + 4);
```

Solution

The output generated by the above program segment is

```
7
false
false
```

The first output line is obvious, because 3 + 4 = 7. The remaining output lines are logical values based on the evaluation of the respective relational operations. The result of 'J' > 'K' is false because the Unicode value for 'J' is not greater than the Unicode value for 'K'. Finally, the result of the last expression is false. Here, the evaluation process goes like this:

$$(((3 * 10) \% 3) - 2) > ((20 / 6) + 4) =$$
$$((30 \% 3) - 2) > (3 + 4) =$$
$$0 - 2 > 7 =$$
$$-2 > 7 =$$
false

Notice that the multiplication operation is performed first, followed by the % and / operations, from left to right. Then the addition/subtraction operations are performed, and finally the greater-than operation is performed.

DEBUGGING TIP

To avoid execution problems, it is not a good idea to use the == or != operators to test floating-point values. Rather, you should use <, >, <=, or >= when testing floating-point values.

The equal to, ==, operator in Table 6-1 is used to test simple data types such as integer and character. However, you cannot use it to test the equality of two objects. Remember that an object has data as well as methods associated with it. So, to test the equality of two objects you must have an operation that only looks at the object data for equality. The required method in Java is the *equals()* method. You saw this method back in Chapter 3 when you learned about string objects. The *equals()* method tests to see if its calling object is equal to its argument object. For example, suppose we define two string objects like this:

String myName = "Andy";
String yourName = "Bob";

Then, to test these two objects for equality you would call the *equals()* method like this:

myName.equals(yourName);

Of course, the result would be false, because the two strings are not equal.

> When testing the equality of two objects, such as string objects, you must use the *equals()* method, not the == operator.

Logical Operators

Logical operations also generate Boolean results. The three most common logical operators used in Java are given in Table 6-2. You see from the table that the exclamation symbol (!) is used for NOT, the double vertical bar symbols (||) for OR, and the double ampersand symbols (&&) for AND.

TABLE 6-2 LOGICAL
OPERATORS USED IN JAVA

Operation Name	Symbol
NOT	!
OR	||
AND	&&

The NOT (!) operator is used to negate, or invert, a Boolean value. Because there are only two possible Boolean values (true and false), the negation of one results in the other. For example, suppose we define a Boolean variable A. Then the variable A can take on only two values, true or false. If A is true, then $!A$ is false. Conversely, if A is false, then $!A$ is true. This operation can be shown using a ***truth table***. A truth table simply shows the result of a logic operation on a Boolean value. Here is the truth table for the simple NOT operation:

A	$!A$
true	false
false	true

The OR operator (⸾⸾) is applied to multiple Boolean values. For instance, suppose that A and B are both defined as Boolean variables. Then A and B can be either true or false. The OR operation dictates that if either A or B is true, the result of the operation is true. Another way to say this is that "*any* true results in true." In terms of a truth table,

A	B	A ⸾⸾ B
true	true	true
true	false	true
false	true	true
false	false	false

Notice from the table that A ⸾⸾ B is true whenever A is true or B is true. Of course, if both A and B are true, the result is true.

The AND operator (&&) also operates on multiple Boolean values. Here, if A and B are Boolean variables, then the expression A && B is true only when both A and B are both true. Another way to say this is that "*any* false results in false." In terms of a truth table,

A	B	A && B
true	true	true
true	false	false
false	true	false
false	false	false

The Boolean logical operators can also be applied to logical expressions. For example, consider the following:

$$(-6 < 0) \,\&\&\, (12 >= 10)$$

Is this expression true or false? Well, $-6 < 0$ is true and $12 >= 10$ is true. Consequently, the expression must be true. How about this one?

$$((3 - 6) == 3) \,||\, (\,!(2 == 4))$$

You must evaluate both sides of the expression. If either side is true, then the result is true. On the left side, $3 - 6$ is equal to -3, which is not equal to 3. Thus, the left side is false. On the right side, $2 == 4$ is false, but $!(2 == 4)$ must be true. Consequently, the right side of the expression is true. This makes the result of the ORing operation true.

Observe in the two foregoing expressions that parentheses are used to define the expressions being operated upon. Remember to do this whenever you use a logical operator to evaluate two or more expressions. In other words, *always* enclose the things you are ORing and ANDing within parentheses.

You will see in the next section how these logical operators are used to make decisions that control the flow of a program. For example, using the AND operator, you can test to see if two conditions are true. If both conditions are true, the program will execute a series of statements, while skipping those statements if one of the test conditions is false.

PROGRAMMING NOTE

You should be aware that the single vertical bar, |, and single ampersand symbol, &, also have meaning to Java. So, always be sure to use two vertical bars and two ampersand symbols when you code the logical OR and AND tests, respectively.

Quick Check

1. Operators that allow two values to be compared are called _____ operators.

2. What is the difference between the = operator and the == operator in Java?

3. What value is generated as a result of the following operation?

$$4 > 5 - 2$$

4. What value is generated as a result of the following operation?

$$(5 \mathrel{!=} 5) \mathbin{\&\&} (3 == 3)$$

5. Why should the *equals()* method be used instead of Boolean relational operators when comparing string objects?

PROBLEM SOLVING IN ACTION: BOOLEAN LOGIC

Problem

A common Boolean logic operator that is not available in Java is the NAND (NOT AND) operation. Given two variables, *A* and *B*, the NAND operation is defined as follows:

A	*B*	*A* NAND *B*
true	true	false
true	false	true
false	true	true
false	false	true

Notice that the NAND operation is simply the opposite of the AND operation. In symbols, *A* NAND *B* = NOT(*A* AND *B*). Write a Java program that will display the NAND result of two logical values entered by the user. Let's begin by defining the problem in terms of output, input, and processing.

Defining the Problem

Output: The program must display the logical result of the NAND operation as defined by its truth table.

Input: The user must enter logical values for the input variables, *A* and *B*.

Processing: Although the NAND operation is not available in Java, you can implement it by using the NOT and AND operators, like this:

$$A \text{ NAND } B = {!}\,(A \mathbin{\&\&} B)$$

Because this is a relatively simple problem, we do not need to divide the problem into smaller subproblems. Rather, we will develop a single algorithm from the problem definition. Now, the problem definition requires us to prompt the user to enter two Boolean values for *A* and *B* and apply the foregoing relationship to generate a Boolean result. However, there is one minor difficulty. *You cannot read Boolean values directly from the keyboard.* Instead, you must read character information, test the information for true or false, and then make an assignment to the variables, *A* and *B*. Here's an algorithm that will do the job.

Planning the Solution

BEGIN
    Write a program-description message.
    Write a prompt to enter a logical value of 'T' for true or 'F' for false.
    Read (*entry*).
    If *entry* is 'T' then
        Assign true to *A*.
    Else
        Assign false to *A*.
    Write a prompt to enter a logical value of 'T' for true or 'F' for false.
    Read (*entry*).
    If *entry* is 'T' then
        Assign true to *B*.
    Else
        Assign false to *B*.
    Assign NOT(*A* AND *B*) to NAND.
    Write NAND.
END.

The algorithm shows that a character ('T' or 'F') is read in and then tested to see if it is a 'T' or 'F'. An assignment is then made to the Boolean variable, depending on the test. If the character is a 'T', then true is assigned to the Boolean variable; else false is assigned to the variable. This testing operation is called an **if/else** operation, for obvious reasons. You will learn more about this in the next section. Once the proper Boolean values have been assigned, the NAND operation is performed, and the result is displayed. Here's the program.

Coding the Program

```
/* ACTION 6-1 (ACTION06_01.JAVA)
OUTPUT:       THE PROGRAM MUST DISPLAY THE LOGICAL RESULT OF
              THE NAND OPERATION

INPUT:        THE USER MUST ENTER BOOLEAN VALUES FOR THE
              VARIABLES, A AND B.

PROCESSING: A NAND B = NOT (A AND B) = ! (A && B)
*/
import keyboardInput.*;          //FOR readChar()

public class Action06_01
{
  public static void main(String[] args) throws Exception
  {
  //DEFINE VARIABLES
  char pause = ' ';                     //PAUSE VARIABLE
  char entry = ' ';                     //USER ENTRY
  boolean NAND = false;                 //RESULT OF NAND OPERATION
  boolean A = false;                    //BOOLEAN VALUE
  boolean B = false;                    //BOOLEAN VALUE

  //CREATE KEYBOARD OBJECT
  Keyboard in = new Keyboard();

  //DISPLAY PROGRAM DESCRIPTION MESSAGE
  System.out.println("This program will generate a NAND (not AND) result\n"
                   + "from two Boolean values that you must enter.\n");

  //SET FIRST BOOLEAN VARIABLE
  System.out.print("Enter a Boolean value (T for TRUE or F for FALSE): ");
  entry = in.readChar();

  //TEST USER INPUT FOR TRUE OR FALSE AND
  //MAKE BOOLEAN ASSIGNMENT
  if ((entry == 'T') || (entry == 't'))
    A = true;
  else
    A = false;
```

```
//SET SECOND BOOLEAN VARIABLE
System.out.print("Enter a Boolean value (T for TRUE or F for FALSE): ");
entry = in.readChar();

//TEST USER INPUT FOR TRUE OR FALSE AND
//MAKE BOOLEAN ASSIGNMENT
if ((entry == 'T') || (entry == 't'))
  B = true;
else
  B = false;

//DETERMINE NAND RESULT
NAND = !(A && B);

//DISPLAY RESULT
System.out.println("\n\nThe NAND result is: " + NAND);

//FREEZE DISPLAY
System.out.println("Press ENTER to continue.");
pause = in.readChar();

} //END main()
}//END Action06_01 CLASS
```

This program will generate the NAND (NOT AND) result, given two Boolean values entered by the user. One thing you will notice is that the variables (*A* and *B*) are defined as variables of the **boolean** data type. You see that the variables (*A* and *B*) are assigned **true** *if* the user enters a 'T' or 't'; *else* the variables are assigned **false**. Notice also that the logical OR operator, ||, is employed to test for either a 't' or 'T' input character in order to make the appropriate assignment. Once the variable assignments are made, the NAND expression is evaluated and assigned to the Boolean variable *NAND*. Don't worry about the **if/else** statement syntax now, because it is covered in the next few sections. At this time, it is only important that you understand the program logic. Next, you see the statement NAND = !(A && B) used to determine the NAND result by employing the NOT (!) and AND (&&) operators. Finally, the Boolean value of *NAND* is displayed. Notice that you can display a Boolean value, but you cannot read a Boolean value directly.

6-2 THE **if** STATEMENT

The operation of the **if** statement is illustrated by the diagram in Figure 6-2.

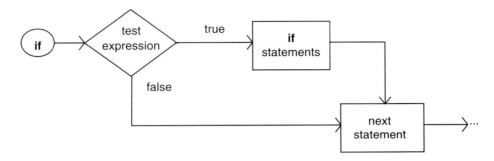

Figure 6-2   The flow of the **if** operation.

The diamond symbol in Figure 6-2 is used to denote a Boolean decision operation, while the rectangles are used to denote processing statements. Observe that the flow of the program is altered, depending on the result of a test expression. The **if** test can be true or false. If the test expression is true, the **if** statements are executed. However, if the result of the test is false, the **if** statements are bypassed and the program flow continues. This is known as a ***decision-making***, or ***selection***, operation, because the program selects, or decides, between one of two possible routes, depending on the conditions that are tested. In summary, the **if** operation can be stated in words like this: "If the test is true, execute the **if** statements." Of course, this implies that if the test is false, the **if** statements are not executed and are then bypassed.

Before we look at the Java format for the **if** statement, let's take a closer look at the test expression. The test expression is a conditional test. This means that one or more conditions are tested to generate a true or false result. To test a single condition, you will use the relational Boolean operators of ==, !=, <, >, <=, and >=. For instance, a typical test might be if (x == y). Here, the single condition, x == y, is tested. If x does in fact equal y, the result of the test is true, and the **if** statements will be executed. If x does not equal y, the **if** statements are bypassed, and the next sequential statement is executed.

To test multiple conditions, you must use the Boolean logical operators of OR and AND. For example, a test such as if ((x != y) && (a < b)) tests two conditions. If x does not equal y *and* if a is less than b, the test result is true, and the **if** statements will be executed. On the other hand, if *x* equals *y* *or* if *a* is *greater than or equal to b*, then the **if** statements are bypassed.

The Java format for the **if** statement is as follows:

if *STATEMENT FORMAT*

```
if (test expression)
{
    statement 1;
    statement 2;
         •                          //COMPOUND STATEMENT
         •
         •
    statement n;
} //END IF
```

First, notice the overall structure of this format. The word **if** and its associated test expression are written on the first line of the statement. The word **if** is a keyword in Java. The test expression follows the **if** keyword and *must* be enclosed within parentheses. The first line is followed by the statements that will be executed if the test is true. This statement block is "framed" by curly braces. A left curly brace, {, signals the beginning of the statement block, and a right curly brace, }, denotes the end of the block. Notice that the beginning curly brace is placed on a separate line, directly below the keyword **if**. The ending curly brace is placed on a separate line, immediately after the last statement in the block and in the same column as the beginning brace. In addition, you should always indent all the block statements two or three spaces in from the curly braces for readability. When this structure is part of a complex program, there is no question which statements belong to the **if** operation. If there is more than one statement to be executed within this block, the entire group of statements is referred to as a ***compound statement***. When a compound statement is encountered within a Java program, the entire group of statements is treated like a single statement. Compound statements must always be framed with curly braces. However, framing is optional when there is only a single statement within the block.

Finally, look at the punctuation syntax of the **if** statement. Notice that there is no semicolon after the test expression in the first line. However, each statement within the statement block is terminated by a semicolon.

PROGRAMMING NOTE

Framing of statements within the **if** control structure using left and right curly braces, {   }, is always required when there is more than one statement, but optional when there is only a single statement. However, framing is a good habit to get into, even when there is only a single statement. This way, if you need to add a statement later on, you will not forget to add the framing.

DEBUGGING TIP

A common error when coding an "equals" test in an **if** statement is to use the assignment symbol, =, rather than the Boolean equals test symbol, ==. Thus, the statement **if** (x = y) will always cause a compiler error and must be corrected to **if** (x == y).

It's probably a good idea to look at some example exercises and programs at this time to get a "feel" for the **if** operation.

Example 6-3

Determine the output for each of the following program segments. Assume that *x* and *y* have the following assignments prior to the execution of *each* **if** operation:

```
int x = 2;
int y = 3;
```

a. if (x < y)
    {
       System.out.println("x = " + x);
       System.out.println("y = " + y);
    }//END IF
b. if (x != 0)
       System.out.println("The value of x is nonzero.");
c.   if (x < y)
     {
        int temp = y;
        y = x;
        x = temp;
        System.out.println("x = " + x);
        System.out.println("y = " + y);
     }//END IF

```
d. if ((x < y) && (y != 10))
   {
      int sum = x + y;
      System.out.println("x = " + x);
      System.out.println("y = " + y);
      System.out.println("sum = " + sum);
   }//END IF
e. if ((x > y) || (x - y < 0))
   {
      ++x;
      --y;
      System.out.println("x = " + x);
      System.out.println("y = " + y);
   }//END IF
f. if ((x > y) || (x * y < 0))
   {
      ++x;
      --y;
    System.out.println("x = " + x);
    System.out.println("y = " + y);
   }//END IF
   System.out.println("x = " + x);
   System.out.println("y = " + y);
g. if (x % y == 0)
      System.out.println("x is divisible by y.");
      System.out.println("x is not divisible by y.");
```

Solution

a. The value of x is less than the value of y. Thus, the output is

```
x = 2
y = 3
```

b. Here, the test is on the value of x. If x is zero, the test is false. When x is a nonzero value, the test is true and the *println()* statement is executed, producing an output of

```
The value of x is nonzero.
```

c. The value of x is less than y, so the compound statement is executed and the output is

```
x = 3
y = 2
```

Notice that the values of x and y have been swapped using a temporary variable called *temp*. Why is this temporary variable required?

d. The value of x is less than y *and* the value of y is not equal to 10. As a result, the two values are added and the output is

```
x = 2
y = 3
sum = 5
```

e. Here, the value of x is not greater than the value of y, but $x - y$ is less than 0. Thus, the test result due to the OR operator is true, and the compound statement is executed, resulting in an output of

```
x = 3
y = 2
```

Notice that the compound statement increments x and decrements y.

f. This time the test is false. Thus, the compound statement is bypassed. As a result, the values of x and y remain unchanged, and the output is

```
x = 2
y = 3
```

g. This is a tricky one. Here, the test is false, because y does not divide evenly into x. So, what happens? There are no curly braces framing the block, so the compiler takes only the first *println()* statement to be the **if** statement. As a result, the first *println()* statement is bypassed, and the second one is executed to produce an output of

```
x is not divisible by y.
```

Remember, the logical flow of the program always goes to the next statement outside the **if** when the test is **false**. What would happen if the test expression were true? In this case, both *println()* statements would be executed, generating an output of

```
x is divisible by y.
x is not divisible by y.
```

But, this logic doesn't make sense. You want only one of the *println()* statements executed, not both. To solve this dilemma, we need a different decision control structure called the **if/else** control structure. The **if/else** control structure is discussed next.

Quick Check

1. True or false: The logical opposite of greater-than is less-than.

2. True or false: When a test expression in an **if** statement evaluates to true, the related **if** statements are bypassed.

3. What is wrong with the following **if** statement?
   ```
   if (x = y)
       System.out.println("There is a problem here");
   ```

4. What Boolean operator must be employed to test if all conditions are true?

5. What Boolean operator(s) must be employed to test if one or more of several conditions is false?

6. What Boolean operator must be employed to test if one of several conditions is true?

7. For what values of *x* will the *println()* statement in the following code be skipped?
   ```
   if(x > 50)
       System.out.println("Hello World");
   ```

6-3 THE if/else STATEMENT

The operation of the **if/else** statement is illustrated by the diagram in Figure 6-3. Here, you see that there are two sets of statements that can be executed, depending on whether the test expression is true or false. If the test result is true, the **if** statements are executed. Conversely, if the test result is false, the **else** statements are executed. In words, "If the test expression is true, then execute the **if** statements; otherwise, execute the **else** statements." As compared to the **if** operation, you could say **if/else** is a two-way decision process, and **if** is a one-way decision process.

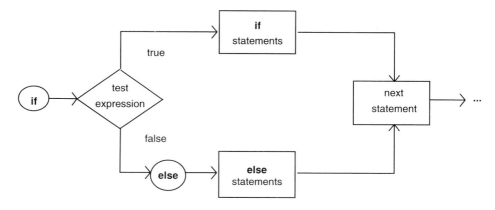

Figure 6-3 The flow of the **if/else** operation.

The Java format for the **if/else** operation is as follows:

if/else *STATEMENT FORMAT*

if (*test expression***)**
{
   statement 1;
   statement 2;
      •
      •
      •
   statement n;
} //END IF
else
{
   statement 1;
   statement 2;
      •
      •
      •
   statement n;
} //END ELSE

As you can see, the **else** option is included after the **if** statement. If the test expression is true, the **if** statements are executed, and the **else** statements are ignored. However, if the test expression is false, the **if** statements are ignored, and the **else** statements are executed.

A few words about syntax: First, observe that both the **if** and **else** statements are "framed" using curly braces. However, you can eliminate the curly braces in either section when only a single statement is required. Second, notice the indentation scheme. Again, such a scheme makes your programs self-documenting and readable.

Example 6-4

Determine when the **if** statements will be executed and when the **else** statements will be executed in each of the following program segments.

```
a.  if (x < y)
        sum = x + y;
    else
        difference = x – y;
b.  if (x != 0)
        sum = x + y;
    else
        difference = x – y;
c.  if (x = 0)
        sum = x + y;
    else
        difference = x – y;
d.  if ((x < y) && (2*x – y == 0))
        sum = x + y;
    else
        difference = x – y;
e.  if ((x < y) || (2*x – y == 0))
        sum = x + y;
    else
        difference = x – y;
f.  if (x > 2*y)
        sum = x + y;
        Product = x * y;
    else
        difference = x – y;
```

Solution

a. The **if** statement is executed when x is less than y, and the **else** statement is executed when x is greater than or equal to y. Remember, the opposite of less than is greater than *or equal to*.

b. The **if** statement is executed when x is nonzero. The **else** statement is executed when the value of x is zero.

c. This is a syntax error, because the Boolean test is coded as $x = 0$ and must be coded as $x == 0$.

d. This segment employs the Boolean AND (&&) operator. Here, the **if** statement is executed when the value of x is less than the value of y *and* the value of $2x - y$ is equal to zero. The **else** statement is executed when the value of x is *greater than or equal to* the value of y *or* the value of $2x - y$ is not equal to zero.

e. This segment employs the Boolean OR (⋮) operator. Here, the **if** statement is executed when the value of x is less than the value of y *or* the value of $2x - y$ is equal to zero. The **else** statement is executed when the value of x is *greater than or equal to* the value of y *and* the value of $2x - y$ is not equal to zero.

f. This segment of code will not compile because of a dangling, or misplaced, **else**. The **if** statements must be framed in order for the segment to compile. When the **if** statements are framed, they will be executed when the value of x is greater than the value of $2y$. The **else** statement will execute when the value of x is *less than or equal to* the value of $2y$.

Comparing Strings

The standard string compare method, *compareTo()*, should be used when comparing strings rather than Boolean relational operators because Boolean relational operators do not give you what you expect when comparing strings. For example, the following code will generate a compile error:

```
String s1 = "Andy";
String s2 = "Janet";
if (s1 < s2)
    System.out.println("String s1 is less than string s2");
else
    System.out.println("String s1 is not less than string s2");
```

To prevent a compiler error, you must call the *compareTo()* method within the **if/else** statement like this:

```
String s1 = "Andy";
String s2 = "Janet";
if (s1.compareTo(s2) < 0)
    System.out.println("String s1 is less than string s2");
else
    System.out.println("String s1 is not less than string s2");
```

This code is valid because the *compareTo()* method actually subtracts the individual ASCII values of the two strings one character at a time from left to right until an unequal condition occurs or it runs out of characters. If all the characters in the two strings are the same, the result of subtracting character-by-character is zero. If a given character in the first string is larger than the corresponding character in the second string, the subtraction result is positive. If a given character in the first string is smaller than the corresponding character in the second string, the subtraction result is negative. Thus, in the foregoing code, if strings *s1* and *s2* are equal, *compareTo()* returns a 0. If string *s1* is less than string *s2*, *compareTo()* returns a negative value. If string *s1* is greater than string *s2*, *compareTo()* returns a positive value. Here, the string "Andy" is less than the string "Janet", since the character 'A' is less than the character 'J' in the Unicode table. Thus, the *compareTo()* method generates a negative result, making the Boolean test true.

If you are just interested in string equality, use the standard *equals()* method like this:

```
String s1 = "Andy";
String s2 = "Janet";
if (s1.equals(s2))
    System.out.println("The strings are equal");
else
    System.out.println("The strings are not equal");
```

Here, by definition, the *equals()* method returns a Boolean result of **true** or **false**. As a result, you do not have to test it against 0 to prevent a compiler error.

Use *compareTo()* to see if one string is alphabetically less than or greater than another string. The *compareTo()* method returns an integer value that must be tested against 0. Use *equals()* to test if two strings are equal or not equal. The *equals()* methods returns a Boolean value and, therefore, must not be tested against 0.

Quick Check

1. True or false: An **else** must always have a corresponding **if**.

2. Why does the following pseudocode need an **else** statement?
    If Day is Friday
       Write("It's pay day")
    Write("It's not pay day")

3. True or false: Framing with curly braces can be eliminated when an **if** or **else** statement section has only a single statement.

4. The *compareTo()* method actually performs a _____ operation on two strings.

5. True or false: The *compareTo()* method returns a Boolean value.

6. True or false: The *equals()* method returns a Boolean value.

6-4 NESTED if's

Until now, you have witnessed one-way and two-way decisions using the **if** and **if/else** statements, respectively. You can achieve additional decision options by using nested **if** statements. A nested **if** statement is simply an **if** statement within an **if** statement. To illustrate this idea, consider the diagram in Figure 6-4. Here, a temperature is being tested to see if it is within a range of 0 to 100 degrees Celsius. If it is within this range, you get water. However, if it is outside the range, you get steam or ice, depending on whether it is above or below the range, respectively.

Let's follow through the diagram. The first test-expression operation checks to see if the temperature is greater than 0 degrees. If the test result is false, the temperature must be less than or equal to 0 degrees, resulting in ice. However, if the test result is true, a second test is made to see if the temperature is greater than or equal to 100 degrees. If this test result is true, you get steam. However, if this second test result is false, you know that the temperature must be somewhere between 0 degrees and 100 degrees, resulting in water. Notice how the second test is "nested" within the first test. The first test result must be true before the second test is performed.

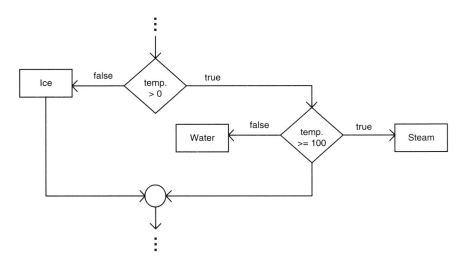

Figure 6-4   A nested **if** operation.

Let's develop a program to implement the nested decision-making operation illustrated in Figure 6-4. We begin with the problem definition.

Defining the Problem

Output: The word "WATER", "STEAM", or "ICE".

Input: Temperature in degrees Celsius from the user keyboard.

Processing: Determine if the temperature constitutes water, steam, or ice.

Now for the algorithm. Here is one that will work.

Planning the Solution

BEGIN
    Write a program description message.
    Write a user prompt to enter the *temperature* in degrees Celsius.
    Read (*temperature*).
    If *temperature* > 0
      If *temperature* $>= 100$
        Write "STEAM."

```
      Else
          Write "WATER."
      Else
          Write "ICE."
END.
```

This algorithm is constructed by simply following the diagram in Figure 6-4. Notice how the second **if/else** operation is nested within the first **if/else** operation. If the *temperature* is not greater than 0 degrees, the nested **if** operation is not performed. However, if the *temperature* is greater than 0, the nested **if** operation is performed to see if the *temperature* results in steam or water.

To code the program, you simply follow the algorithm, like this:

Coding the Program

```
/*  OUTPUT:           DISPLAY THE WORD "STEAM", "ICE", OR "WATER",
                      DEPENDING ON TEMPERATURE TO BE ENTERED
                      BY THE USER.

    INPUT:            A CELSIUS TEMPERATURE FROM THE USER.

    PROCESSING:       TEST TEMPERATURE VALUE AGAINST
                      A RANGE OF 0 TO 100 DEGREES CELSIUS.
*/

import keyboardInput.*;          //FOR readDouble()

public class Test
{
  public static void main(String[] args)
  {
  //DEFINE VARIABLES
  double temperature = 0.0;      //TEMPERATURE VALUE FROM USER

  //CREATE KEYBOARD OBJECT
  Keyboard in = new Keyboard();

  //DISPLAY PROGRAM DESCRIPTION MESSAGE TO USER
  System.out.println("This program will evaluate a temperature to see if\n"
                  + "it produces ice, water, or steam. ");
```

```
//GET THE TEMPERATURE FROM USER
System.out.println("Enter a temperature in degrees Celsius:");
temperature = in.readDouble();

//TEST IF TEMPERATURE IS  WATER, STEAM, OR ICE
if (temperature > 0)
      if (temperature >= 100)
          System.out.println("STEAM");
      else
          System.out.println("WATER");
  else
     System.out.println("ICE");
 } //END main()
} //END temperature
```

Notice how the program flow can be seen by the indentation scheme. However, you do not see any curly brace pairs framing the **if** or **else** blocks. Remember that you do not need to frame a code block when it consists of only a single statement. But, you say that the first **if** block looks as if it consists of several statements. Well, the first **if** block contains a single **if/else** statement. Because the compiler sees this as a single statement, it does not need to be framed. Of course, if you are in doubt, it does no harm to frame the block, like this:

```
//TEST IF TEMPERATURE IS  WATER, STEAM, OR ICE
  if (temperature > 0)
  {
       if (temperature >= 100)
           System.out.println("STEAM");
       else
           System.out.println("WATER");
  } //END IF TEMPERATURE > 0
  else
     System.out.println("ICE");
```

PROGRAMMING NOTE

There are different ways to construct nested **if/else** logic. For example, some might see the temperature algorithm logic as follows:

If *temperature* <= 0
    Write "ICE"

Else
  If *temperature* > = 100
    Write "STEAM."
  Else
    Write "WATER."

Here you see the inner **if/else** operation nested inside of the outer **else** operation. This logic will also accomplish the required decision task. Both methods are correct and adhere to good programming style. We will refer to this method as the **if-else-if-else** form and the earlier method as the **if-if-else-else** form. It's simply a matter of personal choice and how you view the logic of the problem. In general, the **if-else-if-else** form should be used when a number of *different* conditions need to be satisfied before a given action can occur, and the **if-if-else-else** form should be used when the *same* variable is being tested for different values and a different action is taken for each value. This latter reason is why we first chose to use the **if-if-else-else** form. Notice also that indentation is extremely important to determine the nested logic.

Example 6-5

Determine when "Red", "White", and "Blue" will be written in each of the following program segments.

a.
```java
if (x < y)
    if (x == 0)
        System.out.println("Red");
    else
        System.out.println("White");
else
    System.out.println("Blue");
```

b.
```java
if (x >= y)
    System.out.println("Blue");
else
    if (x == 0)
        System.out.println("Red");
    else
        System.out.println("White");
```

c.
```java
if ((x < y) && (x == 0))
    System.out.println("Red");
if ((x < y) && (x != 0))
    System.out.println("White");
if (x >= y)
    System.out.println("Blue");
```

Solution

All three segments of code will produce the same results. "Red" will be written when the value of x is less than the value of y and the value of x is zero. "White" will be written when the value of x is less than the value of y and the value of x is not equal to zero. "Blue" will be written when the value of x is greater than or equal to the value of y, regardless of whether or not the value of x is zero. Desk-check the logic of each code segment.

Example 6-6

Convert the following series of **if** statements to nested **if/else** statements using the **if-else-if-else** form and the **if-if-else-else** form.

```
if (year == 1)
    System.out.println("Freshman");
if (year == 2)
    System.out.println("Sophomore");
if (year == 3)
    System.out.println("Junior");
if (year == 4)
    System.out.println("Senior");
if (year > 4)
    System.out.println("Graduate");
```

Solution

a. To convert to the **if-else-if-else** form, we use the logic that if the year is greater than 4, then we know to write "Graduate"; else we test to see if the year is greater than 3. If the year was not greater than 4 but is greater than 3, its value must be 4, so we write "Senior"; else we test to see if the year is greater than 2. If it passes this test, you know that the year was not greater than 4 and not greater than 3 but is greater than 2, so its value must be 3, and we write "Junior". We continue this logic to produce "Sophomore" and "Freshman" for year values of 2 and 1, respectively. Here's the resulting code:

```
if (year > 4)
    System.out.println("Graduate");
else
    if (year > 3)
        System.out.println("Senior");
    else
        if (year > 2)
            System.out.println("Junior");
        else
            if (year > 1)
                System.out.println("Sophomore");
            else
                System.out.println("Freshman");
```

b. To convert to the **if-if-else-else** form, we use the logic that if the year is greater than 1, we test to see if the year is greater than 2, then 3, then 4. If it passes all of these tests, we know to write "Graduate". However, if the year was not greater than 1 in the first test, we know to write "Freshman", which forms the **else** part of the first **if** test. Next, if the year is greater than 1, but fails the second **if** test (>2), we know to write "Sophomore", which forms the **else** part of the second **if** test. This logic continues to produce "Junior" and "Senior" for year values of 3 and 4, respectively. Here's the resulting code:

```
if (year > 1)
   if (year > 2)
      if (year > 3)
         if (year > 4)
            System.out.println("Graduate");
         else
            System.out.println("Senior");
      else
         System.out.println("Junior");
   else
      System.out.println("Sophomore");
else
   System.out.println("Freshman");
```

DEBUGGING TIP

Always remember to frame your **if/else** statements with curly braces, { }, when you have more than one statement to execute. If the braces are missing, only the first statement will execute. This could cause a logic error that is very difficult to find. For example, consider the following:

```
if (x < y)
   −−x;
   System.out.println("x is less than y");
else
   System.out.println("x is greater than or equal to y");
```

Here, the compiler "sees" three separate statements, one of them illegal. The first statement is the **if** statement that decrements the value of *x* if the test is true. The second statement is a *println()* statement. Even though this statement is indented under the **if**, the compiler does *not* consider it to be part of the **if** statement, because it is not framed as part of the **if**. The only statement that the compiler recognizes as part of the **if** is the $--x$ statement. This is a logic error and would not be caught by the compiler. Finally, the **else** is all by itself and, therefore, is referred to as a ***dangling***, or ***misplaced***, **else**. An **else** must *always* be associated with a corresponding **if**. This is a syntax error and would be caught by the compiler. The dangling **else** problem often occurs when improper framing is used within nested **if/else** logic.

Quick Check

1. Explain why indentation is important when operations are nested.

2. An **else** that cannot be associated with a corresponding **if** is called a _____.

Consider the following pseudocode to answer questions 3 – 6:

        If *value* < 50
          If *value* > –50
            Write ("Red")
          else
            Write ("White")
        else
          Write ("Blue")

3. What range of values will cause "Red" to be written?

4. What range of values will cause "White" to be written?

5. What range of values will cause "Blue" to be written?

6. Convert the **if-if-else-else** logic to **if-else-if-else** logic.

6-5 THE switch STATEMENT

This last category of decision enables the program to select one of many options, or *cases*. The operation of the **switch** statement is illustrated by the diagram in Figure 6-5. The selection of a particular case is controlled by a matching process. A *selector variable* is first evaluated to produce a value. The selector value is then compared to a series of cases. If the selector value matches one of the case values, the corresponding case statements are executed. If no match is made, the program simply continues in a straight-line fashion, with the first statement following the **switch** statement. Here's the Java format for **switch**:

> **switch** *STATEMENT FORMAT*
>
> **switch** (*selector variable*)
> {
>   **case** *case 1 value* : *case 1 statements*;
>   **break**;
>   **case** *case 2 value* : *case 2 statements*;
>   **break**;
>   •
>   •
>   •
>   **case** *case n value* : *case n statements*;
>   **break**;
> } //END SWITCH

The format requires the selector variable to follow the keyword **switch**. The selector variable must be enclosed within parentheses and must be an integral data type. By an *integral data type*, we mean a data type that is stored as an integer. This basically means that the selector variable must be defined as either an integer or a character. Defining the selector variable as a floating-point variable or string object will cause a compile error.

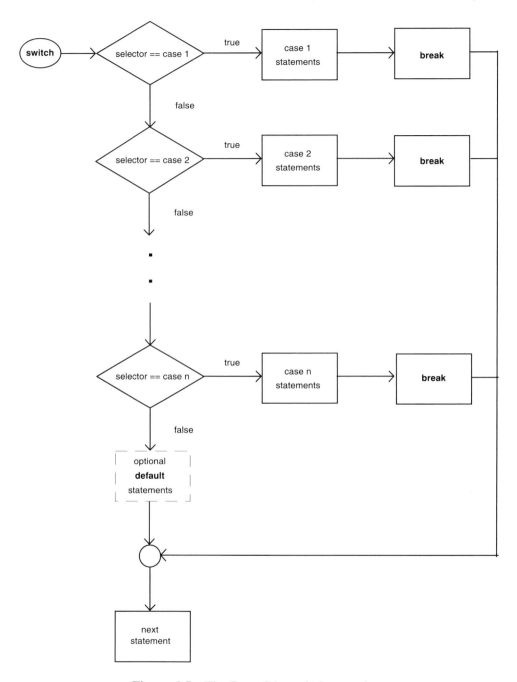

Figure 6-5   The flow of the **switch** operation.

DEBUGGING TIP

When coding a **switch** statement, the selector variable and case values must be the same data type. Only the integral data types (integer or character) are allowed. Any other data type will cause a compiler error.

The **switch** syntax requires the use of curly braces to open and close the **switch** block of **case** statements as shown. The **switch** block is comprised of several cases that are identified using the keyword **case**. An integral case value must be supplied with each case for matching purposes. The **switch** statement attempts to match the value of the selector variable to a given case value. If a match occurs, the corresponding **case** statements are executed. Note that a colon separates the case value from the **case** statements. A given **case** statement block can be any number of statements in length and does not require framing with curly braces. However, the keyword **break** is often inserted as the last statement in a given **case** statement block. If **break** is not used, any subsequent **cases** will be executed after a given **case** match has occurred until a **break** is encountered. This may be desirable at times, especially when multiple **case** values are to "fire" a given set of **case** statements. Again, the idea behind the **switch** statement is easy, if you simply think of it as a matching operation. Some examples should demonstrate this idea.

Suppose the selector variable is the letter grade you made on your last quiz. Assuming that the variable *letterGrade* is defined as a character variable, a typical **switch** statement might go something like this:

```
switch (letterGrade)
{
   case 'A' : System.out.println("Excellent");
            break;
   case 'B' : System.out.println("Superior");
            break;
   case 'C' : System.out.println("Average");
            break;
   case 'D' : System.out.println("Poor");
            break;
   case 'F' : System.out.println("Try Again");
            break;
} //END SWITCH
```

Here, the selector variable is *letterGrade*. The case values are 'A', 'B', 'C', 'D', and 'F'. The value of the selector variable is compared to the list of case values. If a match is found, the corresponding **case** statements are executed. For instance, if the value of *letterGrade* is 'B', the code generates an output of

Superior

Now, suppose you leave out the keyword **break** in each of the previous cases, like this:

```
switch (letterGrade)
{
  case 'A' : System.out.println("Excellent");
  case 'B' : System.out.println("Superior");
  case 'C' : System.out.println("Average");
  case 'D' : System.out.println("Poor");
  case 'F' : System.out.println("Try Again");
} //END SWITCH
```

This time, assuming that *letterGrade* has the value 'B', the code generates an output of

Superior
Average
Poor
Try Again

As you can see from the output, case 'B' was matched and its **case** statement executed. However, all of the **case** statements subsequent to case 'B' were also executed. Surely, you can see the value of using **break** in this application.

Are there times where you might want to eliminate the **break** command? Of course! Consider the following **switch** statement:

```
switch (letterGrade)
{
  case 'a' :
  case 'A' :  System.out.println("Excellent");
              break;
  case 'b' :
  case 'B' :  System.out.println("Superior");
              break;
  case 'c' :
  case 'C' :  System.out.println("Average");
              break;
```

```
        case 'd' :
        case 'D' :  System.out.println("Poor");
                        break;
        case 'f' :
        case 'F' :  System.out.println("Try Again");
                        break;
} //END SWITCH
```

Here, multiple case values need to fire the same **case** statement. So, if *letterGrade* has the value 'b', then a match is made with case 'b'. No **break** is part of this case, so the next sequential case is executed, which will write the word "Superior". Because case 'B' contains a **break**, the **switch** statement is terminated after the output is generated.

What happens if no match occurs? As you might suspect, all the cases are bypassed, and the next sequential statement appearing after the **switch** closing brace is executed.

The default Option

The last thing we need to discuss is the use of the **default** option within a **switch** statement. The **default** option is normally employed at the end of a **switch** statement, like this:

default *OPTION FORMAT*

```
switch (selector variable)
{
   case  case 1 value  : case 1 statements;
                             break;
   case  case 2 value  : case 2 statements;
                             break;
                             •
                             •
                             •
   case  case n value  : case n statements;
                             break;
   default: default statements;

} //END SWITCH
```

The **default** option allows a series of statements to be executed if no match occurs within the **switch**. On the other hand, if a match does occur, the **default** statements are skipped. This provides a valuable protection feature within your program. For instance, suppose that you ask the user to enter a letter grade to be used in a **switch** statement. But, what if the user presses the wrong key and enters a character that is not a valid case value. Well, you can use the **default** option to protect against such invalid entries, like this:

```
switch (letterGrade)
{
   case 'a' :
   case 'A' : System.out.println("Excellent");
            break;
   case 'b' :
   case 'B' : System.out.println("Superior");
            break;
   case 'c' :
   case 'C' : System.out.println("Average");
            break;
   case 'd' :
   case 'D' : System.out.println("Poor");
            break;
   case 'f' :
   case 'F' : System.out.println("Try Again");
            break;
   default  : System.out.println("No match was found for the ENTRY "
                                  + letterGrade );
} //END SWITCH
```

Here, the **default** statement is executed if *letterGrade* is anything other than the listed case characters. For example, if the user entered the character 'E' for *letterGrade*, the foregoing **switch** statement would produce an output of

No match was found for the ENTRY E

You will find that the **default** option in the **switch** statement is extremely useful when displaying menus for user entries.

Example 6-7

A **switch** statement is simply a convenient way to code a series of **if** statements. Convert the following series of **if** statements to a single **switch** statement that employs the **default** option.

```
if (year == 1)
    System.out.println("Freshman");
if (year == 2)
    System.out.println("Sophomore");
if (year == 3)
    System.out.println("Junior");
if (year == 4)
    System.out.println("Senior");
else
    System.out.println("Graduate");
```

Solution

All that needs to be done to convert a series of **if** statements to a single **switch** statement is to use the **if** test variable as the selector variable and the **if** test values as cases within the **switch**. Here's the converted code:

```
switch (year)
{
    case 1: System.out.println("Freshman");
            break;
    case 2: System.out.println("Sophomore");
            break;
    case 3: System.out.println("Junior");
            break;
    case 4: System.out.println("Senior");
            break;
    default: System.out.println("Graduate");
}//END SWITCH
```

Notice how the **default** option is used to write "Graduate". You know to write "Graduate" if no match is made to the previous four cases, right? So, the **else** part of the last **if** test is converted to the **default** in the **switch** statement.

PROGRAMMING NOTE

Be aware that a **switch** statement can only be used to code simple equality tests and *not* relational tests. For instance, you cannot use a **switch** statement to determine if a test score is within a range of values. You must use nested **if/else** logic for such an application.

Quick Check

1. The selection of a particular case in a **switch** statement is controlled by a _____ process.

2. Suppose that you have *n* cases in a switch statement and there are no **break** statements in any of the cases. What will happen when a match is made on the first case?

3. True or false: There are never any times when a case should not contain a **break** statement.

4. A statement that can be inserted at the end of a **switch** statement to protect against invalid entries is the _____ statement.

5. A common application for a **switch** statement is _____.

PROBLEM SOLVING IN ACTION: MENU-DRIVEN PROGRAMS

Problem

The **switch** statement is often used to create menu-driven programs. We're sure you have seen a menu-driven program. It's one that asks you to select different options during the execution of the program. For instance, suppose you must write a menu-driven consumer loan calculator program that will allow the user to determine several things about a loan. The idea will be to generate a menu similar to the one shown in Figure 6-6 that gives the user four options as follows:

- An option to calculate monthly loan payments.
- An option to calculate the total interest of the loan.
- An option to calculate the total amount of the loan.
- An option to quit the program.

We will assume that the user will enter the amount of the loan, the annual interest rate of the loan, and the term of the loan. The program should reject invalid entries.

```
This program will calculate a monthly loan
payment, total loan interest, or total loan amount.

                Enter P to get monthly payment
                Enter I to get total loan interest
                Enter T to get total loan amount
                Enter Q to quit

        Please enter your choice:
```

Figure 6-6   A menu for the consumer loan calculator problem.

Defining the Problem

Output: A program menu that prompts the user to select a monthly payment, total interest, or total loan amount calculation option. The monthly loan payment, total loan interest, or total loan amount, depending on the program option that the user selects. Invalid entry messages as required.

Input: A user response to the menu (P, I, T, or Q).
If P is selected: User enters the loan amount, interest rate, and term.
If I is selected: User enters the loan amount, interest rate, and term.
If T is selected: User enters the loan amount, interest rate, and term.
If Q is selected: Terminate program.

Processing: Calculate the selected option as follows:
Case P: *payment = principle * rate/(1 − (1+rate)$^{-term}$)*
Case I: *interest = term * payment − principle*
Case T: *total = principle + interest*
Case Q: Terminate program.
where: *principle* is the amount of the loan.
    rate is a monthly interest rate in decimal form.
    term is the number of months of the loan.

Planning the Solution

Using a modular program design, we will divide the problem into individual subproblems to solve the overall problem. There are two major tasks that follow directly from the problem definition:

- Display the menu and read the user choice.
- Perform the chosen calculation and display the results.

First, the program must display a menu of choices to the user. The user will enter his or her choice from the menu, and, depending on this choice, one of three calculations will be made to determine the required quantity. The problem solving diagram in Figure 6-7 illustrates the design.

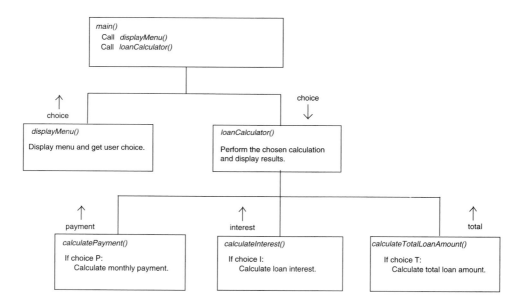

Figure 6-7   A problem solving diagram for the loan problem.

Notice that there are now three levels to solving the problem. At the first level, *main()*, a method is called to display the menu and get the user choice. The *displayMenu()* method accomplishes this task and *returns* the user choice back to *main()* as indicated on the diagram. Method *main()* will then *pass* the choice to a method called *loanCalculator()*, which will call one of three methods, depending on the choice, to perform the required calculation. This is the first time you have seen the *passing* of data between methods. This concept is central to object-oriented program design and the use of methods. From the problem solving diagram you see that the user choice, *choice*, is *passed* from the *displayMenu()* method back to its calling method, *main()*. Then, when *main()* calls the *loanCalculator()* method, *choice* is passed from *main()* to *loanCalculator()*. The *loanCalculator()* method will then use *choice* to determine which calculation method to call. Finally, each of the calculation methods will return the value it calculates back to the *loanCalculator()* method.

The initial algorithm reflects *main()*, which is used to call the *displayMenu()* and *loanCalculator()* methods, as follows:

Initial Algorithm

> *main()*
> BEGIN
>   Call *displayMenu()* method.
>   Call *loanCalculator()* method.
> END.

The first level of refinement shows the contents of the *displayMenu()* and *loanCalculator()* methods, as follows:

First Level of Refinement

> *displayMenu()*
> BEGIN
>   Display a program menu that prompts the user to choose a monthly payment (P), total interest (I), total loan amount (T), or quit (Q) option.
>   Read (*choice*).
>   Return *choice*.
> END.

> *loanCalculator ()*
> BEGIN
>   Case P: Call method *calculatePayment()* and display payment.
>   Case I: Call method *calculateInterest()* and display interest.
>   Case T: Call method *calculateTotalLoanAmount()* and display total loan amount.
>   Case Q: Terminate program.
>   Default: Write an invalid entry message and ask the user to select again.
> END.

Notice that the *displayMenu()* method simply displays the menu and gets the user's choice. The *loanCalculator()* method calls the required calculation method and displays the result, depending on the user's choice. In addition, the *loanCalculator()* method terminates the program if the user chooses to quit and writes an invalid entry message if the user's choice does not reflect one of the choice options.

Now, we need a second level of refinement to show the contents of the calculation methods. Here it is.

Second Level of Refinement

calculatePayment()
BEGIN
    Write a prompt to enter the amount of the loan.
    Read (*principle*).
    Write a prompt to enter the annual interest rate.
    Read (*rate*).
    Write a prompt to enter the term of the loan.
    Read (*term*).
    If *rate* < 0 OR rate > 100
        Write an invalid entry message.
    Else
        Calculate *rate = rate/12/100*.
        Calculate *payment = principle * rate/(1-(1+rate)$^{-term}$)*.
        Return *payment*.
END.

calculateInterest()
BEGIN
    Write a prompt to enter the amount of the loan.
    Read (*principle*).
    Write a prompt to enter the annual interest rate.
    Read (*rate*).
    Write a prompt to enter the term of the loan.
    Read (*term*).
    If *rate* < 0 OR rate > 100
        Write an invalid entry message.
    Else
        Calculate *rate = rate/12/100*.
        Calculate *payment = principle * rate/(1-(1+rate)$^{-term}$)*.

          Calculate *interest = term * payment – principle.*
          Return *interest.*
END.

calculateTotalLoanAmount()
BEGIN
  Write a prompt to enter the amount of the loan.
  Read (*principle*).
  Write a prompt to enter the annual interest rate.
  Read (*rate*).
  Write a prompt to enter the term of the loan.
  Read (*term*).
  If *rate* < 0 OR rate > 100
     Write an invalid entry message.
  Else
     Calculate *rate = rate/12/100.*
     Calculate *payment = principle * rate/(1-(1+rate)$^{-term}$).*
     Calculate *interest = term * payment – principle.*
     Calculate *total = principle + interest.*
     Return *total.*
END.

Each calculation method obtains the data required for the respective calculation. First, notice that each method employs an **if/else** statement to protect against an invalid interest rate entry. An interest rate which is less than 0% or greater than 100% is obviously invalid. If the interest rate is invalid, the user is notified. Otherwise, the method makes the respective calculation and returns the result. Notice also that the annual percentage interest rate must first be converted to a monthly decimal value for use in the subsequent payment calculation. Finally, you see that each method *returns* the result of its calculation to its calling method.

Coding the Program

At this time, we will code the solution using a flat implementation. However, remember what you have learned here, because in Chapter 8 we will modularize the solution by coding and calling the methods individually. Here is the flat implementation of the foregoing program design:

```
/*ACTION 6-2 (ACTION06_02.JAVA)
OUTPUT:   A PROGRAM MENU THAT PROMPTS THE USER TO SELECT A
          MONTHLY PAYMENT, TOTAL INTEREST, OR TOTAL LOAN
          AMOUNT CALCULATION  OPTION.
          INVALID ENTRY MESSAGES AS REQUIRED.
          THE MONTHLY LOAN PAYMENT, TOTAL LOAN INTEREST, OR
          TOTAL LOAN AMOUNT, DEPENDING ON THE PROGRAM
          OPTION THAT THE USER SELECTS. INVALID ENTRY
          MESSAGES AS REQUIRED.

INPUT:    A USER RESPONSE TO THE MENU (P, I, T, OR Q).
          IF P IS SELECTED: USER ENTERS THE LOAN AMOUNT,
          INTEREST RATE, AND TERM.
          IF I IS SELECTED: USER ENTERS THE LOAN AMOUNT,
          INTEREST RATE, AND TERM.
          IF R IS SELECTED: USER ENTERS THE LOAN AMOUNT,
          INTEREST RATE, AND TERM.
          IF Q IS SELECTED: TERMINATE PROGRAM.

PROCESSING: CALCULATE THE SELECTED OPTION AS FOLLOWS:
          CASE P:  PAYMENT = PRINCIPLE * RATE/(1 - (1+RATE)^ -TERM)
          CASE I:   INTEREST = TERM * PAYMENT - PRINCIPLE
          CASE T:  TOTAL = PRINCIPLE + INTEREST
          CASE Q:  TERMINATE PROGRAM.

          WHERE:    PRINCIPLE IS THE AMOUNT OF THE LOAN.
                    RATE IS A MONTHLY INTEREST RATE IN DECIMAL
                    FORM.
                    TERM IS THE NUMBER OF MONTHS OF THE LOAN.
*/

import keyboardInput.*;            //FOR readChar(), readDouble(), readInt()

public class Action06_02
{
  public static void main(String[] args)
  {
  //DEFINE AND INITIALIZE VARIABLES
  char pause = ' ';        //PAUSE VARIABLE
  char choice = 'Q';       //USER MENU ENTRY
  double payment = 0.0; //MONTHLY PAYMENT
  double interest = 0.0;   //TOTAL INTEREST FOR LIFE OF LOAN
  double total = 0.0;      //TOTAL LOAN AMOUNT = PRINCIPLE + INTEREST
```

```
double principle = 0.0; //LOAN AMOUNT
double rate = 0.0;      //INTEREST RATE
int term = 0;           //TERM OF LOAN IN MONTHS

//CREATE KEYBOARD OBJECT
Keyboard in = new Keyboard();

//DISPLAY PROGRAM DESCRIPTION MESSAGE
System.out.println("This program will calculate a monthly loan\n"
            + "payment, total loan interest, or total loan amount.");

//displayMenu() METHOD
System.out.print("\n\n\t\t\tEnter P to get monthly payment"
            + "\n\t\t\tEnter I to get total loan interest"
            + "\n\t\t\tEnter T to get total loan amount"
            + "\n\t\t\tEnter Q to quit"
            + "\n\n\tPlease enter your choice:  ");

//READ USER CHOICE
choice = in.readChar();

//loanCalculator() METHOD
switch (choice)
{
 case 'p':  //calculatePayment() METHOD
 case 'P' : System.out.print("\nEnter the amount of the loan: ");
            principle = in.readDouble();
            System.out.print("\nEnter the duration of the loan in months: ");
            term = in.readInt();
            System.out.print("\nEnter the annual interest rate in percent: ");
            rate = in.readDouble();

            //CHECK FOR INVALID ENTRY
            if ((rate < 0) || (rate > 100))
                System.out.println("\n\nThis is an invalid entry. Please"
                            + " run the program again.");
            else
            {
                rate = rate/12/100;
                payment = principle * rate/(1-Math.pow((1+rate), -term));
                System.out.println("\n\nThe monthly payment is $" + payment);
            }//END ELSE
            break;
```

```
case 'i':    //calculateInterest() METHOD
case 'I' :   System.out.print("\nEnter the amount of the loan: ");
             principle = in.readDouble();
             System.out.print("\nEnter the duration of the loan in months: ");
             term = in.readInt();
             System.out.print("\nEnter the annual interest rate in percent: ");
             rate = in.readDouble();

             //CHECK FOR INVALID ENTRY
             if ((rate < 0) || (rate > 100))
                 System.out.println("\n\nThis is an invalid entry. Please"
                                    + " run the program again.");
             else
             {
                rate = rate/12/100;
                payment = principle * rate/(1-Math.pow((1+rate), –term));
                interest = term * payment - principle;
                System.out.println("\n\nThe total interest is $" + interest);
             }//END ELSE
             break;

case 't':    //calculateTotalLoanAmount() METHOD
case 'T':    System.out.print("\nEnter the amount of the loan: ");
             principle = in.readDouble();
             System.out.print("\nEnter the duration of the loan in months: ");
             term = in.readInt();
             System.out.print("\nEnter the annual interest rate in percent: ");
             rate = in.readDouble();

             //CHECK FOR INVALID ENTRY
             if ((rate < 0) || (rate > 100))
                 System.out.println("\n\nThis is an invalid entry. Please"
                                    + " run the program again.");
             else
             {
                rate = rate/12/100;
                payment = principle * rate/(1-Math.pow((1+rate), –term));
                interest = term * payment - principle;
                total = principle + interest;
                System.out.println("\n\nThe total loan amount is $" + total);
             }//END ELSE
             break;
```

```
        case 'q':  //TERMINATE PROGRAM
        case 'Q':  System.out.println("Program terminated");
                   break;

        //DISPLAY INVALID ENTRY MESSAGE
        default :  System.out.println("\n\nThis is an invalid entry. Please"
                                    + " run the program again.");
    }  //END SWITCH

    //FREEZE DISPLAY
    System.out.println("Press ENTER to continue.");
    pause = in.readChar();
    }  //END main()
}  //END Action06_02 CLASS
```

First, notice how the methods from our design are embedded into this flat implementation. The comments show the location of our methods. Now look at the program closely, and you will find that it incorporates most of the things that you have learned in this chapter. In general, you will find a **switch** statement that contains a **default** option. In addition, notice the **if/else** statements embedded within each **case**. In particular, you should observe the beginnings and endings of the various sections, along with the associated indentation and commenting scheme. As you can see, the program is very readable and self-documenting.

Now for the details. There are eight cases, two for each user-selected option. Notice that the first case in each option allows the user to enter a lowercase character. These cases do not have a **break** statement and, therefore, permit the program to "fall through" to the uppercase character case. This is done to allow the user to enter either a lower- or an uppercase character for each option. Notice that there is a **break** statement at the end of each uppercase case to terminate the **switch** once the case statements are executed.

If the user enters an invalid character from the main menu, the **default** statement is executed, which displays an error message and asks the user to run the program again. Likewise, if the user enters an invalid interest rate within a given case, it is caught by the **if/else** statement, which displays an error message and asks the user to run the program again. As you can see, we have used the **if** part of the **if/else** to catch the invalid entry and the **else** part to proceed with the calculation if the entry is valid. This is typical of the way that many programs are written. Finally, notice how that standard *pow()* method is called using the *Math* object within the payment calculation.

The screen-shot in Figure 6-8 shows the menu generated by the program as well as a sample case execution.

```
This program will calculate a monthly loan
payment, total loan interest, or total loan amount.


                    Enter P to get monthly payment
                    Enter I to get total loan interest
                    Enter T to get total loan amount
                    Enter Q to quit

        Please enter your choice: p↵

Enter the amount of the loan: 1000↵

Enter the duration of the loan in months: 12↵

Enter the annual interest rate in percent: 12↵


The monthly payment is $88.84878867834163
Press ENTER to continue.
```

Figure 6-8   A screen shot produced from the *Action06_02.java* program.

STYLE TIP

As you begin to frame more operations using curly braces, it often becomes
difficult to determine what a closing curly brace is closing. The indentation
scheme helps, but a commenting technique is also used. When several closing
curly braces appear in succession, you should insert a comment after the brace, as
shown at the end of the foregoing program, to indicate what a given brace is
closing. Commenting helps both you and anyone reading your program to readily
see the program framing.

CHAPTER SUMMARY

Boolean operators are those that generate a logical result of true or false. The two categories of Boolean operators in Java are relational and logical operators. Relational operators allow two quantities to be compared. These operators include ==, != , > , < , <=, and >=. Logical operators perform logic operations on Boolean values to generate a Boolean result. The standard logical operators available in Java are NOT (!), OR (¦¦), and AND (&&). Boolean operators are used within your program to test conditions as part of the decision and iteration control structures in Java.

In this chapter, you learned about the decision-making, or selection, control structure available in Java. These include the **if**, **if/else**, and **switch** statements. Each of these operations alters the flow of a program, depending on the result of a Boolean test expression or matching condition.

The **if** statement executes its statements, or *clause*, "if" its test expression is true. If the test result is false, the **if** statements are bypassed and the program continues in a straight-line fashion. The **if** clause can be a single-line statement or a compound statement composed of a series of single-line statements. When using a compound statement, you must frame the entire statement block within curly braces.

The **if/else** statement consists of two separate clauses: an **if** clause and an **else** clause. If the associated test expression is true, the **if** clause is executed; otherwise, the **else** clause is executed when the test result is false. Thus, you could say that **if/else** is a two-way decision operation. Again, compound statements can be used within the **if** or **else** clauses; however, they must be framed within curly braces. Additional selection options can be achieved using nested **if** or **if/else** statements.

The **switch** statement achieves decision using a matching process. Here, the value of an integral selector variable is compared to a series of case values. If the selector value matches one of the case values, the corresponding case statements are executed until a **break** statement is encountered or the **switch** statement terminates. If no match is made, the program simply continues in a straight-line fashion. In addition, Java provides a **default** option with the **switch** statement. When using the **default** option, the **default** statements are executed if no match is made. However, if a match does occur, the corresponding **case** statements are executed, and the **default** statements are skipped. Remember, you must always frame the body of the **switch** statement using curly braces.

QUESTIONS AND PROBLEMS

Questions

1. Evaluate each of the following relational operations:
    a. 7 != 7
    b. −0.75 <= −0.5
    c. 'm' > 'n'
    d. 2 * 5 % 3 − 7 < 16 / 4 + 2
    e. "Andy" == "Andy"
    f. String s1;
        String s2;
        s1 = "Andy";
        s2 = "ANDY";
        s1.equals(s2);

2. Determine the output generated by the following:
    ```
    int x = −7;
    int y = 3;
    System.out.println(!(3*x < 4*y) && (5*x >= y));
    ```

3. Java also provides the *exclusive OR*, XOR logic operation. The caret, ^, symbol is used as syntax for this operation. Given any two Boolean variables, *A* and *B*, here is how the XOR operation is defined:

A	*B*	*A* ^ *B*
true	true	false
true	false	true
false	true	true
false	false	false

    Do you see a pattern in the table that gives a hint to how XOR works? Well, the XOR operation will always produce a **true** result if there is an odd number of **true** variables. Now for the question: Which of the following logical expressions will produce the XOR operation?
    a. !*A* ¦¦ !*B*
    b. (*A* && !*B*) ¦¦ (!*A* && *B*)
    c. !(*A* && !*B*) ¦¦ (!*A* && *B*)
    d. !(!*A* && !*B*)

4. What standard logical operation is performed by the expression in question 3d?

5. Develop a truth table for the following logical expression:

    $$!A \text{ ¦¦ } !B$$

6. Which of the following is equivalent to the logic operation in question 5?
   a. !(A && B)
   b. !(A ¦¦ B)
   c. !A && !B
   d. None of these

7. When will *x* be written as a result of the following **if** statement?
```
if ((x <= 0) && (x % 5 == 0))
    System.out.println(x);
```

8. Convert the single **if** statement in question 7 into two nested **if** statements.

9. Consider the following program segment:
```
Keyboard in = new Keyboard();
System.out.println("Enter a value for x ");
x = in.readInt();
System.out.println("Enter a value for y ");
y = in.readInt();
if x > 0
{
  if y > 0
    −−y;
}//END IF x > 0
else
  ++x;
```
   a. Are there any syntax errors in this code? If so, where are they?
   b. Assuming any syntax errors are corrected, when will *y* be decremented?
   c. Assuming any syntax errors are corrected, when will *x* be incremented?

10. Consider the following segment of code:
```
Keyboard in = new Keyboard();
System.out.println("Enter a value for x ");
x = in.readInt();
System.out.println("Enter a value for y ");
y = in.readInt();
if (x > 0)
{
  if (y > 0)
    −−y;
else
  ++x;
}//END IF x > 0
```
   a. Are there any syntax errors in this code? If so, where are they?
   b. Assuming any syntax errors are corrected, when will *y* be decremented?
   c. Assuming any syntax errors are corrected, when will *x* be incremented?

11. True or false: You must always frame the body of a **switch** statement.

12. Which **if** does the **else** belong to in the following code segment?

```
if (x > 0)
  if (y > 0)
    --y;
else
  ++x;
```

13. True or false: When using a **switch** statement in Java, a no-match condition results in an error.

14. Consider the following segment of code:

```
if (x >= 0)
  if (x < 10)
  {
    y = x * x;
    if (x <= 5)
      x = Math.sqrt(x);
  }//END IF x < 10
  else
      y = 10 * x;
else
  y = x * x * x;
System.out.println("x = " +  x);
System.out.println("y = " +  y);
```

What will be displayed by the program for each of the following initial values of *x*?

a. x = 0;
b. x = 4;
c. x = –5;
d. x = 10;

15. Consider the following **switch** statement:

```
int x = 2;
switch (power)
{
  case 0 :  System.out.println('1');
          break;
  case 1 :  System.out.println(x);
          break;
  case 2 :  System.out.println(x * x);
          break;
  case 3 :  System.out.println(x * x * x);
          break;
  case 4 :  System.out.println(x * x * x * x);
          break;
  default :  System.out.println("No match exists for this power");
} //END SWITCH
```

What will be displayed by the code for each of the following values of *power?*

a. power = 0;
b. power = 1;
c. power = 2;
d. power = 3;
e. power = 4;

16. Consider the following nested **switch** statements:

```
switch (x)
{
  case 2 :
  case 4 :
  case 6 :  switch (y)
            {
               case 1 :
               case 2 :
               case 3 :  x = x + y;
                         break;
               case -1 :
               case -2 :
               case -3 : x = x - y;
                         break;
            }//END SWITCH(y)
            break;
  case 1 :
  case 3 :
  case 5 :  switch (y)
            {
               case 2 :
               case 4 :
               case 6 : x = x * y;
                        break;
               case -1 :
               case -4 :
               case -6 : x = y * y;
                         break;
            }//END SWITCH(y)
            break;
} //END SWITCH(x)
System.out.println("x = " +  x);
System.out.println("y = " +  y);
```

What will be displayed by the code for each of the following values of *x* and *y?*

a. x = 4;
   y = -2;
b. x = 3;
   y = 6;

    c. x = 1;
       y = –4;
    d. x = 7;
       y = –2;
    e. x = 2;
       y = 5;

17. Prove or disprove via truth tables that
    !A && !B == !(A && B)

Problems

Least Difficult

1. A part drawing indicates that the length of the part is 3.00 ± 0.25 inch. This means that the minimum acceptable length of the part is 2.75 inches and the maximum acceptable length of the part is 3.25 inches. Write a program to display "ACCEPTABLE" if the part is within tolerance or "UNACCEPTABLE" if the part is out of tolerance. (Note: In Chapter 2, problem 5, you developed an algorithm for this problem. Why not use this algorithm to code the Java program?)

2. Write a program that will calculate weekly gross pay for an employee, given the employee's hourly rate and hours worked. Assume that overtime is paid at "time and a half" for any hours worked in excess of 40 hours.

3. Write a program that will display the corresponding name of a month for an integer entry from 1 to 12. Protect for invalid entries.

4. Write a program to generate a truth table for a NOR operation. A NOR operation is a NOT OR operation. Thus,

$$A \text{ NOR } B = \text{NOT}(A \text{ OR } B)$$

Assume that logical values for *A* and *B* will be entered by the user.

More Difficult

5. Employ nested **if/else** statements to convert a numerical grade to a letter grade according to the following scale:

                90–100   : A

                80–89   : B

                70–79   : C

                60–69   : D

                Below 60 : F

6. Write a program that will determine monthly credit card interest when interest is charged at a rate of 18% for the first $500 of balance and 12% for any balance amount over $500. Assume that the user will enter the account number, customer name, and current balance. Display a statement in a businesslike format.

Most Difficult

7. Ma and Pa are at it again. This time they need a program that will project the profit of their Sporting Goods department. The items in the department are coded with a 1, 2, or 3, depending on the amount of profit for the item. An item with a profit code of 1 produces a 10-percent profit, a code of 2 produces a 12-percent profit, and a code of 3 generates a 15-percent profit. Write a program that will project the profit of the following inventory:

Item	Quantity	Price	Profit Code
Fishing Line	132 spools	$3.95	1
Fish Hooks	97 packages	$0.89	2
Sinkers	123 packages	$0.49	2
Fish Nets	12 ea.	$8.75	1
Spinner Baits	256 ea.	$2.49	3
Jigs	49 ea.	$0.29	3

The program should generate a report of the item, quantity, expected profit in dollars per item, and total expected profit for all items.

8. Besides getting a regular salary, Herb also receives a commission on what he sells at Ma and Pa's General Store. His commission is based on the total dollar sales he makes in one week according to the following schedule:

Sales	Commission (%)
Below $250	0
$250–$499	5
$500–$1000	7.5
Over $1000	10

Write Ma and Pa a program that will determine Herb's sales commission from a user entry of his weekly sales. The program should display the total sales dollars and corresponding sales commission in dollars.

9. Write a menu-driven program that will allow the user to convert between the following units. Provide for invalid user entries.

    1. Degrees Fahrenheit to degrees Centigrade.
    2. Degrees Centigrade to degrees Fahrenheit.
    3. Inches to centimeters.
    4. Centimeters to inches.
    5. Pounds to kilograms.
    6. Kilograms to pounds.

GUI 106: CHOICE AND LIST BOXES

PURPOSE

- *To become familiar with the GUI choice and list box components.*
- *To understand the differences between choice and list boxes.*
- *To add items to choice and list boxes.*
- *To experiment with list box object definitions.*
- *To demonstrate a list box event.*

Introduction

A *choice box* is a GUI component that allows the user to chose one of several items in a *pop-up* menu listing. A *list box* allows the user to chose one *or more* items within a *scrolled* item listing. In this module, you will first load and execute a Java program that produces a choice box, a button, and a text area. You will experiment with the choice box by adding items to it and displaying selected items in the text area when the button is clicked. Then, you will load and execute a program that produces a list box, a button, and a text area. You will experiment with the list box by selecting multiple items and displaying the selected items in the text area when the button is clicked. You will add items to the list box and set the number of visible items. Finally, you will load and execute a third program that uses a list box event, rather than a button event, to display the selected list box items in a text area.

Procedure

1. Load and execute the *GUI106_1.java* program contained on the CD that accompanies this book, or download it from www.prenhall.com. You should see a window similar to the one shown in Figure 1. The window contains a choice box, a button, and a text area.

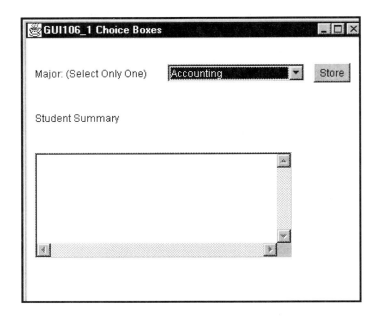

Figure 1 A frame with a choice box, a button, and a text area.

2. Notice that the choice box shows the single visible item, "Accounting". This item is highlighted, indicating that it is selected, by default. Click the *Store* button and notice that the *Accounting* major appears in the text area.

3. Click the down-arrow button on the checkbox and notice that a menu pops up to show several more selectable items.

4. Click on any of the items and notice that the pop-up menu disappears and the item you selected appears highlighted within the checkbox.

5. Click the *Store* button. The item you selected in step 4 will appear in the text area.

6. Try to select more than one item in the box. You will find that this is not possible, because a check box only allows you to select a single item.

Here is the Java code that produced the window in Figure 1:

```
1    import java.awt.*;          //FOR GUI COMPONENTS
2
3    import java.awt.event.*;    //FOR EVENT HANDLING
4
```

```
5    class ChoiceBox extends FrameWithClose implements ActionListener
6    {
7      //DEFINE TEXT AREA OBJECT AS PRIVATE CLASS DATA
8      private TextArea studentArea = new TextArea(7,40);
9
10     //DEFINE CHOICE OBJECT
11     private Choice majorsChoice = new Choice();
12
13     //CONSTRUCTOR
14     public ChoiceBox (String title)
15     {
16      //CALL SUPERCLASS CONSTRUCTOR
17      super(title);
18
19      //SET FRAME LAYOUT MANAGER
20      setLayout(new FlowLayout(FlowLayout.LEFT,10,30));
21
22      //DEFINE LABEL OBJECT
23      Label majorsLabel = new Label("Major: (Select Only One)");
24      Label summaryLabel = new Label("Student Summary");
25
26      //DEFINE BUTTON OBJECT
27      Button storeButton = new Button("Store");
28
29      //ADD ITEMS TO CHOICE BOX
30      majorsChoice.addItem("Accounting");
31      majorsChoice.addItem("Business");
32      majorsChoice.addItem("Computer Info. Systems");
33      majorsChoice.addItem("Computer Science");
34      majorsChoice.addItem("Economics");
35      majorsChoice.addItem("Undecided");
36
37      //ADD COMPONENTS TO FRAME
38      add(majorsLabel);
39      add(majorsChoice);
40      add(storeButton);
41      add(summaryLabel);
42      add(studentArea);
43
44      //REGISTER LISTENERS
45      storeButton.addActionListener(this);    //BUTTON LISTENER
46     }//END ChoiceBox()
47
```

```
48   //PROCESS BUTTON EVENT
49   public void actionPerformed(ActionEvent e)
50   {
51     //DID A BUTTON CAUSE EVENT?
52     if (e.getSource() instanceof Button)
53     {
54       //DISPLAY IN TEXT FIELD DATA IN TEXT AREA
55       studentArea.append("\nMajor:\t" + majorsChoice.getSelectedItem());
56     }//END IF
57   }//END actionPerformed()
58 }//END ChoiceBox CLASS
59
60 //APPLICATION CLASS TO TEST ChoiceBox CLASS
61 public class GUI106_1
62 {
63   public static void main(String[] args)
64   {
65     //DEFINE FRAME OBJECT
66     ChoiceBox window = new ChoiceBox("GUI106_1 Choice Boxes");
67
68     //SET FRAME SIZE
69     window.setSize(400,350);
70
71     //MAKE FRAME VISIBLE
72     window.setVisible(true);
73   }//END main()
74 }//END GUI106_1 CLASS
```

7. In line 11 of the program, we defined a choice box object called
    majorsChoice. Then in lines 30-35 we use this object to call the *addItem()*
    method to add choice items to the box. Using the syntax you see in lines 30-
    35, use line 36 to add another item to the box.

8. Execute the program again and verify that the item you added in line 36
    appears in the choice box and is a selectable item.

Discussion

A choice box provides a pop-up menu of choices. In Java, choice boxes are
provided by the *Choice* class and include a pop-up menu of selectable items. The
items are added to the menu by calling the *addItem()* method with the choice box
object. The item to be added is provided as a string argument of the *addItem()*

method. By definition, a choice box can only be used to select a single item. But, what if you need to select more than one item, such as more than one major in the majors item listing? Well, to select more than one item you need a list box.

Procedure (continued)

9. Load and execute the *GUI106_2.java* program contained on the CD that accompanies this book, or download it from www.prenhall.com. You should see a window similar to the one shown in Figure 2. The window contains a list box, a button, and a text area.

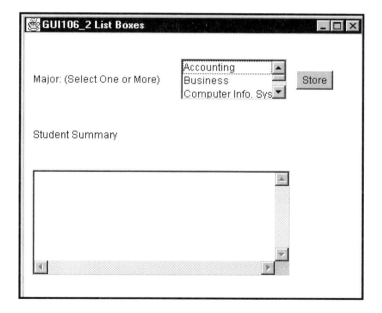

Figure 2 A frame with a list box, a button, and a text area.

10. Notice that the list box shows three visible items, none of which is highlighted. In addition, notice the scrollbar to the right of the item listing. Scroll through the items and select two or more items by clicking on the items. Each time you select an item, the item will be highlighted within the listing

11. Click the *Store* button and notice that all the items you selected appear in the text area.

12. You can deselect an item by clicking on it after it has been selected (highlighted). Deselect an item and select another item. Click on the *Store* button and you will notice that the newly selected items appear in the text window.

Here is the Java code that produced the window in Figure 2:

```
1    import java.awt.*;              //FOR GUI COMPONENTS
2
3    import java.awt.event.*;        //FOR EVENT HANDLING
4
5    class ListBox extends FrameWithClose implements ActionListener
6    {
7      //DEFINE TEXT AREA OBJECT AS PRIVATE CLASS DATA
8      private TextArea studentArea = new TextArea(7,40);
9
10     //DEFINE LIST OBJECT
11     private List majorsList = new List(3,true);
12
13     //DEFINE MAJORS ARRAY
14     private String majors[];
15
16     //CONSTRUCTOR
17     public ListBox (String title)
18     {
19       //CALL SUPERCLASS CONSTRUCTOR
20       super(title);
21
22     //SET FRAME LAYOUT MANAGER
23     setLayout(new FlowLayout(FlowLayout.LEFT,10,30));
24
25     //DEFINE LABEL OBJECT
26     Label majorsLabel = new Label("Major: (Select One or More)");
27     Label summaryLabel = new Label("Student Summary");
28
29     //DEFINE BUTTON OBJECT
30     Button storeButton = new Button("Store");
31
32     //ADD ITEMS TO LIST BOX
33     majorsList.addItem("Accounting");
34     majorsList.addItem("Business");
35     majorsList.addItem("Computer Info. Systems");
36     majorsList.addItem("Computer Science");
```

```
37    majorsList.addItem("Economics");
38    majorsList.addItem("Undecided");
39
40    //ADD COMPONENTS TO FRAME
41    add(majorsLabel);
42    add(majorsList);
43    add(storeButton);
44    add(summaryLabel);
45    add(studentArea);
46
47    //REGISTER LISTENERS
48    storeButton.addActionListener(this);    //BUTTON LISTENER
49    }//END ListBox()
50
51    //PROCESS BUTTON EVENT
52    public void actionPerformed(ActionEvent e)
53    {
54      //DID A BUTTON CAUSE EVENT?
55      if (e.getSource() instanceof Button)
56      {
57        //GET SELECTED MAJORS
58        majors = majorsList.getSelectedItems();
59        studentArea.append("\nMajor(s):\t");
60        for (int index = 0; index < majors.length; ++index)
61        {
62          studentArea.append(majors[index]);
63          studentArea.append("\n\t");
64        }//END FOR
65      }//END IF
66    }//END actionPerformed()
67  }//END ListBox CLASS
68
69  //APPLICATION CLASS TO TEST ListBox CLASS
70  public class GUI106_2
71  {
72    public static void main(String[] args)
73    {
74      //DEFINE FRAME OBJECT
75      ListBox window = new ListBox("GUI106_2 List Boxes");
76
77      //SET FRAME SIZE
78      window.setSize(400,350);
79
```

```
80     //MAKE FRAME VISIBLE
81     window.setVisible(true);
82   }//END main()
83  }//END GUI106_2 CLASS
```

13. In line 11 of the program, we defined a list box object called *majorsList*. Then in lines 33-38 we use this object to call the *addItem()* method to add items to the box. Using the syntax you see in lines 33-38, use line 39 to add another item to the list box.

14. Execute the program again a verify that the item you added in line 39 appears in the list box and is a selectable item.

15. The list box object, called *majorsList*, was defined in line 11, as follows:

    private List majorsList = new List(3,true);

    Change the object definition, as follows:

    private List majorsList = new List(2,false);

16. Execute the program again and observe the window. You should find that only the first two list items are visible. (Why?)

17. Use the scrollbars as before and try to select more than one item. You should find that you can only select a single item. Any ideas why you are now limited to selecting only a single item?

18. Click the *Store* button and you will see the selected item appear in the text area.

Discussion

A list box provides scrollable list of items from which to select. In Java, list boxes are provided via the *List* class and include an active scrollbar when the number of items in the list exceed that visible portion of the list box. The visible portion of the list box is set when the list box object was defined in line 11 of the foregoing program. At first, the number of visible items was set to 3. Then, you changed the object definition is step 15 and set the number of visible items to 2. A list box also allows more than one item to be selected. However, to accomplish this, the list box object definition must include the Boolean value **true** to allow multiple selections. A value of **false** will only permit a single selection, as in a choice box. Items are added to the list by calling the *addItem()* method with the choice box object. The item to be added is provided as string argument to the *addItem()* method.

Procedure (continued)

19. Load and execute the *GUI106_3.java* program contained on the CD that accompanies this book, or download it from www.prenhall.com. You should see a window that contains a list box and a text area. Observe that there is no *Store* button. So, how can we select list box items? The list box program has been changed to allow the list box to generate its own event, without using a button event.

20. Select one or more items using a single-click on the item, then double-click on any of the items that you selected. You find that the selected items appear in the text area after the double-click.

Discussion

Here is the *GUI106_3.java* source code:

```
1   import java.awt.*;          //FOR FRAME CLASS
2   import java.awt.event.*;    //FOR EVENT HANDLING
3
4   class ListBox2 extends FrameWithClose implements ActionListener
5   {
6     //DEFINE TEXT AREA OBJECT AS PRIVATE CLASS DATA
7     private TextArea studentArea = new TextArea(7,40);
8
9     //DEFINE LIST OBJECT
10    private List majorsList = new List(3,true);
11
12
13    //DEFINE MAJORS ARRAY
14    private String majors[];
15
16    //CONSTRUCTOR
17    public ListBox2(String title)
18    {
19      //CALL SUPERCLASS CONSTRUCTOR
20      super(title);
21
22      //SET FRAME LAYOUT MANAGER
23      setLayout(new FlowLayout(FlowLayout.LEFT,10,30));
24
```

```
25    //DEFINE LABEL OBJECT
26    Label majorsLabel = new Label("Major: (Select One or More)");
27    Label summaryLabel = new Label("Student Summary");
28
29    //ADD ITEMS TO LIST BOX
30    majorsList.addItem("Accounting");
31    majorsList.addItem("Business");
32    majorsList.addItem("Computer Info. Systems");
33    majorsList.addItem("Computer Science");
34    majorsList.addItem("Economics");
35    majorsList.addItem("Undecided");
36
37    //ADD COMPONENTS TO FRAME
38    add(majorsLabel);
39    add(majorsList);
40    add(summaryLabel);
41    add(studentArea);
42
43    //REGISTER LISTENERS
44    majorsList.addActionListener(this);    //LIST BOX LISTENER
45  }//END ListBox2()
46
47  //PROCESS BUTTON EVENT
48  public void actionPerformed(ActionEvent e)
49  {
50   //DID A BUTTON CAUSE EVENT?
51   if (e.getSource() instanceof List)
52   {
53    //GET SELECTED MAJORS
54    majors = majorsList.getSelectedItems();
55    studentArea.append("\nMajor(s):\t");
56    for (int index = 0; index < majors.length; ++index)
57    {
58     studentArea.append(majors[index]);
59     studentArea.append("\n\t");
60    }//END FOR
61   }//END IF
62  }//END actionPerformed()
63 }//END ListBox2 CLASS
64
65 //APPLICATION CLASS TO TEST ListBox CLASS
66 public class GUI106_3
67 {
```

```
68    public static void main(String[] args)
69    {
70      //DEFINE FRAME OBJECT
71      ListBox2 window = new ListBox2("GUI106_3 List Boxes");
72
73      //SET FRAME SIZE
74      window.setSize(400,350);
75
76      //MAKE FRAME VISIBLE
77      window.setVisible(true);
78    }//END main()
79  }//END GUI106_3 CLASS
```

A list box can be made to generate its own event by registering the list box object as a listener as we did in line 44. Then, the *actionPerformed()* method is coded to look for an "instance of List" in line 51 rather than an "instance of Button" as in the previous program. A list box event is triggered by double-clicking any of the list box items.

7

LOOPING OPERATIONS: ITERATION

OBJECTIVES

When you are finished with this chapter, you should have a good understanding of the following:

- Pretest, posttest, and fixed repetition iteration control structures.
- The Java iteration control structures of **while**, **do/while**, and **for**.
- How to detect an infinite loop condition.
- How to desk-check a loop for correct number of iterations and termination.
- How to initialize product and sum variables.
- How to construct a sentinel controlled loop for data entry.
- How to construct loop-controlled menu-driven programs.
- How to test for invalid user entries in a program using loops.
- When to use the **break** and **continue** options in a loop statement.
- Nested loop structures.
- Down-to loop structures.
- When to use one Java loop structure over another.

INTRODUCTION

In Chapter 6, you learned about the decision control structure. It is now time to explore the third and final control structure employed by Java: *iteration*. Iteration simply means doing something repeatedly. In programming, this is called *looping* because the iteration control structure causes the program flow to go around in a loop. Of course, there must be a way to get out of the loop, or the computer would loop forever! Such a situation is called an *infinite loop*, for obvious reasons. To prevent infinite looping, all iteration control structures test a condition to determine when to exit the loop. *Pretest* loops test a condition before each loop is executed. *Posttest* loops test condition after each loop execution. And, finally, *fixed repetition* loops cause the loop to be executed a predetermined number of times.

    The three iteration control structures employed by Java are the **while**, **do/while**, and **for**. As you will learn in this chapter, each provides a means for you to perform repetitive operations. The difference between them is found in the means by which they control the exiting of the loop. The **while** is a pretest loop, the **do/while** is a posttest loop, and the **for** is a fixed repetition loop. Let's begin our discussion with the **while** loop.

7-1 THE while LOOP

You can see from Figure 7-1 that the **while** loop is a pretest loop because a Boolean test is made *before* the loop body can ever be executed. If the test expression is true, the loop body is executed. If the test expression is false the loop body is bypassed, and the next sequential statement after the loop is executed. As long as the test expression is true, the program continues to go around the loop. In other words, the loop is repeated "while" the test expression is true. To get out of the loop, something must change within the loop that makes the test expression false. If such a change does not take place, you have an infinite loop. In addition, the diagram shows that *if the test expression is false the first time it is encountered, the loop body will never be executed.* This is an important characteristic of the **while** control structure.

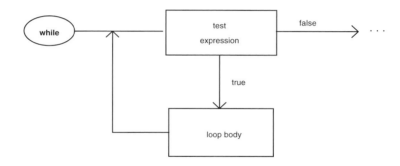

Figure 7-1   The while loop operation.

The Java format for the **while** statement is as follows:

while *STATEMENT FORMAT*

while (*test expression*)
{
   statement 1;
   statement 2;
        •
        •   *//LOOP BODY*
        •
   statement n;
} //END WHILE

The first line of the statement contains the keyword **while** followed by a test expression within parentheses. To test a single condition, you will often use the Boolean operators of ==, !=, <, >, <=, >=, and !. To test multiple conditions, you must use the logical operators of OR (||) and AND (&&). Notice that the loop body is framed using curly braces. This forms a compound statement, which consists of the individual loop body statements. An indentation scheme is also used so that the loop body can be easily identified. Finally, you should be aware that the loop body does not have to be framed if it consists of only a single statement. However, the CPU will execute just this single statement during the loop. Any additional statements are considered to be outside the loop structure. Let's see how the **while** loop works by looking at a few simple examples.

DEBUGGING TIP

Always remember to frame the body of a loop with curly braces, { }, if it contains more than one statement. For example, consider the following:

```
count = 0;
while (count < 10)
  System.out.println(count);
  ++count;
```

The body of this loop obviously consists of two statements, as shown by the indentation. However, the loop body is not framed. As a result, you have an infinite loop. (Why?)

Example 7-1

What will be displayed by the following segments of code?

a.

```
int number = 5;
int sum = 0;
while (number > 0)
{
  sum += number;
  --number;
} //END WHILE
System.out.println("The sum is " + sum);
```

Here, the ***loop control variable***, *number*, is first assigned the value 5, and the variable *sum* is assigned the value 0. The **while** loop body will be executed as long as *number* is greater than 0. Observe that each time the loop is executed, the value of *number* is added to *sum*. In addition, the value of *number* is decremented by 1. Let's desk-check the code by tracing through each iteration to see what is happening, keeping track of the values of *number* and *sum* after each iteration:

1st Iteration:	*sum* is 5
	number is 4
2nd Iteration:	*sum* is 9
	number is 3
3rd Iteration:	*sum* is 12
	number is 2
4th Iteration:	*sum* is 14
	number is 1
5th and Final Iteration:	*sum* is 15
	number is 0

The looping stops here because the value of *number* is zero. As a result, the loop body is bypassed and the *println()* statement is executed, producing a display of

The sum is 15

In summary, you could say that the program segment computes the sum of integers from 1 through 5.

DEBUGGING TIP

Always initialize a variable that is accumulating a sum to 0. On the other hand, always initialize a variable that is accumulating a product to 1 *not* 0. What will be the result if such a product variable is initialized to 0?

b.

```
int sum = 0;
while (number > 0)
{
  sum += number;
  --number;
```

```
} //END WHILE
System.out.println("The sum is " + sum);
```

What has been changed in this segment of code versus the previous segment in part a? Well, notice that the loop control variable, *number*, has not been initialized prior to the loop test. As a result, *number* will initially have some arbitrary value from memory. This condition will result in an indeterminate number of looping iterations, often producing an infinite loop for all practical purposes.

DEBUGGING TIP

Make sure the loop control variable always has a meaningful value prior to entering the **while** loop statement. The **while** loop is a pretest loop and, therefore, must have a legitimate value to test the first time the loop test is executed.

c.

```
int number = 5;
int sum = 0;
while (number > 0)
{
  if (number % 2 != 0)
     sum += number;
  −−number;
} //END WHILE
System.out.println("The sum is " + sum);
```

Here, an **if** statement has been included within the loop so that *number* is added to *sum* only if *number* is odd. Why will the calculation be performed when *number* is odd? Well, the remainder of any odd number divided by 2 is 1, right? Since 1 is not equal to 0, the test is true and *number* is added to *sum*. If *number* is even, the remainder operation generates a 0 result. This makes the **if** test false and the calculation statement is bypassed. This program segment computes the sum of odd integers from 1 through 5, resulting in a display of

The sum is 9

d.

```
int number = 5;
int sum = 0;
while (number > 0)
{
```

```
   if (number % 2 == 0)
      sum += number;
   --number;
} //END WHILE
System.out.println("The sum is " + sum);
```

This time, the program computes the sum of even integers from 1 through 5, because *number* is added to *sum* only if *number* is even. (Why?) As a result, the display is

The sum is 6

---

e.

```
int maxNumber = 5;
int number = 0;
double sum = 0;
while (number != maxNumber)
   sum += number;
System.out.println("The average of the first " + maxNumber
                   + "positive integers is :  " + sum/maxNumber);
```

This is an infinite loop. Notice that the loop is executed as long as *number* and *maxNumber* are not equal. The initial value of *number* is 0, and the initial value of *maxNumber* is 5. However, these values are never changed within the loop. Thus, *number* is always not equal to *maxNumber*, resulting in an infinite loop. No display is generated, and with many systems you must turn off the computer in order to get out of the loop. To correct this problem, you must change the loop control variable somewhere within the loop so that the loop test will eventually become false. In this segment of code, you need to increment *number* within the body of the loop, like this:

```
int maxNumber = 5;
int number = 0;
double sum = 0;
while (number != maxNumber)
{
   ++number;
   sum += number;
} //END WHILE
System.out.println("The average of the first " + maxNumber
                   + " positive integers is :  " + sum/maxNumber);
```

The loop will now produce a result of

The average of the first 5 positive integers is: 3.0

By the way, why was *sum* defined as a floating-point value?

f.

What would happen if *number* were incremented by 2 in part e? This modification
would also result in an infinite loop, because the value of *number* would skip over
the value of *maxNumber* and the two would always be unequal.

DEBUGGING TIP

Remember, an infinite loop is the result of a logical error in your program. ***The
compiler will not detect an infinite loop condition***. For this reason, you should
always ***desk-check*** your loop structures very closely prior to coding and
execution. A little time desk-checking will save you a lot of time at the keyboard.

g.
```
boolean positive = true;        //DEFINE BOOLEAN FLAG VARIABLE
int number = 0;
int sum = 0;
Keyboard in = new Keyboard();
while (positive == true)
{
  System.out.println("Enter an integer value: ");     //GET A NUMBER
  number = in.readInt();
  if (number < 0)              //SET FLAG TO FALSE IF NUMBER < 0
  {
     positive = false;
     System.out.println("Loop terminated");
  }//END IF
  else                          //ADD NUMBER TO SUM AND DISPLAY
  {
    sum = sum + number;
    System.out.println("The sum is now: " + sum + "\n\n");
  }//END ELSE
}//END WHILE
```

This is an example of a *flag controlled loop*. A *flag* is a Boolean variable that is
used to control the flow of a program. We first initialize the flag to **true**, then
change it to **false** when a given event has occurred within the program. Here, we
have started out by defining a variable for the **boolean** class called *positive*. The
variable *positive* is then initialized to the value **true**. The loop will continue to
execute as long as the value of *positive* remains **true**. With each iteration, the
program will display the sum of the integers entered by the user. However, when
the user enters a negative number, *positive* is set to **false**, and the loop will
terminate. Why? Here is a typical output produced by the loop:

```
Enter an integer value:
1↵
The sum is now 1

Enter an integer value:
2↵
The sum is now 3

Enter an integer value:
3↵
The sum is now 6

Enter an integer value:
-1↵
Loop terminated
```

Data Entry Using while

There are many situations in which you will want to use a looping operation to read data. One common example is to read strings of data. The idea is to read a single data element, such as a character, each time the loop is executed. Then break out of the loop when the data string is terminated. For instance, consider the following program:

```
//COUNT THE CHARACTERS
import keyboardInput.*;            //FOR readChar()
public class CharacterCount
{
  //DECLARE PERIOD CONSTANT
  static final char PERIOD = '.';
  public static void main(String[] args)
  {
    char inChar = ' ';                    //USER ENTRY VARIABLE
    int charCount = 0;                    //CHARACTER COUNT
    Keyboard in = new Keyboard();         //CREATE KEYBOARD OBJECT
    System.out.println("Enter several characters, pressing ENTER after each\n"
                + "entry. Terminate the input with a period.\n");
    inChar = in.readChar();               //READ A CHARACTER
    while (inChar != PERIOD)              //CHARACTER A PERIOD?
    {
      ++charCount;                        //INCREMENT CHARACTER COUNT
      inChar = in.readChar();             //READ ANOTHER CHARACTER
    } //END WHILE
```

```
    System.out.println("The number of characters entered was "+ charCount);
  } //END main()
} //END CharacterCount
```

The general idea of this program is to read a string of characters, one character at a time, until a period, '.', is encountered. The period is called a **sentinel value**, because it ends the input string but is not part of that string. The input variable is *inChar*. The **while** loop is executed as long as *inChar* is not equal to a period. With each iteration, a counter (*count*) is incremented to count the number of characters that were entered before the period. Here is what you will see when the program is executed:

```
Enter several characters, pressing ENTER after each
entry. Terminate the input with a period.
a.⏎
b.⏎
c.⏎
d.⏎
..⏎
The number of characters entered was 4
```

Here the user has entered five characters, including the sentinel. The program counts the number of characters entered, excluding the sentinel value.

Now, let's look at the program a bit closer. First, notice that a character is read just prior to the **while** statement because the **while** statement tests the variable *inChar* to see that it is not a period. Without the first read operation, *inChar* would not have a value and, therefore, could not be tested. Remember that the variable being tested in the **while** statement must always have a value prior to the first test. This is a common source of error when writing **while** loops. Why didn't the program count the period? Well, the loop is broken and *count* is not incremented for the period character.

> A **sentinel** controlled loop is a loop that terminates when a given sentinel value is entered by the user.

PROGRAMMING TIP

When using a sentinel-controlled loop, always provide a prompt that instructs the user what to enter as the sentinel value. The prompts for data entry must continually remind the user of the sentinel value in a clear, unambiguous manner. Never use a sentinel value that the user could confuse with the normal data items being entered.

 Quick Check

1. True or false: A **while** loop repeats until the test expression is true.

2. True or false: The **while** loop is a posttest loop.

3. What is wrong with the following code?

   ```
   int x = 10;
   while (x > 0)
      System.out.println("This is a while loop.");
      - -x;
   ```

4. Correct the code in question 3.

5. How many times will the following loop execute?

   ```
   int x = 1;
   while (x <= 0)
   {
      System.out.println("How many times will this loop execute?");
      ++x;
   }//END WHILE
   ```

6. How many times will the following loop execute?

   ```
   int x = 1;
   while (x >=0)
   {
      System.out.println("How many times will this loop execute?");
       ++x;
   }//END WHILE
   ```

7-2 THE do/while LOOP

The flow of the **do/while** loop can be seen in Figure 7-2.

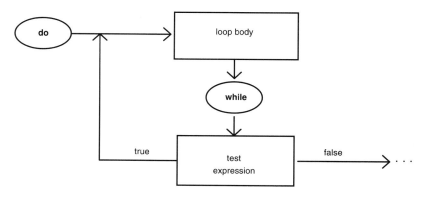

Figure 7-2   The **do/while** loop operation.

If you compare Figure 7-2 to the flow of **while** in Figure 7-1, you will find that the test is made at the end of the loop, rather than the beginning of the loop. This is the main difference between the **while** and the **do/while** loops. Because the **do/while** is a posttest loop, *the loop body will always be executed at least once.* To break the loop, the test expression must become false. Thus, if the test condition is initially true, something must happen within the loop to change the condition to false; otherwise, you have an infinite loop. Here's the required Java syntax:

do/while *STATEMENT FORMAT*

```
do
{
  statement 1;
  statement 2;
        •
        •          //LOOP BODY
        •
  statement n;
}//END DO/WHILE
while (test expression);
```

This format shows that the operation must begin with the single keyword **do**. This is followed by the loop body, which is followed by the keyword **while** and the test expression enclosed within parentheses. You must always frame the loop body with curly braces if it contains multiple statements. However, no framing is required when there is only a single loop statement within the body of the loop. In addition, notice that there is no semicolon after the keyword **do** in the first line, but a semicolon is required after the test expression in the last line. Look at the program segments in Example 7-2, and see if you can predict their results.

Example 7-2

What will be displayed by the following segments of code?

a.

```
int number = 5;
int sum = 0;
do
{
  sum += number;
  --number;
}//END DO/WHILE
while (number > 0);
System.out.println("The sum is " + sum);
```

In this segment, the value of *number* is initially set to 5, and the value of *sum* to 0. Each time the loop is executed, the value of *number* is added to *sum*. In addition, the value of *number* is decremented by 1. The looping will end when *number* has been decremented to 0. The resulting display is

The sum is 15

Notice that this **do/while** loop computes the sum of integers 1 through 5, as did the **while** loop in Example 7-1a.

b.

```
int number = 0;
int sum = 0;
do
{
  sum += number;
  ++number;
}//END DO/WHILE
while (number != 5);
System.out.println("The sum is " + sum);
```

In this segment, both *number* and *sum* are initially 0. Again, you might suspect that the loop computes the sum of the integers 1 through 5. But, it actually computes the sum of integers 1 through 4. Why? Notice that *number* is incremented after the *sum* is calculated. Thus, when *number* increments to 5, the loop is broken, and the value 5 is never added to *sum*. The resulting display is

The sum is 10

How would you change the loop to sum the integers 1 through 5? One way is to change the test expression to *while(number != 6)*. Another, more preferred, way is to reverse the two loop statements so that *number* is incremented prior to the *sum* calculation.

---

c.

```
int maxNumber = 5;
int number = 0;
double sum = 0;
do
{
   --number;
   sum += number;
}//END DO/WHILE
while (number != maxNumber);
System.out.println("The average of the first " + maxNumber
              + " positive integers is :  " + sum/maxNumber);
```

In this segment, *maxNumber* begins with the value 5, and both *number* and *sum* are initialized to 0. The loop is broken when the value of *number* equals the value of *maxNumber*. How many times will the loop execute? If you said "five," you are wrong! Notice that *number* is decremented each time the loop is executed. Theoretically, the loop will execute an infinite number of times. However, because the range of integers in Java is normally from −2,147,483,648 to +2,147,483,647 the loop will execute 4,294,967,291 times. How did we get this figure? Well, 2,147,483,648 loops will have executed when *number* reaches −2,147,483,648. The next looping operation will decrement *number* to +2,147,483,647, because two's complement signed values "wrap-around." It then takes 2,147,483,642 loops to decrement *number* to 5. Notice that 2,147,483,648 + 1 + 2,147,483,642 = 4,294,967,291. Of course, this is infinite for all practical purposes!

---

d.

```
int maxNumber = 5;
int number = 0;
double sum = 0;
```

```
do
{
  ++number;
  sum += number;
}//END DO/WHILE
while (number != maxNumber);
System.out.println("The average of the first " + maxNumber
                   + " positive integers is :  " + sum/maxNumber);;
```

Here, the loop in part c has been corrected so that the value of *number* is incremented by 1 with each iteration. When *number* reaches 5, it equals the value of *maxNumber*, and the loop is broken. The resulting display is

The average of the first 5 positive integers is: 3.0

---

e.

```
static final char PERIOD = '.';         //DECLARE PERIOD CONSTANT

Keyboard in = new Keyboard();           //CREATE KEYBOARD OBJECT
char inChar = ' ';                      //DEFINE USER ENTRY VARIABLE
int charCount = 0;                      //DEFINE CHAR COUNTER

System.out.println("Enter several characters, pressing ENTER after each\n"
                   + "entry. Terminate the input with a period.\n");
do
{
    ++charCount;
    inChar = in.readChar();             //READ A CHARACTER
}//END DO/WHILE
while (inChar != PERIOD);               //CHARACTER A PERIOD?
System.out.println("The number of characters entered was " + --charCount);
```

This program segment shows how a sentinel value can be employed to break a **do/while** loop. Notice that each iteration reads a single character from the keyboard until the period key is pressed. When this operation was performed using a **while** loop, you had to read the first character prior to the loop structure, so there was an initial value to test. This is because the Boolean test is made at the beginning of **while**. On the other hand, a **do/while** loop performs the Boolean test at the end of the loop. As a result, you do not have to read the first character prior to the loop structure, because the loop body will always be executed at least once and *inChar* will have a legitimate value before the loop test is made.

Now, look at the *println()* statement. The value being displayed is *−−charCount*. Why? Observe that *charCount* will be incremented, even for the last loop iteration that reads the period sentinel value. Therefore, *charCount* must be decremented to get the correct number of characters entered, excluding the sentinel value. This is required because of the posttest nature of **do/while**.

Assuming the user enters the string "abcd.", the display would be

```
Enter several characters, pressing ENTER after each
entry. Terminate the input with a period.
a.↵
b.↵
c.↵
d.↵
..↵
The number of characters entered was 4
```

PROBLEM SOLVING IN ACTION: LOOP-CONTROLLED MENU-DRIVEN PROGRAMS

Problem

In the last chapter, you saw that the **switch** statement is used to create menu-driven programs. It is often desirable to allow the user to select a menu option, perform the task associated with that option, then return to the menu to select another option without terminating the program until a quit option is chosen. Such a program would require the menu to be displayed repeatedly until the quit option is chosen. This is an ideal application for looping. We will encase our menu within a loop so that the menu and associated tasks will keep repeating until the user chooses to terminate the program. We will apply this technique to the menu-driven loan program developed in the last chapter. Let's revisit the problem.

Defining the Problem

Output: A program menu that prompts the user to select a monthly payment, total interest, or total loan amount calculation option.
The monthly loan payment, total loan interest, or total loan amount, depending on the program option that the user selects.
Invalid entry messages as required.

Input: A user response to the menu (P, I, T, or Q).
If P is selected: User enters the loan amount, interest rate, and term.
If I is selected: User enters the loan amount, interest rate, and term.
If T is selected: User enters the loan amount, interest rate, and term.
If Q is selected: terminate program.

Processing: Calculate the selected option as follows:
Case P: *payment = principle * rate/1 − (1+rate)* $^{-term}$
Case I: *interest = term * payment − principle*
Case T: *total = principle + interest*
Case Q: terminate program.

where: *principle* is the amount of the loan.
rate is a monthly interest rate in decimal form.
term is the number of months of the loan.

Planning the Solution

Using the program design developed in the last chapter, we divided the problem into two subproblems to solve the overall problem. They were:

- Display the menu and read user choice.
- Perform the chosen calculation and display results.

The problem solving diagram for this solution is shown again in Figure 7-3.

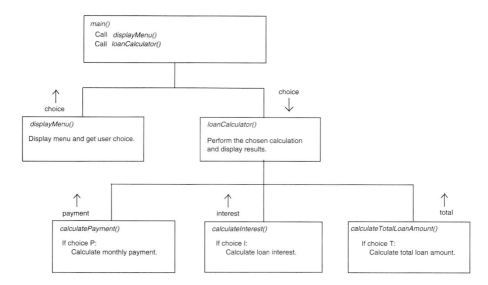

Figure 7-3   A problem solving diagram for the loan problem.

Recall that there were three levels to solving the problem. At the first level, *main()*, a method is called to display the menu and get the user choice. The *displayMenu()* method accomplishes this task and sends the user choice back to *main()*, as indicated on the diagram. Method *main()* will then send the choice to a method called *loanCalculator()*, which will call one of three methods, depending on the choice, to perform and return the required calculation. Now, the process description requires that we add a loop control feature to the program. Here is the revised set of algorithms through the first level of refinement:

Initial Algorithm

> *main()*
> BEGIN
>   do
>   Call *displayMenu()* method.
>   Call *loanCalculator()* method.
>   while *choice* ≠ 'q' AND *choice* ≠ 'Q'
> END.

First Level of Refinement

> *displayMenu()*
> BEGIN
>   Display a program menu that prompts the user to choose a monthly payment (P), total interest (I), total loan amount (T), or quit (Q) option.
>   Read (*choice*).
> END.

> *loanCalculator()*
> BEGIN
>   Case P: Call method *calculatePayment()* and display payment.
>   Case I: Call method *calculateInterest()* and display interest.
>   Case T: Call method *calculateTotalLoanAmount()* and display total loan amount.
>   Case Q: terminate program.
>   Default: Write an invalid entry message and ask the user to select again.
> END.

Notice that the loop control feature is added to the initial algorithm level, *main()*. The *displayMenu()* and *loanCalculator()* algorithms at the first level of refinement have not changed much from our earlier solution. So, let's focus on the loop control in *main()*. Now, recall that the *displayMenu()* method obtains the user's menu choice. If the user enters a 'q' or 'Q' to quit the program, the loop will break, and the program terminates. But, is there something wrong here? We said if the "user enters a 'q' *or* 'Q' to quit the program …"; however, the loop test employs the AND operation. So, why have we used the Boolean AND operation rather than the OR operation to perform this test? This is a classic candidate for desk-checking the algorithm logic *before* coding the program. Ask yourself: "When will the loop break?" Any Java loop breaks when the condition tested is false, right? Remember that the result of an AND operation is false when any one of its conditions is false. As a result, the loop will break when *choice* is a 'q' *or* a 'Q'. The loop will continue when both sides of the AND operation are true. Therefore, the loop will continue as long as *choice* is not a 'q' *and choice* is not 'Q'. Isn't this what we want to do? What would happen if you mistakenly used the OR operation in the foregoing loop test? An OR operation produces a true result when any one of its conditions is true. One of these conditions would always be true, because *choice* cannot be both a 'q' and a 'Q'. The result of this oversight would be an infinite loop.

Another point needs to be made here. This application is a classic candidate for a **do/while** loop rather than a **while** loop, because you always want the menu to be displayed at least once to allow for a user choice.

DEBUGGING TIP

A common mistake when developing loop control logic is to use an OR operation rather than an AND operation, or vice versa. This mistake almost always results in an infinite loop. The lesson to be learned here is to *always* desk-check your loop control logic before coding the program.

We will not repeat the second level of refinement, because it has not changed from the solution developed in the last chapter. Now that we have desk-checked our loop control logic, we are ready to code the program.

Coding the Program

Here is the flat implementation of the foregoing program design:

```
/* ACTION 7-1 (ACTION07_01.JAVA)
OUTPUT:   A PROGRAM MENU THAT PROMPTS THE USER TO SELECT A
          MONTHLY PAYMENT, TOTAL INTEREST, OR TOTAL LOAN
          AMOUNT CALCULATION   OPTION.
          INVALID ENTRY MESSAGES AS REQUIRED.
          THE MONTHLY LOAN PAYMENT, TOTAL LOAN INTEREST, OR
          TOTAL LOAN AMOUNT, DEPENDING ON THE PROGRAM
          OPTION THAT THE USER SELECTS. INVALID ENTRY
          MESSAGES AS REQUIRED.

INPUT:    A USER RESPONSE TO THE MENU (P, I, T, OR Q).
          IF P IS SELECTED: USER ENTERS THE LOAN AMOUNT,
          INTEREST RATE, AND TERM.
          IF I IS SELECTED: USER ENTERS THE LOAN AMOUNT,
          INTEREST RATE, AND TERM.
          IF R IS SELECTED: USER ENTERS THE LOAN AMOUNT,
          INTEREST RATE, AND TERM.
          IF Q IS SELECTED: TERMINATE PROGRAM.

PROCESSING: CALCULATE THE SELECTED OPTION AS FOLLOWS:
          CASE P: PAYMENT = PRINCIPLE * RATE/(1 - (1+RATE)^ -TERM)
          CASE I:  INTEREST = TERM * PAYMENT - PRINCIPLE
          CASE T:  TOTAL = PRINCIPLE + INTEREST
          CASE Q:  TERMINATE PROGRAM.

          WHERE:   PRINCIPLE IS THE AMOUNT OF THE LOAN.
                   RATE IS A MONTHLY INTEREST RATE IN DECIMAL
                   FORM.
                   TERM IS THE NUMBER OF MONTHS OF THE LOAN.
*/

import keyboardInput.*;            //FOR readChar(), readDouble(), readInt()
public class Action07_01
{
  public static void main(String[] args)
  {
  //DEFINE VARIABLES
  char pause = ' ';          //PAUSE VAR TO FREEZE DISPLAY
  char choice = 'Q';         //USER MENU ENTRY
  double payment = 0.0;      //MONTHLY PAYMENT
  double Interest = 0.0;     //TOTAL INTEREST FOR LIFE OF LOAN
  double total = 0.0;        //TOTAL LOAN AMOUNT = PRINCIPLE + INTEREST
  double principle = 0.0;    //LOAN PRINCIPLE
```

```
        double rate = 0.0;        //ANNUAL INTEREST RATE
        int term = 0;             //TERM OF LOAN IN MONTHS

    //CREATE KEYBOARD OBJECT
    Keyboard in = new Keyboard();

    //DISPLAY PROGRAM DESCRIPTION MESSAGE
    System.out.println("This program will calculate a monthly loan interest\n"
                    + "payment, total loan interest, or total loan amount.");

    do                //BEGIN MENU CONTROL LOOP
    {
      //displayMenu() METHOD
      System.out.print("\n\n\t\t\tEnter P to get monthly payment"
                    + "\n\t\t\tEnter I to get total loan interest"
                    + "\n\t\t\tEnter T to get total loan amount"
                    + "\n\t\t\tEnter Q to quit"
                    + "\n\tPlease enter your choice:  ");
      //READ USER CHOICE
      choice = in.readChar();

      //LOAN CALCULATION METHOD
      switch (choice)
      {
       case 'p':  //calculatePayment() METHOD
       case 'P' : System.out.print("\nEnter the amount of the loan: ");
                  principle = in.readDouble();
                  System.out.print("\nEnter the duration of the loan in months: ");
                  term = in.readInt();
                  System.out.print("\nEnter the annual interest rate: ");
                  rate = in.readDouble();

                  //CHECK FOR INVALID RATE
                  if ((rate < 0) || (rate > 100))
                     //DISPLAY INVALID ENTRY MESSAGE
                     System.out.println("\n\nThis is an invalid entry.");
                  else
                  {
                     rate = rate/12/100;
                     payment = principle * rate/(1-Math.pow((1+rate),-term));
                     System.out.println("\n\nThe monthly payment is $" + payment);
                  }//END ELSE
                  break;
```

```
case 'i':    //calculateInterest() METHOD
case 'I' :   System.out.print("\nEnter the amount of the loan: ");
             principle = in.readDouble();
             System.out.print("\nEnter the duration of the loan in months: ");
             term = in.readInt();
             System.out.print("\nEnter the annual interest rate: ");
             rate = in.readDouble();

             //CHECK FOR INVALID RATE
             if ((rate < 0) || (rate > 100))
                //DISPLAY INVALID ENTRY MESSAGE
                System.out.println("\n\nThis is an invalid entry.");
             else
             {
                rate = rate/12/100;
                payment = principle * rate/(1-Math.pow((1+rate),-term));
                Interest = term * payment - principle;
                System.out.println("\n\nThe total interest is $" + Interest);
             }//END ELSE
             break;

case 't':    //CalculateTotalLoanAmount() METHOD
case 'T':    System.out.print("\nEnter the amount of the loan: ");
             principle = in.readDouble();
             System.out.print("\nEnter the duration of the loan in months: ");
             term = in.readInt();
             System.out.print("\nEnter the annual interest rate: ");
             rate = in.readDouble();

             //CHECK FOR INVALID RATE
             if ((rate < 0) || (rate > 100))
                //DISPLAY INVALID ENTRY MESSAGE
                System.out.println("\n\nThis is an invalid entry.");
             else
             {
                rate = rate/12/100;
                payment = principle * rate/(1-Math.pow((1+rate),-term));
                Interest = term * payment - principle;
                total = principle + Interest;
                System.out.println("\n\nThe total loan amount is $" + total);
             }//END ELSE
             break;
```

```
case 'q':  //TERMINATE PROGRAM
case 'Q':  System.out.println("Program terminated");
           break;

           //DISPLAY INVALID ENTRY MESSAGE
default :  System.out.println("\n\nThis is an invalid entry. ");
} //END SWITCH

//DISPLAY CONTINUE MESSAGE
System.out.println("Press ENTER to continue.");
pause = in.readChar();

} //END DO/WHILE
while ((choice != 'q') && (choice != 'Q'));
} //END main()
}//END Action07_01 CLASS
```

The major change here is the **do/while** loop control feature that we added in our solution planning. Notice how the conditional loop test is coded at the end of the program. The entire test must be within parentheses. The variable *choice* is tested twice; both tests must be enclosed within parentheses. The results of both tests are combined via the Boolean AND (&&) operation.

DEBUGGING TIP

A common mistake when coding a compound Boolean test on a variable is to forget to code it so that each side of the compound test produces a Boolean result. For example, suppose that we coded the foregoing loop test as

```
while (choice != 'q' && 'Q');
```

This code will always produce a compiler error, because the right side of the AND operation does not produce a Boolean result. It might make sense for you to code it this way, but it doesn't make sense to the compiler!

Another feature that has been added to this program is the use of a "dummy" entry variable to pause the display until the user presses the **ENTER** key. Notice that *pause* has been defined as a single character variable. Then, the statement

```
pause = in.readChar();
```

is inserted into the program just before the loop test. The *readChar()* method simply freezes the display until the user presses the **ENTER** key. This happens when the program must continue to redisplay the menu. The frozen display gives the user a chance to read any information generated by the program before the menu is displayed again. Remember this little trick, because it often comes in handy.

 Quick Check

1. True or false: A **do/while** repeats until the loop test is true.

2. True or false: The **do/while** loop is a posttest loop.

3. What is wrong with the following code?

    ```
    int x = 10;
    do
        System.out.println("This is a do/while loop");
    while (x > 0);
    ```

4. Correct the code in question 3.

5. How many times will the following loop execute?

    ```
    int x = 1;
    do
        System.out.println("This is a do/while loop");
        ++x;
    while (x <= 0);
    ```

6. How many times will the following loop execute?

    ```
    int x = 1;
    do
    {
        System.out.println("This is a do/while loop");
        ++x;
    }//END DO/WHILE
    while (x >=0);
    ```

7-3 THE for LOOP

The **for** loop is called a *fixed repetition* loop because the loop is repeated a fixed number of times. You would use it in place of a **while** or **do/while** loop when it is known in advance, by you or the program, exactly how many times the loop must repeat itself.

    You can see from Figure 7-4 that the first thing that takes place before the loop body is executed is the initialization of a loop counter. Initialization means setting a counter variable to some initial, or beginning, value. A test expression is then executed to test the counter value. If the result of this test is true, the loop body is executed. Each time the loop body is executed, the counter value must be incremented or decremented. The test expression is evaluated again before the loop body is executed another time. The loop is repeated as long as the result of the test expression is true. In other words, the counter is incremented/decremented, tested, and the loop is repeated *until* the test expression is false. When this occurs, the loop body is not executed again, and the loop is broken. Control of the program then goes to the next sequential statement following the loop.

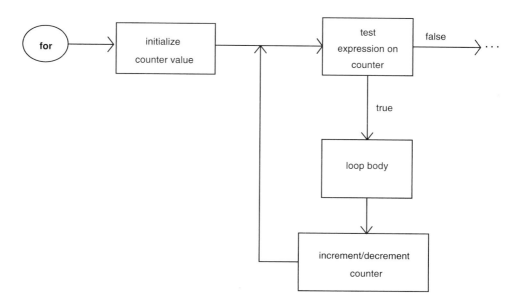

Figure 7-4 The **for** loop operation.

Here's the Java syntax:

for *STATEMENT FORMAT*

```
for (int Counter = initial value; Counter  test expression;
      Increment/Decrement Counter)
{
   statement 1;
   statement 2;
      •
      •                        //LOOP BODY
      •
   statement n;
} //END FOR
```

The statement begins with the keyword **for**. This is followed by *three* separate statements: an *initialization* statement, a *test expression*, and an *increment/decrement* statement, all enclosed within a single set of parentheses. The loop counter is initialized by assigning an initial value to the counter variable. The counter variable will almost always be an **int** but can be any simple data type, except a floating-point type. The counter variable can be defined before the **for** statement or within the **for** statement as part of the initialization step, like this:

for (int *count* = 1; ...

If defined within the **for** statement, it is only valid within the **for** statement in which it is defined. Thus, as far as Java is concerned, the counter variable doesn't exist outside of the **for** statement in which it is defined.

The test expression is used to test the value of the loop counter against some predetermined value. The loop body will be executed until the result of the test expression becomes false.

The increment/decrement statement is used to change the value of the loop counter so that the test expression becomes false after a fixed number of iterations. If the value of the loop counter is never changed, you have an infinite loop. It is important to note that the increment/decrement statement is not executed until *after* the loop body is executed in a given iteration. Thus, *if the initial test expression is true, the loop body will be executed at least once.* However, *if the initial test expression is false, the loop body is never executed.* This means that the **for** loop acts very much like the **while** loop. In fact, a **for** loop and a **while** loop are really one and the same looping structure, just coded differently. Think about it!

One last point about the loop counter variable: *Never* alter the counter variable within the body of the loop. The counter variable can be used within the body of the loop, but its value should not be altered. In other words, never use the counter variable on the left side of the assignment symbol (=) within the loop.

DEBUGGING TIP

A common programming error is to increment the loop counter inside a **for** loop like this:

```
for (int count = 0; count != 5; ++count)
{
    System.out.println(count);
    ++count;
}
```

This code will not produce a compiler error, but will produce an infinite loop! Why? Because *count* is incremented twice during each loop thereby skipping completely over the value 5 and creating an infinite loop condition. The lesson to be learned here is "don't mess with the loop counter inside a **for** loop."

Finally, notice from the above format that the loop body is framed within the curly braces. This is always required when there is more than one loop statement. The framing can be eliminated when there is only a single loop statement. Here are a few examples; see if you can predict the results.

Example 7-3

What will be displayed by the following segments of code?

a.

```
for (int count = 1; count != 11; ++count)
    System.out.println(count);
```

The loop counter variable, *count*, ranges from 1 to 11. How many iterations will there be? Eleven, right? Wrong! The *++count* statement increments the value of *count* <u>after</u> each loop iteration. When the value of *count* reaches 11, the test expression is false and the loop is broken. As a result, there is no eleventh iteration. With each loop iteration, the *println()* statement displays the value of *count*, like this:

```
1
2
3
4
5
6
7
8
9
10
```

DEBUGGING TIP

When desk-checking a loop, always check the *loop boundaries*. The loop boundaries occur at the initial and final value of the loop control variable. Checking these values will help prevent *off-by-one* errors, where the loop executes one time more or one time less than it is supposed to. Also, when desk-checking a loop, try to imagine circumstances where the loop might execute 0 times, 1 time, or *n* times.

b.

```
for (int count = 10; count != 0; --count)
    System.out.println(count);
```

Here, the value of *count* ranges from 10 to 0. The *--count* statement decrements the value of *count* after each loop iteration. When the value of *count* reaches zero, the loop is broken. This type of loop is sometimes referred to as a "down-to" loop. The output generated by this loop is

```
10
9
8
7
6
5
4
3
2
1
```

c.

```
for (int count = 0; count != 5; ++count)
  {
    sum = sum + count;
    System.out.println("The sum in the first iteration is " + sum);
    ++count;
  }//END FOR
```

This is an infinite loop! Notice that the loop counter is incremented within the body of the loop. What actually happens is that the loop counter is incremented twice, once within the body of the loop by the increment statement and then automatically by the **for** statement. As a result, the value of *count* skips over the value 5, creating an infinite loop. The lesson to be learned here is this: *Never change a **for** loop counter within the body of the loop.*

d.

```
for (int count = -5; count < 6; ++count)
    System.out.println(count);
```

Here, *count* ranges from –5 to 6. Because the loop is broken when *count* reaches 6, the *println()* loop statement is executed for values of *count* from –5 to 5. How many times will the loop be executed? Ten, right? Wrong! There are 11 integers in the range of –5 to 5, including 0. As a result, the loop is executed eleven times to produce an output of

```
-5
-4
-3
-2
-1
0
1
2
3
4
5
```

e.

```
System.out.println("\n\tNumber\tSquare\tCube");
System.out.println("\t------\t------\t----");
for (int count = 1; count < 11; ++count)
    System.out.println("\t" + count + "\t" + count * count
                    + "\t" + count * count * count);
```

This **for** loop is being used to generate a table of squares and cubes for the integers 1 through 10. Notice how the counter variable *count* is squared and cubed within the *println()* loop statement. However, observe that at no time is the value of *count* altered within the loop. The resulting display is

number	Square	Cube
1	1	1
2	4	8
3	9	27
4	16	64
5	25	125
6	36	216
7	49	343
8	64	512
9	81	729
10	100	1000

f.

```
for (char character = 'A'; character <= 'Z'; ++character)
    System.out.print(character);
```

The counter variable in this loop is the character variable *character*. Recall that the character data type is ordered so that 'A' is smaller than 'Z'. Notice that the test expression, *character* <= 'Z' forces the loop to execute for the last time when the value of *character* is 'Z'. Consequently, the loop is executed 26 times as *character* ranges from 'A' to 'Z'. The value of *character* is displayed each time using a *println()* statement to produce an output of

ABCDEFGHIJKLMNOPQRSTUVWXYZ

g.

```
static final int MAX_COUNT = 100;
double sum = 0.0;
double average = 0.0;
for (int count = 1; count <= MAX_COUNT; ++count)
    sum = sum + count;
average = sum / MAX_COUNT;
System.out.println("The average of the first " + MAX_COUNT
                + " positive integers is:  " + average);
```

Here, the counter value is being added to the floating-point variable *sum* each time through the loop. Thus, the loop adds all the positive integers within the defined range of the counter variable. The range of *count* is from 1 to *MAX_COUNT*. Notice that *MAX_COUNT* has been declared a constant with a value of 100. Therefore, *count* will range from 1 to 100 + 1, or 101. However, because the loop is broken when *count* reaches the value 101, this value is never added to *sum*. This results in a summing of all integers within the range of 1 to *MAX_COUNT*. After the loop is broken, the value of *sum* is divided by *MAX_COUNT* to calculate the *average* of all integers from 1 to 100. Here's what you would see:

The average of the first 100 positive integers is: 50.5

Notice that the variable *sum* was defined as a floating-point value, so that the division operator, /, produces a floating-point quotient. If both *sum* and *MAX_COUNT* were defined as integer values, the division operator would produce an erroneous integer result of 50. Also, you should be aware that constants like *MAX_COUNT* are often used as shown here for the initial or final counter values in a **for** loop. The reason is this: If the constant value needs to be changed for some reason, you need to change it in only one place, at the beginning of the program within the **final** declaration. This changes its value any place it is used within the program.

---

h.

```
static final int MAX_COUNT = 100;

for (int i = 1; i <= MAX_COUNT; ++i)
{
    if (i % 17 == 0)
        System.out.println("The value " + i + " is divisible by 17.");
} //END FOR
```

An **if** statement is used in this loop to determine when the counter value, *i*, is divisible by 17. Thus, the loop displays all the values between 1 and *MAX_COUNT* (100) that are divisible by 17. Do you understand how the test expression is working in the **if** statement? Here is what you would see when it is executed:

The value 17 is divisible by 17.
The value 34 is divisible by 17.
The value 51 is divisible by 17.
The value 68 is divisible by 17.
The value 85 is divisible by 17.

PROGRAMMING TIP

Suppose that a loop must execute *n* times and you create a loop control variable called *count*. In Java, if the loop control variable begins with the value 0, the loop test would use the *less than* (<) operator, like this: *count < n*. If the application requires you to begin the loop control variable with the value 1, the test would use the *less than or equal to* (<=) operator, like this: *count <= n*. When the application does not require otherwise, it is standard practice to initialize Java loop control variables with the value 0 and use the *less than* test.

Nested Loops

Many applications require looping operations within loops. This is called ***nested looping***. To get the idea, think about the seconds, minutes, and hours of a 12-hour digital timer. Isn't each a simple counter? The seconds count from 0 to 59, the minutes from 0 to 59, and the hours from 0 to 11. For every 60 seconds, the minutes counter is incremented. Likewise, for every 60 minutes, the hours counter is incremented. Thus, the seconds count is "nested" within the minutes count, and the minutes count is "nested" within the hours count. Here's how a digital timer might be coded in a Java program using nested **for** loops:

```java
public class Timer
{
  public static void main(String[] args)
  {
   //DISPLAY HEADINGS
   System.out.println(" \t\t\tHours\tMinutes\tSeconds");
   //START TIMER
   for (int hours = 0; hours < 12; ++hours)
     for (int minutes = 0; minutes < 60; ++minutes)
       for (int seconds = 0; seconds < 60; ++seconds)
       {
         System.out.print("\t\t\t\r");               //BLANK DISPLAY
         System.out.print("\t\t\t" + hours           //DISPLAY TIME
                          +"\t"  + minutes
                          + "\t" + seconds + "\r");
       } //END SECONDS LOOP
   } //END main()
} //END Timer
```

As you can see, the seconds **for** loop is part of the minutes loop, which is part of the hours loop. The *outer* **for** loop begins by initializing the *hours* counter to 0. The statement within this loop is another **for** loop that begins by initializing the *minutes* counter to 0. This leads to the seconds loop, where the *seconds* counter is initialized to 0. Once the *seconds* counter is initialized, the seconds loop is executed 60 times, as *seconds* ranges from 0 to 59. Each time the seconds loop is executed, the *hours, minutes*, and *seconds* count values are displayed. After the seconds loop is executed 60 times, the *minutes* count is incremented, and the seconds loop is entered again and executed 60 more times.

So, the seconds loop is executed 60 times for each iteration of the minutes loop. Likewise, because the minutes loop is nested within the hours loop, the minutes loop is executed 60 times for each iteration of the hours loop. After 60 iterations of the minutes loop (3600 iterations of the seconds loop), the *hours* count is incremented and displayed. The hours loop is not broken until it has been executed 12 times, from 0 to 11. Of course, this requires $12 \times 60 = 720$ iterations of the minutes loop and $12 \times 60 \times 60 = 43,200$ iterations of the seconds loop. We say that the seconds loop is the *innermost* loop, and the hours loop is the *outermost* loop. It is important to observe that the index of an outer loop controls how many times its inner loop statement is entered. For instance, since the hours loop executes 12 times, the minutes loop statement is entered 12 times. Since the minutes loop executes 60 times, the seconds loop statement is entered 60 times.

Notice that *no* framing is required for the hours and minutes loops because the hours loop consists of a single **for** statement, which is the minutes loop, and the minutes loop consists of a single **for** statement, which is the seconds loop. An indentation scheme becomes important here, because it is the indentation that really shows the nesting. The seconds loop requires framing because it consists of two *print()* statements. The first *print()* statement "blanks" the output values prior to displaying the time values in the second *print()* statement. Blanking is required so that the time values appear correctly on the screen. Notice that the '\r' escape sequence is employed in both *print()* statements so that a given output overwrites the previous output.

To make the digital timer work, the *seconds* counter must be incremented precisely once every second. This requires a time delay routine within the seconds loop to slow down the seconds count accordingly. This will be left as an exercise at the end of the chapter.

Aside from counting, nested **for** loops are commonly used in graphics applications for line drawing, pattern drawing, and graphing things like histograms.

Before we leave the topic of nested loops, you should be aware that **while** and **do/while** loops can also be nested. You will find examples of this in the questions at the end of the chapter.

DEBUGGING TIP

A common error when coding a **for** loop is to place a semicolon at the end of the **for** statement like this:

```
for(int count = 1; count <= 5; ++count);
   System.out.println(System.out.println("Hello World");
```

Here, the programmer obviously wanted to display "Hello World" down the screen five times. However, the string is only displayed once. Why? Because the semicolon at the end of the **for** statement terminates the statement and the *println()* statement is seen as a single statement all by itself. The **for** loop actually executes five times but does not do anything since it has no statement section. It just sits there and "spins its wheels."

There might be an application where this is desirable within a program. Can you think of one? How about creating time delays within a program? You could simply use a very large final test value and force the program to loop enough times to create a noticeable delay. Of course, the precise amount of delay would depend on your system performance, right?

Down-to for Loops

In most of the **for** loops you have seen so far, the loop counter has been incremented from some initial value to some final value. You can also begin the loop counter at some value, then decrement it down to a final value. Such a loop is called a "down-to" loop, for obvious reasons. The digital timer program segment could be easily revised to employ down-to loops, like this:

```
public class Timer
{
  public static void main(String[] args)
  {
   //DISPLAY HEADINGS
   System.out.println(" \t\t\tHours\tMinutes\tSeconds");
```

```
//START TIMER
   for (int hours = 11; hours >= 0; --hours)
      for (int minutes = 59; minutes >= 0; --minutes)
         for (int seconds = 59; seconds >= 0; --seconds)
         {
            System.out.print("\t\t\t\r");                      //BLANK DISPLAY
            System.out.print("\t\t\t" + hours                   //DISPLAY TIME
                             +"\t"  + minutes
                             + "\t" + seconds + "\r");
         } //END SECONDS LOOP
   } //END main()
} //END Timer
```

The differences here are that the initial and final values of the respective loop counters have been changed so that the timer counts down from 11:59:59 and times out when the count reaches 00:00:00. The test expressions are simply the counter values, and the counters are being decremented rather than incremented. When a given counter value reaches zero, the loop test becomes false and the respective loop is broken. The net effect is still the same: There are 60 iterations of the seconds loop for each iteration of the minutes loop and 60 iterations of the minutes loop for each iteration of the hours loop. Of course, the timer counts down rather than counting up as in the previous program.

 Quick Check

1. List the three things that must appear in the first line of a **for** loop structure.

2. True or false: The loop counter in a **for** loop is altered after the loop body is executed in a given iteration.

3. True or false: A **for** loop can always be replaced by a **while** loop, because both are basically the same looping structure, just coded differently.

4. How many times is the following loop executed?

   ```
   for (int x = 0; x > 0; ++x)
      System.out.println("How many times will this loop execute?");
   ```

5. How many times is the following loop executed?

   ```
   for (int x = 0; x <= 10; ++x)
      System.out.println("How many times will this loop execute?");
   ```

6. When must the body of a **for** loop be framed?

7. Suppose that you have two nested loops. The inner loop executes five times and the outer loop executes ten times. How many total iterations are there within the nested loop structure?

8. In a down-to loop, the loop counter is always _____.

7-4 THE break AND continue OPTIONS

The **break** and **continue** statements can be used to alter the execution of predefined control structures, such as loops, when certain conditions occur. In general, the **break** statement is used to immediately terminate a loop, and the **continue** statement is used to skip over a single loop iteration.

The break Statement

You observed the use of the **break** statement within the **switch** statement in the last chapter. Recall that the **break** statement forced the **switch** statement to terminate. The same is true when you use the **break** statement inside a loop structure. When Java executes the **break** statement within a loop, the loop is immediately terminated, and control is passed to the next statement following the loop. The **break** statement is usually used as part of an **if** statement within the loop to terminate the loop structure if a certain condition occurs. The action of the **break** statement within a **while** loop can be illustrated like this:

THE **break** *OPTION*

```
while (test expression)
{
   statement 1;
   statement 2;
      •
      •
      •
   if (test expression)
      break;
      •
      •
```

```
      statement n;
   } //END WHILE
   Next statement after while;
```

Consider the following program segment:

```
int number = 1;                    //LOOP CONTROL VARIABLE
while (number < 11)
{
  if (number == 5)
      break;
  System.out.println("In the while loop, number is now:  " + number);
  ++number;
} //END WHILE

System.out.println("The loop is now terminated and the value of number is:  "
                   + number);
```

This **while** loop employs a **break** statement to terminate the loop when *number* reaches the value of 5. Here is what you would see as a result of the loop execution:

```
In the while loop, number is now:  1
In the while loop, number is now:  2
In the while loop, number is now:  3
In the while loop, number is now:  4
The loop is now terminated and the value of number is:  5
```

As you can see, even though the final value of *number* is 5, the *println()* statement within the loop is not executed when *number* reaches 5 because the **break** statement forces the loop to terminate for this value. Normally, you would not break out of a loop as a result of a natural loop counter value. Doing so would indicate that you have coded your loop test incorrectly. This was done only to illustrate how the **break** statement works. You will use the **break** statement primarily to break out of a loop when the potential for an infinite loop exists. Such an application could be to interrupt the digital timer loops given in the last section as the result of a user entry to stop the timer.

The continue Statement

You have not seen the use of the **continue** statement before this, because it is used primarily to skip a single iteration within a loop if a certain condition occurs. Like the **break** statement, the **continue** statement is normally employed within a loop as part of an **if** statement. We can illustrate the operation of **continue** within a **for** loop, like this:

THE **continue** *OPTION*

```
for (Counter = initial value; Counter test expression;
    Increment/Decrement Counter)
{
    statement 1;
    statement 2;
        •
        •
    if (test expression)
        continue;
        •
        •
    statement n;
} //END FOR
Next statement after for;
```

Here you see that when the **if** statement test expression is true, the **continue** statement is executed, forcing the current iteration to terminate. It is important to remember that *only the current iteration is terminated* as the result of **continue**. All subsequent iterations will be executed, unless, of course, they are terminated by executing a **break** or **continue**. The following program segment demonstrates how **continue** works:

```
int value = 0;
for(int number = 1;number < 11; ++number)
 {
    if (number == 5)
         continue;
    System.out.println("In the while loop, number is now:  " + number);
    value = number;
 } //END FOR
```

System.out.println("The loop is now terminated and the value of number is: "
+ value);

Here is the result of executing the program segment:

```
In the for loop, number is now: 1
In the for loop, number is now: 2
In the for loop, number is now: 3
In the for loop, number is now: 4
In the for loop, number is now: 6
In the for loop, number is now: 7
In the for loop, number is now: 8
In the for loop, number is now: 9
In the for loop, number is now: 10
The loop is now terminated and the value of number is: 10
```

You see here that the fifth iteration is skipped because of the execution of the **continue** statement. All subsequent iterations are performed, and the loop is broken naturally when *number* reaches the value of 11.

The foregoing program segment also illustrates something you need to remember about a **for** loop counter. That is, when a **for** loop counter is actually defined within the **for** loop, it has no meaning outside the **for** loop in which it is defined. This is why we defined the integer variable *value* prior to the loop. *value* acts as a placeholder for *number* during the loop execution. This way, the final value of *number* can be displayed via the variable *value* after the loop terminates. You could not display *number* after the loop terminates, because *number* is not defined outside **for** the loop. Of course, you could have defined *number* prior to the loop statement, not within the loop statement, to avoid the need for an extra variable in this situation.

PROGRAMMING TIP

We *strongly* urge you to only use a **break** or **continue** statement within a loop as a last resort. If your loops are well thought out, there should very few times that you would need to use **break** or **continue**. If you find yourself using **break** or **continue** too often, you might not be thoroughly thinking through the loop logic. Overuse of **break** and **continue** makes the logic hard to follow.

Quick Check

1. The statement that will cause only the current iteration of a loop to be terminated is the _____ statement.

2. The **break** and **continue** statements are normally used as part of a(n) _____ statement within a loop structure.

3. How many times will the following loop execute?

```
x = 0;
while (x <10)
{
  System.out.println("How many times will this loop execute?");
  if (x > 0)
    break;
  ++x;
} //END WHILE
```

PROBLEM SOLVING IN ACTION: COMPUTING YOUR TEST AVERAGE

Problem

Let's close this chapter by writing a program that will allow a user to compute his or her test average. We will solve the problem using the **while** loop structure. Then, you will be asked to convert the solution to a **do/while** and a **for** loop solution in the problems at the end of the chapter. As usual, let's define the problem in terms of output, input, and processing.

Defining the Problem

Output: The program must first prompt the user to enter the number of test scores to average. A prompt will then be generated to enter each test score value separately. The final output will be a display of the test average.

Input: The number of test scores to average and the individual test score values.

Processing: Each time a test score value is entered, a new test total will be recalculated as follows:

$$testTotal = testTotal + score$$

Then, the average of all the test scores will be calculated as follows:

$$average = testTotal/number$$

Now, using this problem definition, we are ready for the algorithm. Let's employ the **while** iteration control structure to repeatedly calculate the test total each time a score value is entered.

Planning the Solution

So as not to distract from concentrating on iteration, we will not stepwise refine the problem solution. Rather, we will employ a flat solution to the problem.

BEGIN
    Set *count* = 0.
    Set *testTotal* = 0.
    Write a user prompt to enter the number of test scores to be averaged.
    Read (*number*).
    While (*number* <= 0)
        Write an invalid entry message.
        Write a user prompt to enter the number of test scores to be averaged.
        Read (*number*).
    While (*count* < *number)*
        Set *count* = *count* + 1.
        Write prompt to enter test score #*count*.
        Read (*score*).
        While (*score* < 0) OR (*score* > 100)
            Write an invalid entry message.
            Write prompt to enter test score #*count*.
            Read(*score*).
        Calculate *testTotal* = *testTotal* + *score*.
    Calculate *average* = *testTotal/number*
END.

Wow! Here you see three **while** loops. Why three loops? Well one loop is used to calculate the test total as expected, and two additional loops are used to force the user to provide valid entries. The first loop is used to force the user to enter a valid number for the number of scores. If the value of *number* entered by the user is less than or equal to 0, the loop will repeat until the user enters a value which is greater than 0, right? A negative value for *number* is not reasonable and a value of zero will cause a divide-by-zero error later in the program.

The second loop is used to add up the individual test scores. Each time the loop is executed, an additional score value is entered, and the test total is calculated. However, a nested loop is provided which forces the user to enter valid scores. Notice how the OR test is employed to test the score value. If the entered score value is less than 0 or greater than 100, the user is prompted again and must enter a value between 0 and 100 to get out of the loop. Remember this loop trick to force the user to enter correct values—it often comes in handy.

Observe that a loop counter (*count*) must be initialized to 0 prior to the second loop. The value of *count* must then be incremented with each loop iteration to prevent an infinite loop. The looping continues until the value of *count* equals the number of test scores (*number*). When this happens, the loop body is not executed again and control is passed to the next sequential statement which calculates the average. Also notice how the value of *count* is used as part of the prompt to instruct the user which score to enter. Next, it is important to initialize the value of *testTotal* to zero prior to the second loop. Why? Finally, notice that the pseudocode indentation clearly shows which statements go with which loop.

Following the algorithm, you can easily code a Java program, like this.

Coding the Program

/*ACTION 7-2 (ACT07_02.JAVA)

OUTPUT: THE PROGRAM MUST FIRST PROMPT THE USER TO
ENTER THE NUMBER OF TEST SCORES TO AVERAGE.
A PROMPT WILL THEN BE GENERATED TO ENTER EACH
TEST SCORE VALUE SEPARATELY.
THE FINAL OUTPUT WILL BE A DISPLAY OF THE
TEST AVERAGE.

INPUT: THE NUMBER OF TEST SCORES TO AVERAGE AND THE
INDIVIDUAL TEST SCORE VALUES.

```
PROCESSING: EACH TIME A TEST SCORE VALUE IS ENTERED, A NEW
            TEST TOTAL WILL BE CALCULATED AS FOLLOWS:

            TEST TOTAL = TEST TOTAL + SCORE

            THEN, THE AVERAGE OF ALL THE TEST SCORES WILL BE
            CALCULATED AS FOLLOWS:

            AVERAGE = TEST TOTAL / NUMBER
*/

import keyboardInput.*;  //FOR readInt() AND readDouble()

public class Action07_02
{
  public static void main(String[] args)
  {
  //DEFINE VARIABLES
  char pause = ' ';              //FREEZE VARIABLE
  int count = 0;                 //LOOP COUNTER
  int number = 0;                //NUMBER OF TEST SCORES TO AVERAGE
  double score = 0.0;            //INDIVIDUAL TEST SCORE VALUES
  double testTotal = 0.0;        //TOTAL OF TEST SCORES ENTERED
  double average = 0.0;          //FINAL TEST AVERAGE

  //CREATE KEYBOARD OBJECT
  Keyboard in = new Keyboard();

  //WRITE PROGRAM DESCRIPTION MESSAGE
  System.out.println("This program will calculate average of any number\n"
                  + "of test scores that you enter.\n\n");

  //GET NUMBER OF SCORES TO AVERAGE
  System.out.print("Enter the number of scores to average:  ");
  number = in.readInt();

  //LOOP UNTIL VALID NUMBER IS ENTERED
  while (number <= 0)
  {
    System.out.println("Invalid entry.");
    System.out.print("Enter the number of scores to average:  ");
    number = in.readInt();
  } //END INVALID ENTRY WHILE
```

```
//READ IN THE SCORES AND ADD THEM UP USING WHILE
while (count < number)
{
    ++count;
    System.out.print("Enter the value for score #" + count + ": ");
    score = in.readDouble();

    //LOOP UNTIL VALID SCORE IS ENTERED
    while ((score < 0) || (score > 100))
    {
        System.out.println("Invalid entry.");
        System.out.print("Enter the value for score #" + count + ": ");
        score = in.readDouble();
    }//END INVALID ENTRY WHILE

    //ADD SCORE TO TEST TOTAL
    testTotal = testTotal + score;
} //END TEST TOTAL WHILE

//CALCULATE THE TEST AVERAGE
average = testTotal/number;
System.out.println("\n\nThe average of the scores you entered is: "
                    + Math.round(average));


    //FREEZE DISPLAY
    System.out.println("Press ENTER to continue.");
    pause = in.readChar();

  } //END main()
} //END Action07_02 CLASS
```

Here is what you would see on the display when this program is executed:

```
This program will calculate average of any number
of test scores that you enter.

Enter the number of test scores to average: 0↵
Invalid entry.
Enter the number of test scores to average: 3↵
Enter the value for score #1  87.5↵
Enter the value for score #2  105.3↵
Invalid entry.
```

Enter the value for score #2 **95.3**↵
Enter the value for score #3 **78**↵

The average of the scores you entered is: 87

You should now have no problem understanding the foregoing code. One final point—observe the use of the *round()* method to round off the test average to the closest integer value.

CHAPTER SUMMARY

In this chapter, you learned about the three iteration control structures employed by Java: **while**, **do/while**, and **for**. The **while** is a pretest looping structure, the **do/while** a posttest looping structure, and the **for** a fixed repetition looping structure. As a result, the following general guidelines should be considered when deciding which looping structure to use in a given situation:

- Use **while** whenever there is a possibility that the loop body will not need to be executed.
- Use **do/while** when the loop body must be executed at least once.
- Use **for** when it can be determined exactly how many times the loop body must be executed. Thus, if the number of loop iterations is predetermined by the value of a variable or constant, use a **for** loop.

The **break** and **continue** statements can be used to interrupt loop iterations. Execution of the **break** statement within a loop forces the entire loop structure to terminate immediately and pass control to the next statement following the loop structure. Execution of the **continue** statement within a loop terminates only the current loop iteration.

QUESTIONS AND PROBLEMS

Questions

1. Name the three iteration control structures employed by Java.
2. Which iteration control structure(s) will always execute the loop at least once?

3. Which iteration control structure(s) evaluates the test expression before the loop is executed?

4. Which iteration control structure(s) should be employed when it can be determined in advance how many loop repetitions there should be?

5. What will the following loop do?

    ```
    while (count < 10)
      System.out.println("Hello");
    ```

6. Explain the difference between the execution of **break** and **continue** within a loop.

In questions 7–17, determine the output generated by the respective program segment.

7.
    ```
    int a = 1;
    while (17 % a != 5)
    {
      System.out.println(a  + "  " + 17 % a );
      ++a;
    }//END WHILE
    ```

8.
    ```
    int b = 2;
    do
    {
      System.out.println(b + "  " + b / 5);
      b *= 2;
    }//END DO/WHILE
    while (b != 20);
    ```

9.
    ```
    int b = 2;
    do
    {
      System.out.println(b + "  " + b / 5);
      b *= 2;
    }//END DO/WHILE
    while (b != 32);
    ```

10.
    ```
    int number = 1;
    int product = 1;
    do
    {
      ++number;
      product *= number;
    }//END DO/WHILE
    while (number < 5);
    System.out.println("The product is:  " + product);
    ```

11.
```java
int count = -3;
while (count < 3)
{
   if (count == 0)
      continue;
   System.out.print(count + "\t");
   ++count;
}//END WHILE
```

12.
```java
int count = -3;
while (count < 3)
{
   ++count;
   if (count == 0)
      continue;
   System.out.print(count + "\t");
}//END WHILE
```

13.
```java
int count = -3;
while (count < 3)
{
   ++count;
   if (count == 0)
      break;
   System.out.print(count + "\t");
}//END WHILE
```

14.
```java
System.out.println("Angle\tSin\tCos" );
System.out.println("-----\t---\t---");
for (int angle = 0; angle <= 90; angle += 5)
   System.out.println(angle + "\t" + Math.sin(angle * Math.PI/180)
                         + "\t" + Math.cos(angle * Math.PI/180));
```

15.
```java
for (int row = 1; row < 6; ++row)
{
   for (int col = 1; col < 11; ++col)
      System.out.print(row + "," + col + "\t");
   System.out.println();
}//END FOR
```

16.
```java
int count = 0;
static final int MAX_COUNT = 5;
while (count < MAX_COUNT)
{
   for (int i = 1; i < MAX_COUNT + 1; ++i)
      System.out.print(i);
```

```
        System.out.println();
        ++count;
    }//END WHILE
```

17. `static final int MAX_COUNT = 5;`
```
    int times = 3;
    do
    {
        int count = 0;
        while (count < MAX_COUNT)
        {
            for (int J = 1; J < count + 1; ++J)
                System.out.print(J);
            ++count;
            System.out.println();
        }//END WHILE
        System.out.println();
        --times;
    }//END DO/WHILE
    while (times != 0);
```

18. When will the following loop terminate?

```
    Keyboard in = new Keyboard();  //CREATE KEYBOARD OBJECT
    boolean flag = true;           //DEFINE BOOLEAN VARIABLE
    int number = 0;                //INPUT VARIABLE
    int sum = 0;                   //SUM VARIABLE
    char query = 'N';              //CONTINUE QUERY

    while (flag == true)
    {
        System.out.print("Enter an integer number: ");
        number = in.readInt();
        System.out.print("Want to continue (y/n)? ");
        query = in.readChar();
        if ((query == 'n') || (query == 'N'))
        {
            flag = false;
            System.out.println("Loop terminated");
        }//END IF
        else
        {
            sum = sum + number;
            System.out.println("The sum is now " + sum);
        }//END ELSE
    }//END WHILE
```

Problems

Least Difficult

1. Revise the *Action07_02.java* program to employ **do/while** loops.

2. Revise the *Action07_02.java* program to employ **for** loops.

3. Expand the *Action07_02.java* program to include an average for lab scores and a composite average which weights tests at 70% and labs at 30%.

4. Write a Java program that will ask the user for a number, then display a box of asterisks whose dimension is the number entered. Place the routine within a loop that allows the user to repeat the task until he or she wants to quit.

5. In Chapter 6 you wrote a program for Ma and Pa's Sporting Goods department that would calculate expected profit based on profit codes for each item in the department. The items in the department are coded with a 1, 2, or 3, depending on the amount of profit for the item. An item with a profit code of 1 produces a 10 percent profit, a code of 2 produces a 12 percent profit, and a code of 3 generates a 15 percent profit. Rewrite the program to allow the user to enter sales item information until the user decides to quit. The required sales item information includes an item description, quantity on hand, price, and profit code. For example, a typical entry dialog might appear as follows:

   Enter Item Name: **Fishing Line** ↵

   Enter Quantity on Hand: **125** ↵

   Enter Price: **5.25** ↵

   Enter Profit Code: **1** ↵

   Have another item to enter? (y/n) **y** ↵

   The program should generate a tabular report of the item, quantity, expected profit in dollars per item, and total expected profit for all items at the end of the report.

6. Using the formula $C = 5/9(F - 32)$, generate a Celsius conversion table for all even temperatures from 32 degrees to 212 degrees Fahrenheit.

7. The subway system in Java City, USA has three fee classifications: student (17 years old or less), adult, and senior (65 years old or more). Write a program that counts how many of each fee classification rode the subway on a given day. Assume that the subway conductor has a laptop PC that runs your program. The conductor enters the age of each customer as the subway is under way. Your user instructions tell the conductor to enter a sentinel value

of −1 at the end of the day to terminate the entry process. After the sentinel value is entered, the program must display the number of customers in each fee category.

More Difficult

8. Write a program that will obtain any two integers between 2 and 10 from the user and display a multiplication a table. For example, if the user enters the values 4 and 5, the table would be:

1	2	3	4	5
2	4	6	8	10
3	6	9	12	15
4	8	12	16	20

9. Write a program that will calculate the mean ($\overline{x}$) and standard deviation (σ) of a series of numbers. The mean of a series of numbers is the same as the average of the numbers. The standard deviation of a series of numbers is found using the following formula:

$$\sigma = \sqrt{\frac{(x_1 - \overline{x})^2 + (x_2 - \overline{x})^2 + \cdots + (x_n - \overline{x})^2}{n}}$$

10. Some programming languages, like BASIC, allow you to use a STEP command within a **for** statement, like this:

FOR counter = <initial value> TO <final value> STEP N DO

The STEP command allows the loop counter to increment by some value (N), other than the value 1, with each loop iteration.

Write a **for** loop in Java that will emulate this STEP operation. Provide for user entry of any desired step value. To demonstrate its operation, use your step loop to display every fifth integer, from 1 to 100.

11. To make the digital timer program given in this chapter work properly, you must insert a time delay within the seconds loop so that the seconds counter is incremented precisely once every second. To do this, you can insert a **for** loop that simply decrements a large counter, like this:

```
for(long timer = 4000000; timer > 0; − −timer);
```

This loop will not do anything but waste time. However, the amount of time delay is dependent on the initial counter value and the clock speed of your system CPU. Insert such a delay loop into the timer program given in this chapter, and, by trial and error, determine a counter value that will provide a one-second delay for your system. Compile, execute, and observe the program output.

12. Using the ideas you saw in the digital timer program in this chapter, write a Java program to display the output of a 4-bit binary counter. A 4-bit binary counter simply counts in binary from 0000 to 1111. The first count value is 0000, the second is 0001, the third is 0010, and so on, until it reaches the final count value of 1111. Insert a delay in the program so that the counter increments once every two seconds. Change the delay value and observe the effect on the count frequency. (*Hint:* You will need four nested loops, one for each bit within the count value.)

13. Write a tax program that will figure depreciation using the *straight-line* method. With the straight-line method, the cost of the item is depreciated each year by $1/n$, where n is the number of years to depreciate. Assume that the user will enter the original cost of the item and the number of years to depreciate the item. The program should display a table showing the depreciated value at the end of each year, the amount depreciated for each year, and the total accumulated depreciation at the end of each year.

Most Difficult

14. Write a program that will determine the value of a bank account balance that is compounded monthly. Assume that the user will enter the beginning balance, annual interest rate, and number of years to compound. As an example, suppose that the beginning balance was $1000 and the annual interest rate is 12%. Then, at the end of the first month, the balance would be $1010. At the end of the second month, the balance would be $1020.10, and so on. Notice that at the end of each month, the interest is added to the old balance to form a new balance that will be used in the next month's calculation.

15. Ma and Pa have asked you to write a program for their Bass Boat department. The program is to read the price of the boat from the user and, using an interest rate of 1% per month, display a table showing the monthly payment, amount of principle, amount of interest, and remaining loan balance for each month over the number of months specified by the user.

GUI 107: CHECKBOXES AND RADIO BUTTONS

PURPOSE

- *To become familiar with the GUI checkbox and radio button components.*
- *To understand the differences between a checkbox and a radio button.*
- *To learn how to define checkbox and radio button objects.*
- *To learn how to process checkbox and radio button events.*

Introduction

Both the ***checkbox*** component and ***radio button*** component are referred to as ***state buttons***, because they represent a Boolean state of on/off, true/false. A ***checkbox*** is a GUI component that allows the user to select one of two possible states: checked or unchecked. The user clicks the box, placing a checkmark inside of it, or once checked, clicks the box to remove the checkmark. Any number of checkboxes can be checked at any given time, since checking one box has no effect on another, unless underlying logic is develop to prevent multiple selection. Class *Checkbox* is used to create checkboxes.

A ***radio button*** is also a type of checkbox and is created using the *Checkbox* class. However, radio buttons are grouped using the *CheckboxGroup* class so that only one radio button within the group can be on, or true, at any given time. Selecting one radio button within a group turns all other radio buttons within that group off, or false.

In this module, you will load and execute a program that produces several checkboxes. You will experiment with the checkboxes by selecting/deselecting them and displaying the checkbox status in a text area when a store button is clicked. You will also create an additional checkbox for the GUI. Next, you will load and execute a program that produces a group of radio buttons. Again, you will experiment by selecting/deselecting them and displaying the radio button status within a text area. You will create an additional radio button for the group and add logic to proces the additional button.

Procedure

1. Load and execute the *GUI107_1.java* program contained on the CD that accompanies this book, or download it from www.prenhall.com. You should see a window similar to the one shown in Figure 1. The window includes four checkboxes, a button, and a text area.

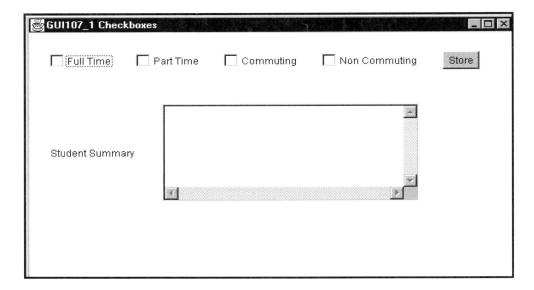

Figure 1 A frame with four checkboxes, a button, and a text area.

2. Notice that each checkbox has a label that indicates a student's status when the box is checked. Select a box and notice that a checkmark appears inside the box, indicating that it is selected. Deselect the same box and notice that the checkmark disappears.

3. Select any number of boxes and click the *Store* button. You should see the student status information represented by the selected boxes within the text area, unless you selected both full-time and part-time or both commuting and noncommuting. A student cannot be both full-time and part-time or both commuting and noncommuting, right? We have added logic to our event processing code that displays a message to the user if these pairs of checkboxes are selected.

Here is the class code that produced the GUI and processes the button event:

```
1    class CheckBoxes extends FrameWithClose implements ActionListener
2    {
3      //DEFINE TEXT AREA OBJECT
4      private TextArea studentArea = new TextArea(7,40);
5
6      //DEFINE CHECK BOX OBJECTS
7      private Checkbox fullTimeBox = new Checkbox("Full Time");
8      private Checkbox partTimeBox = new Checkbox("Part Time");
9      private Checkbox commutingBox = new Checkbox("Commuting");
10     private Checkbox nonCommutingBox = new Checkbox("Non-Commuting");
11
12   //CONSTRUCTOR
13   public CheckBoxes(String title)
14   {
15     //CALL SUPERCLASS CONSTRUCTOR
16     super(title);
17
18     //SET FRAME LAYOUT MANAGER
19     setLayout(new FlowLayout(FlowLayout.LEFT));
20
21     //DEFINE LABEL OBJECTS
22     Label summaryLabel = new Label("Student Summary");
23
24     //DEFINE BUTTON OBJECT
25     Button storeButton = new Button("Store");
26
27     //DEFINE PANELS
28     Panel panel1 = new Panel();
29     Panel panel2 = new Panel();
30
31     //SET PANEL LAYOUT MANAGERS
32     panel1.setLayout(new FlowLayout(FlowLayout.LEFT,20,20));
33     panel2.setLayout(new FlowLayout(FlowLayout.LEFT,20,20));
34
35     //ADD COMPONENTS TO panel1
36     panel1.add(fullTimeBox);
37     panel1.add(partTimeBox);
38     panel1.add(commutingBox);
39     panel1.add(nonCommutingBox);
40
41     panel1.add(storeButton);
```

```
42
43    //ADD TEXT AREA TO panel2
44    panel2.add(summaryLabel);
45    panel2.add(studentArea);
46
47    //ADD PANELS TO FRAME
48    add(panel1);
49    add(panel2);
50
51    //REGISTER LISTENERS
52    storeButton.addActionListener(this);     //BUTTON LISTENER
53  }//END Checkboxes()
54
55  //PROCESS BUTTON EVENT
56  public void actionPerformed(ActionEvent E)
57  {
58    //CLEAR TEXT AREA
59    studentArea.setText("Student Status:");
60
61    //DID A BUTTON CAUSE EVENT?
62    if (E.getSource() instanceof Button)
63    {
64      //PROCESS CHECK BOXES
65      if ((fullTimeBox.getState()) && (partTimeBox.getState()))
66        studentArea.append("\nCANNOT SELECT BOTH FULL TIME\n"
67                           + "AND PART TIME");
68      else
69      {
70        if (fullTimeBox.getState())
71          studentArea.append("\nFull Time");
72        if (partTimeBox.getState())
73          studentArea.append("\nPart Time");
74      } //END ELSE
75      if ((commutingBox.getState()) && (nonCommutingBox.getState()))
76        studentArea.append("\nCANNOT SELECT BOTH COMMUTING\n"
77                           + "AND NON-COMMUTING");
78      else
79      {
80        if (commutingBox.getState())
81          studentArea.append("\nCommuting");
82        if (nonCommutingBox.getState())
83          studentArea.append("\nNon Commuting");
84      }//END ELSE
```

```
85
86
87     }//END IF BUTTON
88     }//END actionPerformed()
89   }//END CheckBoxes CLASS
```

4.   You see that our four checkbox objects are defined in lines 7-10. Notice that the checkbox label is part of the object definition. As a result, checkboxes do not need a separate label object to identify them as do text fields and text areas. Define a checkbox object in line 11 to add a "My Box" checkbox to the GUI using the syntax you see in lines 7-10. Name your object *myBox*.

5.   Execute the program again and verify that the item you added appears on the GUI. What? It isn't there? The reason its not there is because it was not added to the frame. Add your checkbox to the frame by adding it to *panel1* in line 40, using the same syntax that you see the other checkboxes added in lines 36-39.

6.   Execute the program again and notice that your checkbox appears as the last checkbox within the group, just prior to the *Store* button.

7.   Select your new checkbox and click the *Store* button. Observe that its status is not reflected within the text area. Why?

8.   Add the following statement in lines 85-86:

```
if (myBox.getState())
     studentArea.append("\nMy Box Selected");
```

9.   Execute the program again and select your checkbox. You should see its status reflected in the text area.

Discussion

A checkbox allows the user to select one of two possible states: checked or unchecked which represents on/off, true/false. Any number of checkboxes can be selected at any given time, unless there is underlying logic that prevents multiple selections. This is exactly what we did in lines 65-84 in the foregoing program. Notice that the **if/else** logic prevents both the full-time and part-time or commuting and noncommuting boxes to be selected at the same time. Look at the logic and convince yourself that this is the case. Notice that to get the Boolean state of a given checkbox, its respective object is used to call the *getState()* method. The *getState()* method returns **true** if the object's checkbox is selected or **false** is the object's checkbox is deselected.

A checkbox object is created using the *Checkbox* class. In line 11, you added a new checkbox object, but found that it did not appear unless the object was added to the frame via a panel. Then, you found that selecting your checkbox had no effect until you added an **if** statement in line 85 of the *actionPerformed( )* method to get the state of the checkbox and append its status to the text area.

Procedure (continued)

10. Load and execute the *GUI107_2.java* program contained on the CD that accompanies this book, or download it from www.prenhall.com. You should see a window similar to the one shown in Figure 2. The window contains two radio buttons, a button, and a text area.

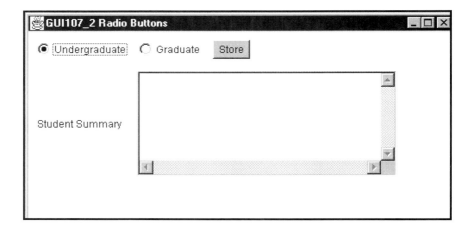

Figure 2 A frame with two radio buttons, a button, and a text area.

11. First, notice that a radio button appears differently than a checkbox. The radio button is round, and is either filled in or not filled in. A filled-in radio button means that it is selected. Observe that the *Undergraduate* button is selected and the *Graduate* button is not selected in Figure 2. Click the *Store* button and notice that the undergraduate status appears in the text window, indicating that this is the selected radio button.

12. Click the *Graduate* button and notice that it becomes filled in while the *Undergraduate* button does not. This demonstrates that only a single radio button can be selected at any given time.

13. Click the *Store* button and notice that the selected radio button status appears in the text area.

Here is the class code that produced the GUI and processes the button event:

```
1    class RadioButton extends FrameWithClose implements ActionListener
2    {
3      //DEFINE TEXT AREA OBJECT
4      private TextArea studentArea = new TextArea(7,40);
5
6      //DEFINE RADIO BUTTON GROUP
7      private CheckboxGroup RadioButtons = new CheckboxGroup();
8
9      //DECLARE RADIO BUTTON OBJECTS
10     private Checkbox undergraduate =
11                 new Checkbox("Undergraduate",RadioButtons,true);
12     private Checkbox graduate =
13                 new Checkbox("Graduate",RadioButtons,false);
14
15
16
17     //CONSTRUCTOR
18     public RadioButton(String Title)
19     {
20      //CALL SUPERCLASS CONSTRUCTOR
21      super(Title);
22
23      //SET FRAME LAYOUT MANAGER
24      setLayout(new FlowLayout(FlowLayout.LEFT));
25
26      //DEFINE PANELS
27      Panel panel1 = new Panel();
28      Panel panel2 = new Panel();
29
30      //SET PANEL LAYOUT MANAGERS
31      panel1.setLayout(new FlowLayout(FlowLayout.LEFT));
32      panel2.setLayout(new FlowLayout(FlowLayout.LEFT));
33
34      //DEFINE LABEL OBJECTS
35      Label summaryLabel = new Label("Student Summary");
36
```

```
37    //DEFINE BUTTON OBJECT
38    Button storeButton = new Button("Store");
39
40    //ADD COMPONENTS TO panel1
41    panel1.add(undergraduate);
42    panel1.add(graduate);
43
44    panel1.add(storeButton);
45
46    //ADD TEXT AREA TO panel2
47    panel2.add(summaryLabel);
48    panel2.add(studentArea);
49
50    //ADD PANELS TO FRAME
51    add(panel1);
52    add(panel2);
53
54    //REGISTER LISTENERS
55    storeButton.addActionListener(this);    //BUTTON LISTENER
56    }//END RadioButton()
57
58    //PROCESS BUTTON EVENT
59    public void actionPerformed(ActionEvent e)
60    {
61      //CLEAR TEXT AREA
62      studentArea.setText("Student Status:");
63
64      //DID A BUTTON CAUSE EVENT?
65      if (e.getSource() instanceof Button)
66      {
67        if (undergraduate.getState())
68          studentArea.append("\nUndergraduate");
69        else
70          studentArea.append("\nGraduate");
71      }//END IF BUTTON
72    }//END actionPerformed()
73  }//END RadioButton CLASS
```

14. Add the following radio button object definition in lines 14-15:

```
private Checkbox myButton =
                  new Checkbox("My Button",RadioButtons,false);
```

15. Add the *myButton* component to *panel1* in line 43 as follows:

```
panel1.add(myButton);
```

16. Execute the program and notice that a third radio button, called *My Button* appears on the GUI.

17. Select *My Button* and click the *Store* button. What's this? You selected the *My Button*, but the *Graduate* button status appears in the text area. There must be something wrong with the event logic, right?

18. Look at the **if/else** logic in lines 67-70. Notice that the **else** portion of the **if/else** statement will always append the text area with "Graduate" when the *undergradate* object is not selected. Thus, selecting *My Button* forces the **else** clause to execute, reflecting the *graduate* object status. So, more logic must be added to handle our new *myButton* object. Here's the required logic:

```
if (undergraduate.getState())
     studentArea.append("\nUndergraduate");
else
     if (graduate.getState())
                 studentArea.append("\nGraduate");
           else
                 studentArea.append("\nMy Button");
```

19. Change lines 67-70 to reflect the foregoing logic.

20. Execute the program again and select any of the radio buttons, followed by the *Store* button. You should observe the selected button status reflected in the text area.

Discussion

You see that the two original radio button objects are defined in lines 10-13. Like checkbox objects, radio button objects are created from the *CheckBox* class. Notice that the radio button label is part of the object definition. As a result, radio buttons, like checkboxes, do not need a separate label object to identify the button. However, unlike a checkbox, a radio button object needs to know the *CheckBoxGroup* to which it belongs. Notice that, in line 7, the *CheckBoxGroup* class is used to define a *RadioButtons* object. This object must be referenced in each radio button object definition to indicate the group to which the button belongs. Lastly, a radio button object needs to be set to a Boolean state of **true** or **false**. A **true** state means that the respective button is selected, by default. A **false** state means the button is deselected by default. Of course, only one button within a group can be initially set to **true**. So we defaulted the *undergraduate* object to **true** and the rest to **false**. In step 14, you added code to define a third radio button object called *myButton*. This object belongs to the same *RadioButtons* group as the other two objects and is initially set to a **false** state. After adding the *myButton* object to the GUI, you found that logic had to be added to handle this new object within the *actionPerformed( )* method. The nested **if/else** statements that you added in step 18-19 provided the necessary logic. Make sure you understand how this logic will cause the status of any selected button to appear in the text area.

8

METHODS IN-DEPTH

OBJECTIVES

When you are finished with this chapter, you should have a good understanding of the following:

- How to construct your own methods in Java.
- The difference between a nonvoid method and a void method.
- The difference between a class method and an instance method.
- How to call nonvoid versus void methods.
- How to develop method signatures.
- The significance of a method interface.
- The scope, or visibility, of a variable.
- The difference between an argument and a parameter.
- Overloaded methods and the concept of polymorphism.

INTRODUCTION

Methods are a major part of programming in Java. As you already know, all classes in Java contain methods that provide for the behavior of the class. In addition, the class methods provide the only way of communicating with the class.

You have already used built-in, or predefined, methods in your programs. All of these methods are part of the various classes included with Java. Now it is time to develop your own methods. Methods that you create for your own use in a program are called ***programmer-defined*** methods.

> A ***programmer-defined method*** is a block of statements, or a subprogram, that is written to perform a specific task required by you, the programmer.

In this chapter and the next chapter, you will begin building true object-oriented programs as collections of classes employing collections of methods to perform the activities of the program. A method is given a name and ***called***, or ***invoked***, using its name each time the task is to be performed within the program. We will refer to the code in which a method call is made as the ***calling program***.

Up to this point, you have employed one method, *main()*, within a single program class. However, commercial object-oriented programs are written as a collection of classes, with each class containing its own collection of data and methods. Writing a program as a collection of methods within classes has several advantages, as follows:

- Methods eliminate the need for duplicate statements within a program. Given a task to be performed more than once, the statements are written just once for the method. Then, the method is called each time the task must be performed.
- Methods make the program easier to design, since the program activities and class behaviors (algorithms) are modularized as individual methods, whose combined execution solves the problem at hand.
- Methods make the program easier to code and test, since you can concentrate on a single method at a time, rather than one big *main()* method.
- Methods allow for *software reusability*, where existing methods can be reused to create new programs.
- Methods make the program more clear and readable, thus making the program easier to maintain.
- And most important, the use of methods provides the basis for us to construct classes in object-oriented programming.

The bottom line is that without methods, a class has no behavior, and therefore, is useless. In fact, without methods you cannot even access the data within a class. So this chapter is crucial to your learning about object-oriented programming in general and programming in the Java language in particular.

In Java, a method can be made to serve two roles. A method can be made to return a single value to the calling program. This type of method is referred to as a **nonvoid** method. In addition, methods can also be written to perform specific tasks or operate on class data. This type of method is called a **void** method.

8-1 NONVOID METHODS

You have already had some experience with methods that return a single value in Java. Recall the standard methods that you have already learned, such as *compareTo(), sqrt(), sin()*, and *length()*, just to mention a few. You found that Java included several predefined mathematical, string, and I/O methods that are part of standard classes in the Java language. However, suppose you want to perform some operation that is not a predefined method in Java, such as cubing a value. Because Java does not include any standard method for the cube operation, you could code the operation as a statement in your program, like this:

```
cube = x * x * x;
```

Then, you insert this statement into your program each time the value of x must be cubed. However, wouldn't it be a lot easier simply to insert the command *cube(x)* each time x is to be cubed, where Java knows what to do just as it knows how to execute *sqrt(x)*? You can do this by defining your own programmer-defined *cube()* method. A programmer-defined method is a subprogram that, when called, produces a single value (nonvoid method) or performs some task (void method). Thus, if *cube()* is a method that will cube a value, say, x, the statement System.out.println(cube(x)) will call the method and cause the cube of x to be displayed. Here, the *cube()* method is a nonvoid method that produces a single value which is the cube of x. Now you need to learn how to create such methods.

Here is the format that you must use when defining your own methods:

METHOD FORMAT

//METHOD SIGNATURE
modifier return type method name **(***parameter list***)**

{ //BEGIN METHOD BODY
   method statement #1;
   method statement #2;
       •
       •   **//METHOD BODY**
       •
   method statement #n;
   return *return value*;
} //END METHOD BODY

The method definition format consists of two main parts: a ***method signature*** and a ***method body***. For example, here is the *cube()* method code that we are about to develop:

```
//THIS METHOD RETURNS THE CUBE OF AN INTEGER
static long cube(int x)    //METHOD SIGNATURE
{
  return x * x * x;        //METHOD BODY
} //END cube()
```

The Method Signature

The *method signature* provides the data *interface* for the method.

> A *method signature*, or *interface*, is a statement that forms a common boundary between the method and its calling program.

This idea is illustrated by Figure 8-1. Notice that the signature dictates what data the method will *accept* from the calling program and what data the method will *return* to the calling program, if any. When developing method signatures, your perspective needs to be relative to the method. You must ask yourself two things:

1. What data must the method accept from the outside in order to perform its designated task?
2. What data, if any, must the method return in order to fulfill its designated task?

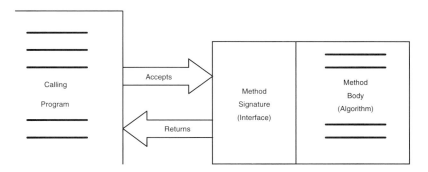

Figure 8-1 The method signature forms the interface between the calling program and the method.

In general, the method signature consists of the following four parts:

- Optional modifiers that declare the *scope* of the method.
- The data type of the value to be returned by the method, if any.
- The name of the method.
- A parameter listing.

The Modifier

The first thing that appears in the method signature is the modifier. The modifier determines the *scope* of the method. The scope of a method defines to what extent the method can be called within the program. This is sometimes referred to as *visibility*, since the scope of a method determines the portion of a program in which the method is visible.

> The *scope*, or *visibility*, of a method defines to what extent the method can be called within the program.

A method can be declared static using the keyword **static** or nonstatic by omitting the keyword **static**. A **static** modifier declares the method as a *class method*. A static, or class, method is a method that is *not* called by an object. Rather, a class method is simply called by referencing its name if called within the class in which it is defined, or using the class name and a dot operator if called outside the class in which it is defined. An example is the *sqrt()* method in the standard *Math* class. To call the *sqrt()* method you must use its class name, like this: Math.sqrt(x).

A nonstatic method is called an *instance method*. An object is always required to call a nonstatic, or instance, method. Thus, to call an instance method, an object (instance) must be created; then this object must be used to call the method. An example is the *length()* method of the *String* class. To call this method you must create a string object, say *s*, and then call the method like this: s.length().

> *Class methods* are declared using the **static** modifier and are not called by an object. *Instance methods* are not static and must be called by an object.

In addition to being static or nonstatic, a method can also be **public**, **private**, or **protected**. Again, these control the visibility of the method outside of its class. A **public** method is visible anywhere outside of its resident class, while a **private** method is only visible within its resident class. A **protected** method is visible to its resident class as well as any subclasses of its resident class when using inheritance. More about this later.

A summary of these method modifiers is provided in Table 8-1.

TABLE 8-1 METHOD MODIFIERS

Modifier	Description
abstract	Body of method must appear in subclass (inheritance).
final	Cannot be overridden in a subclass (inheritance).
private	Visible only in its resident class.
protected	Visible to its resident class as well as any subclasses of its resident class (inheritance).
public	Visible anywhere outside of its resident class.
static	A class method. Does not require an object to call.

In this chapter, the only modifier that we will be using is the **static** modifier. You will work with the other modifiers when you learn about classes in-depth and inheritance in later chapters. So, don't let all of this modifier stuff confuse you at this point. It should become clear as you progress through the text.

The Return Type

The return type can be **void** or nonvoid. A **void** return type indicates that that method does not return anything. If a method is nonvoid, the return type indicates the type of data the method will return. A nonvoid method, such as our *cube()* method, will always return a single value. Thus, the return type will be any of the simple data types discussed earlier, such as **int**, **double**, **char**, and so on. For example, suppose that a *cube()* method returns the cube of an integer. Because the cube of an integer is an integer, the method will return an integer value. As a result, the return type must be **int** or **long** and specified in the method signature, like this:

static long cube(*parameter listing*)

On the other hand, if our *cube()* method were to cube a double floating-point value, the return type would have to be **double**, and the signature would look like this:

static double cube(*parameter listing*)

A nonvoid method always returns a single value. You can think of this value as replacing the method name wherever the name appears in a calling program. For example, the statement System.out.println(cube(2)) is actually seen as the statement System.out.println(8). The value that replaces the method name in the calling program, 8 in this example, is referred to as the ***return value***.

A void method does not return anything to the calling program. To indicate this, Java requires that the return type be **void**, like this:

modifier **void** voidMethod(*parameter listing*)

Void methods are procedural-type methods that are used to perform specific tasks or operate on class data. More about these types of methods later.

PROGRAMMING NOTE

You should be aware that any method, upon completion, always returns control back to the calling program. Nonvoid methods return a value along with control, while void methods only return control to the calling program when they are finished executing.

The Method Name

The method name should be a verb or a verb phrase in mixed lower- and uppercase. Like a variable name, the first letter of the name should be lowercase and the first letter of any subsequent word uppercase. The method name should be descriptive of the operation that the method performs, just as *cube* describes the cubing of a value. You will use this name when you call, or invoke, the method within your calling program.

Three things to remember:

1. The method name can never be used as a variable *inside of the method*. In other words, the following statement inside the *cube()* method will generate an error:

    cube = x * x * x;

    There is one exception to this rule called ***recursion***, which will be discussed in a later chapter.

2. The method name can never be used on the left side of the assignment symbol *outside of the method*. Therefore, the following statement will cause an error in the calling program:

   cube = x * x * x;

3. All logical paths within a nonvoid method must always lead to a **return** statement. For example, if you have an **if/else** statement within the method and the **if** clause leads to a **return** statement, the **else** clause must also lead to a **return** statement.

DEBUGGING TIP

A nonvoid method *must always* return a value, or a compiler error will result. So, regardless of the path of execution a nonvoid method takes, it must lead to a **return** statement.

The Parameter Listing

The method parameter listing includes variables, called ***parameters***, that will be *passed* from the calling program and evaluated by the method. Think of a parameter as a method variable, waiting to receive a value from the calling program when the method is called. To determine the method parameters, ask yourself: What data must the method *accept* to perform its designated task? Suppose that our *cube( )* method will cube integer values. Then, the method must accept an integer value from the calling program and return an integer value to the calling program. Thus, our *method interface* can be described as follows:

Method *cube( )*: Cubes an integer.
Accepts: An integer value.
Returns: An integer value.

Let's designate *x* as the integer variable that the method will accept. In Java, a given *parameter* must be specified in the method signature by indicating its data type followed by its identifier. As a result, the appropriate parameter listing for the *cube( )* method would be *(int x)*. Putting everything together, the complete signature would be

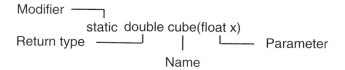

Notice that we have used an **int** for the integer parameter type and **long** for the integer return type. Why? Because cubing will always generate a result of more magnitude than the value being cubed.

If the *cube()* method were to cube floating-point values, an appropriate signature would be

Here, we have used **double** as the return type and **float** as the parameter type. (Why?)

Example 8-1

Suppose you want to write a programmer-defined method to calculate the gross pay for an employee. Write an appropriate method signature.

Solution

Let's call the method *grossPay()*, because this is what the method must return to the calling program each time the method is called.

To develop the method signature, we will treat the method like a black box and ask ourselves the following two questions: (1) What data must the method *accept* from the calling program in order to perform its designated task? (2) What must the method *return* to the calling program? The answers to these questions will dictate the method signature, or interface. To answer the first question, think about what the method must evaluate. In order to calculate gross pay, the method must evaluate two things: hours worked and rate of pay. So let's use the names *hours* and *rate* as our parameters. Of what data type should the parameters be? The obvious choice is floating-point, because you want to allow the method to evaluate decimal values of hours and rate. Thus, the method must accept a floating-point value of *hours* and a floating-point value of *rate*.

Next, you must decide what data the method must *return* to the calling program. Because the method is evaluating floating-point values, it makes mathematical sense that the returned value should also be a floating-point value.

Now, the method interface can be described as follows:

Method *grossPay()*: Calculates the gross pay of an employee.
Accepts: A floating-point value for *hours* and a floating-point
                       value for *rate*.
Returns: A floating-point value for *grossPay*.

Once you have decided what the method accepts and returns, the method
signature is easily constructed in Java syntax as follows:

```
static double grossPay (double hours, double rate)
```

At this point, we will assume that the method is a static method and, therefore,
does not need to be called by an object. In this chapter, all of our methods will be
static methods.

The Method Body

The body of the method includes those statements that the method must execute to
return a value to the calling program. The entire method body must be framed
with curly braces. After the opening curly brace, you should begin by defining any
variables and objects that will be used only within the method. Any variables
listed here are called ***local***, because they are defined only for local use within the
method itself. Local variables have no meaning outside of the method in which
they are defined. *You do not duplicate any of your method parameters here.* You
list only additional variables that the method might require during its execution. A
common example of a local variable is a loop counter that is employed as part of a
while, **do/while**, or **for** loop within the method. Actually, you can define local
variables anyplace within the method as long as they are listed prior to their use.
However, good style dictates that they be defined at the beginning of method body.

CAUTION

Do not confuse local variables with method parameters. A local variable is defined
after the opening brace of a method for use within that method to temporarily store
values during the method execution. A method parameter is defined in the method
signature as a place holder for argument values passed to the method when the
method is called. It will also be used within the method to supply data from the
calling program to the method.

The executable statements of the method follow any local definitions. Any
logical path within a nonvoid method must lead to a **return** statement. The **return**

statement is used when a single value must be returned to the calling program. So, if our *cube()* method must return the cube of *x*, an appropriate return statement would be

return x * x * x;

Combining the method signature with the method body gives us the complete method as follows:

```
static long cube(int x)    //METHOD SIGNATURE
{
  return x * x * x;        //METHOD BODY
} //END cube()
```

This is a relatively simple method that doesn't require any local definitions or additional logic.

Example 8-2

Complete the *grossPay()* method whose signature was developed in Example 8-1.

Solution

To calculate gross pay, we must multiply hours by rate if the hours are less than 40. If the hours are greater than 40, we must multiply the amount of hours exceeding 40 by one and one-half times the rate and add this to 40 times the rate to provide for overtime. Thus, the statement section of our method requires an **if/else** statement. By putting it all together, the complete method becomes

```
static double grossPay(double hours, double rate)
{
  if (hours <= 40.0)
    return hours * rate;
  else
    return rate * 40.0 + (1.5 * rate * (hours – 40.0));
}/ /END grossPay()
```

Notice that both logical paths of the **if/else** statement lead to a **return** statement.

DEBUGGING TIP

A possible source of error in coding a nonvoid method is to make an assignment to the method name within the method, as follows:

```
static double grossPay(double hours, double rate)
{
```

```
  if (hours <= 40.0)
    return grossPay = hours * rate;
  else
    return grossPay = rate * 40.0 + (1.5 * rate * (hours − 40.0));
}//END grossPay()
```

This will always cause a compiler error, because you are attempting to return the method name. You must return a value, which, in this case, is a calculation involving *hours* and *rate*.

Example 8-3

Write a method to return the sum of all integers from 1 to some maximum integer value, called *max*. The method must obtain the value of *max* from the calling program.

Solution

Let's call this method *sum()*. Now, the method must *accept* an integer value, called *max*, from the calling program. Because the method is to sum all the integers from 1 to *max*, it must return an integer value. Thus, our method interface can be described as follows:

Method *sum()*:	Sums all integers from 1 to *max*.
Accepts:	An integer value, *max*.
Returns:	An integer value.

Using this information, the method signature becomes

```
static int sum(int max)
```

The next step is to determine what control structures are needed within the method. You can use a loop to calculate the sum of integers from 1 to *max*, because it is a simple repetitive process to sum consecutive values. We will use the **for** loop. Why a **for** loop? Because the method knows exactly how many values it needs to sum via the parameter, *max*. In addition, the **for** statement requires a local counter variable. We will call this variable *count*. Next, you also need a temporary variable within the **for** loop to keep a running subtotal of the sum each time the loop executes. Let's call this local variable *subTotal*. Using these ideas, the complete method becomes:

```
static int sum(int max)
{
  int subTotal = 0;    //LOCAL SUBTOTAL VARIABLE
  for (int count = 1; count <= max; ++count)
```

```
    subTotal = subTotal + count;
  return subTotal;
}//END sum()
```

Notice that *subTotal* is defined as a local variable for the method and *count* is defined locally inside the **for** loop. Why can't you use *sum* instead of *subTotal* within the method **for** loop? This would cause an error during compilation. The reason? *sum* is the method name and cannot appear within the body of the method except when used as part of a recursive operation (to be discussed later).

Calling a Nonvoid Method

You call, or invoke, a nonvoid method just as you call many of the standard methods in Java. For example, you can call a method by using an assignment operator or a *println()* statement, like this:

```
long y = 0;
y = cube(2);
```

or

```
System.out.println(cube(2));
```

In both cases, the value 2 is passed to the method to be cubed. Thus, in our *cube()* method, the parameter *x* takes on the value 2. The method will return the cube of 2, which is 8. With the assignment statement, the variable *y* will be assigned the value 8, and the *println()* statement causes the value 8 to be displayed on the monitor.

Here are two other ways that our *cube()* method can be called:

```
long y = 0;
int a = 2;
y = cube(a);
```

or

```
System.out.println(cube(a));
```

In these cases, the method is cubing the variable *a*, where *a* has been previously assigned the value 2. Thus, the value of *a*, or 2, is passed to the method. In our *cube()* method, the parameter *x* takes on the value of *a*. This value is cubed and assigned to *y* in the first example and displayed via a *println()* statement in the second example.

Nonvoid methods can also be called as part of arithmetic expressions or relational statements. For instance, our *cube()* method can be called as part of an arithmetic expression, like this:

```
long y = 0;
int a = 2;
y = 1 + cube(a) * 2;
```

What will be assigned to *y*? Well, Java evaluates the *cube()* method first to get 8, then performs the multiplication operation to get 16, and finally adds 1 to 16 to get 17.

You also can use methods as part of relational operations, like this:

```
if (cube(a) >= 27)
```

When will the relationship be true? When *a* is greater than or equal to 3, right? When *a* is greater than or equal to 3, *cube(a)* is greater than or equal to 27. Just remember that when a method is designed to return a single value to the calling program, the *value returned replaces the method name wherever the name appears in the calling program.*

PROGRAMMING NOTE

You will normally call nonvoid methods within your program using an assignment statement, a *println()* statement, or as part of an arithmetic expression. Remember to think of the method call as a *value*. That is, a value replaces the method call where it appears in the program. Ask yourself: "Does a *value* make sense here?" For example, the following statements all make sense, because a value can easily be substituted for the method call:

```
Result = cube(a);
System.out.println(cube(a));
Solution = 2 * cube(a) + 5;
```

On the other hand, the following statement would not make sense and would cause a compile error, because the compiler sees just a single value coded as an executable statement.

```
cube(a);
```

Arguments versus Parameters

Some terminology is appropriate at this time. In the foregoing *cube( )* example, the variable *a* used in the calling program is called an ***argument***. On the other hand, the corresponding variable *x* used in the method signature is called a ***parameter***.

> ***Arguments*** are values/variables used within the method call, and ***parameters*** are variables used within the method signature that receive the argument values.

Thus, we say that the parameter in our *cube( )* method, *x*, takes on the value of the argument, *a*, used in the method call. Here are some things that you will want to remember about arguments and parameters:

- Argument variables must be defined in the calling program. This will be method *main( )*, unless methods are calling other methods.
- The data type of the corresponding arguments and parameters should be the same.
- Parameters are place holders for the argument values during the execution of the method. Parameters are always listed in the parameter section of the method signature.
- The number of arguments used during the method call must be the same as the number of parameters listed in the method signature.
- The correspondence between arguments and parameters is established on a one-to-one basis according to the respective listing orders.
- Although the argument and parameter variables often have different variable names, they can be the same. When this is the case, the respective variables must still be defined in the calling program and must also appear in the parameter listing of the method.

DEBUGGING TIP

- Always remember to check that the number and data types of the arguments in a method call match the number and data types of the parameters in the method signature on a one-to-one basis, according to their respective listing orders. Each argument in the method call *must* correspond to one and only one parameter in the method signature, and the respective ordering *must* be the same. You will always get a compiler error if the number of arguments does not match the number of parameters. However, you will often not get a compiler error if their data types do not match or the respective ordering is different. The result here will be garbage, and its source might be very difficult to locate.

- The names of the arguments do not have to match the names of the parameters and often do not match. For instance, suppose we have a method signature as follows:

static void foo(int a, int b, int c)

Then, a method call of

foo(x,y,z);

is perfectly legal. Here, *a* takes on the value of *x*, *b* takes on the value of *y*, and *c* takes on the value of *z* within the body of the method. Of course, the variables *x*, *y*, and *z* must be defined as **int** prior to the method call. Note that *foo()* is a void method and, therefore, is called differently than a nonvoid method.

 Quick Check

1. List four advantages of using methods in a Java program.
2. The two different kinds of methods provided by Java are _____ and _____ methods.
3. The two parts of a method are the method _____ and the method _____.
4. All logical paths in a nonvoid method must lead to a _____ statement.
5. What two things must be considered when developing a method signature?
6. What is the purpose of the method signature in a Java program?
7. List the four parts of a method signature.
8. A method variable, waiting to receive a value from the calling program, is called a _____.
9. What is the purpose of a **return** statement in a method?

10. Explain the difference between an argument in a calling program and a parameter in a method signature.

11. Write a signature for a nonvoid method called *loanPayment()* that will return a monthly loan payment, given the loan amount, interest rate, and term.

8-2 VOID METHODS

Methods that do not return a single value to the calling program are often written to perform some procedural task or operate directly on class data. These are called *void methods*.

> A *void method* is a method that performs some procedural task or operates directly on class data, rather than returning a single value to the calling program.

When a method is not returning a single value to the calling program, you must use the keyword **void** as the return type. In addition, these methods may or may not require parameters. When no parameters are required, you simply leave the parameter listing blank to indicate to the compiler that the method does not need to receive any values from the calling program. Methods that do not return a value or do not require any parameters are the simplest type of methods in Java. For example, suppose that you want to write a method that will display the following heading on the monitor each time it is called:

NAME   STREET   ADDRESS   STATE   CITY   ZIP
_____   _____   _____   _____   ____   ___

Let's call this method *displayHeading()*. To develop the method signature, ask yourself what the method must *accept* to perform its designated task and what it must *return*. In this case, the method is simply displaying constant header information and does not need to accept any data or return any data. Thus, our method interface can be described as follows:

Method *displayHeading()*:   Displays fixed heading information.
Accepts: Nothing.
Returns: Nothing.

Using this information, the method signature becomes

```
static void displayHeading()
```

Look at the method signature and you will see the keyword **void** used as the method return type. The keyword **void** used here indicates to the compiler that there is no return value. Furthermore, notice that there are no parameters required by this method, because the parameter listing is left blank. In other words, the method does not return a value and does not require any arguments to evaluate. It simply performs a given task, in this case displaying a heading. To display the heading, all you need is a couple of *println()* statements in the body of the method. Putting everything together, the method becomes

```
static void displayHeading()
{
 System.out.println("\tNAME\tSTREET ADDRESS\tCITY\tSTATE\tZIP");
 System.out.println("\t____\t_____\t____\t____\t___");
}//END displayHeading()
```

Finally, you do not see a **return** statement at the end of the method, because no single value is being returned by the method.

How would you call this method in your program? Simple; just use the method name as a statement within the calling program each time the heading must be displayed, like this:

```
displayHeading();
```

No arguments are listed in the method call, because no arguments need to be evaluated by the method.

PROGRAMMING NOTE

When calling a void method, simply list the method name and required arguments as a single statement within your program. Do *not* call a void method with an assignment operator or *println()* statement as you do nonvoid methods. The following calls on *displayHeading()* would, at best, cause a compiler error,

```
Heading = displayHeading();              //ERROR
System.out.println(displayHeading());     //ERROR
```

The correct call is simply

```
displayHeading();
```

Example 8-4

Write a method called *display()* that could be used to display a name, address, and telephone number obtained from the calling program. Write a statement to call the *display()* method.

Solution

The first chore in writing a method is to write the method signature. To do this, you must decide what the method accepts and returns. Here is a description of the required interface:

Method *display()*:	Displays a name, address, and telephone number obtained from the calling program.
Accepts:	Three strings representing a name, address, and telephone number.
Returns:	Nothing

To pass a string to a method, you simply define a string object in the method parameter listing. Our method requires that three strings be passed to it. Thus, the method signature becomes:

static void display(String nam, String addr, String ph)

Notice that the method return type is **void**. (Why?) Once the method signature is determined, the method body is developed. This method only requires *println()* statements. The complete method then becomes:

```
static void display(String nam, String addr, String ph)
{
   System.out.println(nam);
   System.out.println(addr);
   System.out.println(ph);
} //END display()
```

How do you suppose this method will be called? Well suppose we define three string objects in *main()* like this:

```
String name = "Andrew C. Staugaard, Jr.";
String address = "Java City, USA";
String phone = "(123) 456-7890";
```

Then, to call the method you simply use the string identifiers as arguments as follows:

```
display(name, address, phone);
```

Notice that the string object identifiers in the method call are different from those used in the parameter listing. Is there a problem here? No! In fact, the argument identifiers used in a method call are often different from the identifiers employed in the method parameter listing. This allows the method parameters to be more general, as you will see shortly. The only requirement is that the number and types of the arguments be the same and that they be listed in the same respective order.

PROGRAMMING NOTE

Is it possible to place a **return** statement within a void method to return control to the calling program? Yes! For instance, consider the following method:

```
static void processIfEven(int value)
{
  // IS value ODD?
  if (value % 2 == 1)
     return;                //YES, RETURN CONTROL TO CALLING PROGRAM
  else                      //NO, VALUE IS EVEN, PROCESS VALUE
  {
     //PROCESS value
         •
         •
         •
  }//END else
}//END processIfEven()
```

This method will only process the value that it receives if *value* is even. If *value* is odd, control is *returned* to the calling program via the **return** statement.

 Quick Check

1. What must be used as the return type when a method does not return a single value to the calling program?

2. What two things must be considered when developing a method signature?

3. How must you call a void method?

4. True or false: A void method can be called with an assignment operator.

5. When might you want to use a **return** statement within a void method?

6. Write a signature for a method called *displayEmployee()* that would display an employee's name, social security number, number of years employed, and annual salary, all obtained from the calling program.

8-3 LOCATING STATIC METHODS WITHIN YOUR PROGRAM

When writing Java application programs where your methods are **static** and called by *main()*, you will locate your methods just after the closing brace of *main()*, as shown in Figure 8-2. There is no limit on the number of programmer-defined methods that can be used in a program. To call a method that returns a single value, you must insert the method name and any required arguments where you want the value to be returned. To call a void method, you simply list its name and any required arguments as a statement within the calling program, usually *main()*. In addition, the number of arguments used in the method call must be the same as the number of parameters defined in the respective method signature.

Notice the block structure of the overall program in Figure 8-2. Method *main()* forms the overall outer program block, and the programmer-defined methods form the inner blocks that are nested within method *main()* via the method calls. This is why Java could be called a ***block-structured language***. From now on, when we develop Java programs, we will attempt to divide the overall programming problem into a group of simpler subproblems whose combined solution solves the original problem. How will these subproblems be coded? You've got it—as methods! This is the essence of modular programming and top-down software design.

```
public class < Name>
{
  public static void main(String[] args)
  {
    Call method1(<arguments>);
    Call method2(<arguments>);
  } //END main()

      static method1(<parameters>)
      {
        _____
        _____
        _____

      } //END method1( )


      static method2(<parameters>)
      {
        _____
        _____
        _____

      } //END method2( )

} //END <class Name>
```

Figure 8-2   Static methods called by *main()* are usually placed after *main()* in a Java program.

Quick Check

1. Where is the body of a **static** method normally located in an application program when the method is called by *main()*?

2. Where must variables be defined when used as arguments for methods being called by *main()*?

3. Where must variables be defined when used locally by a method?

4. What is the scope of a **static** method?

8-4 METHOD OVERLOADING

The idea of method overloading is important to programming in Java. When a method is overloaded, it is designed to perform differently when it is supplied with a different number of arguments or argument data types. In other words, the same method exhibits different *behavior* with a different number of arguments or argument data types. Thus, a given method might *behave* one way when supplied one argument and an entirely different way when supplied two arguments. For example, consider the following program:

```
public class Overload
{
  public static void main(String[] args)
  {
    //DEFINE METHOD ARGUMENT VARIABLES
    int side = 3;
    int length = 4;
    int width = 5;
    double radius = 6.25;

    //METHOD CALLS
    System.out.println("The area of the square is:  " + area(side));
    System.out.println("The area of the rectangle is: " + area(length,width));
    System.out.println("The are of the circle is: " + area(radius));
  } //END main()

  //THIS METHOD FINDS THE AREA OF A SQUARE
  static int area(int s)
  {
    return s * s;
  } //END area(int)

  //THIS METHOD FINDS THE AREA OF A RECTANGLE
  static int area(int l, int w)
  {
    return l * w;
  } //END area(int,int)

  //THIS METHOD FINDS THE AREA OF A CIRCLE
  static double area(double r)
  {
    return 3.14159 * r * r;
  } //END area(double)
} //END Overload
```

Look at the method signatures. The first thing you see is three different signatures for *area()*. In the first signature, *area()* requires a single integer argument and returns an integer value. In the second signature, *area()* requires two integer arguments and returns an integer value. In the third signature, *area()* requires a single double floating-point argument and returns a double floating-point value. Thus, the single method *area()* is defined three different times to do three different things. The way *area()* will *behave* is determined by the number and types of the arguments supplied when it is called. If a single integer argument is provided when *area()* is called, it will return the area of a square. If two integer arguments are supplied in the call, *area()* will return the area of a rectangle, which is not square. However, if a single floating-point argument is supplied in the call, *area()* will return the area of a circle. Here is the result of the program execution:

The area of the square is: 9

The area of the rectangle is: 20

The area of the circle is: 122.718

You could say that *area()* is *overloaded* with work, because it is performing three different tasks, depending on the number and data types of the arguments used in its call. Overloading is used where the tasks are very similar, differing only in the number of arguments required by the method or the data types of the arguments. Without overloading, you would have to invent different names for each similar task instead of just one, thus requiring you and your program users to remember all of them.

Overloaded methods cannot be distinguished by their return type. Two methods with the same name that have the same parameter list but different return types, are not overloaded and will cause a compiler error. For example, suppose that we change the parameter for the area of a square method to be a double floating-point value, the same as the area of a circle method, like this:

```
static int area(double s);
static double area(double r);
```

Here, both *area()* methods have a double floating-point parameter but have different return types. The corresponding method calls might be:

```
System.out.println("The area is:  " + area(x));
System.out.println("The area is: " + area(x));
```

The argument *x* must be defined as double floating-point variable. Could *you* decide from the method calls which *area( )* method to execute, the area of a square or the area of a circle? Of course not, since both methods operate on a floating-point value. Well, if you can't decide which method to execute, neither can the compiler. As a result, the compiler will generate an error message. Thus, overloaded methods must have different parameter listings.

Method overloading is related to the concept of ***polymorphism***, which is one of the cornerstones of object-oriented programming, as you will find out later. Polymorphism is used extensively in commercial programs. A common example is the print method used in a word processor. The print button on the tool bar of a typical word processor invokes a polymorphic print method to perform the printing task. Do you have a separate print button for a memo document, one for a fax document, one for a text document, and so on? Of course not! A single print button is provided for printing any type of document. You expect the single print button to print the document, regardless of the document format. Thus, we say that the printing operation is polymorphic. We are introducing polymorphism here so that you understand the concept. You will see how it is applied when you learn about OOP in a later chapter.

 Quick Check

1. When overloading a method, what determines how the method will behave?

2. Why is method overloading important in commercial programs.

3. True or false: Method overloading can be distinguished by the method return type as well as parameter listings.

4. Method overloading relates to an important concept in object-oriented programming called _____.

PROBLEM SOLVING IN ACTION: PROGRAMMING WITH METHODS

Problem

In previous chapters, we developed a loop-controlled, menu-driven loan program. However, although we developed a modular design, we have employed a flat implementation when coding the design. It is now time to do it right and employ modular programming via methods to implement the modular design. Here is the problem definition that we developed earlier:

Defining the Problem

Output:
A program menu that prompts the user to select a monthly payment, total interest, or total loan amount calculation option.
The monthly loan payment, total loan interest, or total loan amount, depending on the program option that the user selects.
Invalid entry messages as required.

Input:
A user response to the menu (P, I, T, or Q).
If P is selected: User enters the loan amount, interest rate, and term.
If I is selected: User enters the loan amount, interest rate, and term.
If T is selected: User enters the loan amount, interest rate, and term.
If Q is selected: Terminate program.

Processing:
Calculate the selected option as follows:
Case P: *payment = principle * rate/(1-(1+rate)$^{-term}$)*
Case I: *interest = term * payment − principle*
Case T: *total = principle + interest*
Case Q: Terminate program.

where: *principle* is the amount of the loan.
            rate is a monthly interest rate in decimal form.
            term is the number of months of the loan.

Planning the Solution

The problem solving diagram we developed earlier is shown again in Figure 8-3.

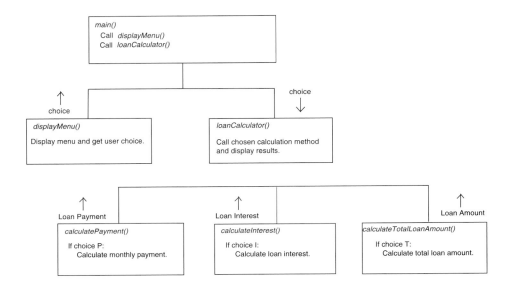

Figure 8-3   A problem solving diagram for the loan problem.

Now, here is the set of algorithms we developed earlier:

Initial Algorithm

> *main( )*
> BEGIN
>   do
>   Call *displayMenu( )* method.
>   Call *loanCalculator( )* method.
>   while *choice* ≠ 'q' AND *choice* ≠ 'Q'
> END.

First Level of Refinement

> *displayMenu( )*
> BEGIN

Display a program menu that prompts the user to choose a monthly payment (P), total interest (I), total loan amount (T), or quit (Q) option. Read (*choice*).
END.

loanCalculator( )
BEGIN
  Case P: Call method *calculatePayment( )* and display payment.
  Case I: Call method *calculateInterest( )* and display interest.
  Case T: Call method *calculateTotalLoanAmount( )* and display total loan amount.
  Case Q: Terminate program.
  Default: Write an invalid entry message and ask the user to select again.
END.

Coding the Program

Now, to implement the design, we need to construct the methods. The main task here is to develop the method interfaces, or signatures. To do this, we must develop a problem definition for *each* method. The problem definition developed earlier addresses output, input, and processing for the overall application program. This is still needed to define the problem for the program as a whole. However, to construct the method signatures, we must address problem definition from the perspective of the method. In other words, we must consider the output, input, and processing of each individual method. The *input* to the method is what the method must *accept* in order to perform its designated task, the *output* from the method is what the method *returns*, and the processing is the task, or algorithm, the method will perform.

We will start with the *displayMenu( )* method. You must ask yourself two questions: 1) "What does the method need to *accept* (input) to perform its designated task?" and 2) "What does the method need to *return* (output) to the calling program?" The task of the *displayMenu( )* method is to display the menu and return the user's choice to its calling method, *main( )*. Thus, this method does not need to accept anything from *main( )* to perform its task but needs to return a single value to *main( )*, which is the user's menu choice. This is shown in the problem solving diagram by the variable *choice* coming out of *displayMenu( )*. Notice that nothing is going into this method. Here is the problem definition from the perspective of this method:

Method *displayMenu( )*:   Display menu and get user entry.
Accepts: Nothing.
Returns: Menu choice obtained from user.

The method definition describes the method interface. The first decision you need to make is whether to use a void method or a nonvoid method. Use a nonvoid method if the method produces a single value that is returned to the calling program. Use a void method if the method does not return anything to the calling program. In other words, if the problem solving diagram indicates that a single value is being produced by the method, use a nonvoid method. If the problem solving diagram indicates nothing is being returned by the method, use a void method. These guidelines are summarized in Table 8-2. Because our *displayMenu( )* method accepts nothing but returns the user's menu choice, it must be a nonvoid method. So, the return type must be **char**, because the user's choice will be a character from the menu.

TABLE 8-2 METHOD RETURN TYPE

Returns	Return Type
A single value	Nonvoid
Nothing	Void

Next, we must decide the method parameters. No parameters are required for *displayMenu( )*, because it does not accept anything. Thus, the method signature is simply

```
static char displayMenu()
```

DEBUGGING TIP

When deciding what a method must accept, you only include those items that need to be accepted from the *calling program*. Since *choice* is entered by the user, and not received from the calling program, it is not a parameter in the foregoing *displayMenu( )* method.

Now, we simply place the *displayMenu( )* code developed earlier inside the method. Here is the complete method:

```
//DISPLAY MENU METHOD
static char displayMenu()
{
  //DISPLAY MENU
  System.out.print("\n\n\t\t\tEnter P to get monthly payment"
                 + "\n\t\t\tEnter I to get total loan interest"
                 + "\n\t\t\tEnter T to get total loan amount"
                 + "\n\t\t\tEnter Q to quit"
                 + "\n\tPlease enter your choice:  ");

  //READ AND RETURN USER CHOICE
  return in.readChar();
}//END displayMenu()
```

The method begins by displaying the menu. Then, a **return** statement is executed to return the user entry to the calling program. Notice that our *in* object is used to call the *readChar()* method, which reads the user entry. This object will be defined as a **static** class object prior to *main()*. The **return** statement then returns the entry read by the *in* object.

Next, let's develop the *loanCalculator()* method. We begin by developing the method interface. From the problem solving diagram, it is easy to see the following:

Method *loanCalculator()*: Perform chosen calculation and display results.
Accepts: Menu entry, *choice*, obtained from *main()*.
Returns: Nothing.

From the interface description, it is easy to see that we must use a void method, because nothing is returned by the method. Even though the method is displaying the result, it *is not* returning any values to its calling method, *main()*. However, this method needs to accept the menu choice from *main()*. This means that we need a method parameter. The required parameter is a character, so the method signature becomes

```
static void loanCalculator(char choice)
```

Now, inserting our switch statement code into the body of the method, the complete method becomes:

```
//LOAN CALCULATION METHOD
static void loanCalculator(char choice)
{
  switch (choice)
  {
    case 'p':  //CALL calculatePayment() METHOD
    case 'P':  System.out.println("The monthly loan payment is $"
                                    + calculatePayment());
          break;

    case 'i':  //CALL calculateInterest() METHOD
    case 'I' : System.out.println("The monthly loan payment is $"
                                    + calculateInterest());
          break;

    case 't':  //CALL calculateTotalLoanAmount() METHOD
    case 'T':  System.out.println("The monthly loan payment is $"
                                    + calculateTotalLoanAmount());
          break;

    case 'q':  //TERMINATE PROGRAM
    case 'Q':  System.out.println("Program terminated.");
          break;

               //DISPLAY INVALID ENTRY MESSAGE
    default :  System.out.println("\n\nThis is an invalid entry.");
  } //END SWITCH
}//END loanCalculator()
```

Notice that the body of the method employs our earlier **switch** statement, which acts on the user choice, *choice*, received as a parameter from the calling method, *main()*. Next, you see that each **case** calls another method as part of a *println()* statement to calculate the required loan payment, interest, or total loan amount, depending on the value of *choice*. Each method will return a single value of monthly payment, interest, or total loan amount, depending on which **case** is executed. Does this give you a hint as to what type of methods these will be (void or nonvoid)? Finally, notice that there is no **return** statement in our *loanCalculator()* method, because it is a void method.

Here are the interface descriptions for each of the loan methods:

Method *calculatePayment()*:   Get loan principle, rate, and term from user and calculate the loan payment.

Accepts:	Nothing.
Returns:	Loan payment.

Method *calculateInterest()*:	Get loan principle, rate, and term from user and calculate the loan interest.
Accepts:	Nothing.
Returns:	Loan interest.

Method *calculateTotalLoanAmount()*:	Get loan principle, rate, and term from user and calculate the total loan amount.

Accepts:	Nothing.
Returns:	Loan amount.

Each of these methods will have the same interface, except, of course, for the method name. Each method will be a nonvoid method, because a single value is being produced and returned by the method. No parameters are required, because none of the methods needs to accept any data from the calling method, *loanCalculator()*. You are probably thinking each method needs the three unknown quantities in order to make the required calculation, right? However, these quantities will be obtained from the user within each of the methods and not from the *loanCalculator()* calling method. As a result, these values are *not* passed to any of the methods. Here are the resulting method signatures:

```
static double calculatePayment()
static double calculateInterest()
static double calculateTotalLoanAmount()
```

Now, here is each complete method:

```
//CALCULATE PAYMENT METHOD
static double calculatePayment()
{
  //DEFINE LOCAL VARIABLES
  double principle = 0.0;     //LOAN PRINCIPLE
  double rate = 0.0;          //ANNUAL INTEREST RATE
  int term = 0;               //TERM OF LOAN IN MONTHS

  //GET LOAN DATA FROM USER
  System.out.print("\nEnter the amount of the loan: ");
  principle = in.readDouble();
  System.out.print("\nEnter the duration of the loan in months: ");
```

```
      term = in.readInt();
      System.out.print("\nEnter the annual interest rate: ");
      rate = in.readDouble();

      //CHECK FOR INVALID RATE
      while ((rate < 0) || (rate > 100))
      {
        //DISPLAY INVALID ENTRY MESSAGE
        System.out.println("\n\nThis is an invalid entry.");
        System.out.print("\nEnter the annual interest rate: ");
        rate = in.readDouble();
      }//END WHILE

      //CALCULATE PAYMENT
      rate = rate/12/100;
      return principle * rate/(1-Math.pow((1+rate),-term));
    }//END calculatePayment()

    //CALCULATE INTEREST METHOD
    static double calculateInterest()
    {
      //DEFINE LOCAL VARIABLES
      double payment = 0.0;       //MONTHLY PAYMENT
      double principle = 0.0;     //LOAN PRINCIPLE
      double rate = 0.0;          //ANNUAL INTEREST RATE
      int term = 0;               //TERM OF LOAN IN MONTHS

      //GET LOAN DATA FROM USER
      System.out.print("\nEnter the amount of the loan: ");
      principle = in.readDouble();
      System.out.print("\nEnter the duration of the loan in months: ");
      term = in.readInt();
      System.out.print("\nEnter the annual interest rate: ");
      rate = in.readDouble();

      //CHECK FOR INVALID RATE
      while ((rate < 0) || (rate > 100))
      {
        //DISPLAY INVALID ENTRY MESSAGE
        System.out.println("\n\nThis is an invalid entry.");
        System.out.print("\nEnter the annual interest rate: ");
        rate = in.readDouble();
      }//END WHILE
```

```
  //CALCULATE INTEREST
  rate = rate/12/100;
  payment = principle * rate/(1-Math.pow((1+rate),-term));
  return term * payment - principle;
}//END calculateInterest()

//CALCULATE TOTAL LOAN AMOUNT METHOD
static double calculateTotalLoanAmount()
{
  //DEFINE LOCAL VARIABLES
  double payment = 0.0;      //MONTHLY PAYMENT
  double interest = 0.0;     //TOTAL INTEREST FOR LIFE OF LOAN
  double principle = 0.0;    //LOAN PRINCIPLE
  double rate = 0.0;         //ANNUAL INTEREST RATE
  int term = 0;              //TERM OF LOAN IN MONTHS

  //GET LOAN DATA FROM USER
  System.out.print("\nEnter the amount of the loan: ");
  principle = in.readDouble();
  System.out.print("\nEnter the duration of the loan in months: ");
  term = in.readInt();
  System.out.print("\nEnter the annual interest rate: ");
  rate = in.readDouble();

  //CHECK FOR INVALID RATE
  while ((rate < 0) || (rate > 100))
  {
    //DISPLAY INVALID ENTRY MESSAGE
    System.out.println("\n\nThis is an invalid entry.");
    System.out.print("\nEnter the annual interest rate: ");
    rate = in.readDouble();
  }//END WHILE

  //CALCULATE TOTAL LOAN AMOUNT
  rate = rate/12/100;
  payment = principle * rate/(1-Math.pow((1+rate),-term));
  interest = term * payment - principle;
  return principle + interest;
 }//END calculateTotalLoanAmount()
```

Notice that each method obtains the data required for the calculation from the user. The interest rate value is tested. If invalid, a loop is entered which writes an invalid entry message and continues to iterate until the user enters a valid interest rate.

We are now ready to combine everything into a complete program. Here it is:

```
/* ACTION 8_1 (ACTION08_01.JAVA)
OUTPUT:   A PROGRAM MENU THAT PROMPTS THE USER TO SELECT A
          MONTHLY PAYMENT, TOTAL INTEREST, OR TOTAL LOAN
          AMOUNT CALCULATION   OPTION.
          INVALID ENTRY MESSAGES AS REQUIRED.
          THE MONTHLY LOAN PAYMENT, TOTAL LOAN INTEREST, OR
          TOTAL LOAN AMOUNT, DEPENDING ON THE PROGRAM
          OPTION THAT THE USER SELECTS. INVALID ENTRY
          MESSAGES AS REQUIRED.

INPUT:    A USER RESPONSE TO THE MENU (P, I, T, OR Q).
          IF P IS SELECTED: USER ENTERS THE LOAN AMOUNT,
          INTEREST RATE, AND TERM.
          IF I IS SELECTED: USER ENTERS THE LOAN AMOUNT,
          INTEREST RATE, AND TERM.
          IF R IS SELECTED: USER ENTERS THE LOAN AMOUNT,
          INTEREST RATE, AND TERM.
          IF Q IS SELECTED: TERMINATE PROGRAM.

PROCESSING: CALCULATE THE SELECTED OPTION AS FOLLOWS:
          CASE P:  PAYMENT = PRINCIPLE * RATE/(1 - (1+RATE)^ -TERM)
          CASE I:   INTEREST = TERM * PAYMENT - PRINCIPLE
          CASE T:  TOTAL = PRINCIPLE + INTEREST
          CASE Q:  TERMINATE PROGRAM.


WHERE:    PRINCIPLE IS THE AMOUNT OF THE LOAN.
          RATE IS A MONTHLY INTEREST RATE IN DECIMAL FORM.
          TERM IS THE NUMBER OF MONTHS OF THE LOAN.
*/

import keyboardInput.*; //FOR KeyBoard CLASS
public class Action08_01
{
  //CREATE STATIC INPUT OBJECT
  static Keyboard in = new Keyboard();

  public static void main(String[] args)
  {
```

```
          //DEFINE VARIABLES
          char choice = 'Q';            //USER MENU ENTRY
          char pause = ' ';             //DISPLAY FREEZE VAR

          //DISPLAY PROGRAM DESCRIPTION MESSAGE
          System.out.println("This program will calculate a monthly loan interest\n"
                        + "payment, total loan interest, or total loan amount.");

          do              //BEGIN MENU CONTROL LOOP
          {
            choice = displayMenu();
            loanCalculator(choice);

            //FREEZE DISPLAY BEFORE LOOPING AGAIN
            System.out.println("Press ENTER to continue");
            pause = in.readChar();
          } //END DO/WHILE
          while ((choice != 'q') && (choice != 'Q'));
       } //END main()

  //DISPLAY MENU METHOD
  static char displayMenu()
  {
    //DISPLAY MENU
    System.out.print("\n\n\t\t\tEnter P to get monthly payment"
                        + "\n\t\t\tEnter I to get total loan interest"
                        + "\n\t\t\tEnter T to get total loan amount"
                        + "\n\t\t\tEnter Q to quit"
                        + "\n\tPlease enter your choice:  ");

    //READ AND RETURN USER CHOICE
    return in.readChar();
  }//END displayMenu()

  //LOAN CALCULATION METHOD
  static void loanCalculator(char choice)
  {
    switch (choice)
    {
      case 'p':  //CALL calculatePayment() METHOD
      case 'P':  System.out.println("The monthly loan payment is $"
                                + calculatePayment());
                 break;
```

```
   case 'i':   //CALL calculateInterest() METHOD
   case 'I' :  System.out.println("The total loan interest is $"
                                      + calculateInterest());
             break;

   case 't':   //CALL calculateTotalLoanAmount() METHOD
   case 'T':   System.out.println("The total loan amount is $"
                                      + calculateTotalLoanAmount());
             break;

   case 'q':   //TERMINATE PROGRAM
   case 'Q':   System.out.println("Program terminated.");
             break;

   //DISPLAY INVALID ENTRY MESSAGE
   default :   System.out.println("\n\nThis is an invalid entry.");
 } //END SWITCH
}//END loanCalculator()

//CALCULATE PAYMENT METHOD
static double calculatePayment()
{
 //DEFINE LOCAL VARIABLES
 double principle = 0.0;      //LOAN PRINCIPLE
 double rate = 0.0;           //ANNUAL INTEREST RATE
 int term = 0;                //TERM OF LOAN IN MONTHS

 //GET LOAN DATA FROM USER
 System.out.print("\nEnter the amount of the loan: ");
 principle = in.readDouble();
 System.out.print("\nEnter the duration of the loan in months: ");
 term = in.readInt();
 System.out.print("\nEnter the annual interest rate: ");
 rate = in.readDouble();

//CHECK FOR INVALID RATE
 while ((rate < 0) || (rate > 100))
 {
   //DISPLAY INVALID ENTRY MESSAGE
   System.out.println("\n\nThis is an invalid entry.");
   System.out.print("\nEnter the annual interest rate: ");
   rate = in.readDouble();
 }//END WHILE
```

```
  //CALCULATE PAYMENT
  rate = rate/12/100;
  return principle * rate/(1-Math.pow((1+rate),-term));
}//END calculatePayment()

//CALCULATE INTEREST METHOD
static double calculateInterest()
{
  //DEFINE LOCAL VARIABLES
  double payment = 0.0;    //MONTHLY PAYMENT
  double principle = 0.0;  //LOAN PRINCIPLE
  double rate = 0.0;       //ANNUAL INTEREST RATE
  int term = 0;            //TERM OF LOAN IN MONTHS

  //GET LOAN DATA FROM USER
  System.out.print("\nEnter the amount of the loan: ");
  principle = in.readDouble();
  System.out.print("\nEnter the duration of the loan in months: ");
  term = in.readInt();
  System.out.print("\nEnter the annual interest rate: ");
  rate = in.readDouble();

  //CHECK FOR INVALID RATE
  while ((rate < 0) || (rate > 100))
  {
    //DISPLAY INVALID ENTRY MESSAGE
    System.out.println("\n\nThis is an invalid entry.");
    System.out.print("\nEnter the annual interest rate: ");
    rate = in.readDouble();
  }//END WHILE

  //CALCULATE INTEREST
  rate = rate/12/100;
  payment = principle * rate/(1-Math.pow((1+rate),-term));
  return term * payment - principle;
}//END calculateInterest()

//CALCULATE TOTAL LOAN AMOUNT METHOD
static double calculateTotalLoanAmount()
{
  //DEFINE LOCAL VARIABLES
  double payment = 0.0;    //MONTHLY PAYMENT
  double interest = 0.0;   //TOTAL INTEREST FOR LIFE OF LOAN
```

```
double principle = 0.0;      //LOAN PRINCIPLE
double rate = 0.0;           //ANNUAL INTEREST RATE
int term = 0;                //TERM OF LOAN IN MONTHS

//GET LOAN DATA FROM USER
System.out.print("\nEnter the amount of the loan: ");
principle = in.readDouble();
System.out.print("\nEnter the duration of the loan in months: ");
term = in.readInt();
System.out.print("\nEnter the annual interest rate: ");
rate = in.readDouble();


//CHECK FOR INVALID RATE
while ((rate < 0) || (rate > 100))
{
  //DISPLAY INVALID ENTRY MESSAGE
  System.out.println("\n\nThis is an invalid entry.");
  System.out.print("\nEnter the annual interest rate: ");
  rate = in.readDouble();
}//END WHILE

//CALCULATE TOTAL LOAN AMOUNT
  rate = rate/12/100;
  payment = principle * rate/(1-Math.pow((1+rate),-term));
  interest = term * payment - principle;
  return principle + interest;
}//END calculateTotalLoanAmount()
}//END Action08_01 CLASS
```

One of the first things you see at the top of the program is a static definition for the keyboard input object, *in*. A static object definition was used prior to *main()* so that the object is visible within the entire program. Thus, you could say that the *in* object is global to the entire class. As a result, our *in* object can be used by any method within the class. Next, you should be impressed by the simplicity of method *main()*. All that needs to be done here is to write a program description message and call our two methods within a program control loop. Most of the real work of the program is being done within the methods. The rest of the program contains each of the methods that we discussed earlier.

DOCUMENTATION NOTE

It's a good idea to include any program documentation that you have created within the program listing. Then, anyone looking at the listing can readily see the program design through the problem definitions and algorithms, without having to go through the code. We suggest that our students place the appropriate interface description and algorithm for each method in comments, just prior to the method in the program code. This means that the original problem definition and initial algorithm should be placed in comments just prior to *main()*. Then, each method interface description and algorithm should be placed in comments just prior to the respective method code. This way, there are no doubts about what the various parts of the program are doing.

PROBLEM SOLVING IN ACTION: BANKING

In Chapter 3, we employed stepwise refinement to design a solution for a bank account application. We coded the solution using a flat implementation because, at that time, you did not know how to implement a design using Java methods. Let's revisit this application with our newly gained knowledge of methods.

Here's the problem statement again:

Problem

Your local bank has contracted you to design a Java application program that will process savings account data for a given month. Assume that the savings account accrues interest at a rate of 12% per year and that the user must enter the current account balance, amount of deposits, and amount of withdrawals. Develop a problem definition, set of algorithms, and Java program to solve this problem.

Here is how we defined the overall problem in terms of output, input, and processing.

Defining the Problem

Output: The program must display a report showing the account transactions and balance for a given savings account in a given month.

Input: To process a savings account, you need to know the initial balance, amount of deposits, amount of withdrawals, and interest rate. We will assume that these values will be entered by the program user, with the exception of the interest rate, which will be coded as a constant.

Processing: The program must process deposits and withdrawals and calculate interest to determine the monthly balance.

This will serve as our problem definition for the initial algorithm, *main( )*.

Planning the Solution

Next, using stepwise refinement we constructed the problem solution diagram in Figure 8-4 along with the following set of related algorithms.

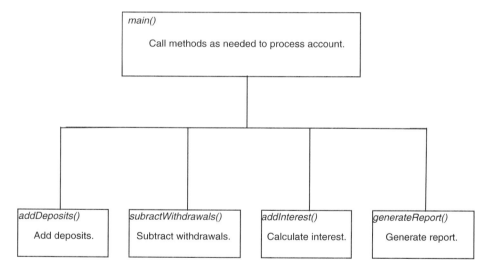

Figure 8-4   A problem solution diagram for the banking problem.

Initial Algorithm

main( )
BEGIN
    Get the transaction data from the user.
    Call the method to add the account deposits.
    Call the method to subtract the account withdrawals.

Call the method to calculate the account interest.
Call the method to generate the account report.
END.

First Level of Refinement

addDeposits( )
BEGIN
   Return *balance + deposits.*
END.

subtractWithdrawals( )
BEGIN
   Return *balance − withdrawals.*
END.

addInterest( )
BEGIN
   Return *balance + (balance ∗ interest).*
END.

generateReport( )
BEGIN
   Write(*balance*).
   Write(*deposits*).
   Write(*withdrawals*).
END.

With our new-found knowledge of methods, we can modify the problem solution diagram, as shown in Figure 8-5. Notice what has been added. First, the box at the top is labeled *main( )* and simply calls the individual methods in the order that they are needed to solve the problem. Second, data being passed to/from the methods are shown on the lines connecting *main( )* to the methods. Data the method accepts are shown to the left of the connecting line, and data the method returns are shown to the right of the line. Using this diagram, we can make the following conclusions:

- If a given data item goes into the method, it is a parameter.
- If a given data item goes out of the method, it is a return value.
- If a method has a return value, it is a nonvoid method; otherwise, it is a void method.

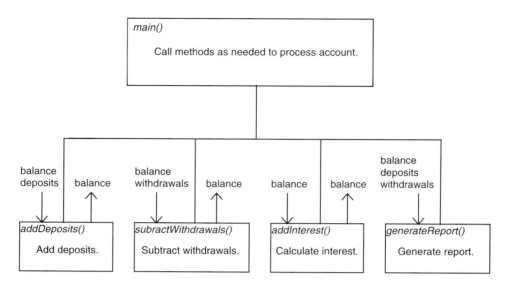

Figure 8-5 An expanded problem solving diagram shows data items flowing to/from the bank account methods.

To construct the expanded problem solution diagram, you must consider a problem definition for each method by describing the method interface in terms of what it accepts and returns. Let's begin with the *addDeposits()* method.

The *addDeposits()* method interface can be described as follows:

Method *addDeposits()*:   Add deposits to the current balance.
Accepts: The current account balance and deposits.
Returns: The sum of balance and deposits.

This method must receive the current account balance and deposits in order to calculate and return the new account balance. As a result, the balance and deposits are accepted by the method, and the method returns the value obtained by adding the balance and deposits as shown in the diagram. Therefore, the resulting method signature must be

static double addDeposits(double balance, double deposits)

The *subtractWithdrawals()* method must receive the current account balance and withdrawals, then return the value obtained by subtracting the withdrawals from the balance. With this information, its interface can be described as follows:

Method *subtractWithdrawals( )*:   Subtract withdrawals from the current balance.

Accepts: The current account balance and withdrawals.

Returns: The difference of balance and withdrawals.

The resulting method signature is

```
static double subtractWithdrawals(double balance, double withdrawals)
```

Next, the *addInterest( )* method must receive the account balance and return a value which adds the monthly interest to the account balance. This method can be described as follows:

Method *addInterest( )*:   Add monthly interest to account balance.
Accepts: The current account balance.
Returns: A sum of balance and monthly interest

Here, the account balance is accepted by the method. The method returns the sum of the balance and the monthly interest. The resulting interface is

```
static double addInterest(double balance)
```

Notice that the interest percentage is *not* passed to the method, because it will be coded as a global constant within the program. You always should declare constants as globally as possible so that they can be used by any methods within the program.

Finally, the *generateReport( )* method must receive the account balance, deposits, and withdrawals in order to generate the required account report. This method can, therefore, be described as follows:

Method *generateReport( )*:   Generate account report.
Accepts: The current account balance, deposits, and withdrawals.
Returns: Nothing.

In order to generate the account report, the method must receive the account balance, deposits, and withdrawals from *main( )*. However, these values are simply being displayed as part of the report by the method. Thus, the problem solution diagram in Figure 8-5 indicates *balance*, *deposits*, and *withdrawals* going into the method and nothing being returned. As a result, this method must be a void method. The resulting method signature is

static void generateReport(double balance, double deposits, double withdrawals)

Make sure that you see how the interface description for each method is illustrated on the problem solution diagram and how the diagram in Figure 8-5 is translated directly into the foregoing Java signature code.

Finally, using the method signatures, algorithms, and combining everything, we get the following code.

Coding the Program

```
//ACTION8-2 (ACTION08-02.JAVA)
//THIS PROGRAM WILL PROCESS A SAVINGS ACCOUNT DATA INTO A
//MONTHLY STATEMENT

import keyboardInput.*;          //FOR Keyboard CLASS
public class Action08_02
{
  //DEFINE INTEREST CONSTANT
  static final double INTEREST = 0.01;  //MONTHLY INTEREST
                                        //RATE IN DECIMAL FORM
  //CREATE KEYBOARD OBJECT
  static Keyboard in = new Keyboard();

  public static void main(String[] args)
  {
   //DEFINE METHOD ARGUMENT VARIABLES
   double balance = 0.0;        //ACCOUNT BALANCE
   double deposits = 0.0;       //MONTHLY DEPOSITS
   double withdrawals = 0.0;    //MONTHLY WITHDRAWALS
   char pause = ' ';            //FREEZE VARIABLE

   //DISPLAY PROGRAM DESCRIPTION MESSAGE
   System.out.println("This program will generate a banking account report based"
                   + "on information entered by the user\n\n");

   //SET VARIABLES TO USER DATA
   System.out.print("Enter the account balance:  $");
   balance = in.readDouble();
   System.out.print("Enter the deposits this month:  $");
   deposits = in.readDouble();
   System.out.print("Enter the withdrawals this month:  $");
   withdrawals = in.readDouble();
```

```
//CALL METHODS
balance = addDeposits(balance,deposits);
balance = subtractWithdrawals(balance,withdrawals);
balance = addInterest(balance);
generateReport(balance,deposits,withdrawals);

//PAUSE DISPLAY
System.out.println("Press ENTER to continue");
pause = in.readChar();
} //END main()

//THIS METHOD ADDS THE MONTHLY DEPOSITS
//TO THE ACCOUNT BALANCE
static double addDeposits(double balance, double deposits)
{
    return balance + deposits;
} //END addDeposits()

//THIS METHOD SUBTRACTS THE MONTHLY WITHDRAWALS
//FROM THE ACCOUNT BALANCE
static double subtractWithdrawals (double balance, double withdrawals)
{
    return balance - withdrawals;
} //END subtractWithdrawals()

//THIS METHOD ADDS MONTHLY INTEREST
//TO THE ACCOUNT BALANCE
static double addInterest(double balance)
{
    return balance + (balance * INTEREST);
} //END addInterest()

//THIS METHOD DISPLAYS THE MONTHLY ACCOUNT REPORT
static void generateReport(double balance, double deposits, double withdrawals)
{
 System.out.println("The account balance, with interest, is currently:  $" + balance);
 System.out.println("Deposits were:  $" + deposits );
 System.out.println("Withdrawals were:  $" + withdrawals);
 } //END generateReport()
} //END Action08_02 CLASS
```

That's it! You should now have the knowledge to understand all facets of this problem, from the modular design to the modular Java application program.

CHAPTER SUMMARY

In this chapter, you learned how to write and use methods in Java. A method is created by writing a method signature, which includes the method modifier, the return type, the method name, and a parameter listing. The body, or statement section, of the method then follows the method signature. Methods in Java can be **nonvoid** methods which return a single value to the calling program or **void** methods that perform some specific task. When a nonvoid method is designed to return a single value to the calling program, the value returned replaces the method name wherever the name is used in the calling program. Thus, the method name can appear as part of an assignment operator, a *println()* statement, an arithmetic operator, or a conditional test statement. When a void method is designed to perform a specific task, the method is called by using the method name (followed by a list of arguments) as a statement in the program.

Arguments are data passed to the method when the method is called. Parameters are defined within the method signature and take on the value(s) of the arguments when the method is called.

In addition to parameters, methods can operate with local variables that are defined within the method body. Such local variables are visible only for use within the method in which they are defined. Local variables are destroyed once the method execution is terminated. Global constants and objects are available for use by any methods in a given program and must be defined prior to *main()*. The scope of a constant or variable refers to the largest block in which it is visible. Variables always should be defined as locally as possible, whereas constants should be declared as globally as possible.

QUESTIONS AND PROBLEMS

Questions

1. What four things must be specified in a method signature?
2. Four possible modifiers for Java methods are _____, _____, and _____, _____.
3. Explain the difference between a **static** method and a nonstatic method.
4. Explain the difference between an argument and a parameter.
5. Which of the following are invalid method signatures? Explain why they are invalid.

    a. static double average (num1, num2)

    b. static int largest (x,y : int)

    c. static double smallest (double a,b)

    d. static String display(String name)

6. Write the appropriate signatures for the following methods:

    a. Inverse of x: $1/x$

    b. *tan (x)*

    c. Convert a decimal test score value to a letter grade.

    d. Convert degrees Fahrenheit to degrees Celsius.

    e. Compute the factorial of any integer n ($n!$).

    f. Compute the average of three integer test scores.

    g. Display the average of three integer test scores.

7. True or false: When a method does not have a return type, you must indicate this with the keyword **null**.

8. When passing an argument to a method parameter,

    a. The argument takes on the parameter value.

    b. The parameter takes on the argument value.

    c. The argument reflects any changes to the parameter after the method execution.

    d. a and b

    e. b and c

    f. a and c

9. When using an assignment operator to call a method, the method must include a _____ statement.

10. Which of the following are invalid method signatures? Explain why they are invalid.

    a. static void print()

    b. static boolean error(float num1, char num2)

    c. static void getData(int amount, char date)

    d. static double average (int number, float total)

    e. static char sample (int, char, float);

11. True or false: A nonstatic variable defined in *main()* has visibility in all methods called by *main()*.

12. Explain the difference between calling a nonvoid method and calling a void method.

13. Write the appropriate signatures for the following methods:

    a. A method called *sample()* that must return a floating-point value and receive an integer, a floating-point value, and a character (in that order) when it is called.

       b. A method called *skip()* that will cause the printer to skip a given number of lines where the number of lines to skip is obtained from the calling program.

       c. A method called *myMethod()* that accepts a string and returns a Boolean value.

       d. A method called *hypot()* that will return the hypotenuse of a right triangle, given the values of the two sides from the calling program.

       e. A method called *yourMethod()* that accepts a Boolean value and returns a string value.

14. Write Java statements that will call the methods in question 13.

15. Explain the difference between a local and global variable.

16. What is meant by the scope of a variable or method?

17. True or false: Variables should be defined as locally as possible and constants as globally as possible.

18. Suppose that a method must have access to a variable defined in *main()*. How must this be accomplished?

Problems

Least Difficult

Write methods to perform the following tasks. Test your methods in a Java application program.

1. Convert a temperature in degrees Fahrenheit to degrees Celsius.

2. Find x^y, where x is a real value and y is an integer value.

3. Calculate $tan(\theta)$, for some angle θ in degrees.

4. Find the inverse $(1/x)$ of any real value x.

5. Find the maximum of two integer values.

6. Find the minimum of two integer values.

7. Examine a range of values, and return the Boolean value true if a value is within the range and false if the value is outside of the range.

8. Find your bank balance at the end of any given month for some initial deposit value and interest rate. Define the number of months, deposit, and interest rate variables in *main()* and pass them to your method.

9. Display your name, class, instructor, and hour. To display your name and instructor, the method must accept a string object. To make the method accept a string, you simply provide a string object as a parameter in your method

signature. For example, suppose that you define a string object in *main()* to hold your name, as follows:

String name = "Andy";

To receive this string object from *main()*, you simply repeat the string object definition in your method signature, like this:

static void display(String name, ...

Of course, parameters for the instructor's name and class hour must be added to the signature. To call the method, simply pass the required string objects as arguments to the method like this:

display(name, ...

10. Cause the cursor on the display to skip a given number of lines, where the number of lines to be skipped is passed to the method.

More Difficult

Use methods to solve the following problems 11–14:

11. Revise the payroll program you developed for Ma and Pa in problem 8 of Chapter 5 to employ methods. Recall that the payroll program will calculate Herb's net pay given the following information:

> Employee's name
> Number of weekly hours worked
> Hourly rate of pay
> FICA (7.15%)
> Federal withholding (28%)
> State withholding (10%)

Ma or Pa will be required to enter only the first three items when running the program. The program must generate a report using the following format:

> Employee Name: XXXXXXXXXXXXXXXXXXXXX

Rate of Pay:	$XXXXX
Hours Worked:	XXXXX
Gross Pay:	$XXXXX
Deductions:	
FICA	$XXXXX
Federal withholding	$XXXXX
State withholding	$XXXXX

Total Deductions	$XXXXX
Net Pay:	$XXXXX

12. Find the height at which the ladder in Figure 8-6 makes contact with the wall, given the length of the ladder and the distance the base of the ladder is from the wall.

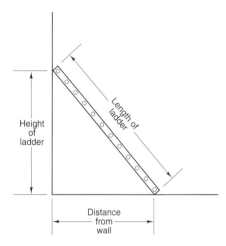

Figure 8-6   A ladder for problem 12.

Most Difficult

13. Table 8-3 provides the 1997 federal income tax schedule for single tax payers. Write a program that calculates the federal income tax, given the taxable income from the user. Use three methods: one to obtain the taxable income from the user, one to calculate the income tax, and one to display the taxable income and corresponding income tax.

TABLE 8-3 1997 FEDERAL TAXABLE INCOME RATES FOR SINGLE TAX PAYERS

If the amount on Form 1040 line 38, is: *Over ---*	*But not over*	Enter on Form 1040, line 39		*of the amount over -*
$0	$24,650		15%	**$0**
24,650	59,750	**3,697.50 +**	**28%**	**24,650**
59,750	124,650	**13,525.50 +**	**31%**	**59,750**
124,650	271,050	**33,644.50 +**	**36%**	**124,650**
271,050		**86,348.50 +**	**39.6%**	**271,050**

14. McJava's coffee shop sells expresso coffee for $1.25 a cup, bagels for $1.50 and Danish pastries for $2.25. Write a cash register program to compute a customer's bill. Use methods to obtain the quantity of each item ordered, calculate the subtotal of the bill, calculate the total cost of the bill, including a 7% sales tax, and display an itemized bill as follows:

Item	Quantity	Price
Coffee	3	$3.75
Bagels	2	$3.00
Danish	1	$2.25
Sub total		$9.00
Sales Tax		$ .63
Total		$9.63

GUI 108: MENUS AND FONT CONTROL

- *To become familiar with menus.*
- *To understand the purpose of a menu bar.*
- *To learn how to add menu items to a menu.*
- *To learn how to add menus to a menu bar.*
- *To understand the logic required to process menu events.*
- *To demonstrate and experiment with font control.*
- *To learn how to set the foreground and background color of a text area.*

Introduction

A ***menu*** consists of a set of selectable options located at the top of a window within a ***menu bar***. Menus are widely used in window applications because they make selection easier and do not clutter up the GUI. Menus are created in Java by creating menu objects. Selectable options are added to the menu object and the menu is added to a menu bar object, which is set on a frame. Thus, a frame is a container for a menu bar, which is a container for one or more menus.

Java allows you to control the ***font*** within a text component. A font consists of a ***font name***, ***font style***, and ***font size***. The font name is the type of font, such as Courier, Helvetica, or Times Roman. There are literally hundreds of different font types available within the computer industry. The font types that are available for a given Java program are those that are supported within the host operating environment. As long as the host operating environment, like Windows 98® or Mac, supports it, a given font type is available to a Java program running within that environment. The font style can be either plain, *italic*, or **bold**. In addition ***bold-italic*** can be generated by combining **bold** with *italic*. The font size is measured in points, where one point is approximately 1/72 of an inch. For example, the font that you are now reading is Times Roman, plain, 11 point. Java allows you to set the font name, style, and size within a text component, such as a text area.

In this module, you will load and execute a program that produces a menu bar with a font menu. The font menu will allow you to set the font type for any text displayed within a text area. You will experiment with the menu by selecting different font types and observing the selected font within a text area. You will also create an additional font type and add it to the menu. Then, you will experiment with different styles and sizes of font. Finally, you will experiment with setting the foreground and background color of a text area.

Procedure

1. Load and execute the *GUI108_1.java* program contained on the CD that accompanies this book, or download it from www.prenhall.com. You should see a window similar to the one shown in Figure 1. At the top of the window you see a menu bar with a *Font type* menu. A text area appears in the middle of the window.

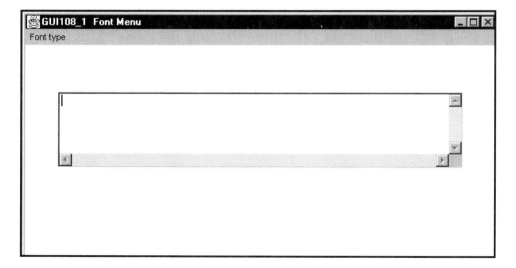

Figure 1 A frame with a single menu and text area.

2. Click on the *Font type* menu and notice that is drops down, providing several selectable menu items. Click on any of the font types and observe the font displayed within the text area. The selected font will be displayed along with a message that indicates the name, style, and size of the font being displayed. Also notice that once a given font is selected, the menu disappears.

3. Select the *Font type* menu again with your mouse, then use the up/down arrow keys on your keyboard to highlight a given font type. Press the **ENTER** key to select the highlighted font.

Here is the class code that produced the GUI in Figure 1 and processes a menu event:

```
1    class FontMenu extends FrameWithClose implements ActionListener
2    {
3
4      //DEFINE TEXT AREA OBJECT
5      private TextArea textArea = new TextArea(5,70);
6
7      //CONSTRUCTOR
8      public FontMenu(String Title)
9      {
10     //CALL SUPERCLASS CONSTRUCTOR
11     super(Title);
12
13     //SET FRAME LAYOUT MANAGER
14     setLayout(new FlowLayout(FlowLayout.CENTER,10,60));
15
16     //DEFINE MENU OBJECT
17     Menu fontTypeMenu = new Menu("Font type");
18
19     //ADD ITEMS TO FONT TYPE MENU
20     fontTypeMenu.add(new MenuItem("Courier"));
21     fontTypeMenu.add(new MenuItem("Helvetica"));
22     fontTypeMenu.add(new MenuItem("Times Roman"));
23
24     //DEFINE MENU BAR OBJECT
25     MenuBar bar = new MenuBar();
26
27     //ADD MENU TO MENU BAR
28     bar.add(fontTypeMenu);
29
30     //SET MENU BAR
31     setMenuBar(bar);
32
33     //ADD TEXT AREA TO FRAME
34     add(textArea);
35
```

```
36    //REGISTER LISTENERS
37     fontTypeMenu.addActionListener(this);
38    }//END FontMenu()
39
40    //PROCESS MENU EVENT
41    public void actionPerformed(ActionEvent e)
42    {
43     //DID MENU CAUSE EVENT?
44     if (e.getSource() instanceof MenuItem)
45     {
46      //GET MENU ITEM SELECTED
47      String item = e.getActionCommand();
48
49      //CHECK FOR COURIER ITEM
50      if (item.equals("Courier"))
51      {
52       //CREATE NEW COURIER FONT OBJECT
53       Font newFont = new Font("Courier",Font.PLAIN,12);
54       //SET TEXT AREA TO NEW FONT
55       textArea.setFont(newFont);
56       //DISPLAY NEW FONT IN TEXT AREA
57       textArea.setText("\n\nTHE FONT IS NOW:\n" + newFont.toString());
58      }//END IF COURIER
59
60      //CHECK FOR HELVETICA ITEM
61      if (item.equals("Helvetica"))
62      {
63       //CREATE NEW HELVETICA FONT OBJECT
64       Font newFont = new Font("Helvetica",Font.PLAIN,12);
65       //SET TEXT AREA TO NEW FONT
66       textArea.setFont(newFont);
67       //DISPLAY NEW FONT IN TEXT AREA
68       textArea.setText("\n\nTHE FONT IS NOW:\n" + newFont.toString());
69      }//END IF HELVETICA
70
71      //CHECK FOR TIMES ROMAN ITEM
72      if (item.equals("Times Roman"))
73      {
74       //CREATE NEW TIMES ROMAN FONT OBJECT
75       Font newFont = new Font("TimesRoman",Font.PLAIN,12);
76       //SET TEXT AREA TO NEW FONT
77       textArea.setFont(newFont);
```

```
78        //DISPLAY NEW FONT IN TEXT AREA
79        textArea.setText("\n\nTHE FONT IS NOW:\n" + newFont.toString());
80      }//END IF TIMES ROMAN
81
82
83
84
85
86
87
88
89
90
91      }//END IF MENU ITEM
92    }//END actionPerformed()
93  }//END FontMenu CLASS
```

4. You see that a font menu object called *fontTypeMenu* is defined in line 17. The menu title appears in quotation marks within the object definition. Look at lines 20-22 and you will see the selectable menu items being added to the *fontTypeMenu* object. In line 23, add a "Bookman" font to the menu object using the same syntax you see in lines 20-22.

5. Execute the program again, click the menu, and notice that the *Bookman* option appears at the bottom of the menu. Select the *Bookman* font type. What? It isn't displayed within the text area? Why?

6. Look at lines 43-80 in the program. This is where the menu items are processed as part of the *actionPerformed()* method. Notice that once a menu item event is detected in line 44, a series of nested **if** statements are used to determine which menu item was selected and to set the text area font accordingly. However, we have not added any code to process the *Bookman* menu item. Add the following statements in lines 81-90:

```
//CHECK FOR BOOKMAN ITEM
if (item.equals("Bookman"))
{
    //CREATE NEW BOOKMAN FONT OBJECT
    Font newFont = new Font("Bookman",Font.PLAIN,12);
    //SET TEXT AREA TO NEW FONT
    textArea.setFont(newFont);
    //DISPLAY NEW FONT IN TEXT AREA
    textArea.setText("\n\nTHE FONT IS NOW:\n" + newFont.toString());
}//END IF BOOKMAN
```

7. Execute the program again and select the *Bookman* menu item. You should see it is reflected in the text area.

8. Notice that within each menu item **if** statement, there is a statement that creates a *newFont* object. This statement sets the font name to the type of font selected in the menu. In addition, the font style and font size are set within this statement. For example, notice that in line 53, the *newFont* object is set to "Courier," with a style of plain, and a size of 12 points. Then, in line 55 the text area is set with the *newFont* object by calling the *setFont()* method . This changes the font of the text area to the font selected on the menu. Now, change the style and/or size of any font within its respective *newFont* object definition statement. To change the font style you must use the syntax Font.PLAIN, Font.ITALIC, or Font.BOLD. Note that there is a dot between the word Font and its style. The style must be in all caps.

9. Execute the program again, click the menu items whose font style and/or size you changed and observe the changes within the text area.

10. Change one of the font styles to Font.BOLD + Font.ITALIC.

11. Execute the program again and select the font the you changed. Observe the style of this font is now ***bold-italic***.

Discussion

A menu is a GUI component located at the top a window that contains several user-selectable menu items. A menu bar is a container for menus. Menu objects are created with the *Menu* class and menu bar objects are created using the *MenuBar* class. Once a menu object is created, items are added to the menu using the *MenuItem* class. A menu is made part of a frame by adding the menu object to a menu bar object using the *add()* method, then setting the menu bar object to the frame using the *setMenuBar()* method. Menu events are processed by adding a listener for the menu object and handling the event within the *actionPerformed()* method.

Font objects are created using the *Font* class. A font object has three characteristics: its name, or type, its style, and its size. The font name can be any type of font supported by the operating environment. The font style can be either plain, **bold**, *italic*, or ***bold-italic***. The font size can be any reasonable value and is measured in points, where one point is approximately 1/72 of an inch. Once a font object is created, it can be applied to a text component such as a text field or text area using the *setFont()* method.

Procedure (continued)

12. Load and execute the *GUI108_2*.java program contained on the CD that accompanies this book, or download it from www.prenhall.com. You should see a window similar to the one shown in Figure 2. This window contains two menus and a text area.

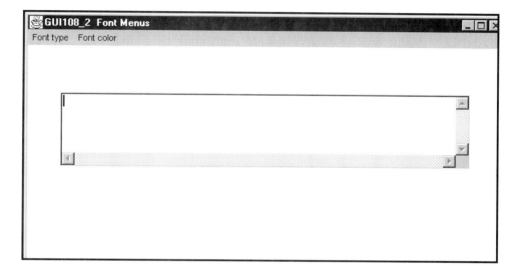

Figure 2 A frame with two menus and a text area.

13. Select a font from the *Font type* menu, then select a color from the *Font color* menu. You should find that the text displayed in the text area reflects the font type and color that you selected from the two menus.
14. Select a different font color from the *Font color* menu and notice that the text reflects the selected color.

Here is the class code that produced the GUI in Figure 2 and processes the two menus:

```
1   class FontColorMenu extends FrameWithClose implements ActionListener
2   {
3
4       //DEFINE TEXT AREA OBJECT
5       private TextArea textArea = new TextArea(5,70);
6
```

```
7    //CONSTRUCTOR
8    public FontColorMenu(String Title)
9    {
10   //CALL SUPERCLASS CONSTRUCTOR
11   super(Title);
12
13   //SET FRAME LAYOUT MANAGER
14   setLayout(new FlowLayout(FlowLayout.CENTER,10,60));
15
16   //DEFINE MENU OBJECTS
17   Menu fontTypeMenu = new Menu("Font type");
18   Menu fontColorMenu = new Menu("Font color");
19
20   //ADD ITEMS TO FONT TYPE MENU
21   fontTypeMenu.add(new MenuItem("Courier"));
22   fontTypeMenu.add(new MenuItem("Helvetica"));
23   fontTypeMenu.add(new MenuItem("Times Roman"));
24
25   //ADD ITEMS TO FONT COLOR MENU
26   fontColorMenu.add(new MenuItem("Red"));
27   fontColorMenu.add(new MenuItem("Blue"));
28   fontColorMenu.add(new MenuItem("Green"));
29   fontColorMenu.add(new MenuItem("Black"));
30
31
32   //DEFINE MENU BAR OBJECT
33   MenuBar bar = new MenuBar();
34
35   //ADD MENUS TO MENU BAR
36   bar.add(fontTypeMenu);
37   bar.add(fontColorMenu);
38
39   //SET MENU BAR
40   setMenuBar(bar);
41
42   //ADD TEXT AREA TO FRAME
43   add(textArea);
44
45   //REGISTER LISTENERS
46   fontTypeMenu.addActionListener(this);
47   fontColorMenu.addActionListener(this);
48   }//END FontColorMenu()
49
```

```
50    //PROCESS MENU EVENT
51    public void actionPerformed(ActionEvent e)
52    {
53     //DID MENU CAUSE EVENT?
54     if (e.getSource() instanceof MenuItem)
55     {
56      //GET MENU ITEM SELECTED
57      String item = e.getActionCommand();
58
59      //FIND COLOR ITEM AND CHANGE FOREGROND COLOR
60      if (item.equals("Red"))
61       textArea.setForeground(Color.red);
62      if (item.equals("Blue"))
63       textArea.setForeground(Color.blue);
64      if (item.equals("Green"))
65       textArea.setForeground(Color.green);
66      if (item.equals("Black"))
67       textArea.setForeground(Color.black);
68
69
70
71
72      //CHECK FOR COURIER ITEM
73      if (item.equals("Courier"))
74      {
75        //CREATE NEW COURIER FONT OBJECT
76        Font newFont = new Font("Courier",Font.PLAIN,12);
77        //SET TEXT AREA TO NEW FONT
78        textArea.setFont(newFont);
79        //DISPLAY NEW FONT IN TEXT AREA
80        textArea.setText("\n\nTHE FONT IS NOW:\n" + newFont.toString());
81      }//END IF COURIER
82
83      //CHECK FOR HELVETICA ITEM
84      if (item.equals("Helvetica"))
85      {
86        //CREATE NEW HELVETICA FONT OBJECT
87        Font newFont = new Font("Helvetica",Font.PLAIN,12);
88        //SET TEXT AREA TO NEW FONT
89        textArea.setFont(newFont);
90        //DISPLAY NEW FONT IN TEXT AREA
91        textArea.setText("\n\nTHE FONT IS NOW:\n" + newFont.toString());
92      }//END IF HELVETICA
```

```
93      //CHECK FOR TIMES ROMAN ITEM
94      if (item.equals("Times Roman"))
95      {
96        //CREATE NEW TIMES ROMAN FONT OBJECT
97        Font newFont = new Font("TimesRoman",Font.PLAIN,12);
98        //SET TEXT AREA TO NEW FONT
99        textArea.setFont(newFont);
100       //DISPLAY NEW FONT IN TEXT AREA
101       textArea.setText("\n\nTHE FONT IS NOW:\n" + newFont.toString());
102     }//END IF TIMES ROMAN
103    }//END IF MENU ITEM
104   }//END actionPerformed()
105 }//END FontColorMenu CLASS
```

There are 13 different colors available in the Java *Color* class, as follows:

- black
- blue
- cyan
- darkGray
- gray
- green
- lightGray
- magenta
- orange
- pink
- red
- white
- yellow

15. Add a new color to the *Font color* menu in line 30, using syntax similar to that which you see in lines 26-29.

16. Execute the program again and select a font from the *Font type* menu. Now select the *Font color* menu and notice that the color you added appears at the bottom of the menu. Select the new color. Why didn't the text in the text area reflect the new color? You're right! We have not added any logic to process the new color in the *actionPerformed()* method.

17. Add an **if** statement in lines 68-69 similar to those you see in lines 60-67 to process your new color.

18. Execute the program again, select a font type and your new font color. Notice that the text in the text area now reflects your new font color.
19. Change line 67 as follows:

    textArea.setBackground(Color.black);

20. Execute the program again and select a font from the *Font type* menu. Now select "Black" from the *Font color* menu. Notice that the *background* of the text area changes from white to black.

Discussion

The foreground and background color of a frame button, text field, or text area component can be set using any of the 13 colors available in the Java *Color* class. The foreground of a component object is set using the *setForeground()* method, while its background is set using the *setBackground()* method. The default foreground color is black, while the default background color is white.

CLASSES AND OBJECTS IN-DEPTH

INTRODUCTION

This chapter will introduce you to the important topic of object-oriented programming (OOP) and is intended to prepare you for further study of the topic.

With object-oriented programming, you construct complex programs from simpler program entities called *objects*, which are real instances, or specimens, of abstract *classes*. Object-oriented programs are organized as a collection of objects that cooperate with each other. Thus, object-oriented programming employs objects, rather than algorithms, as the fundamental building blocks for program development.

Object-oriented programming facilitates the extension and reuse of general-purpose classes in new applications with minimal modification to the original code. Although this can be accomplished with ordinary methods in algorithmic programming, OOP provides an important feature called *inheritance*, which is a mechanism for deriving new classes from existing ones. As a result, classes are related to each other to create a hierarchy of classes through inheritance. This inheritance feature also allows new applications to "inherit" code from existing applications, thereby making the programming chore much more productive.

In summary, the goals of OOP are to improve programmer productivity by managing software complexity via the use of classes and their associated objects that provide for reusable code via the class inheritance feature.

Up to this point you have been learning how to construct programs using a modular approach based on methods. This has been a top-down design strategy. Although the overall design of any software is a top-down process, writing object-oriented programs requires a different approach. You create object-oriented programs from the inside out by expanding on classes. For example, you might approach a banking problem by creating a bank account class that defines the basic data that all accounts must contain (account number, balance, etc.) as well as the fundamental operations that are performed on bank accounts (deposit, withdrawal, etc.). This basic bank account class can then be expanded into classes that define specific types of bank accounts, such as checking accounts, super-now accounts, savings accounts, and so on.

There are four concepts central to OOP: *encapsulation with information hiding*, *inheritance*, *polymorphism*, and *dynamic binding*. You have already had experience with polymorphism when you learned about overloaded methods. In this chapter, you will be exposed to the idea of encapsulation and information hiding. The next chapter is devoted entirely to inheritance. The concept of dynamic binding is beyond the scope of this text and, as a result, will only be covered lightly in the next chapter.

Object-oriented programming has its own unique terminology. Be sure to grasp the terminology as you progress through the chapter. A glossary of OOP terms is provided at the end of this text for quick reference.

OBJECTIVES

When you are finished with this chapter, you should have a good understanding of the following:

- How to construct your own Java classes and objects.
- Classes at the abstract as well as the implementation level.
- Encapsulation and information hiding.
- Private versus public class members.
- Constructor and access methods.
- Overloaded constructor methods.
- Scoping inside methods.
- How to develop your own class packages.

9-1 CLASSES AND OBJECTS

A thorough understanding of classes and objects is essential to developing object-oriented code. You have been working with the standard Java classes and objects since Chapter 2, so you should now have a good feeling for the class/object concept. It is now time to learn how to create your own classes and objects that provide all the ADT characteristics of the standard classes. Before we get into the details, let's reinforce your class/object knowledge with a real-world example of how they might be used in a commercial program.

The Idea of Classes and Objects

For now, you can think of a class as a model, or pattern, for its objects. If you have used a word processor, you are aware that most word processing programs include templates for business letters, personal letters, interoffice memos, press releases, etc. (*Note*: Be aware that OOP uses the term *template* in a different sense than it is used here in word processing.) The idea is to first open one of the built-in general-purpose template files when you want to generate, let's say, an interoffice memo. An example of such a template is provided in Figure 9-1.

As you can see, the template provides the accepted interoffice memo formatting, the memo type style, and any fixed information, such as headings and the date. Using this template, you fill in all the *object* information required for the memo, including the text of the memo as shown in Figure 9-2.

InterOffice Memo

To:	Recipient
From:	Sender
Date:	May 16, 1999
Subject:	The Subject of the Memo

CC:

Figure 9-1 A *class* can be thought of as a model, or pattern, like this memo template in a word processor.

InterOffice Memo

To:	All Java Students
From:	Prof. Andrew C. Staugaard, Jr.
Date:	January 5, 1999
Subject:	Classes and Objects

This memo represents an object of the class shown in Figure 9-1. The class provides a general framework from which objects are created. It is important that you understand this concept.

CC:
    Your Instructor

Figure 9-2 An *object* is a particular instance, or specimen, of a class, as this memo is an instance of the memo template of Figure 9-1.

In other words, you provide the details that might make one memo different from another. You can think of a class as the memo template and the actual memo that you generate as an object of that template. Different memos made from the same memo template would represent unique objects of the same class. The class template provides the framework for each of its object memos. All the object memos would have the same general format and type style defined by the class template but would have different text information defined by a given object memo. You could load in another template file, let's say for a business letter, that would represent a different class. Then using this template, you could construct different object business letters from the business letter template.

The word *class* in OOP is used to impart the notion of classification. Objects defined for a class share the fundamental framework of the class. Thus, the class is common to the set of objects defined for it. In the preceding example, the interoffice memo template defines the characteristics that are common to all interoffice memos created by the word processor. In fact, many current word processing programs employ classes and objects for this purpose. A given class provides the foundation for creating specific objects, each of which shares the general *attributes*, or *characteristics*, and *behavior* of the class.

> A class provides the foundation for creating specific objects, each of which shares the general **attributes**, or **characteristics**, and **behavior** of the class.

As you can see from this example, classes and objects are closely related. In fact, it is difficult to discuss one without the other. The important difference is that a class is only an **abstraction**, or pattern, whereas an object is a real entity. The interoffice memo class is only an abstraction for the real memo object that can be physically created, printed, and mailed. As another example, think of a class of fish. The fish class describes the general characteristics and behavior of all fish. However, the notion of a fish only provides an abstraction of the real thing. To deal with the real thing, you must consider specific fish objects such as a Charlie the tuna, or my goldfish Skippy, and so on. A fish, in general, behaves as you would expect a fish to behave but a particular *instance* of a fish has its own unique behavior and personality.

Classes

In order to completely understand the nature of a class, we must consider two levels of definition: the **abstract** level and the **implementation** level.

The Abstract Level

The abstract level of a class provides the outside view of the class, without concern for the inner structure and workings of the class. Here's how we define a class at the abstract level.

> At the abstract level, a ***class*** can be described as an *interface* that defines the behavior of its objects.

An ***interface*** is something that forms a common boundary, or barrier, between two systems. The interface for a class is provided by its methods. The method signatures of a class define how data must be presented to the class. At the abstract level, all you need to be concerned about are the method interfaces, or signatures, and not the inner workings of the class. A good analogy to this idea would be the postal system. You do not have to know how the postal system works to mail a letter and get it to its destination. All you need to know is how to present the required data (address and a stamp) and place the letter in a mail box. The postal system defines how the letter must be addressed (data presentation) just as the method signatures of a class define how data must be presented to the class. The class methods also define the behavior of the class through their designated operations. In this way, we say a class defines the behavior common to all of its objects. By behavior, we mean how an object of a given class acts and reacts when it is accessed via one of its methods.

The abstract view of a class as an interface provides its *outside* view while hiding its internal structure and behavioral details. Thus, an object of a given class can be viewed as a black box, as shown in Figure 9-3. As you can see, the operation, or method, interface provides a communications channel to and from the class object. The application program generates an operation request to the object, and the object responds with the desired result. The interface dictates *what* must be supplied to the object and *how* the object will respond. As a result, a class, through its operation interfaces, defines how its objects will behave. At the client application level, you treat the class object as a black box because you do not care about what goes on inside the object. All you care about is how to work with the object.

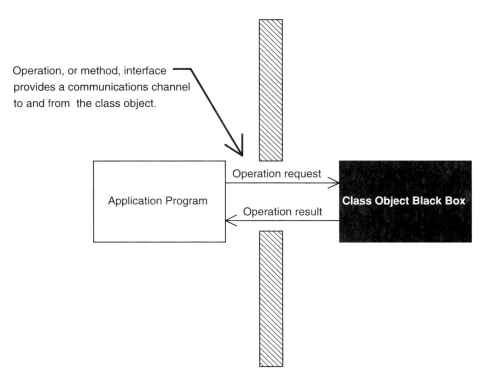

Operation, or method, interface provides a communications channel to and from the class object.

Application Program

Operation request

Operation result

Class Object Black Box

Figure 9-3 At the abstract level, a class is an interface that defines the behavior of its objects.

The Implementation Level

The class implementation provides its *inside* view, showing the secrets of its data organization and method implementation. As a result, the class implementation reveals the secrets of its behavior, because it is primarily concerned with the operations that define the abstract level, or interface.

At the implementation level, a ***class*** is a syntactical unit that describes a set of data and related operations that are common to its objects.

The implementation of a class consists of two types of ***members***: (1) ***data members*** and (2) ***method members***. Any item declared in a class is called a class ***member***. Consequently, to implement a class we create data members and method members.

The Data Members

The data members of the class provide the class attributes, or characteristics. The data members of the class are usually the variables defined within the class. We say that these members are "private" because they are *accessible only by the method members declared for the class*. This means that the data members can be changed only by the method members in the class.

The Method Members

The method members of the class consist of methods that operate on the data members of the class. These methods are usually "public" because they can be accessed anywhere within the scope of a given class. In other words, method members can be called from outside the class, as long as the class is visible at the time of access. As you might suspect, it is the public method members that form the interface and exhibit the behavior of the class objects.

There is nothing special about public member methods, except that they are used to operate on the data members of the class. The important thing to remember is that *no methods outside a given class can access the private data members of the class*.

The Class Declaration

The implementation level of a class can be clearly seen by its declaration format, as follows:

CLASS DECLARATION FORMAT

```
class class name
{
   //DATA MEMBERS
   private data type  variable 1;
   private data type  variable 2;
              .
   private data type  variable n;
```

```
        //METHOD MEMBERS
        public return type  method 1 name (method 1 parameter listing)
        {
                //METHOD 1 STATEMENTS
        }

        public return type  method 2 name (method 2 parameter listing)
        {
                //METHOD 2 STATEMENTS
        }

                                •
                                •
                                •

        public return type  method n name (method n parameter listing)
        {
                //METHOD n STATEMENTS
        }

    } //END CLASS
```

The declaration begins with the keyword **class**, followed by the class name. The class name should be a noun or a noun phrase that is descriptive of its purpose. The first letter of each word within the name should be capitalized. The entire class declaration is enclosed in a set of curly braces. Normally, the data members of the class are specified first, followed by the method members of the class. The data members of the class consist of *private instance variables*. An instance variable is a variable that will be created for any given object of the class. Each instance variable is prefixed with the keyword **private**. A private member of a class is visible within that class and, therefore, can only be accessed by methods within the class. The method members of the class consist of **public** and **private** *instance methods*. An instance method is a method that will be available to any given object of the class. To declare a method as a class member, you list the method signature, followed by the code for the method. The access modifier for a class method is usually **public**. Public methods form the interface to the class, because they can be accessed, or called, from outside the class. Methods can also be **private** but then they are only accessible within the class and cannot be called outside the class. Such methods are referred to as *utility methods*, since they are often used within the class to perform housekeeping, or utility, operations.

A **private** class member is only accessible within the class by methods of the same class. The **public** class methods form the interface to the class and are accessible from outside the class. Public methods are used to provide access to and manipulate the private class members.

The diagram in Figure 9-4 illustrates the idea of the **public** class methods providing the interface, or boundary, to access the **private** class members. The data members of a class should always be designated as **private**. Why? Because making the data members private enforces *encapsulation* with *information hiding*.

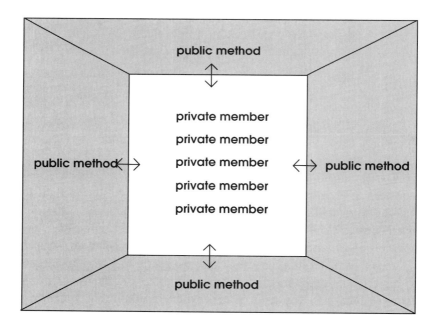

Figure 9-4 The **private** class members can only be accessed via the **public** class methods, which provide the interface, or boundary, of the class.

Encapsulation and Information Hiding

Encapsulation is simply the idea of packaging things together in a well-defined programming unit. A record, or table, in a database program is encapsulated because it is a collection of data that are combined into a well-defined unit, the record, or table. The class in Java obviously provides for encapsulation by packaging both data and methods into a single class unit.

> **Encapsulation** means to package data and/or operations into a single well-defined programming unit.

The idea of encapsulation can be enhanced with **information hiding**.

> **Information hiding** means that there is a binding relationship between the information, or data, and its related operations so that operations outside the encapsulated unit cannot affect the information inside the unit.

With information hiding, there is a *binding* relationship between the information and the operations that are performed on that information. The class provides for information hiding in Java. The public methods provide the class interface that is accessible from outside the class, and the private data members provide the information that is accessible only from within the class itself. Only the methods declared for the class can operate on the private class members. Thus, the private data members of a class provide the information hiding. Without encapsulation and information hiding, there is no such binding relationship. In programming languages that do not support information hiding, you define data structures and the code that operates on those data structures separately. Then, you place both in a single source code file while attempting to treat the data and code as separate modules within the file. Although such an approach seems reasonable, it can create problems. Because there is no defined, or explicit, binding relationship between the data and the code, another programmer could write methods to access and inadvertently change the data.

For instance, suppose that you are writing a program for a bank that calculates bank account interest. To write such a program, you would define an account balance variable, among others, and write methods to change the balance based on deposits, withdrawals, interest earned, and so on. These methods would be written according to the policies dictated by the bank—and the government, for that matter. Would you want another programmer to be able to write methods that would affect the account balances differently than yours? Even worse, would you want the transactions of one account to affect the balance of another account? Of course not!

With information hiding, you can truly separate the account data and the methods operating on those data into two separate categories, private and public but bind them tightly together in an encapsulated class unit. Only public methods can operate on the private account data. This means that outside methods written by another programmer cannot corrupt the data. Thus, only the operations that you have defined for a given type of account can be applied to that type of account and no others. In addition, these same operations applied to one account cannot affect another account of the same type. The class dictates the data format and legal operations for all accounts of a given type. Then, individual accounts of the same type are created as objects of the account class. A class in Java inherently enforces information hiding.

There is a cost, however. You must use a method call to access the private data. This reduces the efficiency of the code slightly. On the other hand, using the compiler to enforce the rules that relate data to code can pay off in a big way when it comes time to debug a large program. In addition, object-oriented code is much easier to maintain because the classes and their objects closely match the application. Finally, once object-oriented code is developed for a given application program, it can be easily reused in another program that has a similar application. Consider a windows program. All windowing programs employ the same window classes. To create a new windows application program, you simply "inherit" the general window classes and customize them to the new application.

The ideas of encapsulation and information hiding are not new. Only languages like Ada, Modula II, C++, and Java, which easily and efficiently provide for encapsulation and information hiding, are new. These concepts have been around as long as computers. Common examples of information hiding include those data and routines that are part of BIOS to control a PC keyboard, monitor, and file access. Also, the file handling routines built into most compilers employ information hiding. Imagine what would happen if you could inadvertently corrupt these data and routines (system crash, lost unrecoverable files, etc.). You can use these built-in routines just by knowing how to operate them but you cannot get at the inner workings of the routines. Likewise, you can operate your CD player via its controls without worrying about the inner workings of the player. Imagine what might happen if a nontechnical user could get to the inner workings of your CD player. This is why it is so important to think of a class in the abstract sense of an interface.

You should be aware that some texts equate encapsulation with information hiding. However, remember that encapsulation does not necessarily relate to information hiding. Each language permits various parts of a programming entity to be accessible to the outside world. Those parts that are not visible to the outside world represent the information hiding aspect of encapsulation. COBOL records, for example, are encapsulated and permit all member data to be visible and manipulated by outside operations and, therefore, do not provide any information hiding. Java classes are encapsulated, but in addition, provide information hiding through the private members of the class.

Now, let's declare our first class. Suppose you are working for a bank, and they want you to convert an old COBOL program to a Java application program. The program is a savings account program that contains an account balance and account interest rate. The operations within that program allow the user to add deposits, subtract withdrawals, add interest, and report the current balance.

The first thing you should do when writing an object-oriented program is to develop a problem statement and look for the nouns and verbs within the statement. The nouns will suggest classes as well as data members for those classes. The verbs will suggest methods, or interfaces, for the classes. Here is the foregoing problem statement again, with the applicable noun and verb phases underlined.

"Convert an old COBOL program to a Java application program. The program is a <u>savings account</u> program that contains an <u>account balance</u> and <u>account interest rate</u>. The program allows the user to <u>add deposits</u>, <u>subtract withdrawals</u>, <u>add interest</u>, and <u>report the current balance</u>."

Now, there are three noun phrases: *savings account*, *account balance*, and *account interest*. Do you see a hierarchy within these? Of course, the main noun phrase is *savings account*. The other two, *account balance* and *account interest*, are part of the *savings account*, right? Thus, the class will be a savings account class, which includes data members of account balance and account interest.

The four verb phrases within the problem statement are: *add deposits*, *subtract withdrawals*, *add interest*, and *report balance*. Each of these phrases suggests an action to be performed on the account data and therefore will form the method members of the class. So, here is the class specification:

    Class: *SavingsAccount*
      Data Members: *balance*
                interestRate

Method Members: *addDeposit()*
                 subtractWithdrawal()
                 addInterest()
                 currentBalance()

This class specification is depicted by the diagram in Figure 9-5. An arrow pointing toward the private members indicates that the method is operating on one or more members, while an arrow pointing away from the private members indicates that the method is returning one or more of the private member values.

SavingsAccount Class

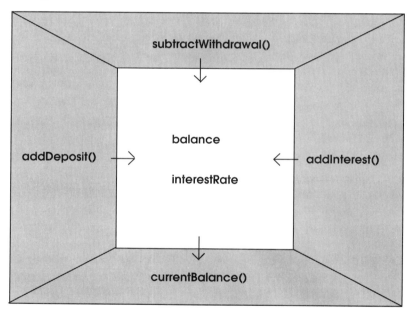

Figure 9-5   The *SavingsAccount* class consists of private *balance* and *interestRate* members and public *addDeposit()*, *subtractWithdrawal()*, *addInterest()*, and *currentBalance()* methods that form the class interface, or boundary.

Once you decide that class composition, the class can be easily coded as follows:

```
class SavingsAccount
{
 //DATA MEMBERS
 private double balance = 0.0;          //ACCOUNT BALANCE
 private double interestRate = 0.0;     //MONTHLY INTEREST RATE

 //METHOD MEMBERS

 //INITIALIZE PRIVATE DATA
 public void initialize(double bal, double rate)
 {
   balance = bal;
   interestRate = rate;
 }//END initialize()

 //ADD MONTHLY INTEREST
 public void addInterest()
 {
   balance = balance + balance * interestRate;
 }//END addInterest

 //ADD DEPOSIT
 public void addDeposit(double amount)
 {
   balance = balance + amount;
 } //END addDeposit()

 //SUBTRACT WITHDRAWAL
 public void subtractWithdrawal(double amount)
 {
   balance = balance - amount;
 }//END subtractWithdrawal()

 //RETURN BALANCE
 public double currentBalance()
 {
   return balance;
 }//END currentBalance()
} //END SavingsAccount
```

The class declaration begins with the keyword **class**, followed by our class name, *SavingsAccount*. Next, you find a listing of the private class members. There are two private floating-point members, *balance* and *interestRate,* each initialized with the value zero.

The method members follow the data members of the class. This class contains five public method members. All the methods operate on the private data members. The *initialize()* method initializes the private members to beginning values received from the calling program but does not return any data to the calling program. We have added this method so that the user can "set" the *balance* and *interestRate* variables. This is why such methods are often called *set methods*. Notice that this method has two parameters which are assigned to the private data members within the method. Because of encapsulation, this is the only way that the calling program can assign values to the private class members. Thus, the private class members cannot be arbitrarily changed. In addition, the method does not have any return type, since it is operating directly on the private members of the class. The *initialize()* method must be called to accomplish this task. The *addInterest()* method calculates a new balance from the current private member values and, therefore, does not require any parameters. The *addDeposit()* method adds an amount received from the calling program to the account balance. The amount to be added must be supplied as an argument when the method is called. The *subtractWithdraw()* method subtracts an amount received from the calling program from the account balance. The amount to be subtracted must be supplied as an argument when the method is called. Finally, the *currentBalance()* method returns the value of the account balance to the calling program. Again, because of encapsulation, this is the only way the *balance* can be accessed for reporting purposes. That's all there is to it! See how everything is nice and tight within the class structure. The class data define the attributes of the class while the class methods define the class behavior.

Example 9-1

Write class declarations for the following:

a. A rectangle class that consists of the rectangle length and width with methods to initialize the private members, calculate the perimeter of the rectangle, and calculate the area of the rectangle.

b. A circle class that consists of the circle radius with methods to initialize the private member, calculate the circumference of the circle, and calculate the area of the circle.

Solution

a. The rectangle class requires two private data members, *length* and *width*, and three public methods: *initialize()*, *perimeter()*, and *area()*. Here's the declaration:

```
class Rectangle
{
    //DATA MEMBERS
    private double length = 0.0;              //RECTANGLE LENGTH
    private double width  = 0.0;              //RECTANGLE WIDTH

    //METHOD MEMBERS
    public void initialize(float l, float w)  //INITIALIZE PRIVATE DATA
    {
      length = l;
      width = w;
    }//END initialize()

    public double perimeter()                 //RETURN PERIMETER
    {
      return 2*(length + width);
    }//END perimeter()

    public double area()                      //RETURN AREA
    {
      return length * width;
    }//END area()
} //END Rectangle
```

The *initialize()* method receives length and width values from the calling program. This method does not require any return type, because it is operating directly on the private members of the class. The *perimeter()* and *area()* methods do not receive any data from the calling program, but both will return floating-point values to the calling program. Because the private data and public methods are so tightly bound within the class, you *do not pass the private data to the public methods.*

PROGRAMMING NOTE

Remember, when method members of a class operate directly on private data members of the class, you *do not* pass the member data to the methods. The reason is that the method and data members are so tightly bound within the class that passing of class data is not necessary.

---

b. The circle class requires three public member methods: one to initialize the radius, one to calculate the circumference, and one to calculate the area. The only private member required is the circle radius. Here's the declaration:

```
class Circle
{
    //DATA MEMBERS
    private double radius = 0.0;      //CIRCLE RADIUS

    //METHOD MEMBERS
    public void initialize(double r)   //INITIALIZE PRIVATE DATA
    {
      radius = r;
    }//END initialize()

    public double circumference()  //RETURN CIRCUMFERENCE
    {
      return 2 * Math.PI * radius;
    }//END circumference()

    public double area()               //RETURN AREA
    {
      return Math.PI*radius*radius;
    }//END area()
}//END Circle
```

The *initialize()* method receives an initializing radius value from the calling program and doesn't return any values, because it is operating directly on the private data member. The *circumference()* and *area()* methods do not receive any parameters from the calling program but return the circumference and area of the circle, respectively. The single private member is the circle radius, which is declared as a double floating-point value.

STYLE TIP

When naming method members to be used in Java classes, you should use a verb when the purpose of the method is to perform some designated task and a noun when the method returns a value. For instance, in the foregoing example, the method that performs the initialization task of the private class members was named *initialize()*, and the method that returned the area of the rectangle and circle was named *area()*.

Objects

You should now have a pretty good handle on what an object is. Here is a technical definition for your reference.

> An ***object*** is an instance, or specimen, of a given class. An object of a given class has the structure and behavior defined by the class that is common to all objects of the same class.

An object is a real thing that can be manipulated in a program. An object must be defined for a user-defined class to use the class, just as an object must be defined for the standard **String** class to use the class. An object defined for a class has the structure and behavior dictated by the class which are common to all objects defined for the class. You see from the foregoing definition that an object is an "instance" of a class. The word *instance* means an example or specimen of something. In this case, you could say that an object is an example or specimen of a class. If you have a class of dogs, then my dog *Randy* is an example or specimen of a dog. The same idea applies between Java objects and classes.

Defining Objects

Here is the required object definition format:

FORMAT FOR DEFINING CLASS OBJECTS

class name object name **=** **new** *class name*(*constructor args.*)**;**

When defining objects, you simply list the object name after the class name, followed by an = symbol, the reserved word **new**, then the class name followed by any required constructor arguments. When the object is defined, memory is allocated to store the class for which the object is defined. Many different objects can be defined for a given class with each object made up of the data described by the class and responding to methods defined by the class. However, the private member data are hidden from one object to the next, even when multiple objects are defined for the same class. Objects are usually nouns. This means that they are persons, places, or things, like a *square* object for a *Rectangle* class, a *checkbook* object for a *BankAccount* class, and so on.

Example 9-2

Define a *square* object for a class called *Rectangle* and a *mySavings* object for a class called *SavingsAccount*.

Solution

The *square* object definition is

Rectangle square = **new** Rectangle();

The *mySavings* object definition is

SavingsAccount mySavings = **new** SavingsAccount();

Neither of these object definitions require any constructor arguments within the parentheses. You will learn all about constructors in the next section. Then, we will define objects that require constructor arguments.

Be aware that not all classes require objects to be instantiated in order to access the class methods. Remember the standard *Math* class in Java? You access methods of this class by referencing the class name as in *Math.sqrt(x)* rather than first creating an object and then using the object to access the class methods. However, our programmer-defined classes will always require that objects be defined for them.

 Quick Check

1. What do we mean when we say that a class defines the behavior of its objects?

2. True or false: Encapsulation ensures information hiding.

3. True or false: Private class members can be accessed only via public method members.

4. Combining data with the operations that are dedicated to manipulating the data so that outside operations cannot affect the data is known as _____.

5. True or false: A class is an encapsulated unit.

6. Information hiding is provided by the _____ members of a class.

7. The behavioral secrets of a class are revealed at the _____ level.

8. Write a class declaration for a checking account class that contains an account balance, minimum balance to avoid a check cashing charge, and a check cashing charge amount. The class must have provision to make a deposit, cash a check, and report the current balance.

In questions 9 – 11, assume that no constructor arguments are required.

9. Define an object called *myAccount* for the class in question 8.

10. Define an object called *pickUp* for a class called *Truck*.

11. Define an object called *convertible* for a class called *Automobile*.

9-2 CLASS METHODS

The method members of a class provide the interface to the class objects, because the private data within an object can only be manipulated by calling the public class methods. Recall that to include a member as part of a class declaration, you list the method signature followed by the method body, or **implementation**. Class methods are generally designated as **public** so they can be called from code outside their resident class. However, class methods can be **private** when they perform special "housekeeping" tasks for the class. Such tasks normally support the operation of a public method. Private class methods are referred to as **utility methods**. You will see an example of such a method shortly. Another type of class method that needs to be discussed is the **constructor method**.

Constructors

A constructor is a special class method that is used to initialize an object automatically when the object is defined. Although a constructor is a method used to initialize an object, it is often used to open files, call any special utility methods, and generally get an object ready for processing. In several previous examples, you have seen the *initialize()* method used to set the private class members to initial values. However, to set the values of a given object using this method, you would have to call the *initialize()* method someplace in the program code. The advantage of using a constructor is that the constructor method is called automatically when an object is defined for the class in which the constructor resides.

> A ***constructor*** is a special class method that is used to initialize an object automatically when the object is defined.

Here are the rules governing the creation and use of constructors:

- The name of the constructor is always the same as the name of the class.
- The constructor cannot have a return type, not even **void**.
- A class cannot have more than one constructor; however, the constructor is often overloaded.
- Constructors should *not* be developed for tasks other than to initialize an object for processing.

To illustrate how to set up a constructor, consider the following *Rectangle* class declaration:

```
class Rectangle
{
  //DATA MEMBERS
  private double length = 0.0;              //RECTANGLE LENGTH
  private double width = 0.0;               //RECTANGLE WIDTH

  //METHOD MEMBERS
  //CONSTRUCTOR
  public Rectangle(float l, float w)
  {
    length = l;
    width = w;
  }//END Rectangle()

  //PERIMETER METHOD
  public double perimeter()
  {
    return 2 * (length + width);            //RETURN PERIMETER
  }//END perimeter()

  //AREA METHOD
  public double area()
  {
    return length * width;                  //RETURN AREA
  }//END area()
} //END Rectangle
```

This is the declaration for the *Rectangle* class that you saw earlier, with one big difference: It includes a constructor. Here, the constructor is *Rectangle()*, which takes the place of the *initialize()* method that you observed earlier. Aside from the comment, you can recognize the constructor because it has the same name as the class and does not have any return type, not even **void**. The format of the *Rectangle()* constructor signature is illustrated in Figure 9-6.

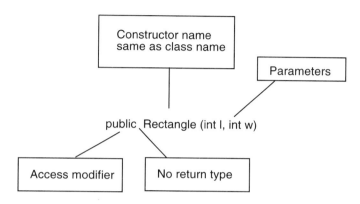

Figure 9-6   The format of a constructor signature.

The statement section of the *Rectangle()* constructor shows that the two private class members, *length* and *width*, are being initialized to the values received by the constructor parameters, *l* and *w*, respectively, just as in our former *initialize()* method.

Now, the next question is: How is the constructor called? Well, the reason for using a constructor over a regular method to initialize an object is that the constructor is called automatically when an object is defined. So, let's define two objects for the *Rectangle* class and therefore automatically call the constructor.

```
Rectangle  smallBox = new Rectangle(2,3);
Rectangle  largeBox = new Rectangle(10,20);
```

Here, *smallBox* and *largeBox* are defined as objects of the *Rectangle* class. Notice that two argument values are passed to each object. The *smallBox* object receives the argument values (2,3) and the *largeBox* receives the argument values (10,20). What do you suppose happens with these arguments? You're right; the argument values are passed to the constructor, which is automatically called to set the *length* and *width* of the *smallBox* object to 2 and 3, respectively. Likewise, the *length* and *width* of the *largeBox* object are initialized to the values 10 and 20, respectively. So, the idea is to list the constructor arguments in parentheses after the class name when the object is defined. This passes the arguments to the constructor, which is automatically called to perform its initializing task.

PROGRAMMING NOTE

In the foregoing *Rectangle* class example, the constructor was only used to initialize the private members, *length* and *width*, of the object. It was not used to calculate the perimeter or area of the object. Separate methods were developed for these tasks. Good practice dictates that constructors only be used initialize the object prior to additional processing by other object members.

Overloaded Constructors

Any method, even a constructor, can be overloaded. Recall from Chapter 8 that an overloaded method is one that performs different tasks depending on the number and/or type of arguments that it receives. Let's overload our *Rectangle()* constructor as follows:

```
class Rectangle
{
   //DATA MEMBERS
   private double length = 0.0;          //RECTANGLE LENGTH
   private double width = 0.0;           //RECTANGLE WIDTH

   //METHOD MEMBERS

   //CONSTRUCTORS
   //THIS CONSTRUCTOR REQUIRES NO ARGUMENTS
   public Rectangle()
   {
   } //END Rectangle()

   //CONSTRUCTOR FOR A SQUARE, REQUIRES ONE ARGUMENT
   public Rectangle(double s)
   {
      length = width = s;
   } //END Rectangle(double)
```

```
//CONSTRUCTOR FOR A RECTANGLE, REQUIRES TWO ARGUMENTS
public Rectangle(double l, double w)
{
   length = l;
   width = w;
}//END Rectangle(double,double)

//PERIMETER METHOD
public double perimeter()
{
   return 2 * (length + width);         //RETURN PERIMETER
}//END perimeter()

//AREA METHOD
public double area()
{
   return length * width;               //RETURN AREA
}//END area()
} //END Rectangle CLASS
```

You are probably thinking that there are three constructors in the foregoing declaration. No, there is a single constructor called *Rectangle()*, which is overloaded. You can tell that the *Rectangle()* constructor is overloaded, because it has three different sets of parameters. The first constructor does not have any parameters and, therefore, does not initialize the *length* and *width* members. Such a constructor is sometimes referred to as a ***parameterless constructor***. When this constructor is called, the *length* and *width* members each remain at their default values of 0. The second constructor is for a square and the third for a nonsquare rectangle. The square constructor sets the *length* and *width* members of the rectangle equal to the same value, *s*, that is received when the constructor is called. The nonsquare constructor sets the *length* and *width* to two different values, *l* and *w*, when the constructor is called. What determines which version of the constructor is used? Well, if an object is created with no arguments, the first version is executed. If an object is created with a single argument, the square constructor is executed. If an object is created with two arguments, the nonsquare version of the constructor is executed. Here are some sample object definitions:

```
Rectangle box1 = new Rectangle();        //box1 OBJECT DEF
Rectangle box2 = new Rectangle(2);       //box2 OBJECT DEF
Rectangle box3 = new Rectangle(3,4);     //box3 OBJECT DEF
```

Here, three objects, *box1*, *box2*, and *box3*, are defined. Notice that no argument is passed to *box1*, a single argument of 2 is passed to *box2*, and a double argument of 3,4 is passed to the *box3* object. What do you suppose happens? When the *box1* object is defined, the *length* and *width* remain at 0. When the *box2* object is defined, the second constructor is executed, setting the *length* and *width* of the *box2* object to the same value, 2. When the *box3* object is defined, the third constructor is executed, setting the *length* to 3 and the *width* to 4.

Scoping Inside Methods

There can be a problem using a constructor, or any class method for that matter, when the private member names are the same as the method parameter names. For instance, suppose that we declare a simple *Circle* class that contains a private member called *radius*. You then decide to use the *radius* name as a parameter for the constructor. Here is the appropriate class declaration:

```
class Circle
{
  //DATA MEMBERS
  private double radius;          //CIRCLE RADIUS

  //METHOD MEMBERS
  public Circle(double radius)    //CONSTRUCTOR
  {
     radius = radius;
  }//END Circle()
} //END Circle
```

The problem arises in the constructor implementation. The implementation will compile; however, it will initialize *radius* to garbage! Look at the statement within the constructor implementation and you will see ambiguity in the use of the *radius* name. It appears that *radius* is being assigned to itself. How does the compiler know what *radius* to use? Is *radius* the variable defined as the private class member, or is *radius* the value received by the constructor, or both? We must tell the compiler that the *radius* on the left side of the assignment operator is the private class member and the *radius* on the right side of the assignment operator is the value received by the constructor. There is a simple way to solve this problem: by using the **this** reference.

The "this" Reference

All the objects of a class carry with them an invisible reference, called **this**, that locates the object that called the method. The use of the **this** reference can be used to prevent ambiguity problems like the one in the foregoing *Circle( )* constructor. Here is how the **this** reference is employed in the constructor implementation to solve an ambiguity problem:

```
public Circle(double radius)        //CONSTRUCTOR
{
   this.radius = radius;
}//END Circle()
```

The compiler knows that **this** references the object that called the constructor, and it knows what class the object belongs to from the class reference in the object definition. As a result, this.radius references the private member *radius* of the *Circle* class. Now there is no ambiguity between the two *radius* names. Notice that the dot operator is employed to apply the **this** reference to the class member.

PROGRAMMING TIP

A simple solution to the use of duplicate names in a program is to make sure that you employ different names to avoid any ambiguity. For instance, the radius of a circle could be named *radius*, *rad*, or *r*, depending on where it is used in the program. Thus, the *Circle( )* constructor could be coded like this:

```
public Circle(double r)             //CONSTRUCTOR
{
   radius = r;
}//END Circle()
```

This represents much better overall programming style and is less confusing to anyone looking at the code. However, this solution is not always possible in order to keep the code readable and self-documenting. This is why we have introduced the **this** reference at this time.

Example 9-3

Declare a *Point* class that defines an (*x,y*) coordinate for a cursor position on the monitor. Provide a constructor to initialize the coordinate when an object is defined for *Point*. The default coordinate should be (0,0). Include a method, called *plot()*, as part of the class that will display the string "Java" at the (*x,y*) coordinate location. Finally, code a statement required to define an object, *p*, of the *Point* class, and initialize this object to point to the middle of the monitor screen. Also, write a statement to call the *plot()* method.

Solution

First, the class declaration:

```
//Point CLASS DECLARATION
class Point
{
 //DATA MEMBERS
 private int x = 0;                    //X-COORDINATE
 private int y = 0;                    //Y-COORDINATE

 //METHOD MEMBERS

 //CONSTRUCTOR
 public Point(int x, int y)
 {
   this.x = x;
   this.y = y;
 }//END Point()

 //PLOT POINT(x,y)
 public void plot()
 {
   for(int i = 0; i < y; ++i)         //MOVE CURSOR DOWN y LINES
     System.out.println();
   for (int i = 0; i < x; ++i)        //MOVE CURSOR OVER x LINES
     System.out.print(' ');
   System.out.println("Java");        //DISPLAY "Java"
 } //END plot()
}//END Point
```

This declaration should be straightforward. The *Point* class consists of two private integer members, *x* and *y*, that will form the coordinate. The default coordinate is (0,0). A constructor method is included to initialize the *x* and *y* values to a coordinate received when an object is defined for the class. Notice that the constructor implementation uses the **this** reference to prevent ambiguity between the *x,y* class members and the *x,y* constructor parameters. The *plot()*

method uses the *x,y* class members within **for** loops to position the cursor at the (*x,y*) position on the monitor. Once the cursor is positioned, the final *println()* statement within the method displays the string "Java" at the cursor position.

A statement to define an object, *p*, of the *Point* class and initialize *p* to point to the middle of the screen is

Point p = **new** Point(40,12);

This statement defines an object, *p*, and calls the constructor to initialize the (*x,y*) coordinate to (40,12), which is the approximate middle of the screen. The following statement will call the *plot()* method to move the cursor to the (*x,y*) coordinate position and display the string.

p.plot();

To call a nonconstructor method, you simply list the object, a dot, and then the method name with any required arguments. Of course, the *plot()* method doesn't require any arguments, because it operates directly from the private members of the object.

Access Methods

Remember that the only way to access the private members of class are with a public method member of the same class. Even if we simply want to examine the private members of a class object, we need to use a public method that is declared within the same class. Such a method needs to return only the private member(s) to the calling program. Access methods, sometimes called **get** methods, are used for this purpose.

> An ***access***, or ***get***, ***method*** is a method that returns only the values of the private members of an object.

Let's revisit one of our *Rectangle* class declarations, adding access methods to it, as follows:

```
class Rectangle
{
  //DATA MEMBERS
  private double length = 0.0;        //RECTANGLE LENGTH
  private double width = 0.0;         //RECTANGLE WIDTH
```

```
//METHOD MEMBERS
//CONSTRUCTORS
//THIS CONSTRUCTOR REQUIRES NO ARGUMENTS
public Rectangle()
{
}//END Rectangle()

//CONSTRUCTOR FOR A SQUARE, REQUIRES ONE ARGUMENT
public Rectangle(double side)
{
  length = width = side;
}//END Rectangle(double)

//CONSTRUCTOR FOR A RECTANGLE, REQUIRES TWO ARGUMENTS
public Rectangle(double l, double w)
{
  length = l;
  width = w;
}//END Rectangle(double,double)

//PERIMETER METHOD
public double perimeter()
{
  return 2 * (length + width);           //RETURN PERIMETER
}//END perimeter()

//AREA METHOD
public double area()
{
  return length * width;                 //RETURN AREA
}//END area()

//LENGTH ACCESS METHOD
public double currentLength()
{
  return length;                         //ACCESS LENGTH
}//END currentLength()

//WIDTH ACCESS METHOD
public double currentWidth()
{
  return width;                          //ACCESS WIDTH
}//END currentWidth()
} //END Rectangle
```

Two new member methods called *currentLength()* and *currentWidth()* have been added here to return the *length* and *width* private member values, respectively. The only purpose of an access method is to return the value of a private member, so the implementation requires only a **return** statement as shown.

When either of these methods is executed, the respective private member value is returned to the calling program. So, if we define *box* to be an object of *Rectangle*, you can call either access member using the ***dot operator*** to examine the private members. For instance, to display the member values of *box*, the access methods could be called as part of *println()* statements, like this:

```
System.out.println("The length of the box is:  " + box.currentLength());
System.out.println("The width of the box is:  " + box.currentWidth());
```

Messages

> A *message* is a call to an object method.

The term ***message*** is used for a call to an object method with the idea that when we are calling a method, we are sending a message to its object. The object responds to the calling program by sending back return values, if required. This idea is illustrated in Figure 9-7. As you might suspect, objects communicate with each other using messages.

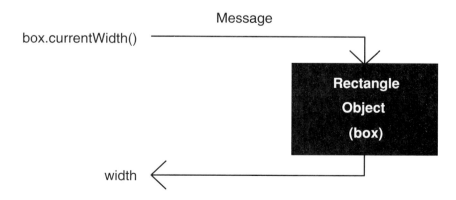

Figure 9-7 Messages are the means of communicating with an object. Here, the *currentWidth()* method sends a message to the *box* object of the *Rectangle* class, which returns the *width* of the object.

To generate a message to an object, you must call one of its public member methods. You call a member method by using the dot operator. The required format is

> ### SENDING A MESSAGE USING THE DOT OPERATOR
>
> *object name* • *method name* (*argument listing*);

Let's define three objects for our *Rectangle* class called *box1*, *box2*, and *box3*. Here are the required definitions:

```
//DEFINE OBJECTS
Rectangle box1 = new Rectangle();          //box1 OBJECT DEF
Rectangle box2 = new Rectangle(2);         //box2 OBJECT DEF
Rectangle box3 = new Rectangle(3,4);       //box3 OBJECT DEF
```

Next, let's send messages to all the methods of the three boxes using *println()* statements. We will use a separate *println()* statement for each message so that you can easily observe the required syntax. Here are the messages:

```
//DISPLAY LENGTH, WIDTH, PERIMETER, AND AREA OF box1 OBJECT
  System.out.println("\nThe length of box1 is:  " + box1.currentLength());
  System.out.println("The width of box1 is:  " + box1.currentWidth());
  System.out.println("The perimeter of box1 is:  " + box1.perimeter());
  System.out.println("The area of box1 is:  " + box1.area());

//DISPLAY LENGTH, WIDTH, PERIMETER, AND AREA OF box2 OBJECT
  System.out.println("\nThe length of box2 is:  " + box2.currentLength());
  System.out.println("The width of box2 is:  " + box2.currentWidth());
  System.out.println("The perimeter of box2 is:  " + box2.perimeter());
  System.out.println("The area of box2 is:  " + box2.area());

//DISPLAY LENGTH, WIDTH, PERIMETER, AND AREA OF box3 OBJECT
  System.out.println("\nThe length of box3 is:  " + box3.currentLength());
  System.out.println("The width of box3 is:  " + box3.currentWidth());
  System.out.println("The perimeter of box3 is:  " + box3.perimeter());
  System.out.println("The area of box3 is:  " + box3.area());
```

Observe that each group of four *println()* statements deals with a different box object. Each group sends messages to its respective object via the dot operator. That's all there is to it!

Putting Everything Together in a Complete Program

We now have all the ingredients to build a complete program. Here it is:

```
//Rectangle CLASS DECLARATION
class Rectangle
 {
   //DATA MEMBERS
   private double length = 0.0;          //RECTANGLE LENGTH
   private double width = 0.0;           //RECTANGLE WIDTH

   //METHOD MEMBERS

   //CONSTRUCTORS
   //THIS CONSTRUCTOR REQUIRES NO ARGUMENTS
   public Rectangle()
   {
   }//END Rectangle()

   //CONSTRUCTOR FOR A SQUARE, REQUIRES ONE ARGUMENT
   public Rectangle(double s)
   {
     length = width = s;
   }//END Rectangle(double)

   //CONSTRUCTOR FOR A  RECTANGLE, REQUIRES TWO ARGUMENTS
   public Rectangle(double l, double w)
   {
     length = l;
     width = w;
   }//END Rectangle(double,double)

   //PERIMETER METHOD
   public double perimeter()
   {
     return 2 * (length + width);        //RETURN PERIMETER
   }//END perimeter()
```

```
    //AREA METHOD
    public double area()
    {
      return length * width;            //RETURN AREA
    }//END area()


    //LENGTH ACCESS METHOD
    public double currentLength()
    {
      return length;                    //ACCESS LENGTH
    }//END currentLength()


    //WIDTH ACCESS METHOD
    public double currentWidth()
    {
      return width;                     //ACCESS WIDTH
    }//END currentWidth()
} //END Rectangle

//APPLICATION CLASS DECLARATION
public class RectangleTest
{
  public static void main(String[] args)
  {
  //DEFINE OBJECTS
  Rectangle box1 = new Rectangle();          //box1 OBJECT DEF
  Rectangle box2 = new Rectangle(2);         //box2 OBJECT DEF
  Rectangle box3 = new Rectangle(3,4);       //box3 OBJECT DEF


  //DISPLAY LENGTH, WIDTH, PERIMETER, AND AREA OF BOX1 OBJECT
  System.out.println("\nThe length of box1 is:  " + box1.currentLength());
  System.out.println("The width of box1 is:  " + box1.currentWidth());
  System.out.println("The perimeter of box1 is:  " + box1.perimeter());
  System.out.println("The area of box1 is:  " + box1.area());


  //DISPLAY LENGTH, WIDTH, PERIMETER, AND AREA OF BOX2 OBJECT
  System.out.println("\nThe length of box2 is:  " + box2.currentLength());
  System.out.println("The width of box2 is:  " + box2.currentWidth());
  System.out.println("The perimeter of box2 is:  " + box2.perimeter());
  System.out.println("The area of box2 is:  " + box2.area());
```

```
//DISPLAY LENGTH, WIDTH, PERIMETER, AND AREA OF BOX3 OBJECT
System.out.println("\nThe length of box3 is:  " + box3.currentLength());
System.out.println("The width of box3 is:  " + box3.currentWidth());
System.out.println("The perimeter of box3 is:  " + box3.perimeter());
System.out.println("The area of box3 is:  " + box3.area());
} //END main()
}//END RectangleTest
```

First notice the overall structure of the program. Two classes are declared: *Rectangle* and *RectangleTest*. Method *main()* resides within the *RectangleTest* class. Our *Rectangle* class is declared first which includes two private members and five public method members (the single *Rectangle()* constructor method is overloaded). The methods consist of an overloaded constructor, two methods that return the perimeter and area of the rectangle, and two access methods, Next, a class called *RectangleTest* is declared. The *RectangleTest* class has a single method, *main()*. The sole purpose of the *RectangleTest* class is to provide a class for *main()* to reside. Remember, all Java application programs must include *main()* and, since *main()* is a method, it must reside within a class. Within *main()* you see our *Rectangle* class objects defined and used to call the various methods Three objects are defined for the *Rectangle* class, and then messages are sent to the objects by calling all their respective methods. Here is the output from the program:

```
The length of box1 is:  0
The width of box1 is:  0
The perimeter of box1 is:  0
The area of box1 is:  0

The length of box2 is:  2
The width of box2 is:  2
The perimeter of box2 is:  8
The area of box2 is:  4

The length of box3 is:  3
The width of box3 is:  4
The perimeter of box3 is:  14
The area of box3 is:  12
```

Quick Check

1. Write a signature for a method called *wheels()* that will return the number of wheels from a class called *Truck*. Assume that the number of wheels is a private member of the class.

2. A method member that is used specifically to initialize object data is called a _____.

3. How do you know which method in a class is the constructor method?

4. True or false: The return type of a constructor method is optional.

5. How is a constructor called?

6. True or false: A constructor cannot be overloaded.

7. How do you call a nonconstructor method of a class?

8. A method that returns only the values of the private class members is called a _____ method.

9. Why is the term "message" associated with a call to a method of an object?

10. Write a signature for a constructor of a class called *MyClass* that initializes two integer members of the class.

11. Write a statement to define an object called *myObject* for *MyClass* in question 10. Assume that the two integer members of the class must be initialized to the values 5 and 6.

PROBLEM SOLVING IN ACTION: BUILDING PROGRAMS USING CLASSES AND OBJECTS

Professional baseball has heard about Java and they have hired you to write a simple program for their pitchers. The program must store the pitcher's name, team, wins, losses, winning percentage, and earned run average (ERA). In addition, a provision must be provided for the user to enter a given pitcher's stats as well as display a given pitcher's stats. Develop such a program using classes and objects.

The first thing to be done when developing an object-oriented program is to identify the nouns and verbs in the problem statement. Remember, the nouns suggest private data for the class and the verbs suggest methods for the class.

Here is the problem statement again with the important nouns and verbs underlined:

The program must store the pitcher's <u>name</u>, <u>team</u>, <u>wins</u>, <u>losses</u>, <u>winning percentage</u>, and <u>ERA</u>. In addition, provision must be provided for the user to <u>enter</u> a given pitcher's data as well as <u>display</u> a given pitcher's data. Develop such a program using classes and objects.

From the nouns and verbs, we develop a class specification as follows:

Class: *Pitcher*
    Data Members: *name*
                 team
                 wins
                 losses
                 winningPercentage
                 era

    Method Members: *setStats( )*
                   getStats( )

Now, we are ready to code the class. Here it is:

```
class Pitcher
{
 //DATA MEMBERS
 private String name = " ";          //PITCHER'S NAME
 private String team = " ";          //PITCHER'S TEAM
 private int wins = 0;               //NUMBER OF WINS
 private int losses = 0;             //NUMBER OF LOSSES
 private double winPercent = 0.0;    //WIN PERCENTAGE
 private double era = 0.0;           //EARNED RUN AVERAGE

 //METHOD MEMBERS
 //CONSTRUCTOR THAT DOES NOT INITIALIZE ANYTHING
 public Pitcher()
 {
 }//END Pitcher()

 //CONSTRUCTOR THAT INITIALIZES ONLY PITCHER NAME
 public Pitcher(String n)
 {
    name = n;
 }//END Pitcher(String)
```

```
//CONSTRUCTOR THAT INITIALIZES ALL PITCHER DATA EXCEPT WIN %
public Pitcher(String n,String t, int w, int l, double era)
{
   name = n;
   team = t;
   wins = w;
   losses = l;
   this.era = era;
   calculateWinPercent();
 }//END Pitcher(String,String,int,int,double)

//UTILITY METHOD TO CALCULATE winPercent
private void calculateWinPercent()
{
   if ((wins + losses) == 0)
      winPercent = 0.0;
   else
      winPercent = (double)wins/(wins + losses) * 100;     //TYPE CASTING
}//END calculateWinPercent

//SET PITCHER STATS TO USER ENTRIES
public void setStats()
{
   //CREATE KEYBOARD OBJECT
   Keyboard in = new Keyboard();

   //PROMPT AND READ PITCHER STATS
   System.out.print("Enter the pitcher's name: ");
   name = in.readString();
   System.out.print("Enter the pitcher's team: ");
   team = in.readString();
   System.out.print("Enter the number of wins for " + name + ": ");
   wins = in.readInt();
   System.out.print("Enter the number of losses for " + name + ": ");
   losses = in.readInt();
   System.out.print("Enter the era " + name + ": ");
   era = in.readDouble();
   calculateWinPercent();
}//END setStats()
```

```
//GET AND DISPLAY STATS
  public void getStats()
  {
    System.out.println("Pitcher name: " + name);
    System.out.println("\tTeam: " + team);
    System.out.println("\tNumber of wins: " + wins);
    System.out.println("\tNumber of losses: " + losses);
    System.out.println("\tWinning percentage: " + winPercent);
    System.out.println("\tERA: " + era);
  }//END getStats()
}// END pitcher
```

First, look at the data members of the class. Here you see all the data members that we found in the problem statement. Each member is initialized with a default value and designated as **private** to enforce information hiding.

Next, look at the method members of the class. The first thing you see is an overloaded constructor. The first version of the constructor does not have any arguments and, therefore, will allow an object to be defined without supplying constructor arguments. Of course, if no arguments are supplied, the class data are initialized with their default values. The second version of the constructor requires only the pitcher's name. Notice that the single constructor parameter is a string object. The third version of the constructor requires arguments for each of the data members, except the winning percentage. Thus, values for each argument must be supplied when an object is defined in order for this constructor to execute. When the constructor is executed, the argument values are assigned to their respective data members. But what about the *winPercent* member? Well, the winning percentage is calculated from the *wins* and *losses* members. To accomplish this task, we have created a utility method called *calculateWinPercent( )*. This method calculates the winning percentage using the *wins* and *losses* data members. This is an ideal application for a utility method, because it will only be called within the class to calculate the *winPercent* data member and does not need to be called from outside the class. Notice that the constructor calls this method to initialize the *winPercent* data member.

Now, look at the *calculateWinPercent( )* method. First, you see that it is a **private** method and, therefore, cannot be called from outside the class. Second, you see that it contains an **if/else** statement. Why? Because if both *wins* and *losses* were zero, a run-time error would occur and the program would crash. So, the **if/else** statement protects against division by zero. Last, you see something that you have not seen before. The statement winPercent = (double)wins/(wins + losses) * 100;   //TYPE CAST

includes what is called a ***type cast***. A type cast temporarily converts data of one type to a different type. The type cast is created by the code (double) in the preceding statement. Without the type cast to double, the calculation would always be 0. Why? Because *wins* and *losses* are both integers. When you divide two integers, you get an integer. Since (wins + losses) will always be greater than *wins*, integer division will always give you a result of 0. The type cast forces a double floating-point result, which is what we need for our *winPercent* member. Remember this little trick, because it often comes in handy. We should caution you, however, that type casting should only be used when really necessary as in the above application. If you find yourself doing a lot of type casting, then you have probably not data-typed your variables properly when they were defined. This is why we have not discussed type casting until now.

PROGRAMMING NOTE

A ***type cast*** converts data of one type to a different type, temporarily. You can convert data of one type to another type by preceding the data variable/expression with the type to convert to within parentheses like this: (double). The conversion is not permanent, since it is only in effect for the statement in which it resides. Type casting should be used sparingly, when a legitimate need for its use arises. Too much type casting within a program indicates a problem in the way in which the program variables have been typed when they were defined.

The next method, *setStats()*, prompts the user and reads the user entries for the private members. Again, notice that the *calculateWinPercent()* method is called to determine *winPercent* member value. Also, notice that we had to create a *Keyboard* class object to read the user entries. Of course, the *keyboardInput* package must be imported to use this class.

The last method, *getStats()*, simply displays the pitcher data stored by the private data members of the class. The diagram in Figure 9-8 illustrates the class members and interface.

Pitcher Class

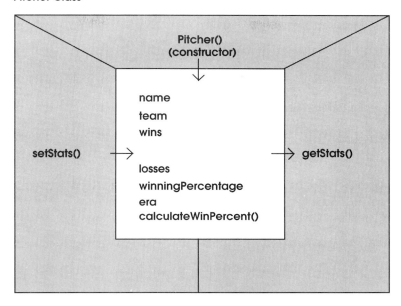

Figure 9-8 The *Pitcher* class consists of private members for the pitcher stats as well as a private method to calculate the winning percentage. The public interface includes the class constructor and methods to get the stats from the user and display the stats.

Now, the last thing to do is to create an application program to exercise our *Pitcher* class. Here is the complete program:

```
//ACTION 9-1(ACTION09_01.JAVA)
import keyboardInput.*;          //FOR Keyboard CLASS

class Pitcher
{
 //DATA MEMBERS
 private String name = " ";              //PITCHER'S NAME
 private String team = " ";              //PITCHER'S TEAM
 private int wins = 0;                   //NUMBER OF WINS
 private int losses = 0;                 //NUMBER OF LOSSES
 private double winPercent = 0.0;        //PERCENTAGE OF WINS
 private double era = 0.0;               //EARNED RUN AVERAGE
```

```
//METHOD MEMBERS
//CONSTRUCTOR THAT DOES NOT INITIALIZE ANYTHING
public Pitcher()
{
}//END Pitcher()

//CONSTRUCTOR THAT INITIALIZES ONLY PITCHER NAME
public Pitcher(String n)
{
   name = n;
}//END Pitcher()

//CONSTRUCTOR INITIALIZES ALL PITCHER STATS EXCEPT WIN %
public Pitcher(String n,String t, int w, int l, double era)
{
   name = n;
   team = t;
   wins = w;
   losses = l;
   this.era = era;
   calculateWinPercent();
 }//END Pitcher(String,String,int,int,double)

//UTILITY METHOD TO CALCULATE winPercent
private void calculateWinPercent()
{
   if ((wins + losses) == 0)
       winPercent = 0.0;
   else
       winPercent = (double)wins/(wins + losses) * 100;
}//END calculateWinPercent()

//SET PITCHER STATS TO USER ENTRIES
public void setStats()
{
   //CREATE KEYBOARD OBJECT
   Keyboard in = new Keyboard();

   //PROMPT AND READ PITCHER STATS
   System.out.print("Enter the pitcher's name: ");
   name = in.readString();
   System.out.print("Enter the pitcher's team: ");
   team = in.readString();
```

```
        System.out.print("Enter the number of wins for " + name + ": ");
        wins = in.readInt();
        System.out.print("Enter the number of losses for " + name + ": ");
        losses = in.readInt();
        System.out.print("Enter the era " + name + ": ");
        era = in.readDouble();
        calculateWinPercent();
    }//END setStats()

    //GET AND DISPLAY STATS
    public void getStats()
    {
        System.out.println("Pitcher name: " + name);
        System.out.println("\tTeam: " + team);
        System.out.println("\tNumber of wins: " + wins);
        System.out.println("\tNumber of losses: " + losses);
        System.out.println("\tWinning percentage: " + winPercent);
        System.out.println("\tERA: " + era);
    }//END getStats()
}// END Pitcher CLASS

public class Action09_01
{
 public static void main(String[] args)
 {
    //DEFINE VARIABLES
    char pause = ' ';                        //FREEZE VARIABLE

    //CREATE KEYBOARD OBJECT
    Keyboard in = new Keyboard();

    //DEFINE PITCHER OBJECT
    Pitcher JohnSmoltz = new Pitcher("John Smoltz");

    //CALL PITCHER METHODS
    JohnSmoltz.setStats();
    JohnSmoltz.getStats();

    //PAUSE DISPLAY
    System.out.println("\nPress ENTER to continue.");
    pause = in.readChar();
  }//END main()
}//END Action09_01 CLASS
```

The application class is called *Action09_01*. Notice that a *JohnSmoltz* object is defined for our *Pitcher* class inside of *main()*. (Which constructor is executed?) The *JohnSmoltz* object is then used to call the *setStats()* and *getStats()* methods to allow the user to enter the pitcher data and display the data, respectively. That's it! Now you are ready to build your own object-oriented programs.

This case study summarizes most of what has been covered in the last two sections. Before going on, study the program to make sure that you understand everything in it. Many important OOP concepts are demonstrated here.

PROBLEM SOLVING IN ACTION: BUILDING PROGRAMS USING PACKAGES

You have been importing Java packages, such as *keyboardInput*, into your programs when prewritten classes are needed to perform some task. Java provides packages as a way to group related classes to together. For example, the *keyboardInput* package contains the *Keyboard* class and the *KeyboardReadException* class.

All files that make up a given package must be stored in a subdirectory whose name is the same as the package name. So, the *Keyboard.class* and the *KeyboardReadException.class* files must be stored in a subdirectory called *keyboardInput*.

> All files that make up a given package must be stored in a directory whose name is the same as the package name.

As you build your programs, it is convenient to create your own packages to hold related classes, just as we created the *keyboardInput* package to hold the keyboard classes. You can compile the classes independently and import them when needed into an application program or applet. For example, you might want to create a *SavingsAccount* class and a *CheckingAccount* class and place them in a *banking* package. Well, we're about to do just that! Together, we will create a *banking* package that includes a *SavingsAccount* class and a *CheckingAccount* class to process those types of banking transactions. However, before getting into the details, let's learn a "bit" more about Java packages in general.

Recall that the name of the package directory must be the same name as the package. So, our *banking* package will be placed in a directory called *banking*. This way, when you reference the *SavingsAccount* class of the *banking* package, Java knows to look in the *banking* directory.

As you know, Java was designed to be totally platform independent. To support platform independence, Java requires that the operating system set a *classpath* variable to determine where to begin looking for user-defined packages. Setting the *classpath* variable differs between operating systems, such as UNIX versus Windows. In Windows, for example, a *set classpath* statement is required in the *autoexec.bat* file. The parameters for the statement are the path where the user-defined packages will be found. For instance, the statement

set classpath= C:\mypackages

would tell Windows to look in the *mypackages* directory for the user-defined package directories. Thus, you would locate your *banking* directory within the *mypackages* directory.

> Check your operating systems manual for details on setting the *classpath* variable, because the requirements differ between operating systems.

Once we create a package directory, the separate *.java* files will be compiled in the normal way from within this directory. The compiler will produce *.class* files and store them in the package directory. Thus, we will save our *SavingsAccount.java* and *CheckingAccount.java* source files in a *banking* directory and compile these class files independently. The compiler will produce byte-code files called *SavingsAccount.class* and *CheckingAccount.class* and place them in the *banking* directory. We can then write an application or applet program and import these classes using an **import** statement at the beginning of the program.

Package Naming

Sun has recommended certain naming conventions for packages in order to encourage consistency within the industry. Here they are:

- The first word in a package name should begin with a lowercase letter; all subsequent words should begin with an uppercase letter.
- Package names must not begin with the word *java*, because this is reserved for naming standard Java packages.
- For Internet programs, package names should begin with the Internet domain name, only reversed. Thus, if your Internet domain name is *domain.COM*, your package name should begin with *COM.domain*.

Notice that *COM* is capitalized. It is suggested that domain categories, such as *COM*, *EDU*, *GOV*, and the like always be capitalized. However, if a package is only for local system use, such a prefix would be inappropriate.

- Always be consistent with case when naming and referring to packages. Windows systems are not case sensitive, but other operating systems, such as UNIX, are case sensitive.

These are only guidelines and the Java compiler does not enforce them. However, when used consistently in developing your programs, you are likely to avoid naming conflicts, especially across multiple systems and platforms.

Now, let's get back to our *banking* package. First we will create two separate classes, *SavingsAccount* and *CheckingAccount*. Each will be placed within its own separate *.java* file within the *banking* directory and compiled independently. We will use the *SavingsAccount* class specification and code developed earlier in this chapter. Here they are:

Class: *SavingsAccount*
    Data Members: *balance*
                interestRate

    Method Members: *addDeposit( )*
                subtractWithdrawal( )
                addInterest( )
                currentBalance( )

```
package banking;
public class SavingsAccount
{
 //DATA MEMBERS
 private double balance = 0.0;          //ACCOUNT BALANCE
 private double interestRate = 0.0;     //MONTHLY INTEREST RATE

 //METHOD MEMBERS
 public SavingsAccount()
 {
 }//END SavingsAccount()

 //INITIALIZE balance
 public SavingsAccount(double bal)
 {
    balance = bal;
 }//END SavingsAccount(double)
```

```
//INITIALIZE balance AND interestRate
public SavingsAccount(double bal, double rate)
{
   balance = bal;
   interestRate = rate;
}//END SavingsAccount(double,double)

//ADD MONTHLY INTEREST
public void addInterest()
{
   balance = balance + balance * interestRate;
}//END addInterest()

//ADD DEPOSIT
public void addDeposit(double amount)
{
   balance = balance + amount;
} //END addDeposit()

//SUBTRACT WITHDRAWAL
public void subtractWithdrawal(double amount)
{
   balance = balance - amount;
}//END subtractWithdrawal()

//RETURN BALANCE
public double currentBalance()
{
   return balance;
}//END currentBalance()
} //END SavingsAccount
```

There are three major differences between this code and the code we developed earlier. First, and most important, you see the statement

package banking;

as the first line in the program. This statement tells Java that the *SavingsAccount* class is part of the *banking* package. Second, you see that we have declared the class **public**. This allows the class to be accessible outside the package in which it resides. Third, we have replaced our earlier *initialize()* method with an overloaded *SavingsAccount()* constructor. Notice that the first version does not require any argument, the second version requires a single argument to initialize *balance*, and the third version requires two arguments to initialize both *balance* and *interestRate*. The remaining parts of the code are the same as the code we used earlier. The class diagram in Figure 9-9 depicts the class members and interface.

SavingsAccount Class

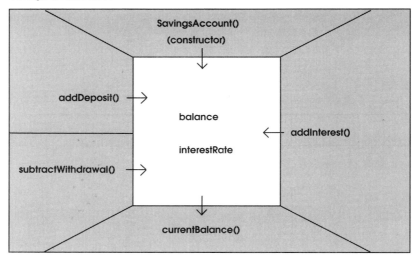

Figure 9-9 The *SavingsAccount* class consists of private *balance* and *interestRate* members and public *addDeposit()*, *subtractWithdrawal()*, *addInterest()*, and *currentBalance()* methods as well as a constructor that form the class interface.

Declaring a class **public** allows the class to be visible outside the package in which the class resides.

Next, we will "spec-out" our *CheckingAccount* class as follows:

Class: *CheckingAccount*
    Data Members: *balance*
                   minimum
                   charge

    Method Members: *addDeposit()*
                    cashCheck()
                    currentBalance()

The class has three data members: *balance*, *minimum*, and *charge*. The *balance* is self-explanatory. The *minimum* data member will be the minimum account balance required to avoid a check cashing charge. If the balance goes below this minimum, an additional charge will be made to cash a check. The amount of the charge is stored in the *charge* data member.

The *addDeposit()* method does exactly what is says: adds a deposit to the balance. The *cashCheck()* method subtracts the amount of the check from the balance and also subtracts a check cashing charge, if applicable. Finally, the *currentBalance()* method will return the current account balance. The class diagram in Figure 9-10 depicts the *CheckingAccount* class members and interface.

CheckingAccount Class

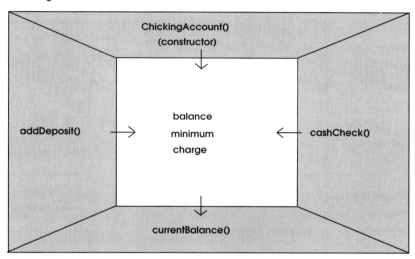

Figure 9-10 The *CheckingAccount* class consists of private *balance*, *minimum*, and *charge* members along with public *addDeposit()*, *cashCheck()*, and *currentBalance()* methods as well as a constructor that form the class interface.

Here's the class code:

```
package banking;
public class CheckingAccount
{
  //DATA MEMBERS
  private double balance = 0.0;          //ACCOUNT BALANCE
  private double minimum = 500.00;       //MINIMUM BALANCE TO
                                         //AVOID CHECK CHARGE
  private double charge = 0.5;           //PER-CHECK CHARGE
```

```
//METHOD MEMBERS
//CONSTRUCTORS
//DO NOT INITIALIZE ANYTHING
public CheckingAccount()
{
}//END CheckingAccount()

//INITIALIZE balance
public CheckingAccount(double bal)
{
    balance = bal;
}//END CheckingAccount(double)

//INITIALIZE balance, minimum, AND charge
public CheckingAccount(double bal, double min, double chg)
{
    balance = bal;
    minimum = min;
    charge = chg;
}//END CheckingAccount(double,double,double)

//ADD DEPOSIT
public void addDeposit(double amount)
{
    balance = balance + amount;
} //END addDeposit()

//CASH A CHECK
public void cashCheck(double amt)
{
    //TEST FOR OVERDRAW
    if (amt > balance)
        System.out.println("Cannot cash check, account overdrawn.");

    //CASH CHECK
    else
        //CHECK FOR MINIMUM BALANCE
        if (balance < minimum)
            balance = balance - (amt + charge); //DEBIT BALANCE WITH
                                                //CHECK AMOUNT
                                                //AND CHARGE
        else                                    //DEBIT BALANCE WITH
            balance = balance - amt;            //CHECK AMOUNT
} //END cashCheck()
```

```
//RETURN BALANCE
public double currentBalance()
{
   return balance;
}//END currentBalance()
} //END CheckingAccount
```

Most of this code should be self-explanatory by now. Again you see the **package** statement as the first line in the program. You also see that the class is declared as a **public** class. (Why?) Look at the *cashCheck()* method a minute. Notice that it receives an amount (*amt*) from the calling object and generates an error message if this amount exceeds the account balance. Otherwise, the check is cashed, and the account balance is debited accordingly. Notice that a check-cashing charge is applied if the amount of the check is less than the required minimum balance.

The last thing we need to do is to create an application program that tests our banking classes. In this program, we must import the *banking* package and create objects of the banking classes. We can then write statements to process banking transactions and generate a report using the class methods. Here is such a program:

```
import banking.*;       //FOR SavingsAccount, CheckingAccount CLASSES
import keyboardInput.*;  //FOR Keyboard CLASS
public class Action09_02
{
  public static void main(String[] args)
  {
   //DEFINE VARIALBES
   char pause = ' ';                 //FREEZE VARIABLE

   //CREATE BANKING OBJECTS
   SavingsAccount GraceHopper1 = new SavingsAccount(5000);
   CheckingAccount GraceHopper2 = new CheckingAccount(1000);

   //CREATE KEYBOARD OBJECT
   Keyboard in = new Keyboard();

   //PROCESS TRANSACTIONS
   GraceHopper1.subtractWithdrawal(501.25);
   GraceHopper1.addDeposit(300.52);
   GraceHopper2.cashCheck(200);
   GraceHopper2.addDeposit(352.90);
   GraceHopper2.cashCheck(25.37);
```

```
//GENERATE STATEMENT
System.out.println("\nYour savings account balance is: $"
                    + GraceHopper1.currentBalance());
System.out.println("Your checking account balance is: $"
                    + GraceHopper2.currentBalance());

//PAUSE DISPLAY
System.out.println("\nPress ENTER to continue.");
pause = in.readChar();

}//END main()
}//END Action09_02 CLASS
```

The first thing you see is an **import** statement that imports our *banking* package. The application class name is *Action09_02* and, therefore, the application file name is *Action09_02.java*. The class has one method, *main()*. Within main you see that we have defined two objects, *GraceHopper1* and *GraceHopper2*, as objects of our imported *SavingsAccount* class and *CheckingAccount* class, respectively. When each object is defined, a single argument is provided which will initialize the respective account balances. Then, several transactions are made by calling the various class methods. Finally, each object calls its *currentBalance()* method to report the balance after the account transactions were processed. Here is the output produced by the program:

Your savings account balance is: $4799.27
Your checking account balance is: $1127.53

As you can now see, method *main()* simply acts as a coordinator, or control panel, for objects within a Java application program. Objects are created in *main()* and messages are sent to those objects via calls to the object methods. Make sure to review the foregoing package and application program code to assure that you understand all the coding details. From now on, many of our application programs will be built using packages.

The real purpose of method *main()* in a Java application program is to act as a coordinator, or control panel, for objects that make up the program.

Project Managers

Most commercial Java compilers on the market today allow you to easily build your own multifile programs. By a multifile program, we mean one which links several packages and classes together to build a complete workable program using a ***project manager***. When using a project manager, you specify the files required to build an application program. This information is kept in a ***project file***.

A ***project file*** identifies the files that need to be compiled and linked to create a workable Java program.

In the foregoing banking program we had three separate source files: *SavingsAccount.java*, *CheckingAccount.java*, and *Action09_02.java*. Using a project manager, you code and compile the banking account class files separately, then open a project file. Once a project file is open, you can add and delete class files and packages to and from the project. For this project, all we did was to add the *Action09_02.java* application file. When the project manager detected the **import** statement in this file, it added the *banking* package class files to the program. Figure 9-11 illustrates the composition of our project file.

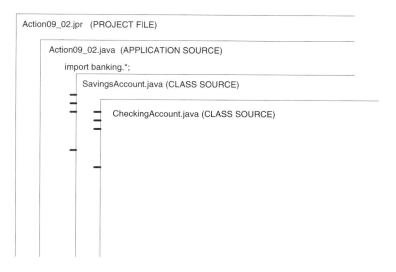

Figure 9-11   A project file includes all the files needed to create a workable Java program.

At this point, it might be a good idea to build, compile, and execute your own project for the banking program, using the code we developed and your compiler's project manager.

CHAPTER SUMMARY

Object-oriented programs are developed from the inside out by expanding on simple classes. The fundamental components of any object-oriented program are the class and its objects. At the abstract level, a class can be described as an interface, because its methods provide a boundry and define the behavior common to all of its objects. At the implementation level, a class is a construct that describes a set of data and related operations that are common to its objects. The abstract level provides an outside view of a class, whereas the implementation level provides the inside view of the class, disclosing its behavioral secrets. At the implementation level, a class is comprised of public and private members. The private class members are hidden from the outside, because they can only be accessed using the public method members. This provides for information hiding within the class.

Encapsulation is the idea of packaging things together in a well-defined programming unit. A COBOL record is encapsulated, because it consists of a collection of data members. A class in Java is also encapsulated, because it consists of a collection of data members and related methods. However, a COBOL record does not provide information hiding, whereas a Java class does provide information hiding through its private members.

An object is an instance, or specimen, of a class. Thus, an object of a given class has the attributes and behavior defined by the class. The private data of a given object provide for the object attributes, while the public methods of the object provide for the behavior of the object.

There are various types of class methods, including constructor methods and access methods. It is the class methods that provide a means of communication with objects defined for the class. Messages are sent to an object by calling its methods to perform a given task on the hidden object data. The object responds via the values returned by the method members.

Object-oriented programs are normally constructed using packages. A package is a directory where related classes are stored. To include a package in a Java program, you simply use the **import** statement. Once a package is imported, you can create and manipulate objects for the classes declared within the package.

Most commercial Java compilers include a project manager that makes it easier to build Java programs. When using the project manager, you specify all the files required to build an application program. This information is kept in a *project file*. A *project file* identifies the files that need to be compiled to create a workable Java program. Typically, the project file will identify the application and class source files required for the program.

QUESTIONS AND PROBLEMS

Questions

1. Define the following OOP terms:
    Class at the abstract level
    Class at the implementation level
    Encapsulation
    Information hiding
    Object
    Instance
    Member
    Instance variable
    Instance method
    Set method
    Get method
    Constructor
    Access method
    Utility method
    Overloaded constructor
    Message

2. What are the two things that make up a class declaration?

3. What is the scope of a private class member?

4. What is the scope of a public class member?

5. The concept of combining data with a set of operations that are dedicated to manipulating the data so tightly that outside operations cannot affect the data is called _____.

6. A computer window can be considered an object of a window class. What data and operations might be part of this object?

7. True or false: Only public members of a given class can access the private members of that class.

8. Why are classes *declared* and objects *defined*?

9. True or false: Utility methods are declared as **private** methods.

10. At the abstract level, a class can be described as an _____ that defines the behavior of its objects.

11. At the implementation level, a class consists of _____ and _____ members.

12. True or false: The abstract view of a class provides its inside view, showing the secrets of its data organization and method implementation.

13. What is meant by the term "behavior" relative to a class object?

14. OOP provides an important feature called _____, which is a mechanism for deriving new classes from existing ones

15. A method that simply displays the value of class data member is called a _____ method.

16. What is the purpose of a constructor?

17. Write a constructor for a class called *MyClass* that does not initialize any members of the class.

18. Define an object called *myObject* for the class in question 17.

19. How do you provide default values for the private data members of a class?

20. A private method of a class is often called a _____ method.

Use the following class declaration to answer questions 21–27:

```
class Student
{
  //DATA MEMBERS
  private String name = " ";          //STUDENT NAME
  private String major = " ";         //STUDENT MAJOR
  private long studentNumber = 0;     //STUDENT NUMBER
  private double gpa = 0.0;           //STUDENT GPA

  //METHOD MEMBERS
  //CONSTRUCTOR WITH NO INITIALIZING VALUES
  public Student()
  {
  }//END Student()

  //CONSTRUCTOR WITH INITIALIZING VALUES
  public Student(String nam, String maj, long num, double gpa)
  {
    name = nam;
    major = maj;
```

```
            studentNumber = num;
            this.gpa = gpa;
        }//END Student

        //INITIALIZE FROM USER ENTRIES
        public void setStats()
        {

        }//END setStats()

        //ACCESS STUDENT DATA
        public void getStats()
        {

        }//END getStats()
    } //END Student
```

21. What is the name of the constructor method?

22. Write a statement to define a student named John Doe as a student object that will be initialized to the default values in the class.

23. Jane Doe (student #456) is a Computer Information Systems major with a GPA of 3.58. Write a statement to define Jane Doe as a student object that will be initialized to the proper data values.

24. Write statements for the *setStats()* method that will allow the user to enter the data values from the keyboard.

25. Write a statement that will allow the user to initialize the Jane Doe object from the keyboard.

26. Write statements for the *getStats()* method, assuming that this method will display the student data.

27. Write a statement that will display the data in a *JohnDoe* student object.

28. Why does defining a data member of a class as **public** defeat the concept of information hiding?

29. True or false: A constructor never has a return type, not even void.

30. Suppose that you have a class called *Circle*. What will be the corresponding constructor name?

31. Given the following method implementation:

```
public Dogs(int legs)
{
    legs = legs;
} //END Dogs()
```

   a. What special type of method is this?

   b. What problem would the compiler encounter when attempting to compile
      this method?

   c. Rewrite the method to correct any problems.

32. What operator is used to send a message to an object?

33. Explain why you should use packages when developing Java programs.

34. A package called *accounting* must be stored in a directory called _____.

35. What is the classpath variable and how is it associated with packages?

Problems

Least Difficult

1. Develop a class to store a person's name and address. The address should be
   divided into separate fields of street, city, state, and zip code. In addition,
   provision must be provided for the user to enter a given person's name and
   address as well as display a given person's data.

2. Write an application program that contains the class you developed in
   problem 1 and defines an object to test the class methods. Compile and
   execute your program.

3. Professional basketball has heard about Java and they have hired you to write
   a program for their players' statistics. The program must store the player's
   name, team, total points scored, number of games played, average points per
   game, number of assists, number of rebounds, average field goal percentage.
   In addition, provision must be provided for the user to enter a given player's
   stats as well as display a given player's stats. Develop the required program
   using classes and objects.

More Difficult

4. Ma and Pa were reading the latest issue of *Wired* and ran across an article on
   OOP. They were so excited that they contracted you to write a object-oriented
   payroll program. They want the program to include an *Employee* class to
   store the employee's name, hourly rate, and hours worked. The class is to
   have operations that perform the following tasks:

   - An operation to initialize the hourly rate to a minimum wage of $6.00
     per hour and the hours worked to 0 when an employee object is defined.

   - An operation to get the employee's name, hourly rate, and hours
     worked from the user.

- An operation to return weekly pay, including overtime pay, where overtime is paid at a rate of time-and-a-half for any hours worked over 40.

- An operation to display all the employee information, including the employee's pay for a given week.

Most Difficult

5. Create a Java application program to process one line of an invoice. Assume that the invoice must include the following data and operations:

   Data:
   - Quantity Ordered
   - Quantity Shipped
   - Part Number
   - Part Description
   - Unit Price
   - Extended Price (Qty. Ordered * Unit Price)
   - Sales Tax rate
   - Sales Tax amount
   - Shipping
   - Total

   Operations:
   - An operation to initialize all the data items to 0, except the Sales Tax rate, which should be initialized to 7%.
   - An operation to allow the user to initialize all the data items from the keyboard.
   - An operation to calculate the extended price of the item.
   - An operation to calculate the sales tax amount of the item.
   - An operation to calculate the total amount of the invoice.
   - An operation to display the invoice data with header information in a businesslike format.

6. Write a 12-hour clock program that declares a *Clock* class to store hours, minutes, seconds, A.M., and P.M. Provide methods to perform the following tasks:

   - Set hours, minutes, seconds to 00:00:00 by default.
   - Initialize hours, minutes, seconds, A.M., and P.M. from user entries.

- Allow the clock to tick by advancing the seconds by one and at the same time correcting the hours and minutes for a 12-hour clock value of A.M. or P.M.

- Display the time in hours:minutes:seconds A.M./P.M. format.

Write an application program that allows the user to set the clock and tick the clock at 1-second intervals while displaying the time.

7. Add a *SuperNow* class to the *banking* package developed in this chapter. A super-now account is simply an interest-bearing checking account. Assume that interest will be credited to the account at the end of each month if the balance exceeds $1000.

CLASS INHERITANCE

INTRODUCTION

One of the most important properties of object-oriented programming is *inheritance*. In fact, some believe that a program that doesn't employ inheritance is not an object-oriented program.

> **Inheritance** is that property of object-oriented programming that allows one class, called a **subclass**, or **derived class**, to share the structure and behavior of another class, called a **superclass**, or **base class**.

The natural world is full of inheritance. All living things inherit the characteristics, or traits, of their ancestors. Although you are different in many ways from your parents, you are also the same in many ways because of the genetic traits that you have inherited from them. In object-oriented programming, inheritance allows newly created classes to inherit members from existing classes. These new *derived*, or *sub-*, classes will include their own members and members inherited from the *base*, or *super-*, class. In Java, the term *superclass* is used to denote a base class and the term *subclass* is used to denote a subclass. You can view a collection of classes with common inherited members as a *family* of classes, just like the family that you belong to. Classes are related to each other through inheritance. Such inheritance creates a class family hierarchy.

In this chapter, we will first explain why inheritance is important and then illustrate its use via a practical example. Finally, we will discuss two more important aspects of OOP: *polymorphism* and *dynamic binding*.

OBJECTIVES

When you are finished with this chapter, you should have a good understanding of the following:

- The concepts of inheritance, polymorphism, and dynamic binding.
- Why inheritance is important to object-oriented programming.
- Class hierarchies and families.
- How to build class families within Java packages.

- The IS-A relationship between a subclass and its superclass.
- The difference between a private, protected, and public class member.
- When to declare a class as a public class.
- How to call a superclass constructor within a subclass constructor.
- How to use a Venn diagram to represent a class family hierarchy.
- The difference between static and dynamic binding.
- The difference between overloaded methods and polymorphic methods.
- When and how to use abstract classes and methods.

10-1 WHY USE INHERITANCE?

One reason to use inheritance is that it allows you to reuse the code from a previous programming project without starting from scratch to reinvent the code. Many times the code developed for one program can be reused in another program. Although the new program might be slightly different from the old, inheritance allows you to build on what was done previously. Why reinvent the wheel?

Another reason for using inheritance is that it allows you to build a *hierarchy* among classes. The classes that include those things that are most commonly inherited are at the top of the hierarchy, just as your ancestors are at the top of your genetic family hierarchy. Take a banking situation, for example. A general bank account class is used to define variables, such as an account number and account balance, and methods, such as deposit, that are common to all bank accounts. Then, classes that define a checking account, super-now account, and savings account can all be derived from the bank account *superclass*. This way, they will inherit the account number and balance members as well as the deposit method of the general bank account class. Although the subclasses may have their own unique members, they all include the bank account superclass as part of their structure and behavior. Thus, a general bank account class would be at the top of a banking class hierarchy. This idea is illustrated by the hierarchy diagram in Figure 10-1. In fact, the left side of the hierarchy diagram in Figure 10-1 shows two levels of inheritance. The *BankAccount* class is inherited by both the *Checking* class and the *Savings* class. In addition, the *Checking* class is inherited by the *SuperNow* class. Notice that the *SuperNow* class inherits the *BankAccount* class indirectly through the *Checking* class. A family of classes related like this is referred to as a *class hierarchy*.

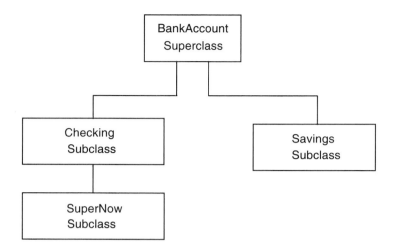

Figure 10-1 The *Checking* and *Savings* classes are derived from the *BankAccount* superclass, which has data and methods common to both of these subclasses. The *SuperNow* class is derived from the *Checking* class and will inherit data and methods from both the *Checking* and *BankAccount* classes.

PROGRAMMING TIP

The important relationship between a subclass and its superclass is the IS-A relationship. The IS-A relationship must exist if inheritance is used properly. For instance, a checking account IS-A bank account. A super-now account IS-A checking account. However, a savings account IS **NOT** A checking account; it IS-A banking account. Thus, a savings account should *not* be derived from a checking account but from a more general bank account class. Always consider the IS-A relationship when creating inheritance. If there is no IS-A relationship, inheritance should not be used.

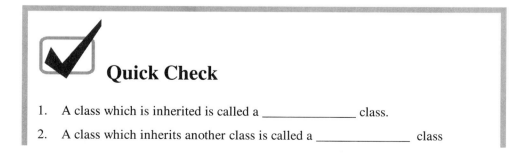

Quick Check

1. A class which is inherited is called a _____ class.

2. A class which inherits another class is called a _____ class

3. A collection of classes with common inherited members is called a _____.

4. List at least two reasons for using inheritance.

5. The important link between a subclass in its superclass is the _____ link.

6. True or false: The proper use of inheritance would allow a line class to be derived from a point class.

7. True or false: The proper use of inheritance would allow a pixel class to be derived from a point class.

8. True or false: The proper use of inheritance would allow a pick-up truck class to be derived from a truck class.

10-2 DECLARING AND USING SUBCLASSES

A subclass is declared using the following format:

> **FORMAT FOR DECLARING SUBCLASSES**
>
> **class** *subclass name* **extends** *superclass name*
> **{**
>
>   *Subclass Data Members*
>
>   *Subclass Method Members*
>
> **}** //END CLASS

Let's illustrate inheritance via the classes of bank accounts shown in Figure 10-1. Look at the figure again. You see that the *Checking* and *Savings* classes are derived directly from the *BankAccount* superclass, and the *SuperNow* class is derived indirectly from the *BankAccount* superclass through the *Checking* class. Here is how we will set up the various account classes.

BankAccount Class

The *BankAccount* class is at the top of the hierarchy diagram and, therefore, will be the superclass for the entire family. It will contain member data and methods that are common to all types of bank accounts. The composition of this class will be as follows:

Data Members
- An account number.
- An account balance.

Method Members
- A method to make deposits.
- A method to access the account number.
- A method to access the account balance.

Checking Account Class

The *Checking* account class will inherit the *BankAccount* class members. In addition, it will contain the following members:

Data Members
- A minimum balance value that will dictate when a per check charge is to be made.
- A value that will be charged on each check cashed when the account balance is less than the minimum required balance.

Method Members
- A constructor method to initialize the *Checking* account data members.
- A method that will cash a check by receiving a check amount and debit the account balance accordingly.

SuperNow Checking Account Class

A super-now account is simply an interest-bearing checking account. As a result, this class will inherit the *Checking* account class members and, therefore, will also inherit the *BankAccount* class members. In addition, the *SuperNow* account class will contain the following members:

Data Members
- An annual interest rate value that is credited to the account balance on a monthly basis, if the account balance remains above a minimum required level.

Method Members
- A constructor method to initialize the *SuperNow* checking account data members.
- A method that will credit interest to the account if the balance is above the required minimum.

Savings Account Class

The savings account class is derived from the original *BankAccount* superclass. In addition to the *BankAccount* class members, the *Savings* account class will contain the following:

Data Members
- An annual interest rate value that is credited to the account balance on a monthly basis.

Method Members
- A constructor method to initialize the *Savings* account data members.
- A method that will credit interest to the account.
- A method that will debit the account for a withdrawal.

Now, we begin our program construction by declaring our *BankAccount* superclass, as follows:

```
package bankaccounts;

//SUPERCLASS FOR ALL BANK ACCOUNTS
public class BankAccount
{
  //DATA MEMBERS
  protected int accountNumber;        //ACCOUNT NUMBER
  protected double balance;           //ACCOUNT BALANCE

  //METHOD MEMBERS

  //CONSTRUCTOR TO INITIALIZE DATA MEMBERS
  public BankAccount(int acctNum, double bal)
  {
    accountNumber = acctNum;
    balance = bal;
  } //END BankAccount(int,double)
```

```
//deposit() METHOD
public void deposit(double amount)
{
  balance = balance + amount;
} //END deposit()

//accountNum() ACCESS METHOD
public int accountNum()
{
  return  accountNumber;            //RETURN ACCOUNT NUMBER
} //END accountNumber()

//currentBalance() ACCESS METHOD
public double currentBalance()
{
  return  balance;                  //RETURN ACCOUNT BALANCE
} //END currentBalance()
} //END BankAccount
```

First, you see that the class declaration is part of a package called *bankaccounts*. The *bankaccounts* package will be used to hold all of our bank account classes. Looking at the class declaration, you see that it contains two data members and four method members. The data members of the *BankAccount* superclass are *accountNumber* and *balance*. Notice that they are declared as **protected members** using the keyword **protected**.

> A **protected member** of a class is a member that is accessible to both the superclass and any subclasses of the superclass in which it is declared. Thus, a protected member of a superclass is accessible to any descendent subclass within the family but not accessible to things outside the class family.

You could say that a protected member of a superclass has accessibility that is somewhere between that of a **private** member and a **public** member. If a member is a **private** member of a superclass, it is *not* accessible to a subclass. It is only accessible to methods in the superclass. However, a **protected** member of a superclass is accessible to any of its subclasses. On the other hand, a protected member is "protected" from being accessed outside the class family, thereby preserving information hiding within the family.

Another option that you will have for both data or methods relative to inheritance is declaring them **final** or nonfinal. A **final** data or method member cannot be overridden in a subclass. In other words, you can redefine a nonfinal member in a subclass and the subclass method will override the superclass definition. However, a **final** member of a superclass can never be redefined, or overridden, in a subclass. Classes can be **final** also. A **final** class cannot be extended, or inherited, by another class.

PROGRAMMING TIP

You will avoid confusion about when to use the keywords **private**, **protected**, and **public** relative to inheritance if you remember the following points:

- Use the keyword **private** when declaring a member of a class if you *do not* want the member of the class to be inherited by another class. A **private** class member is only accessible by **public** methods of the *same* class.
- Use the keyword **protected** when declaring a member of a class if you want to allow access to the member by a subclass. A protected member will be accessible within all descendent subclasses of the class in which it is defined but not outside the class family.
- Use the keyword **public** when declaring a *member* if you want the member to be accessible anywhere the class is visible. Of course, data members should never be declared **public**; otherwise, the whole purpose of information hiding is defeated.
- Use the keyword **public** when declaring a *class* if you want the class to be accessible outside the package in which it resides.

The **private**, **protected**, and **public** options are provided in Java to provide flexibility during inheritance and packaging. With the proper use of these options, you can specify precisely which class members are to be inherited by other classes. If you *do not* want a member of a class inherited, declare it as **private**. If you *do* want a member of a class inherited, declare it as **protected** or **public**. If you *do not* want a class in a package to be visible outside the package, do not use the keyword **public** in the class declaration. If you *do* want a class to be visible outside its package, declare it as **public**.

The public methods are *BankAccount()*, *deposit()*, *accountNum()*, and *currentBalance()*. The constructor, *BankAccount()*, is used to initialize the two data members. The *deposit()* method will be used to make a deposit to the

account. The *accountNum()* and *currentBalance()* methods are access methods
that are used to return the account number and balance, respectively. Why do you
suppose a *deposit()* method is included in the superclass. Well, any type of bank
account allows for a deposit where the deposit amount is simply added to the
balance, right? Thus, a deposit operation is common to all bank accounts, just as
an account number and balance are common to all accounts. When developing a
superclass, you include those data and operations that are common to all classes
within the family. So, you're thinking that a withdrawal operation is also common
to all types of bank accounts? Well, it is but each different type of account might
withdraw funds a different way. For instance, a checking account withdrawal
might add a check cashing charge, whereas a savings account withdrawal does
not. Thus, each derived bank account class will have its own unique *withdrawal()*
method.

The class diagram in Figure 10-2 shows the *BankAccount* superclass
structure and interface. Now, let's declare our first subclass. This class, called
Checking, will be derived from the *BankAccount* class, as follows:

```
package bankaccounts;

//SUBCLASS Checking INHERITS BankAccount CLASS
public class Checking extends BankAccount
{
  //DATA MEMBERS
  protected double minimum = 500;      //MINIMUM BALANCE TO
                                       //AVOID CHECK CHARGE
  protected double charge = 0.5;       //PER CHECK CHARGE

  //METHOD MEMBERS
  //PARAMETERLESS CONSTRUCTOR
  public Checking()
  {
     super(0000,0.0);
  }//END Checking()

  //CONSTRUCTOR TO INITIALIZE ACCOUNT NUMBER AND BALANCE
  public Checking(int acctNum, double bal)
  {
     super(acctNum,bal);
  }//END Checking(int,double)

  //CONSTRUCTOR TO INITIALIZE ALL PRIVATE DATA
  public Checking(int acctNum, double bal, double min, double chg)
```

```
   {
      super(acctNum,bal);
      minimum = min;
      charge = chg;
   } //END Checking(int,double,double,double)

   //cashCheck() METHOD
   public void cashCheck (double amt)
   {
      if (amt > balance)              //TEST FOR OVERDRAW
         System.out.println("Cannot cash check, account overdrawn.\n");
      else                            //CASH CHECK
         if (balance < minimum)              //CHECK FOR MIN BALANCE
            balance = balance - (amt + charge);
         else
            balance = balance - amt;
   } //END cashCheck()
}//END Checking
```

BankAccount Superclass

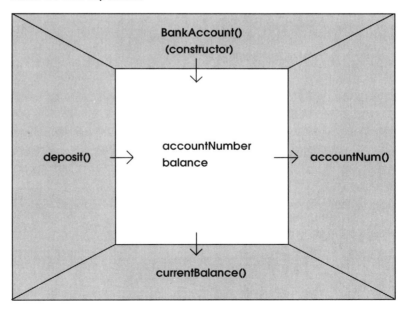

Figure 10-2 The *BankAccount* superclass consists of protected *accountNumber* and *balance* members along with public *deposit()*, *accountNumber()*, and *currentBalance()* methods as well as a constructor that form the class interface.

Again, the *Checking* class declaration is also included in the *bankaccounts* package. Looking at the class declaration, you see that the *Checking* class is derived from the *BankAccount* class. This is indicated by the class header line which includes the code **extends** BankAccount. The keyword **extends** is used to tell Java the this class is to be derived from the *BankAccount* class. Furthermore, notice the use of the keyword **public** prior to the subclass name. Recall that this designation makes the *Checking* class public to all classes outside the package. As a result, an application program class has access to the *Checking* class.

> Declaring a class **public** allows the class to be visible outside the package in which the class resides.

You see that the *Checking* class has two protected data members, *minimum* and *charge*. The *minimum* data member will be used to store a minimum balance value, whereby no per check charge is made if the account balance is above the stored minimum value. The *charge* data member will be used to store a per check charge for writing checks if the account balance is less than *minimum*. Notice that both *minimum* and *charge* are designated as protected members, because they will be inherited by the *SuperNow* class (see Figure 10-1). Also, observe that each data member has a default value. Of course, because *Checking* is derived from *BankAccount*, the protected *BankAccount* class members, *accountNumber* and *balance*, are inherited by the *Checking* class. Thus, *Checking* actually has four data members, *accountNumber* and *balance*, which are inherited from *BankAccount*, as well as *minimum* and *charge*, which are declared in *Checking*.

Two method members are declared for the *Checking* class: *Checking()* and *cashCheck()*. The *Checking()* method is an overloaded constructor. The first version is a ***parameterless*** constructor. The parameterless constructor is executed when an object is created without supplying any arguments in the object definition. You see that its body contains a statement that you have not seen before, as follows:

super(0000,0.0);

This statement tells the compiler to call the superclass constructor. The keyword **super** calls the superclass constructor, which requires two arguments to initialize the *accountNumber* and *balance*. Here, we have supplied arguments of 0000 and 0.0 to initialize *accountNumber* and *balance*, respectively. Maybe you noticed in the *BankAccount* class declaration that we did not initialize its data members. This is because they will be initialized automatically by a call to the superclass constructor within a subclass constructor when any object is created for a subclass. The superclass constructor is not inherited by the subclass but can be called by the subclass constructor using the keyword **super**. One thing you need to remember is that the call to the superclass constructor must be the first statement in the subclass constructor.

> A superclass constructor is called by a subclass constructor using the keyword **super** and supplying the argument values required by the superclass constructor. The call to the superclass constructor must be the first statement in the subclass constructor.

Now, look at the second version for the *Checking()* constructor. Do you see what it is doing? You're right if you thought that it is initializing the *accountNumber* and *balance* data members with values received by the constructor. Notice that these values are passed on to the superclass constructor via the **super**(acctNum,bal) call. How about the third version of the constructor? Here you see the *accountNumber* and *balance* being initialized by calling the superclass constructor, followed by assignments to *minimum* and *charge* to initialize these data members. Of course, the constructor requires four parameters to initialize all four data members, right? (Why does this class have four data members, when only two are shown in the foregoing declaration?) Because we have three different versions of the *Checking()* constructor, we can define an object for the *Checking* class three different ways. Here are some examples:

```
Checking AndrewStaugaard = new Checking();
Checking MichaelJordan = new Checking(0010,10000);
Checking BillGates = new Checking(0020,100000,100,0.25);
```

With what values have each of the four data members been initialized for each object in the foregoing definitions? Think about it, since this will be left as an exercise at the end of this section.

Finally, the *cashCheck()* method is used to debit the account balance by cashing a check. It receives an amount (*amt*) from the calling object and generates an error message if this amount exceeds the account balance. Otherwise, the check is cashed, and the account balance is debited accordingly. Notice that a check-cashing charge is applied if the amount of the check is less than the required minimum balance.

The class diagram in Figure 10-3 shows the *Checking* subclass structure and interface.

Checking Subclass

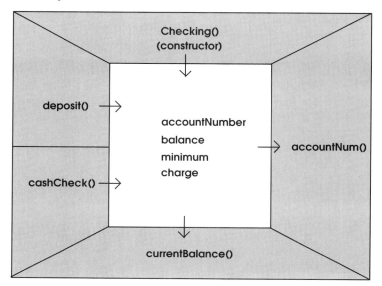

Figure 10-3 The *Checking* subclass inherits the *BankAccount* superclass members and adds its own protected members of *minimum* and *charge* as well as a public method called *cashCheck* and a constructor.

Looking back at Figure 10-1, you see that a *SuperNow* class is derived from the *Checking* class. A super-now account is one where you get interest on your checking account if you maintain a minimum balance. In addition, no per-check charge is made if the balance stays above the minimum. This is a perfect place to declare a subclass of the *Checking* class, because the *SuperNow* class can inherit the *minimum* and *charge* data members as well as the *cashCheck()* method of the *Checking* class. So, let's develop a subclass called *SuperNow* like this:

```
package bankaccounts;

//SUBCLASS SuperNow INHERITS Checking CLASS
public class SuperNow extends Checking
{
```

```
//DATA MEMBERS
protected double interestRate = 0.0;    //ANNUAL INTEREST RATE

//METHOD MEMBERS
//PARAMETERLESS CONSTRUCTOR
public SuperNow()
{
   super(0000,0.0);
}//END SuperNow()

//CONSTRUCTOR TO INITIALIZE ACCOUNT NUMBER AND BALANCE
public SuperNow(int acctNum, double bal)
{
   super(acctNum,bal);
}//END SuperNow(int)

//CONSTRUCTOR TO INITIALIZE ALL DATA
public SuperNow (int acctNum,
                 double bal,
                 double min,
                 double chg,
                 double rate)
{
   super(acctNum,bal);
   minimum = min;
   charge = chg;
   interestRate = rate;
} //END SuperNow(int,double,double,double,double)

//IMPLEMENTATION FOR addInterest() METHOD
public void addInterest()
{
   double interest = 0.0;         //LOCAL VARIABLE TO CALC. INTEREST
   if (balance >= minimum)
   {
       interest = balance * (interestRate/12/100);
       balance = balance + interest;
   } //END IF
 } //END addInterest()
}//END SuperNow
```

First, you see that this class is part of our *bankaccounts* package, because of the statement package bankaccounts; The *SuperNow* class declaration uses the keyword **public** so it is accessible outside the *bankaccounts* package. As you can see, this class inherits the *Checking* class, which inherits the *BankAccount* class. The only data member unique to this class is *interestRate*, which specifies the annual interest rate to be applied to the account. However, through inheritance, there are four additional data members. What are they? Well, *accountNumber* and *balance* are inherited from the *BankAccount* class via the *Checking* class, and *minimum* and *charge* are inherited directly from the *Checking* class.

There are two additional methods declared for this class: the *SuperNow()* constructor method, which initializes the data members of the class; and the *addInterest()* method, which will credit the account balance with interest at a rate specified by the *interestRate* data member. As you can see, the *SuperNow()* constructor method is overloaded three ways. Observe how each version of the constructor uses **super** to call the superclass constructor. The *addInterest()* method adds monthly interest to the account if the account balance is greater than or equal to the minimum required balance.

The class diagram in Figure 10-4 shows the *SuperNow* subclass structure and interface. Now, the last class that we need to declare for our family is the *Savings* account class. Here's the declaration:

```
package bankaccounts;
//SUBCLASS Savings INHERITS BankAccount CLASS
public class Savings extends BankAccount
{
 //DATA MEMBERS
 protected double interestRate = 0.0;     //ANNUAL INTEREST RATE

 //METHOD MEMBERS
 //PARAMETERLESS CONSTRUCTOR
 public Savings()
 {
    super(0000,0.0);
 }//END Savings()

 //CONSTRUCTOR TO INITIALIZE ACCOUNT NUMBER AND BALANCE
 public Savings(int acctNum,double bal)
 {
    super(acctNum,bal);
 }//END Savings(int,double)

 //CONSTRUCTOR TO INITIALIZE ALL PRIVATE DATA
 public Savings(int acctNum, double bal, double rate)
 {
```

```
        super(acctNum,bal);
        interestRate = rate;
    }//END Savings(int,double,double)

    //withdraw() METHOD
    public void withdraw(double amt)
    {
        balance = balance - amt;
    }//END withdraw()

    //IMPLEMENTATION FOR addInterest() METHOD
    public void addInterest()
    {
        double interest;
        interest = balance * (interestRate/12/100);
        balance = balance + interest;
    } //END addInterest()
}//END Savings
```

SuperNow Subclass

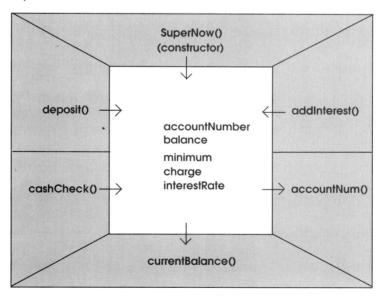

Figure 10-4 The *SuperNow* subclass inherits the *Checking* class members and adds its own protected member of *interestRate* as well as a public method called *addInterest( )* and a constructor.

The *Savings* class also inherits the *accountNumber* and *balance* data members from the *BankAccount* class. In addition, an *interestRate* data member is defined for this class. The *interestRate* data member will store an annual savings account interest rate value. There are three additional methods defined for the *Savings* class. The overloaded *Savings()* constructor method is used to initialize the class data members. The *addInterest()* method is used to credit the account balance with monthly interest earnings. The *withdraw()* method is used to debit the account balance when a savings withdrawal is made. Moreover, because the *Savings* class is derived from the *BankAccount* class, it inherits the *deposit()* method. The method implementations should be self-explanatory by now. Notice, however, that this *addInterest()* method differs from the *addInterest()* method in the *SuperNow* class. The *Savings* class *addInterest()* method does not depend on a minimum balance, whereas the *SuperNow* class *addInterest()* method does. The class diagram in Figure 10-5 shows the *Savings* subclass structure and interface.

We can use the **Venn diagram** shown in Figure 10-6 to summarize the bank account class family hierarchy. Notice how the class inheritance patterns can be seen by the intersections between the classes.

Savings Subclass

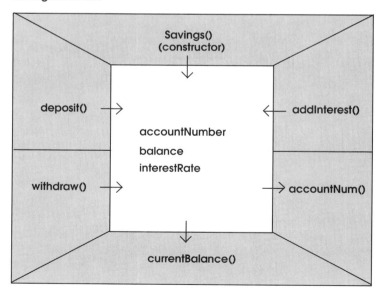

Figure 10-5 The *Savings* subclass inherits the *BankAccount* superclass members and adds its own protected member of *interestRate* as well as public methods called *withdraw(), addInterest(),* along with a constructor.

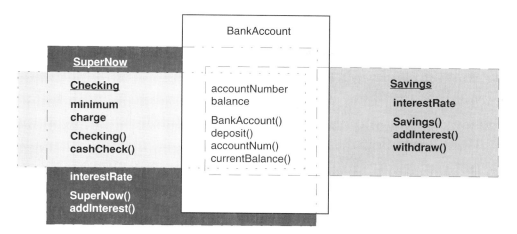

Figure 10-6 A Venn diagram shows the shared members of a class family hierarchy.

Finally, we need an application class to exercise our class family. Here is one that will demonstrate most of the family features:

```
import bankaccounts.*;        //FOR BANKING ACCOUNT CLASSES
import keyboardInput.*;       //FOR readChar()

public class Transactions
{
  public static void main(String[] args)
  {
  //DEFINE VARIABLES
  char pause = ' ';    //FREEZE VARIABLE

  //DEFINE KEYBOARD OBJECT
  Keyboard in = new Keyboard();

  //DEFINE BANKING ACCOUNT OBJECTS
   Checking BjarneStroustrup1 = new Checking(0001,0);
   SuperNow JohnMcCarthy1 = new SuperNow(0002,1050);
   Savings GraceHopper1 = new Savings(0003,2500);
   Checking GraceHopper2 = new Checking(0004,0);
   Savings AndrewStaugaard = new Savings();

  //MONTHLY CHECKING ACCOUNT TRANSACTIONS
  BjarneStroustrup1.deposit(2500);
  BjarneStroustrup1.cashCheck (500.00);
  BjarneStroustrup1.cashCheck (500.00);
```

```
BjarneStroustrup1.cashCheck (700.75);
BjarneStroustrup1.cashCheck (200.00);
GraceHopper2.deposit(2500);
GraceHopper2.cashCheck(25.75);
GraceHopper2.cashCheck(75.25);

//MONTHLY SUPER-NOW ACCOUNT TRANSACTIONS
JohnMcCarthy1.deposit(2000.00);
JohnMcCarthy1.cashCheck(200.00);

//MONTHLY SAVINGS ACCOUNT TRANSACTIONS
GraceHopper1.deposit(2000.00);
GraceHopper1.withdraw(350);

//MONTHLY REPORT OF ACCOUNT BALANCES
JohnMcCarthy1.addInterest();
GraceHopper1.addInterest();
System.out.println("\n\t\t\tAccount Statement\n");
System.out.println("Account number:  "
                    + BjarneStroustrup1.accountNum()
                    + "\tBjarne Stroustrup:  $"
                    + BjarneStroustrup1.currentBalance());

System.out.println("\n\n\t\t\tAccount Statement\n");
System.out.println("Account number:  "
                    + JohnMcCarthy1.accountNum()
                    + "\tJohnMcCarthy:  $"
                    + JohnMcCarthy1.currentBalance());

System.out.println("\n\n\t\t\tAccount Statement\n");
System.out.println("Account number:  "
                    + GraceHopper1.accountNum()
                    + "\tGraceHopper1:  $"
                    + GraceHopper1.currentBalance());

System.out.println("\n\n\t\t\tAccount Statement\n");
System.out.println("Account number:  "
                    + GraceHopper2.accountNum()
                    + "\tGraceHopper2:  $"
                    + GraceHopper2.currentBalance());
```

```
System.out.println("\n\n\t\t\tAccount Statement\n");
System.out.println("Account number:  "
                    + AndrewStaugaard.accountNum()
                    + "\tAndrewStaugaard:  $"
                    + AndrewStaugaard.currentBalance());

//FREEZE DISPLAY
System.out.println("\nPress ENTER to continue.");
pause = in.readChar();
} //END main()
}//END Transactions
```

The application class is called *Transactions* and begins by importing all of the bank account classes contained in the *bankaccounts* package. Looking at method *main()* within the class, you see that several objects are defined for the various banking account classes. The object name corresponds to the customer name. A suffix is added to the customer name so that the same customer can have more than one bank account. For instance, you see that *GraceHopper1* is a checking account object, and *GraceHopper2* is a savings account object. Notice also that a unique account number and an initial account balance are specified when each object is defined, except for the last object. As a result, the customer account number and balance are initialized with these values. All other data members will take on their respective default. The last object is defined without any initializing values. Therefore, its account number and balance are initialized with zeros.

Next, monthly transactions are listed for each type of account. Can you determine what should happen in each transaction? Finally, a monthly balance report of each account is generated on the display monitor. What will be the balance for each account at the end of the month, using the indicated transactions in the order that they appear?

 Quick Check

1.   True or false: When declaring a subclass, the subclass name is listed first followed by the keyword **extends** followed by the superclass name.

2.   You must use the keyword _____ to call the superclass constructor in a subclass constructor.

3. True or false: A protected superclass member is protected from any use by the subclasses of that superclass.

4. Explain the difference between a **private**, **protected**, and **public** member of a class.

5. What would be wrong with deriving the *Savings* class from the *SuperNow* class in the program discussed in this section?

6. Given the following object definitions for the *Checking* class declared in this section:

    Checking AndrewStaugaard = new Checking();
    Checking MichaelJordan = new Checking(0010,10000);
    Checking BillGates = new Checking(0020,100000,100,0.25);

    To what values will each of the object data members be initialized?

10-3 POLYMORPHISM AND DYNAMIC BINDING

In the Chapter 10 introduction, it was stated that there are four concepts central to OOP: encapsulation with information hiding, inheritance, polymorphism, and dynamic binding. We have thoroughly explored the first two. For completeness, we will now briefly discuss the latter two concepts of polymorphism and dynamic binding.

Polymorphism

The term "polymorphic" is Greek meaning "of many forms." Polymorphism is associated with methods, as indicated in the following definition:

> A *polymorphic* method is one that has the same name for different classes of the same family but has different implementations for the various classes.

As you can see, polymorphism allows methods of the same name to behave differently within a class family. You have just seen an example of a polymorphic method in our bank account class family. Can you identify which method it is from the class declarations? You're right if you thought the *addInterest()* method. Notice that this method is defined in both the *SuperNow* and *Savings* classes. The method interface is identical in both classes; however, the implementation is different in each class. In effect, we are hiding alternative operations behind the common *addInterest( )* interface. This means that two objects defined for these classes will respond to the common operation, *addInterest( )*, in different ways. Languages that do not support polymorphism, such as COBOL and C, require large switch/case statements to implement this effect.

Polymorphism allows objects to be more independent, even though they are members of the same class family. Moreover, new classes can be added to the family without changing existing ones. This allows systems to evolve over time, meeting the needs of a changing application. Consider a word processing program where the system is required to print many different types of documents. Recall from Chapter 9 that many such programs employ classes to define the structure and behavior of a given type of document. Each document class will have a *print( )* method to print a specific document in its correct format. Such a method would be a polymorphic method, because it would have a common interface but behave differently for different document objects. Polymorphism allows one method name to be shared throughout the class family, with each class implementing the method in a way that is appropriate to its own purpose.

Polymorphism is accomplished using ***overloaded methods*** or ***polymorphic methods***. Overloaded methods were discussed earlier in Chapter 8. However, polymorphic methods are something new. The difference between the two has to do with the different techniques that are used by Java to call the method. Overloaded methods are called using ***static binding***, and polymorphic methods are called using ***dynamic binding***.

Dynamic versus Static Binding

Binding relates to the actual time when the code for a given method is attached, or bound, to the method.

> ***Dynamic***, or ***late***, ***binding*** occurs when a method is defined for several classes in a family but the actual code for the method is not attached, or bound, until execution time. Such a method is called a ***polymorphic method***.

Dynamic binding is implemented in Java through ***polymorphic methods***. With dynamic binding, the selection of code to be executed when a method is called is delayed until execution time. This means that when a method is called, the executable code determines at run time which version of the method to call.

As an example of dynamic binding consider what happens when you double-click a mouse. The double-clicking action generates an *event*, which calls upon a poloymorphic method. If you double-click on a file folder, a directory listing opens. If you double-click on an application icon, a program is executed. If you double-click on a document, a word processing program is launched and the document is opened. So, the double-clicking event resulted in a different behavior each time. This is polymorphism and it surely happens at execution time.

> ***Static binding*** occurs when a method is defined with the same name but with different signatures and implementations. The actual code for the method is attached, or bound, at compile time. Overloaded methods are statically bound.

Static binding, on the other hand, occurs when the method code is "bound" at compile time. This means that when an overloaded method is called, the compiler determines at compile time which version of the method to call. Overloaded methods are statically bound, whereas polymorphic methods are dynamically bound. With overloaded methods, the compiler can determine which method to call based on the number of and data types of the method parameters. However, polymorphic methods have the same signature within a given class family. Therefore, hidden ***pointers*** must be used during run time to determine which method to call. Fortunately, you don't have to worry about how the binding is accomplished, because this is taken care of automatically by the compiler.

> A ***pointer*** is a direct program reference to an actual physical address in memory. Java uses pointers extensively to implement programs but does not allow you, the programmer, to use pointers. This can be an advantage or a disadvantage. Languages that allow the use of pointers, such as C and C++, provide more flexibility for the programmer, because the programmer can create a pointer to point to anything in memory, even the operating system memory. But, of course, this could be very hazardous to your system if not used properly. Because pointers can be dangerous when used improperly, Java simply does not support them, providing you protection from errors commonly associated with pointers. Another reason for Java's not supporting pointers is that Java was meant to be a totally portable language across all platforms.

Abstract Classes and Methods

You have probably noticed that with inheritance, superclasses are very abstract and become more concrete as subclasses are created. In other words, a superclass starts off as very general while its subclasses become more specific, or refined, with each succeeding subclass in the class hierarchy. In fact, when inheritance is used properly, there should never be any objects defined for the superclass, since the superclass is too general, or abstract. When no objects can be created for a class, the class is called an ***abstract class***. A subclass of an abstract class is referred to as ***concrete class***, since objects can be created for the subclass.

An ***abstract*** class is a superclass for which objects will never be created.

A ***concrete class*** is a subclass for which objects will always be created.

To declare a superclass as an abstract superclass in Java, you must use the keyword **abstract** in the class header line. When would you want to declare a superclass as abstract? Well, when you have a situation where no objects will ever be created for the superclass. Actually, our *BankAccount* class is a good candidate for an abstract class, since no objects would ever be created for this class. A given bank account can only be a checking, super-now, savings, or some other type of account, right? As another example, consider an employee package. Such a package would most likely have one class for hourly employees and another class for salaried employees. Both classes would have common data members, such as the employee's name and number, and both classes would have common operations, or methods, such as one to determine weekly pay. Thus, you would likely create an employee superclass with two subclasses as shown in Figure 10-7. So, let's specify an *Employee* superclass like this:

Class: *Employee*
    Data Members: *employeeName*
                  employeeNumber

    Method Members: *getName()*
                  getNumber()

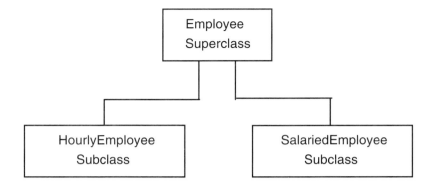

Figure 10-7 This employee class family consists of an abstract superclass called *Employee* and two concrete subclasses called *HourlyEmployee* and *SalariedEmployee*.

The class diagram in Figure 10-8 illustrates this superclass. Should the *Employee* class be an abstract class? Of course it should, because no object will ever be created for this class. An employee must either be an hourly employee or a salaried employee. So, let's declare an abstract class called *Employee* as follows:

```
package employees;

//ABSTRACT SUPERCLASS FOR ALL EMPLOYEES
public abstract class Employee
{
 //DATA MEMBERS
 protected String employeeName;        //EMPLOYEE NAME
 protected int employeeNumber;         //EMPLOYEE NUMBER

 //METHOD MEMBERS
 //CONSTRUCTOR
 public Employee(String name, int number)
 {
   employeeName = name;
   employeeNumber = number;
 }//END Employee()

 //ACCESS METHOD FOR name
 public String getName()
 {
   return employeeName;                //RETURN EMPLOYEE NAME
 }//END getName()
```

```
//ACCESS METHOD FOR employeeNumber
public int getNumber()
{
  return employeeNumber;          //RETURN EMPLOYEE NUMBER
}//END employeeNumber()

//ABSTRACT METHOD TO RETURN WEEKLY PAY
  public abstract double weeklyPay();
}//END Employee CLASS
```

Employee Superclass

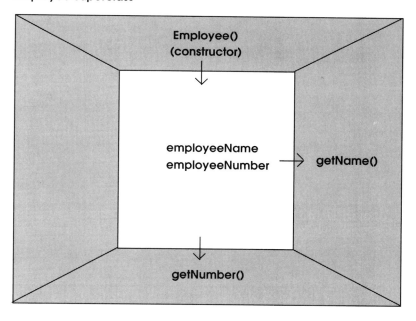

Figure 10-8 The *Employee* superclass consists of protected *employeeName* and *employeeNumber* members along with public access methods of *getName()* and *getNumber()* as well as a constructor that form the class interface.

Most of the *Employee* class code should be familiar to you by now. The class is part of a package called *employees*. Notice that the class is declared as an abstract class by including the keyword **abstract** in the class header line. This means that no objects can ever be created for this class. The class has two protected data members, *employeeName* and *employeeNumber*, to store the employees name and number, respectively. The class has four methods: an

Employee() constructor method, two access methods that return the employees name and number, and an ***abstract method*** called *weeklyPay()* that will return the weekly pay for a given employee. An abstract method is a polymorphic method whose signature is placed in the superclass, along with the keyword **abstract**. Notice that only the signature for the *weeklyPay()* method is provided in the *Employee* class declaration. A semicolon follows the signature with no implementation provided. The implementation will be provided in the subclass declarations. Why? Because the process of determining the weekly pay for an hourly employee differs from that of determining the weekly pay for a salaried employee, right? Observe that we have added the keyword **abstract** within the method signature to specify it as an abstract method. This tells the compiler to look for the method implementation in the subclasses. By the way, an **abstract** method can never be **static**, **final**, or **private**.

> An ***abstract method*** is a polymorphic method in a superclass whose behavior will be defined in the subclasses.

DEBUGGING TIP

It is a syntax error to create an object for an abstract class. Thus, the statement

Employee BobJones = new Employee();

will not compile. An employee object must be either an hourly employee object or a salaried employee object in this example.

Now, let's declare our two subclasses. First the *HourlyEmployee* class as follows needs to have the following members:

    Class: *HourlyEmployee*
       Data Members: *rate*
                           hours

       Method Members: *weeklyPay()*

The class diagram in Figure 10-9 illustrates this subclass.

HourlyEmployee Subclass

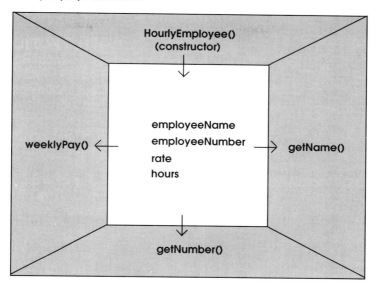

Figure 10-9 The *HourlyEmployee* superclass consists of *rate* and *hours* data members and *weeklyPay()* method member in addition to the members inherited from the *Employee* superclass.

Following the class specification, the class code becomes:

```
package employees;

public class HourlyEmployee extends Employee
{
  //DATA MEMBERS
  private double rate = 0.0;          //HOURLY PAY RATE
  private double hours = 0.0;         //WEEKLY HOURS WORKED

  //METHOD MEMBERS

  //PARAMETERLESS CONSTRUCTOR
  public HourlyEmployee()
  {
    super(" ",0000);
  }//END HourlyEmployee()
```

```
//CONSTRUCTOR TO INITIALIZE EMPLOYEE NAME AND NUMBER
public HourlyEmployee(String name, int number)
{
  super(name,number);
}//END HourlyEmployee(String,int)

//CONSTRUCTOR TO INITIALIZE ALL PRIVATE DATA
public HourlyEmployee(String name, int number, double rate, double hours)
{
  super (name,number);
  this.rate = rate;
  this.hours = hours;
}//END HourlyEmployee(String,int,double,double)

//METHOD TO RETURN WEEKLY PAY
public double weeklyPay()
{
  if (hours <= 40)
    return rate * hours;
  else
    return 40 * rate + ((hours - 40) * 1.5 * rate);
}//END weeklyPay()
}//END HourlyEmployee
```

This class has two additional private members for the hourly rate and weekly hours. There are two methods: an overloaded constructor which should be self-explanatory at this point, and our polymorphic *weeklyPay()* method. Here is where you find the implementation required to calculate the weekly pay of an hourly employee.

Next we have the *SalariedEmployee* class specification as follows:

Class: *SalariedEmployee*
    Data Members: *annualSalary*

    Method Members: *weeklyPay()*

The class diagram in Figure 10-10 illustrates this subclass.

SalariedEmployee Subclass

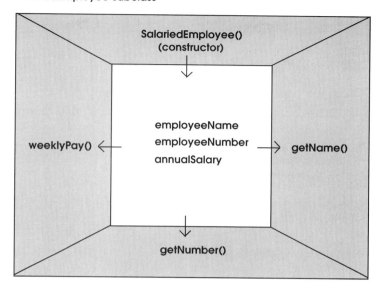

Figure 10-10 The *SalariedEmployee* superclass consists of an *annualSalary* data member and *weeklyPay()* method member in addition to the members inherited from the *Employee* superclass.

Here's the class code:

```
package employees;
public class SalariedEmployee extends Employee
{
  //DATA MEMBERS
  private double annualSalary = 0.0;      //ANNUAL SALARY

  //METHOD MEMBERS

  //PARAMETERLESS CONSTUCTOR
  public SalariedEmployee()
  {
    super(" ",0000);
  }//END SalariedEmployee()
```

```
//CONSTRUCTOR TO INITIALIZE EMPLOYEE NAME AND NUMBER
public SalariedEmployee(String name, int number)
{
  super(name,number);
}//END SalariedEmployee(String,int)

//CONSTRUCTOR TO INITIALIZE ALL PRIVATE DATA
public SalariedEmployee(String name, int number, double salary)
{
  super (name,number);
  annualSalary = salary;
}//END SalariedEmployee(String,int,double)

//METHOD TO RETURN WEEKLY PAY
public double weeklyPay()
{
  return annualSalary/52;
}//END weeklyPay()
}//END SalariedEmployee
```

Here you see an additional data member called *annualSalary*. Again, we have an overloaded constructor and the *weeklyPay()* method. However, the implementation of this *weeklyPay()* method is that which is required to calculate the weekly pay of a salaried employee from an annual salary figure versus that of an hourly employee.

How do you suppose that the compiler knows which *weeklyPay()* method to use? You're right if you thought that it doesn't until an object is defined in an application class. If an object is defined as a *HourlyEmployee* object, the hourly implementation is executed, while a *SalariedEmployee* object will cause the salary implementation to be executed. This will happen at run time, making the *weeklyPay()* method truly a polymorphic method. Here is the application class that we used to test the *Employee* class family:

```
import employees.*;          //FOR EMPLOYEE CLASSES
import keyboardInput.*;       //FOR readChar()

public class Payroll
{
  public static void main(String[] args)
  {
   //DEFINE VARIABLES
   char pause = ' ';    //FREEZE VARIABLE
```

```
        //DEFINE KEYBOARD OBJECT
        Keyboard in = new Keyboard();

        //DEFINE EMPLOYEE OBJECTS
        HourlyEmployee BobJones= new HourlyEmployee("Bob Jones",0001,
                                        10.00,45.0);

        SalariedEmployee BillGates = new SalariedEmployee("Bill Gates",0002,
                                                10000000.00);


        //DISPLAY WEEKLY PAY
        System.out.println("The weekly pay for " + BobJones.getName()
                        + " is $" + BobJones.weeklyPay());

        System.out.println("The weekly pay for " + BillGates.getName()
                        + " is $" + BillGates.weeklyPay());

        //FREEZE DISPLAY
        System.out.println("Press ENTER to continue.);
        pause = in.readChar();
    }//END main()
}//END Payroll
```

Here is the output produced by the program:

```
The weekly pay for Bob Jones is $475.00
The weekly pay for Bill Gates is $192307.69
```

Do you think there is any disparity between the two weekly pay figures?

 Quick Check

1. True or false: An overloaded method is polymorphic.

2. True or false: All overloaded methods are dynamically bound.

3. True or false: A polymorphic method interface is identical for each version of the method in a given class family.

4.   Overloaded methods are _____ bound.

5.   Polymorphic methods are _____ bound.

6.   The implementation code for a dynamically bound method is determined at _____.

7.   What is the difference between an abstract class and a concrete class?

8.   True or false: An abstract method is always polymorphic.

9.   Where is the implementation found for an abstract method?

CHAPTER SUMMARY

Inheritance is an important property of object-oriented programming that allows one class, called a subclass, to share the structure and behavior of another class, called a superclass. The subclass should always be related to its superclass via the IS-A relationship. You control the amount of inheritance by designating the members as private, protected, or public in the class declarations. You control the amount of class inheritance by designating the class as public or nonpublic (by default) in the subclass declaration. Classes are designated as subclasses in Java by using the keyword **extends** within the class header line.

Polymorphism has to do with methods and objects that have the same name but different behavior within a class family. Polymorphism allows methods and objects to be more independent and class families to be more flexible. Overloaded methods and polymorphic methods are both polymorphic. Overloaded methods are statically bound to their code during compile time, whereas polymorphic methods are dynamically bound to their code during run time.

When inheritance is used properly, there should never be any objects defined for a superclass, since the superclass is too general, or abstract. When no objects can be created for a class, the class is called an abstract class. A subclass of an abstract class is referred to as concrete class, since objects are normally created for subclasses. An abstract method is truly polymorphic, since its implementation differs from subclass to subclass within a class family. Both abstract classes and methods are designated as such in Java by using the keyword **abstract** within the class header line or method signature.

QUESTIONS AND PROBLEMS

Questions

1. Define the following terms:
   Superclass
   Subclass
   Inheritance
   IS-A
   Polymorphism
   Abstract class
   Concrete class
   Abstract method
   Dynamic binding
   Static binding

2. Suggest several real-world applications for the use of inheritance.

3. What relationship must be considered between a potential subclass and its superclass when developing inheritance?

4. Given a superclass called *Point*, write the class declaration header line for a subclass called *Pixel*. Assume that the *Pixel* class is to be accessible outside of its package.

5. Why doesn't Java support pointers?

6. Explain the difference between a **private**, **protected**, and **public** member of a class.

7. When should you use the keyword **public** in a subclass declaration?

8. Why is an overloaded method polymorphic?

9. Explain the difference between static binding and dynamic binding.

10. Draw a Venn diagram for the employee class family developed in this chapter.

11. When should a superclass be declared as an abstract superclass?

12. When should a method be declared as an abstract method?

13. Where are the implementations found for an abstract method?

Problems

Least Difficult

1. Determine the output generated by the application class *(Transactions)* given in this chapter.

2. Code the files for the banking program given in this chapter. Then, write your own application program to exercise the class family in different ways. See if you can predict the results of your banking transactions.

3. Rewrite the *BankAccount* class given in this chapter as an abstract class. This class can be found in the *BankAccount.java* file of the *bankaccounts* package on the CD that came with this book or downloaded from www.prenhall.com. Make the *deposit()* method an abstract method and define its implementation in the respective subclasses that employ its use. Then, write your own application program to exercise the class family in different ways. See if you can predict the results of your banking transactions.

4. Code the files for the employee program given in this chapter. The *Employee* class family is within the *employees* package on the CD that accompanies this book and is also at www.prenhall.com. Then, write your own application class to exercise the class family in different ways.

More Difficult

5. Add a *CreditCard* class to the *BankAccount* class family developed in this chapter. The *BankAccount* class family is within the *bankaccounts* package on the CD which accompanies this book and is also at www.prenhall.com. The *CreditCard* class should inherit the *BankAccount* class directly. Provide methods to debit monthly charges and interest from the account balance. Write an application class to exercise a *CreditCard* class object and report the balance due.

6. Add a *PartTimeEmployee* class to the *Employee* class family developed in this chapter. The *Employee* class family is within the *employees* package on the CD that accompanies this book and is also at www.prenhall.com. The *PartTimeEmployee* class should have a *weeklyPay()* method that does not calculate overtime. Write an application class to exercise a *PartTimeEmployee* class object and report the weekly pay for this object.

More Difficult

7. Create a *persons* package that contains a family of classes of persons. Think of the persons that make up your institution. For example, a student is a person, a staff member is a person, a faculty member is a person, and an administrator is a person (some of the time). Each of these persons has

common as well as unique attributes and behaviors. For instance, both a student and a faculty member have a name and address. However, a student has a GPA, while a faculty member has a rank

Build, compile, and test your person family using an application class. Be creative and try different things—this is when you really learn how to program in Java, as well as any other language for that matter.

Most Difficult

8. Declare an *Insurance* superclass that contains the following members:

    Class: *Insurance*

    Data Members

    - An insurance account number.
    - An insurance policy number.
    - The name of the insured.
    - Annual premium.

    Method Members

    - A set method that will allow the user to enter the values of the data members.
    - A get method that will display the data member values.

9. Declare two subclasses called *Automobile* and *Home* that inherit the *Insurance* superclass declared in problem 8. Provide the following methods in these subclasses:

    Class: *Automobile*

    Data Members

    - Make of automobile.
    - Model of automobile.
    - Automobile VIN number.
    - Amount of liability coverage
    - Amount of comprehensive coverage.
    - Amount of collision coverage.

    Method Members

    - *Set and get methods for the specific automobile data members.*

    Class: *Home*

    Data Members

    - House square footage.

- • Amount of dwelling coverage.
- • Amount of contents coverage.
- • Amount of liability coverage

Method Members

- • *Set and get methods for the specific home data members.*

10. Write an application class that defines an automobile and home insurance object from the classes declared in problems 8 and 9. Include statements in the program that will exercise the object methods.

Applet 101: APPLETS

PURPOSE

- *To become familiar with Java applets.*
- *To demonstrate that applets have all the generic window features of a frame, including the closing feature.*
- *To show how to create a simple applet from the Applet class in Java.*
- *To demonstrate the use of the paint() method.*
- *To show how to set the font and color of graphical objects within an applet window.*
- *To show how to draw a string within an applet window.*
- *To show how to set the status bar of an applet window.*

Introduction

As you are now aware, you can build ***application*** or ***applet*** programs in Java. As a piglet is a little pig, an applet is a little application. The term applet has nothing to do with the Apple computer company. Application programs are created for general system and shrink-wrapped commercial software, while applets are created to run on the Internet when called by an HTML page. As a result, applets can be run from a "Java-enabled" Web browser. An applet provides for dynamic user interaction and graphical animation on a Web page through its graphical user interface. Without applets, static HTML Web pages would be very boring.

Everything that you have learned to date can be applied to applets, except for frames. This is because a frame is a container for GUI components within an application program, while the applet itself is a container for GUI components within an applet program. Like frames in applications, applets are used as containers to hold GUI components. When you create an applet program, it is, by definition, a GUI program. Furthermore, a Java application program has a *main()*

method which is called when the program starts. Applet programs, on the other hand, do not have a *main()* method. Rather, applets rely on the Web browser to call certain other methods that we will discuss shortly.

In this module, you will load and execute a simple Java applet. You will modify the code and observe the effect on the window generated by the applet.

Procedure

1. Load and execute the *Applet101_1.java* program contained on the CD that accompanies this book or download it from www.prenhall.com. Use your Java compiler to compile the program as an applet, then execute the program through your compiler or a Web browser. You should observe the window shown in Figure 1.

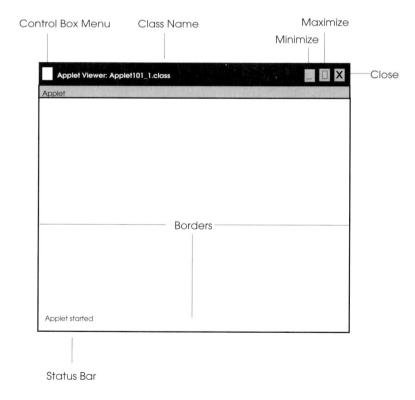

Figure 1 The simple window generated by the *Applet101_1.java* applet program in a Windows environment.

2. Resize the window to different sizes by grabbing and moving the window borders.

3. If you are in a Windows environment, minimize the window by clicking the Minimize button in the upper-right-hand corner of the window. Restore the window by switching to the *Applet101_1.java* task (*Alt-Tab*).

4. Close the window by clicking the *Close* button in the upper-right-hand corner of the window (Windows), or upper-left-hand corner of the window (Mac).

Discussion

Here is the code that produced the applet window:

```
1   import java.applet.Applet;  //FOR APPLET CLASS
2
3   public class Applet101_1 extends Applet
4   {
5
6   }//END APPLET
```

Wow, what a simple program! Notice that the standard Java *Applet* class is imported and then our *Applet101_1* class is declared as a subclass of this standard *Applet* class. Our *Applet101_1* class is empty and, therefore, does not do anything but create the applet window in Figure 1. All the work of creating this generic window is being done by the standard *Applet* superclass. Notice our applet window has inherited all the standard features of any window, such as borders, maximize, minimize, closing, resizing, and so on. In addition, an applet window contains a *status bar* at the bottom of the window to indicate the current status of the applet. Here, the status bar indicates the applet has started running.

So, an applet is like a frame which provides a window container for GUI components; however, unlike a frame, an applet includes a status bar and the window close feature. Recall that the window closing feature had to be added to a simple frame.

5. Load and execute the *Applet101_2.java* program contained on the CD that accompanies this book or download it from www.prenhall.com. Use your Java compiler to compile the program as an applet and then execute the program through your compiler or a Web browser. You should observe the window shown in Figure 2.

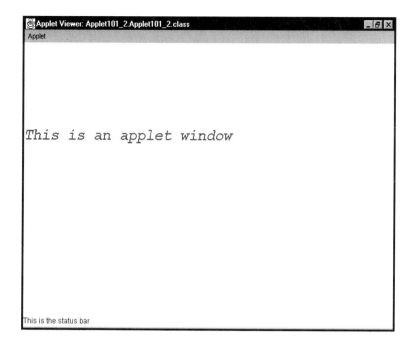

Figure 2 The window generated by the *Applet101_2.java* applet .

Here is the code that produced the applet window in Figure 2:

```
1     import java.applet.Applet;            //FOR APPLET CLASS
2     import java.awt.*;                    //FOR GRAPHICS CLASS
3
4     public class Applet101_2 extends Applet
5     {
6
7       public void paint(Graphics g)
8       {
9         //DEFINE FONT OBJECT AND SET FONT
10        Font f = new Font("Courier",Font.ITALIC + Font.BOLD,25);
11        g.setFont(f);
12
13        //SET COLOR
14        g.setColor(Color.red);
15
```

```
16     //DRAW STRING
17     g.drawString("This is an applet window",0,150);
18
19     //DISPLAY STATUS MESSAGE
20     showStatus("This is the status bar");
21   }//END paint()
22 }//END APPLET
```

6. Notice a red string is displayed within the window and a status bar message is displayed at the bottom of the window. Looking at the code, you find a font object, *f*, defined in line 10. Change the font type, style, or size. Then execute the applet again and notice that the applet font is changed accordingly.

7. In line 14 you find the color of the text set to red via the *setColor()* method. Change the text color to any of the 13 colors supported by Java. Execute the program again and notice that the text string color is changed accordingly.

8. In line 17 of the program, you find a call to the *drawString()* method that contains the message displayed in the window. After the message string, you see two numbers that provide the coordinate for the message. The first number is its horizontal position in pixels, while the second number is its vertical position in pixels. Of course, this coordinate is with reference to (0,0), which is the top left-hand corner of the window. Change the message coordinate and execute the program again. Notice that the message is repositioned accordingly.

9. In line 20 of the program, you find a call to the *showStatus()* method. As you probably suspect, this method sets the message displayed within the status bar at the bottom of the applet window. Change the message and execute the applet again. The status bar should reflect your new message.

Discussion

We have one method in this applet called *paint()*. The *paint()* method is called automatically during the execution of an applet and is used to draw strings and geometric shapes. Because it is called automatically, you will never call *paint()* directly from within your applet. You must call *repaint()* within your applet if you want to refresh the images displayed by the *paint()* method. Furthermore, the *paint()* method is not used to display GUI components; it is only used to display strings and geometric shapes. You will learn how to display GUI components in a future *Applet10X* module. The *paint()* method has a single parameter which is an object, *g*, of the standard *Graphics* class. This object is used within *paint()* to call methods of the *Graphics* class, such as *setColor()*, *setFont()*, and *drawString()* as shown in lines 11, 14, and 17 of the applet.

The *setFont()* method sets the font for all subsequent text operations to the font object specified in its argument. Note that, in line 10, we defined a font object, *f*, which is passed to the *setFont()* method.

The *setColor()* method of the *Graphics* class sets the color of all subsequent graphical objects to the color specified in its argument. In line 14 we have specified a color of red.

The *drawString()* method draws the text of the specified string using the current font and color. The first character of the string is placed at the coordinate specified in the method. For example, the *drawString()* method in line 17 places the first character of the string at coordinate (0,150). Of course, the point of reference is (0,0) which is the top left-hand corner of the window. Remember most display screens are 640 pixels wide by 480 pixels high. So, the coordinate of the lower-right-hand corner of the window is (640,480).

Finally, the *showStatus()* method is used to display a string in the status bar at the bottom of the window. This method is a member of the *Applet* class, not the *Graphics* class and, therefore, is called directly and not with a graphics object.

11
GRAPHICAL USER INTERFACES: GUIs

INTRODUCTION

Up to this point, you have been programming using text-based I/O. By text-based, we mean that all input has been generated from the keyboard and all output has been generated as text characters on the display monitor. A graphical user interface, or GUI, is window-based. Input and output are provided via graphical **components**. Components include menus, buttons, checkboxes, text fields, and radio buttons, just to mention a few. You have been familiarized with most of these components through the *GUI 10X* series of modules in previous chapters. In this chapter, you will learn how to design and code your own GUIs using the components demonstrated within these modules. GUI design is a big area, not only in computer information systems, but in psychology and graphic arts as well. If this material interests you, you might want to take additional courses in these fields as well as advanced graphics courses in computer information systems or computer science.

As you know, the background for a GUI component is the window. In Java, a window is referred to as a **container**. The term container is used to denote the idea that its purpose is to hold, or contain, window components. A special type of container that we will use to build our GUIs is the **frame**. We will first create a frame which provides a generic window background. Next, we will add the required GUI components to the frame using a **layout manager**. A layout manager provides a standard, predefined way to lay out, or place, our components onto the frame, or window. Finally, we will add **event handlers** to our GUI code in order to capture events generated by the mouse or keyboard.

This chapter will provide you with the basic techniques required to design and build GUIs. Make sure that you get plenty of practice by coding the examples in this chapter, doing the problems at the end of the chapter, and experimenting on your own. This is how you will become proficient in building graphical user interfaces. The material in this chapter employs **event listeners** which are a Java 1.1+ issue. So, to implement event listeners in your Java program you must have Java, version 1.1, or greater.

OBJECTIVES

When you are finished with this chapter, you should have a good understanding of the following:

- How to design and build a GUI.
- The use of frames as containers for GUI components.

- The basic GUI components found in the Java Abstract Windowing Toolkit (AWT).
- The use of a layout manager to place GUI components onto a window.
- How to capture GUI component events using listeners and event handlers.

11-1 FRAMES

As stated in the chapter introduction, a ***frame*** is a container used to hold GUI components. A frame is used to generate a generic window that inherits all the general characteristics of any window. These include a window title, window border, window sizing as well as window maximizing and minimizing. All graphical components in a Java *application program* must be placed in a frame; however, this differs from the requirements of a Java applet. In a Java applet program, the applet itself acts as the container for GUI components. A window created from a frame is nothing more than an object of the standard *Frame* class. The *Frame* class is found in the *java.awt* package. To create a simplified frame you must do three things as follows:

- Define a frame object and provide a frame, or window, title.
- Set the size of the frame, or window, in pixels.
- Make the frame visible to the user.

Here is the required code:

```
//DEFINE FRAME OBJECT
Frame  window = new Frame("This is a frame");

//SET FRAME SIZE WIDTH, HEIGHT
window.setSize(500,300);

//MAKE FRAME VISIBLE
window.setVisible(true);
```

Here, an object called *window* is defined from the standard *Frame* class. The *Frame* class has two constructors as follows:

```
//CREATE A FRAME WITHOUT A TITLE
public Frame();

//CREATE A FRAME WITH A TITLE
public Frame(String title);
```

Notice that the only difference is that the second constructor requires a string argument, while the first does not. The string argument is the frame, or window, title. Thus, the first constructor does not provide any title for the resulting window. In the foregoing frame code, we have employed the second constructor to generate a window title of "This is a frame".

In the second line of code our *window* object calls the *setSize()* method to set the size of the frame, in pixels (picture elements). The first argument of *setSize()* is the width of the frame and the second argument is the height of the frame. Thus, the size of our frame is 500 pixels wide by 300 pixels high. A typical display monitor is 640 pixels wide by 480 pixels high.

The third line of code makes the frame visible. The frame is not displayed until the *setVisible()* method is called by the frame object. Notice that the argument *true* must be provided to make it visible.

Now, let's organize this code into an application program and use inheritance to create our own customized frame class as follows:

```
import java.awt.*;       //FOR FRAME CLASS

//CLASS INHERITS THE FRAME CLASS AND CUSTOMIZES
//THE FRAME AS DESIRED
class SimpleFrame extends Frame
{
  //CONSTRUCTOR
  public SimpleFrame(String title)
  {
   super(title);                        //CALL SUPERCLASS CONSTRUCTOR
   setBackground(Color.white);  //SET WINDOW BACKGROUND COLOR
  }//END SimpleFrame()
}//END SimpleFrame

//CLASS TO TEST SimpleFrame CLASS
public class FrameTest
{
  public static void main(String[] args)
  {
   //DEFINE FRAME OBJECT
   SimpleFrame window = new SimpleFrame("This is a frame");

   //SET FRAME SIZE
   window.setSize(500,300);
```

```
   //MAKE FRAME VISIBLE
   window.setVisible(true);
 }//END main()
}//END FrameTest
```

There is nothing new here; we are simply using the application program format developed earlier. Notice the overall organization of the program. We have created a *SimpleFrame* class that inherits, or extends, the standard *Frame* class. Of course, we have to import the *java.awt* package in order to inherit the *Frame* class. All GUI containers and components are provided in the Java **Abstract Windowing Toolkit**, or **AWT**. The Java AWT is found in the *java.awt* package. As a result, any GUI code must import this package. The *SimpleFrame* class is used to customize the frame the way we want it. Next, a *FrameTest* class is created that uses *main()* to test our frame. Here is where the frame object is defined and used to call the *setSize()* and *setVisible()* methods.

Now, back to the *SimpleFrame* class. All this class consists of is a constructor to customize the frame the way we want it. You see that the constructor calls the superclass constructor. Since the superclass is *Frame*, a call to its constructor will pass the string, *title*, required to set the frame title. Next, the *setBackground()* method is called to set the background color of the frame. This method is also provided in the *java.awt* package. The argument required for this method is a reference to the *Color* class followed by a dot and the desired color. There are 13 different colors possible. Check your on-line help or Java documentation for additional colors. The default color of the frame is white. So, if you desire a white window, you do not need to call the *setBackground()* method. We are just showing it here for example purposes. That completes our custom frame class.

The next class, *FrameTest*, includes *main()* where we first define an object called *window* of our *SimpleFrame* class. When the object is defined, the *SimpleFrame* constructor is called automatically, which will set the frame title and background color. Next, the *window* object is used to call the *setSize()* and *setVisible()* methods as discussed earlier. Code and execute the above program. The window produced by *SimpleFrame* class is shown in Figure 11-1.

Figure 11-1 A simple frame consists of a title bar with title, borders, maximize, minimize, and close buttons. However, the close button is not active. This frame was generated by the *SimpleFrame* class.

If you execute the program, you will find that the window which it creates has all the features of a standard window, except one important feature. You can maximize, minimize, and resize the window, but you cannot close it. To close the window you would normally click the close button in the upper-right-hand corner or select the close option in the control box menu in the upper-left-hand corner. However, even though the close button and menu are part of the window, closing requires a mouse event. Our program does not yet include the code to handle such an event. In a Windows environment, you must *Ctrl-Alt-Delete* at this point and end the program task. So, let's talk about how to handle events. In a Mac environment, you end the task with *option-command-escape*.

Event Handling

Until now, your programs have been employing procedural control of the program logic, whereby control statements, such as decision and loop statements, control the flow of the program. Even though your programs have been object-oriented programs, they have all employed procedural control. Windowed programs, on the other hand, are event-driven programs, whereby the flow of the program logic is dictated by external events. These events usually are the result of a mouse action, such as clicking or movement, or a keyboard stroke.

Java defines several types of events which are summarized in Table 11-1. Notice that each different type of event is associated with a given ***source object***. As its name implies, a source object is the object responsible for the event. Of course, each type of source object responds to a certain action by the user.

TABLE 11-1 EVENTS DEFINED BY JAVA

Event Class	Source Object(s)	User Action
WindowEvent	A window	Window opened/closed.
ActionEvent	A button	Click button.
	A text field	Press return.
	A menu item	Select menu item.
ItemEvent	A checkbox	Select/deselect item.
	A choice box	Select/deselect item.
	A list box	Select/deselect item.
TextEvent	A text component	Change text.
AdjustmentEvent	A scrollbar	Move the scrollbar.
KeyEvent	A key	Key pressed or released.
MouseEvent	A mouse	Move or click mouse.

Event Listeners

The event that we are interested in at this time is *WindowEvent*, because this event is associated with the closing of a window. Now, when an event occurs, the source object triggers the predefined event. Thus, when the close button is clicked in a window, the window source object generates a *WindowEvent*. To detect the event, you need to "register" the source object as a ***listener***. If the object is not registered as a listener, no event handling can occur. Registering an object as a listener is accomplished with an associated *add_____Listener()* method. The blank, _____, in the forgoing method name is the type of event for which to listen. For example, the *addWindowListener()* method is used to register a window object as a listener, the *addActionListener()* method is used to register a button or text field object, the *addItemListener()* method is used to register a checkbox or choice object, and so on.

Now when an event occurs, all the registered listeners will be notified. The registered listeners reference their respective listener class. For instance, a window listener references the *WindowListener* class, an action listener references the *ActionListener* class, and so on. Each class has several predefined abstract methods to handle the event. For example, the *WindowListener* class includes the *windowClosed()*, method and the *ActionListener* class includes the *actionPerformed()* method. These methods are called automatically to handle the event. The listeners and corresponding methods are listed in Table 11-2.

TABLE 11-2 LISTENER CLASSES AND CORRESPONDING METHODS

Listener Class	Method(s)
WindowListener	*windowClosing(WindowEvent e)* *windowOpened(WindowEvent e)* *windowClosed(WindowEvent e)* *windowIconified(WindowEvent e)* *windowDeiconified(WindowEvent e)* *windowActivated(WindowEvent e)* *windowDeactivated(WindowEvent e)*
ActionListener	*actionPerformed(ActionEvent e)*
ItemListener	*itemStateChanged(ItemEvent e)*
TextListener	*textValueChanged(TextEvent e)*
AdjustmentListener	*adjustmentValueChanged(AdjustmentEvent e)*
KeyListener	*keyPressed(KeyEvent e)* *keyReleased(KeyEvent e)* *keyTyped(KeyEvent e)*
MouseListener	*mouseClicked(MouseEvent e)* *mousePressed(MouseEvent e)* *mouseReleased(MouseEvent e)* *mouseEntered(MouseEvent e)* *mouseExited(MouseEvent e)*

Remember, all of the methods in Table 11-2 are abstract methods. Therefore, they are not implemented within their respective class. You must implement them in your subclasses to handle a given type of event. If all of this sounds very complicated, it is! Maybe the flowcharts in Figures 11-2 and 11-3 will help. The flowchart in Figure 11-2 illustrates the programming process of creating a GUI component object, registering the object as a listener, and processing an object event by implementing an event method. Notice from Figure 11-2 that you must first define an object for a component class, then add a listener for the object, then write the implementation code for one of the standard listener class methods to process, or handle, the event.

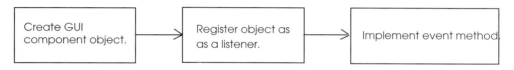

Figure 11-2 The steps required by you, the programmer, to create a GUI component and process the component event.

The flowchart in Figure 11-3 shows how Java detects and handles an event. Notice here that the user action generates an event which is detected by a listener which has been registered for the component object that generated the event. An event object is then passed to the listener class methods which are called to handle the event.

Figure 11-3 The event processing provided by Java.

Let's look at some code that will allow us to handle a window closing event. Here is the frame class we developed earlier:

```
//INHERITS AND CUSTOMIZES FRAME CLASS TO ADD DESIRED FEATURES
class FrameWithClose extends Frame implements WindowListener
{
  //CONSTRUCTOR
  public FrameWithClose(String title)
  {
    //CALL SUPERCLASS CONSTRUCTOR
    super(title);
```

```
    //SET BACKGROUND WINDOW COLOR
    setBackground(Color.white);

    //ADD LISTENER FOR THIS FRAME
    addWindowListener(this);
 }//END FrameWithClose()

public void windowClosing(WindowEvent e)
{
   System.exit(0);        //EXIT TO OPERATING SYSTEM
 }//END windowClosing()

 public void windowClosed(WindowEvent e)
 {
 }
 public void windowDeiconified(WindowEvent e)
 {
 }
 public void windowIconified(WindowEvent e)
 {
 }
 public void windowActivated(WindowEvent e)
 {
 }
 public void windowDeactivated(WindowEvent e)
 {
 }
 public void windowOpened(WindowEvent e)
 {
 }
}//END FrameWithClose
```

The code that has been added is printed in bold type. Of course, the class name has been changed to *FrameWithClose* to reflect its new capability. First, notice that that class header line includes the code implements WindowListener. This is required to use the *WindowListener* class. The next change that you see is the statement addWindowListener(this). This statement adds a listener for the object. But, which object? Well, "this" object. The **this** reference is used so that, when an object is created for the class, a listener will be created for "this" object. Does this make sense? Finally you see that all of the *WindowListener* methods have been implemented. When a class defines several abstract methods, such as *WindowListener* does (Ref. Table 11-2), you must implement all the methods in any subclass. Even though we do not need all the methods to process a window closing, we must implement every method. Notice that only the *WindowClosing()* method includes code, while the other methods do not. The code required in the *WindowClosing()* method is simply System.exit(0).

Here's how it works: When a window event occurs, *WindowListener* calls *WindowClosing()*, passing the event source object to the method. The event source object within the method is *e*. Notice that the method parameter is *e*, which is an object of the *WindowEvent* class. The *WindowClosing()* method executes, forcing the system to exit and, therefore, close the window. All of the other *WindowListener* methods are also called but do not perform any meaningful action in this application. Now, here is a complete application program that tests our new *FrameWithClose* class.

```
import java.awt.*;              //FOR FRAME CLASS
import java.awt.event.*;        //FOR EVENT HANDLING

//INHERITS AND CUSTOMIZES FRAME CLASS TO ADD DESIRED FEATURES
class FrameWithClose extends Frame implements WindowListener
{
 //CONSTRUCTOR
 public FrameWithClose(String title)
 {
  super(title);               //CALL SUPERCLASS CONSTRUCTOR
  setBackground(Color.white); //SET WINDOW BACKGROND COLOR
  addWindowListener(this);    //ADD LISTENER FOR THIS FRAME
 }//END FrameWithClose()

 //WindowListener METHODS
 public void windowClosing(WindowEvent e)
 {
  System.exit(0);        //EXIT TO OPERATING SYSTEM
 }//END windowClosing()

 public void windowClosed(WindowEvent e)
 {
 }
 public void windowDeiconified(WindowEvent e)
 {
 }
 public void windowIconified(WindowEvent e)
 {
 }
 public void windowActivated(WindowEvent e)
 {
 }
```

```
  public void windowDeactivated(WindowEvent e)
  {
  }
  public void windowOpened(WindowEvent e)
  {
  }
}//END FrameWithClose

//CLASS TO TEST FrameWithClose CLASS
public class FrameWithCloseTest
{
  public static void main(String[] args)
  {
   //DEFINE FRAME OBJECT
   FrameWithClose window = new FrameWithClose("This is a frame with close");

   //SET FRAME SIZE
   window.setSize(500,300);

   //MAKE FRAME VISIBLE
   window.setVisible(true);

  }//END main()
}//END FrameWithCloseTest
```

The only addition here is the importation of the *java.awt.event* package. This is required for event handling. Notice that our application class has not changed, except for its name. All we do is to define an object of our *FrameWithClose* class, set the frame size, and make the frame visible. That's all there is to it!

The methods used in this section and associated with the *Frame* class are summarized in Table 11-3.

As stated earlier, a window in nothing more than a frame with the desired components. The various GUI components provided by Java are listed in Table 11-4. We will not cover all these components here, only the more common ones. Once your learn how to deal with one component, all the others are similar. Let's begin with the button.

TABLE 11-3 SUMMARY OF METHODS USED IN THIS SECTION

Method	Description
*addWindowListener(**this**)*	Registers a listener for this window object.
Frame( )	Constructs new frame without title.
Frame(String)	Constructs new frame with *String* title.
setSize(int, int)	Sets frame size to width by height in pixels.
setVisible(boolean)	Makes frame visible or invisible (true/false).
setBackground(Color)	Sets frame background color to *Color.c*.
windowClosing(WindowEvent)	Handles a window closing event.

TABLE 11-4 STANDARD GUI COMPONENTS PROVIDED BY JAVA

Component	Description
Button	An area that generates an event when clicked.
Checkbox	A set of selectable buttons that can be toggled on or off.
Choice box	A single button that displays a list of choices when selected.
Label	A noneditable text area.
List	A list of selectable items with a scrollbar.
Menu	A set of selectable options located at the top of a window on a menu bar.
Panel	A container in which components can be placed and subsequently added to a frame.
Radio buttons	A set of selectable buttons whereby only one button can be selected at any one time.
Scrollbar	A sliding bar to control position.
Text field	An editable line of text.
Text area	An editable or noneditable area consisting of one or more lines of text with scrollbars.

Quick Check

1. What package must be imported into a program to use the GUI components available in the Java Abstract Windowing Toolkit?

2. The container used to hold GUI components in a Java application program is the
    _____.

3. Write a statement to create a frame object called *myFrame* that will generate a window with a title of "This is my first frame".

4. Write a statement to set the size of *myFrame* to 450 by 250 pixels.

5. Write a statement to make *myFrame* visible.

6. What three things must you do as a programmer to setup a window component and process an event generated by that component.

7. What method is used to handle a window closing event?

8. Write a statement to register a listener for a frame that you have created.

9. What package must be imported into a program to handle a window event?

11-2 THE BUTTON

To create a button, or any GUI component for that matter, we must first create a subclass of *Frame* as we did earlier. We will then create a button object within our subclass and add it to the frame. Here is the class we developed earlier, with the code required for a button shown in bold type:

```
class FrameWithButton extends FrameWithClose implements ActionListener
{
 //CONSTRUCTOR
 public FrameWithButton(String title)
 {
  super(title);                    //CALL SUPERCLASS CONSTRUCTOR
  setBackground(Color.white);      //SET WINDOW BACKGROUND COLOR
  setForeground(Color.black);      //SET COMPONENT FOREGROUND COLOR
```

```
//DEFINE BUTTON OBJECT
Button beepButton = new Button("Click Here");

//ADD BUTTON TO FRAME
add(beepButton);

//ADD EVENT LISTENER FOR THIS BUTTON
beepButton.addActionListener(this);

}//END FrameWithButton()

//PROCESS EVENT
public void actionPerformed(ActionEvent e)
 {
   final char SOUND = 7;              //DECLARE SOUND CONSTANT
   //DID A BUTTON CAUSE EVENT?
   if (e.getSource() instanceof Button)
     //IF SO, BEEP
     System.out.println(SOUND);
 }//END actionPerformed
}//END FrameWithButton
```

The first change you see, besides the frame name, is that our *FrameWithButton* class inherits our *FrameWithClose* class. Why reinvent the wheel? We have already developed a class that will produce a blank frame with a the close feature, so why not use it here? This way, we do not have to register a window listener or implement all the abstract window listener methods, since this is all inherited. Next, you see the inclusion of *ActionListener* in the class header line. We must implement *ActionListener* since a button generates an action event (Ref. Table 11-1). *ActionListener* is the listener class for an action event, just as *WindowListener* is the listener class for a window event.

Next, you see the additional statement setForeground(Color.black). The *setForeground()* method will set the color of any components added to the frame. As a result, the program will generate a button with a black label inside of it. The next statement we added creates a button object. Our button is called *beepButton* and is an object of the standard *Button* class. The *Button* class has two versions of its constructor as follows:

```
//CREATES A BUTTON WITHOUT A LABEL
Button()
```

```
//CREATES A BUTTON WITH A LABEL
Button(String label)
```

526 Graphical User Interfaces: GUIs Chap. 11

526   Graphical User Interfaces: GUIs   Chap. 11

As you can see, the first version does not provide for any button label, while the second one does. So, the statement Button beepButton = new Button("Click Here") will create a button object called *beepButton* with a label of "Click Here". Next, we need to add the *beepButton* object to the frame. This is accomplished by calling the standard *add()* method and providing *beepButton* as its argument. Finally, we must register a listener for our *beepButton* object. This is done with the statement beepButton.addActionListener(this). Notice that we use our *beepButton* object to call the *addActionListener()* method providing **this** as an argument. (Why?) Observe that all of this code is part of the frame constructor. As a result, both the frame and its button are created when an object is defined in *main()* for our *FrameWithButton* class.

Now, we are almost there. From Table 11-2 you see that the *ActionListener* class has a single abstract method called *actionPerformed()*. We must implement this method to handle a button event. You see that the *actionPerformed()* method receives an *ActionEvent* object, *e*. This object carries with it information about the event. The statement if (e.getSource() instanceof Button) uses the event object, *e*, to call the *getSource()* method. This method returns the source of the event. The keyword **instanceof** tests to see if the event source object is an "instance of" the *Button* class. If it is, the statement is true and the System.out.println(SOUND) is executed. Notice that *SOUND* is declared as a constant with the value 7. This is the UNICODE/ASCII value for the beeper in your computer. Thus, clicking the button will cause the computer to beep. Now, all we need is an application class to test our new *FrameWithButton* class. Here is the complete program:

```
import java.awt.*;            //FOR FRAME CLASS
import java.awt.event.*;      //FOR EVENT HANDLING

//A FRAME CLASS WITH A SINGLE BUTTON
class FrameWithButton extends FrameWithClose implements ActionListener
{
  //CONSTRUCTOR
  public FrameWithButton(String title)
  {
    super(title);                      //CALL SUPERCLASS CONSTRUCTOR
    setBackground(Color.white); //SET WINDOW BACKGROUND COLOR
    setForeground(Color.black); //SET COMPONENT FOREGROUND COLOR
```

```
//DEFINE BUTTON OBJECT
Button beepButton = new Button("Click Here");

//ADD BUTTON TO FRAME
add(beepButton);
//ADD EVENT LISTENER THIS BUTTON
beepButton.addActionListener(this);
}//END FrameWithButton()

//ActionListener METHOD
public void actionPerformed(ActionEvent e)
{
  final char SOUND = 7;                    //DECLARE SOUND CONSTANT
  //DID BUTTON CAUSE EVENT?
  if (e.getSource() instanceof Button)
    //IF SO, BEEP
    System.out.println(SOUND);
}//END actionPerformed
}//END FrameWithButton

//APPLICATION CLASS TO TEST FrameWithButton
public class FrameWithButtonTest
{
  public static void main(String[] args)
  {
  //DEFINE FRAME OBJECT
  FrameWithButton window = new FrameWithButton("This is a frame with a button");

  //SET FRAME SIZE
  window.setSize(500,300);

  //MAKE FRAME VISIBLE
  window.setVisible(true);

}//END main()
}//END FrameWithButtonTest
```

Nothing is new here, except our application class name. Method *main( )* still creates a frame object, sets the size of the frame, and makes the frame visible just as before. The difference is that our frame now has a button component. The window produced by the *FrameWithButton* class is shown in Figure 11-4.

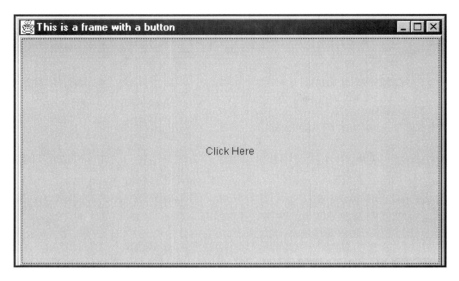

Figure 11-4   A frame with a single button generated by the *FrameWithButton* class.

Wow, what a button! Our button fills up the entire window! It works fine, generating a beep when clicked. However, do you suppose that we intended to fill up the entire window with a single button? Of course not! That brings us to out next discussion—layout managers.

The methods used in this section and associated with the *Button* class are summarized in Table 11-5.

TABLE 11-5 SUMMARY OF METHODS USED IN THIS SECTION

Method	Description
add(Component)	Adds specified component to container.
*addActionListener(**this**)*	Registers a listener for calling action object.
actionPerfomed()	Processes a button event.
Button()	Constructs a new button without label.
Button(String)	Constructs a new button with *String* label.
getSource()	Returns object source of an event.
setForeground(Color)	Sets foreground color to *Color.c*.

Quick Check

1. Write a statement to create a button called *myButton* with a label of "Store".

2. Write a statement to add the button in question 1 to a frame.

3. Write a statement to register a listener for the button in question 1.

4. What method is used to handle a button event?

5. Write an **if** statement that will test if a button generated an event using an event object called *event*.

11-3 LAYOUT MANAGERS

A layout manager does exactly what it says: lays out the components within a frame. The layout managers that we will discuss in this sections are listed in Table 11-6.

TABLE 11-6 LAYOUT MANAGERS DISCUSSED IN THIS SECTION

Layout Manager	Description
FlowLayout	Arranges components from left to right within a frame or panel in the order they are added.
GridLayout	Arranges components into rows and columns within a frame or panel in the order they are added.
BorderLayout	Arranges components into North, South, East, West, and Center areas within a frame or panel.

Flow Layout

All we need to do to our *FrameWithButton* class to make the button more manageable is to add the following statement to the *FrameWithButton()* constructor:

```
setLayout(new FlowLayout());
```

This single line invokes the *FlowLayout* manager to generate the window shown in Figure 11-5.

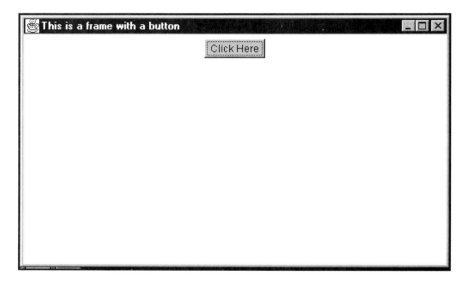

Figure 11-5 A frame with a single button generated by the *FrameWithButton* class using the *FlowLayout* manager.

Now, that's more like it! Here we have a single "Click Here" button centered at the top of the window. So, what is this *FlowLayout* stuff anyway? Well, *FlowLayout* is one of several layout managers provided by Java. The *FlowLayout* manager arranges components sequentially, from left to right, as they are added to a frame. There are three versions of the *FlowLayout* class constructor as follows:

```
//DEFAULT CENTER ALIGNMENT AND 5 PIXEL GAP
FlowLayout()
```

//CENTER, LEFT, or RIGHT ALIGN
FlowLayout(int alignment)

//CENTER, LEFT, or RIGHT ALIGN, HORIZONTAL GAP, VERTICAL GAP
FlowLayout(int alignment, int hGap, int vGap)

Each version of the constructor provides different component alignment and gapping options. Alignment relates to justification. Left alignment means that the components will be left-justified across the window, while right alignment means that the components will be right-justified across the window. Center alignment means the components will be justified equally left and right. Gapping is measured in pixels (picture elements). You can set the horizontal gap between the components as well as the vertical component gap. The first constructor uses a default center alignment and default gapping of 5 pixels. The second constructor allows you to specify center, left, or right alignment. Finally, the third constructor allows you to specify both alignment and component gapping. Here is an example that will specify a left alignment, a horizontal gap of 10 pixels, and a vertical gap of 20 pixels:

setLayout(new FlowLayout(FlowLayout.LEFT,10,20));

Notice that the alignment must be specified using the standard *FlowLayout* class followed by a dot, followed by the constant *CENTER*, *LEFT*, or *RIGHT*. Here, a *FlowLayout* object is created and passed as an argument to the *setLayout()* method. Now, let's expand our single button class and develop a frame class that incorporates five buttons as follows:

```
//A FRAME CLASS WITH FIVE BUTTONS
class FrameWithButtons extends FrameWithClose implements ActionListener
{
 //CONSTRUCTOR
 public FrameWithButtons(String title)
 {

 //CALL SUPERCLASS CONSTRUCTOR
 super(title);

 //SET FLOWLAYOUT, LEFT ALIGNMENT, 10 HORIZ. GAP, 20 VERT. GAP
 setLayout(new FlowLayout(FlowLayout.LEFT,10,20));

 //DEFINE BUTTON OBJECTS
 Button yellowButton = new Button("Yellow");
 Button blueButton = new Button("Blue");
 Button cyanButton = new Button("Cyan");
```

```
Button redButton = new Button("Red");
Button greenButton = new Button("Green");

//ADD BUTTONS TO FRAME
add(yellowButton);
add(blueButton);
add(cyanButton);
add(redButton);
add(greenButton);

//ACTIVATE EVENT LISTENERS FOR BUTTONS
yellowButton.addActionListener(this);
blueButton.addActionListener(this);
cyanButton.addActionListener(this);
redButton.addActionListener(this);
greenButton.addActionListener(this);
 } //END FrameWithButtons()
} //END FrameWithButton CLASS
```

None of this code is new to you. We have simply created a frame subclass called *FrameWithButtons* which employs the *FlowLayout* manager. The button components will be left-justified across the frame, with horizontal spacing of 10 pixels and vertical spacing of 20 pixels. As you can see, five button objects have been defined and added to the frame. Also, an event listener has been added for each button object. The window which is generated when an object is created for this class is shown in Figure 11-6.

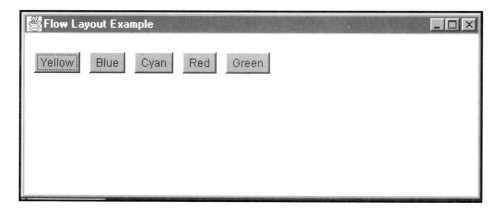

Figure 11-6 A frame with five buttons generated by the *FrameWithButtons* class using the *FlowLayout* manager.

Now, the question is: If a button is clicked, which button is it? Well, to determine this, we must add some logic to the *actionPerformed( )* method as follows:

```
//PROCESS EVENT
  public void actionPerformed(ActionEvent e)
  {
   //GET LABEL OF EVENT OBJECT
   String buttonLabel = e.getActionCommand();

   //DID A BUTTON CAUSE EVENT?
   if (e.getSource() instanceof Button)
    //IF SO, WHICH BUTTON?
    if (buttonLabel.equals("Yellow"))
    {
     setBackground(Color.yellow);
     repaint();
    }//END IF "Yellow"
    if (buttonLabel.equals("Blue"))
    {
     setBackground(Color.blue);
     repaint();
    }//END IF "Blue"
    if (buttonLabel.equals("Cyan"))
    {
     setBackground(Color.cyan);
     repaint();
    }//END IF "Cyan"
    if (buttonLabel.equals("Red"))
    {
     setBackground(Color.red);
     repaint();
    }//END IF "Red"
    if (buttonLabel.equals("Green"))
    {
     setBackground(Color.green);
     repaint();
    }//END IF "Green"
  }//END actionPerformed()
```

Again, the additional code is shown in bold type. Notice that a string object called *buttonLabel* is defined and assigned the value returned by a call to the *getActionCommand( )* method via the event object, *e*. The *getActionCommand( )*

method will return the label of the component associated with the event object, *e.* Of course, this will be the label of the button which was clicked. Notice that the logic compares *buttonLabel* to all possible labels using the standard *String* class *equals()* method. When a match is made, the background color of the window is set to a color which corresponds to the button label and the window is "repainted" by calling the *repaint()* method. The *repaint()* method simply refreshes the window. You will normally call this method when you have new things to display. So, once an event occurs, the *actionPerformed()* method is executed. The first **if** test determines if the event was a button event. Then, the nested **if**s determine which button generated the event. What should happen when a given button is clicked?

Grid Layout

The next layout manager we need to discuss is the *GridLayout* manager. This layout manager places components in a grid with a specified number of rows and columns. You will use one of the following versions of the *GridLayout* constructor to specify the number of rows and columns in the grid:

```
//NUMBER ROWS, COLUMNS
GridLayout(int rows, int cols)
```

```
//NUMBER ROWS, COLUMNS, HORIZONTAL GAP, VERTICAL GAP
GridLayout(int rows, int cols, int hGap, int vGap)
```

In the first constructor you simply specify the number of rows and columns desired for the grid. In the second constructor you specify the horizontal and vertical component gap in addition to the number of rows and columns. As an example, the following statement will set the layout to *GridLayout* with 2 rows and 3 columns. Horizontal and vertical gapping is set to 10 pixels.

```
setLayout(new GridLayout(2,3,10,10));
```

If this statement were inserted into the previous *FrameWithButtons* class, you would see the window shown in Figure 11-7 upon execution of the application program.

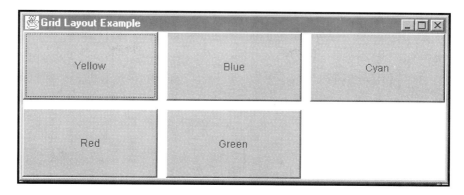

Figure 11-7 A frame with five buttons generated by the *FrameWithButtons* class using the *GridLayout* manager with 2 rows and 3 columns.

You should be aware that if you specify zero rows and columns, Java will throw an exception. However, if the number of rows and/or columns specified is too small for the number of components, Java will make room to accommodate all the components by adding more columns. The rows are always filled-up first, then the columns. For instance, suppose we insert the following constructor into our *FrameWithButtons* class:

setLayout(new GridLayout(5,2,10,10));

This constructor specifies a grid of 5 rows and 2 columns, or 10 cells total. However, our *FrameWithButtons* class only contains five buttons. The window shown in Figure 11-8 is what you would see when the program executes.

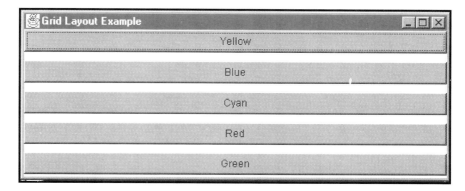

Figure 11-8 A frame with five buttons generated by the *FrameWithButtons* class using the *GridLayout* manager with 5 rows and 2 columns.

Observe that the rows are filled up first with our five buttons and the second column in each row is not even used, or visible for that matter.

Border Layout

The last layout manager that we will discuss is *BorderLayout*. This layout manager divides the window into five predefined regions of *North*, *South*, *East*, *West*, and *Center* as illustrated in Figure 11-9.

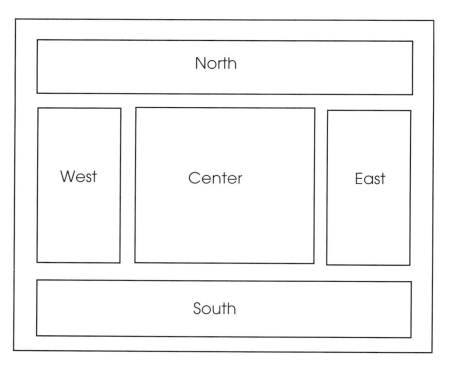

Figure 11-9 The *BorderLayout* manager divides the window into five predefined regions of *North*, *South*, *East*, *West*, and *Center*.

There are two versions of the *BorderLayout* constructor as follows:

```
//SET BORDER LAYOUT WITH NO GAP
BorderLayout()
```

//SET BORDER LAYOUT WITH HORIZONTAL, VERTICAL GAP
BorderLayout(int hGap, int vGap)

As an example, suppose we insert the following constructor into our *FrameWithButtons* class:

setLayout(new BorderLayout(10,10));

This constructor specifies *BorderLayout* with a 10-pixel horizontal and vertical gap. Now, to use *BorderLayout* you must specify the region of the component when it is added to the frame. Thus, we must modify the *add()* method arguments in our *FrameWithButtons* class like this:

//ADD BUTTONS TO FRAME
add(yellowButton,"North");
add(blueButton,"West");
add(cyanButton,"East");
add(redButton,"Center");
add(greenButton,"South");

As you can see, we must specify the component region as the second argument in the *add()* method. You can only place one component in a given region. The window shown in Figure 11-10 is what you would see upon execution of an application program containing this frame class.

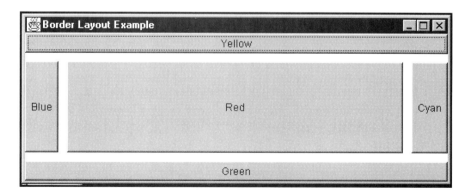

Figure 11-10 A frame with five buttons generated by the *FrameWithButtons* class using the *BorderLayout*.

You see that the size of each component is governed by the size of the component region. The *North* and *South* components are as wide as the window, while the *East* and *West* components are as tall as the distance between the *North* and *South* components, minus any specified gap. The *Center* component fills in the space between the other four components, minus any specified gap.

No Layout Manager

If you do not like the standard layout managers available in Java, you can choose not to use them and do your own layout. Take note, however, that this can be a "bit tricky." Also, such layouts will not be consistent across different platforms. The reason is that you must specify your component positions and sizes in pixels. Not all platform monitors, or even monitors within a given platform for that matter, have the same number of pixels. In addition, if the window is resized smaller than its original frame size, cropping will occur.

> GUIs that do not employ a layout manager will not be consistent across different platforms. The reason is that you must specify your component positions and sizes in pixels. Not all platform monitors, or even monitors within a given platform for that matter, have the same number of pixels. In addition, if the window is resized smaller than its original frame size, cropping will occur.

To do your own layout, you must first tell Java that no standard layout manager is required. This is accomplished by setting the layout to **null** as follows:

setLayout(null);

Then, you use the *setLocation( )* and *setSize( )* methods to set the component location and size, respectively, as desired. The signatures for these methods are as follows:

//SETS COMPONENT LOCATION h PIXELS TO RIGHT, v PIXELS DOWN
public void setLocation(int hLoc, int vLoc)

//SETS COMPONENT SIZE w PIXELS WIDE BY h PIXELS HIGH
public void setSize(int w, int h)

The arguments in the *setLocation( )* method provide the screen coordinates for the *upper-left-hand corner* of the component. The point of reference is the top-left-hand corner of the window, which has a coordinate of (0,0). Thus, a coordinate of (10,30) places the upper-left-hand corner of the component 10 pixels to the right and 30 pixels down from the upper-left-hand corner of the window. The arguments in the *setSize( )* method provide the width and height measurements of the component in pixels. For example, consider the following code:

```
myComponent.setLocation(10,30);   //10 PIXELS TO RIGHT, 30 PIXELS DOWN
myComponent.setSize(50,20);       //50 PIXELS WIDE BY 20 PIXELS HIGH
```

The first statement tells Java to set the location of *myComponent* 10 pixels horizontal and 30 pixels vertical, placing the component in the upper-left-hand corner of the window. (*Note*: For the component to be visible, it must be located below the window title bar. This is why a vertical coordinate of 30 pixels was used in the preceding example.) The second statement sets the size of *myComponent* to 50 pixels wide by 20 pixels high. Remember the five-button code developed earlier? Let's rewrite the class constructor to lay out the buttons without a layout manager. Consider the following:

```
public NoLayout(String title)
{
   //CALL SUPERCLASS CONSTRUCTOR
   super(title);

   //SET LAYOUT MANAGER TO NULL
   setLayout(null);

   //DEFINE BUTTON OBJECTS
   Button yellowButton = new Button("Yellow");
   Button blueButton = new Button("Blue");
   Button cyanButton = new Button("Cyan");
   Button redButton = new Button("Red");
   Button greenButton = new Button("Green");

   //SET LOCATION AND SIZE
   yellowButton.setLocation(10,30);    //UPPER LEFT CORNER
   yellowButton.setSize(50,20);
   blueButton.setLocation(590,30);     //UPPER RIGHT CORNER
   blueButton.setSize(40,40);
   cyanButton.setLocation(10,370);     //LOWER LEFT CORNER
   cyanButton.setSize(50,100);
```

```
   redButton.setLocation(530,450);    //LOWER RIGHT CORNER
   redButton.setSize(100,20);
   greenButton.setLocation(220,140); //CENTER
   greenButton.setSize(200,200);

   //ADD BUTTONS TO FRAME
   add(yellowButton);
   add(blueButton);
   add(cyanButton);
   add(redButton);
   add(greenButton);

   //ACTIVATE EVENT LISTENERS FOR BUTTONS
   yellowButton.addActionListener(this);
   blueButton.addActionListener(this);
   cyanButton.addActionListener(this);
   redButton.addActionListener(this);
   greenButton.addActionListener(this);
}//END NoLayout()
```

Of course, the constructor name has changed to reflect the new class description. First you see that the layout manager is set to **null**. Next you find the location and size of each button component explicitly set using the *setLocation()* and *setSize()* methods. The rest of the code is identical to that developed earlier. The resulting window is shown in Figure 11-11. The figure indicates the component coordinates and sizes specified in the constructor. Notice that the window size is 640 pixels wide by 480 pixels high. This is the size of a typical PC screen. However, if the screen size were different, the layout would *not* be the same. So, be careful when doing your own layout. It might look fine on the system that you are using but might look totally different on another system.

Panels

It is often difficult to get the look you desire using a single frame container. For this reason, *panels* are provided so that you can achieve presentable layouts. A panel is a container for components that does not create a window of its own. Rather, you place components on separate panels and then add the panels to a frame to create a window.

A panel is a container for components that does not create a window of its own

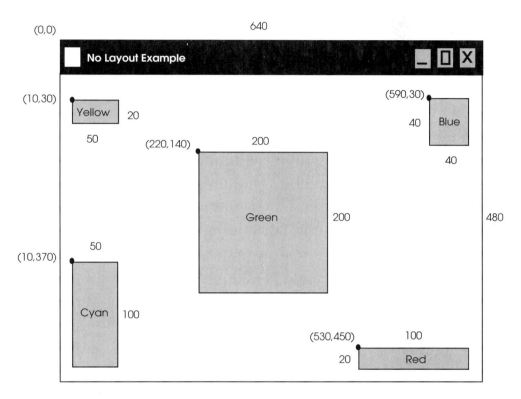

Figure 11-11 The window resulting from the *NoLayout( )* constructor which sets the location and size of the button components using coordinates in lieu of a layout manager.

It's probably best at this point to just look at an example. Figure 11-12 shows a window produced from a frame containing two easily identifiable panels. The top panel has three buttons and employs left-justified flow layout. The bottom panel has two buttons and employs center-justified flow layout. The frame employs border layout with the top panel located in the *Center* region and the bottom panel located in the *South* region.

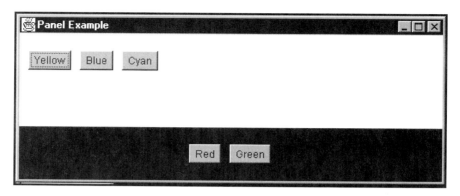

Figure 11-12 A frame created from two panels. The top panel contains three buttons and employs left-justified flow layout, while the bottom panel contains two buttons and employs center-justified flow layout.

To create the window in Figure 11-12, we developed a subclass called *Panels* of the *Frame* superclass. Here's the *Panels* class code:

```
class Panels extends FrameWithClose implements ActionListener
{
  //DEFINE PANELS AS PRIVATE MEMBERS
  private Panel panel1 = new Panel();
  private Panel panel2 = new Panel();

  //CONSTRUCTOR
  public Panels(String title)
  {
  //CALL SUPERCLASS CONSTRUCTOR
  super(title);

  //SET FRAME LAYOUT MANAGER
  setLayout(new BorderLayout());

  //SET PANEL LAYOUT MANAGERS
  panel1.setLayout(new FlowLayout(FlowLayout.LEFT,10,20));
  panel2.setLayout(new FlowLayout(FlowLayout.CENTER,10,20));

  //SET PANEL BACKGROND COLORS
  panel1.setBackground(Color.white);
  panel2.setBackground(Color.black);
```

```
//DEFINE BUTTON OBJECTS
Button yellowButton = new Button("Yellow");
Button blueButton = new Button("Blue");
Button cyanButton = new Button("Cyan");
Button redButton = new Button("Red");
Button greenButton = new Button("Green");

//ADD BUTTONS TO PANELS
panel1.add(yellowButton);
panel1.add(blueButton);
panel1.add(cyanButton);
panel2.add(redButton);
panel2.add(greenButton);

//ADD PANELS TO FRAME
add(panel1,"Center");
add(panel2,"South");

//ACTIVATE EVENT LISTENERS FOR BUTTONS
yellowButton.addActionListener(this);
blueButton.addActionListener(this);
cyanButton.addActionListener(this);
redButton.addActionListener(this);
greenButton.addActionListener(this);
}//END Panels()

//PROCESS ACTION EVENTS
public void actionPerformed(ActionEvent e)
{
  //GET LABEL OF EVENT OBJECT
  String buttonLabel = e.getActionCommand();
  //DID A BUTTON CAUSE EVENT?
  if (e.getSource() instanceof Button)
    //IF SO, WHICH BUTTON?
    if (buttonLabel.equals("Yellow"))
    {
      panel1.setBackground(Color.yellow);
      repaint();
    }//END IF "Yellow"
    if (buttonLabel.equals("Blue"))
    {
      panel1.setBackground(Color.blue);
      repaint();
    }//END IF "Blue"
```

```
                if (buttonLabel.equals("Cyan"))
                {
                  panel1.setBackground(Color.cyan);
                  repaint();
                }//END IF "Cyan"
                 if (buttonLabel.equals("Red"))
                {
                  panel2.setBackground(Color.red);
                  repaint();
                }//END IF "Red"
                 if (buttonLabel.equals("Green"))
                {
                  panel2.setBackground(Color.green);
                  repaint();
                }//END IF "Green"
              }//END actionPerformed
          }//END Panels
```

As before, the statements of interest are highlighted in bold type. You first see the panel objects, *panel1* and *panel2*, defined as private members of the class. The reason they are defined as private data members and not local objects within the constructor is that these objects need to be accessible outside of the constructor, within the *actionPerformed()* method as you will see shortly. Notice that *panel1* and *panel2* are objects of the *Panel* class.

PROGRAMMING NOTE

You must define a component object as **private** within a frame subclass when that object must be visible to another method within the class, such as the *actionPerformed()* method. Otherwise, you can define the component object as a local object within the frame class constructor.

Next you find the *Panels* class constructor. The first thing new within this constructor is the setting of the layout managers for the frame as well as the panels. Observe that the frame is set to *BorderLayout*, while the two panels are set to *FlowLayout*, with *panel1* left-justified and *panel2* center-justified. After setting the panel layout managers, the background color of each panel is set when the respective panel object calls the *setBackground()* method. We have defined five button objects as before but, rather than adding them to the frame, we have added the first three buttons to *panel1* and the last two buttons to *panel2*. Finally, the panels are added to the frame via the statements add(panel1,"Center") and add(panel2,"South"). Notice that the first argument of the *add()* method is the panel object and the second argument is the region of the frame in which to add the panel. Remember, the frame employs the *BorderLayout* manager. That's it for the constructor.

When an object is created for the *Panels* class in an application program and made visible, you will get the window shown in Figure 11-12. Following the constructor, we have implemented the *actionPerformed()* method as before to handle the button events. The only change here is the use of the panel objects to set the background color of their respective panels when a given button is clicked. Notice that the respective panel object must be used to call the *setBackground()* method to change the background color of the panel. Look over the above *Panels* class code again and make sure you understand all of its features. The following application class was used to test the *Panels* class.

```
//APPLICATION CLASS TO TEST Panels
public class PanelsTest
{
  public static void main(String[] args)
  {
    //DEFINE FRAME OBJECT
    Panels window = new Panels("Panel Example");

    //SET FRAME SIZE
    window.setSize(500,200);

    //MAKE FRAME VISIBLE
    window.setVisible(true);
  }//END main()
}//END PanelsTest
```

There is nothing new here. We have just created an object for our *Panels* class called *window*, set the size of *window*, and made it visible. That's all there is to it! The methods used in this section are summarized in Table 11-7.

TABLE 11-7 SUMMARY OF METHODS USED IN THIS SECTION

Method	Description
BorderLayout()	Constructs new border layout with no gaps.
BorderLayout(int,int)	Constructs new border layout with hGap, vGap.
FlowLayout()	Constructs new flow layout, center, 5-pt. gap.
FlowLayout(int)	Constructs new flow layout with alignment.

TABLE 11-7 (CONTINUED) SUMMARY OF METHODS USED IN THIS SECTION

Method	Description
FlowLayout(int,int,int)	Constructs new flow layout with alignment, hGap, and vGap.
getActionCommand( )	Returns the command name associated with this event.
GridLayout(int,int)	Constructs new grid layout with rows and cols.
GridLayout(int,int,int,int)	Constructs new grid layout with rows, cols., hGap, and vGap.
Panel( )	Constructs new panel.
Panel(Layout Manager)	Constructs new panel with this layout manager.
setLayout(Layout Manager)	Sets layout for this layout manager.
setLocation(int,int)	Sets component upper-left corner location to (x,y).
setSize(int,int)	Sets component size to width, height.

 Quick Check

1. The layout manager that arranges components from left to right within a frame or panel in the order they are added is _____ layout manager.

2. The layout manager that arranges components into rows and columns within a frame or panel in the order they are added is _____ layout manager.

3. Write a statement to set the layout for a frame to flow layout, left-justified, with a 20-point horizontal gap and 10-point vertical gap.

4. What are the five regions designated by the *BorderLayout* manager?

5. Write a statement to designate no layout manager.

6. Where is the origin, (0,0), of a window located?

7. Write a statement to locate a button called *myButton* at screen coordinate (20,30).

8. Write a statement to set the size of a button called *myButton* to 50 pixels high and 25 pixels wide.

9. What method can be called by an event object to return the command name associated with an event?

10. Write a statement to set the layout for a frame to border layout with 20-pixel gapping between all components.

11. Write a statement to place a panel, called *panel*, in the center region of the frame in question 10.

11-4 MORE COMPONENTS

You now have the basic concepts of frames, listeners, event handlers, and layout managers that are required to build GUIs in Java. All you need to learn about now are the additional components that are available in the Java AWT. All these additional components are handled much like the button component that you have already studied. So, let's see what additional components are available to build Java GUIs. In this section, you will actually build the student GUI with which you experimented back in the *GUI101* module.

Labels

A label is a noneditable text area that is used to label other components, usually text fields and text areas. There are three label constructors, as follows:

```
//CREATES A BLANK LABEL
public Label();

//CREATES A LABEL WITH TEXT
public Label(String text);

//CREATES A LABEL WITH TEXT AND
//LEFT, RIGHT, OR CENTER ALIGNMENT
public Label(String text, int alignment);
```

The alignment in the third constructor can be *Label.LEFT*, *Label.CENTER*, or *Label.RIGHT*. Here is some code that will create three label objects and add them to a panel.

```
//DEFINE LABEL OBJECTS
Label nameLabel = new Label("Student name");
Label numberLabel = new Label("Student Number");
Label gpaLabel = new Label("GPA");

//ADD LABELS TO panel1
panel1.add(nameLabel);
panel1.add(numberLabel);
panel1.add(gpaLabel);
```

Of course, this code assumes that *panel1* has been previously defined. That's all we have to say about labels for now. You will see how the foregoing code is used to label text fields and text areas in the discussions that follow

Text Fields and Text Areas

A text field is a single line of text, while a text area is several lines of text. Text fields and areas allow the user to enter string data or the system to display text data. An editable text field or area allows the user to enter data, while a non-editable text field or area is used to display data. There are four versions of the *TextField* class constructor, and four versions of the *TextArea* class constructor as follows:

```
//CREATES TEXT FIELD WITHOUT TEXT
public TextField()

//CREATES TEXT FIELD WITH TEXT
public TextField(String text)

//CREATES TEXT FIELD WITHOUT TEXT AND SETS COLUMNS
public TextField(int columns)

//CREATES TEXT FIELD WITH TEXT AND SETS COLUMNS
public TextField(String text, int columns)

//CREATES TEXT AREA WITHOUT TEXT
public TextArea()

//CREATES TEXT AREA WITH TEXT
public TextArea(String text)

//CREATES TEXT AREA  WITHOUT TEXT AND SETS ROWS AND COLUMNS
public TextArea(int rows, int columns)
```

//CREATES TEXT AREA WITH TEXT AND SETS ROWS AND COLUMNS
public TextArea(String text, int rows, int columns)

Remember, a text field is just one line of text, while a text area is several lines of text. This is why two of the *TextField()* constructors allow you to specify the number of field columns (width), and two of the *TextArea()* constructors allow you to specify both the number of text area rows (height) and columns (width). Also, you have the option of initializing both with a text string.

Look at Figure 11-13. This window contains three panels clearly identified by the different shading. The top panel contains a label and a single text field. The middle panel contains two labels, two text fields, and a button. The bottom panel contains a label and text area. The text fields are for user entry of the labeled student data. When the *Store* button is clicked, the information entered in the text fields is displayed in the text area. Notice that the text area has scrollbars. Scrollbars are provided by default with the text area constructor. This allows the user to scroll through the text if it is too large for the area. You should be aware that there is an additional version of the *TextArea()* constructor that allows you to eliminate the scrollbars or specify other scrollbar options. Check your Java on-line help or reference material if you are interested in using this constructor.

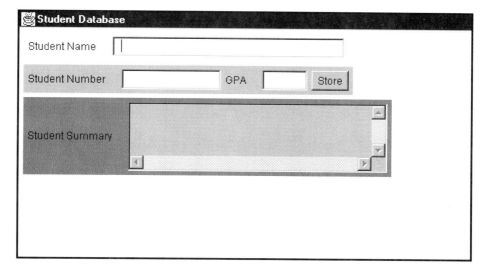

Figure 11-13 A frame created from three panels. The top panel contains a label and a single text field. The middle panel contains two labels, two text fields, and a button. The bottom panel contains a label and text area.

Now, here is the code that produced the window in Figure 11-13.

```java
import java.awt.*;        //FOR GUI COMPONENTS
import java.awt.event.*;  //FOR EVENT HANDLING

class StudentGUI extends FrameWithClose implements ActionListener
{
  //DEFINE TEXT FIELD OBJECTS AS PRIVATE CLASS DATA
  private TextField nameField = new TextField(35);
  private TextField numberField = new TextField(13);
  private TextField gpaField = new TextField(4);
  private TextArea studentArea = new TextArea(4,40);

  //CONSTRUCTOR
  public StudentGUI (String title)
  {
   //CALL SUPERCLASS CONSTRUCTOR
   super(title);

   //SET FRAME LAYOUT MANAGER
   setLayout(new FlowLayout(FlowLayout.LEFT));

   //DEFINE PANELS
   Panel panel1 = new Panel();
   Panel panel2 = new Panel();
   Panel panel3 = new Panel();

   //SET PANEL LAYOUT MANAGERS
   panel1.setLayout(new FlowLayout(FlowLayout.LEFT));
   panel2.setLayout(new FlowLayout(FlowLayout.LEFT));
   panel3.setLayout(new FlowLayout(FlowLayout.LEFT));

   //SET PANEL SHADING
   panel2.setBackground(Color.lightGray);
   panel3.setBackground(Color.gray);

   //DEFINE LABEL OBJECTS
   Label nameLabel = new Label("Student name");
   Label numberLabel = new Label("Student Number");
   Label gpaLabel = new Label("GPA");
   Label summaryLabel = new Label("Student Summary");

   //DEFINE BUTTON OBJECT
   Button storeButton = new Button("Store");
```

```
//ADD COMPONENTS TO panel1
panel1.add(nameLabel);
panel1.add(nameField);

//ADD COMPONENTS TO panel2
panel2.add(numberLabel);
panel2.add(numberField);
panel2.add(gpaLabel);
panel2.add(gpaField);
panel2.add(storeButton);

//ADD COMPONENTS TO panel3
panel3.add(summaryLabel);
panel3.add(studentArea);

//ADD PANELS TO FRAME
add(panel1);
add(panel2);
add(panel3);

//REGISTER BUTTON LISTENER
storeButton.addActionListener(this);
}//END StudentGUI()

//PROCESS BUTTON EVENT
public void actionPerformed(ActionEvent e)
{
 //DID A BUTTON CAUSE EVENT?
 if (e.getSource() instanceof Button)
 {
  //DISPLAY TEXT FIELD DATA IN TEXT AREA
  studentArea.setText("This is an example of data stored"
                    + " in the student database.\n");
  studentArea.append("\nStudent name: " + nameField.getText());
  studentArea.append("\nStudent Number: " + numberField.getText());
  studentArea.append("\nGPA: " + gpaField.getText());
 }//END IF
}//END actionPerformed()
}//END StudentGUI
```

We intend to discuss only those statements that are pertinent to text fields and text areas. First you see the text fields and text area defined as private members of the class. They are defined here as private members, rather than within the class constructor, so that they will be visible to the *actionPerformed()*

method later on. We have used the text field and text area constructors that allow us to set the number of the text field columns, and the number of text area rows and columns. The size of each should be consistent with the amount of data to be entered or displayed. Next comes the *StudentGUI()* constructor which, as before, is responsible for displaying the window. Within the constructor, three panels are defined, along with the other component objects (labels and button). Flow layout is employed for the frame, as well as for the three panels. All the component objects, including the text field and text area objects, are added to their respective panel using the *add()* method as before. Finally, the constructor adds the panels to the frame and a listener is registered for the *storeButton* object. Nothing new here.

Now, look at the *actionPerformed()* method. As before, an **if** statement is used to test an event for a button event. When a button event occurs, the *studentArea* object calls the *setText()* and *append()* methods to write information into the text area. Both *setText()* and *append()* write string data to the text area when called by the text area object. The data to be written is formatted the same way as that used within the *println()* method. The *setText()* method must be called first to write the initial information, followed by calls to the *append()* method to "append" additional information to the text area. If you use *setText()* repeatedly, any information displayed previously is overwritten. Now, notice that within each *append()* call, there is a call to *getText()* by the respective text field object. The *getText()* method does exactly what it says—gets the text entered into the object text field. Thus, the statement

studentArea.append("\nStudent name: " + nameField.getText());

appends the *studentArea* text area with the string data obtained from the *nameField* text field.

So, the user enters data into the student text fields, clicks the *Store* button and the data appears in the text area as shown in Figure 11-14. In this program, the event we are looking for is a button event. However, be aware that text fields generate their own events which can be handled individually. A text field event is triggered by pressing the **ENTER** key (Ref. Table 11-1). Like a button, the *ActionEvent* class is also used to handle text field events. So, to handle a text field event you must first register the text field object as a listener using the *addActionListener()* method and then process the event within the *actionPerformed()* method much as we did the button event.

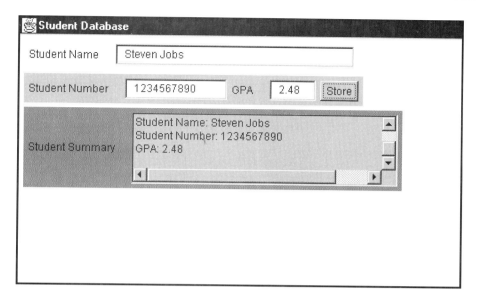

Figure 11-14 The text area shows the student data entered by the user, after clicking the *Store* button.

STYLE TIP

As your GUIs begin to get more complex, you will have several labels, fields, areas, etc., as part of a single frame. To make your code more readable and therefore less confusing, we suggest that you tag each component name with its component class. For instance, the text fields in the foregoing program are named *nameField*, *numberField*, and *gpaField*, while the text area is named *studentArea*. The component class designation allows anyone reading the program to tell which type of component a given name refers to. In addition, notice that the labels are named *nameLabel*, *numberLabel*, and so on, to indicate which component the label belongs to, as well as the fact the component is a label component. This is much better than *Label1*, *Label2*, and so on.

Choice and List Boxes

Choice boxes and list boxes are similar components in their appearance as well as the way in which they are handled in Java. Both a choice box and a list box are a listing of several selectable items. However, you can only select one item in a choice box, while one or more items can be selected in a list box. In Figure 11-15 we have added a choice box to our previous student database window.

> A ***choice box*** allows you to select one of several items in a listing, while a ***list box*** allows you to select one or more items in a listing.

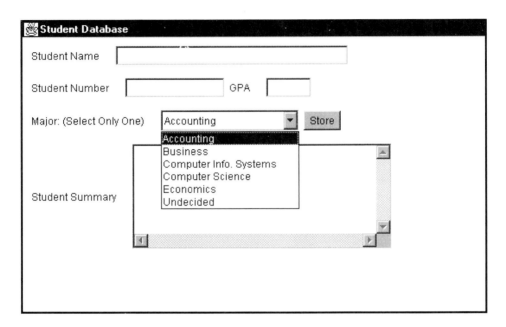

Figure 11-15 A choice box is added to our student GUI..

As you can see, the choice box allows the user to select a major for the given student. By default, the choice box includes a button that allows the user to see the choice items. Only the first choice item appears until the button is clicked. When the button is clicked, all possible choice items appear as shown in the figure. The first thing we had to do to create our choice box was to create a choice box object using the *Choice* class like this:

```
//DEFINE PRIVATE CHOICE BOX OBJECT
private Choice majorsChoice = new Choice();
```

The choice box class is *Choice*, with a single constructor *Choice()*. The constructor does not require any arguments. So, the first line in the foregoing statement simply defines *majorsChoice* as an object of the *Choice* class. Notice that *majorsChoice* is defined as a private member, because we will need it to be visible in the *actionPerformed()* method of the class. Next, we added items to the *majorsChoice* object as follows:

```
//ADD ITEMS TO CHOICE BOX AS PART OF FRAME CONSTRUCTOR
majorsChoice.addItem("Accounting");
majorsChoice.addItem("Business");
majorsChoice.addItem("Computer Info. Systems");
majorsChoice.addItem("Computer Science");
majorsChoice.addItem("Economics");
majorsChoice.addItem("Undecided");
```

Here, our *majorsChoice* object calls the *addItem()* method for each item to be added to the box. This all takes place in the frame constructor. The next task is to add our choice box object to a panel like this:

```
//ADD CHOICE BOX TO PANEL AS PART OF FRAME CONSTRUCTOR
panel1.add(majorsChoice);
```

Of course, this code assumes that *panel1* has already been defined. Again, the code is placed within the frame constructor.

Finally, a choice box selection must be processed in the *actionPerformed()* method, because the selected major must appear in the text area when the *Store* button is clicked. Here is the code we placed in *actionPerformed()*:

```
//PLACE CHOICE IN TEXT AREA AS PART OF actionPerformed()
studentArea.append("\nMajor: " + majorsChoice.getSelectedItem());
```

This code appends the text area with the item chosen from the choice box. To do this, the *studentArea* object must call the *append()* method, which requires our *majorsChoice* object to call the *getSelectedItem()* method. The *getSelectedItem()* method is part of the *Choice* class and returns the string representation of the selected choice.

List Boxes

A list box is like a choice box but allows the user to select one *or more* items within the item listing. There are three list box constructors as follows:

```
//CREATES LIST BOX WITH ONE VISIBLE ITEM
public List()
```

//CREATES LIST BOX WITH SEVERAL VISIBLE ITEMS
public List(int visible)

//CREATES LIST BOX WITH SEVERAL VISIBLE ITEMS AND ENABLES
//MULTIPLE ITEM SELECTION
public List(int visible, boolean enable)

As you can see, the list box class is *List*. The first constructor provides a box much like a choice box. Several items are initially shown in the box, but only one item can be selected. Scrollbars are added automatically if the number of items shown is less than the total number of items. The second constructor allows you to specify how many items are initially shown in the box. Again, scrollbars are added automatically if this number is less than the total number of items. Also, like the first constructor, you can only select one item from the list. The third constructor allows you to specify the number of items shown initially and enables multiple-item selection. Of course, if the second argument were **false**, this constructor would act just like the second constructor. For example, consider the following code:

private List majorsList = new List(3,true);

This object definition specifies that the first three items will be initially visible and that multiple-item selection is enabled.

In Figure 11-16, we have replaced the choice box of Figure 11-15 with a list box to allow the user to select one or more majors using the foregoing *majorsList* object definition.

Here are the statements that are pertinent to the task.

//DEFINE PRIVATE LIST OBJECT
private List majorsList = new List(3,true);

//DEFINE PRIVATE MAJORS ARRAY
private String majors[];

//ADD ITEMS TO LIST BOX AS PART OF FRAME CONSTRUCTOR
majorsList.addItem("Accounting");
majorsList.addItem("Business");
majorsList.addItem("Computer Info. Systems");
majorsList.addItem("Computer Science");
majorsList.addItem("Economics");
majorsList.addItem("Undecided");

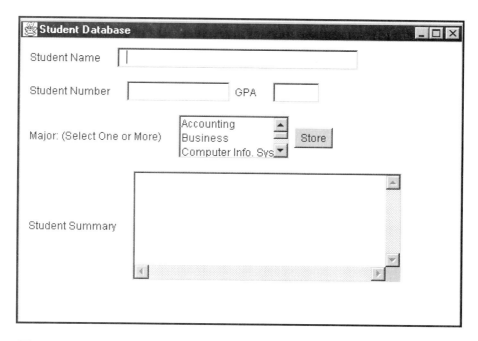

Figure 11-16 A list box is added to our student GUI, replacing the choice box of Figure 11-15 to allow the user to select more than one major.

```
//ADD LIST BOX TO PANEL AS PART OF FRAME CONSTRUCTOR
panel3.add(majorsList);

//GET SELECTED ITEMS FROM LIST AND APPEND TO TEXT AREA
//AS PART OF actionPerformed()
majors = majorsList.getSelectedItems();
studentArea.append("\nMajors:\t");
for (int index = 0; index < majors.length; ++index)
{
  studentArea.append(majors[index]);
  studentArea.append("\n\t");
}//END FOR
```

The first statement defines a list object called *majorsList*, making three items visible and enabling multiple selection. The second statement defines an array of string objects. Later on we will have to determine which of several list items have been selected. The *majors[ ] array* will be used for this purpose. An **array** is a **data structure** that can be used to hold multiple items. Arrays are discussed in detail in a later chapter. For now, just assume that the array will hold the list items selected by the user. Next you see the items added to the list via calls to the *addItem()* method, just the way we added items to a choice box earlier. Once the items are added, the entire list is added to a panel.

Now we must add code to the *actionPerformed()* method to handle the list items that were selected. This is the purpose of the *getSelectedItems()* method. This method returns the selected items of a list in an array of strings. So, the statement

```
 majors = majorsList.getSelectedItems();
```

places the selected item strings in the *majors[]* array defined earlier. Now all we have to do is extract the strings from the array and append them to the text area. This is the purpose of the **for** loop. Notice that the loop test calls the *length()* method of the *String* class to determine how many strings are in the array. Thus, the loop will continue to execute as long as strings remain in the array. With each loop execution, a string is appended to the text area via the statement

```
studentArea.append(majors[index]);
```

The second loop statement simply provides formatting for the appended strings. In the above discussion, we have handled both the choice and the list boxes within the *actionPerformed()* method, since the primary event we are interested in handling is the clicking of the *Store* button. This triggers the *actionPerformed()* method where all of our component processing logic appears. You should be aware that choice and list box items generate their own events. To process these events separately you must add a listener for each choice and list box object using the *addItemListener()* method, which triggers the *itemStateChanged()* method. If you want to process choice and list box events separately, your processing logic must appear within the *itemStateChanged()* method.

Checkboxes and Radio Buttons

Checkboxes and radio buttons are called ***state buttons*** because they can be turned on and off, representing one of two possible Boolean states, true or false. The difference between a checkbox and a radio button is that any number of checkboxes within a group can be selected at a given time, while only one radio button within a group can be selected at any one time. Both checkboxes and radio buttons require the use the *Checkbox* class. However, radio buttons also require the use of the *CheckboxGroup* class, as you will see shortly. The window in Figure 11-17 shows that both checkboxes and radio buttons have been added to our student GUI. The checkboxes allow the user to select full-time, part-time, commuting, or noncommuting status. The radio buttons allow the user to select undergraduate or graduate status. Let's consider checkboxes first.

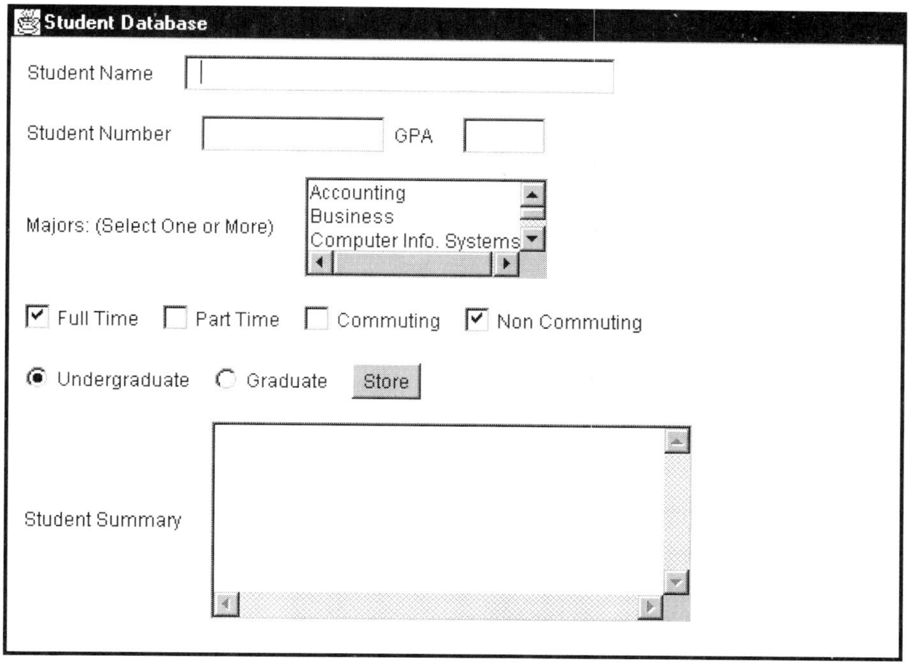

Figure 11-17 Check boxes and radio buttons are added to our student GUI..

There are four versions of the *Checkbox* class constructor as follows:

```
//CHECKBOX WITHOUT LABEL
public Checkbox();

//CHECKBOX WITH LABEL
public Checkbox(String label);

//CHECKBOX WITH LABEL AND SET TO A GIVEN STATE
public Checkbox(String label, boolean state);

//RADIO BUTTON WITH LABEL
public Checkbox(String label, CheckboxGroup g, boolean state);
```

The first three versions of the constructor are used to create checkbox objects, while the fourth version is used to create radio button objects. Here is the code that we used to create the four checkboxes shown in Figure 11-17.

```
//DEFINE CHECKBOX OBJECTS AS PRIVATE
private Checkbox fullTimeBox = new Checkbox("Full Time");
private Checkbox partTimeBox = new Checkbox("Part Time");
private Checkbox commutingBox = new Checkbox("Commuting");
private Checkbox nonCommutingBox = new Checkbox("Non Commuting");
```

Here, we have created four *Checkbox* objects which will be private members of our frame subclass. The second constructor given above is used so that each checkbox has its own label. Once the checkbox objects are created, they must be added to a panel, like this:

```
//ADD CHECKBOXES TO PANEL AS PART OF FRAME CONSTRUCTOR
panel4.add(fullTimeBox);
panel4.add(partTimeBox);
panel4.add(commutingBox);
panel4.add(nonCommutingBox);
```

That's it! All you have to do to create checkboxes on your GUI is to (1) define the *Checkbox* object(s), and (2) add the objects to a panel or frame. Of course, if you are using panels, the panel must be added to the frame. The objects are defined as private, since they must be visible in *actionPerformed( )*, while the objects are added to the panel as part of the frame constructor.

Now, we need some logic to process our checkboxes. In our student database application, we will simply write the student status represented by the selected checkboxes within the student summary text area when the *Store* button is clicked. As a result, the checkbox logic will appear in the *actionPerformed( )* method along with the logic that processes the other components within this window. Now, think about the checkbox logic for a minute. It should not be possible for the user to select both full-time and part-time status, right? Also, we need to prevent the user from selecting both commuting and noncommuting status. Any other combination of items is okay. This requires some **if/else** logic as follows:

```
//PROCESS CHECKBOXES AS PART OF actionPerformed()
if ((fullTimeBox.getState()) && (partTimeBox.getState()))
    studentArea.append("\nCANNOT BE FULL TIME AND PART TIME STATUS");
```

```
    else
    {
      if (fullTimeBox.getState())
         studentArea.append("\nFull Time");
      if (partTimeBox.getState())
         studentArea.append("\nPart Time");
    } //END ELSE

    if ((commutingBox.getState()) && (nonCommutingBox.getState()))
      studentArea.append("\nCANNOT BE COMMUTING AND NON-COMMUTING STATUS");
    else
    {
      if (commutingBox.getState())
         studentArea.append("\nCommuting");
      if (nonCommutingBox.getState())
         studentArea.append("\nNon Commuting");
    }//END ELSE
```

The key ingredient here is the *getState( )* method. This method is part of the *Checkbox* class and returns the Boolean state of its calling checkbox object. In the first **if** statement, *getState( )* is called by both the *fullTimeBox* and *partTimeBox* objects. If *getState( )* returns true for both objects, the AND (&&) test is true, resulting in an error message being appended to the text area. Otherwise, the **else** clause is executed to determine which one, if any, of these two items have been selected. If either the full-time or part-time checkbox has been selected, but not both, the student status is appended to the text area. The same logic is then applied to the *commutingBox* and *nonCommutingBox* objects.

Here, we have handled the checkboxes within the *actionPerformed( )* method, since the primary event we are interested in handling is the clicking of the *Store* button. This triggers the *actionPerformed( )* method where all of our component processing logic appears. You should be aware that, like choice boxes and list boxes, checkboxes generate their own events. To process these events separately you must add a listener for each checkbox object using the *addItemListener( )* method, which triggers the *itemStateChanged( )* method. If this were the case, your checkbox processing logic must appear within the *itemStateChanged( )* method and not the *actionPerformed( )* method.

Now, look at the two radio buttons in Figure 11-17. Radio buttons require the use of both the *Checkbox* class and the *CheckboxGroup* class. You must first define a checkbox group object using the *CheckboxGroup* class like this:

```
//DEFINE RADIO BUTTON GROUP AS PRIVATE
private CheckboxGroup radioButtons = new CheckboxGroup();
```

Now, when a *Checkbox* object is defined as part of this group, it becomes a radio button within the group such that only one of the buttons within the group can be "on" at any given time. So, we will use the fourth version of the *Checkbox* class constructor from above to define our radio button objects, designating *radioButtons* as the group to which they belong, like this:

```
//DEFINE PRIVATE RADIO BUTTONS FOR GROUP
private Checkbox undergraduate = new Checkbox("Undergraduate",
                                                radioButtons,true);

private Checkbox graduate = new Checkbox("Graduate",radioButtons,false);
```

Notice the three constructor arguments in each radio button object definition. The first argument is the button label, the second argument is the checkbox group to which the object belongs, and the third argument sets the button **true** (on) or **false** (off). Of course, only one of the buttons within any given group should be set to **true**. If you set more than one button to **true**, Java will turn the last button you set **true** on and all others off.

> A *Checkbox* class object becomes a radio button when it is defined as part of a checkbox group.

The logic required to handle the radio buttons within the *actionPerformed()* method is rather straightforward. Here it is:

```
if (undergraduate.getState())
     studentArea.append("\nUndergraduate");
else
     studentArea.append("\nGraduate");
```

All we need here is a single **if/else** statement because we are only dealing with two radio buttons. If one button is on, the other is off and vice versa. If we had more than two buttons in our group, we would use multiple **if** statements. You see that the *getState()* method is employed within the **if** test to determine that Boolean state of a given button.

Again, radio buttons generate their own events. To handle a radio button event separately you must register each radio button object as a listener with the *addItemListener()* method and process the event within the *itemStateChanged()* method. That's it! Now, let's complete our student GUI with a discussion of menus.

Menus and Submenus

A ***menu*** consists of a set of selectable options located at the top of a window within a ***menu bar***. Menus are widely used in window applications because they make selection easier and do not clutter up the GUI. A *Color* menu has been added to our student GUI, as shown in Figure 11-18.

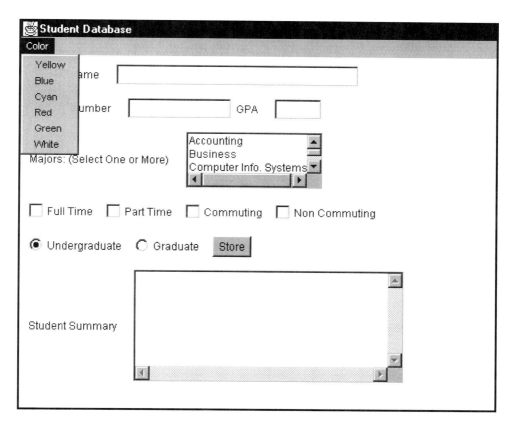

Figure 11-18 The student GUI containing a *Color* menu.

Notice the ***menu bar*** at the top of the window, just under the title bar. We have added a single *Color* menu to the menu bar. The color menu has six selectable color items. The purpose of the *Color* menu is to set the background color of the *Student Summary* text area.

Here is what you have to do to create a menu:

- Define a menu bar object.
- Define menu and submenu objects.
- Add menu items to the menus.
- Add submenus to the main menus.
- Add main menus to the menu bar.
- Set the menu bar on the frame.

There are three classes that control the creation and use of menus. They are *MenuBar*, *Menu*, and *MenuItem*. All menus require a **menu bar**. The menu bar is a separate GUI component located under the title bar at the top of a window. The menu bar component is a container for menus. It has its own separate class called *MenuBar*. There is a single constructor for the *MenuBar* class that does not require any arguments. Thus, the following statement will create a menu bar object called *bar*:

```
//DEFINE MENU BAR OBJECT AS PART OF FRAME CONSTRUCTOR
MenuBar bar = new MenuBar();
```

Creating a menu bar object is the first step in creating a menu. The next step is to create menu and submenu objects using the *Menu* class. There are three versions of the *Menu* class constructor, as follows:

```
//CONSTRUCTS A NEW MENU WITHOUT A LABEL
public Menu()
```

```
//CONSTRUCTS A NEW MENU WITH A LABEL
public Menu(String label)
```

```
//CONSTRUCTS A NEW MENU WITH A LABEL AND TEAR-OFF
public Menu(String label, boolean tearOff)
```

We will use the last constructor because it allows us to create a menu label as well as a ***tear-off*** menu. The tear-off feature allows a menu, once selected, to be displayed after the mouse button has been released. If you have ever worked with a window application that does not have this feature, you know it can be annoying when the menu disappears after releasing the mouse button. You should be aware, however, that not all implementations of Java support this feature. If your implementation does not, it will simply ignore the tear-off argument without creating any problems. Here is the statement we used to created our *colorMenu* object:

//DEFINE COLOR MENU OBJECT AS PART OF FRAME CONSTRUCTOR
Menu colorMenu = new Menu("Color",true);

Notice that the menu label is "Color" and we have enable the tear-off feature. The next thing to do is add the menu items to the menu. We will use our *colorMenu* object to call the *add()* method to accomplish this task as follows:

//ADD MENU ITEMS TO MENU AS PART OF FRAME CONSTRUCTOR
colorMenu.add(new MenuItem("Yellow"));
colorMenu.add(new MenuItem("Blue"));
colorMenu.add(new MenuItem("Cyan"));
colorMenu.add(new MenuItem("Red"));
colorMenu.add(new MenuItem("Green"));
colorMenu.add(new MenuItem("White"));

Observe that the *MenuItem* class is used within the *add()* method argument to create a menu item object with the specified color label. Since this menu does not contain any submenus, the next task is to call the *add()* method with our *bar* object to add our *colorMenu* to the menu bar like this:

//ADD MENU TO MENU BAR AS PART OF FRAME CONSTRUCTOR
bar.add(colorMenu);

Finally, we must set the menu bar on the frame. This is accomplished with the *setMenuBar()* method as follows:

//SET MENU BAR
setMenuBar(bar);

Up to this point, we have only created a menu for the GUI. We must now develop the code to handle a menu event. A menu event occurs when one of the menu items is selected. Selection can occur by pointing and clicking the mouse on an item or by using the keyboard arrow and **ENTER** keys. Either way, a menu event is generated. To handle the event, we must register an action listener for our *colorMenu* object like this:

//REGISTER MENU LISTENER AS PART OF FRAME CONSTRUCTOR
colorMenu.addActionListener(this);

The *addActionListener()* method is employed, because a menu event is an action event. Of course, the **this** argument is used, because we will register the object as a listener within the frame constructor. All of the foregoing menu code resides in our *StudentGUI()* frame constructor.

Now, since a menu item generates an action event, the menu processing logic must appear inside the *actionPerformed()* method. The purpose of the *Color* menu is to set the background color of our *Student Summary* text area, so, we have to first determine if a menu event was generated (versus a button event), then determine which menu item generated the event. Once this is determined, we can set the background color of the text area to the color selected on the menu. Here is the required logic:

```
//DID MENU CAUSE EVENT?
if (e.getSource() instanceof MenuItem)
{
  //GET MENU ITEM SELECTED
  String item = e.getActionCommand();

  //FIND ITEM AND CHANGE BACKGROND COLOR
  if (item.equals("Yellow"))
    studentArea.setBackground(Color.yellow);
  if (item.equals("Blue"))
    studentArea.setBackground(Color.blue);
  if (item.equals("Cyan"))
    studentArea.setBackground(Color.cyan);
  if (item.equals("Red"))
    studentArea.setBackground(Color.red);
  if (item.equals("Green"))
    studentArea.setBackground(Color.green);
  if (item.equals("White"))
    studentArea.setBackground(Color.white);
```

Here, the event object, *e*, calls the *getSource()* method to get the source of the event. If the event object is an instance of *MenuItem*, the **if** test is **true** and a local string variable called *item* is defined and set to the name of the menu item, or color, that generated this event. Notice that the code e.getActionCommand() will return the name of the menu item that generated the event. Finally, a series of **if** statements are used to compare *item* to all possible item labels and set the text area background accordingly.

Submenus

We will refer to the foregoing *Color* menu as a main menu, because it appears on the menu bar. A ***submenu*** is a menu within a menu. You build submenus just as you build main menus. You must define a submenu object, add items to the submenu, then add the submenu to a main menu. Let's suppose that we want to use a menu to control the type and style of the character font within our *Student Summary* text area of our student GUI as shown in Figure 11-19. Notice that the main menu is *Font*, which contains two submenus called *Font type* and *Font style*. As you can see, the *Font style* submenu contains three selectable items: *Plain*, *Bold*, and *Italic*.

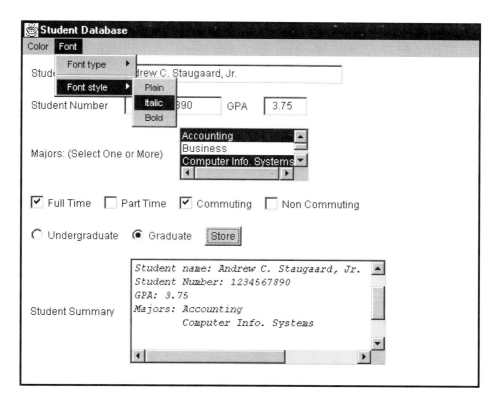

Figure 11-19 The student GUI containing a *Font* menu which contains *Font type* and *Font style* submenus.

The font type is the font name, such as Courier, **Helvetica**, Times Roman, and so forth. The font style controls how a given font will appear, such as plain, *italic*, or **bold**. So, we need to create a main menu object called *fontMenu* and then create two submenu objects called *fontTypeMenu* and *fontStyleMenu* like this:

```
//DEFINE MENU OBJECTS AS PART OF FRAME CONSTRUCTOR
Menu fontMenu = new Menu("Font",true);
Menu fontTypeMenu = new Menu("Font type",true);
Menu fontStyleMenu = new Menu("Font style",true);
```

Nothing new here. We have simply created three menu objects, given them a label, and enabled the tear-off feature. Next, we need to add items to each menu as follows:

```
//ADD ITEMS TO SUBMENUS AS PART OF FRAME CONSTRUCTOR
fontTypeMenu.add(new MenuItem("Courier"));
fontTypeMenu.add(new MenuItem("Helvetica"));
fontTypeMenu.add(new MenuItem("Times Roman"));

fontStyleMenu.add(new MenuItem("Plain"));
fontStyleMenu.add(new MenuItem("Italic"));
fontStyleMenu.add(new MenuItem("Bold"));
```

We have only used three font types to keep it simple, but as you will see shortly, there are many more that could be applied. Once the menu items are added, we must add each submenu to the main menu like this:

```
//ADD SUBMENUS TO MAIN MENU AS PART OF FRAME CONSTRUCTOR
fontMenu.add(fontTypeMenu);          //ADD FONT TYPE SUBMENU
fontMenu.add("-");                   //ADD SEPARATOR BAR
fontMenu.add(fontStyleMenu);         //ADD FONT STYLE SUBMENU
```

Here, the main menu object, *fontMenu*, is used to call the *add()* method which references the submenu object as its argument. Notice that a dash, "-", appears as the argument in the second *add()* statement. This is called a **menu separator** and creates the line between the *Font type* and *Font style* labels in Figure 11-19. Finally, we need a statement to add the main menu to the menu bar, like this:

```
//ADD FONT MENU TO MENU BAR AS PART OF FRAME CONSTRUCTOR
bar.add(fontMenu);
```

Here, we have used the same menu bar object, *bar*, that we used earlier for the *Color* menu. Of course, we still must set the menu bar to the frame using *setMenuBar()* as before.

The next task is to process a *fontMenu* event. Again, we will add logic to the *actionPerformed()* method to handle the event. However, before an event can be handled the event objects must be registered as listeners. Here's the required code:

```
//REGISTER LISTENERS AS PART OF FRAME CONSTRUCTOR
fontTypeMenu.addActionListener(this);    //FONT TYPE MENU LISTENER
fontStyleMenu.addActionListener(this);   //FONT STYLE MENU LISTENER
```

Notice that the submenu objects are registered and not the main menu object. The reason is that the main menu object is not generating an event; only the submenu objects are generating events.

Here is the code that must appear in the *actionPerformed()* method to handle a *fontTypeMenu* or *fontStyleMenu* event.

```
//DID MENU CAUSE EVENT?
if (e.getSource() instanceof MenuItem)
{
    //GET MENU ITEM SELECTED
    String item = e.getActionCommand();

    //FIND ITEM AND CHANGE BACKGROND COLOR
    if (item.equals("Yellow"))
      studentArea.setBackground(Color.yellow);
    if (item.equals("Blue"))
      studentArea.setBackground(Color.blue);
    if (item.equals("Cyan"))
      studentArea.setBackground(Color.cyan);
    if (item.equals("Red"))
      studentArea.setBackground(Color.red);
    if (item.equals("Green"))
      studentArea.setBackground(Color.green);
    if (item.equals("White"))
      studentArea.setBackground(Color.white);

    //CHECK FOR COURIER ITEM
    if (item.equals("Courier"))
    {
      Font oldFont = studentArea.getFont();  //GET CURRENT TEXT AREA FONT
      int style = oldFont.getStyle();         //GET CURRENT FONT STYLE
      int size = oldFont.getSize();           //GET CURRENT FONT SIZE
      //CREATE NEW COURIER FONT OBJECT
      Font newFont = new Font("Courier",style,size);
      //SET TEXT AREA TO NEW FONT
      studentArea.setFont(newFont);
    }//END IF COURIER
```

```
//CHECK FOR HELVETICA ITEM
if (item.equals("Helvetica"))
{
   Font oldFont = studentArea.getFont();  //GET CURRENT TEXT AREA FONT
   int style = oldFont.getStyle();          //GET CURRENT FONT STYLE
   int size = oldFont.getSize();            //GET CURRENT FONT SIZE
   //CREATE NEW HELVETICA FONT OBJECT
   Font newFont = new Font("Helvetica",style,size);
   //SET TEXT AREA TO NEW FONT
   studentArea.setFont(newFont);
}//END IF HELVETICA

//CHECK FOR TIMES ROMAN ITEM
if (item.equals("Times Roman"))
{
   Font oldFont = studentArea.getFont();  //GET CURRENT TEXT AREA FONT
   int style = oldFont.getStyle();          //GET CURRENT FONT STYLE
   int size = oldFont.getSize();            //GET CURRENT FONT SIZE
   //CREATE NEW TIMES ROMAN FONT OBJECT
   Font newFont = new Font("TimesRoman",style,size);
   //SET TEXT AREA TO NEW FONT
   studentArea.setFont(newFont);
}//END IF TIMES ROMAN

//CHECK FOR PLAIN STYLE
if (item.equals("Plain"))
{
  Font oldFont = studentArea.getFont();  //GET CURRENT TEXT AREA FONT
  String name = oldFont.getName();        //GET CURRENT FONT NAME
  int size = oldFont.getSize();            //GET CURRENT FONT SIZE
   //CREATE NEW PLAIN FONT OBJECT
  Font newFont = new Font(name,Font.PLAIN,size);
   //SET TEXT AREA TO NEW FONT
  studentArea.setFont(newFont);
}//END IF "Plain"

if (item.equals("Italic"))
{
  Font oldFont = studentArea.getFont();  //GET CURRENT TEXT AREA FONT
  String name = oldFont.getName();        //GET CURRENT FONT NAME
  int size = oldFont.getSize();            //GET CURRENT FONT SIZE

   //CREATE NEW ITALIC FONT OBJECT
  Font newFont = new Font(name,Font.ITALIC,size);
```

```
  //SET TEXT AREA TO NEW FONT
  studentArea.setFont(newFont);
}//END IF "Italic"

if (item.equals("Bold"))
{
  Font oldFont = studentArea.getFont();   //GET CURRENT TEXT AREA FONT
  String name = oldFont.getName();        //GET CURRENT FONT NAME
  int size = oldFont.getSize();           //GET CURRENT FONT SIZE
  //CREATE NEW BOLD FONT OBJECT
  Font newFont = new Font(name,Font.BOLD,size);
  //SET TEXT AREA TO NEW FONT
  studentArea.setFont(newFont);
}//END IF "Bold"
}//END IF MENU ITEM
```

Font Control

Okay, we have added our font processing logic to the color processing logic developed earlier. As you can see, both are part of an **if** statement that determines if the event is a menu event. The string, *item*, is assigned the menu item which generated the event. Then *item* is tested as before for a color item, followed by a test for a font item. First, notice that there is a separate **if** statement for each font item, just as for each color item. Now we need to analyze the contents of these **if** statements. This requires us to learn about Java font control. For example, here is the **if** statement used to test for a font type of Helvetica:

```
//CHECK FOR HELVETICA ITEM
if (item.equals("Helvetica"))
{
    Font oldFont = studentArea.getFont();   //GET CURRENT TEXT AREA FONT
    int style = oldFont.getStyle();         //GET CURRENT FONT STYLE
    int size = oldFont.getSize();           //GET CURRENT FONT SIZE

    //CREATE NEW HELVETICA FONT OBJECT
    Font newFont = new Font("Helvetica",style,size);

    //SET TEXT AREA TO NEW FONT
    studentArea.setFont(newFont);
}//END IF HELVETICA
```

The first statement creates an object called *oldFont* of the standard Java *Font* class. The Java *Font* class can be used to control three main font properties within a GUI: the *font type*, or *name*, the *font style*, and the *font size*. The font name can be any font supported by the system within which the program is running. Typical font names include Arial, Courier, Century Gothic, Helvetica, Sans Serif, and Times Roman, just to mention a few. In fact, some systems, like Windows 98, support over 100 different font types, or names. The font styles provided within the *Font* class are plain, italic, and bold. These styles are declared as constants within the class and are accessed via *Font.PLAIN*, *Font.ITALIC*, and *Font.BOLD*. Finally, the font size is specified in *points*, where one point is 1/72 of an inch. For example, the font of the text you are now reading is Times Roman, plain, 11 point. Table 11-8 summarizes the properties of a font.

TABLE 11-8 FONT PROPERTIES

Property	Description
name or type	Any font typeface supported by the underlying operating system.
style	Font.PLAIN, Font.ITALIC, Font.BOLD.
size	Specified in points, where one point is 1/72 of an inch.

Now back to the code. When the *oldFont* object is created, it is assigned the current font name, style, and size of the *studentArea* text area from our student GUI. Notice that the *studentArea* object is used to call the *getFont()* method. This method gets the font name, style, and size of the calling object. Since *oldFont* is a font object which now has the font properties of our *studentArea* object, we can extract the name, style, or size of the font from this object by calling *getName()*, *getStyle()*, or *getSize()*, respectively. The *getName()* method returns a string, while *getStyle()* and *getSize()* return integers. Here, we are getting the current font style and size, since these will not change. Only the font name will change to "Helvetica." Next, a new font object called *newFont* is created which uses the *Font* class constructor to set the object to "Helvetica," *style*, and *size*, where *style* and *size* are the style and size of the current text area font, respectively. Finally, the *studentArea* object is used to call the *setFont()* method which sets the text area font to the properties of the *newFont* object. Table 11-9 summarizes some of the methods available in the *Font* class. See your on-line help or Java reference documentation for more information on these and other font-related methods.

TABLE 11-9 FONT METHODS

Method	Description
getFont()	Returns a font object representing the current font of the calling object..
getName()	Returns a string which is the current font name.
getSize()	Returns an integer which is the current font size.
getStyle()	Returns an integer which represents the current font style.
isBold()	Returns **true** if the font is bold.
isItalic()	Returns **true** if the font is italic.
isPlain()	Returns **true** if the font is plain.
setFont()	Sets the font of the calling component object.

Now, we have to process the font style menu items. Here is the **if** statement that processes the plain font style:

```
if (item.equals("Plain"))
{
   Font oldFont = studentArea.getFont();      //GET CURRENT TEXT AREA FONT
   String name = oldFont.getName();           //GET CURRENT FONT NAME
   int size = oldFont.getSize();              //GET CURRENT FONT SIZE
   //CREATE NEW PLAIN FONT OBJECT
   Font newFont = new Font(name,Font.PLAIN,size);
   //SET TEXT AREA TO NEW FONT
   studentArea.setFont(newFont);
}//END IF "Plain"
```

The only difference here is that we need to obtain the text area font name via *getName()*, rather than the font style, because we are changing the style to plain. The rest of the logic is the same as that discussed for the font type menu. There you have it! You should now know how to create menus and submenus as well as control the font of a GUI component. The methods used in this section are summarized in Table 11-10.

TABLE 11-10 SUMMARY OF COMPONENT METHODS USED IN THIS SECTION

Method	Description
addItem(String)	Adds *String* item to calling choice or list object.
*addItemListener(**this**)*	Registers a listener for calling item object.
append(String)	Appends *String* to text of calling text object.
Checkbox()	Constructs a new checkbox without a label.
Checkbox(String)	Constructs a new checkbox with *String* label.
Checkbox(String, boolean)	Constructs a new checkbox with *String* label, set to a given boolean state.
Checkbox(String,CheckBoxGroup, boolean)	Constructs new checkbox with *String* label, in the specified checkbox group, set to specified boolean state.
Choice()	Constructs a new empty choice box.
getSelectedItem()	Returns selected choice item of calling choice object.
getSelectedItems()	Returns selected list items of calling list object in an array of strings.
getState()	Returns the boolean state of the calling checkbox object.
getText()	Returns text contained in calling text object.
Label()	Constructs a new empty label.
Label(String)	Constructs a new label with *String* text.
Label(String, int)	Constructs a new label with *String* text and specified alignment.
List()	Constructs a new empty list box.
List(int)	Constructs a new empty list box with specified number of items visible.
List(int, boolean)	Constructs a new empty list box with specified number of items visible, and true/false enabling multiple item selection or not.
Menu()	Creates a new menu without a label.
Menu(String)	Creates a new menu with *String* label.
Menu(String, boolean)	Creates a new menu with *String* label and tear-off enabled/disabled (true/false).

TABLE 11-10 (CONTINUED) SUMMARY OF COMPONENT METHODS USED
IN THIS SECTION

Method	Description
MenuItem(String)	Creates a new menu item with *String* label.
MenuBar()	Creates a new menu bar.
processItemEvent()	Processes an item event.
setMenuBar(MenuBar)	Sets *MenuBar* object to frame.
setText(String)	Sets text of calling text object to *String*.
TextField()	Constructs a new empty text field.
TextField(Sting)	Constructs a new text field initialized with *String*.
TextField(int)	Constructs a new empty text field with specified number of columns.
TextField(String, int)	Constructs a new text field initialized with *String* with specified number of columns.
TextArea()	Constructs a new empty text area.
TextArea(Sting)	Constructs a new text area initialized with *String*.
TextArea(int, int)	Constructs a new empty text area with specified number of rows and columns.
TextArea(String, int, int)	Constructs a new text area initialized with *String* with specified number of rows and columns.

 Quick Check

1. Write statements to create a "This is my label" label object called *myLabel* and add it to a panel called *myPanel*.

2. Write a statement to define a text field object called *myTextField* which is 20 columns wide.

3. Write a statement to define a text area object called *myTextArea* which is 10 rows high and 50 columns wide.

4. Write a statements to add the objects in questions 2 and 3 to a panel called *myPanel*.

5. What is the difference between a choice box and a list box?

6. What method is used to determine the state of a checkbox or radio button?

7. What is the purpose of a menu bar?

8. Write a statement to create a menu bar called *myMenuBar*.

9. Write a statement to create a menu object called *myMenu* with a label of "My Menu" and the tear-off feature enabled.

10. Write a statement to add the menu in question 9 to the menu bar in question 8.

11. Write a statement to add the menu bar in question 8 to a frame.

12. What are the general properties associated with a font?

13. What is the size of a font point?

14. Write a statement to create a 16-point Arial bold font called *myFont*.

15. Write a statement to set the font of the text area in question 3 to the font in question 14.

PROBLEM SOLVING IN ACTION: DESIGNING AND BUILDING GUIs

Problem

In previous chapters, we have developed text interfaces for our programs. It is now time to develop GUI interfaces. We will deal with a problem that has been dealt with before, so that we can concentrate, not on the problem itself, but on the user interface. The problem is that of determining monthly payments and interest on a consumer loan. Recall that we need the user to enter the loan amount, term of the loan, and loan interest rate. The program will then determine the monthly payments, total loan interest, and total loan amount.

Defining the Problem

Based on the problem statement, our problem definition addresses the output produced by the program, the input required to produce the output, and the processing required to determine the output from the given input as follows:

Output: The monthly loan payment, total loan interest, and total loan amount, including interest.

Input: Loan principle, term of the loan, and annual interest rate.

Processing: Calculate the following:

$$payment = principle * rate/(1-(1+rate)^{-term})$$
$$interest = term * payment - principle$$
$$total = principle + interest$$

Planning the Solution

So far, nothing in our approach to problem solving is new. But, here is where things change. We must now think of the problem in terms of a GUI interface and object-orientation. The first thing we must do is to visualize the interface. We can do this with a *window layout chart* like the one shown in Figure 11-20.

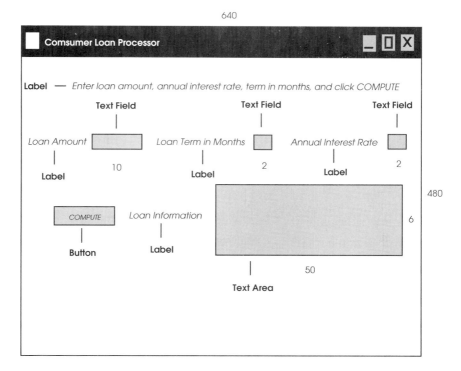

Figure 11-20 A window layout chart is a sketch of the window, showing the GUI components and their locations.

Notice that the window layout chart is simply a drawing, or sketch, of the GUI components and their layout, or location, on the window. In addition, each component is labeled as to its type and size, if necessary. Notice also that the text of each label component is written just as it will be seen by the user and coded by you, the programmer. Since no component coordinates are shown, you can assume that we are going to use a layout manager. If you do not use a layout manager, the window layout chart must show the component coordinates in addition to their sizes. From the layout, you can visualize that three panels are needed if we use the flow layout manager. The instruction label at the top will go in one panel, the text fields with go in the middle panel, and the button and text area will be added to the bottom panel. It is also clear from the layout that the user will enter the text field data and click the *COMPUTE* button. The calculated values will then be displayed in the text area. Window layout charts are a must when developing GUIs. Don't be tempted to work without one. It's like anything else you try to build—you always need to start with a good plan.

Now, the algorithms we develop will relate not only to processing, but also to the construction of the GUI. We will create a subclass of *Frame* called *LoanProcessor* that will generate the GUI and process any component events. As you already know, the GUI will be generated by the *LoanProcessor()* frame constructor and the button event will be processed in the *actionPerformed()* method. Of course, *main()* will be used to define the frame object, set its size, and make is visible. As result, we must develop an algorithm for *main()*, *LoanProcessor()*, and *actionPerformed()*. Here is the first level of each:

Initial Algorithms

main()
BEGIN
    Define frame object.
    Define frame font.
    Set frame font.
    Set frame size.
    Make frame visible.
END.

LoanProcessor() Constructor
BEGIN
    Call superclass constructor.
    Register frame as a listener for a closing event.
    Set frame layout.
    Define panels.

Set panel layout.
Define components.
Add components to panels.
Add panels to frame.
Register listeners.
END.

actionPerformed( )
BEGIN
Determine which type of component generated an event.
Get event data.
Process data.
Generate any required output.
END.

Now, the foregoing algorithms are so general that they could be applied to any GUI program. The initial algorithm for *main()* is at a codeable level; however, the *LoanProcessor()* and *actionPerformed()* algorithms need some refinement. So, let's refine them to fit our program task, as follows:

First Level of Refinement

LoanProcessor( )
BEGIN
Call superclass constructor.
Register frame as a listener for closing event.
Set frame layout to flow layout.
Define three panels.
Set each panel to flow layout, center justified, with 10 point gapping.
Define user instruction label.
Define loan amount text field label.
Define loan term text field label.
Define loan interest text field label.
Define loan information text area label.
Define compute button.
Add user instruction label to first panel.
Add loan amount, term, and interest labels and text fields to second panel.
Add compute button, text area label, and text area to third panel.
Add all three panels to frame.
Register button object as a listener.
END.

> *actionPerformed( )*
> BEGIN
>> If a button caused the event
>>> Read *principle* from loan amount text field.
>>> Read *term* from term text field.
>>> Read *rate* from interest rate text field.
>>> Calculate *payment = principle * rate/(1-(1+rate)$^{-term}$)*.
>>> Calculate *interest = term * payment − principle*.
>>> Calculate *total = principle + interest*.
>>> Append text area with *payment*.
>>> Append text area with *interest*.
>>> Append text area with *total*.
> END.

Now, let's look at the *LoanProcessor( )* constructor algorithm first. Most of these steps should be familiar to you and reflect the GUI in Figure 11-20 that we must create. However, notice that the text fields are not defined here. Why? Because the text field objects need to be visible to the *actionPerformed( )* method to process the data they contain. Therefore, the text fields must be defined outside of the constructor as private class members. Now, you should have no trouble coding the constructor algorithm at this point. Here's the code:

```
//CONSTRUCTOR
 public LoanProcessor(String title)
 {
 //CALL SUPERCLASS CONSTRUCTOR
 super(title);

 //REGISTER LISTENER FOR THIS FRAME
 addWindowListener(this);

 //SET FRAME LAYOUT MANAGER
 setLayout(new FlowLayout());

 //DEFINE THREE PANELS
 Panel panel1 = new Panel();
 Panel panel2 = new Panel();
 Panel panel3 = new Panel();

 //SET EACH PANEL TO FLOW LAYOUT, CENTER JUSTIFIED, 10 PT. GAPPING
 panel1.setLayout(new FlowLayout(FlowLayout.CENTER,10,10));
 panel2.setLayout(new FlowLayout(FlowLayout.CENTER,10,10));
 panel3.setLayout(new FlowLayout(FlowLayout.CENTER,10,10));
```

```
//DEFINE LABEL OBJECTS
Label userInstruction = new Label("Enter loan amount,"
                              + " annual interest rate, term in months,"
                              + " and click COMPUTE");
Label principleLabel = new Label("Loan Amount");
Label termLabel = new Label("Loan Term in Months");
Label rateLabel = new Label("Annual Interest Rate");
Label loanInfoLabel = new Label("Loan Information");

//DEFINE BUTTON OBJECT
Button computeButton = new Button("COMPUTE");

//ADD COMPONENTS TO PANELS
panel1.add(userInstruction);
panel2.add(principleLabel);
panel2.add(principleField);
panel2.add(termLabel);
panel2.add(termField);
panel2.add(rateLabel);
panel2.add(rateField);
panel3.add(computeButton);
panel3.add(loanInfoLabel);
panel3.add(loanInfoArea);

//ADD PANELS TO FRAME
add(panel1);
add(panel2);
add(panel3);

//REGISTER BUTTON LISTENER
computeButton.addActionListener(this);
}//END LoanProcessor()
```

Nothing new here, you have seen all of this before. Now for the *actionPerformed()* method. First, the algorithm looks pretty straightforward and you might suspect that it can be easily coded. In most programming languages this would be true; however, Java presents a problem when reading numerical data. Remember when we had to create a special *keyboardInput* package to read keyboard data? Well, we are now about to "unwrap" this package and explain some of the things that need to be done to get numerical data into your program. We will leave the algorithm as is, assuming that it is at a codeable level. Here is how it must be coded in Java:

```
//actionPerformed METHOD
  public void actionPerformed(ActionEvent e)
  {
    //DID A BUTTON CAUSE EVENT?
    if (e.getSource() instanceof Button)
    {
      //IF SO, READ DATA AND CALCULATE LOAN INFORMATION
      //DEFINE WRAPPER CLASS OBJECTS AND GET TEXT FIELD DATA
      Double p = new Double(principleField.getText().trim());
      Double t = new Double(termField.getText().trim());
      Double r = new Double(rateField.getText().trim());

      //CONVERT Double TO double
      double principle = p.doubleValue();
      double term = t.doubleValue();
      double rate = r.doubleValue();

      //MAKE LOAN CALCULATIONS
      rate = rate/12/100;
      double payment = principle * rate/(1-Math.pow((1+rate), -term));
      double interest = term * payment - principle;
      double total = principle + interest;

      //DISPLAY IN TEXT AREA
      loanInfoArea.setFont(new Font("TimesRoman",Font.ITALIC + Font.BOLD,14));
      loanInfoArea.setText("CONSUMER LOAN AMOUNTS");
      loanInfoArea.append("\n\nMonthly Payment: $" + String.valueOf(payment));
      loanInfoArea.append("\nTotal Interest : $" + String.valueOf(interest));
      loanInfoArea.append("\nTotal Loan Amount: $" + String.valueOf(total));
    }//END IF
  }//END actionPerformed
```

The first line should be familiar. We simply use an **if** statement to test for a button event. Then comes the problem: reading numeric data from the text fields. Java "sees" all input as string input. As a result, we must convert the text field strings to numeric values. To do this, we must first create a ***wrapper object*** for each value. Java includes several numeric wrapper classes which correspond to the primitive numeric data types. They are **Integer**, **Long**, **Float**, **Double**, **Character**, and **Boolean**. We say that the wrapper classes "wrap" a value of a primitive data type as an object. In other words, a wrapper class allows an object to be created for a primitive data type. Furthermore, the wrapper class contains methods that allow the primitive data type to be converted to and from a string. This is why we need a wrapper class for input. The idea will be to read the string data from a text field, and assign it to a **Double** wrapper object and then convert the object to the primitive **double** data type so that we can use the value in a calculation. For example, consider the following line of code:

```
Double p = new Double(principleField.getText().trim());
```

Here, we have created an object, *p*, of the **Double** wrapper class. In creating the object, the *Double()* class constructor is called. This constructor takes a string argument and converts it to a floating-point value, initializing the object with this value. Notice that the argument uses our *principleField* object to call the *getText()* method to get the text field string. The *trim()* method is a member of *String* class that "trims," or removes, any leading or trailing whitespace from the string. So, can this method be called here? Sure, since the code principleField.getText() returns a string object, which is used to call the *trim()* method. At this point, our wrapper object, *p*, contains the floating-point representation of the string data obtained from the *principleField* text field. However, this object *cannot* be manipulated within an arithmetic expression. It must first be converted to a **double** primitive data type. In other words, we need to convert **Double** to **double**. This is the purpose of the following statement:

```
double principle = p.doubleValue();
```

Here we have defined a **double** floating-point variable, called *principle*, and assigned it the value returned from p.doubleValue(). The *doubleValue()* method is a member of the **Double** class that returns the **double** equivalent of the calling object value. Now, after all of this, the **double** variable *principle* contains a numerical floating-point value that can be used in an arithmetic expression. That's a lot of work just to read-in a numeric value, but that's Java!

So, you can see from the foregoing *actionPerformed()* method code that each text field string is read and converted to a **double** primitive data type variable in this manner. Then, the variables are used as before to make the required calculations. Finally, the *loanInfoArea* text area is appended with the results. Note that the *String* class is used to call the *valueOf()* method to convert the primitive data back to a string for display within the text area.

Now, let's put everything together in a complete program. Here it is:

```
//ACTION 11-1  (ACTION11_01.JAVA)
//THIS PROGRAM WILL GENERATE AND PROCESS A GUI FOR THE
//CONSUMER LOAN PROBLEM

import java.awt.*;              //FOR FRAME CLASS
import java.awt.event.*;        //FOR EVENT HANDLING
```

```
class LoanProcessor extends FrameWithClose implements ActionListener
{
  //DEFINE TEXT FIELD AND AREA OBJECTS AS PRIVATE CLASS DATA
   private TextField principleField = new TextField(10);
   private TextField termField = new TextField(2);
   private TextField rateField = new TextField(2);
   private TextArea  loanInfoArea = new TextArea(6,50);

  //CONSTRUCTOR
  public LoanProcessor(String title)
  {
  //CALL SUPERCLASS CONSTRUCTOR
   super(title);

  //SET FRAME LAYOUT MANAGER
   setLayout(new FlowLayout());

  //DEFINE THREE PANELS
   Panel panel1 = new Panel();
   Panel panel2 = new Panel();
   Panel panel3 = new Panel();

  //SET EACH PANEL TO FLOW LAYOUT, CENTER JUSTIFIED, 10 PT. GAPPING
   panel1.setLayout(new FlowLayout(FlowLayout.CENTER,10,10));
   panel2.setLayout(new FlowLayout(FlowLayout.CENTER,10,10));
   panel3.setLayout(new FlowLayout(FlowLayout.CENTER,10,10));

  //DEFINE LABEL OBJECTS
   Label userInstruction = new Label("Enter loan amount,"
                                  + " annual interest rate, term in months,"
                                  + " and click COMPUTE");
   Label principleLabel = new Label("Loan Amount");
   Label termLabel = new Label("Loan Term in Months");
   Label rateLabel = new Label("Annual Interest Rate");
   Label loanInfoLabel = new Label("Loan Information");

  //DEFINE BUTTON OBJECT
   Button computeButton = new Button("COMPUTE");

  //ADD COMPONENTS TO PANELS
   panel1.add(userInstruction);
   panel2.add(principleLabel);
   panel2.add(principleField);
   panel2.add(termLabel);
   panel2.add(termField);
   panel2.add(rateLabel);
```

```
    panel2.add(rateField);
    panel3.add(computeButton);
    panel3.add(loanInfoLabel);
    panel3.add(loanInfoArea);

    //ADD PANELS TO FRAME
    add(panel1);
    add(panel2);
    add(panel3);

    //REGISTER BUTTON LISTENER
    computeButton.addActionListener(this);
    }//END LoanProcessor()

    //PROCESS BUTTON EVENT
    public void actionPerformed(ActionEvent e)
    {
      //DID A BUTTON CAUSE EVENT?
      if (e.getSource() instanceof Button)
      {
        //IF SO, READ DATA AND CALCULATE LOAN INFORMATION
        //DEFINE WRAPPER CLASS OBJECTS AND GET TEXT FIELD DATA
        Double p = new Double(principleField.getText().trim());
        Double t = new Double(termField.getText().trim());
        Double r = new Double(rateField.getText().trim());

        //CONVERT Double TO double
        double principle = p.doubleValue();
        double term = t.doubleValue();
        double rate = r.doubleValue();

        //MAKE LOAN CALCULATIONS
        rate = rate/12/100;
        double payment = principle * rate/(1-Math.pow((1+rate), -term));
        double interest = term * payment - principle;
        double total = principle + interest;

        //DISPLAY IN TEXT AREA
        loanInfoArea.setFont(new Font("TimesRoman",Font.ITALIC + Font.BOLD,14));
        loanInfoArea.setText("CONSUMER LOAN AMOUNTS");
        loanInfoArea.append("\n\nMonthly Payment: $" + String.valueOf(payment));
        loanInfoArea.append("\nTotal Interest : $" + String.valueOf(interest));
        loanInfoArea.append("\nTotal Loan Amount: $" + String.valueOf(total));
      }//END IF
    }//END actionPerformed()
}//END LoanProcessor CLASS
```

```
//APPLICATION CLASS TO TEST loanProcessor CLASS
public class Action11_01
{
  public static void main(String[] args)
  {
    //DEFINE FRAME OBJECT
    LoanProcessor window = new LoanProcessor("Consumer Loan Processor");

    //SET FONT FOR FRAME
    window.setFont(new Font("Arial",Font.ITALIC,12));

    //SET FRAME SIZE TO MAXIMIZE
    window.setSize(640,480);

    //MAKE FRAME VISIBLE
    window.setVisible(true);
  }//END main()
}//END Action11_01 CLASS
```

As you can see, our *LoanProcessor* class appears first, along with its constructor and the *actionPerformed()* method. Prior to the constructor, we have defined the text field and text area objects as private, because they need to be visible within the *actionPerformed()* method. Of course, we have also inherited our earlier *FrameWithClose* class to handle the window closing event. The *LoanProcessor* class is followed by an application test class called *Action11_01*. The application class contains *main()*, which defines a frame object called *window*, sets the frame font, sizes the frame, and makes the frame visible. Observe that here we have set the font of our frame to Arial, *italic*, 12 point using the statement:

window.setFont(new Font("Arial",Font.ITALIC,12));

Our frame object, *window*, is used to call the *setFont()* method with an argument that creates a font. However, notice that in the *actionPerformed()* method we change the font of the text area with the following statement:

loanInfoArea.setFont(new Font("TimesRoman",Font.ITALIC + Font.BOLD,14));

Here, our *loanInfoArea* object calls the *setFont()* method to create a font of Times Roman, ***italic/bold***, 14 point for the text area. Notice how italic and bold are combined using the '+' concatenation operator.

That's it! You should now be ready to design and build your own GUIs. Make sure that you do the programming problems that follow. The more practice you get, the better you will get at designing and building GUIs. You will find that it's a lot of fun.

CHAPTER SUMMARY

In this chapter you learned how to design and build your own graphical user interfaces, or GUIs, within a Java application program. You found that the Java Abstract Windowing Toolkit, or AWT, provided you with all the components necessary to build a GUI. The component classes in the AWT allow you to create frames, labels, text fields, text areas, choice boxes, list boxes, checkboxes, and menus.

To design a GUI, you employ a window layout chart to lay out the components as they will appear on the window. You should indicate the type of component as well as its location and size, if applicable. Then, you employ algorithms and stepwise refinement to outline the steps required to create the GUI. Method *main()* in your application program will create a frame object from your frame subclass, set the frame font, set the size of the frame, and make the frame visible. You create your own frame subclass by inheriting the standard *Frame* class. Most of the GUI components are created within your frame subclass constructor, except those that must be visible to other methods within the subclass. You need to do the following within your frame subclass constructor:

- Call the superclass *Frame* constructor and set the window title.
- Register the frame as a listener for a closing event.
- Set the frame layout.
- Define any required panels.
- Set the layout for each panel.
- Define the GUI object components.
- Add the GUI component objects to the panels.
- Add the panels to the frame.
- Register any required component object listeners.

To process a GUI component event, you must first register the component object as a listener. Then, implement your event logic within the required event method. Each type of component is associated with a given event class and listener class. Each listener class contains its own abstract method(s) that must be implemented within your frame subclass to process an event. The following general tasks are normally performed within an event method:

- Determine which type of component generated the event.
- Get the event data.

- Process the event data.
- Generate any required output.

Of course, these tasks must be stepwise refined to show the logic required to process a particular type of event.

QUESTIONS AND PROBLEMS

Questions

1. List the three tasks that must be performed within *main()* to create a visible frame in a Java application program.

2. Explain why you must create your own subclass of the standard *Frame* class to generate a window.

3. Explain the difference between procedural-controlled and event-driven programs.

4. List at least three GUI events defined by Java.

5. Explain the purpose of a listener.

6. Where is the event handling logic located for an action event?

7. The layout manager that arranges components into geographical regions is the _____ layout manager.

8. Write a statement to set the layout for a panel object, called *panel*, to grid layout, with 5 rows, and 3 columns.

9. Explain why using no layout manager can be a problem for portability.

10. Explain the purpose of a panel.

11. Most of the events handled in this chapter were handled by the *actionPerformed()* method, because a button triggered the event. What GUI components generate events handled by the *processItemEvent()* method?

12. Explain the functional difference between using *setText()* and *append()* when placing text in a text area.

13. What is the difference between a group of checkboxes and a group of radio buttons?

14. Write the code required to perform the following tasks:

    - Create a button object called *StoreButton* with a label of "STORE".
    - Create a "Midwestern States" label object called *StatesLabel*.

- Create a choice box object called *midStatesChoice* which contains the following choice items: "Arkansas", "Missouri", "Iowa", "Kansas".
- Add the label and choice box objects to a panel called *statesPanel*.

15. Write the statements required to determine if a button event has occurred and, if so, determine which choice item in question 14 was selected.

16. List the things that you must do to create a menu.

17. What is the difference between a font name and a font style?

Problems

Least Difficult

1. Write an application program that contains the *FrameWithButtons* class developed in this chapter. This class can be found in the *GUI103_2.java* file on the CD or downloaded from www.prenhall.com. Compile and execute your program. What happens when the various buttons are clicked?

2. Change the *FrameWithButtons* class developed in this chapter to employ different *FlowLayout* alignment and component gapping. This class can be found in the *GUI103_2.java* file on the CD or downloaded from www.prenhall.com. Compile and execute your program and notice the effect of the different alignment and gapping.

3. Change the *FrameWithButtons* class developed in this chapter to employ different *GridLayout* cell arrangement (rows/columns) and component gapping. This class can be found in the *GUI103_2.java* file on the CD or downloaded from www.prenhall.com. Compile and execute your program and notice the effect of the different cell arrangement and gapping.

4. Use the *PanelsTest* class given in this chapter to test the *Panels* class given in the chapter. This class can be found in the *PanelsTest.java* file on the CD or downloaded from www.prenhall.com. Compile and execute your program and observe the effect of clicking the buttons. Change the *Panels* class code to employ different layouts, colors, etc., and observe the results by executing the program.

5. Code the *StudentGUI* class given in this chapter. This class can be found in the *StudentGUI.java* file on the CD or downloaded from www.prenhall.com. Write an application class to test the class. Change the *StudentGUI* class code to employ different layouts, field sizes, etc., and observe the results by exercising the program.

6. Place the choice box code given in this chapter within the *StudentGUI* class code. This class can be found in the *StudentGUI.java* file on the CD or downloaded from www.prenhall.com. Write a Java application program to test the class and verify the operation of the choice box.

7. Place the list box code given in this chapter within the *StudentGUI* class code. This class can be found in the *StudentGUI.java* file on the CD or downloaded from www.prenhall.com. Write a Java application program to test the class and verify the operation of the list box.

8. Place the checkbox code given in this chapter within the *StudentGUI* class code. This class can be found in the *StudentGUI.java* file on the CD or downloaded from www.prenhall.com. Write a Java application program to test the class and verify the operation of the checkboxes.

9. Place the radio button code given in this chapter within the *StudentGUI* class code. This class can be found in the *StudentGUI.java* file on the CD or downloaded from www.prenhall.com. Write a Java application program to test the class and verify the operation of the radio buttons.

10. Place the color menu code developed in this chapter within the *StudentGUI* class code. This class can be found in the *StudentGUI.java* file on the CD or downloaded from www.prenhall.com. Write a Java application program to test the class and verify the operation of the menus.

11. Place the font menu code developed in this chapter within the *StudentGUI* class code. This class can be found in the *StudentGUI.java* file on the CD or downloaded from www.prenhall.com. Write a Java application program to test the class and verify the operation of the menus.

12. Code and execute the consumer loan processor GUI developed in this chapter This class can be found in the *Action11_01.java* file on the CD or downloaded from www.prenhall.com.

More Difficult

13. Add a menu to the consumer loan processor GUI developed in this chapter that will allow the user to select the color of the text appearing in the text area. This class can be found in the *Action11_01.java* file on the CD or downloaded from www.prenhall.com.

14. Add a menu to the consumer loan processor GUI developed in this chapter that will allow the user to select the font type, style, and size of the text area. This class can be found in the *Action11_01.java* file on the CD or downloaded from www.prenhall.com.

Most Difficult

15. Design and build an ATM GUI that will process a banking transaction. The GUI is to have the following components and capabilities, at a minimum:

    •   User instruction label(s).

- Text fields and associated labels for the user's personal identification number (PIN), and amount deposited or withdrawn.
- Radio buttons to select between a checking or savings account transaction.
- Button to process the transaction.
- Logic to calculate a new balance, assuming the initial balance was $1000.00.
- A text area to display the new balance and a "Thank you" message, or a polite message, requesting the user to enter a different amount if they attempt to withdraw more than $300.00.

16. Design and build a loan application GUI. The GUI is to have the following components and capabilities, at a minimum:

- Text fields and associated labels that will allow the user to enter their name, address, telephone number, and social security number.
- Text fields and associated labels that will allow the user to enter the amount of the loan and term for which they are applying.
- Text field and associated label for annual income.
- Radio buttons for married/single status.
- Text area to display the loan information.
- Menu to set the text area font type, style, and size.
- A store/calculate button that will display the loan applicant information as well as monthly payment based on an interest rate of 10% in a text area as well as "APPROVED" or "NOT APPROVED" based on the following criteria:
    - For loan amounts <= $1,000, annual income must be at least $10,000.
    - For loan amounts between $1,000 and $10,000, annual income must be at least $25,000.
    - For loan amounts between $10,000 and $25,000, annual income must be at least $50,000.
    - We do not make loans above $25,000.

17. Design and build a stock buy/sell GUI. The GUI is to have the following components and capabilities, at a minimum:

- Text fields and associated labels for account number, number of shares to buy/sell, stock "ticker" symbol, and trading password.
- Radio button group for type of transaction: buy or sell.
- Radio button group for price: market or stop order. A market order is an order to buy or sell at the current market price. A stop order becomes a market order when the stock price reaches the price you specify in an associated text field.
- Choice box for items of "good for a day" or "good until canceled".

- Buttons to preview order or cancel order. If preview order is clicked, a text area must display the type of transaction, quantity of shares, stock symbol, and total price which includes a $14.95 commission. If the order is a "buy" order, the commission is added to the total price of the order. If the order is a "sell" order, the commission is subtracted from the gross proceeds realized from the sale. For a market order, assume the price is $25.00 per share. For a stop order, the price per share is the amount entered by the user in the text field associated with the stop order radio button.
- Do not accept an order if either the account number or trading password is not entered.

Applet 102: GRAPHICS I

PURPOSE

- *To become familiar with the graphical components contained within the Java Graphics class.*
- *To learn how to create graphical images using rectangles, ovals, arcs, lines, and strings.*
- *To employ the paint() method within an applet to receive a graphics object and use this object to paint graphical components.*
- *To experiment with graphics color and location.*
- *To understand the difference between a filled graphic and a nonfilled graphic.*
- *To understand how complex graphics and pictures can be constructed from simple graphical components.*
- *To learn how to use graphics in both applet and application programs.*

Introduction

In this module, you will use the Java *Graphics* class with the *paint()* method to experiment with graphical components. These components include rectangles, ovals, arcs, lines, and strings. You will load and execute an applet that draws graphical components within its *paint()* method. You will modify the code and observe the effect on the graphics generated by the applet. Now, let's have some fun.

Procedure

1. Load and execute the *Applet102_1.java* program contained on the CD that accompanies this book or download it from www.prenhall.com. Use your Java compiler to compile the program as an applet; then execute the program through your compiler or a Web browser. You should observe the applet shown in Figure 1.

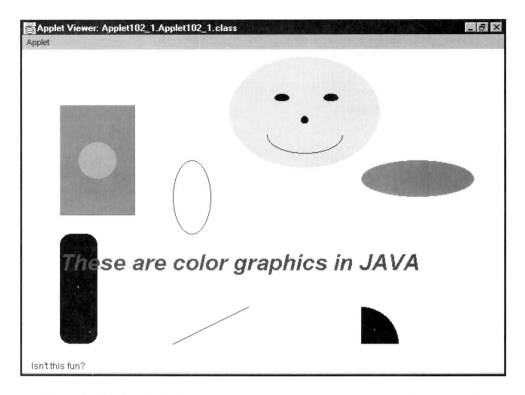

Figure 1 The simple window generated by the *Applet101_1.java* applet program in a Windows environment.

2. Maximize the window. Wow, what an applet! The graphics you see are composed of several graphical components, as follows:

    *   A filled 3D rectangle implemented by method *fill3DRect( )*

    *   A filled rounded rectangle, implemented by method *fillRoundRect( )*

    *   A filled oval, implemented by method *fillOval( )*

    *   A nonfilled oval, implemented by method *drawOval( )*

    *   An arc, implemented by method *drawArc( )*

    *   A line, implemented by method *drawLine( )*

    *   A filled arc, implemented by method *fillArc( )*

    See if you can identify each of these graphics in Figure 1.

Here is the code that produced the applet window:

```
1   import java.awt.*;           //FOR GRAPHICS CLASS
2   import java.awt.event.*;     //FOR EVENT CLASS
3   import java.applet.*;        //FOR APPLET CLASS
4
5
6   public class Applet102_1 extends Applet
7   {
8     //DEFINE RGB COLORS
9     private int red = 250;
10    private int green = 100;
11    private int blue = 100;
12
13    public void paint(Graphics g)
14    {
15
16      //RGB COLOR AND RECTANGLES
17      //SET RGB COLOR
18      g.setColor(new Color(red,green,blue));
19
20      //FILL 3D RECTANGLE
21      g.fill3DRect(50,75,100,150,true);
22
23      //SET COLOR TO BLACK
24      g.setColor(Color.black);
25
26      //FILL ROUNDED RECTANGLE
27      g.fillRoundRect(50,250,50,150,30,30);
28
29      //OVALS
30      //FILL CYAN OVAL
31      g.setColor(Color.cyan);
32      g.fillOval(75,125,50,50);
33
34      //DRAW BLUE OVAL
35      g.setColor(Color.blue);
36      g.drawOval(200,150,50,100);
37
38      //FILL GREEN OVAL
39      g.setColor(Color.green);
40      g.fillOval(450,150,150,50);
41
42      //DRAW SMILING FACE
43      //USE FILLED OVAL FOR FACE
```

```
44    g.setColor(Color.yellow);        //SET FACE COLOR TO YELLOW
45    g.fillOval(275,10,200,150);
46
47    //USE FILLED OVAL FOR EYES
48    g.setColor(Color.black);
49    g.fillOval(335,60,20,10);        //LEFT EYE
50    g.fillOval(400,60,20,10);        //RIGHT EYE
51
52    //USE FILLED OVAL FOR NOSE
53    g.fillOval(370,90,10,10);
54
55    //ARCS
56    //USE ARC FOR MOUTH OF SMILING FACE
57    g.drawArc(325,90,100,50,0,-180);
58
59    //FILLED AN ARC
60    g.fillArc(400,325,75,75,0,135);
61
62    //LINES
63    //DRAW A LINE
64    g.drawLine(200,400,300,350);
65
66    //FONTS AND STRINGS
67    //DRAW RED FONT STRING
68    g.setColor(Color.red);
69    g.setFont(new Font("Helvetica",Font.ITALIC + Font.BOLD,30));
70    g.drawString("These are color graphics in JAVA",50,300);
71
72    //SHOW APPLET STATUS
73    showStatus("  Isn't this fun?");
74   }//END paint()
75 }//END APPLET
```

The preceding code is divided into sections for each major type of graphic as indicated by the bold comment lines. Our procedure and associated discussion will relate to these graphical divisions.

RGB Color and Rectangles

3. The first thing you see in the *Applet102_1* class are three private members named *red*, *blue*, and *green*. These members control the amount of red, green, and blue color for the reddish filled rectangle with a circle inside of it in the upper-left-hand side of the window. Each color value can range from 0

to 255. Since red, green, and blue are primary colors, you can produce any color from these three primaries. Change each color value to 0 and execute the program again. You should see a black rectangle, because black is the total absence of any color.

4. Change each color value to 255 and execute the program again. Now the rectangle cannot be seen, but it is there. It can't be seen because it is now a white rectangle on a white background. However, you can see the right and bottom edges of the rectangle. These edges are produced by the *fill3DRect()* method to give the rectangle a three-dimensional (3D) look.

5. Adjust the color values to produce any color you desire. The larger the value for a given color, the more amount of that color is added to the image.

6. In line 21 of the program, you see that the rectangle is produced by using the graphics object, *g*, to call the *fill3DRect()* method. Experiment with the method argument values and determine their purpose. What is the difference between a fifth argument of **true** versus **false**? The first two arguments in the *fill3DRect()* method are the horizontal and vertical coordinates for the upper-left-hand corner of the rectangle. The second two arguments are the width and height of the rectangle. The third argument produces a *raised* 3D rectangle with a value of **true** and a *sunken* 3D rectangle with a value of **false**.

7. Using the code you see in line 21, add another rectangle to the applet.

8. In line 24, you see that the color of the graphics object, *g*, is set to black rather than a red-green-blue, or ***RGB***, color. You can use any of the 13 colors provided by Java in lieu of RGB values. Of course, you can achieve more control over the color by using RGB values. In line 27, the graphics object calls the *fillRoundRect()* method. This creates the filled rounded black rectangle in the lower-left-hand corner of Figure 1. Notice that the corners of the rectangle are rounded. This is why its called a "rounded" rectangle. The method requires six arguments. The first two values represent the horizontal and vertical coordinates of the upper-left-hand corner of the rectangle. The next two arguments control the width and height of the rectangle. The last two arguments control that amount of roundness of the rectangle corners. The first of these sets the horizontal diameter of the arc at the four corners, while the second sets the vertical diameter of the arc at the four corners. Change the rectangle location by changing the first two arguments in the *fillRoundRect()* method and execute the program again. Remember, most screens are 640 pixels wide by 480 pixels high.

9. Change the rectangle size by changing the second two arguments in the *fillRoundRect()* method and execute the program again.

10. Change the rectangle corner diameters to 0,0 and execute the program again. Notice that the corners are square, because their diameters are set to 0.

11. Change the rectangle corner diameters by changing the last two arguments in the *fillRoundRect()* method to any reasonable values and execute the program again. How did your values affect the rectangle corners?

12. Load and execute the *Applet102_1.java* program again so that you have a fresh applet as shown in Figure 1.

13. Change the name of the *fillRoundRect()* method in line 27 to *drawRoundRect()* and execute the program again. What is the difference between the *fillRoundRect()* method and the *drawRoundRect()* method?

Discussion

We have one method in this applet called *paint()*. The *paint()* method is called automatically when an applet begins execution, after the *init()* and *start()* methods. The *paint()* method is not called again, unless the applet is resized or the user leaves and then moves back to the HTML page containing the applet. You cannot call the *paint()* method directly within your program. However, you can call it indirectly by calling the *repaint()* method when you need to refresh the applet window. The *repaint()* method calls the *update()* method which clears the component window and calls the *paint()* method. The *paint()* method is primarily used to draw strings and graphical objects. Notice that, by definition, the *paint()* method receives an object of the *Graphics* class that we have called *g*. This allows object *g* to call any of the methods in the *Graphics* class. This class contains a wealth of methods that can be used to draw geometric shapes. The first thing you did in this exercise was to set the red, green, and blue (RGB) color of the graphics object, *g*. Each color value can range from 0 to 255. Since red, green, and blue are primary colors, you can produce any desired color from these three primaries. To set the color of a graphical component, you simply use the graphics object to call the *setColor()* method. This method sets the color of any subsequent graphical components to the color specified within its argument as an RGB value or one of the 13 constant colors defined by Java. In line 21 we used our graphics object, *g*, to call the *fill3DRect()* method. This method produces a raised or sunken rectangle to give it a 3D look. Here is the signature for this method:

```
public void fill3DRect(int x,          //HORIZONTAL COOR.
                       int y,          //VERTICAL COOR.
                       int width,      //RECT. WIDTH
                       int height,     //RECT. HEIGHT
                       boolean raised) //RAISED OR SUNKEN
```

In line 24, we set the color of the graphics object to black and then used the object to call the *fillRoundRect()* method. Here is the signature for this method:

```
public void fillRoundRect(int x,          //HORIZONTAL COOR.
                          int y,          //VERTICAL COOR.
                          int width,      //RECT WIDTH
                          int height,     //RECT HEIGHT
                          int arcWidth    //CORNER HORIZ. DIAM.
                          int arcHeight)  //CORNER VERT. DIAM.
```

After experimenting with these methods, you should have a pretty good idea of how the method arguments control the shape of the rectangle being displayed. Finally, you found that the *drawRoundRect()* method employed the same arguments as the *fillRoundRect()* method, but painted an empty, unfilled, rectangle.

Ovals

14. In lines 31 and 32, a cyan filled oval is added to the applet, inside the rectangle. This time the color is set to cyan in line 31 using the *Color* class. The filled oval is created by calling the *fillOval()* method with the graphics object. Change the method arguments and observe the effect on the oval. Why was the oval a circle at the beginning? Why does the oval appear inside the rectangle? What do the method arguments represent?

15. In lines 35 and 36, a blue nonfilled oval is added to the applet. This time the color is set to blue in line 35 using the *Color* class. The oval is created by calling the *drawOval()* method with the graphics object. Change the method arguments and observe the effect on the oval. What do the method arguments represent?

16. In lines 39 and 40, a green filled oval is added to the applet. This oval is created by calling the *fillOval()* method with the graphics object. Change the method arguments and observe the effect on the oval. What do the method arguments represent?

17. Now, how do you suppose we constructed the smiling face in Figure 1? You are right if you thought mostly with ovals. The face itself, as well as the eyes and nose are all filled ovals created in lines 44-53 of the program. The mouth, however, was created with an arc using the *drawArc()* method in line 57. Can you correlate the oval code with the graphic components it creates? Change the method arguments for the ovals and notice that affect on the face.

Discussion

Ovals are created using two methods from the *Graphics* class: *fillOval()* and *drawOval()*. As with rectangles, a filled oval, created by *fillOval()*, is filled with the color set for the *Graphics* class object, while a nonfilled oval, created by *drawOval()*, is simply a line drawing with the line reflecting the color of the *Graphics* class object. Here are the signatures for these methods:

public abstract void fillOval(int x,   //HORIZONTAL COOR.
                           int y,   //VERTICAL COOR.
                           int width,   //OVAL WIDTH
                           int height)   //OVAL HEIGHT

public abstract void drawOval(int x,   //HORIZONTAL COOR.
                           int y,   //VERTICAL COOR.
                           int width,   //OVAL WIDTH
                           int height)   //OVAL HEIGHT

Here you see that the first two arguments for both methods provides the pixel (*x*,*y*) coordinate for the oval. Imagine the oval contained within a rectangle as shown in Figure 2. The (*x*,*y*) coordinate for the oval is the upper-left-hand corner of this rectangle.

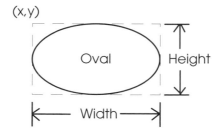

Figure 2 Imagine an oval inside of a rectangle where the upper-left-hand corner of the rectangle provides the oval coordinate and the width and height of the rectangle provide the size and shape of the oval.

The length an width of the rectangle in Figure 2 provide for the size and shape of the oval. Notice that you get a circle when the width and height of the oval are the same, as in the cyan oval created in line 32 of the program.

Arcs

18. A nonfilled arc is used to create the mouth of the smiling face in Figure 1. Look at the code that was used to create the mouth arc in line 57 of the program. Change the code in line 57 as follows:

g.drawArc(325,90,100,50,0,180);

Can you predict the results of this change?

19. Execute the program again and notice that this new arc creates a frowning face. The only change to the code was to change the last argument in the *drawArc()* method from −180 to 180. This changes the direction in which the arc is drawn. However, the mouth is positioned too high. Why? Imagine the bounding rectangle around the mouth arc and you will realize that the vertical coordinate of the rectangle must be increased. Increase the vertical coordinate by changing the second method argument from 90 to 110. Execute the program again an the mouth should be positioned properly.

20. A filled arc is shown in the lower right-hand corner of Figure 1. This arc is created by the *fillArc()* method in line 60 of the program. Notice that the arc is *swept counterclockwise* about 135°, beginning at the three o'clock position. Change the last argument in the method from 135 to −135 and execute the program again. Notice that the arc is now swept clockwise about 135°, beginning at the three o'clock position.

21. Change the arguments in the *fillArc()* method on line 60 one at a time, executing the program after each change. Notice the affect on the filled arc.

Discussion

Like rectangles and ovals, arcs can be filled for nonfilled. Filled arcs, like the one in the bottom-right-hand corner of Figure 1, are created using the *fillArc()* method, while nonfilled arcs, like the mouth on the smiling face, are created using the *drawArc()* method. Here are the signatures of each:

```
public abstract void fillArc(int x,          //HORIZONTAL COOR.
                             int y,           //VERTICAL COOR.
                             int width,       //ARC WIDTH
                             int height,      //ARC HEIGHT
                             int start,       //START ANGLE
                             int arcAngle)    //ARC ANGLE FROM START
```

public abstract void drawArc(int x,   //HORIZONTAL COOR.
                                int y,   //VERTICAL COOR.
                                int width,   //ARC WIDTH
                                int height   //ARC HEIGHT
                                int start,   //START ANGLE
                                int arcAngle)   //ARC ANGLE FROM START

Notice that the both arc signatures are the same. To see how an arc works, imagine that the arc is bounded by a rectangle, as shown in Figure 3. The first pair of arguments specify the (*x,y*) coordinate of the upper-left-hand corner of the bounding rectangle. The second pair of arguments specify the bounding rectangle width and height, which would be the actual arc width and height if the arc swept 360° to form a complete circle. The third pair of arguments control the arc angle based on a polar coordinate system where 0° is at the three o'clock position. The first argument in this pair is called the ***start angle*** and specifies where the arc will start within this coordinate system. The second argument in the pair is called the ***arc angle*** and specifies how many degrees the arc will sweep from its starting point. A *positive arc angle* will force the arc to be swept in a *counterclockwise* direction, while a *negative arc angle* will force the arc to be swept in a *clockwise* direction. In Figure 3a, the arc starts at 0° and has a +90° counterclockwise arc angle. Thus, the start angle argument would be 0 and the arc angle argument would be 90. The arc in Figure 3b starts at 0° and has a –90° arc clockwise arc angle. Therefore, the start angle argument would be 0 and the arc angle argument would be –90. By changing the arc width, height, start angle, and arc angle you can achieve just about any filled or non-filled arc you desire.

Lines

22. In the bottom center of Figure 1, you find a simple line. The line is created from the *drawLine()* method in line 64 of the program. Change the method arguments, execute the program again, and observe the affect on the line. What is the purpose of each method argument.

23. Change the color of the line by adding a statement to set the color of the graphics object. Add this statement just before the line is drawn in the program.

Discussion

Lines are drawn by using the graphics object to call the *drawLine()* method. This method has the following signature:

```
public abstract void drawLine(int x1,    //X COOR. OF START OF LINE
                              int y1,    //Y COOR. OF START OF LINE
                              int x2,    //X COOR. OF END OF LINE
                              int y2)    //X COOR. OF END OF LINE
```

You see that the first pair of method arguments specify the coordinate for the start of the line, while the second pair of arguments specify the coordinate for the end of the line.

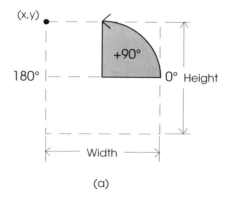

(a)

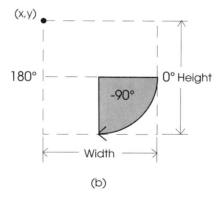

(b)

Figure 3 Imagine an arc inside a rectangle where the upper-left-hand corner of the rectangle provides the arc coordinate and the width and height of the rectangle provide the size of the arc. The arc in (a) has a start angle of 0°, and an arc angle of 90°. The arc in (b) has a start angle of 0°, and an arc angle of –90°.

Strings

24. The last graphic that we need to talk about in Figure 1 is the string. Strings are drawn by using the graphics object to call the *drawString()* method. The string that is drawn will take on the font and color to which the graphics object has been set. The font and color of the string are set in lines 68 and 69 of the program. Change the string font and color and execute the program. Notice that the string reflects the changes you made.

25. The string in drawn by using the graphics object to call the *drawString()* method in line 70 of the program. Here you see that the string text is the first argument of the method. What do you suppose the second pair of arguments represent? Change the method arguments, execute the program again, and observe the affect on the string.

Discussion

String are drawn by using the graphics object to call the *drawString()* method. This method has the following signature:

public abstract void drawString(String text,   //TEXT OF STRING
                                          int x,   //X COOR. OF STRING
                                          int y)   //Y COOR. OF STRING

The *drawString()* signature is straightforward. The only thing the you might note is that the last two arguments specify the coordinate of the **baseline**, or bottom, of the string. If you imagine the string contained within a rectangle, then the *string coordinate is the lower-left-hand corner of the rectangle*.

By the way, you can also use the *paint()* method in an application program just like we did here in an applet.

Graphics and Applications

26. Graphics can also be included within a frame in an application program. Load and execute the *ApplicationGraphics.java* application program contained on the CD that accompanies this book or download it from www.prenhall.com. You should observe the frame shown in Figure 4.

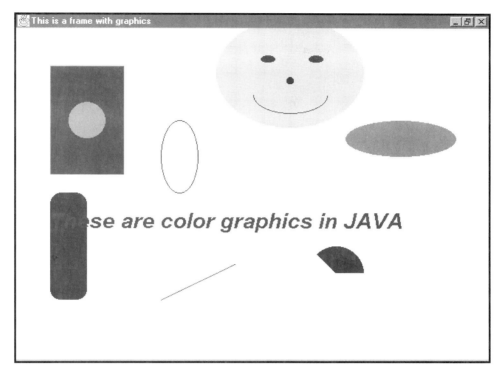

Figure 4 A frame in an application program containing graphical components.

Discussion

Here is the program that produced the frame in Figure 4:

```
1    import java.awt.*;                    //FOR FRAME CLASS
2
3    //A FRAME CLASS WITH A SINGLE BUTTON
4    class GraphicsDemo extends FrameWithClose
5    {
6      //CONSTRUCTOR
7      public GraphicsDemo(String title)
8      {
9        //CALL SUPERCLASS CONSTRUCTOR
10       super(title);
11       //CALL paint() VIA repaint() TO GENERATE GRAPHICS
12       repaint();
13     }//END GraphicsDemo()
```

```
14      public void paint(Graphics g)
15      {
16       //RGB COLOR AND RECTANGLES
17       //SET RGB COLOR
18       int red = 250;
19       int green = 100;
20       int blue  = 100;
21
22       g.setColor(new Color(red,green,blue));
23
24       //FILL 3D RECTANGLE
25       g.fill3DRect(50,75,100,150,true);
26
27       //SET COLOR TO BLACK
28       g.setColor(Color.black);
29
30      //FILL ROUNDED RECTANGLE
31       g.fillRoundRect(50,250,50,150,30,30);
32
33      //OVALS
34      //FILL CYAN OVAL
35       g.setColor(Color.cyan);
36       g.fillOval(75,125,50,50);
37
38      //DRAW BLUE OVAL
39       g.setColor(Color.blue);
40       g.drawOval(200,150,50,100);
41
42      //FILL GREEN OVAL
43       g.setColor(Color.green);
44       g.fillOval(450,150,150,50);
45
46      //DRAW SMILING FACE
47      //USE FILLED OVAL FOR FACE
48       g.setColor(Color.yellow);        //SET FACE COLOR TO YELLOW
49       g.fillOval(275,10,200,150);
50
51      //USE FILLED OVAL FOR EYES
52       g.setColor(Color.black);
53       g.fillOval(335,60,20,10);       //LEFT EYE
54       g.fillOval(400,60,20,10);       //RIGHT EYE
55
56      //USE FILLED OVAL FOR NOSE
57       g.fillOval(370,90,10,10);
```

```
58      //ARCS
59      //USE ARC FOR MOUTH OF SMILING FACE
60      g.drawArc(325,90,100,50,0,-180);
61
62      //FILLED AN ARC
63      g.fillArc(400,325,75,75,0,135);
64
65      //LINES
66      //DRAW A LINE
67      g.drawLine(200,400,300,350);
68
69       //FONTS AND STRINGS
70       //DRAW RED FONT STRING
71       g.setColor(Color.red);
72       g.setFont(new Font("Helvetica",Font.ITALIC + Font.BOLD,30));
73       g.drawString("These are color graphics in JAVA",50,300);
74      }//END paint()
75    }//END FRAME SUBCLASS
76
77    //APPLICATION CLASS TO TEST GraphicsDemo CLASS
78    public class ApplicationGraphics
79    {
80      public static void main(String[] args)
81      {
82        //DEFINE FRAME OBJECT
83        GraphicsDemo window = new GraphicsDemo("This is a frame with
84                                                graphics");
85
86        //SET FRAME SIZE
87        window.setSize(500,300);
88
89        //MAKE FRAME VISIBLE
90        window.setVisible(true);
91      }//END main()
92    }//END ApplicationGraphics
```

You see that we have created a frame subclass called *GraphicsDemo* and included our *paint()* method as a method within this class. However, we have eliminated the call to the *showStatus()* method at the end of *paint()*, since frames do not have a status bar, and therefore do not support the *showStatus()* method. The test class which includes *main()* simply defines a frame object, sets that size of the frame, and makes the frame visible. Within the frame constructor, a call is made to the *repaint()* method, which calls the *paint()* method within our

GraphicsDemo class. Remember, you cannot call *paint( )* directly. You must call *repaint( )* which indirectly calls *paint( )*. That's all there is to it!

You might notice a slight difference between the graphical windows produced by the applet versus the application (Figure 1 versus Figure 4). The obvious difference is that the applet contains a status bar, while the frame does not. Another difference is the frame coordinate system places (0,0) at the upper-left-hand corner of the frame, or window, while the applet coordinate system places (0,0) just below the title bar of the applet. Notice how the head of the smiling face is cut off slightly by the title bar in Figure 4. This is because the (0,0) origin is at the corner of the frame, and not below the title bar, so the same component coordinates produce a slightly different vertical positioning of the components within a frame verus an applet.

FILE I/O AND EXCEPTION HANDLING

INTRODUCTION

In data processing applications, a *file* is a collection of related *records*, or classes. Each record is made up of related *fields*, or members, that contain the file information. Of course, we implement a record in Java using the class, whose private members represent the fields of the record. For example, a student file might consist of a student name field, a student number field, a gpa field, and so on. All of these fields encapsulated together for a given student form a record. Several student records stored together on a disk form a file. In a typical college computer center you might find student files, faculty files, staff files, inventory files, transcript files, and so on. Several related files form a *database*. As an example, a college employee database might consist of faculty files, staff files, and administrator files.

All the data types and structures you have learned about so far have provided a means of organizing and storing data in primary memory. However, recall that primary memory is relatively small and, more importantly, volatile. In other words, when the system is turned off or power is lost for any reason, all information stored in primary memory goes to "bit heaven." The obvious solution to this problem is to store any long-term data in secondary memory, because secondary memory is nonvolatile. Furthermore, secondary memory provides a means of storing data between program runs. A file is a secondary memory storage structure.

In this chapter, you will learn how to create and manipulate your own disk files in Java. There are three basic operations that you will need to perform when working with disk files:

- Open the file for input or output.
- Process the file, by reading from or writing to the file.
- Close the file.

In addition, since working with files requires that you communicate with a peripheral device, there is always the possibility that something unexpected could happen such as a disk could be write-protected during a write operation, a disk file might not exist during a read operation, and so on. To protect your program from terminating prematurely during file operations, you must learn how to handle such events. This, together with the aforementioned file operations, forms the topics of this chapter.

OBJECTIVES

When you are finished with this chapter, you should have a good understanding of the following:

- How to use the Java files stream classes to create, or open, disk files.
- How to use the Java data stream classes to write primitive data types to files and read primitive data from files.
- The concept of streams and the role they play in communicating with I/O devices.
- How to handle I/O errors, which generate exceptions in Java.
- The checked exceptions provided in Java.
- The use of **try** and **catch** blocks in your program to handle exceptions.
- How to develop classes to read/write sequential files that provide for exception handling.

12-1 FUNDAMENTAL CONCEPTS AND IDEAS

A *file* is a data structure that consists of a sequence of components.

A file is a *sequence* of components. This means that the data elements, called **components**, are arranged within the file sequentially, or serially, from the first component to the last component. As a result, when accessing files, the file components must be accessed in a sequential manner from one component to the next. A common analogy for a file is an audio cassette tape. Think of the songs on the tape as the file components. How are they stored on the tape? You're right, sequentially from the first song to the last. How must you access a given song? Right again, by sequencing forward or backward through the tape until the desired song is found. Thus, like a cassette tape, a file is a sequential, or serial, storage medium. This makes file access relatively slow as compared to other random-access storage mediums, like primary memory.

You might be tempted to think of a file as a one-dimensional array, but there are some important differences. First, files provide a means for you to store information within a program run as you do with arrays. But, unlike arrays, files also allow you to store information between program runs. Second, many compilers require you to access the file components in sequence, starting with the first file component. You cannot jump into the middle of a file as you can an array to access a given component. However, Java does provide a means of semi-random direct access using the *seek* operations. Third, files are not declared with a specific dimension as are arrays. Once you create a file, its size is theoretically unlimited. Of course, the file size is actually limited by the amount of storage space available in secondary memory, such as a disk.

In Java all I/O, including file I/O, is based on the concept of ***streams***.

> A ***stream*** provides a channel for data to flow between your program and the outside world.

In particular, a file stream provides a channel for the flow of data from some source to some destination. Think about what happens when you are typing characters on the keyboard when prompted by a program. You can think of the characters as flowing, or streaming, from the keyboard into the program. Likewise, when your program generates a character display, you can easily visualize the characters streaming from the program to the display. Java provides standard streams for the keyboard and display. However, you must create separate streams to read and write disk files.

Classes Provide the Basis for Java Files

All program I/O is supported by files that operate on predefined classes in Java. The familiar *System* class that you have been using in your programs for display output is a class included in Java that provides for standard input and output. When you called the *print()* or *println()* methods to display something, you called either method using the code *System.out*. Here, *System* references the standard *System* class in Java and *out* specifies the standard output stream. The "standard" output stream is *attached* to the system display. Likewise, you can use the *System* class for keyboard input, although it is awkward to do so. In this case, you would call a standard keyboard input method, such as *read()*, using the code *System.in.read()*. Again, *System* references the standard *System* class in Java and *in* specifies the standard input stream, which is attached to the system keyboard. Thus, we say that standard input is read from the *in stream* and standard output is written to the *out stream*. Of course, the only files that you can access conveniently with *System.in* and *System.out* are the keyboard and display files that are "attached" to these file streams.

You will use four classes to access disk files in Java: *FileOutputStream*, *DataOutputStream*, *FileInputStream*, and *DataInputStream*. All of these classes are part of the *java.io* package which must be imported into your program. The first two classes are used to perform output, or write, operations on disk files; and the second two are used to perform input, or read, operations on disk files. Class inheritance provides the basis for these classes. A hierarchy diagram of the Java file class family is given in Figure 12-1. Notice that all four of these classes are derived from the Java *Object* class. In fact, the *Object* class is the **root** class of the entire Java class hierarchy. In other words, *Object* is a superclass to all classes in Java. The *InputStream* and *OutputStream* classes are derived directly from *Object*. These classes provide the basis for all classes that deal with input streams and output streams, respectively. Next you see *FileInputStream* and *FileOutputStream* derived from *InputStream* and *OutputStream*, respectively. *FileInputStream* provides a stream for reading data from a disk file, while *FileOutputStream* provides a stream for writing data to a disk file. The *DataInputStream* and *DataOutputStream* classes are also derived from *InputStream* and *OutputStream*, respectively. These classes provide a means to read/write primitive data types from/to the file streams. The four classes that we will use to read/write disk files are summarized in Table 12-1. Be aware that there are a wealth of file stream classes provided by Java to support other types of file access, such as semi-random access. Check your on-line help or Java reference material for these additional classes.

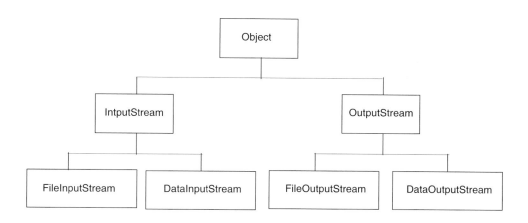

Figure 12-1   The file class hierarchy in Java.

TABLE 12-1 SOME FILE STREAM CLASSES PROVIDED BY JAVA

Class	Purpose
DataInputStream	To read primitive data from a stream.
DataOutputStream	To write primitive data to a stream.
FileInputStream	To open an input stream and attach it to a physical disk file.
FileOutputStream	To open an output stream and attach it to a physical disk file.

Creating File Streams in Java: Opening Files

To create a file stream, you must do two things:

1. Using one of the *File_____Stream* classes, create a file stream and *attach* it to a physical disk file to *open* the file.
2. Define a file stream object for one of the *Data _____Stream* classes.

The *File_____Stream* classes contain a constructor to create a file stream and attach it to a physical disk file as illustrated in Figure 12-2. The constructor requires a string argument which is the name of the disk file to be read or written. For example, the code

FileOutputStream("student.dat")

will create an output file stream and attach it to the *student.dat* disk file, while the code

FileInputStream(myFile)

will create an input file stream and attach it to the disk file represented by the string object *myFile*. Of course, this assumes that *myFile* has been previously defined as a string object and contains a valid file name.

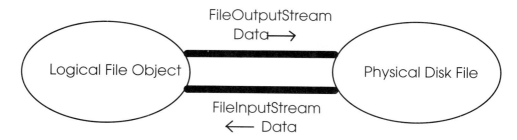

Figure 12-2 The *FileOutputStream* and *FileInputStream* classes are used to create file streams that attach a logical program object to a physical disk file.

The *Data_____Stream* classes contain a constructor that prepares an object to read/write data from/to a specified stream The constructor requires a *File_____Stream* object as its argument. Thus, the statement

outFile = new DataOutputStream(new FileOutputStream("student.dat"));

defines an object called *outFile* and prepares it to write data to the output file stream attached to the *student.dat* disk file. Likewise the statement

inFile = new DataInputStream(new FileInputStream(myFile));

defines an object called *inFile* and prepares it to read data from the input file stream attached to the disk file name contained in the *myFile* string object. Notice that, in each of the above cases, a *File_____Stream* object is provided to the *Data_____Stream* constructor by calling the *File_____Stream()* constructor within the argument of the *Data_____Stream()* constructor. This is referred to as **chaining** of objects. Chaining of objects simply means that the constructor of one class calls the constructor of another class as its argument. Here, the physical disk file name is supplied to the *File_____Stream()* constructor, which supplies an object for the *Data_____Stream()* constructor, which is used to create an object that can be manipulated within a program. Thus, a communication path is established between the logical program object and the physical disk file. We say that this process **opens** a file for processing.

Let's incorporate the foregoing file stream definitions into methods for opening input or output files. We will name these methods *openInputFile()* and *openOutputFile()*, respectively. Here is the code:

```
//CREATE AN INPUT STREAM AND ATTACH IT TO A PHYSICAL DISK FILE
public void openInputFile(String s)
{
   inFile = new DataInputStream(new FileInputStream(s));
}//END openInputFile()
```

```
//CREATE AN OUTPUT STREAM AND ATTACH IT TO A PHYSICAL DISK FILE
public void openOutputFile(String s)
{
     outFile = new DataOutputStream(new FileOutputStream(s));
}//END openOutputFile()
```

Here, we have simply placed our *inFile* and *outFile* object definitions inside two methods so that the files can be easily opened by calling a method. Each method receives a string object, *s*, which is the disk file to be opened. But, what if the file, *s*, doesn't exist for whatever reason? In the case of an input file, a non-existing file would cause an **exception**, or error, to be generated and result in a program crash if the exception was not *caught* by the program. Here is where Java forces you to protect yourself from such errors. In fact, neither of the above methods will compile. An error message such as "*unreported exception … must be caught or declared to be thrown*" would be generated by the Java compiler. So we must add some error protection to our file opening methods. Such protection is called **exception handling**, and the topic of the next section.

Example 12-1

Write statements to create the following file objects:

a. A file object called *read* that will read from a disk file called *sample.doc*.
b. A file object called *write* that will write to a disk file whose name is stored in a string named *fileName*

Solution

a.   read = new DataInputStream(new FileInputStream("sample.doc"));
b.   write = new DataOutputStream(new FileOutputStream(fileName));

 Quick Check

1.   True or false: A file is a random-access data structure.

2. What happens when a disk file is opened?

3. A channel where data can flow between your Java program and the outside world is called a _____.

4. Standard output in Java is written to the _____ file stream.

5. What class is used to create an input file stream and attach it to a disk file?

6. What class is used to write primitive data to an output file stream?

7. What is specified by the code *System.out*?

8. Write a statement to define *myFile* as an output file stream object and attach it to a disk file called *"myFile.txt"*.

9. Write a statement to define *yourFile* as an input file stream object and attach it to a disk file whose name is stored in a string called *yourFileName*.

10. What standard Java package must be imported to use the file classes?

12-2 EXCEPTION HANDLING

We have put off a discussion of exception handling long enough. Now we are really forced by Java to provide it to protect our programs from crashing when working with files. Exception handling has to do with error handling. To handle an error, the error condition must first be detected and then control must be transferred from the point where the error occurred to an error handling routine that can deal with error. What types of errors might you want to deal with? Well, user input is always a possible source of error, since Murphy's law usually applies. Users do not always enter data the way the program expects to see it. Another general source of error is when you exceed the storage capacity of things like primary memory or disk space. However one of the most common sources of error is related to I/O devices. I/O errors occur when an I/O device presents the program with an unexpected condition. A printer could be off-line or run out of paper, a disk could be write-protected during a write operation, a disk file might not exist during a read operation, and so on.

When an error occurs at run time, a Java method can be made to ***throw*** an exception. When an exception is thrown, Java has detected an error condition. In order to prevent program failure, an exception that is thrown must be ***caught***. When an exception is caught, control is transferred to a routine that can deal with the error. This throwing and catching of exceptions is referred to as ***exception handling***. If a thrown exception is not caught, an error message is displayed and the program will terminate.

PROGRAMMING NOTE

An exception that is not caught will cause abnormal termination of a program. The one "exception" to this rule is a Java applet or application program employing a GUI. If a thrown exception is not caught in a GUI program, an error message is generated but the program is not terminated and control returns to normal event processing.

To throw and catch exceptions, you must include statements that have the potential of throwing an exception within a **try** block. A **try** block consists of a framed block of code appearing after the keyword **try**. The **try** block is followed immediately with zero or more **catch** blocks of code. A **catch** block consists of a framed block of code appearing after the keyword **catch**. Any code required to handle the exception(s) is contained within the **catch** block(s). Thus, the **catch** blocks are referred to as *exception handlers*. The **catch** blocks can be followed by an optional **finally** block. A **finally** block is a framed block of code appearing after the keyword **finally**. A **finally** block always executes, whether or not an exception is thrown within the **try** block or handled within a **catch** block. Here's the general format for the **try/catch/finally** sequence:

```
try
{
   //STATEMENTS THAT MIGHT THROW EXCEPTIONS
}

catch(ExceptionClass exception object)
{
   //STATEMENTS TO HANDLE EXCEPTIONS THROWN BY try STATEMENT
}

finally
{
   //STATEMENTS THAT WILL EXECUTE WHETHER OR NOT EXCEPTION IS
   //THROWN OR CAUGHT
}
```

You will place statements that might throw exceptions within the **try** block. Then you will create one or more **catch** blocks that contain statements required to handle any exceptions thrown by the **try** block. Each **catch** block specifies the type of exception that it will catch. You cannot have a **try** block without a corresponding **catch** block, unless you have a **finally** block. When an exception is thrown within the **try** block, Java searches for a **catch** block that will handle that type of exception. In the search, Java tries to match the type of exception thrown with the exception parameter listed in one of the **catch** blocks. When the correct exception parameter is found, control is transferred to the respective **catch** block and its code is executed. A compiler error results if a match is not found, unless you have a **finally** block of code. A **finally** block is always executed, regardless of whether an exception is thrown or not.

As a practical example, let's revise the foregoing *openInputFile( )* method code to include exception handling. One of the most common errors associated with opening an input file is a *file-not-found* error. We can use a **try** block when opening the file and a corresponding **check** block to catch a file-not-found exception as follows:

```
//CREATE AN INPUT STREAM AND ATTACH IT TO A PHYSICAL DISK FILE
public void openInputFile(String s)
{
    //TRY TO OPEN FILE BY ATTACHING INPUT STREAM TO A DISK FILE
    try
    {
     inFile = new DataInputStream(new FileInputStream(s));
     textArea.setText("FILE OPEN");
    }//END try()

    //CATCH EXCEPTION IF FILE CANNOT BE OPENED
    catch(IOException io)
    {
      textArea.setText("\n\nFILE NOT FOUND ERROR\n" + io.toString());
    }//END catch()
}//END openInputFile()
```

When the file to be opened cannot be found for whatever reason, the *FileInputStream( )* constructor throws an *IOException* object. This is a predefined exception, often called a ***checked*** exception, in Java. To prevent the program from terminating, we have placed the statement that defines our *inFile* object within a **try** block. Then, if the file is not found, the *FileInputStream( )* constructor throws an *IOException* object. Notice that the **catch** block of code has an *IOException* object as its parameter. Since the thrown object matches this exception parameter, the object is caught and control passes to the **catch** block. The caught object takes on the name *io* within the **catch** block. Within the **catch** block, an error message is displayed within a text area of the program GUI. In addition, notice that the *io* object is used to call the *toString()* method. The thrown object carries with it information about the error that can be converted to a string by using it to call the *toString()* method. So, the code io.toString() concatenates more information about the exception to the error message already being displayed. At this point, control is passed back to the GUI. The user has been notified that a file-not-found error has occurred and can take corrective action before attempting to open the file again.

Now, what happens if an error does not occur and an exception is not thrown? Well, the statement that will cause an exception to be thrown is the first statement within the **try** block that defines our *inFile* object. If this creates an exception, control is passed to the **catch** block immediately, without executing the remaining statements within the **try** block. However, if opening the file does not create an exception, the remaining statements within the try block are executed and the **catch** block is skipped. If an exception is not generated, the foregoing **try** block simply displays a "FILE OPEN" message in the GUI text area.

PROGRAMMING NOTE

Once an exception is thrown from within a **try** block, control is passed immediately out of the **try** block without executing the remaining statements in the **try** block. Control *never* returns to the **try** block, whether the exception is caught or not.

Next, let's expand our *openOutputFile()* method to include exception handling. Here's the expanded code:

```
//CREATE AN OUTPUT STREAM AND ATTACH IT TO A PHYSICAL DISK FILE
public void openOutputFile(String s)
{
   //TRY TO OPEN FILE BY ATTACHING OUTPUT STREAM TO A DISK FILE
   try
   {
    outFile = new DataOutputStream(new FileOutputStream(s));
    textArea.setText("FILE OPEN");
   }//END try()
   //CATCH EXCEPTION IF FILE CANNOT BE OPENED
   catch(IOException io)
   {
     textArea.append("\n\nFILE NOT FOUND ERROR\n"+ io.toString() );
   }//END catch() IOException
 }//END openOutputFile
```

Here again, we have included our file opening statement within a **try** block. A **catch** clock is again created to catch an *IOException* object and notify the user if there is any problem opening the file.

We will be using exception handling throughout our discussion of files, because errors often occur when working with files. You should be aware, however, that Java includes a wealth of checked exceptions that you can use to prevent programs from terminating prematurely, some of which are listed in Table 12-2. Check your on-line help or compiler documentation for more information on these and other checked exceptions.

TABLE 12-2 CHECKED EXCEPTIONS PROVIDED BY JAVA

Exception	Description
ArithmeticException	Thrown when an arithmetic error has occurred, such as division by zero.
ArrayIndexOutOfBoundsException	Thrown when an array has been accessed with an index which is negative or greater than or equal to the size of the array.
Exception	Thrown for any checked exception.
EOFException	Thrown when the end of a file has been reached.
FileNotFoundException	Thrown when a file cannot be found.
InterruptedIOException	Thrown when an I/O operation has been interrupted.
IOException	Thrown when an I/O error has occurred.
NullPointerException	Thrown when a program tries to use **null** when an object is required.
NumberFormatException	Thrown when a program tries to convert a string to a numeric data type when the string does not have the correct format.
StringIndexOutOfBoundsException	Thrown by *String* class methods when a string has been accessed with an index which is negative or greater than or equal to the size of the string.

Notice from Table 12-2 that there is a *FileNotFoundException* that we could have used within our file open methods. The *FileNotFoundException* class is a subclass of the *IOException* class. The *FileInputStream* class constructor throws this exception directly when a problem is encountered opening an input file and we could have caught a *FileNotFoundException* in place of the *IOException* and accomplished the same goal. However, the *FileOutputStream* class constructor throws an *IOException* directly and a *FileNotFoundException* indirectly. This is because the *IOException* class is a superclass to the *FileNotFoundException* class. As a result, to catch a *FileNotFoundException* we must also catch an *IOException*. This would require two catch blocks in our *openOutputFile()* method. It is just simpler to catch an *IOException*, knowing it had to be the result of a file not being found for whatever reason.

PROGRAMMING NOTE

Through inheritance, it is possible that several types of exceptions will thrown for the same error condition. For instance, a file-not-found error will cause a *FileNotFoundException* as well as an *IOException* to be thrown when opening a file for output, since the *FileNotFoundException* class is a subclass of the *IOException* class. If a **catch** block is coded to catch the subclass exception, it must also be coded before the superclass exception **catch** block. If it is not, the subclass **catch** block will be unreachable and result in a compiler error. Thus, a *FileNotFoundException* **catch** block must be coded before an *IOException* **catch** block.

There is one catch-all exception called *Exception*. The *Exception* class is the superclass of all exception classes. Thus, the following **catch** block will catch any checked exception:

```
catch(Exception e)
{
   // STATEMENTS TO HANDLE ANY CHECKED EXCEPTION
}
```

Of course, if you catch this exception, you might not know what type of exception has occurred. Therefore, you should always catch one of the more specific subclass exceptions if possible. If you catch this exception in addition to any of its subclass exceptions, you must catch it after all **catch** blocks that catch the subclass exceptions, or a syntax error will occur.

Quick Check

1. The process of throwing and catching exceptions is know as _____.

2. Why is exception handling required when opening files?

3. A predefined exception in Java is referred to as a _____ exception.

4. True or false: An exception that is not caught in a non-GUI program will cause the program to terminate prematurely.

5. True or false: An exception that is not caught in a GUI program will cause the program to terminate prematurely.

6. To handle a checked exception, you must place any statements that have the potential of generating an exception within a _____ block.

7. True or false: You can have more than one **check** block for a given **try** block.

8. What Java exception class throws a divide-by-zero exception?

9. True or false: A **finally** block only executes when an exception is thrown and no **catch** block is found for the exception.

10. True or false: A subclass exception handler must always be coded before its superclass exception handler.

12-3 READING AND WRITING SEQUENTIAL FILES

We have a lot to talk about here, so make yourself comfortable. In order to effectively demonstrate file operations, we will wrap our file handling within two GUI classes, one called *WriteStudentFile* that will write student records to a file and another called *ReadStudentFile* that will read student records from a sequential file. Before we begin, take a look at Figures 12-3 and 12-4. These figures show the GUIs created by the two classes just mentioned. Notice that both classes generate a GUI that requires the user to enter the file name and click an *Open File* button.

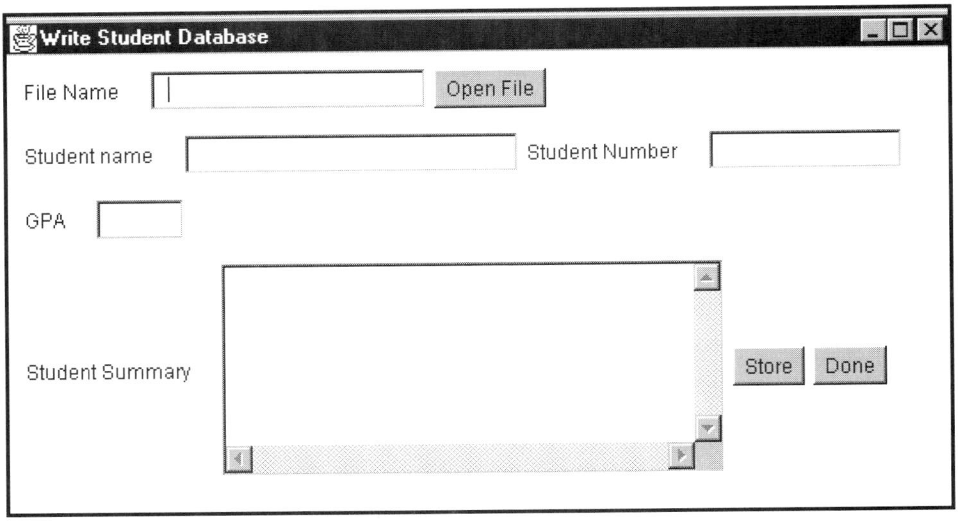

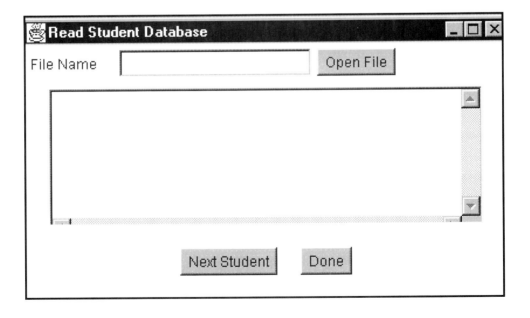

Figure 12-3   The GUI created by the *WriteStudentFile* class.

Figure 12-4   The GUI created by the *ReadStudentFile* class.

To create a file, the user will use the *WriteStudentFile* class and enter the student name, student number, and gpa in the appropriate text fields and then click the *Store* button shown in Figure 12-3. When the *Store* button is clicked, the student data will be written to the file. In addition, the student data will be displayed in the text area and the text fields will be blanked to allow another student record entry. The user can enter as many student records as desired, entering the data in the text fields, and clicking the *Store* button for each entry. When there are no more records to enter, the user must click the *Done* button. This event **closes** the file and terminates the program. You will learn shortly that *all* files must be closed after they have been processed.

To read a file, the user will use the *ReadStudentFile* class. Again, the user must enter the file name to read and click the *Open File* button. Once the file is open, the user simply clicks the *Next Student* button, which displays each student record, one at a time, within the text area. The program will terminate when the end of the file is reached or the *Done* button is clicked.

Now, you already have a pretty good idea of how to build the GUIs shown in Figures 12-3 and 12-4, so, let's concentrate on the file stuff. First the files must be opened when a file name is entered by the user and the *File Open* button is clicked. We have used the two open methods discussed in the last section to accomplish this task within each respective file class. Here's the method code we developed earlier:

```
//CREATE AN OUTPUT STREAM AND ATTACH IT TO A PHYSICAL DISK FILE
 public void openOutputFile(String s)
 {
   //TRY TO OPEN FILE BY ATTACHING OUTPUT STREAM TO A DISK FILE
   try
   {
    outFile = new DataOutputStream(new FileOutputStream(s));
    studentArea.setText("FILE OPEN, BEGIN STORING RECORDS");
   }//END try()

   //CATCH EXCEPTION IF FILE CANNOT BE OPENED
   catch(IOException io)
   {
     studentArea.append("\n\nFILE NOT FOUND ERROR\n" + io.toString() );
   }//END catch() IOException
 //END openOutputFile
```

```
//CREATE AN INPUT STREAM AND ATTACH IT TO A PHYSICAL DISK FILE
public void openInputFile(String s)
{
   //TRY TO OPEN FILE BY ATTACHING INPUT STREAM TO A DISK FILE
   try
   {
     inFile = new DataInputStream(new FileInputStream(s));
     studentArea.setText("FILE OPEN, PRESS Next Student BUTTON");
   }//END try()

   //CATCH EXCEPTION IF FILE CANNOT BE OPENED
   catch(IOException io)
   {
     studentArea.setText("\n\nFILE NOT FOUND ERROR\n" + io.toString());
   }//END catch()
}//END openInputFile()
```

As you might suspect, each method is called when an event is generated by the user clicking the *File Open* button within its respective GUI. There is nothing new here.

> When a file is open for output via the *FileOutputStream* class, its contents are destroyed and will be replaced by any subsequent data written to the file.

Next, we must develop methods to write student records to a file and read student records from a file. We have chosen to call these methods *writeStudentRecord()* and *readStudentRecord()*, respectively. Of course, the *writeStudentRecord()* method will appear in the *WriteStudentFile* class and the *readStudentRecord()* method will appear in the *ReadStudentFile* class. Let's examine the *writeStudentRecord()* method first. Here's its code:

```
//METHOD TO WRITE A STUDENT RECORD TO AN OPENED DISK FILE
public void writeStudentRecord()
{
   //TRY TO WRITE STUDENT RECORD TO FILE
   try
   {
     outFile.writeUTF(nameField.getText());
     outFile.writeUTF(numberField.getText());
     outFile.writeDouble((new Double(gpaField.getText().trim())).doubleValue());
   } //END try() TO WRITE RECORD
```

```
//CATCH NUMBER FORMAT EXCEPTION FOR GPA FIELD
catch (NumberFormatException nfe)
{
  studentArea.append("\n\nWRITE FILE ERROR\n"
                     + "MAKE SURE GPA IS CORRECT\n"
                     + nfe.toString());
}//END NumberFormatcatch()

//CATCH ANY EXCEPTIONS WRITING TO FILE
catch (IOException io)
{
  studentArea.append("\nWRITE FILE ERROR\n" + io.toString());
} //END IO catch()

//CLEAR TEXT FIELDS
numberField.setText("");
nameField.setText("");
gpaField.setText("");
}//END writeStudentRecord()
```

The first thing you see is a **try** block which contains three statements that write the student name, student number, and gpa, respectively, to the opened file. We include these statements within a **try** block, since there is a potential for an I/O error when writing to a file. Here, we use our *outFile* object to call two standard methods: *writeUTF()* and *writeDouble()*. These methods are members of the *DataOutputStream* class of which our object was created in the *openOutputFile()* method. Remember that the *DataOutputStream* class was used so that primitive data could be written to the output file stream. Other methods contained in this class are listed in Table 12-3. The *writeUTF()* method is used to write a string to the output stream using UTF-8 character encoding format. This is a byte-oriented character coding format that is a machine-independent format for writing to files. Notice that the argument for the method is simply the string obtained from a given text field using the *getText()* method. The *writeDouble()* method writes a double floating-point value to the output file stream. However, the *gpaField* object contains a string that must be converted to a **double** before it is written to the file. As a result, you see that the *writeDouble()* method contains an argument of

```
(new Double(gpaField.getText().trim())).doubleValue()
```

Remember doing this conversion in the GUI chapter? Just to review, the *gpaField* object is used to call the *getText()* method which returns the string contained in the gpa text field. The *trim()* method of the *String* class is called to "trim," or remove, any whitespace from the string. The resulting string is used as an argument for the *Double()* class constructor. Recall that the constructor takes a string argument and creates a **Double** floating-point object. At this point, we have a **Double** floating-point wrapper object which contains the floating-point representation of the string data obtained from the *gpaField* text field. However, this object *cannot* be written directly to the output stream using the *writeDouble()* method, because this method requires a primitive data type of **double** as its argument. In other words, we need to convert **Double** to **double**. So, the *doubleValue()* method is called by the new **Double** object, resulting in a primitive **double** value. Now we have something that can be used by the *writeDouble()* method.

TABLE 12-3 SOME STANDARD *DataOutputStream* METHODS FOR WRITING FILES

Method	Description
writeBoolean(boolean b)	Writes a Boolean value to the output stream as a 1-byte value.
writeByte(byte b)	Writes a **byte** to the output stream.
writeChar(char c)	Writes a Unicode **char** to the output stream as a 2-byte value, high byte first.
writeDouble(double f)	Writes a **double** to the output stream as an 8-byte value, high byte first.
writeFloat(float f)	Writes a **float** to the output stream as a 4-byte value, high byte first.
writeInt(int i)	Writes an **int** to the output stream as a 4-byte value, high byte first.
writeLong(long l)	Writes a **long** to the output stream as an 8-byte value, high byte first.
writeShort(short s)	Writes a **short** to the output stream as a 2-byte value, high byte first.
writeUTF(String s)	Writes a string to the output stream using UTF-8 encoding.

You see two **catch** blocks in the *writeStudentRecord( )* method. The first block catches a *NumberFormatException*, while the second block catches an *IOException*. The *Double* class constructor throws a *NumberFormatException*. The exception is thrown if its argument does not contain a valid string. For example, a blank field or a string containing any alpha characters would cause a *NumberFormatException* to be thrown. Notice that our **catch** block notifies the user that the *gpa* text field could have a problem. The second **catch** block is used to catch a general *IOException* generated by the *writeUTF( )* or *writeDouble( )* methods. Such an exception will be generated if there are any errors writing to the file.

The *readStudentRecord( )* method code is as follows:

```
//METHOD TO READ A STUDENT RECORD FROM AN OPENED DISK FILE
public void readStudentRecord()
{
  //TRY TO READ FILE
  try
  {
    //DISPLAY STUDENT RECORD DATA IN TEXT AREA
    studentArea.append("\n\nStudent Name: " + inFile.readUTF());
    studentArea.append("\nStudent Number: " + inFile.readUTF());
    studentArea.append("\nGPA:  " + String.valueOf(inFile.readDouble()));
  } //END try() READ

  //CATCH UTF EXCEPTION
  catch (UTFDataFormatException utf)
  {
    studentArea.append("\nINCORRECT DATA IN FILE");
    System.exit(1);
  }//END CATCH UTF

  //CATCH NO RECORD TO READ EXCEPTION
  catch (NullPointerException np)
  {
    studentArea.append("\nREAD ERROR, MAKE SURE FILE IS OPEN\n");
  }//END CATCH NULL POINTER

  //CATCH END OF FILE EXCEPTION
  catch (EOFException eof)
  {
    studentArea.append("\n\nTHERE ARE NO MORE RECORDS IN FILE");
  }//END CATCH EOF
```

```
//CATCH GENERAL READ EXCEPTION AND EXIT PROGRAM
catch (IOException io)
{
   studentArea.append("\n\nGENERAL FILE READ ERROR");
   System.exit(1);
}//END CATCH IO
}//readStudentRecord()
```

Again, you see that all the file action is coded within a **try** block. However, this time we are using our *inFile* object to call the *readUTF()* and *readDouble()* methods. These methods, along with others listed in Table 12-4, are part of the *DataInputStream* class. You see that the *DataInputStream* methods listed in Table 12-4 are simply the counterparts of the *DataOutputStream* methods listed in Table 12-3. Now, note from the foregoing program that the *readUTF()* and *readDouble()* methods are called as part of an argument for the text area *append()* method so that the values read from the file will be appended to the GUI text area.

TABLE 12-4 SOME STANDARD *DataInputStream* METHODS FOR READING FILES

Method	Description
readBoolean()	Reads a Boolean value from the data input stream.
readByte()	Reads a signed 8-bit value from the data input stream.
readChar()	Reads a Unicode character from the data input stream.
readDouble()	Reads a **double** from the data input stream.
readFloat()	Reads a **float** from the data input stream.
readInt()	Reads an **int** from the data input stream.
readLong()	Reads a **long** from the data input stream.
readShort()	Reads a **short** from the data input stream.
readUTF()	Reads a UTF string from the data input stream.

The *readUTF( )* method is the counterpart of the *writeUTF( )* method. This method will read a string in UTF-8 format and convert it to a Unicode Java string. The method is called twice in succession to read the student name and student number strings stored previously in the file via our *writeStudentRecord( )* method. The *readDouble( )* method is the counterpart of the *writeDouble( )* method. It reads a primitive **double** value. However, this value must be converted to a string before it can be appended to the text area. This is why the *valueOf( )* method is called within the argument of the *append( )* method.

Note that there are four **catch** blocks in our method. The first block is used to catch at *UTFDataException*. This exception is thrown by the *readUTF( )* method when the data it reads are not in proper UTF format. Such a situation might occur if the user opened the wrong file. Notice that the handler appends an error message to the text area then terminates the program via the statement System.exit(1). A call to the *exit( )* method by the *System* class terminates program execution. A nonzero argument within the *exit( )* method notifies the operating system of an abnormal termination due to an error, while an argument of zero indicates a normal termination. The second **catch** block is used to catch a *NullPointerException*. This exception is thrown by the *readUTF( )* or *readDouble( )* methods when there is no value to read. This will happen when the user tries to read a record before opening the file. Notice that the handler notifies the user to open the file and try again. The third block catches an *EndOfFileException*. This exception is thrown when the end of the file is reached, indicating that no more records are available. The handler notifies the user of this condition by appending a message to the text area. Finally, the last block catches a general *IOException*. This block is required because both the *readUTF( )* and *readDouble( )* methods throw an *IOException*. If a general *IOException* occurs, the handler will exit the program, notifying the operating system of an abnormal termination.

Closing a File

The last thing that needs to be done is to develop methods to close both our input and output files. You must always close a file when the file processing is complete, otherwise you cannot assure the integrity of the file for future processing. Our two file closing methods are similar. One is called *closeOutputFile( )* while the other is called *closeInputFile( )*. These methods are executed when the user clicks the *Done* button in Figures 12-3 and 12-4, respectively. Here they are:

```java
//CLOSE OUTPUT FILE
 public void closeOutputFile()
 {
   //TRY TO CLOSE FILE
   try
   {
     outFile.flush();
     outFile.close();
     studentArea.append("\nFILE CLOSED");
     System.exit(0);
   }//END try()

   //CATCHES EXCEPTION OF NO FILE EXISTS TO CLOSE
   catch (NullPointerException np)
   {
     studentArea.append("\nNO FILE TO CLOSE\n" + np.toString());
   } //END CATCH NULL POINTER

   //CATCH GENERAL IO EXCEPTION
   catch(IOException io)
   {
     studentArea.append("\nFILE CLOSING ERROR\n" + io.toString());
     System.exit(1);
   }//END CATCH IO
 }//END closeOutputFile()


//CLOSE INPUT FILE
public void closeInputFile()
{
    //TRY TO CLOSE FILE
    try
    {
     inFile.close();
     studentArea.append("\nFILE CLOSED");
     System.exit(0);
    }//END try()

    //CATCH NO FILE TO CLOSE EXCEPTION
    catch(NullPointerException np)
    {
     studentArea.append("\nNO FILE TO CLOSE\n" + np.toString());
    }//END CATCH NULL POINTER
```

```
//CATCH CLOSE EXCEPTION
catch(IOException io)
{
  studentArea.append("\nFILE CLOSING ERROR\n" + io.toString());
  System.exit(1);
}//END CATCH GENRERAL IO
}//END closeInputFile()
```

As you can see, both methods attempt to close the file within a **try** block. Both methods use their respective objects to call the standard *close()* method available in the *File_____Stream* classes. In addition, notice that the *closeOutputFile()* method calls the *flush()* method prior to closing the file. The *FileOutputStream* class inherits the *flush()* method from the *OutputStream* class. This method "flushes" the output stream, causing any internally buffered data to be written to the file. Both file closing methods call the *exit()* method with an argument of zero to terminate the program normally.

Each closing method has two identical **catch** blocks. The first block catches a *NullPointerException* which will occur if the user tries to close a file that has not been opened. The second block catches a general *IOException* which will occur if the operating system has trouble closing the file for any reason. If this happens, the handler terminates the program abnormally.

 Quick Check

1. True of false: The *DataInputStream* class provides methods to write primitive data types to files.

2. Which general exception is always thrown when an exception error occurs?

3. What method was used in this text to write strings to disk files?

4. Write a statement that will obtain a string from a text field object called *myName* and write it to a disk file attached to an object called *myOutputFile*.

5. Write a statement to read a string from a file attached to an object called *myInputFile* and display it in a text area called *displayText*.

6. Write a statement that will obtain a string from a text field called *myAge*, convert it to an **int**, and write it to a file attached to an object called *myOutputFile*.

7. Write a statement to read an **int** from a file attached to an object called *myInputFile* and display it in a text area called *displayText*.

8. The last thing that needs to be done when processing a disk file is to _____ the file.

9. What is the purpose of calling the *flush()* method when closing an output file?

12-4 PUTTING IT ALL TOGETHER

Now we have all the ingredients for our file processing classes. The *WriteStudentFile* class will contain the *openOutputFile()*, *writeStudentRecord()*, and *closeOutputFile()* methods, and the *ReadStudentFile* class will contain the *openInputFile()*, *readStudentRecord()*, and *closeInputFile()* methods. Of course these classes must also contain all of the respective GUI code.

A Class to Write a Sequential File

Encapsulating the file write methods and GUI code into a single class gives us the following:

```
//CLASS TO WRITE A STUDENT FILE
class WriteStudentFile extends FrameWithClose implements ActionListener
{
   //DECLARE OUTPUT FILE STREAM OBJECT
   private DataOutputStream outFile;

   //DEFINE TEXT FIELD OBJECTS AS PRIVATE CLASS DATA
   private TextField nameField = new TextField(25);
   private TextField numberField = new TextField(13);
   private TextField gpaField = new TextField(4);
   private TextField fileNameField = new TextField(20);
   private TextArea studentArea = new TextArea(7,40);

   //CONSTRUCTOR
   public WriteStudentFile(String Title)
   {
```

```
//CALL SUPERCLASS CONSTRUCTOR
super(Title);

//SET FRAME LAYOUT MANAGER
setLayout(new FlowLayout(FlowLayout.LEFT));

//DEFINE PANELS
Panel panel1 = new Panel();
Panel panel2 = new Panel();
Panel panel3 = new Panel();
Panel panel4 = new Panel();

//SET PANEL LAYOUT MANAGERS
panel1.setLayout(new FlowLayout(FlowLayout.LEFT));
panel2.setLayout(new FlowLayout(FlowLayout.LEFT));
panel3.setLayout(new FlowLayout(FlowLayout.LEFT));
panel4.setLayout(new FlowLayout(FlowLayout.LEFT));

//DEFINE LABEL OBJECTS
Label nameLabel = new Label("Student name");
Label numberLabel = new Label("Student Number");
Label gpaLabel = new Label("GPA");
Label summaryLabel = new Label("Student Summary");
Label fileNameLabel = new Label("File Name");

//DEFINE BUTTON OBJECTS
Button openFileButton = new Button("Open File");
Button storeButton = new Button("Store");
Button doneButton = new Button("Done");

//ADD COMPONENTS TO panel1
panel1.add(fileNameLabel);
panel1.add(fileNameField);
panel1.add(openFileButton);

//ADD COMPONENTS TO panel2
panel2.add(nameLabel);
panel2.add(nameField);
panel2.add(numberLabel);
panel2.add(numberField);
panel3.add(gpaLabel);
panel3.add(gpaField);
```

```
  //ADD COMPONENTS TO panel3
  panel4.add(summaryLabel);
  panel4.add(studentArea);
  panel4.add(storeButton);
  panel4.add(doneButton);

  //ADD PANELS TO FRAME
  add(panel1);
  add(panel2);
  add(panel3);
  add(panel4);

  //REGISTER LISTENERS
  openFileButton.addActionListener(this);      //OPEN FILE BUTTON LISTENER
  storeButton.addActionListener(this);         //STORE BUTTON LISTENER
  doneButton.addActionListener(this);          //DONE BUTTON LISTENER
}//END WriteStudentFile()

 //PROCESS EVENT
 public void actionPerformed(ActionEvent e)
 {
   //DID A BUTTON CAUSE EVENT?
   if (e.getSource() instanceof Button)
   {
     //IF SO, WHICH BUTTON?
     String item = e.getActionCommand();

     //DID OPEN FILE BUTTON CAUSE EVENT?
     if (item.equals("Open File"))
     {
       //IF SO, OPEN FILE
       openOutputFile(fileNameField.getText());
     }//END IF OPEN FILE

     //DID STORE BUTTON CAUSE EVENT?
     if (item.equals("Store"))
     {
       //DISPLAY IN TEXT FIELD DATA IN TEXT AREA
       studentArea.setText("");
       studentArea.append("\nStudent name: " + nameField.getText());
       studentArea.append("\nStudent Number: " + numberField.getText());
       studentArea.append("\nGPA: " + gpaField.getText());

       //CALL METHOD TO WRITE STUDENT RECORD
       writeStudentRecord();
     }//END IF STORE BUTTON
```

```
                //DID DONE BUTTON CAUSE EVENT?
                if (item.equals("Done"))
                {
                  closeOutputFile();
                }//END IF DONE BUTTON
              }//END IF BUTTON
            }//END actionPerformed()

//CREATE AN OUTPUT STREAM AND ATTACH IT TO A PHYSICAL DISK FILE
public void openOutputFile(String s)
{
  //TRY TO OPEN FILE BY ATTACHING OUTPUT STREAM TO A DISK FILE
  try
  {
    outFile = new DataOutputStream(new FileOutputStream(s));
    studentArea.setText("FILE OPEN, BEGIN STORING RECORDS");
  }//END try()

  //CATCH EXCEPTION IF FILE CANNOT BE OPENED
  catch(IOException io)
  {
    studentArea.append("\n\nFILE NOT FOUND ERROR\n" + io.toString() );
  }//END catch() IOException
}//END openOutputFile

public void writeStudentRecord()
{
//TRY TO WRITE STUDENT RECORD TO FILE
try
{
  outFile.writeUTF(nameField.getText());
  outFile.writeUTF(numberField.getText());
  outFile.writeDouble((new Double(gpaField.getText().trim())).doubleValue());
} //END try() TO WRITE RECORD

//CATCH NUMBER FORMAT EXCEPTION FOR GPA FIELD
catch (NumberFormatException nfe)
{
  studentArea.append("\n\nWRITE FILE ERROR\n"
                    + "MAKE SURE GPA IS CORRECT\n"
                    + nfe.toString());
}//END NumberFormatcatch()
```

```
    //CATCH ANY EXCEPTIONS WRITING TO FILE
    catch (IOException io)
    {
      studentArea.append("\nWRITE FILE ERROR\n" + io.toString());
    } //END IO catch()

    //CLEAR TEXT FIELDS
    numberField.setText("");
    nameField.setText("");
    gpaField.setText("");
   }//writeStudentRecord

  //CLOSE OUTPUT FILE
  public void closeOutputFile()
  {
    //TRY TO CLOSE FILE
    try
    {
      outFile.flush();
      outFile.close();
      studentArea.append("\nFILE CLOSED");
      System.exit(0);
    }//END try()

  //CATCHES EXCEPTION OF NO FILE EXISTS TO CLOSE
    catch (NullPointerException np)
    {
      studentArea.append("\nNO FILE TO CLOSE\n" + np.toString());
    } //END CATCH NULL POINTER

    //CATCH GENERAL IO EXCEPTION
    catch(IOException io)
    {
      studentArea.append("\nFILE CLOSING ERROR\n" + io.toString());
      System.exit(1);
    }//END CATCH IO
  }//END closeOutputFile()
}//writeStudentFile CLASS
```

A Class to Read a Sequential File

Encapsulating the file read methods and GUI code into a single class gives us the
following:

```
//CLASS TO READ A STUDENT FILE
class ReadStudentFile extends FrameWithClose implements ActionListener
{
  //DECLARE INPUT FILE STREAM OBJECT
  private DataInputStream inFile;

  //DEFINE TEXT FIELD OBJECTS
  private TextField fileNameField = new TextField(20);
  private TextArea studentArea = new TextArea(7,50);

  //DEFINE BUTTON OBJECTS
  private Button openFileButton = new Button("Open File");
  private Button nextStudentButton = new Button("Next Student");
  private Button doneButton = new Button("Done");

  //CONSTRUCTOR
  public ReadStudentFile(String Title)
  {
  //CALL SUPERCLASS CONSTRUCTOR
  super(Title);

  //SET FRAME LAYOUT MANAGER
  setLayout(new BorderLayout());

  //DEFINE PANELS
  Panel panel1 = new Panel();
  Panel panel2 = new Panel();
  Panel panel3 = new Panel();

  //SET PANEL LAYOUT MANAGERS
  panel1.setLayout(new FlowLayout(FlowLayout.LEFT));
  panel2.setLayout(new FlowLayout(FlowLayout.CENTER));
  panel3.setLayout(new FlowLayout(FlowLayout.CENTER,20,20));

  //DEFINE LABEL OBJECTS
  Label fileNameLabel = new Label("File Name");

  //ADD COMPONENTS TO panel1
  panel1.add(fileNameLabel);
  panel1.add(fileNameField);
  panel1.add(openFileButton);

  //ADD COMPONENTS TO panel2
  panel2.add(studentArea);

  //ADD COMPONENTS TO panel3
  panel3.add(nextStudentButton);
  panel3.add(doneButton);
```

```
   //ADD PANELS TO FRAME
   add(panel1,"North");
   add(panel2,"Center");
   add(panel3,"South");

   //REGISTER LISTENERS
   openFileButton.addActionListener(this);       //OPEN BUTTON LISTENER
   nextStudentButton.addActionListener(this);  //STUDENT BUTTON LISTENER
   doneButton.addActionListener(this);            //DONE BUTTON LISTENER
 }//END ReadStudentFile()

//PROCESS BUTTON EVENT
public void actionPerformed(ActionEvent e)
{
  //DID A BUTTON CAUSE EVENT?
  if (e.getSource() instanceof Button)
  {
    //IF SO, WHICH BUTTON?
    String item = e.getActionCommand();

    //DID OPEN FILE BUTTON CAUSE EVENT?
    if (item.equals("Open File"))
    {
      //IF SO, OPEN FILE
      openInputFile(fileNameField.getText());
    }//END IF OPEN FILE

    //DID NEXT STUDENT BUTTON CAUSE EVENT?
    if (item.equals("Next Student"))
    {
      readStudentRecord();
    }//END IF NEXT STUDENT

    //DID DONE BUTTON CAUSE EVENT?
    if (item.equals("Done"))
    {
      closeInputFile();
    }//END IF DONE
  }//END IF BUTTON
}//END actionPerformed()

//CREATE AN INPUT STREAM AND ATTACH IT TO A PHYSICAL DISK FILE
public void openInputFile(String s)
{
```

```
//TRY TO OPEN FILE BY ATTACHING INPUT STREAM TO A DISK FILE
try
{
  inFile = new DataInputStream(new FileInputStream(s));
  studentArea.setText("FILE OPEN, PRESS Next Student BUTTON");
}//END try()

//CATCH EXCEPTION IF FILE CANNOT BE OPENED
catch(IOException io)
{
  studentArea.setText("\n\nFILE NOT FOUND ERROR\n" + io.toString());
}//END catch()
}//END openInputFile()

public void readStudentRecord()
{
  //TRY TO READ FILE
  try
  {
    //DISPLAY STUDENT RECORD DATA IN TEXT AREA
    studentArea.append("\n\nStudent Name: " + inFile.readUTF());
    studentArea.append("\nStudent Number: " + inFile.readUTF());
    studentArea.append("\nGPA:  " + String.valueOf(inFile.readDouble()));
  } //END try() READ

  //CATCH UTF EXCEPTION
  catch (UTFDataFormatException utf)
  {
    studentArea.append("\nINCORRECT DATA IN FILE");
    System.exit(1);
  }//END CATCH UTF

  //CATCH NO RECORD TO READ EXCEPTION
  catch (NullPointerException np)
  {
    studentArea.append("\nREAD ERROR, MAKE SURE FILE IS OPEN\n");
  }//END CATCH NULL POINTER

  //CATCH END OF FILE EXCEPTION
  catch (EOFException eof)
  {
    studentArea.append("\nTHERE ARE NO MORE RECORDS IN THIS FILE");
  }//END CATCH EOF
```

```
//CATCH GENERAL READ EXCEPTION AND EXIT PRORGRAM
catch (IOException io)
{
  studentArea.append("\n\nGENERAL FILE READ ERROR");
  System.exit(1);
}//END CATCH IO
}//readStudentRecord()

//CLOSE INPUT FILE
public void closeInputFile()
{
//TRY TO CLOSE FILE
try
{
  inFile.close();
  studentArea.append("\nFILE CLOSED");
  System.exit(0);
}//END try()

//CATCH NO FILE TO CLOSE EXCEPTION
catch(NullPointerException np)
{
  studentArea.append("\nNO FILE TO CLOSE\n" + np.toString());
}//END CATCH NULL POINTER

//CATCH CLOSE EXCEPTION
catch(IOException io)
{
  studentArea.append("\nFILE CLOSING ERROR\n" + io.toString());
  System.exit(1);
}//END CATCH GENRERAL IO
}//END closeInputFile()
}//END ReadStudentFile CLASS
```

There you have it. Take a close look at each class and make sure you understand all of the details. You now have the knowledge required to read/write your own sequential disk files.

CHAPTER SUMMARY

In data processing applications, a file is a collection of related records, or classes. Each record is made up of related fields, or members, that contain the file information. A file can be viewed as a data structure that consists of a sequence of components. Files provide a means for your program to communicate with the outside world. Any I/O operations performed by your program, even keyboard input and display output, are handled via streams. A stream provides a channel for data to flow between your program and the outside world. You will use four classes to access disk files in Java: *FileOutputStream*, *DataOutputStream*, *FileInputStream*, and *DataInputStream*. All of these classes are part of the *java.io* package which must be imported into your program. The first two classes are used to perform output, or write, operations on disk files; and the second two are used to perform input, or read, operations on disk files. The *File_____Stream* class constructors are used to open a file, creating a file stream which attaches a logical program file object to a physical disk file. The methods in the *Data _____Stream* classes are use to read/write primitive data types, including strings, from/to file streams.

There are three basic operations that you will need to perform when working with disk files:

- Open the file for input or output.
- Process the file, by reading from or writing to the file.
- Close the file.

You use the *File_____Stream* class constructors to open a file and the *Data _____Stream* class methods to read/write the file. See Table 12-3 and Table 12-4 for the various *Data _____Stream* class methods. Finally, you must call the *close()* method of the *File_____Stream* classes to close a file when the file processing is complete.

Working with files requires that your program communicate with a peripheral device. When communicating with a peripheral device, there is always the possibility that something unexpected could happen such as a disk could be write-protected during a write operation, a disk file might not exist during a read operation, and so on. As a result, you must provide exception handling to protect your program from terminating prematurely during file operations, as well as other possible sources of error. Exception handling in Java is provided by coding any statements that have a potential of causing an error within a **try** block. One or more **catch** blocks must then be coded to catch and handle any exception thrown from within the **try** block.

You will wrap your file opening, processing, and closing methods along with the required exception handling and GUI code into separate classes to read or write a given file. Although they look complex, such classes are easy to build once you understand the basics of file I/O, exception handling and GUI construction. You now have this knowledge.

QUESTIONS AND PROBLEMS

Questions

1. List the three major operations that must be performed in order to process files.
2. What is a file stream?
3. What is the purpose of opening a file?
4. What predefined classes does Java provide to create a stream and attach it to a physical disk file?
5. What predefined classes does Java provide to read/write primitive data values from/to a disk file?
6. Write a statement to create a file stream object called *fileIn* that will read a disk file called *mydata.txt*.
7. Write a statement to create a file stream object called *fileOut* that will write to a file whose name is stored in a string called *fileName*.
8. Statements that have the potential for throwing an exception are placed within a _____ block.
9. When an exception is thrown, it must be caught by a _____ block in order to handle the exception.
10. List and describe at least four checked exceptions that are defined in Java.
11. True or false: Once an exception is caught and processed by the handler, control returns to the **try** block that threw the exception.
12. True or false: A subclass exception handler must be coded prior to its superclass exception handler.
13. What problem is encountered when catching the generic *Exception* class exception to catch any and all exceptions?

14. What happens in a non-GUI program when an exception is thrown, but not caught?

15. What happens in a GUI program when an exception is thrown, but not caught?

16. True or false: You can have more than one **catch** block for a given **try** block.

17. Write a **catch** block to notify the user that a divide-by-zero error has occurred.

18. Write a statement that gets a string from a text field called *doubleField* and converts it to a primitive **double** data type.

19. What is UTF format and what type of data uses this format for file I/O?

20. What exception must be caught when reading data in UTF format?

21. Write a statement to close a file attached to a file object called *myFile*.

22. What exception should be caught when closing a file?

23. What *DataInputStream* method would you use to read a Unicode character from a disk file?

24. Write a statement that will obtain a string from a text field called *employeeSalary*, convert it to a **double**, and write it to a file attached to an object called *employeeFile*.

25. Write a statement to read a **double** from a file attached to an object called *employeeFile* and display it in a text area called *employeeData*.

Problems

Least Difficult

1. Place the *WriteStudentFile* class and the *ReadStudentFile* class discussed in this chapter inside two separate application programs. The class source code can be found on the CD that accompanies this book or can be downloaded from www.prenhall.com. All the application class needs to do is to create an object for the given class, then use this object to set the size of the GUI frame and make it visible. Don't forget to import the *java.io* package for the file stream classes. You must also have the *FrameWithClose* class available for the file classes to inherit. This class is also available on your CD or can be douwnloaded. Execute your application programs and experiment with the classes by writing then reading disk files. Make sure to test the exception handling features of the classes.

More Difficult

Refer to the student database GUI shown in Figure 12-5 for problems 2-4 .

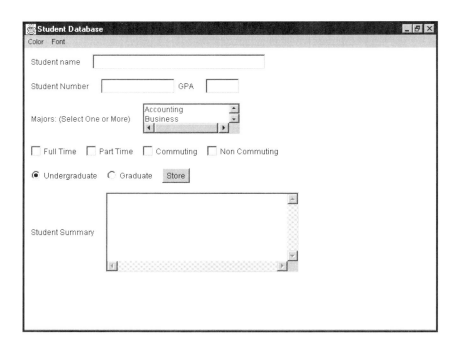

Figure 12-5 A GUI for problems 2 – 4.

2.   Add a student majors list box similar to the one shown in Figure 12-5 to the *WriteStudentFile* GUI. Modify the *WriteStudentFile* and *ReadStudentFile* classes given in this chapter to write/read the student's major(s) selected from the added list box.

3.   Add student status checkboxes similar to those shown in Figure 12-5 to the *WriteStudentFile* GUI. Modify the *WriteStudentFile* and *ReadStudentFile* classes given in this chapter to write/read the student's full-time/part-time and commuting status selected from the added checkboxes.

4.   Add student status radio buttons similar to those shown in Figure 12-5 to the *WriteStudentFile* GUI. Modify the *WriteStudentFile* and *ReadStudentFile* classes given in this chapter to write/read the student's undergraduate/graduate status selected from the added radio buttons.

Most Difficult

5. Using the techniques discussed in this chapter, develop classes that will process a parts inventory file of the following information:
   - Part name
   - Part number
   - Part price
   - Quantity on hand

   Develop one class that will allow a user to create the parts inventory file and another class that will read and display the file. Make sure to provide a GUI interface for both classes. Place your classes in two separate application programs to execute and test your code.

6. Using the techniques discussed in this chapter, develop classes that will process an employee file containing the following information:
   - Employee name
   - Employee number
   - Employee type: salaried, commissioned, or hourly
   - Employee gender: male or female
   - Employee wage: annual salary, commission rate, or hourly rate

   Develop one class that will allow a user to create the employee file and another class that will read and display the file. Make sure to provide a GUI interface for both classes. Place your classes in two separate application programs to execute and test your code.

Applet 103: Applets and GUIs

PURPOSE

- *To learn how to add components and process events within an applet GUI.*
- *To demonstrate how an applet acts as a container for GUI components, much as frames do for applications.*
- *To show how the applet init( ) method is used like a frame constructor in applications to construct applet GUIs.*
- *To demonstrate the use of the FlowLayout and BorderLayout managers in an applet.*
- *To demonstrate the use of panels in an applet.*
- *To learn how to control the echo character generated in a text field.*

Introduction

In the earlier GUI modules and in Chapter 11, you learned how to create application program GUIs. Almost everything you learned about application program GUIs can be applied to creating GUIs for applets, with the exception of using a frame as the GUI component container. In an application program, the *Frame* class is inherited to produce a generic window and provide a container for the GUI components that make up a window. In an applet program, the *Applet* class in inherited to produce a generic window and provide a container for the GUI components.

By definition, an applet is a GUI container. You simply cannot create a non-GUI applet program, as you can an application program. Of course, an applet can only be executed from a Java compiler or a Java-enabled Web browser and, therefore, is primarily an Internet-based program. All Java programs for non-Internet applications must be Java application programs. A classic example of when an application is required over an applet is when the program must operate on disk files. Since an applet is primarily created for use over the Internet, Java applets do not even support file handling. This is part of the inherent security built into Java. Would you want someone else's applet to have access to your disk files?

In this module, you will load, compile, and execute applets that contain GUI components. You will experiment with layout managers, font control, and add your own components to the GUI. The last applet in this module is a GUI for an on-line stock investing program. Such investing is becoming very popular over the Internet. Why do you suppose we didn't use the *student database GUI* program developed previously for a Java application program? You're right, because such a GUI might be used to build a local database of student files and Java applets do not support file access.

Procedure

1. Load and execute the *Applet103_1.java* program contained on the CD that accompanies this book or download it from www.prenhall.com. Use your Java compiler to compile the program as an applet, then execute the program through your compiler or a Web browser. You should observe the applet shown in Figure 1.

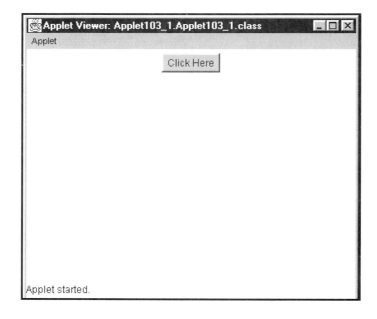

Figure 1 The applet generated by the *Applet103_1.java* program.

2. Click the button and observe that the background color of the applet changes to black. Also, observe the status bar message at the bottom of the window.

3. Minimize the window, then restore the window. Notice that the applet has restarted and the window changes to a white background.

Discussion

Here is the code that produced the applet window:

```
1    import java.applet.Applet;  //FOR APPLET CLASS
2    import java.awt.*;          //FOR GRAPHICS CLASS
3    import java.awt.event.*;    //FOR EVENT PROCESSING
4
5    public class Applet103_1 extends Applet implements ActionListener
6    {
7      //INITIALIZE APPLET
8      public void init()
9      {
10     //DEFINE BUTTON OBJECT
11     Button colorButton = new Button("Click Here");
12
13     //ADD BUTTON TO APPLET
14     add(colorButton);
15
16     //ADD EVENT LISTENER THIS BUTTON
17     colorButton.addActionListener(this);
18    }//END init()
19
20     //PROCESS EVENT
21     public void actionPerformed(ActionEvent e)
22     {
23      //DID BUTTON CAUSE EVENT?
24      if (e.getSource() instanceof Button)
25      {
26       //IF SO, CHANGE COLOR TO BLACK COLOR
27       setBackground(Color.black);
28       showStatus("Background color changed to black via " + e.getSource());
29      }//END IF
30     }//END actionPerformed()
```

```
31    //SET BACKGROUND BACK TO WHITE ON RESTART
32    public void start()
33    {
34      setBackground(Color.white);
35    }//END start()
36  }//END APPLET
```

Recall that, in an application, the GUI was constructed as part of a frame subclass constructor, since the constructor is the first thing executed when a frame object is created in *main()*. An applet, on the other hand, does not employ a frame as a container class for the GUI components. The applet itself is the container class for the components. There are several standard methods that an applet calls automatically when it is started, one of which is the *paint()* method that you have seen in the previous *Applet10X* modules. There are three more methods that are called automatically if they exist within an applet. They are the *init()*, *start()*, *stop()*, and *destroy()* methods. These methods are summarized in Table 1.

TABLE 1 STANDARD METHODS CALLED BY AN APPLET

Method	Description
init()	Called when the applet is first loaded for execution and also when the applet is reloaded.
start()	Called after *init()* and when the applet is reactivated or when the user moves back to the Web page containing the applet.
paint()	Called automatically after *init()*, and by *repaint()* when the applet must be repainted. Receives an object from the standard *Graphics* class to create applet graphics.
stop()	Called when the user leaves the Web page containing the applet.
destroy()	Called after *stop()* only when applet is being removed from memory, such as when the use of the browser is terminated. Used to release any system resources that were allocated by the applet.

The method of interest at this point is the *init()* method. The *init()* method is the first method to be called if it exists within an applet. Thus, *init()* acts like a constructor for the applet. Like a constructor, *init()* is used to initialize the applet, so to build an applet GUI you place your GUI code within the *init()* method, rather than a constructor method as we did when we built application GUIs. Look at lines 8-18 and you will find that we have defined our button object, added the object to the applet container, then registered the object as an event listener all within the *init()* method.

Following the *init()* method we begin the *actionPerformed()* method in line 21. Here, we simply use an **if** statement as we did earlier in an application program to determine if the event was a button event. If so, the applet background color is set to black. In addition, a status bar message is generated which uses the event object, *e*, to call the *getSource()* method. The event object carries with it information about the event. The *getSource()* method extracts this information which includes the fact that a button generated the event as well as the label of the button that caused the event.

When you minimized and then restored the applet, you restarted the applet. Whenever an applet is restarted like this, or returned to as you might if you go back and forth between Web pages, the applet automatically calls its *start()* method if one exists. The *start()* method that we coded in lines 32-35 simply sets the applet background color to white when it is restored.

Procedure (continued)

4. Load and execute the *Applet103_2.java* program contained on the CD that accompanies this book or download it from www.prenhall.com. Use your Java compiler to compile the program as an applet, then execute the program through your compiler or a Web browser. You should observe the applet shown in Figure 2.

5. Click any of the color buttons and notice that the applet background color is changed accordingly. Notice also the message in the status bar at the bottom of the window.

6. Minimize then restore the window. The restored window should appear with a white background.

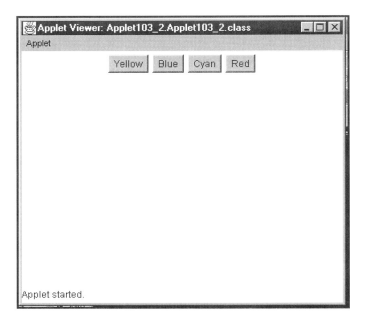

Figure 2 The window generated by the *Applet103_2.java* applet .

Discussion

Here is the code that produced the applet window:

```
1     import java.applet.Applet;      //FOR APPLET CLASS
2     import java.awt.*;              //FOR GUI COMPONENTS
3     import java.awt.event.*;        //FOR EVENT PROCESSING
4
5     public class Applet103_2 extends Applet implements ActionListener
6     {
7       //DEFINE BUTTON OBJECTS
8       private Button yellowButton = new Button("Yellow");
9       private Button blueButton = new Button("Blue");
10      private Button cyanButton = new Button("Cyan");
11      private Button redButton = new Button("Red");
12
13      //INITIALIZE APPLET WITH GUI COMPONENTS
14      public void init()
15      {
16
```

```
17      //SET LAYOUT TO FLOW LAYOUT
18      setLayout(new FlowLayout());
19
20      //ADD BUTTONS TO APPLET
21      add(yellowButton);
22      add(blueButton);
23      add(cyanButton);
24      add(redButton);
25
26      //ACTIVATE EVENT LISTENERS FOR BUTTONS
27      yellowButton.addActionListener(this);
28      blueButton.addActionListener(this);
29      cyanButton.addActionListener(this);
30      redButton.addActionListener(this);
31      greenButton.addActionListener(this);
32      }//END init()
33
34      //PROCESS EVENT
35      public void actionPerformed(ActionEvent e)
36      {
37      //GET LABEL OF EVENT OBJECT
38      String buttonLabel = e.getActionCommand();
39
40      //DID A BUTTON CAUSE EVENT?
41      if (e.getSource() instanceof Button)
42       //IF SO, WHICH BUTTON?
43       if (buttonLabel.equals("Yellow"))
44       {
45         setBackground(Color.yellow);
46         showStatus("Background color changed to yellow via "+e.getSource());
47       }//END IF "Yellow"
48       if (buttonLabel.equals("Blue"))
49       {
50         setBackground(Color.blue);
51         showStatus("Background color changed to blue via " + e.getSource());
52       }//END IF "Blue"
53       if (buttonLabel.equals("Cyan"))
54       {
55         setBackground(Color.cyan);
56         showStatus("Background color changed to cyan via " + e.getSource());
57       }//END IF "Cyan"
```

```
58        if (buttonLabel.equals("Red"))
59        {
60          setBackground(Color.red);
61          showStatus("Background color changed to red via " + e.getSource());
62        }//END IF "Red"
63      }//END actionPerformed()
64
65      //SET BACKGROUND BACK TO WHITE ON RESTART
66      public void start()
67      {
68        setBackground(Color.white);
69      }//END start()
70    }//END APPLET
```

In this applet, we have first defined five button objects as private members of the applet *Applet103_2* subclass. The buttons are defined outside the *init()* method as private class members because we must have access to them in the subsequent *actionPerformed()* method. The *init()* method simply sets the layout manager of the applet to *FlowLayout* the same way that we set the layout manager for an application frame in the previous GUI modules. The buttons are then added to the applet and each button is registered as a listener. The *actionPerformed()* method processes the button events as you have seen in the past. The *start()* method is used as before to reset the background color to white when the applet is restarted for any reason.

Procedure (continued)

7. Add a green button to the applet using code similar to that which you see for the other buttons.

8. Execute the revised program to verify that your green button is working.

9. Change the layout manager to *BorderLayout* with a component gapping of 30 pixels and add a button to each of the five *BorderLayout* regions.

10. Execute the revised program to verify that the applet produces a border layout.

Discussion

In step 7 you added a green button to the applet. To do this, you must define a private green button object, add the button to the applet, and register a listener for the button object in the *init()* method, then add the required logic to the *actionPerformed()* method to process an event generated by the green button object. In step 9 you changed the applet layout to *BorderLayout*. You found that applets also support the *BorderLayout* manager. In fact, applets support any of the layout managers that are supported by frames, including no layout.

Procedure (continued)

11. Load and execute the *Applet103_3.java* program contained on the CD that accompanies this book or download it from www.prenhall.com. Use your Java compiler to compile the program as an applet, then execute the program through your compiler or a Web browser. Maximum the window. You should observe the applet shown in Figure 3.

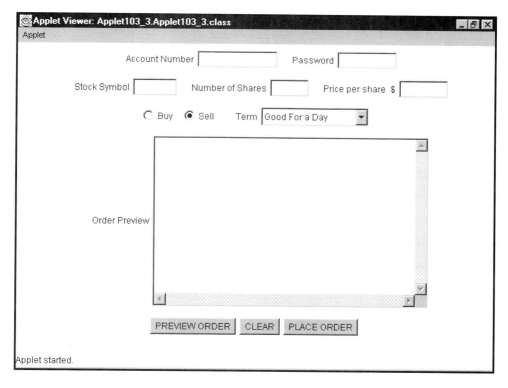

Figure 3 The stock buy/sell GUI generated by the *Applet103_3.java* applet .

12. Exercise the applet by entering the required text field information, selecting buy or sell, and selecting an item from the choice box. Click the *PREVIEW ORDER* button and notice that the stock order is summarized in the text area. A sample order preview is shown in Figure 4.

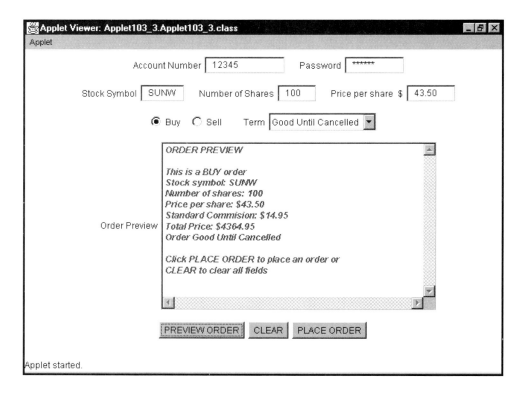

Figure 4 A sample stock order generated by the *Applet103_3.java* applet .

13. Make a change to any of the stock buy/sell information and click the *PREVIEW ORDER* button again. The text area should reflect any changes made.

14. Click the *PLACE ORDER* button and notice that the text area indicates that the order has been placed.

15. Click the *CLEAR* button and notice that all the text fields and the text area are cleared to allow for new entries.

Discussion

Here is the applet code:

```
1    package Applet103_3;
2
3    import java.applet.Applet;      //FOR APPLET CLASS
4    import java.awt.*;              //FOR GUI COMPONENTS
5    import java.awt.event.*;        //FOR EVENT PROCESSING
6
7    public class Applet103_3 extends Applet implements ActionListener
8    {
9      //DEFINE BUTTON OBJECTS
10     private Button previewButton = new Button("PREVIEW ORDER");
11     private Button cancelButton = new Button("CLEAR");
12     private Button orderButton = new Button("PLACE ORDER");
13
14     //DEFINE TEXT FIELD OBJECTS
15     private TextField accountNumberField = new TextField(12);
16     private TextField stockSymbolField = new TextField(5);
17     private TextField numberSharesField = new TextField(4);
18     private TextField priceField = new TextField(6);
19     private TextField passwordField = new TextField(8);
20     private TextArea previewArea = new TextArea(14,50);
21
22     //DEFINE CHOICE BOX OBJECT
23     private Choice termChoice = new Choice();
24
25     //DEFINE RADIO BUTTON OBJECTS
26     private CheckboxGroup transactionGroup = new CheckboxGroup();
27     private Checkbox buy = new Checkbox("Buy",transactionGroup,false);
28     private Checkbox sell = new Checkbox("Sell",transactionGroup,true);
29
30     //INITIALIZE APPLET WITH GUI COMPONENTS
31     public void init()
32     {
33     //DEFINE TEXT AREA FONT AND COLOR
34     Font f = new Font("Helvetica",Font.BOLD + Font.ITALIC,12);
35     previewArea.setFont(f);
36     previewArea.setForeground(Color.red);
37
```

```
38    //DEFINE PANELS
39    Panel panel1 = new Panel();
40    Panel panel2 = new Panel();
41    Panel panel3 = new Panel();
42    Panel panel4 = new Panel();
43    Panel panel5 = new Panel();
44
45    //SET PANEL LAYOUT MANAGERS
46    panel1.setLayout(new FlowLayout(FlowLayout.LEFT));
47    panel2.setLayout(new FlowLayout(FlowLayout.LEFT));
48    panel3.setLayout(new FlowLayout(FlowLayout.LEFT));
49    panel4.setLayout(new FlowLayout(FlowLayout.LEFT));
50    panel5.setLayout(new FlowLayout(FlowLayout.LEFT));
51
52    //DEFINE LABEL OBJECTS
53    Label accountNumberLabel = new Label("Account Number",Label.RIGHT);
54    Label passwordLabel = new Label("Password",Label.RIGHT);
55    Label stockSymbolLabel = new Label("Stock Symbol",Label.RIGHT);
56    Label numberSharesLabel = new Label("Number of Shares",Label.RIGHT);
57    Label priceLabel = new Label("Price per share  $",Label.RIGHT);
58    Label termLabel = new Label("Term",Label.RIGHT);
59    Label previewLabel = new Label("Order Preview",Label.RIGHT);
60
61    //ADD ITEMS TO CHOICE BOX
62    termChoice.addItem("Good For a Day");
63    termChoice.addItem("Good Until Cancelled");
64
65    //ADD COMPONENTS TO panel1
66    panel1.add(accountNumberLabel);
67    panel1.add(accountNumberField);
68    panel1.add(passwordLabel);
69    panel1.add(passwordField);
70
71    //ADD COMPONENTS TO panel2
72    panel2.add(stockSymbolLabel);
73    panel2.add(stockSymbolField);
74    panel2.add(numberSharesLabel);
75    panel2.add(numberSharesField);
76    panel2.add(priceLabel);
77    panel2.add(priceField);
78
79    //ADD COMPONENTS TO panel3
80    panel3.add(buy);
```

```
81   panel3.add(sell);
82   panel3.add(termLabel);
83   panel3.add(termChoice);
84
85   //ADD COMPONENTS TO panel4
86   panel4.add(previewLabel);
87   panel4.add(previewArea);
88
89   //ADD COMPONENTS TO panel5
90   panel5.add(previewButton);
91   panel5.add(cancelButton);
92   panel5.add(orderButton);
93
94   //ADD PANELS TO APPLET
95   add(panel1);
96   add(panel2);
97   add(panel3);
98   add(panel4);
99   add(panel5);
100
101  //SET * ECHO CHARACTER FOR PASSWORD TEXT FIELD
102  passwordField.setEchoChar('*');
103
104  //REGISTER LISTENERS
105  previewButton.addActionListener(this);
106  orderButton.addActionListener(this);
107  cancelButton.addActionListener(this);
108 }//END init()
109
110 //PROCESS BUTTON EVENT
111 public void actionPerformed(ActionEvent e)
112 {
113   //DID A BUTTON CAUSE EVENT?
114   if (e.getSource() instanceof Button)
115   {
116     //IF SO, WHICH BUTTON
117     if(e.getActionCommand().equals("PREVIEW ORDER"))
118     {
119       previewArea.setText("ORDER PREVIEW\n");
120       //BUY OR SELL?
121       if (buy.getState())
122         previewArea.append("\nThis is a BUY order");
```

```
123        else
124          previewArea.append("This is a SELL order");
125
126        //DISPLAY ORDER INFO
127        previewArea.append("\nStock symbol: "
128                               +stockSymbolField.getText());
129        previewArea.append("\nNumber of shares: "
130                               +numberSharesField.getText());
131        previewArea.append("\nPrice per share: $" + priceField.getText());
132        previewArea.append("\nStandard Commision: $14.95");
133
134        //GET PRICE DATA AND CONVERT TO DOUBLE
135        Double price = new Double(priceField.getText().trim());
136        double p = price.doubleValue();
137        Double shares = new Double(numberSharesField.getText().trim());
138        double s = shares.doubleValue();
139
140        //CALCULATE AND DISPLAY TOTAL
141        double total = p*s + 14.95;
142        previewArea.append("\nTotal Price: $" + String.valueOf(total));
143
144       previewArea.append("\nOrder " + termChoice.getSelectedItem());
145       previewArea.append("\n\nClick PLACE ORDER to place an order or\n"
146                               + "CLEAR to clear all fields");
147      }//END IF PREVIEW
148
149      if(e.getActionCommand().equals("CLEAR"))
150      {
151       accountNumberField.setText("");
152       stockSymbolField.setText("");
153       numberSharesField.setText("");
154       priceField.setText("");
155       passwordField.setText("");
156       previewArea.setText("");
157      }//END IF CANCEL
158
159      if(e.getActionCommand().equals("PLACE ORDER"))
160      {
161        previewArea.setText("ORDER PLACED");
162      }//END IF ORDER
163     }//END IF BUTTON
164    }//END actionPerformed()
165 }//END APPLET
```

As you can see, most of the GUI code resides in the applet *init( )* method, which is called when the applet is initially started. In an application program GUI, this code would be placed within the frame subclass constructor. Of course, any component object that must be accessed outside the *init( )* method must be defined as a private member of the applet subclass. This is why all the component objects, except the labels, are defined as private class members. These objects must be visible in the *actionPerformed( )* method. You should be able to understand most of the code at this point. Here are a few features that you might want to take note of:

- The text area font is set in lines 34-36.
- Applets support panels just as frames do in applications.
- In line 102, we set the echo character of the *passwordField* to an asterisk by calling the *setEchoChar( )* method. As a result, the user, and anyone looking over his/her shoulder, will only observe asterisks in the password field as the password is entered. However, the text field will actually contain the password string that was entered.
- The number of shares and price per share are converted to a primitive **double** data type in lines 135-138 so that they can be used to calculate the total order price in line 141.
- The resulting price is converted to a string in line 142 for display within the text area.
- All the text fields and the text area are set with a blank string in lines 151-156 if the user clicks the *CLEAR* button.

ONE-DIMENSIONAL ARRAYS

OBJECTIVES

When you are finished with this chapter, you should have a good understanding of the following:

- How to define one-dimensional arrays in Java.
- How to access one-dimensional arrays using direct assignment, reading/writing, and loops.
- How to pass arrays to methods.
- How to pass individual array elements to methods.
- How to search an array for a given element.
- How to sort an array.
- How to initialize an array with elements

INTRODUCTION

This chapter will introduce you to a very important topic in any programming language: *arrays*. The importance of arrays cannot be overemphasized, because they lend themselves to so many applications.

> An *array* is an *indexed* data structure that is used to store data elements of the same data type or class.

Arrays simply provide an organized means for locating and storing data, just as the post office boxes in your local post office lobby provide an organized means of locating and storing mail. This is why an array is referred to as a *data structure*. The array data structure can be used to store just about any type or class of data, including integers, floats, characters, arrays, and objects. In addition, arrays are so versatile that they can be used to implement other data structures that you will learn about later, such as stacks, queues, linked lists, and binary trees. In fact, in some languages like FORTRAN, the array is the only data structure available to the programmer, because most other structures can be implemented using arrays.

We will cover *one-dimensional* arrays in this chapter, because they are the most commonly used arrays in Java programs. You will most likely learn about arrays of more dimensions, called *multidimensional arrays*, in a future data structures course.

13-1 THE STRUCTURE OF A ONE-DIMENSIONAL ARRAY

An array is a data structure. In other words, an array consists of data elements that are organized, or structured, in a particular way. This array data structure provides a convenient means of storing large amounts of data in primary, or user, memory. There are both one-dimensional and multidimensional arrays. In this chapter, you will learn about one-dimensional arrays. Then, in a later course, you will literally expand this knowledge into multidimensional arrays.

To get the idea of an array, look at the illustration in Figure 13-1. Here you see a single row of post office boxes as you might find in any common post office lobby. As you know, each box has a post office (P.O.) box number. In Figure 13-1, our P.O. box numbers begin with 0 and go up to some finite number N. How do you locate a given box? By using its P.O. box number, right? However, the P.O. box number has nothing to do with what's inside the box. It is simply used to locate a given box. Of course, the contents of a given box is the mail delivered to that box. The reason the postal service uses the P.O. box method is that it provides a convenient, well-organized method of storing and accessing the mail for its postal customers. An array does the same thing in a computer program; it provides a convenient, well-organized method of storing and accessing data for you, the programmer. By the way, how many post office boxes are there in Figure 13-1? Because the first box number is 0 and the last is N, there must be $N + 1$ boxes.

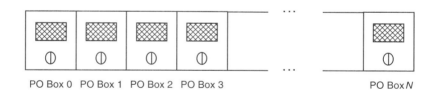

PO Box 0 PO Box 1 PO Box 2 PO Box 3   PO Box N

Figure 13-1 A one-dimensional array is like a row of post office boxes.

You can think of a one-dimensional array, like the one shown in Figure 13-2, as a row of post office boxes. The one-dimensional array consists of a single row of storage locations, each labeled with a number called an ***index***. The data stored at a given index location is referred to as an array ***element***. Thus, a one-dimensional array is a sequential list of storage locations that contain individual data elements that are located, or accessed, via indices.

INDICES

Figure 13-2   A one-dimensional array, or list, is a sequential list of storage locations that contain data elements that are located via indices.

The two major components of any array are the elements stored in the array and the indices that locate the stored elements. Don't get these two array components confused! Although array elements and indices are related, they are completely separate quantities, just as the contents of a post office box is something different from its P.O. box number. With this in mind, let's explore array elements and indices a bit further.

The Array Elements

The elements of an array are the data stored in the array. These elements can be any type of data that you have seen so far. Thus, a given array can store integer elements, floating-point elements, character, and Boolean elements. In addition to these standard data-type elements, an array can also be used to store objects. In fact, the elements in an array even can be other arrays. However, there is one major restriction that applies to the array elements: *The elements in a given array all must be of the same data type or class.*

As you will see shortly, arrays must be defined before they can be used to store data in a Java program. Part of the definition is to specify the type or class of the elements that the array will store. Once a given array is defined for a certain data type or class, only elements of that type or class can be stored in that array.

The Array Indices

The array indices locate the array elements. In Java, the compiler automatically assigns integer indices to the array element list beginning with index [0]. So, the first element of the array in Figure 13-2 is located at index [0], and the last element is located at index [N]. The indices begin with 0 and go to N, so there must be $N + 1$ elements in the array. Also, because this is a one-dimensional array, or **list**, we say that it has a ***dimension*** of $1 \times (N + 1)$, meaning that there is one row of $N + 1$ elements. The dimension of an array indicates the size of the array, just as the dimension of a piece of lumber indicates its size.

Quick Check

1. The two major components of an array are the _____ and _____.

2. True or false: The elements within a given array can be any combination of data types.

3. Suppose the last element of a Java array is located at index [10]. What is the dimension of the array?

13-2 DEFINING ONE-DIMENSIONAL ARRAYS IN JAVA

All arrays in Java must be defined. In order to define an array, you must specify three things:

1. The data type or class of the array elements.
2. The name of the array.
3. The size of the array.

Here's the general format:

ONE-DIMENSIONAL ARRAY DEFINITION FORMAT

element data type or class **[ ]** *array name* **=**
new *element data type or class* **[***number of array elements***]**;

The first thing you see in the definition is the data type or class of the array elements. This is followed by empty square brackets, [], to indicate an array definition. Then comes the array identifier, or name, which is followed by an equals symbol and the keyword **new**. The element type or class follows **new**, followed by the number of elements that the array will store enclosed within square brackets. A semicolon terminates the definition. For instance, the following code defines an array of 10 characters whose name is *characters*.

char[] characters = new char[10];

Example 13-1

Write definitions for the following arrays:

a. An array called *integers* that will store 10 integers.
b. An array called *reals* that will store 5 double floating-point values.
c. An array called *characters* that will store 11 characters.
d. An array called *strings* that will store 15 string objects.

Solution

a. int[] integers = new int[10];
b. double[] reals = new double[5];
c. char[] characters = new char[11];
d. String[] strings = new String[15];

Each definition should be fairly self-explanatory, except perhaps the *strings* array definition. In this definition, the class of the array is *String*. Thus, the definition specifies that the *strings* array will store 15 string objects.

 Quick Check

1. Define an array called *testScores* that will store up to 15 decimal test scores.

2. What is the dimension of the array in question 1?

3. What is the index of the first element of the array in question 1?

4. What is the index of the last element of the array in question 1?

5. Suppose that the index of the last element in an array is [25]. How many elements will the array store?

13-3 ACCESSING ONE-DIMENSIONAL ARRAYS

Accessing the array means to insert elements into the array for storage or to get stored elements from the array.

Inserting Elements into One-Dimensional Arrays

There are basically three major ways to insert elements into an array: by using a *direct assignment* statement, by *reading*, or by using *loops*.

Direct Assignment

Here's the general format for inserting an element into an array using a direct assignment:

> ### DIRECT ASSIGNMENT FORMAT (INSERTING ARRAY ELEMENTS)
>
> *array name* [*array index*] *= element value*;

Using the following array definitions,

```
char[] characters = new char[6];
int[] integers = new int[3];
```

direct assignments might go something like this:

```
characters[0] = 'H';
characters[5] = '$';
integers[0] = 16;
integers[2] = –22;
```

In each of these instances, an element is placed in the first and last storage positions of the respective array. The character 'H' is placed in the first position of the *characters* array, and a dollar sign is placed in the last position of this array. Recall that the first position of an array is always [0], and the last array position is always one less than the array size. The integer 16 is placed in the first position of the *integers* array, and the integer –22 placed in the last position of this array.

Observe that the respective array name is listed, followed by the array index within brackets. An assignment operator (=) is then used, followed by the element to be inserted. The data type or class of the element being inserted should be the same as the data type or class defined for the array elements; otherwise, you could get unpredictable results when working with the array elements.

DEBUGGING TIP

Remember that Java array indices are integer values. This means that any specified index is converted to its integer equivalent. For instance, you can specify an index as a character, like this: *array*['A']; however, Java sees this as *array*[65], because the integer equivalent of the character 'A' is 65 from the UNICODE/ASCII character set. To avoid confusion and potential problems, we suggest that you always use integer values for your indices, unless the application specifically dictates otherwise.

Reading Elements into the Array

You can also use any of the methods found in the *keyboardInput* package to insert array elements from a keyboard entry, like this:

```
characters[1] = in.readChar();
integers[0] = in.readInt();
```

Here, the user must type the respective array element value on the keyboard and press the **ENTER** key to execute each statement. A character should be entered for the first statement and an integer for the second statement. (Why?) The character entered from the keyboard will be stored in the second position (index [1]) of the *characters* array, whereas the integer entered from the keyboard will be stored in the first position (index [0]) of the *integers* array.

Inserting Array Elements Using Loops

The obvious disadvantage to using direct assignments to insert array elements is that a separate assignment statement is required to fill each array position. You can automate the insertion process by using a loop structure. Although any of the three loop structures (**while**, **do/while**, **for**) can be employed, the **for** structure is the most common. Here's the general format for using a **for** loop:

INSERTING INTO A ONE-DIMENSIONAL ARRAY USING A for *LOOP*

```
for (int index = 0; index < array size;  ++index)
        assign or read to array[index]
```

Consider the following program:

```
//FILLING AN ARRAY USING A FOR LOOP
import keyboardInput.*;          //FOR readInt()

public class Test
{
  //DECLARE ARRAY SIZE
  static final int SIZE = 10;
  public static void main(String[] args)
  {
    int[] sample = new int[SIZE];        //DEFINE INTEGER ARRAY
    Keyboard in = new Keyboard();        //DEFINE KEYBOARD OBJECT

    //INSTRUCTIONS TO USER
    System.out.println("Enter a list of " + SIZE +" elements and press"
                        + " the ENTER key after each entry.");

    //READ ELEMENTS FROM KEYBOARD INTO THE ARRAY
    for (int index = 0; index < SIZE; ++index)
        sample[index] = in.readInt();
  } //END main()
}//END Test
```

First, you see a constant called *SIZE* declared. Notice where *SIZE* is used in the program. It is the array-size value and the final counter value in the **for** loop. Using a constant like this allows you to change the size of the array easily. Here, the array size is 10 elements. To change the size of the array, you only need to make a change one place in the program under the constant declaration.

Next, look at the array definition. The array *sample* is defined as an array of integer elements. The user is told to "Enter a list of *SIZE* (where *SIZE* is 10) values and press the **ENTER** key after each entry." Once this prompt is displayed, the program enters a **for** loop. The loop counter variable is *index*, which ranges from 0 to *SIZE*. When the loop counter reaches the value of *SIZE*, the loop is broken, because the loop test is *index* < *SIZE*. It is important to use the "less than" (<) test here rather than the "less than or equal to" (<=) test; otherwise, the loop will execute one too many times. (Why?) The loop counter is employed as the index value for the array. With each loop iteration, a single *readInt()* statement is executed to insert an element into the array at the respective position specified by the loop counter, *index*.

Let's analyze the *readInt()* statement. First, the identifier *sample* is listed with the loop counter variable *index* as the array index in brackets. What does *index* do with each loop iteration? It increments from 0 to *SIZE*, right? As a result, the first loop iteration reads a value into *sample*[0], the second iteration reads a value into *sample*[1], and so on, until the last loop iteration reads a value into the last array position *sample*[*SIZE* − 1]. When the loop counter increments to the value of *SIZE* at the end of the last loop iteration, the loop is broken and no more elements are inserted into the array. That's all there is to it! The array is filled!

You can also use loops for assigning values to array elements. For instance, using the foregoing definitions, consider this loop:

```
for (int index = 0; index < SIZE; ++index)
    sample[index] = 2 * index;
```

This time, the array elements are assigned twice the loop counter value with each loop iteration. What values are actually inserted into the array? How about the 10 even integers from 0 through 18?

DEBUGGING TIP

Be careful not to specify an array index that is out of bounds. Such an index would be one that is less than zero or greater than the maximum index value. For example, suppose that you define an array like this:

```
int[] array = new int[SIZE];
```

A common mistake using this definition would be to attempt to access the element *array*[*SIZE*]. However, remember that array indices in Java begin with 0; therefore, *SIZE* specifies one position beyond the maximum index value of the array. The maximum index in this array is [*SIZE* − 1]. In a loop situation, the following loop statement would create an out of bounds error:

```
for (int index = 0; index <= SIZE; ++index)
    System.out.println( array[index]);
```

Again, the last loop iteration specifies an array index of [*SIZE*], which is out of the index range. To prevent this error, the test must be *index* < *SIZE*. Of course, the test could also be *index* <= *SIZE* − 1, but this is a bit more awkward. When an array index is out of bounds, you *will not* get a compiler error. Java will throw an exception and, if not caught, your program will crash. So, be safe and make sure that your indices are always within their specified bounds.

Extracting Elements from One-Dimensional Arrays

First, let me caution you that the word *extract* is not a good term here. Why? Because, in general, the word *extract* means to remove something. When we extract an element from an array, we don't actually remove it! We simply *copy* its value. The element remains stored in the array until it is replaced by another value using an insertion operation. As with insertion, you can extract array elements using one of three general methods: *direct assignment*, *writing*, or *looping*.

Direct Assignment

Extracting array elements using assignment statements is just the reverse of inserting elements using an assignment statement. Here's the general format:

> ### *DIRECT ASSIGNMENT FORMAT (EXTRACTING ARRAY ELEMENTS)*
> *variable identifier* **=** *array name* **[***array index***]**;

As an example, suppose we make the following definitions:

```
static final int SIZE = 10;
int[] sample = new int[SIZE];
int value = 0;
```

As you can see, the array *sample[ ]* consists of 10 integer elements. Now, assuming the array has been filled, what do you think the following statements do?

```
value = sample[0];
value = sample[SIZE − 1];
value = sample[3] * sample[5];
value = 2 * sample[2] − 3 * sample[7];
```

The first statement assigns the element stored in the first array position to the variable *value*. The second statement assigns the element stored in the last array position to the variable *value*. The third statement assigns the product of the elements located at indices [3] and [5] to *value*. Finally, the fourth statement assigns two times the element at index [2] minus three times the element at index [7] to *value*. The last two statements illustrate how arithmetic operations can be performed using array elements.

In all of the foregoing cases, the array element values are not affected by the assignment operations. The major requirement is that *value* should be defined as the same data type as the array elements so that you don't get unexpected results.

As a final example, consider these assignment statements:

```
sample[0] = sample[SIZE – 1];
sample[1] = sample[2] + sample[3];
```

Can you determine what will happen here? In the first statement, the first array element is replaced by the last array element. Is the last array element affected? No, because it appears on the right side of the assignment operator. In the second case, the second array element at index [1] is replaced by the sum of the third and fourth array elements at indices [2] and [3]. Again, the third and fourth array elements are not affected by this operation, because they appear on the right side of the assignment operator.

Writing Array Elements

A *print()* or *println()* statement can be used to display array elements. Let's use the same array to demonstrate how to write array elements. Here's the array definition again:

```
static final int SIZE = 10;
int[] sample = new int[SIZE];
```

Now what do you suppose the following statements will do?

```
System.out.println(sample[0]);
System.out.println(sample[SIZE – 1]);
System.out.println(sample[1] / sample[2]);
System.out.println(Math.sqrt(sample[6]));
```

The first statement will display the element contained at index [0] of the array. The second statement will display the last element of the array, located at index [*SIZE* – 1]. The third statement will divide the element located at index [1] by the element located at index [2] and display the integer quotient. Finally, the fourth statement will display the square root of the element located at index [6]. None of the array element values is affected by these operations.

Extracting Array Elements Using Loops

As with inserting elements into an array, extracting array elements using loops requires less coding, especially when extracting multiple elements. Again, any of the loop structures can be used for this purpose, but **for** loops are the most common.

Consider the following program:

```
//DISPLAYING AN ARRAY USING A FOR LOOP
public class Test
{
  //DECLARE ARRAY SIZE
  static final int SIZE = 10;

  public static void main(String[] args)
  {
    //DEFINE ARRAY
    int[] sample = new int[SIZE];

    //FILL ARRAY WITH SQUARE OF INDEX
    for (int index = 0; index < SIZE; ++index)
        sample[index] = index * index;

    //DISPLAY ARRAY ACROSS MONITOR
    for (int index = 0; index < SIZE; ++index)
        System.out.print(sample[index] + "\t");
  } //END main()
}//END Test
```

Here again, the array is defined as an array of *SIZE* (10) integer values. The array name is *sample*. Notice that the loop counter variable *index* is used as the array index in both **for** loops. The first loop will fill the array locations with the square of the loop counter. Then, the second loop will display each of the array elements located from index [0] to index [*SIZE* – 1]. A *print()* statement is used to display the array elements horizontally across the face of the display. Notice also that each time an element is displayed, a tab is written after the element to separate it from the next sequential element. Here is what you would see on the display:

0   1   4   9   16   25   36   49   64   81

Quick Check

1. Write a **for** loop that will fill the following array from user entries:

    char[] characters = new char[15];

2. Write a **for** loop that will display the contents of the array in question 1 across the screen, separated by tabs.

13-4 PASSING ARRAYS AND ARRAY ELEMENTS TO METHODS

You can pass an entire array to a method or pass single array elements to a method. The important thing to remember is that to pass the entire array, you must pass the address of the array. In Java, *the array name represents the address of the first element (index* [0]*) of the array*. So, by passing the array name you are passing the address of the array. Let's begin by looking at the required method signature. Here is typical signature for passing a one-dimensional array to a method:

void weird(char[] array)

Looking at the signature, you see that the method does not return a value. There is one character array parameter called *array*. The single set of square brackets after the data type indicates that the parameter is a one-dimensional array. Now, the array identifier "references" the address of the array, so the array is passed **by reference** to the method. A pass by reference means that you are passing the *address* of a variable or data structure to the method. Thus, any operations on the array within the method will affect the original array contents in the calling program because the method is operating on the data stored at the array address. Up to this point, you have been passing variables to methods **by value**. A pass by value passes a *copy* of the variable to the method. As a result, any operations on the variable within the method do not affect its original value because the method is simply operating on a copy.

> Passing a variable by **value** passes a copy of the variable to a method. Any operations on the variable within the method do not affect the original value of the variable within the calling program. In Java, all variables are passed by value to methods. In Java, an array is passed by **reference** to a method. A pass by reference passes the address of the array to the method. Thus, any operations on the array within the method affect the original array values in the calling program.

Next, to call this method and pass the array, you simply use the following statement:

weird(name);

Of course, this call assumes that *name* is a character array in the calling program. (Remember that the actual argument identifier and the formal parameter identifier *can be and are often* different.) The call to *name* references the address of the array, so the array address is passed to the method rather than a copy of the array. Thus, any operations on the array within the method will affect the original array elements. Here's a complete program:

```
//PASSING AN ARRAY TO A METHOD
public class SpaceOdyssey
{
  //DECLARE ARRAY SIZE
  static final int SIZE = 3;

  public static void main(String[] args)
  {
    //DEFINE CHARACTER ARRAY
    char[] name = new char[SIZE];

    //FILL name[] ARRAY WITH CHARACTERS
    name[0] = 'I';
    name[1] = 'B';
    name[2] = 'M';
```

```
    //DISPAY ARRAY BEFORE METHOD CALL
    System.out.print("The contents of name[] before weird() is:  ");
    for(int index = 0;index < SIZE;++index)
        System.out.print(name[index]);

    //CALL METHOD weird()
    weird(name);

    //DISPLAY ARRAY AFTER METHOD CALL
    System.out.print("\nThe contents of name[] after weird() is:  ");
    for(int index = 0;index < SIZE;++index)
        System.out.print(name[index]);
  } //END main()

 //THIS METHOD DECREMENTS EACH OF THE ARRAY ELEMENTS
static public void weird(char[] array)
{
  for (int index = 0; index < SIZE; ++index)
     --array[index];
} //END weird()
}//END SpaceOdyssey
```

The array *name[ ]* is defined as an array of characters and filled using direct assignment with the characters 'I', 'B', 'M' in *main()*. The characters stored in the array are displayed on the monitor using a **for** loop. Then, method *weird()* is called using the array name, *name*, as its argument. This passes the array to method *weird()*, where each of the elements in the array is decremented. After the method call, the array elements are displayed again. What do you suppose the user will see on the monitor after executing the program? Well, this is why things are "weird."

The contents of name[] before weird() is: IBM

The contents of name[] after weird() is: HAL

The point here is that the decrement operation within the method affected the original array elements. Thus, the word *IBM* was converted to the word *HAL*. Is there anything weird here? Recall that HAL was the artificially intelligent computer in the book and movie *2001: A Space Odyssey*. Is there a message here or is this just a coincidence? You will have to ask the author, Arthur Clarke, to find out.

One final point: You cannot pass the entire array by value to a method. If you do not want operations within the method to affect the array elements, you must pass the array to the method, make a temporary local copy of the array within the method using a **for** loop, and then operate on this temporary array.

DEBUGGING TIP

You must use the array bracket syntax within the method signature when passing an array to a method. Thus, to pass a character array to method *weird()*, the signature becomes

void weird(char[] array)

and not

void weird(char array)   //THIS IS AN ERROR

It is a common error to leave off the [ ] syntax. Also, when calling a method and providing an array argument, you *do not* use the [ ] syntax. Rather, you simply provide the array name as the method argument like this:

weird(name);

A common mistake is to call the method using the [ ] syntax as follows

weird(name[ ]);   //THIS IS AN ERROR

Passing Individual Array Elements to Methods

You can also pass individual array elements to a method. Look at the following method signature:

void passByValue(int arrayElement)

The signature says that the method does not return any value and expects to receive a simple integer value from the calling program. Suppose the method were called as follows:

passByValue(scores[0]);

Notice that the actual argument in the method call is *scores*[0]. This will cause a copy of the element stored at index [0] in the *scores[ ]* array to be passed to the method by value. As a result, any operations on this element within the method will not affect the element value in the original *scores[ ]* array. Note that *scores* is the beginning address of the entire array in memory, while *scores*[0] is the single character stored at [0] of the array.

PROBLEM SOLVING IN ACTION: ARRAY PROCESSING USING A STRUCURED VERSUS AN OBJECT-ORIENTED APPROACH

In this case study, we will solve a problem using both a structured and object-oriented approach to programming. The structured approach will employ static methods, using *main()* to define an array and pass the array and other data to and from the methods as required. The object-oriented approach will employ a class to hold the array and its associated methods, then use *main()* to define a class object and call the required class methods. As you will see, the object-oriented approach will require less passing of data to/from the methods because of the tight binding between the class data and its methods.

Problem

Write a program that uses an array to store a maximum of 25 test scores and calculate their average. Use one method to fill the array with the scores, a second method to calculate the average, and a third method to display all the scores along with the calculated average.

A Structured Approach

Defining the Problem

We will begin by developing the signatures for the required methods. Let's call the three methods *setScores()*, *average()*, and *displayResults()*. Now, the *setScores()* method must obtain the test scores from the user and place them in an array. Thus, the method must accept the array structure and return the array containing the test scores. This leads to the following method interface description:

Method *setScores()*:   Obtains test scores from user and places them in an array.

Accepts: A floating-point array, the number of scores to enter, and an object of the *Keyboard* class.

Returns: The array filled with scores entered by the user.

The method signature requires that it must accept and return the array structure. Let's assume that the test scores will be decimal values and, therefore, require a floating-point array. In addition, the method must know the number of scores that will be entered. We will obtain this value from the user prior to the method call, then pass the value to the method. Finally, the method must receive an object of the *Keyboard* class in order to read values from the keyboard. By using these ideas, the method signature becomes:

```
void setScores (double[] scores, int number, Keyboard in)
```

From here, writing the method is easy. We will employ the *readDouble()* method within a **for** loop in the method body to fill the array with the test scores. Here's the entire method:

```
void setScores (double[] scores, int number, Keyboard in)
{
 System.out.println("Enter each score, and press ENTER after each entry.");
 for (int index = 0; index < number; ++index)
 {
   System.out.print("Enter score #" + (index+1) + ": ");
   scores[index] = in.readDouble();
 } //END FOR
} //END setScores()
```

Within the method body you see that the user is prompted to enter each individual score. The scores are entered and placed in the array via a call to the *readDouble()* method within a **for** loop. Notice that the value received by the method for *number* is employed to terminate the **for** loop.

Next, a method called *average()* must be written to average the test scores in the array. This method must accept the array to obtain the test scores along with the number of scores to average. It must return a single floating-point value that is the average of the scores. So, the method interface description is as follows:

Method *average()*:   Computes the average of the test scores.

Accepts: The test scores array and the number of test scores to average.

Returns: A single value that is the average of the test scores.

This time, the array must be passed to the method and the method must return a single value. Therefore, the method signature becomes

```
double average(double[] scores, int number)
```

The body of the method simply adds up all the test scores in the array and divides by their number. Here is the complete method:

```
double average(double[] scores, int number)
{
  double total = 0.0;
  for (int index = 0; index < number; ++index)
    total += scores[index];
  return total/number;
} //END average()
```

There are two local method variables defined: *total* and *index*. The variable *total* will act as a temporary variable to accumulate the sum of the scores, and the variable *index* is the loop counter variable. The variable *total* is first initialized to 0.0. Then the loop is used to obtain the array elements, one at a time, and to add them to *total*. Observe that the loop counter (*index*) acts as the array index within the loop. Thus, the array elements, from index [0] to [*number* − 1], are sequentially extracted with each loop iteration and added to *total*. The last test score is located at index [*number* − 1]. Once the loop calculates the sum total of all the test scores, a **return** statement is used to return the calculated average.

Finally, the *displayResults()* method must display the individual test scores obtained from the user along with their average. To do this, we must pass the array to the method to obtain the test scores along with the number of scores to display. Here's the method description:

Method *displayResults()*: Displays the individual test scores and their average.

Accepts: The test scores array and the number of scores to display

Returns: Nothing.

To display the average, we will simply call the *average()* method within this method as part of a *println()* statement. The entire method then becomes

```
void  displayResults(double[] scores, int number)
{
  System.out.println("\n\nTest scores");
  System.out.println("-----------");
  for (int index = 0; index < number; ++index)
    System.out.println(scores[index]);
  System.out.println("\nThe average of the above scores is:  "
                      + average(scores,number));
} //END displayResults()
```

Again, a **for** loop is employed to display the individual test scores. Notice how the *average()* method is called in the final *println()* statement to calculate the test average.

Coding the Program

Now, putting everything together, we get the following program:

```
//ACTION 13-1  (ACTION13_01.JAVA)
//THIS PROGRAM WILL FILL AN ARRAY WITH SCORES, CALCULATE THE
// AVERAGE AND DISPLAY THE RESULTS

import keyboardInput.*;          //FOR readDouble()

public class Action13_01
{
  //DECLARE ARRAY SIZE
  static final int SIZE = 25;

  public static void main(String[] args)
  {
    //DEFINE SCORES ARRAY
    double[] scores = new double[SIZE];

    //DEFINE NUMBER OF SCORES VARIABLE
    int number = 0;

    //DEFINE FREEZE VARIABLE
    char pause = ' ';
```

```
      //CREATE KEYBOARD OBJECT
      Keyboard in = new Keyboard();

      //DISPLAY PROGRAM DESCRIPTION MESSAGE
      System.out.println("This program will generate obtain test scores, "
                         + "calculate the average and display the results.n\n");

      //GET NUMBER OF SCORES FROM USER
      System.out.print("How many scores do you have to average? ");
      number = in.readInt();

      //CALL METHODS TO GET SCORES AND DISPLAY RESULTS
      setScores(scores, number, in);              //CALL METHOD setScores()
      displayResults(scores, number);             //CALL METHOD displayResults()

      //FREEZE DISPLAY
      System.out.println("Press ENTER to continue.");
      pause = in.readChar();
   } //END main()

   /**************************************************************************

   THIS METHOD WILL GET THE SCORES FROM THE USER
   AND PLACE THEM INTO THE SCORES ARRAY

   **************************************************************************/
   static void setScores (double[] scores, int number, Keyboard in)
   {
    System.out.println("Enter each score, and press ENTER after each entry.");
    for (int index = 0; index < number; ++index)
    {
      System.out.print("Enter score #" + (index+1) + ":  ");
      scores[index] = in.readDouble();
    } //END FOR
   } //END setScores()

   /**************************************************************************

   THIS METHOD WILL RETURN THE AVERAGE OF THE
   SCORES IN THE ARRAY

   **************************************************************************/
   static double average(double[] scores, int number)
   {
     double total = 0.0;
     for (int index = 0; index < number; ++index)
       total += scores[index];
```

```
      return total/number;
   } //END average()

*************************************************************************


THIS METHOD DISPLAYS THE ARRAY SCORES AND THE
FINAL SCORE AVERAGE

*************************************************************************/
   static void  displayResults(double[] scores, int number)
   {
   System.out.println("\n\nTest scores");
   System.out.println("-----------");
   for (int index = 0; index < number; ++index)
     System.out.println(scores[index]);
   System.out.println("\nThe average of the above scores is:  "
                      + average(scores,number));
   } //END displayResults()
}//END Action13_01
```

As you can see, a constant (*SIZE*) is first declared. This will be the maximum number of elements in the array. Now, look at the statement section of *main()*. Are you surprised at its simplicity? Method *main()* is relatively short, because all the work is done in the other methods. All *main()* does is call the two other methods in the order that they are needed. You see that at the beginning of *main()*, a variable called *number* is defined to hold the actual number of test scores entered by the user. This value will be passed to the methods as needed. Then, the array, called *scores[]*, is defined as an array of *SIZE*, or 25, floating-point elements. The array name is *scores,* so this identifier must be used when accessing the array. After the array is defined, the *setScores()* method is called, followed by the *displayResults()* method. Observe that, in both cases, both the *scores[]* array and *number* are passed to the method by listing their names as the method arguments. The method *setScores()* is first called to obtain the scores from the user and to insert them into the array. Next, the method *displayResults()* is called. Again, the test scores array, *scores[]*, and the number of scores, *number*, are passed to the method by listing their respective names as arguments in the method call. This method displays the test scores from the array and calls the *average()* method to return the calculated test average. Here, we have designated the methods as **static** so that they can be called without an object reference.

An Object-Oriented Approach

Defining the Problem

Another way to approach this problem, rather than using static methods, is to use an object-oriented approach and place the array and its methods within a class. The specification for such a class is as follows:

> Class: *Scores*
>> Data Members: *scores array*
>>> *number of scores*
>
>> Method Members: *setScores()*
>>> *average()*
>>> *displayResults()*

When using an object-oriented approach, we always try to first visualize the class composition and its interface developed in the class specification via a class diagram like the one shown in Figure 13-3.

Here, you see a *Scores* class which consists of a private *scores[]* array, a private member to store the number of scores in the array, *number*, and a private utility method, called *average()*, to determine the average of the scores in the array. The public interface consists of a class constructor, a method to set the scores from user entries, *setScores()*, and a method to display the scores and their average, *displayResults()*.

Once the class specification is established, we need to determine the method interfaces, or signatures. First, the *setScores()* simply gets scores from the user and places them in the private array member of the class. Here is its interface description:

Method *setScores()*:   Obtains test scores from user and places them in an array.

Accepts: Nothing

Returns: Nothing

Wow, what a simple interface! Why is nothing being passed to/from the method? Well, the array itself is a private class member, as well as the number of scores held in the array. Remember, if a class method operates directly on a private member of its class, the private member does not get passed to or from the method. This is the great thing about classes! Because of the tight binding between the data and methods of a class, you do not need to pass the class data to/from class methods.

> If a class method operates directly on a private member of its class, the private member does not get passed to or from the method because of the tight binding between the class data and its methods.

So, based on the method interface description, our *setScores()* signature becomes

void setScores()

Scores Class

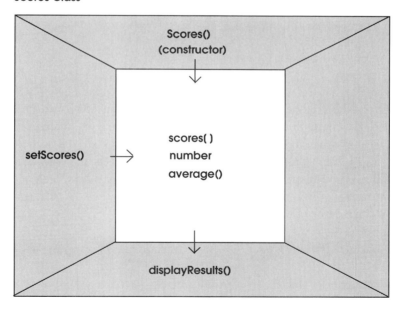

Figure 13-3   The *Scores* class consists of a private *scores[]* array, number of scores in the array, *number*, and utility method, *average()*, to determine the average of the scores in the array. The public interface consists of a constructor, a method to set the scores from user entries, *setScores()*, and a method to display the scores and their average, *displayResults()*.

The body of the method must obtain the number of scores and the scores themselves from the user, setting the class a members to these values. Here's the entire method code:

```
public void setScores ()
{
  //CREATE KEYBOARD OBJECT
  Keyboard in = new Keyboard();

  //GET NUMBER OF SCORES FROM USER
  System.out.print("How many scores do you have to average? ");
  number = in.readInt();

  //FILL ARRAY WITH USER ENTRIES
  System.out.println("Enter each score, and press ENTER after each entry.");
  for (int index = 0; index < number; ++index)
  {
    System.out.print("Enter score #" + (index+1) + ":  ");
    scores[index] = in.readDouble();
  } //END FOR
} //END setScores()
```

Within the method, we must define a *Keyboard* class object, *in*, to read the data entered by the user. We then read the number of scores the user has to enter, then the individual scores the same way we did within our earlier **static** *setScores( )* method.

The next public method we need to define is the *displayResults( )* method. This method displays scores contained in the private scores array and calls the *average( )* utility method to determine the average of the scores. Here is its interface description:

Method *displayResults( )*   Displays the individual test scores and their average.

Accepts: Nothing

Returns: Nothing.

Again, there is nothing to accept because the method has direct access to the *scores* array. Also, there is nothing to return because the method is simply displaying the values. Here is the resulting method signature and body:

```
//METHOD TO DISPLAY RESULTS
public void  displayResults()
{
  System.out.println("\n\nTest scores");
  System.out.println("-----------");
  for (int index = 0; index < number; ++index)
    System.out.println(scores[index]);
  System.out.println("\nThe average of the above scores is:  "
                          + average());
} //END displayResults()
```

Notice that the *average()* method is called in the last line to return the average of the scores stored in the array. The *average()* method will be a private utility method because it does not need to be accessed from outside the class. So, our interface description becomes

Method *average()*:   Computes the average of the test scores.

Accepts: Nothing

Returns: A single value that is the average of the test scores.

Again, the array is not passed (accepted) because it is a private member of the same class as the method. However, the method must return a value to its calling method, since the test average value is not a member of the class. Here is the complete method signature and body:

```
//METHOD TO CALCULATE AVERAGE
private double average()
{
  double total = 0.0;
  for (int index = 0; index < number; ++index)
    total += scores[index];
  return total/number;
} //END average()
```

Now that we have determined the class data and method implementations, the class code becomes

```java
class Scores
{
  //DATA MEMBERS
  private final int SIZE = 25;                      //MAXIMUM ARRAY SIZE
  private double[] scores = new double[SIZE];  //ARRAYS OF TEST SCORES
  private int number = 0;                           //NUMBER OF ARRAY SCORES

  //METHOD MEMBERS
  //PARAMETERLESS CONSTRUCTOR
  public Scores()
  {
  }//END Scores()

  //METHOD TO SET THE ARRAY VALUES TO SCORES ENTERED BY USER
  public void setScores ()
  {
    //CREATE KEYBOARD OBJECT
    Keyboard in = new Keyboard();

    //READ NUMBER OF SCORES FROM USER
    System.out.print("How many scores do you have to average? ");
    number = in.readInt();

    //FILL ARRAY WITH USER ENTRIES
    System.out.println("Enter each score, and press ENTER after each entry.");
    for (int index = 0; index < number; ++index)
    {
      System.out.print("Enter score #" + (index+1) + ":  ");
      scores[index] = in.readDouble();
    } //END FOR
  } //END setScores()

  //METHOD TO CALCULATE AVERAGE
  private double average()
  {
    double total = 0.0;
    for (int index = 0; index < number; ++index)
      total += scores[index];
    return total/number;
  } //END average()

  //METHOD TO DISPLAY RESULTS
  public void  displayResults()
  {
```

```
        System.out.println("\n\nTest scores");
        System.out.println("-----------");
        for (int index = 0; index < number; ++index)
          System.out.println(scores[index]);
        System.out.println("\nThe average of the above scores is:  "
                          + average());
    } //END displayResults()
}//END Scores CLASS
```

The class includes all the data and method members just discussed. In addition, we have added a private constant data member for the array size and a parameterless constructor. To use the class, we must create an application class that includes *main()* to define a *Scores* class object and call the class methods. Here is the application class code:

```
public class Action13_02
{
    public static void main(String[] args)
    {
    //DEFINE FREEZE VARIABLE
    char pause = ' ';

    //DEFINE KEYBOARD OBJECT
    Keyboard in = new Keyboard();

    //DEFINE SCORES CLASS OBJECT
    Scores myScores = new Scores();

    //DISPLAY PROGRAM DESCRIPTION MESSAGE
    System.out.println("This program will generate obtain test scores, "
                      + "calculate the average and display the results.n\n");

    //CALL METHODS TO SET ARRAY SCORES, CALCULATE AVERAGE
    //AND DISPLAY RESULTS
    myScores.setScores();              //CALL METHOD setScores()
    myScores.displayResults();         //CALL METHOD displayResults()

    //FREEZE DISPLAY
    System.out.println("Press ENTER to continue.");
    pause = in.readChar();
    } //END main()
}//END Action13_02 CLASS
```

That's it! You should not have any trouble understanding this code. You have just seen both a structured and an object-oriented approach to solving this problem. Now its up to you and, of course, your instructor as to which approach you will use in the future.

You now have all the ingredients you need to write programs using the versatile one dimensional array. Next, you will learn how to search an array for a given element value as well as sort the elements in an array. What follows are some classic searching and sorting algorithms that are important for you to learn, regardless of the programming language that you are using. Of course, we will implement these classic algorithms using the Java language.

 Quick Check

1. True or false: An array name represents the address of index [1] of the array.

2. Write a signature for a method called *sample()* that must accept and alter the following array:

    char[] characters = new char[15];

    Assume that the method does not return any values except the altered array.

3. Write a statement to call the method in question 2 passing the *characters* array to *sample()*.

4. Write a signature for a method called *test()* that will accept a single array element from the array defined in question 2.

5. Write a statement that will call the *test()* method in question 4 to alter the element stored at index [5] of the *characters[]* array defined in question 2.

PROBLEM SOLVING IN ACTION: SEARCHING AN ARRAY USING ITERATION (SEQUENTIAL SEARCH)

Many applications require a program to search for a given element in an array. Two common algorithms used to perform this task are *sequential*, or *serial*, *search* and *binary search*. Sequential search is commonly used for unsorted arrays, and binary search is used on arrays that are already sorted. In this case study, you will learn about sequential search; then in a later case study, you will learn about binary search.

Problem

Develop a method that can be called to sequentially search an array of integers for a given element value and return the index of the element if it is found in the array.

Defining the Problem

Because we are dealing with a method, the problem definition will focus on the method interface. As a result, we must consider what the method will accept and what the method will return. We will assume that the method must receive an array from outside the class in which it resides and, therefore, we must pass the array to the method. Let's call the method *seqSearch()*. Now, from the problem statement, you find that the method must search an array of integers for a given element value. Thus, the method needs two things to do its job: (1) the array to be searched, and (2) the element for which to search. These will be our method parameters.

Next, we need to determine what the method is to return to the calling program. From the problem statement, you see that the method needs to return the index of the element being searched for if it is found in the array. All array indices in Java are integers, so the method will return an integer value. But, what if the element being searched for is not found in the array? We need to return some integer value that will indicate this situation. Because array indices in Java range from 0 to some finite positive integer, let's return the integer −1 if the element is not found in the array. Thus, we will use −1 to indicate the "not-found" condition, because no array index in Java can have this value. Here is the method interface description:

Method *seqSearch()*:	Searches an integer array for a given element value.
Accepts:	An array of integers and the element for which to search.
Returns:	The array index of the element if found, or the value −1 if the element is not found.

The preceding method interface description provides all the information required to write the method signature. Here it is:

int seqSearch (int[] array, int element)

The signature dictates that the method will accept two things: (1) an array of integer elements, and (2) an integer value, called *element*, that will be the value for which to search.

The next task is to develop the sequential search algorithm.

Planning the Solution

Sequential search does exactly what it says: It *sequentially* searches the array, from one element to the next, starting at the first array position and stopping when either the element is found or it reaches the end of the array. Thus, the algorithm must test the element stored in the first array position, then the second array position, then the third, and so on until the element is found or it runs out of array elements. This is obviously a repetitive task of testing an array element, then moving to the next element and testing again, and so on. Consider the following algorithm that employs a **while** loop to perform the repetitive testing operation:

seqSearch( ) **Algorithm**

seqSearch( )
BEGIN
  Set *found* = false.
  Set *index* = first array index.
  While (*element* is not *found*) AND (*index* <= last array index)
    If (*array*[*index*] == *element*)
      Set *found* = true.
    Else
      Increment *index*.
  If (*found* == true)
    Return *index*.
  Else
    Return −1.
END.

The idea here is to employ a Boolean variable, called *found*, to indicate if the element was found during the search. The variable *found* is initialized to false, and a variable called *index* is initialized to the index of the first element in the array. Notice the **while** loop test. Because of the use of the AND operation, the loop will continue as long as the element is not found *and* the value of *index* is less than or equal to the last index value of the array. Another way to say this is that the loop will repeat until the element is found *or* the value of *index* exceeds the last index value of the array. Think about it!

Inside the loop, the value stored at location [*index*] is compared to the value of *element*, received by the method. If the two are equal, the Boolean variable *found* is set to true. Otherwise, the value of *index* is incremented to move to the next array position. When the loop terminates, either the element was found or not found. If the element was found, the value of *found* will be true, and the value of *index* will be the array position, or index, at which the element was found. Thus, if *found* is true, the value of *index* is returned to the calling program. If the element was not found, the value of *found* will still be false from its initialized state, and the value –1 is returned to the calling program. That's all there is to it!

Coding the Program

Here is the Java code that reflects the foregoing algorithm:

```
//ACTION 13-3 (ACTION13_03.JAVA)
int seqSearch(int[] array, int element)
{
  boolean found = false;        //INITIALIZE found TO false
  int index = 0;                //ARRAY INDEX VARIABLE

//SEARCH ARRAY UNTIL FOUND OR REACH END OF ARRAY
  while ((!found) && (index < SIZE))
  {
    if (array[index] == element)    //TEST ARRAY ELEMENT
      found = true;                 //IF EQUAL, SET found TO TRUE
    else                            //ELSE INCREMENT ARRAY INDEX
      ++index;
  } //END WHILE

//IF ELEMENT FOUND, RETURN ELEMENT POSITION IN ARRAY
//ELSE RETURN -1.
  if (found)
    return index;
  else
    return -1;
} //END seqSearch()
```

There should be no surprises in this code. At the top of the method, you see the signature that is identical to the method interface developed earlier.

The **boolean** variable *found* is defined and set to **false**. We will use the variable *index* as our array index variable. This variable is defined as an integer and set to the first array index, [0]. Remember that arrays in Java always begin with index [0]. The **while** loop employs the AND (&&) operator to test the values of *found* and *index*. The loop will repeat as long as the element is not found (*!found*) and the value of *index* is less than the size of the array, *SIZE*. Remember that when the size of the array is *SIZE*, the last array index is [*SIZE* − 1]. So, when *index* exceeds the maximum array index, [*SIZE* − 1], the loop breaks. When the loop is broken, the value of *found* is tested. If *found* is **true**, the value of *index* is returned; if *found* is **false**, the value −1 is returned to indicate that the element was not found in the array.

PROBLEM SOLVING IN ACTION: SORTING AN ARRAY USING ITERATION (INSERTION SORT)

To sort an array means to place the array elements in either ascending or descending order from the beginning to the end of the array. There are many common algorithms used for sorting. There is *insertion sort*, *bubble sort*, *selection sort*, *quick sort*, *merge sort*, and *heap sort*, just to mention a few. In a data structures course, you will most likely learn about and analyze all of these sorting algorithms. In this problem, we will develop the *insertion sort* algorithm and code it as a method in Java.

Problem

Develop a method that can be called to sort an array of characters in ascending order using the *insertion sort* algorithm.

Defining the Problem

Again, we will code the algorithm as a Java method, so the problem definition will focus on the method interface, leading us to the method signature. Let's call our method *insertSort()*. Think about what *insertSort()* needs to do its job. Well, it must receive an unsorted array of characters and return the same array as a sorted array, right? Does it need anything else? No, additional data are not required by the method, because the only thing being operated upon is the array itself.

What about return values? Does the method need to return a single value? The method does not return any single value but must return the sorted array. Therefore, the return type of the method must be **void**, and the array must be a reference parameter, right? Remember that when arrays are passed to Java methods, they are always treated as reference parameters because the array name represents an address in memory. So, here's our *insertSort()* interface description:

Method *insertSort()*:   Sorts an array of characters in ascending order.

Accepts: An unsorted array of characters.

Returns: A sorted array of characters.

From the preceding description, the method interface is easily coded as

```
void insertSort(char[] array)
```

The signature says that *insertSort()* will receive a character array. The return type is **void**, because no single value is returned. However, because the entire array is being passed to the method, any sorting operations on the array within the method will be reflected in the calling program. Of course, if this method were in the same class as the array, the array would not be passed to the method because of their binding relationship. Now for the insertion sort algorithm.

Planning the Solution

Before we set up the algorithm, let's see how insertion sort works. Look at Figure 13-4. We will assume that we are going to sort a five-character array in ascending order. Before getting into the details, look at the figure from top to bottom and from left to right. The unsorted array is shown at the top of the figure, and the sorted array is shown at the bottom of the figure. Notice that shading is employed in the figure to show the sorting process from top to bottom. As we proceed from the unsorted array at the top, the shading increases, showing the portion of the array that is sorted, until the entire array is shaded at the bottom of the figure.

The top-to-bottom sequence shows that we will make four passes through the array to achieve the sorted array shown at the bottom of the figure. With each pass, an element is placed into its sorted position *relative to the elements that occur before it* in the array. The first pass begins with the first element, 'E', sorted as indicated by the shading. The single character 'E' is considered to be sorted by itself, because it does not have any elements preceding it. Thus, the task in this first pass is to sort the second element, 'D', relative to the character 'E' that precedes it.

The second pass begins with the characters 'D' and 'E' sorted, as indicated by the shading. The task in this pass is to sort the third character, 'C', relative to these two characters. In the third pass, the elements 'C', 'D', and 'E' are sorted, and the task is to sort the character 'B' relative to these characters. Remember, in each pass, the task is to sort the first character of the unsorted portion of the array relative to the characters that precede it in the sorted portion of the array. The process continues until all the characters are sorted, as shown at the bottom of the figure. With each pass, you are essentially repeating what was done in the previous pass. As a result, you can identify a repetitive process, from pass to pass, from the top to the bottom of the figure. This repetition will result in a loop structure in our algorithm.

Now, the question is: What happens during each pass to eventually sort the entire array? Well, during each pass, the first element in the unsorted (unshaded) portion of the array is examined by comparing it to the sorted sequence of elements that precede it. If this element is less than the element preceding it, the two elements are exchanged. Once the element is exchanged with its predecessor, it is compared with its new predecessor element. Again, if it is less than its predecessor, the two elements are exchanged.

This process is repeated until one of two things happens: (1) the element is greater than or equal to its predecessor, or (2) the element is in the first position of the array (index [0]). In other words, the left-to-right compare/exchange process shown in Figure 13-4 ceases when the element under examination has been "inserted" into its proper position in the sorted portion of the array. This compare/exchange process represents repetition from left to right in the figure and will result in another loop structure in our algorithm. So, we can identify two repetitive processes in the figure: one from top to bottom and one from left to right. How are the two repetitive processes related? Well, it seems that for each top-to-bottom pass through the array, the compare/exchange process is executed from left to right. Thus, the left-to-right process must be nested within the top-to-bottom process. This will be reflected in our algorithm by two loop structures: one controlling the left-to-right compare/exchange process that must be nested inside a second loop controlling the top-to-bottom process. Look at the figure again to make sure that you see this nested repetition. Now that you have an idea of how insertion sort works, here is the formal algorithm:

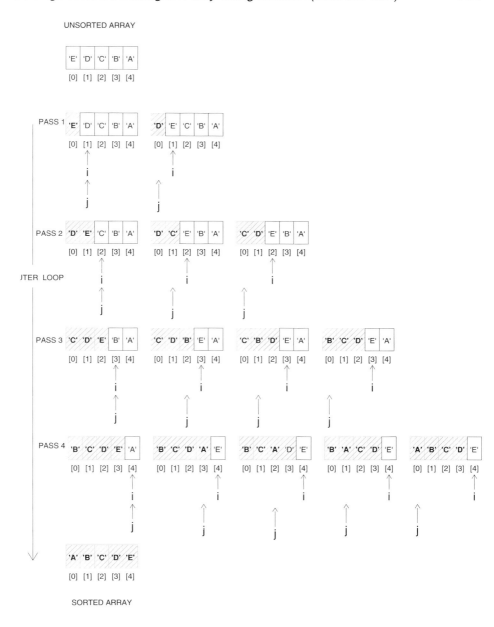

Figure 13-4   Insertion sort is a nested repetition process.

insertSort() **Algorithm**

insertSort()
BEGIN
  Set i = second array index.
  While (i <= last array index)
    Set $j = i$.
    While ((j > first array index) AND (*array*[j] < *array*[$j - 1$]))
      Exchange *array*[j] and *array*[$j - 1$].
      Decrement j.
    Increment i.
END.

    The variables i and j in the algorithm correspond to the i and j shown in Figure 13-4. The variable i controls the outer loop, and j controls the inner loop. Notice that i begins at the second array index. Why not the first array index? Because the first element in the array is always sorted relative to any preceding elements, right? So, the first pass begins with the second array element. The first statement in the outer loop sets j equal to i. Thus, both i and j locate the first element in the unsorted portion of the array at the beginning of each pass. Now, the inner loop will exchange the element located by j, which is *array*[j], with its predecessor element, which is *array*[$j - 1$], as long as j is greater than the first array index *and* element *array*[j] is less than element *array*[$j- 1$]. Once the exchange is made, j is decremented. This forces j to follow the element being inserted into the sorted portion of the array. The exchanges continue until either there are no elements preceding element *array*[j] that are less than element *array*[j] or the element is inserted into the first element position.

    Once the inner loop is broken, element *array*[j] is inserted into its correct position relative to the elements that precede it. Then, another pass is made by incrementing the outer loop control variable i, setting j to i, and executing the inner loop again. This nested looping process continues until i is incremented past the last array position.

    Study the preceding algorithm and compare it to Figure 13-4 until you are sure that you understand *insertSort()*. Now for the Java code.

Coding the Program

We have already developed the *insertSort()* method interface. The algorithm is easily coded as a method in Java, like this:

```
//ACTION 13-4  (ACTION013_04.JAVA)
void insertSort(char[] array)
{
  int i;                   //OUTER LOOP CONTROL VARIABLE
  int j;                   //INNER LOOP CONTROL VARIABLE
  char temp;               //CREATE TEMPORARY VARIABLE
  //SET i TO SECOND ARRAY INDEX
  i = 1;
    //MAKE SIZE - 1 PASSES THRU ARRAY
  while (i < SIZE)
  {
     //j LOCATES FIRST ELEMENT OF UNSORTED ARRAY PORTION
     j = i;

     //COMPARE/EXCHANGE array[j] AND array[j - 1]
     while ((j > 0) && (array[j] < array[j - 1]))
     {
        //EXCHANGE ARRAY ELEMENTS
        temp = array[j];
        array[j] = array[j-1];
        array[j-1] = temp;
        //MAKE j FOLLOW INSERT ELEMENT
        --j;
     }//END INNER WHILE
     //MAKE i LOCATE FIRST ELEMENT OF UNSORTED PORTION
     ++i;
  }//END OUTER WHILE
}//END insertSort()
```

The *insertSort()* code should be straightforward from the algorithm that we just analyzed. Study the code and compare it to the algorithm. You will find that they are identical from a logical and structural point of view.

13-5 INITIALIZING ARRAYS

Before leaving this chapter, you need to know how to initialize arrays at the time they are defined. Arrays, like variables, can be initialized when they are created. The initializing values can be supplied for any array, wherever the array is defined in the program. Let's consider some example array definitions to illustrate how arrays can be initialized.

int[] integers = {10,20,30};

In this definition, an integer array of three elements has been defined. The three integer elements have been initialized to the values 10, 20, and 30, respectively. Notice the syntax. The array definition is followed by an assignment operator, which is followed by the initialization values enclosed within curly braces. Here is what you would see if you inspected the array using a debugger:

DEBUGGER RESULTS

Inspecting *integers*

[0]   10
[1]   20
[2]   30

As you can see, the first initialization value, 10, is placed at index [0] of the array, the value 20 is placed at index [1], and the value 30 is placed at the last index position, which is [2]. With this definition, the compiler will set aside enough storage to hold all the initialization values.

Next, let's consider character arrays. Suppose that you define a character array with initializing values, like this:

char[] characters = {'H','E','L','L','O'};

Again you see that the initialization values are enclosed in curly braces after an assignment operator. Here is what a debugger would reveal:

DEBUGGER RESULTS

Inspecting *characters*

[0]   'H'
[1]   'E'
[2]   'L'
[3]   'L'
[4]   'O'

You see here that the five initialization characters are placed in the array starting at index [0] and ending at the last index position, [4].

Finally, let's consider how to initialize string arrays with string values. Here is how a string array can be initialized with a string values:

String[] strings= {"Bob","Sally","Gayle","Andy"};

Here is what you would see stored in memory via a debugger:

DEBUGGER RESULTS

Inspecting *strings*

   [0]   "Bob"
   [1]   "Sally"
   [2]   "Gayle"
   [3]   "Andy"

Default Initialization of Arrays

If you define an array and don't provide any initialization values, Java will initialize the array with the respective default value (zeros for integer and floating-point arrays, and blanks for character arrays). For instance, suppose you define an integer array and a character array as follows:

int [] integers = new int[5];
char[] characters = new char[5];

Inspecting these arrays with a debugger would reveal the following:

DEBUGGER RESULTS

Inspecting *integers*   Inspecting *characters*

   [0]   0   [0]   ' '
   [1]   0   [1]   ' '
   [2]   0   [2]   ' '
   [3]   0   [3]   ' '
   [4]   0   [4]   ' '

Here is a summary of the foregoing discussion:

- Integer, floating-point, and character arrays are initialized by using an assignment operator after the array definition, followed by a listing of the individual initializing values within curly braces.
- String arrays can be initialized with strings by enclosing the strings within double quotes.
- Arrays are always initialized with the respective default values when no initialization values are supplied in the array definition. The default value for integer and floating-point arrays is zero. The default value for character arrays is a blank.

 Quick Check

1. Define an array called *values[]* and initialize it with the integer values −3 through +3.

2. What is the dimension of the array that you defined in question 1?

3. Define an array called *family[]* and initialize it with the first names of your family members.

4. Suppose that you define a floating-point array without any initializing values. What does the compiler store in the array?

5. Suppose that you define a character array without any initializing values. What does the compiler store in the array?

CHAPTER SUMMARY

An array is an important data structure used to locate and store elements of a given data type or class. The two components of any array are the elements that are stored in the array and the indices that locate the stored elements. Array elements can be any given data type or class, and array indices are always integers ranging from [0] to [*SIZE* − 1], where *SIZE* is the size of the array.

There are both one-dimensional arrays and multidimensional arrays. A one-dimensional array (list or vector) is a single row of elements and has a dimension of $1 \times SIZE$, where *SIZE* is the number of elements in the list. In Java, the maximum index in any dimension is the size of the dimension (*SIZE*) minus 1.

Arrays can be initialized when they are defined by assigning initializing values and listing them within curly braces. When no initializing values are supplied, integer and floating-point arrays are initialized with zeros and character arrays are initialized with blanks.

To access array elements, you must use direct assignment statements, read/write statements, or loops. The **for** loop structure is the most common way of accessing multiple array elements.

Searching and sorting are common operations performed on arrays. *Sequential search* is an iterative search that looks for a given value in an array by sequentially comparing the value to the array elements, beginning with the first array element, until the value is found in the array or until the end of the array is reached.

Many real-world applications require that information be sorted. There are several common sorting algorithms, including *insertion sort*, *bubble sort*, *selection sort*, and *quick sort*. All of these algorithms operate on arrays. The insertion sort algorithm is an iterative process that inserts a given element in the array in its correct place relative to the elements that precede it in the array. You will be acquainted with bubble sort and selection sort in the chapter problems.

QUESTIONS AND PROBLEMS

Questions

1. What three things must be specified in order to define an array?

Use the following array definition to answer questions 2–7.

```
char[] characters = new char[15];
```

2. What is the index of the first array element?

3. What is the index of the last array element?

4. Write a statement that will place the character 'Z' in the third cell of the array.

5. Write a statement that will display the last array element.

6. Write the code necessary to fill the array from keyboard entries. Make sure to prompt the user before each character entry.

7. Write a loop that will display all the array elements vertically on the screen.

8. Show the contents of the following array:

   ```
   int[] integers = {1,2,3};
   ```

9. What is an out-of-bounds error, and how does Java handle it?

10. Write a statement to define a floating-point array of dimension $1 \times SIZE$ that will be initialized with all zeros.

11. Write a statement to define a character array of dimension $1 \times SIZE$ that will be initialized with all blanks.

12. What is wrong with the following definition?

    ```
    int numbers = {0,1,2,3,4};
    ```

13. Given the following array definition:

    ```
    int[] values = new int[10];
    ```

    Write a statement to place the product of the first and second array elements in the last element position.

Use the following array definition to answer questions 14–16:

   ```
   String[] languages = {"Java","C++","COBOL","Visual Basic"};
   ```

14. Write the signature for a method called *stringLength()* that will receive the entire array and return the length of any string object in the array.

15. Write an implementation for method *stringLength()* that would be required to return the length of the last string in the array.

16. Write a *println()* statement to call the method in question 15 and pass the *languages* array to the method.

17. Write a signature for a method called *changeCharacters()* that will receive a character array.

18. Write a statement to call the method in question 17 and pass an array called *characters[ ]* to the method.

19. In general, what element position will be returned by the sequential search method developed in this chapter if there are multiple occurrences of the element in the array?

20. Revise the *insertSort()* algorithm to sort the array in descending order.

Problems

Least Difficult

1. Write a program to fill an array with all the odd integers from 1 to 99. Write one method to fill the array and another method to display the array, showing the odd integers across the screen separated by commas. Test your methods via an application program.

2. Write a method to read the user's name from a keyboard entry and place it in a string array. Use one string to hold the user's first name, another to hold the user's middle initial, and a third to hold the user's last name. Write another method to display the user's name stored in the array. Test your methods via an application program.

3. Write a program to read a list of 25 character elements from a keyboard entry and display them in reverse order. Use one method to fill the list with the entered elements and another method to display the list. Test your methods via an application program.

4. Write a program that uses a string array to store the user's name, street address, city, state, zip code, and telephone number. Provide one method to fill the array and another to display the array contents using proper addressing format. Test your methods via an application program.

More Difficult

5. Write an application program to test the *seqSearch()* method developed in this chapter. Use the *random()* method available in the *Math* class to fill an array with random integer values from 0 to 100 prior to applying *seqSearch()*. For example, the following code will generate *SIZE* random integers between 0 and 100 and place them in an array called *values*:

    ```
    for (int index = 0;index < SIZE; ++index)
        values[index] = (int)(Math.random()*100);
    ```

    Remember that *random()* generates random values between 0 and 1. Therefore, you must scale the range by a factor of 100 to generate values between 0 and 100. Also, notice that you must provide an (int) type cast in order to fill an integer array, because *random()* returns floating-point values.

6. Create a GUI for the *Scores* class given in this chapter.

Most Difficult

7. Another common iterative sorting algorithm is ***bubble sort***. Here's the algorithm:

bubbleSort()
BEGIN
    Set passes = 1.
    Set exchange = true.
    While (passes < number of array elements) AND (exchange == true)
       Set exchange = false.
       For index = (first array index) To (last array index – passes)
         If array[index] > array[index + 1]
            Swap(array[index], array[index + 1]).
            Set exchange = true.
       Set passes = passes + 1.
END.

The bubble sort algorithm makes several passes through the array, comparing adjacent values during each pass. The adjacent values are exchanged if the first value is larger than the second value. The process terminates when $N - 1$ passes have been made (where N is the number of elements in the array) or when no more exchanges are possible.

    Your job is to code the previous algorithm as a Java method called *bubbleSort().* In addition, you will have to code a *swap()* method that can be called by the *bubbleSort()* method to exchange two array elements as shown in the algorithm. Write your methods to sort a character array. Incorporate them into a program that will test the sorting procedure. Why is bubble sort less efficient that insertion sort?

8.   Another common iterative sorting algorithm is ***selection sort.*** The algorithm goes like this:

selectionSort()
BEGIN
    For index1 = (first array index) To (last array index)
       Set position = index1.
       Set smallest = array[position].
       For index2 = (index1 + 1) To (last array index)
         If array[index2] < smallest
            Set position = index2.
            Set smallest = array[position].
       Set array[position] = array[index1].
       Set array[index1] = smallest.
END.

As with bubble sort, selection sort makes several passes through the array. The first pass examines the entire array and places the smallest element in the first array position. The second pass examines the array beginning at the second element. The smallest element in this array segment is found and placed in the second array position. The third pass examines the array beginning at the third element, finds the smallest element in this array segment, and places it in the third element position. The process continues until there are no more array segments left.

Your job is to code the previous algorithm as a Java method called *selectionSort()*. Write your method to sort a character array. Then use it in a program that will test the sorting procedure.

Why is selection sort less efficient than insertion sort?

9. Write a program that will take an *unsorted* integer array and find the location of the maximum value in the array. (*Hint:* Copy the array into another array and sort this second array to determine its maximum value. Then search the original array for this value.)

10. A stack ADT is ideal to implement using a class, because it must include the stack data elements as well as the methods that operate on those elements in a tightly bound manner. As a result, object-oriented programming is perfect for implementing stacks. Here is a description for a *Stack* class:

Class: *Stack*

Data Members: An array to hold the stack elements.
An integer variable called *top* that locates the top of the stack.

Method Members: *Stack()*: A method to initialize the stack.
clearStack(): A method to clear the stack.
emptyStack(): A method to determine if the stack is empty.
fullStack(): A method to determine if the stack is full.
push(element): A method to place *element* on the stack.
pop(): A method to remove an element from the stack.

Assume the stack can hold *MAX* characters. A private member called *top* is declared to access the top element of the stack. Thus, *top* provides the array index of the top element in the stack. The stack is empty when *top* is −1 and the stack is full when *top* is *MAX*−1. Write the stack method implementations according to the following criteria:

- *Stack()* is a constructor method that initializes *top* to −1.

- *clearStack()* sets *top* to −1.

- *emptyStack()* tests to see if *top* = −1.

- *fullStack()* tests to see if *top* = *MAX* − 1 .

- *push(element)* checks to see if the stack is full by calling the *fullStack()* method. Then it must increment *top* and place *element* in the array at the index located to by *top*.

- *pop()* checks to see if the stack is empty by calling the *emptyStack()* method. If the stack is not empty, it returns the character element located at the array index located by *top* and decrements *top*.

Write an application class to completely test your stack class.

Applet 104: GRAPHICS II

PURPOSE

- *To show how to paint a filled polygon, a nonfilled polygon, and a polyline.*
- *To demonstrate how arrays are used to store coordinates for a polygon.*
- *To become familiar with the polygon methods in the Graphics class.*

Introduction

A polygon graphic in Java is simply a multisided rectangle which can be viewed as a series of lines connecting a series of (*x*,*y*) coordinates in a rectangular plane as shown in Figure 1.

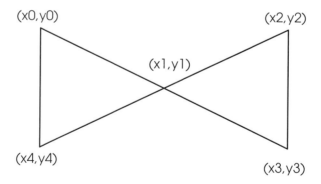

Figure 1 A polygon graphic in Java is simply a multisided rectangle which can be viewed as a series of lines connecting between a series of (*x*,*y*) coordinates in a rectangular plane

Here, our "bow-tie" polygon begins and ends at coordinate $(x0, y0)$. We will assume that the polygon is painted in the numeric order of the coordinates so that the line from $(x0,y0)$ to $(x1,y1)$ is painted first, then the line from $(x1,y1)$ to $(x2,y2)$ is painted, and so on.

If we were to place this polygon within a applet or frame, we must determine values for the (x,y) coordinates in terms of pixels as shown in Figure 2.

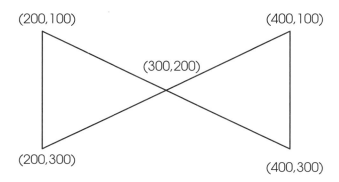

Figure 2 Polygon coordinate values for placement within an applet or frame.

There are three methods in the *Graphics* class used to paint polygons. They are *fillPolygon()*, *drawPolygon()*, and *drawPolyline()*. Each method requires that the polygon coordinate values be stored in two arrays, one array for the *x*-coordinate values, and a second array for the *y*-coordinate values.

In this module, you will load and execute a simple Java program that paints polygons within an applet. You will use arrays to store the polygon coordinates. You will modify the array coordinate values and observe the effect on the polygon generated within the applet.

Procedure

1. Load and execute the *Applet104_1.java* program contained on the CD that accompanies this book or download it from www.prenhall.com. Use your Java compiler to compile the program as an applet; then execute the program through your compiler or a Web browser. Maximize the window and you should observe the nice red "bow-tie" polygon shown in Figure 3.

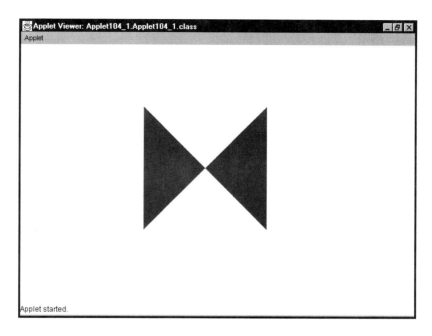

Figure 3 The window generated by the *Applet101_1.java* applet program.

Here is the code that produced the polygon:

```
1    import java.awt.*;              //FOR GRAPHICS CLASS
2    import java.applet.*;           //FOR APPLET CLASS
3
4    public class Applet104_1 extends Applet
5    {
6      public void paint(Graphics g)
7      {
8        //DEFINE POLYGON COORDINATES
9        int [] x = {200,300,400,400,300,200}; //X-COORDINATES
10       int [] y = {100,200,100,300,200,300}; //y-COORDINATES
11
12       //SET GRAPHICS OBJECT COLOR
13       g.setColor(Color.red);
14
15       //PAINT FILLED POLYGON
16       g.fillPolygon(x,y,6);
17     }//END paint()
18   }//END APPLET
```

2. Notice in lines 9 and 10, two arrays are initialize with the coordinate values. The first value in each array forms the (*x0,y0*) coordinate of the polygon, the second value in each array forms that (*x1,y1*) coordinate, and so on. Change the coordinate values within the arrays, execute the program again, and notice the affect on the polygon. You will find that you can get some really weird looking polygons, depending on the coordinate values.

3. Load and execute the *Applet104_1.java* program again from your CD or from www.prenhall.com.

4. Change the last argument in the *fillPolygon()* method to 3. Execute the program again and notice the affect on the polygon. What is the purpose of this argument value?

Discussion

Polygons are painted from (*x,y*) coordinates supplied via two arrays, one supplying the *x*-coordinates and a second supplying the *y*-coordinates. In this program, we employed the *fillPolygon()* method to construct a filled polygon. Here is the signature for this method:

```
public void fillPolygon(int[] x,    //x COORDINATES
                        int[] y,    //y COORDINATES
                        int n)      //NUMBER OF POINTS
```

The method requires two array arguments, one for the *x*-coordinates and one for the *y*-coordinates, plus a third argument which specifies the number of coordinates to use from the two arrays in constructing the polygon. The (*x,y*) coordinates supply the vertices of the polygon perimeter in the order in which they appear within the arrays. Thus, the first pair of (*x,y*) values provide the point of origin for the polygon perimeter. A line is drawn from this point to a point defined by the second pair of (*x,y*) values. Then, a line is drawn from this second point to a point defined by the third pair of (*x,y*) values, and so on. Finally, a line is drawn from the last specified point to the poirt of origin to complete the polygon perimeter. Of course, the *fillPolygon()* method fills the polygon with the color of the graphics object.

Procedure (continued)

5. Change the method call in line 16 to *drawPolygon(x,y,6)*. Execute the program again and notice the affect on the polygon.

6. Change the method call in line 16 to *drawPolyline(x,y,6)*. Execute the program again and notice the affect on the polygon. What is the difference between the three polygon methods?

Discussion

The three methods available to construct polygons are *fillPolygon()*, *drawPolygon()*, and *drawPolyline()*. They all have the same signature, except for their names. The *fillPolygon()* method constructs a filled polygon, while the *drawPolygon()* method constructs a nonfilled polygon. Both of these methods construct a complete polygon, where a connecting line is drawn from the last specified coordinate to the point of origin, which is the first coordinate specified. However, the *drawPolyline()* method constructs a nonfilled polygon but does not connect the last coordinate to the point of origin.

Procedure (continued)

7. It is now time to have some fun. Construct an image that employs all the graphical components that you have learned about in the *Graphics I* and *Graphics II* modules. Make a real scene or something abstract, your choice! Can you combine GUI and graphical components? Of course you can! You now have all the prerequisite knowledge. Have fun and be creative!

INTRODUCTION TO RECURSION, DATA STRUCTURES, AND ADTs

INTRODUCTION

This chapter will begin with a discussion of a very powerful language capability known as ***recursion***. Recursion is a process whereby an operation keeps "cloning" itself until a terminating condition is reached. Although the process of performing recursion is rather complex, it is relatively simple for the programmer, because most of the work is done by the compiler. Many problems are recursive in nature, such as calculating compound interest, among others. This chapter will introduce you to recursion via a practical example, followed by a "Problem Solving in Action" case study on ***binary search***, which is a recursive array searching algorithm.

Abstract data types, or ADTs, provide for data abstraction. You were introduced to data abstraction in an earlier chapter. Recall that the idea behind data abstraction is to combine data with a set of operations that are defined for that data in one neat encapsulated unit called an ADT. The ADT can then be used by knowing what the operations do, without needing to know the details of how the computer system implements the data or its operations. You have been using data abstraction throughout the text as you worked with the standard classes available in Java. In each case, you were not concerned about how the computer stores the data or how the operations were implemented. You could concentrate on their use rather than their implementation. This is especially true in the GUI chapter when you built GUIs using the Java GUI component classes.

Data abstraction is an important software development and programming tool. When developing software with ADTs, you can concentrate on the ADT data and related operations, without worrying about the inner implementation details of the ADT. Data abstraction provides for generality, modularity, and protection when developing software. The Java class is the ideal construct for implementing ADTs. In this chapter, we will use object-oriented programming to build two classic ADTs: the stack and the queue.

OBJECTIVES

When you are finished with this chapter, you should have a good understanding of the following:

- The concept of recursion.
- The concept of a stack and how it is employed by a compiler to perform recursive method calls.

- The recursive binary search algorithm.
- The importance and characteristics of abstract data types, or ADTs.
- The stack ADT and the concept of last-in, first-out.
- The queue ADT and the concept of first-in, first-out.
- How to code a stack ADT using a Java class.
- How to code a queue ADT using a Java class.

14-1 RECURSION

The Java language supports a very powerful process called *recursion*.

> **Recursion** is a process whereby an operation calls itself until a terminating condition is reached.

A recursive method is a method that calls itself. That's right, with the power of recursion, a given method can actually contain a statement that calls, or invokes, the same method, thereby calling itself. By calling itself, the method actually "clones" itself into a new problem which is one step closer to a terminating condition. A recursive method keeps calling, or cloning, itself until the terminating condition is reached.

To get the idea of recursion, consider a typical compound interest problem. Suppose you deposit $1000 in the bank at a 12 percent annual interest rate, but it is compounded monthly. What this means is that the interest is calculated and added to the principle on a monthly basis. Thus, each time the interest is calculated, you get interest on the previous month's interest. Let's analyze the problem a bit closer.

Your initial deposit is $1000. Now, the annual interest rate is 12 percent, which translates to a 1 percent monthly rate. Because interest is compounded monthly, the balance at the end of the first month will be

$$\text{month 1 balance} = \$1000 + (0.01 \times \$1000) = \$1010$$

As you can see, the interest for month 1 is $0.01 \times \$1,000$, or $10.00. This interest amount is then added to the principle ($1,000) to get a new balance of $1010. Using a little algebra, the same calculation can be made like this:

$$\text{month 1 balance} = 1.01 \times \$1000 = \$1010$$

Now, how would you calculate the interest for the second month? You would use the balance at the end of the first month as the principle for the second month calculation, right? So, the calculation for month 2 would be

$$\text{month 2 balance} = 1.01 \times \$1010 = \$1020.10$$

For month 3, the calculation would be

$$\text{month 3 balance} = 1.01 \times \$1020.10 = \$1030.30$$

Do you see a pattern? Notice that to calculate the balance for any given month, you must use the balance from the previous month. In general, the calculation for any month becomes

$$balance = 1.01 \times previous\ balance$$

Let's let *balance(n)* represent the balance of any given month, *n*, and *balance(n − 1)* the previous month's balance. Using this notation, the balance for any month, *balance(n)* is

$$balance(n) = 1.01 \times balance(n - 1)$$

Let's use this relationship to calculate what your balance would be after four months. Here's how you must perform the calculation:

First, the balance for month 4 is

$$balance(4) = 1.01 \times balance(3)$$

However, to find *balance*(4) you must find *balance*(3) like this:

$$balance(3) = 1.01 \times balance(2)$$

Then *balance*(2) must be found like this:

$$balance(2) = 1.01 \times balance(1)$$

Finally, *balance*(1) must be found like this:

$$balance(1) = 1.01 \times balance(0)$$

Now, you know that *balance*(0) is the original deposit of $1000. This is really the only thing known, aside from the interest rate. Therefore, working backwards, you get

$$balance(1) = 1.01 \times \$1000 = \$1010$$

$$balance(2) = 1.01 \times \$1010 = \$1020.10$$

$$balance(3) = 1.01 \times \$1020.10 = \$1030.30$$

$$balance(4) = 1.01 \times \$1030.30 = \$1040.60$$

This is a classic example of recursion, because in order to solve the problem, you must solve the previous problem condition using the same process, and so on, until you encounter a known condition (in our case, the initial $1000 deposit). This known condition is called a ***terminating condition***. Thus, a recursive operation is an operation that calls itself until a terminating condition is reached. Likewise, a recursive method is one that calls, or invokes, itself until a terminating condition is reached.

Now, suppose we wish to express the preceding compound interest calculation as a recursive method. The mathematical expression would be

$$balance(0) = 1000 \text{ and } balance(n) = 1.01 \times balance(n-1) \text{ (for } n > 0)$$

This mathematical expression can be expressed in pseudocode form, like this:

> If n is 0
> $\quad balance(n) = 1000$
> Else
> $\quad balance(n) = 1.01 \times balance(n-1)$

Notice that the terminating condition is tested first. There must *always* be a test for a terminating condition. If the terminating condition exists, the cloning process is halted and the return substitution process begins; otherwise, another recursive call is made to the method.

Next, let's assume the we use a variable called *deposit* to represent the initial deposit and a variable called *rate* to represent the annual interest rate. Then, our balance could be calculated using recursion, as follows:

> If n is 0
> $\quad balance(n) = deposit$
> Else
> $\quad balance(n) = (1 + rate / 12 / 100) \times balance(n-1)$

If a programming language supports recursive operations, a software method can be coded directly from the above algorithm. Because Java employs the power of recursion, the Java method is

```
double balance(double deposit, int month, double rate)
{
    if (month == 0)
      return deposit;
    else
      return (1 + rate / 12 / 100) * balance(deposit,month – 1,rate);
 } //END balance()
```

Here, the deposit, number of months to compound, and annual interest rate are listed as parameters for the method because these values are needed by the method to perform the balance calculation. That's all there is to it! This method will calculate the balance at the end of any month, *month*, passed to the method. Notice how the method calls itself in the **else** clause. Here's how it works. When the computer encounters the recursive call in the **else** clause, it must temporarily delay the calculation to evaluate the recursive method call just as we did as part of the compounded interest calculation. When it encounters the **else** clause a second time, the method calls itself again, and keeps calling itself each time the **else** clause is executed until the terminating condition is reached. When this happens, the **if** clause is executed (because *month* is zero), and the recursive calling ceases.

Now, let's insert this method into a program to calculate compounded interest, as follows:

```
import keyboardInput.* ;          //FOR readInt() and readDouble()

public class Recursion
{
  public static void main(String[] args)
  {
  //DEFINE VARIABLES
  double deposit = 0.0;            //INITIAL DEPOSIT
  double rate = 0.0;               //ANNUAL INTEREST RATE
  int month = 0;                   //NUMBER OF MONTHS AFTER INITIAL
                                   //DEPOSIT TO DETERMINE BALANCE

  //CREATE KEYBOARD OBJECT
  Keyboard in = new Keyboard();
```

```
    //GET DEPOSIT, NUMBER OF MONTHS, AND INTEREST RATE
    System.out.print("Enter the initial balance:  $");
    deposit = in.readDouble();
    System.out.print("Enter the number of months to compound: ");
    month = in.readInt();
    System.out.print("Enter the annual interest rate: ");
    rate = in.readDouble();

    //DISPLAY RESULTS, MAKING RECURSIVE METHOD CALL
    System.out.println("\n\nWith an initial deposit of $" + deposit
                    + " and an interest rate of " + rate
                    + "% \nthe balance at the end of " + month
                    + " months would be $"
                    + balance(deposit,month,rate));
} //END main()

//************************************************************************************
//
//THIS RECURSIVE METHOD WILL CALCULATE A BANK BALANCE
//BASED ON A MONTHLY COMPOUNDED INTEREST RATE
//
//************************************************************************************
static double balance(double deposit, int month, double rate)
{
   if (month == 0)
     return deposit;
   else
     return (1 + rate / 12 / 100) * balance(deposit,month - 1,rate);
} //END balance()
} //END Recursion
```

This program prompts the user to enter the deposit, number of months to compound, and the current annual interest rate. These values are passed to the method. Once the user enters the required values, the recursive calls are made, and the program will write the ending balance. Here is a sample of the program output:

```
Enter the initial deposit:  $1000↵
Enter the number of months to compound:  4↵
Enter the annual interest rate:  12↵

With an initial deposit of $1000 and an interest rate of 12%
the balance at the end of 4 months would be $1040.60
```

During any recursive call, all information required to complete the calculation after the recursive call is saved by the computer in a memory area called a ***stack***. As the recursive calls continue, information is saved on the memory stack until the terminating condition is reached. Then the computer works backward from the terminating condition, retrieving the stack information to determine the final result. The process that the computer goes through is identical to what we did when working the compound interest problem and is illustrated in Figure 14-1. The values shown in the figure assume a $1000.00 initial deposit and an interest rate of 12% per year, compounded monthly. Notice that the last thing placed into the stack is the first thing retrieved from the stack when recursion begins to "unwind." This principle is known as ***last-in-first-out***, or ***LIFO***. All stacks operate using the LIFO principle. Stacks and LIFO are discussed in detail later in this chapter.

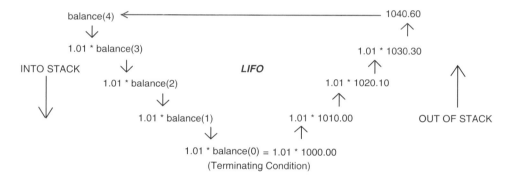

Figure 14-1   As recursion winds up, calculation information is placed into a memory stack until a terminating condition is reached. Recursion then unwinds by retrieving the calculation information out of the stack and using substitution to generate the final result.

CAUTION

A word of caution: A recursive method must always reach a terminating condition. If it does not, the method will keep calling itself forever, resulting in a memory overflow run-time error. (Why?)

Example 14-1

Write a recursive Java method to find the sum of all integers from 1 to some number, n.

Solution

Think about this operation for a minute. Isn't it a classic recursive operation? To find the sum of integers 1 to, say, 5, couldn't you add 5 to the sum of integers from 1 to 4? Then, to find the sum of integers from 1 to 4, you add 4 to the sum of integers from 1 to 3, and so on, right? Expressed in symbols,

$sum(5) = 5 + sum(4)$
$sum(4) = 4 + sum(3)$
$sum(3) = 3 + sum(2)$
$sum(2) = 2 + sum(1)$
$sum(1) = 1$

Notice that $sum(1)$ is the terminating condition, because its value is known. Now, translating this process to a recursive method, you get

$$sum(1) = 1 \ \text{ and } \ sum(n) = n + sum(n-1) \ \ (\text{for } n > 1)$$

This method can be expressed in pseudocode, like this:

> If n is 1
> $sum(n) = 1$
> Else
> $sum(n) = n + sum \ (n-1)$

The recursive Java method is then coded directly from the algorithm as

```java
int sum(int n)
{
  if (n == 1)
    return 1;
  else
    return n + sum(n – 1);
} //END sum()
```

Although recursion is a very powerful feature of any language, you should be aware that it is not always the most efficient method of solving a problem. Whenever we talk about computer efficiency, we must consider two things: *execution speed* and *memory usage*. When using recursion, the computer must keep track of each recursive call in a stack so that it can work backward to obtain a solution. This requires large amounts of both memory and time. As a result, a recursive solution to a problem may not always be the most efficient solution. *All* recursive problems can also be solved nonrecursively using iteration. For instance, consider the sum of integers from 1 to *n* done recursively in Example 14-1. This problem can be solved using an iterative method, like this:

```
int sum(int n)
{
  int subTotal = 0;          //SUM SUBTOTAL
  for (int count = 1; count <= n; ++count)
     subTotal = subTotal + count;
  return subTotal;
} //END sum()
```

So, why use recursion? Probably the main reason is that many recursive solutions are much simpler than iterative solutions. In addition, there are some problems in data structures, such as linked lists and binary trees, where recursion isn't a mere convenience, it is essential to keep the code manageable. Here are two guidelines that should help you decide when to use recursion:

1. Consider a recursive solution only when a *simple* iterative solution is not possible.
2. Use a recursive solution only when the execution and memory efficiency of the solution is within acceptable limits, considering the system limitations.

 Quick Check

1. True or false: There is no way that a Java method can call itself.
2. Explain why we can describe recursion as a "winding" and "unwinding" process.
3. What terminates a recursive method call?
4. A factorial operation, *factorial(n)*, finds the product of all integers from 1 to some positive integer *n*. Thus, 5! = 5 * 4 * 3 * 2 * 1. Write the pseudocode required to find *factorial(n)*, where *n* is any integer. (*Note:* By definition, *factorial(1)* = 1.)
5. True or false: An advantage of recursion is that it does not require a lot of memory to execute.

6. True or false: All recursive problems can also be solved using iteration.

7. Recursion employs a memory data structure called a _____ to save information between recursive calls.

8. Stacks operate on the _____ principle.

PROBLEM SOLVING IN ACTION: SEARCHING AN ARRAY USING RECURSION (BINARY SEARCH)

In this problem, we will develop another popular searching algorithm, called *binary search*. The binary search algorithm that we will develop will employ recursion, although it can also be done using iteration. One of the major differences between binary search and sequential search that you learned about in an earlier chapter is that binary search requires that the array be sorted prior to the search, whereas sequential search does not have this requirement. If, however, you have a sorted array to begin with, binary search is much faster than sequential search, especially for large arrays. For example, if you were to apply sequential search to an array of 1000 integers, the sequential search algorithm would make an *average* of 500 comparisons to find the desired element. Even worse, if the desired element is in the last array position, sequential search will make 1000 comparisons to find the element. On the other hand, a binary search would require a maximum of 10 comparisons to find the element, even if it is in the last array position! Of course, you must pay a price for this increased efficiency. The price you must pay is that of a more complex algorithm. So, when searching a sorted array, the advantage of sequential search is simplicity, whereas the advantage of binary search is efficiency.

Problem

Develop a Java method that can be called to search a sorted array of integers for a given element value and return the index of the element if it is found in the array. Employ a recursive binary search to accomplish this task.

We will be developing a Java method, so our problem definition will again focus on the method signature. However, before we can consider the method signature, we must see how a recursive binary search works, because the search algorithm will dictate our method parameters. So, let's first deal with the algorithm and then develop the method signature.

Planning the Solution

Binary search represents a natural recursive operation. Remember that the idea behind recursion is to divide and conquer. You keep dividing a problem into simpler subproblems of exactly the same type, or cloning itself, until a terminating condition occurs. This is not the same as top-down software design, which divides problems into simpler subproblems. The difference with recursion is that the subproblems are clones of the original problem. For example, suppose that you are searching for a name in a telephone book. Imagine starting at the beginning of the telephone book and looking at every name until you found the right one. This is exactly what sequential search does. Wouldn't it be much faster, on the average, to open up the book in the middle? Then, determine which half of the book contains the name that you are looking for, divide this section of the book in half, and so on, until you obtain the page on which the desired name appears. Here is an algorithm that describes the telephone book search just described

A Recursive Telephone Book Search Algorithm

teleSearch( )
BEGIN
    If (the telephone book only contains one page)
        Look for the name on the page.
    Else
        Open the book to the middle.
        If (the name is in the first half)
            teleSearch(first half of the book for the name).
        Else
            teleSearch(second half of the book for the name).
END.

Do you see how this search is recursive? You keep performing the same basic operations until you come to the page that contains the name for which you are looking. In other words, the *teleSearch( )* algorithm keeps calling itself in the nested **if/else** statement until the correct page is found. The reason that this is called a *binary* search process is that you must divide the book by 2 (*bi*) each time the algorithm calls itself.

Now, let's see how this process can be applied to searching an array of integers. We will call our recursive binary search method *binSearch( )* and will develop our algorithm in several steps. Here is the first-level algorithm.

binSearch( ) **Algorithm: First Level**

binSearch( )
BEGIN
  If (the array has only one element)
    Determine if this element is the element being searched for.
  Else
    Find the midpoint of the array.
    If (the element is in the first half)
      *binSearch(*first half*)*.
    Else
      *binSearch(*second half*)*.
END.

      Notice how this algorithm is almost identical to the *teleSearch( )* algorithm. Here, the recursive searching process continues until the array is reduced to one element that is tested against the element for which we are searching. Do you see how the search keeps calling itself until the terminating condition occurs? Although this algorithm provides the general binary search idea, we need to get more specific in order to code the algorithm. To do this, we must ask ourselves what data *binSearch( )* needs to accomplish its task. Well, like sequential search, it needs an array to search and the element for which to search, right? However, sequential search deals with one array of a given size, whereas binary search needs to deal with arrays of different sizes as it keeps dividing the original array in half. Not only are these arrays of different sizes, but the first and last indices of each half are different. As a result, we must provide *binSearch( )* with the boundaries of the array that it is dealing with at any given time. This can be done by passing the first and last indices of the given array to the method. Let's call these indices *first* and *last*.
      We are now ready to write the method-interface description:

Method *binSearch( )*:   Searches a sorted array of integers for a given value.

Accepts: An array of integers, an element for which to search, the first index of the array being searched, and the last index of the array being searched.
Returns: The array index of the element, if found, or the value −1 if the element is not found.

This description gives us enough information to write the Java method signature, as follows:

int binSearch(int[] array, int element, int first, int last)

Here, *binSearch()* will return an integer value that represents the index of the element being searched for. Again, you will see that the value –1 will be returned if the element is not found in the array. The method receives the integer array being searched (*array[ ]*), the element being searched for (*element*), the first index of the array being searched (*first*), and the last index of the array being searched (*last*).

The next problem is to determine what the value of *first* and *last* will be for any given array during the search. Well, remember that we must divide any given array in half to produce two new arrays each time a recursive call to *binSearch()* is made. Given any array where the first index is *first* and the last index is *last*, we can determine the middle index, like this:

$$mid = (first + last) / 2$$

By using this calculation, the first half of the array begins at *first* and ends at *mid* – 1, and the second half of the array begins at *mid* + 1 and ends at *last*. This idea is illustrated in Figure 14-2.

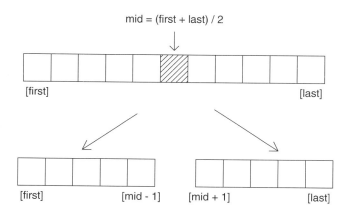

Figure 14-2   Recursive binary search requires that an array be divided in half with each recursive call.

But, notice that neither half of the array contains the middle element. By using this technique, the two halves do not make a whole, right? So, before the split is made, suppose that we test the middle element to see if it is the element that we are looking for. The following test will do the job:

If (array[mid] == element)
Return mid.

If this test is true prior to the split, we have found the element that we are looking for, and we can cease the recursive calls. Otherwise, the element stored in *array*[*mid*] is not the element that we are looking for, and this array position can be ignored during the rest of the search. If this is the case, we will split the array and continue the recursive process. However, we have just added a second terminating condition to our recursive algorithm. Here are the two terminating conditions that we now have:

1. The array being searched has only one element.
2. *array*[*mid*] == *element*.

Either of these terminating conditions will cause the recursive calls to cease. Now, let's consider the first terminating condition more closely. How do we know if the array being searched has only one element? Well, as the recursive calls continue without finding the element, the array will eventually be reduced to a single element. If this is the element that we are looking for, the test *If array*[*mid*] == *element* will be true, and the recursive calls will stop. If this is not the element that we are looking for, the value of *first* will become greater than the value of *last* on the next split. Why? Because if you think about the splitting action of the algorithm, you will realize that each recursive call causes *first* to increase and *last* to decrease. Thus, if the element is not in the array, the value of *first* will eventually become larger than the value of *last*. So we can use this idea to test for the element not being in the array, as well as use it for a terminating condition. Thus, we will replace the original terminating condition with the following statement:

If (first > last)
Return −1

If this condition occurs, the value −1 is returned, indicating that the element was not found, and the recursive calls cease.

Now, let's apply this knowledge to a second-level algorithm. Here it is:

binSearch( ) **Algorithm: Second Level**

```
binSearch(array, element, first, last)
BEGIN
  If (first > last)
    Return −1.
  Else
    Set mid = (first + last) / 2.
    If (array[mid] == element)
      Return mid.
    Else
      If (the element is in the first half)
              binSearch(array, element, first, mid − 1).
      Else
              binSearch(array, element, mid + 1, last).
END.
```

It is much clearer now that our algorithm is performing recursion, because you see the method calling itself in either one of two places, depending on which half of the split array the element is likely to be found. Also, observe where the two terminating conditions are tested. If, at the beginning of any recursive call, *first* > *last*, the element is not in the array, and the recursive calls cease. In addition, if, after calculating *mid*, we find the element at *array*[*mid*], the recursive calls cease. In both cases, the method has finished executing, and a value is returned to the calling program. The last thing our algorithm needs is a way to determine if the element being searched for is likely to be in the first half or the second half of the split array. Here is where the requirement for a sorted array comes in. If the array is sorted, the element will likely be in the first half of the array when *element* < *array*[*mid*]; otherwise, the element is likely to be in the second half of the array. Notice that we are using the term "likely." We cannot guarantee that the element is in either half, because it might not be in the array at all! All we can do is to direct the search to that half where the element is likely to be, depending on the sorted ordering of elements. So, we can now complete our algorithm using this idea. Here is the final algorithm:

binSearch( ) **Algorithm**

```
binSearch(array, element, first, last)
BEGIN
```

If (*first* > *last*)
    Return −1.
Else
    Set *mid* = (*first* + *last*) / 2.
    If (*array*[*mid*] == *element*)
      Return *mid*.
    Else
      If (*element* < *array*[*mid*])
          binSearch(array, element, first, mid − 1).
      Else
          binSearch(array, element, mid + 1, last).
END.

Notice how ***elegant*** the algorithm is. By elegant, we mean that the rather complicated binary search process is reduced to just a few statements. You *know* there is a lot going on here, but recursion allows us to express all of this processing in just a few statements. As you can see, recursive algorithms often provide simple solutions to problems of great complexity, where an equivalent iterative solution might be rather complex. This is not always the case, because some recursive solutions are impractical relative to speed and memory efficiency. Remember the rule of thumb when considering recursion: Consider a recursive solution to a problem only when a simple iterative solution is not possible. You should be aware that binary search has a relatively simple iterative solution. You will code this solution for one of the problems at the end of the chapter.

Coding the Program

The required Java method now can be easily coded from the final algorithm. Here it is:

```
//ACTION 14-1  (ACTION14_01.JAVA)
//THIS METHOD SEARCHES AN INTEGER ARRAY USING RECURSIVE
//BINARY SEARCH
int binSearch(int[] array, int element, int first, int last)
{
    int mid;                          //ARRAY MIDPOINT
    if (first > last)                 //IF ELEMENT NOT IN ARRAY
        return -1;                    //RETURN -1, ELSE CONTINUE
    else
    {
```

```
            mid = (first + last) / 2;          //FIND MIDPOINT OF ARRAY
            if (element == array[mid])         //IF ELEMENT IS IN ARRAY[MID]
                return mid;                    //RETURN MID
            else                               //ELSE SEARCH APPROPRIATE HALF
                if (element < array[mid])
                    return binSearch(array, element, first, mid - 1);
                else
                    return binSearch(array, element, mid + 1, last);
        } //END OUTER ELSE
    } //END binSearch()
```

You should not have any trouble understanding this code, because it reflects the method signature and algorithm just developed. The only difference here is that the recursive calls on *binSearch()* must be part of a **return** statement. Remember that Java requires that all execution paths of a nonvoid method lead to a **return** statement.

14-2 THE CONCEPT OF DATA ABSTRACTION REVISITED

Let's begin with a simple definition for an ADT and then look at some important characteristics of an ADT.

> An ***abstract data type (ADT)*** is a collection of data and related operations.

- *Abstraction*

    The term *abstract* means that the data and related operations are being viewed without considering any of the details of *how* the data or operations are implemented in the computer system. You have been working with abstract data types throughout this book, without knowing it. For instance, consider the **double** data type used in Java. Have you been concerned about how floating-point values are stored in memory? Have you been concerned about how the Java compiler implements floating-point operations? Of course not! All that you are concerned about is the general structure of a floating-point value, what operations are available to be used with floating-point values, and how to use these floating-point operations. The implementation details are left to the Java compiler designer.

This whole idea of abstraction facilitates the design of modular software and the development of algorithms for software design, because abstraction allows us to hide implementation details, thereby facilitating more general thinking.

- *An ADT includes both data and related operations.*

  Think of an ADT as a black box that contains *private* data and *public* operations. Sound familiar? You know what the box does and how to use it through its *public* operations, or interface. However, you are not concerned about what goes on inside the box. The ADT black box concept facilitates modular software design.

  The Data: An ADT defines the data to be operated upon as well as the operations that can be performed on the data. An ADT is not the same thing as a data structure. A data structure provides a way of structuring, or organizing, data within a programming language. You will be concerned about data structures when you implement an ADT, because you will have to decide how to organize and store the ADT data. However, on the surface, you are not concerned with these implementation details in order to access and manipulate the ADT data. The data in an ADT must be private, which means that they are hidden from any operations that are not defined for the ADT.

  The Operations: The ADT includes operations, or methods, that manipulate the ADT data. These operations are public, which means that they are used by outside software to access and manipulate the private ADT data. Again, all you are concerned about at the abstract level is what these operations do and how to use them. As a result, the interface to the operations within the ADT must be complete enough to describe totally the effect that they have on the data. However, you are not concerned about how they do what they do.

- *An ADT provides a means to encapsulate details whereby the data are completely hidden from their surroundings.*

  Recall that *encapsulation* with *information hiding* allows you to combine data with the operations that are dedicated to manipulating the data so tightly that outside operations cannot affect the data. This allows the application program to be oblivious to how the ADT data are stored. In addition, information hiding provides for data protection. Only those operations that are defined for the ADT can operate on the ADT data. As a result, the data cannot be corrupted intentionally or unintentionally by using "unauthorized" operations.

- *ADT operations provide loose coupling to the outside world via a method interface.*

The operations defined for an ADT provide the interface between the outside world and the ADT. In other words, the only way to gain access to the ADT is through the ADT operation, or method, interfaces. Again, the ADT is like a black box that is connected to its surroundings via its method interfaces. The method interfaces provide the communications channel between an application program and the ADT. This idea is illustrated in Figure 14-3. This figure should look familiar to you, because it is basically the same figure used to illustrate a class in an earlier chapter. As you might now suspect, the class in Java provides an ideal implementation of an ADT.

By using ADTs during software development, we gain *modularity*, *generality*, and *protection*. We gain modularity, because ADTs can be thought of as black box building blocks during software development. We gain generality, because algorithms can be developed that depend only on the method interface to the ADT without considering the implementation details of the ADT. In addition, once an ADT is developed, it is available, through inheritance, for general use in many applications without rewriting the ADT code. We gain protection through information hiding. Private data stored within an ADT cannot be corrupted intentionally or unintentionally.

The preceding definition of an ADT completely describes the Java class that we developed in an earlier chapter. Recall that a class includes both data (private members) and related operations (public methods) that are encapsulated. In addition, the private member data are completely hidden from anything outside the class. Finally, the class is coupled to its outside world via the class method interfaces (signatures). That is, to access the class data from the outside, you must invoke the public member methods of the class. This is why Java is ideal for coding ADTs.

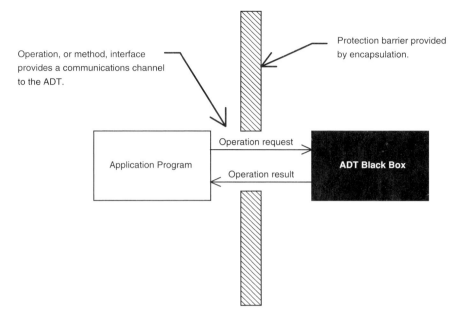

Operation, or method, interface provides a communications channel to the ADT.

Protection barrier provided by encapsulation.

Operation request

Application Program

Operation result

ADT Black Box

Figure 14-3 The ADT is like a black box that is connected to its surroundings via its method interfaces.

The remainder of this chapter is devoted to building some classic ADTs. As you study these ADTs, keep in mind the general ideas of data abstraction presented in this section.

 **Quick Check**

1. What term is used to indicate that data and their related operations are being viewed without considering any of the details of how the data or operations are implemented in the computer system?

2. Give an example of an ADT with which you have been working in the Java language.

3. The ADT black box concept facilitates _____ software design.

4. True or false: A data structure and an abstract data type are the same thing.

5. Data protection in an ADT is provided by _____.

6. The interface to an ADT is through its _____.

7. Why do you gain modularity through the use of ADTs?

8. Why do you gain generality through the use of ADTs?

14-3 THE STACK ADT

You have been introduced to the stack ADT via some of the programming problems in previous chapters as well as the discussion of recursion in this chapter. Now it is time to take a closer look at this important ADT. Stacks are common in a wide variety of applications in computer systems. For example, you observed the use of a stack when you studied recursion earlier. With recursion, a stack is employed to save information as the recursive method calls are made. Once the terminating condition is reached, the stack information is retrieved to determine the final recursive method value.

In general, a stack is used to reverse the order of data placed in it. Now, let's see how a stack works, beginning with a formal definition for a stack:

> A *stack* is a collection of data elements and related operations whereby all the insertions and deletions of elements to and from the stack are made at one end of the stack called the *top*. A stack operates on the *last-in*, *first-out*, or *LIFO*, principle.

To get the idea of a stack, think of a stack of trays in a spring-loaded bin, such as that which you might find in a cafeteria line. Such a stack is illustrated in Figure 14-4. When you remove a tray from the stack, you remove it from the *top* of the stack. If you were to add a tray onto the stack, you would place it on the *top* of the stack. All insertions and deletions of trays to and from the stack are made at the *top* of the stack. In other words, the last tray placed onto the stack will be the first tray removed from the stack. This characteristic is commonly referred to as *last-in*, *first-out*, or simply *LIFO*. Examples of the LIFO principle are hard to find in everyday life. For instance, suppose that you enter a grocery store check-out line. If the line is operating on the LIFO principle, the last person in the line would be the first one to be checked out. It might be quite some time until you were able to pay for your groceries, especially if other people keep entering the line. Think about how unfair such a line would be! To be fair, a grocery store line must operate on a *first-in*, *first-out*, or *FIFO*, principle. This principle is associated with *queues* and will be discussed in the next section. Although the LIFO principle is not very common in everyday life, it is very common in many problems that arise in computer systems.

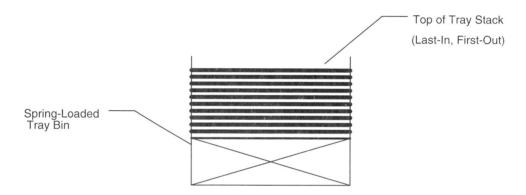

Top of Tray Stack
(Last-In, First-Out)

Spring-Loaded
Tray Bin

Figure 14-4 A stack obeys the last-in, first-out (LIFO) principle, like this stack of cafeteria trays.

Now, let's consider the cafeteria tray stack again. What operations do you suppose could be performed on such a stack? Well, first of all, you can move an empty tray bin into position in preparation for adding trays to the bin. Then, you can begin adding trays to the bin to form a stack of trays. When a single tray is added to the stack, it can only be added at the *top* position and no other position. Adding an element to a stack is referred to as a ***push*** operation. You can remove a tray from the *top* of the stack, and, normally, you can't remove a tray from any position other than the *top* of the stack. Removing an element from a stack is called a ***pop*** operation. You could also inspect the *top* tray, but no others. You could see if the stack of trays were empty, but if not empty, you would not know how many trays were in the stack. Given the situation, you are forced to access the trays from the *top* of the stack. The stack of trays provide a very good analogy to stacks in computer systems, because the operations that can be performed on a stack of trays form the basis for the stack ADT in computer systems. Here is a summary of legal stack operations:

- *createStack( )* ⇒ Creates an empty stack.
- *push( )* ⇒ Places an element on the top of a stack.
- *pop( )* ⇒ Removes an element from the top of a stack.
- *topElement( )* ⇒ Inspects the top element of the stack, leaving the stack unchanged.
- *emptyStack( )* ⇒ Determines if the stack is empty.

Now we are ready to define our stack ADT. Remember, to define an ADT, we must include both a definition for the ADT data as well as any operations that will be needed to manipulate the data. Consider the following ADT definition:

Stack ADT

Data:

A collection of data elements that can be accessed at only one location, called the *top* of the stack.

Operations, or Interface:

createStack( )
    Creates an empty stack.

push( )
    Adds a new element to the top of a stack.

pop( )
    Removes the top element of a stack.

topElement( )
    Copies the top element of the stack, leaving the stack unchanged.

emptyStack( )
    Determines if the stack is empty.

Implementing the Stack ADT

The stack ADT definition provides all the information needed to work with a stack. The operations are clearly defined in order to access and manipulate the stack data. Now it is time to consider the implementation details in order to create stacks in Java. Remember, however, that the following implementation details are not part of the ADT definition. We can always change how we implement the stack ADT, but the stack ADT definition will remain constant.

Creating a Stack Using an Array

It is perfectly natural to use a one-dimensional array to hold a stack. We will create an array of some arbitrary length and create an integer variable called *top* to keep track of the top element on the stack. Remember, we only need to keep track of the top element of the stack, because, by definition, access to the stack elements must be through the top of the stack. To initialize the stack, we will set *top* to the value −1, as shown in Figure 14-5.

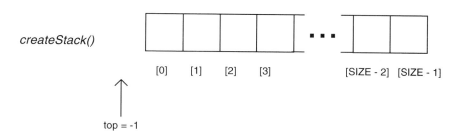

Figure 14-5   Setting *top* to the value −1 will create an empty stack.

First, look at the array. It is defined with indices ranging from [0] to [*SIZE* − 1] and, therefore, can hold *SIZE* elements. The array will be used to hold a stack so that the first stack element will be placed at position [0] in the array, the second stack element at position [1], and so on. We will create an integer variable called *top* that will "point" to the array index that locates the top element in the stack. In Figure 14-5, the value of *top* is set to −1 to indicate that the stack is empty. The value −1 is used to indicate an empty stack condition, because there is no −1 index in the array. So, using this idea, all we have to do to create a new empty stack is to define an array and set *top* to the value −1. How do you know if the stack ever becomes empty when processing the stack data? Of course, the stack is empty if the value of *top* is −1. The algorithm required to create a stack using our array implementation is straightforward. Here it is:

createStack( ) Algorithm

BEGIN
Set *top* = −1.
END.

Now we are ready to start pushing elements onto the stack.

Pushing Elements onto a Stack

The first element pushed onto an empty stack will be placed in position [0] of the array. However, before the first element can be placed into the array, the value of *top* must be incremented to point to position [0]. Let's suppose that we have created a character array to form a stack of characters. Then we execute the following operation:

push('A')

The push operation causes the value of *top* to be incremented from −1 to 0, and then the character 'A' is placed at position [*top*], or [0], of the array. Next, suppose we execute another push operation, like this:

push('B')

This push operation causes *top* to be incremented from 0 to 1, and then the character 'B' is placed on the top of the stack, which is now array position [1]. Lastly, let's execute a third push operation, like this:

push('C')

Now we are pushing the character 'C' onto the stack. Again, the value of *top* is incremented, and this character is placed into array position [*top*], or [2]. This sequence of three push operations is illustrated in Figure 14-6.

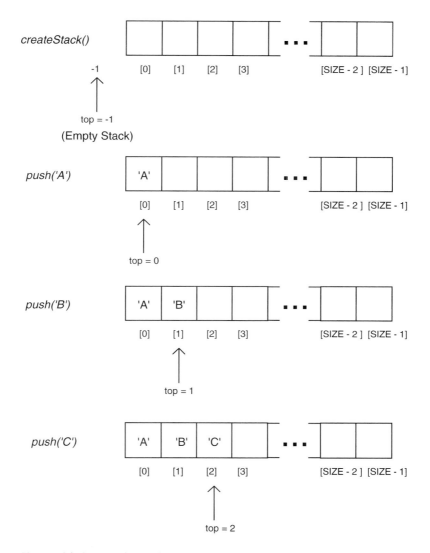

Figure 14-6 The effect of creating a stack and pushing three character elements onto the stack.

It is important to note that the value of *top* must be incremented *prior* to placing the element on the stack. Thus, we say that the *push()* operation preincrements the stack pointer, *top*. Here is an algorithm for *push()*:

push( ) **Algorithm**

BEGIN
   If the stack is not full
      Increment *top*.
      Place element at array position [*top*].
   Else
      Display full stack message.
END.

Notice that a test is made to determine if the stack is full, because you cannot push an element onto a full stack. When would our stack be full? Well, the stack is full when the array is full, right? The maximum array position is $SIZE - 1$, so the stack will be full when *top* has the value $SIZE - 1$.

Popping Elements from a Stack

Now we are ready to illustrate several popping operations. Given the stack in Figure 14-6, suppose that we execute a single pop operation, like this:

pop( )

What happens to the stack? Well, *top* is pointing to the *last* element placed on the stack (the character 'C') so all we need to do is to remove the element at array position [*top*], or [2]. However, once the element is removed, the value of *top* must be decremented to locate the new top of the stack. Thus, in Figure 14-6, the character 'C' at position [2] is removed, and the value of *top* is decremented from 2 to 1 to locate array position [1], which is the new top of the stack.

Next, suppose we execute a second pop operation. This operation removes the character 'B', and *top* is decremented to array position [0]. Finally, if we execute a third pop operation, the character 'A' is removed from the stack, and *top* is decremented to the value −1, indicating an empty stack. This sequence of events is shown in Figure 14-7. Remember that the *pop( )* operation decrements *top* after the element is removed from the stack. Thus, we say that the *pop( )* operation postdecrements the stack pointer. Here is an algorithm for *pop( )*:

pop( ) **Algorithm**

BEGIN
   If the stack is not empty
      Remove element at array position [*top*].
      Decrement *top*.

Else
    Display empty stack message.
END.

Notice that a test must be made to determine if the stack is empty, because you cannot pop an element from an empty stack. How do you know when the stack is empty? Of course, when *top* has the value −1.

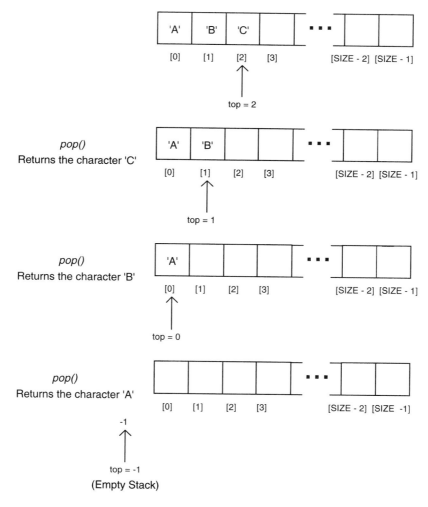

Figure 14-7 The effect of popping three character elements from the stack in Figure 14-6.

One final point: Although the stack is empty after the three popping operations in Figure 14-7, the array still contains the 'A', 'B', and 'C' character elements. These elements could be accessed by reading the array. However, remember that, by definition, an ADT restricts the data access to only those operations defined for the ADT. Therefore, the only possible way to access the array is through the stack operations, *push()* and *pop()*, defined for the stack ADT. Any direct array access would violate the idea of an ADT. This is why object-oriented programming is ideal for implementing ADTs. With object-oriented programming, we can make the array a **private** data member of a class, thereby restricting its access to only those operations defined for the ADT. As a result, the ADT data are completely hidden from the outside world.

Inspecting the Top Element of a Stack

The last operation of our stack ADT that we need to illustrate is the *topElement()* operation. Recall that this operation makes a copy of the top element on the stack, leaving the stack unchanged. So, let's assume that we start with the stack in Figure 14-6 and execute a *topElement()* operation, like this:

topElement()

Like the *pop()* operation, the *topElement()* operation reads the element at array position [*top*]. However, unlike the *pop()* operation, *topElement()* does not decrement the stack pointer, *top*. This operation is illustrated in Figure 14-8.

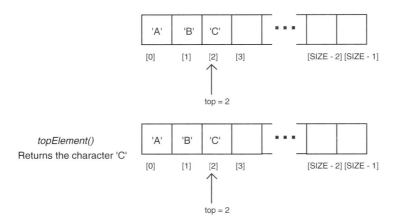

Figure 14-8   The effect of the *topElement()* operation.

The algorithm for *topElement( )* is straightforward. Here it is:

topElement( ) **Algorithm**

BEGIN
   If the stack is not empty
      Copy element at array position [*top*].
   Else
      Display empty message.
END.

Coding the Stack ADT

We are now ready to code our stack ADT. We will code the ADT as a class to enforce encapsulation and information hiding. Here is the stack ADT class coded in a Java file called *Stack.java*

```java
package adts;

//STACK CLASS DECLARATION
public class Stack
{
 //CONSTANT DECLARATIONS
 static final int SIZE = 5;        //MAXIMUM STACK SIZE
 static final int EMPTY = -1;      //DECLARE EMPTY = -1
 static final int FULL = SIZE - 1;  //DECLARE FULL = SIZE - 1

 //DATA MEMBERS
 private char[] stack = new char[SIZE]; //CHARACTER ARRAY TO HOLD
                                        //A STACK OF CHARACTERS

 private int top;                       //top LOCATES TOP STACK ELEMENT

 //METHOD MEMBERS

 //CONSTRUCTOR FOR createStack()
 public Stack()
 {
  top = EMPTY;
 }//END Stack()
```

```
//CHECKS FOR EMPTY STACK
public boolean emptyStack()
{
  if (top == EMPTY)      //IF STACK EMPTY RETURN TRUE
    return true;
  else                   //ELSE RETURN FALSE
    return false;
}//END emptyStack()

//CHECKS FOR FULL STACK
public boolean fullStack()
{
  if (top == FULL)       //IF STACK FULL RETURN TRUE
    return true;
  else                   //ELSE RETURN FALSE
    return false;
}//END fullStack()

//PLACE ELEMENT ON TOP OF STACK
public void push(char character)
{
  if (!fullStack())                //IF STACK NOT FULL, INCREMENT TOP
  {                                //AND ADD ELEMENT TO STACK
    ++top;
    stack[top] = character;
  }//END IF
  else
    System.out.println("The stack is full!");
} //END push()

//REMOVE ELEMENT FROM TOP OF STACK
public char pop()
{
  char character = ' ';
  if (!emptyStack())               //IF STACK NOT EMPTY, RETURN ELEMENT
  {                                //AND DECREMENT TOP
    character = stack[top];
    --top;
    return character;
  } //END IF
  else
  {
    System.out.println("The stack is empty!");
```

```
      return '#';              //ELSE RETURN '#' FOR EMPTY STACK
    } //END ELSE
  } //END pop()

  //INSPECT TOP ELEMENT
  public char topElement()
  {
   if (!emptyStack())      //IF STACK NOT EMPTY, RETURN ELEMENT
     return stack[top];
   else                    //ELSE RETURN '#' FOR EMPTY STACK
   {
     System.out.println("The stack is empty! ");
     return '#';
   } //END ELSE
  } //END topElement()
} //END Stack CLASS
```

First, you see three constants declared. The *SIZE* constant will dictate the maximum size of the array, or stack. We set *EMPTY* to the value −1 to designate an empty stack. Then, we set *FULL* to the value *SIZE* − 1 to designate a full stack. You know why *EMPTY* is set to −1. But why is *FULL* set to *SIZE* − 1? Well, theoretically, the size of a stack is limited only by the amount of memory available in the system to hold the stack. However, because we are using an array to hold the stack, the maximum stack size is limited by the size of the array. The size of this array implementation is *SIZE*, which means that the last array index is [*SIZE* − 1]. Therefore, when the top of the stack is located at array index [*SIZE* − 1], the stack is full.

The stack ADT is defined as a class called *Stack*. The private members of the class are the character array, *stack[ ]*, and the integer variable, *top*. The size of the array is *SIZE*, which means that the stack can hold *SIZE* elements. However, remember that the last array index is [*SIZE* − 1]. It goes without saying that array *stack[ ]* will hold a stack of characters whose top element is located by *top*.

The public members of the class include the operations defined for the stack ADT. First, you see the *Stack()* constructor. This constructor will take the place of the *createStack()* operation. Remember how a constructor works? When an object is defined for a class, the constructor is automatically called to initialize the private members of the class. Here, the constructor method is coded to set the value of *top* to *EMPTY*, or −1. Isn't this what the *createStack()* operation must do? We could not use the name *createStack()*, because a constructor must have the same name as the class.

Next, you see the *emptyStack()* method listed. This method will return **true** if the stack is empty, or **false** if the stack is not empty. What constitutes an empty stack? Of course, when the value of *top* is −1. This is the test that is made in the **if/else** statement. The next method defined is *fullStack()*. This method will be used to determine if the stack is full. The method will return **true** if the stack is full or **false** if the stack is not full. (What constitutes a full stack?) The *fullStack()* implementation is similar to *emptyStack()*. However, *fullStack()* checks to see if the value of *top* is equal to *FULL*. Recall that *FULL* is declared as a constant with the value *SIZE* − 1. This value is the maximum array index value. When *top* reaches *SIZE* − 1, the array is full, thereby making the stack full. You have noticed that in our formal ADT definition, we did not have a *fullStack()* operation, and, in theory, no such operation is needed for the stack ADT. However, *fullStack()* is required in this implementation, because we are using a finite array to hold the stack.

The last three methods defined for the class are *push()*, *pop()*, and *topElement()*. You already know the purpose of these methods. However, take a close look at each method signature. The *push()* method accepts a character, *character*, to be pushed onto the stack. It does not return any value, because it will simply place *character* into the array at the top position. The *pop()* method does not have any formal parameters, because it will read the element at the top position of the stack array. The return type of *pop()* is a character, because it will return the popped element to the calling program. Likewise, the *topElement()* method does not require any formal parameters, because it simply reads the top element of the stack. The return type is character, because it will return a copy of the top element to the calling program.

The implementation of the *push()* method employs an **if/else** statement to check for a full stack condition. You cannot push an element onto a full stack. The condition is checked by calling the *fullStack()* method. If the stack is not full, the value of *top* is incremented, and the character, *character*, received by the method is stored in the stack array at position *stack*[*top*]. If the stack is full, an appropriate message is displayed.

The *pop()* method employs an **if/else** statement to check for an empty stack condition. You cannot pop an element from an empty stack. Here, the *emptyStack()* method is called as part of the **if/else** statement. If the stack is not empty, the element at array position *stack*[*top*] is obtained and assigned to the local variable *character*. (Why is a local variable required here?) The value of *top* is then decremented, and the character, *character*, is returned to the calling program.

Finally, the *topElement( )* method is similar to the *pop( )* method in that it checks for an empty stack condition and, if the stack is not empty, returns the character at array position *stack*[*top*]. Notice, however, that the value of *top* is not altered, thereby leaving the stack unchanged.

PROGRAMMING NOTE

The Java class fully encapsulates the stack ADT. As a result, only those operations defined in the class can operate on the stack data. Even though the stack is being implemented with an array, the stack array is private and, therefore, cannot be corrupted by any operations outside of the class. When using the stack, you are forced to use only those operations defined by the stack ADT. This is why encapsulation and information hiding are so important when creating ADTs. As you can see, the class in Java inherently provides the encapsulation and data hiding required by ADTs.

Now all we need is an application class to test our stack ADT. Here is one that will do the job:

```
import adts.*;              //FOR STACK CLASS
import keyboardInput.*;     //FOR KEYBOARD CLASS

//APPLICATION CLASS TO TEST THE STACK ADT
public class StackTest
{
  public static void main(String[] args)
  {
    char character;       //CHARACTER TO BE STACKED
    int number = 0;       //NUMBER OF CHARACTERS TO BE STACKED
    int count = 0;        //LOOP COUNTER
    char pause = ' ';     //FREEZE VARIABLE

    //DEFINE STACK OBJECT
    Stack stk = new Stack();

    //DEFINE KEYBOARD OBJECT
    Keyboard in = new Keyboard();

    //GET NUMBER OF ELEMENTS TO STACK
    System.out.print("\n\n\nHow many elements do you have to enter? ");
    number = in.readInt();
```

```
//PUSH ELEMENTS ONTO STACK
while (count < number)
{
  ++count;
  System.out.print("\nEnter a character element:  ");
  character = in.readChar();
  stk.push(character);
} //END WHILE

//INSPECT TOP ELEMENT OF THE STACK
System.out.println("\nThe top element of the stack is:  "
                    + stk.topElement());

//POP AND WRITE STACK ELEMENTS
System.out.println("\nThe contents of the stack are:  ");
while (!stk.emptyStack())
  System.out.println(stk.pop());

//ATTEMPT TO POP AN EMPTY STACK
stk.pop();

//FREEZE DISPLAY
System.out.println("\nPress ENTER to continue.");
pause = in.readChar();
  } //END main()
} //END StackTest
```

The program begins by importing a package called *adts*. This is where our *Stack* class resides. There are several local variables declared at the beginning of *main( )*. These variables will be used to process the stack information, as you will see shortly. An object called *stk* is defined for our *Stack* class. The user is first prompted for the number of characters to be entered onto the stack. A **while** loop is used to push the entered characters onto the stack one character at a time. Notice that the **while** loop will execute as long as the number of characters entered is less than the number dictated by the user. The user is prompted within the loop to enter one character at a time. After the character is read from the user, it is pushed onto the stack by calling the *push( )* method.

The next segment of code inspects and displays the top character on the stack with a call to the *topElement( )* method.

The final segment of code pops the entire stack and displays the stack elements one character at a time. A **while** loop is used to pop and display the stack elements. The loop is controlled by making a call to the *emptyStack()* method. As a result, the loop will execute until the stack is empty.

Finally, notice that a single call to *pop()* is made after the stack is emptied. This call is made to test the *pop()* method relative to an empty stack. Here is a sample run of the program:

```
How many elements do you have to enter? 3↵

Enter a character element: A↵

Enter a character element: B↵

Enter a character element: C↵

The top element of the stack is: C

The contents of the stack are:
C
B
A
The stack is empty!

Press ENTER to continue.
```

Observe what has happened. The user entered three characters in the order 'A', 'B', 'C'. The program shows that the last character entered, 'C', is on the top of the stack. Then, the contents of the stack are popped and displayed. Notice that the output order is reversed from the input order because of the LIFO principle. Finally, the attempt to pop an empty stack resulted in the appropriate message to the user, thus verifying the integrity of the *pop()* method.

 Quick Check

1. Suppose that the user filled a stack using the application test class in this section. What would happen if a call was made to the *push()* method after the stack was full?

2. Because we are using an array implementation for a stack, why can't you randomly access the stack elements using array operations, rather than accessing them through *top*?

3. With our array implementation of a stack, a *push()* operation requires that the stack pointer be _____.

4. True or false: With our array implementation of a stack, the stack is full when the value of *top* becomes equal to *SIZE*, where *SIZE* is the maximum number of elements that the array can hold.

5. With our array implementation of a stack, the stack is empty when the value of *top* is _____.

6. What is the functional difference between the *pop()* method and the *topElement()* method?

7. There is no *fullStack()* operation defined for the stack ADT. Why did we have to include a *fullStack()* method in our implementation?

14-4 THE QUEUE ADT

A *queue* is another important ADT in computer systems. There are more examples of queues in the real world than stacks, because queues have the *first-in, first-out*, or *FIFO*, property. For instance, the grocery store line mentioned in the last section is a queue. Aircraft in a holding pattern waiting to land at a busy airport represent a *queuing* operation. As aircraft approach the airport traffic area, they are placed in a holding pattern so that the first one in the pattern is the first one to land. We say that the aircraft are being *queued* into the pattern. A computer scientist would never say that the aircraft are being *stacked* in the pattern, right? Also, print jobs on a network are placed into a print queue for storage until they can be printed by the relatively slow printer. Of course, the jobs are printed in the order they are received. Can you think of other real-world examples of queuing operations?

    Recall that the LIFO property of stacks reverses the order of the stack elements from input to the stack to output from the stack. Queues, on the other hand, exhibit the FIFO property which preserves the order of the elements from input to output. Now for a formal definition of a queue.

A *queue* is a collection of data elements in which all insertions of elements into the queue are made at one end of the queue, called the *rear* of the queue; and all deletions of elements from the queue are made at the other end of the queue, called the *front* of the queue. A queue operates on the *first-in, first-out*, or *FIFO* principle.

From this definition, you see that queue access occurs at one of two ends of the queue. If an element is added to the queue, it is added to the rear of the queue just as in a grocery store checkout line. On the other hand, if an element is removed from the queue, it is removed from the front of the queue, as with the grocery store line. Of course, you can't remove an element from the middle of the queue or from an empty queue. We are now ready to define our queue ADT as follows:

Queue ADT

Data:

A collection of data elements with the property that elements can only be added at one end, called the *rear* of the queue, and elements can only be removed from the other end, called the *front* of the queue.

Operations, or Interface:

createQ
Creates an empty queue.

insert( )
Adds an element to the rear of a queue.

remove( )
Removes an element from the front of a queue.

frontElement( )
Copies the front element of a queue, leaving the queue unchanged.

emptyQ( )
Determines if the queue is empty.

Implementing the Queue ADT

Again we will use the versatile array to implement the queue. However, we need to make use a special array called a *circular*, or *wraparound*, array. Look at the array in Figure 14-9 to see how we can create a queue using a circular array.

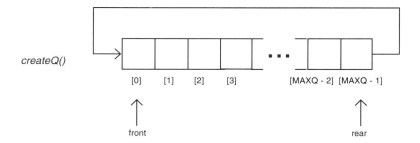

Figure 14-9   Setting *front* to 0 and *rear* to *MAXQ* − 1 will create a queue using a circular array implementation.

Creating a Queue Using a Circular Array

In Figure 14-9 you see an array whose size is *MAXQ* and highest index is *MAXQ* − 1. To make the array hold a queue, we need to initialize two integer variables that locate the front and rear of the queue. Here, *front* is initialized to 0 so that it locates position [0] of the array, and *rear* is initialized to *MAXQ* − 1 so that it locates the last array position. Thus, an appropriate algorithm for *createQ()* is

createQ() **Algorithm**

> BEGIN
>   Set *front* = 0.
>   Set *rear* = *MAXQ* − 1.
> END.

Now, here's the idea behind a circular array. When we are using an external integer variable, such as *front* or *rear*, to locate elements in the array, we will advance the variable through the index range of the array, in our case from 0 to *MAXQ* − 1. When the variable needs to be advanced past the last array index, [*MAXQ* − 1], we will force it to the first array index, [0]. Thus, the variable will be advanced as follows:

$$0, 1, 2, 3, \ldots, (MAXQ - 1), 0, 1, 2, 3, \ldots, (MAXQ - 1), 0, 1, 2, 3, \ldots$$

This way, the advancing process can continue in a circle indefinitely. All we need to accomplish this task is an **if/else** statement, like this:

$$\text{If } rear == MAXQ - 1$$
$$\text{Set } rear = 0.$$
$$\text{Else}$$
$$\text{Set } rear = rear + 1.$$

Here you see that the **else** statement increments *rear*, unless the value of *rear* is $MAXQ - 1$. If this is the case, *rear* is set to 0. Of course, we will do the same thing with *front* to make it wrap around.

Now we are ready to begin inserting and removing elements to and from the queue. Remember, we will insert elements at the rear of the queue and remove elements from the front of the queue.

Inserting Elements into a Queue

To insert an element into the queue, we must first advance *rear* and then place the element at array position [*rear*]. Thus, suppose we start with the array shown in Figure 14-9 and execute the following three insertion operations:

$$insert('A')$$
$$insert('B')$$
$$insert('C')$$

The sequence of events created by these three operations is illustrated in Figure 14-10. We begin with the queue being initialized using *createQ()*. Remember that *createQ()* initializes *front* with the value 0 and *rear* with the value $MAXQ - 1$. When the first character, 'A', is inserted into the queue, the value of *rear* must be advanced prior to the character being placed in the array. However, because *rear* locates the last array index, [$MAXQ - 1$], the value of *rear* is forced to 0 using the wraparound idea. Once *rear* is advanced to 0, the character 'A' is placed at array position [*rear*], or [0]. Notice that both *front* and *rear* locate the character 'A'. This is *always* the case when there is only one element in the queue.

The second character to be inserted is the character 'B'. Again, *rear* is advanced to locate the next array position. This time, however, the value of *rear* is **not** $MAXQ - 1$. Therefore, 1 is added to *rear* so that it locates the next sequential array position, [1]. The character 'B' is then placed at array position [*rear*], or [1].

The third insert operation places that character 'C' at array position [2]. Notice that *front* has not been affected by the insert operations and locates the first character inserted into the queue.

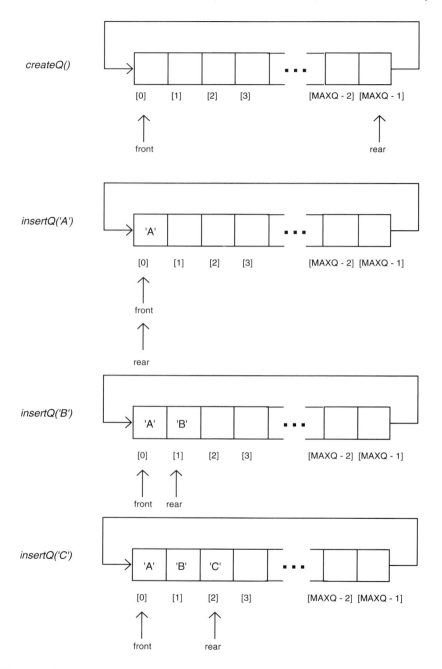

Figure 14-10   The effect of creating a queue and inserting three character elements into the queue.

Here is an algorithm that reflects the *insert()* operation:

insert() **Algorithm**

BEGIN
    If the queue is not full
        If *rear* == *MAXQ* − 1
            Set *rear* = 0.
        Else
            Set *rear* = *rear* + 1.
        Place element at array position [*rear*].
    Else
        Display full queue message.
END.

The first thing that must be done is to check for a full queue. How do you know when the queue is full? Or, for that matter, how do you know when the queue is empty? Well, because we are using an array implementation, the queue is full when the array is full, and the queue is empty when the array is empty, right? But, how can we use *front* and/or *rear* to determine when the array is full or empty? Your first thought might be that the queue is full when an element is placed in the last array position, thereby making *rear* take on the value *MAXQ*−1. But, from Figure 14-9, you see that this condition also reflects an empty queue condition. In fact, because of the circular nature of the array, there is no way to determine a full or empty queue condition using the values of *front* and *rear* unless we alter the nature of our implementation. Think about it!

The simplest way to determine an empty or full queue condition is to count the number of elements being inserted and removed from the queue. When an element is inserted into the queue, we will increment an element counter. When an element is removed from the queue, we will decrement the element counter. In this way, the queue is empty when the counter value is 0 and full when the counter value reaches the size of the array, *MAXQ*. To do this, we must add an additional processing step to our *insert()* algorithm that will increment the element counter. Here is a modified *insert()* algorithm that will check for a full queue condition:

Modified *insert()* Algorithm

BEGIN
    If the queue is not full
        Increment element counter.

If *rear* == *MAXQ* − 1
    Set *rear* = 0.
Else
    Set *rear* = *rear* + 1.
Place element at array position [*rear*].
Else
    Display full queue message.
END.

You should be aware that there is another way to implement a queue using a circular array that doesn't require an element counter to determine the empty/full conditions. However, this implementation requires that you sacrifice one array position by not allowing any queue elements to be placed in this position. This implementation will be left as a programming exercise at the end of the chapter.

Now, back to the algorithm. If the queue is not full, the element counter is incremented, and the **if/else** wraparound statement is executed to advance *rear*. Once *rear* is advanced, the element is placed in array position [*rear*]. Note that *rear* must be advanced prior to placing the element in the array. Of course, if the queue is full, no action is taken on the queue, and an appropriate message is displayed.

Removing Elements from a Queue

Let's remove the three elements that were inserted in Figure 14-10 by executing the following *remove()* operations:

remove()
remove()
remove()

This sequence of events is illustrated in Figure 14-11. Elements are removed from the front of the queue. As a result, the first element to be removed from the queue is the character 'A' at array position [*front*], or [0]. Once the element is removed, *front* is advanced to the next circular array position. Now the character 'B' is at the front of the queue. The second *remove()* operation removes this character and advances *front* to position [2]. Now the only remaining element in the queue is the character 'C'. Notice that both *front* and *rear* locate this character, because it is the only element in the queue. A third *remove()* operation removes the character 'C', leaving an empty queue.

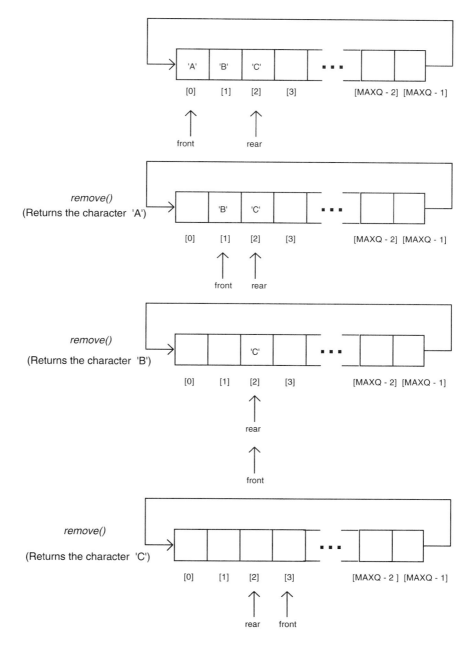

Figure 14-11 The effect of removing three character elements from the queue in Figure 14-10.

How can it be that the queue is empty, because *front* and *rear* are not in their initialized positions? Moreover, *front* has moved ahead of *rear*. Is this a problem? No! Remember how we have defined an empty and a full queue? It does not matter where *front* and *rear* are located in determining the empty or full queue conditions. All that matters is the value of the element counter. If the element counter is 0, the queue is empty. If the element counter is *MAXQ*, the queue is full.

Here is an algorithm for the *remove()* operation:

remove() **Algorithm**

```
BEGIN
    If the queue is not empty
        Decrement element counter.
        Remove the element at array position [front].
        If front == MAXQ − 1
            Set front = 0.
        Else
            Set front = front + 1.
    Else
        Display empty queue message.
END.
```

The algorithm begins by checking for the empty queue condition. If the queue is not empty, the element counter is decremented, and *front* is advanced via the **if/else** wraparound statement. If the queue is empty, an appropriate message is displayed.

Inspecting the Front Element of a Queue

The next thing we need to do is to develop the *frontElement()* operation. Suppose we execute the following statement on the queue created back in Figure 14-10:

frontElement()

The results of this operation are shown in Figure 14-12. Here you find that neither *front* nor *rear* is affected by the *frontElement()* operation. The operation simply returns the front character of the queue. The following algorithm will support this operation:

frontElement( ) **Algorithm**

BEGIN
    If the queue is not empty
        Copy the element at array position [*front*].
    Else
        Display an empty queue message.
END.

If the queue is not empty, the algorithm simply copies the element at the front position of the queue. Comparing this to the *remove( )* algorithm, you find that there is no operation on the element counter or the *front* position locator.

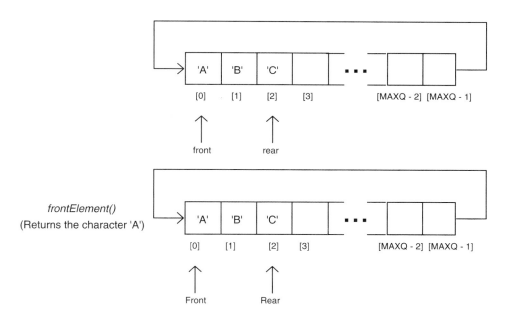

Figure 14-12   The effect of inspecting the queue created in Figure 14-10.

Coding the Queue ADT

We are now ready to code the queue ADT. To assure encapsulation and information hiding, we will code the ADT as a class. Here's the class declaration:

```
package adts;
//QUEUE CLASS DECLARATION
public class Queue
{
   //CONSTANT DECLARATIONS
   public static final int MAXQ = 5;        //MAXIMUM QUEUE SIZE
   public static final int EMPTY = 0;       //DECLARE EMPTY = 0
   public static final int FULL = MAXQ;     //DECLARE FULL = MAXQ

   //DATA MEMBERS
   private char[] queue = new char[MAXQ];   //CHARACTER ARRAY TO HOLD
                                            //A CHARACTER QUEUE
   private int front;                       //FRONT ELEMENT OF QUEUE
   private int rear;                        //REAR ELEMENT OF QUEUE
   private int elementCount;                //ELEMENT COUNTER

   //METHOD MEMBERS

   //CONSTRUCTOR TO IMPLEMENT createQ()
   public Queue()
   {
    front = 0;                    //SET front TO FIRST ARRAY POSITION
    rear = MAXQ - 1;              //SET rear TO LAST ARRAY POSITION
    elementCount = EMPTY;         //SET Q ELEMENT COUNTER TO 0
   } //END Queue()

   //CHECKS TO SEE IF QUEUE IS EMPTY
   public boolean emptyQ()
   {
     if (elementCount == EMPTY) //IF Q  EMPTY, RETURN true
       return true;
     else                       //ELSE RETURN false
       return false;
   } //END emptyQ()

   //CHECKS TO SEE IF QUEUE IS FULL
   public boolean fullQ()
   {
     if (elementCount == FULL)   //IF Q FULL, RETURN true
       return true;
     else                        //ELSE RETURN false
       return false;
   } //END fullQ()
```

```
//ADD ELEMENT TO REAR OF Q
public void insert(char character)
{
  if (!fullQ())                    //IF Q NOT FULL
  {
    ++elementCount;                //ADD ONE TO ELEMENT COUNT
    if (rear == MAXQ - 1)          //INCREMENT REAR USING WRAPAROUND
      rear = 0;
    else
      ++rear;
    queue[rear] = character;       //INSERT CHARACTER INTO Q
  } //END IF
  else
    System.out.println("The queue is full!");
} //END insert()

//REMOVE ELEMENT FROM front
public char remove()
{
  char character;
  if (!emptyQ())                   //IF Q NOT EMPTY
  {
    --elementCount;                //DECREMENT ELEMENT COUNT
    character = queue[front];      //SAVE front ELEMENT
    if (front == MAXQ - 1)         //INCREMENT front USING WRAPAROUND
      front = 0;
    else
      ++front;
    return character;              //RETURN SAVED FRONT ELEMENT
  } //END IF
  else
  {
    System.out.println("The queue is empty");
    return '#';                    //ELSE RETURN '#' FOR EMPTY Q
  } //END ELSE
} //END remove()

//INSPECT front ELEMENT
public char frontElement()
{
  if (!emptyQ())                   //IF Q NOT EMPTY
    return queue[front];           //RETURN front ELEMENT
```

```
    else                              //ELSE RETURN '#' FOR EMPTY Q
    {
      System.out.println("The queue is empty!");
      return '#';
    } //END ELSE
  } //END frontElement()
}//END Queue CLASS
```

The class file is coded as part of the *adts* package. Here, you find the same type of constants that we coded in the *Stack* class. Notice, however, that *EMPTY* is defined with a value of 0, and *FULL* is defined with a value of *MAXQ*. These definitions will be used when testing the element counter for the empty and full conditions, respectively. The private section begins by defining a character array called *queue[]* as a private member. As a result, this queue will store character elements. The size of the array is *MAXQ*, where *MAXQ* has been declared as the constant 5 for example purposes. There are three private integer variables: *front*, *rear*, and *elementCount*. You now should be aware of their use in this implementation. Again, it is important to stress the hiding of these private class members. No operations outside of the class can affect the contents of *queue[]* or the values of *front*, *rear*, or *elementCount*. As a result, any queue object created for this class cannot be corrupted by intentional or unintentional operations outside the queue class.

The public methods that are listed in the class are those defined for the queue ADT, with the exception of the *fullQ()* operation. Why do we need a *fullQ()* operation for our implementation? The same reason that we needed a *fullStack()* operation for our stack implementation. We are dealing with a finite array data structure. Note also that the *createQ()* operation is implemented by the class constructor. All of the queue algorithms discussed earlier have been coded. Compare each coded method to its algorithm so that you understand what's going on. There were no algorithms developed for the *emptyQ()* and *fullQ()* operations, because they are so straightforward. Observe that the code for the *emptyQ()* and *fullQ()* methods simply tests the element counter for an *EMPTY* or *FULL* condition. Recall that *EMPTY* is defined as 0 and *FULL* is defined as *MAXQ*.

The following application class, called *QueueTest*, has been created to test our queue ADT:

```
import adts.*;                     //FOR QUEUE CLASS
import keyboardInput.*;            //FOR KEYBOARD CLASS
//APPLICATION CLASS TO TEST THE QUEUE ADT
public class QueueTest
{
```

```
  public static void main(String[] args)
  {
    char character;      //CHARACTER TO BE QUEUED
    int number = 0;      //NUMBER OF CHARACTERS TO BE QUEUED
    int count = 0;       //LOOP COUNTER
    char pause = ' ';    //FREEZE VARIABLE

    //DEFINE QUEUE OBJECT
    Queue q = new Queue();

    //DEFINE KEYBOARD OBJECT
    Keyboard in = new Keyboard();

    //GET NUMBER OF ELEMENTS TO QUEUE
    System.out.print("\n\n\nHow many elements do you have to enter? ");
    number = in.readInt();

    //INSERT ELEMENTS INTO QUEUE
    while (count < number)
    {
      ++count;
      System.out.print("\nEnter a character element:  ");
      character = in.readChar();
      q.insert(character);
    } //END WHILE

    //INSPECT FRONT ELEMENT OF THE QUEUE
    System.out.println("\nThe front element of the queue is:  "
                       + q.frontElement());

    //REMOVE AND WRITE QUEUE ELEMENTS
    System.out.println("\nThe contents of the queue are:  ");
    while (!q.emptyQ())
      System.out.println(q.remove());

    //ATTEMPT TO REMOVE FROM AN EMPTY QUEUE
    q.remove();

    //PAUSE DISPLAY
    System.out.println("\nPress ENTER to continue.");
    pause = in.readChar();
  } //END main()
} //END QueueTest
```

The test program defines *q* as an object of class *Queue*. Elements are then inserted into *q* one at time from user entries via a **while** loop. Notice that the loop executes as long as the number of elements entered does not exceed the number of elements the user specified for entry. Once the user elements are inserted into the queue, the front element is inspected by a call to the *frontElement()* method. The next segment of code removes and displays the queue elements. If the queue is not empty, a **while** loop is entered to remove and display all of the queue elements one at a time. The termination of the loop is controlled by a call to *emptyQ()*. As a result, the loop statements will execute, removing and displaying one element with each iteration, until the queue is empty. Finally, a single call is made to *removeQ()* in an attempt to remove an element from an empty queue. This call was made to test the *removeQ()* method. Here are the results of executing the test program:

```
How many elements do you have to enter? 3↵

Enter a character element: A↵

Enter a character element: B↵

Enter a character element: C↵

The front element of the queue is: A

The contents of the queue are:
A
B
C
The queue is empty!

Press ENTER to continue.
```

In this test run, the user has entered the characters 'A', 'B', and 'C'. The front character, 'A', is copied and displayed to verify the *frontElement()* method. Then all of the characters of the queue are removed and displayed. Notice that the characters are displayed in the same order in which they were entered, thereby verifying the FIFO principle. The last line on the display verifies that the *remove()* method checks for the empty queue condition.

Quick Check

1. Suppose that the user filled a queue using the application test program in this section. What would happen if a call were made to the *insert()* method after the queue was full?

2. True or false: With our array implementation of a queue, an *insert()* method requires that *front* be advanced prior to placing the element in the array.

3. Write the pseudocode required to advance *front* for the circular array implementation of a queue.

4. True or false: With the circular array implementation of a queue, *front* can never have a higher value than *rear*.

5. Using the circular array implementation of a queue, how can you tell when there is only one element in the queue?

6. Theoretically, the size of a queue is unlimited. Why did we have to include a *fullQ()* method in our implementation?

7. Explain how to determine when the queue is empty and when the queue is full using our array implementation.

CHAPTER SUMMARY

A recursive method is a method that calls itself until a terminating condition is reached. There must always be a terminating condition to terminate a recursive method call; otherwise, a run-time error will occur. Recursive operations are performed as part of an **if/else** statement. The terminating condition forms the **if** clause, and the recursive call is part of the **else** clause of the statement. All recursive operations also can be performed using iteration. Because recursion eats up time and memory as compared to iteration, you should consider recursion only when a simple iterative solution is not possible and when the execution and memory efficiency of the solution are within acceptable limits.

Binary search is a recursive process. Binary search keeps dividing the array in half, directing itself to the half where the value is likely to be found. Binary search requires that the array be sorted, whereas sequential search does not have this requirement. On the other hand, binary search is much faster than sequential search, especially on large sorted arrays.

The definition of an ADT includes the following key concepts:

- *An ADT provides for data abstraction.*
- *An ADT includes both data and related operations.*
- *An ADT provides a means to encapsulate and hide information details whereby the ADT data is completely hidden from its surroundings.*
- *ADT operations provide coupling to the outside world via its method interfaces.*

Data abstraction is an important software development and programming tool. When developing software with ADTs, you can concentrate on the ADT data and related operations, without worrying about the inner implementation details of the ADT. Data abstraction provides for generality, modularity, and protection when developing software.

Two classic ADTs are the stack and the queue. The stack ADT provides for a collection of data elements whereby elements are always added and removed from one end of the stack, called the *top* of the stack. As a result, stacks operate on the last-in, first-out (LIFO) principle, which reverses the ordering of data elements from input to the stack to output from the stack. The queue ADT provides for a collection of data elements whereby elements are always added to the rear of the queue and removed from the front of the queue. Thus, queues operate on the first-in, first-out (FIFO) principle, which preserves the ordering of data elements from input to the queue to output from the queue.

Object-oriented programming is ideal for implementing ADTs because of its data hiding ability. When an ADT is coded as a class, only those operations that are defined for the ADT can be used to access and manipulate the ADT data.

QUESTIONS AND PROBLEMS

Questions

1. Explain recursion.
2. When should you consider a recursive solution to a problem?
3. Recursion employs a data structure called a _____.
4. Why is binary search faster, on the average, than sequential search?
5. When would sequential search be faster than binary search?

6. Why is data abstraction an important software development tool?

7. What three things are gained by using ADTs during software development?

8. Suppose that we implement a queue using a noncircular array. The queue is initialized so that *front* = *rear* = 0. Then, as we add elements to the queue, we increment *rear* and insert the element into the array at position [*rear*]. When we remove elements from the queue, we remove the element at position [*front*] and increment *front*. What problem is encountered with this implementation? Can the problem be corrected? If so, how? What do you suppose the disadvantage is to this implementation versus the one given in this chapter.

9. How do you know that there is only a single element in a queue using the implementation discussed in this chapter?

10. Suggest a way of implementing a queue using a noncircular array. (*Hint*: Always keep *front* at position [0] in the array.) What is the disadvantage of this implementation compared to the circular array implementation?

11. Would a compiler use a stack or a queue to keep track of return addresses for nested method calls?

12. Use the stack ADT to write the pseudocode required to remove the element just below the top element of a stack.

13. How must the stack and queue classes given in this chapter be changed to store integers?

14. How must the stack and queue classes given in this chapter be changed to store double floating-point numbers?

15. How must the stack and queue classes given in this chapter be changed to store objects?

16. Use the queue ADT to write the pseudocode required to move the element at the rear of the queue to the front of the queue.

Problems

Least Difficult

1. Write an application program to test the *binSearch()* method developed in this chapter. Use the standard *random()* method to fill an array with random integer values. Then, apply *insertSort()* to sort the array prior to using *binSearch()*. (*Note*: If you use the *insertSort()* code developed in an earlier chapter, you must change the code to sort an integer array rather than a character array.)

2. Change the stack ADT implementation given in this text to store integers. Write an application program to test your integer stack.

3. Change the queue ADT implementation given in this text to store double floating-point numbers. Write an application program to test your floating-point queue.

4. A palindrome is a word that has the same spelling both forward and backward. Three examples are the words MOM, DAD, and ANNA. Write a program that uses a stack and a queue to determine if a word entered by the user is a palindrome.

5. Write a program that uses only stacks to determine if a word entered by the user is a palindrome. (*Hint:* You will need three stacks. Why?)

More Difficult

6. Here is an iterative solution for the binary search:

binarySearch()
BEGIN
    Set found = false.
    While (!found AND first <= last)
      Set mid = (first + last) / 2.
      If (element == array[mid])
        Set found = true.
      Else
        If (element < array[mid])
          Set last = mid – 1.
        Else
          Set first = mid + 1.
    If (found)
      Return mid.
    Else
      Return –1.
END.

Code this algorithm as a Java method to search for a given element in an integer array. Write an application program to test the method. Remember to sort the array using a sorting method prior to calling the binary search method.

7. Develop an algorithm and code a method to find *n*! using iteration. Write an application program to test your method.

8. Develop an algorithm and code a method to find *n*! using recursion. Write an application program to test your method.

9. Place the methods that you developed in problems 7 and 8 in a menu-driven program that will allow the user to select either an iterative or recursive

solution to *n*!. Execute each option for the same value of *n*, and determine the amount of time it takes to execute each option with the given value of *n*. Repeat this process for increasing values of *n*. What conclusions can you draw about iterative versus recursive solutions?

10. You can implement a queue in a circular array without using an element counter to determine the empty/full conditions. To do this, you must sacrifice an array position so that no element is ever stored in this position. In this implementation, *front* will locate the empty array position, and the empty position will always precede the actual front element in the queue. This idea is shown in Figure 14-13.

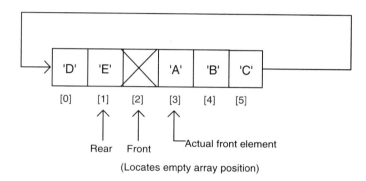

Figure 14-13   An alternative way to implement a queue using a circular array.

With this implementation, the queue is empty when *front* = *rear*, and the queue is full when *rear* + 1 = *front*. To insert an element into the rear of the queue, you must preincrement *rear*. To remove an element from the front of the queue, you must preincrement *front*. The queue can be initialized to an empty condition by setting *front* = *rear* = *MAXQ* − 1.

Develop a class for this implementation. Be sure to write a test program to see if the implementation works.

Does it really matter relative to data abstraction which implementation is used for the queue: this one or the one given in the chapter? Both implementations do the same thing relative to the ADT definition, right?

Most Difficult

11. Provide a GUI for stack class developed in this chapter.

12. Provide a GUI for the queue class developed in this chapter.

13. A Fibonacci sequence of numbers is defined as follows:

$$F_0 = 0$$
$$F_1 = 1$$
$$F_n = F_{n-1} + F_{n-2}, \text{ for } n > 1$$

This says that the first two numbers in the sequence are 0 and 1. Then, each additional Fibonacci number is the sum of the two previous numbers in the sequence. Thus, the first 10 Fibonacci numbers are

$$0, 1, 1, 2, 3, 5, 8, 13, 21, 34$$

Here, we say that the first number occupies position 0 in the sequence, the second number position 1 in the sequence, and so on. Thus, the last position in a 10-number sequence is position 9. Develop a program that employs a recursive method to generate a Fibonacci sequence of all numbers up to some position n entered by the user.

14. Develop a program that employs an iterative method to generate a Fibonacci sequence of all numbers up to some position n entered by the user.

15. Measure the amount of time it takes each of the programs in problems 13 and 14 to generate a Fibonacci sequence of 50 elements. What do you conclude about the efficiency of recursion versus iteration? Why does the recursive program take so long?

Appendix A

QUICK-CHECK SOLUTIONS

CHAPTER 1

SECTION 1-1

1. CPU, memory, and I/O
2. microprocessor
3. Arithmetic: addition, subtraction, multiplication, division

   Logic: equal to, not equal to, less than, greater than, less than or equal to, greater than or equal to
4. arithmetic logic unit (ALU), control unit, and internal registers
5. 16,777,216
6. firmware
7. Instructions are fetched from memory, decoded, executed, and results are stored back into memory.

SECTION 1-2

1. Java is strictly an object-oriented language, while C++ is a hybrid structured and object-oriented language.
2. Enter/edit, save, compile, correct errors, translate Java byte code to machine code.

3. Java byte code is a low-level code which is generic and not specific to any particular CPU.

4. The generic byte codes generated by the Java compiler makes Java an extremely portable language.

5. Java application programs are designed to be run on a computer just like any other application software. Java applets are designed only to be run using an Internet Web browser.

6. A compiler translates the entire program into machine code all at one time, before execution by the CPU. An interpreter translates then executes one high-level program statement at a time.

7. Machine language, assembly language, high-level language.

8. source

9. To manage the resources of the system.

CHAPTER 2

SECTION 2-1

1. pseudocode

2. What output is needed?
   What input is needed?
   What processing is needed to produce the output from the input?

3. Desk-check, compile, debug using a debugger, and run the program.

4. Commenting explains what the program does and self-documents the program, making it easier to read and maintain.

5. A syntax error is any violation of the rules of the programming language.

6. A logic error is an error made by the programmer relative to the way in which the program will execute.

SECTION 2-2

1. To define what steps are needed to produce the desired final result. An algorithm keeps you from "spinning your wheels."

2. Sequence, decision, and iteration.

3. The three decision operations are **if**, **if/else**, and **switch/case**.

4. The three iteration operations are **while**, **do/while**, and **for**.

SECTION 2-3

1. Abstraction allows you to "see the forest over the trees," because it permits you to initially concentrate on the problem at hand, without agonizing over the implementation details of a computer language.

2. Stepwise refinement begins with the initial abstract algorithm and step by step divides it into one or more related algorithms that provide more and more implementation detail.

3. A codeable level of an algorithm is reached when all the statements have been reduced to the pseudocode operations listed in Table 2-1.

CHAPTER 3

SECTION 3-1

1. class

2. standard classes

3. An ADT is an abstract data type, which is implemented by a class to describe the data attributes and behavior of its objects.

4. Primitive data types, standard classes, and programmer defined classes.

5. Behavior, as related to classes and ADTs, describes how the ADT or class will act and react to a given operation.

6. A method is a subprogram that returns a value or performs some specific task related to an algorithm.

7. Because a class allows you to define and code a set of data and operations, or methods, for an ADT.

SECTION 3-2

1. Approximately −2 billion to +2 billion.

2. An overflow error.

3. fixed decimal or exponential

4. The character 'z'.

5. The character 'a'.

6. 28

7. boolean

SECTION 3-3

1. The two reasons for defining constants and variables in a Java program are as follows:
   - The compiler must know the value of a constant before it is used and must reserve memory locations to store variables.
   - The compiler must know the data type of constants and variables to determine their data attributes and behavior.

2. static final char PERIOD = '.' ;

3. static final String BOOK = "Java for CIS";

4. int age = 0;

5. String course = "Accounting" ;

6. System.out.println(course);

SECTION 3-4

1. import, class

2. import myPackage.*;

3. method

4. Immediately after the opening brace of the class.

5. Variables and objects can be defined anywhere in the program as long as they are defined prior to their use. However, good style dictates that they be defined at the beginning of the method or class block in which they are used.

6. *Inventory.java*

7. d. double forward slashes, like this: //COMMENT.

8. At a minimum, the program should include the following comments:

   The beginning of the program should be commented with the programmer's name, date the program was written, date the program was last revised, and the name of the person doing the revision. In other words, a brief ongoing maintenance log should be commented at the beginning of the program.

   The beginning of the program should be commented to explain the purpose of the program, which includes the problem definition. This provides an overall perspective by which anyone, including you, the programmer, can begin debugging or maintaining the program.

   Import statements should be commented as to their purpose.

   Constants, variables, and objects should be commented as to their purpose.

Major sections of the program should be commented to explain the overall purpose of the respective section.

Individual program lines should be commented when the purpose of the code is not obvious relative to the application.

All major subprograms (methods in Java) should be commented just like the main program method.

The end of each program block (right curly brace) should be commented to indicate what the brace is ending.

CHAPTER *4*

SECTION 4-1

1. System.out.println("Andrew C. Staugaard, Jr.");

2. System.out.println(name);

3. '\n'

4. '\t'

5. The *println()* method generates a CRLF after its output to place the cursor on the next line, while the *print()* method does not generate a CRLF.

SECTION 4-2

1. Keyboard myInput = new Keyboard();

2. To allocate, or reserve, storage for the object.

3. A definition reserves storage, while a declaration does not.

4. Keyboard myInput = new Keyboard();
   int value = 0;
   System.out.print("Enter an integer value: ");
   value = myInput.readInt();

5. Keyboard myInput = new Keyboard();
   char character = ' ';
   System.out.print("Enter a single character: ");
   character = myInput.readChar();

6. Examples of whitespace include blanks, tabs, and CRLFs.

7. Keyboard myInput = new Keyboard();

```
char pause = ' ';
System.out.println("Press ENTER to continue. ");
pause = myInput.readChar();
```

8. False, because the *readChar()* method *does* read whitespace.

9. An exception is an error condition generated by a Java program.

10.
```
Keyboard myInput = new Keyboard();
String string = " ";
System.out.print("Enter a string of characters: ");
string = myInput.readString();
```

11. To assure that the input the program actually read is what the programmer expected it to read.

CHAPTER 5

SECTION 5-1

1. The order in which Java performs arithmetic operations is as follows:

    ( ) * / % + −

    Any operations inside of parentheses are performed first, then (from left to right) multiplication, division, and modulus, and then (from left to right) addition and subtraction.

2. The value of x is even.

3. The value of y is divisible by 17.

4. 0

5. 0

6. 1

7. − −x;

8. False because this happens only when both the numerator and denominator operands are *both* integers.

9. The difference between using the preincrement operator versus the postincrement operator on a variable is that a preincrement operator increments the variable before any expression involving the variable is evaluated and a postincrement operator increments the variable after any expression involving the variable is evaluated.

10. The result of 10 / 100 is 0, because both operands are integers, and the / operator generates an integer result when both operands are integers.

11. randomValue = Math.Random * 100;

12. System.out.println(Math.tan(45 * Math.PI/180));

13. pi = Math.PI;

14. The answer to this question depends on your particular Java compiler.

SECTION 5-2

1. x += 5;

2. x /= 10;

3. This expression cannot be written using a compound assignment operator.

4. Because *x* can never be equal to itself plus 5.

CHAPTER 6

SECTION 6-1

1. relational

2. The difference between the = operator and the == operator in Java is that the = operator assigns the value on the right to the variable on the left and the == operator compares two quantities to determine if they are equal.

3. The value boolean value **true**.

4. The boolean value **false** is generated, because (5 != 5) is false, making the entire AND statement false.

5. Because string values are represented as objects, not primitive data types.

SECTION 6-2

1. False, because the logical opposite of greater than is less than or equal to.

2. False, because the **if** statements are executed when the test expression is **true**.

3. The correct **if** statement is:

    if (x == y)
        System.out.println("There is a problem here");

    The test expression needs to be a comparison, not an assignment.

4.   The && (AND) operator must be employed to test if all conditions are true.

5.   The !&& (NOT AND) operators must be employed to test if one or more of several conditions is false.

6.   The ¦¦ (OR) operator must be employed to test if one of several conditions is true.

7.   For all values of x that are less than or equal to 50.

SECTION 6-3

1.   True, an **else** must always have a corresponding **if**.

2.   Because, without an **else** statement, both strings, "It's payday" and "It's not payday", would be written when the **if** test is true.

3.   True, framing can be eliminated when an **if** or **else** has only a single statement.

4.   subtract

5.   False, *compareTo()* returns an integer value that must be tested against 0.

6.   True, the *equals()* method returns a Boolean value.

SECTION 6-4

1.   Indentation is important when operations are nested for code readability and to be able to see at a glance which statements belong to which **if** or **else** statement.

2.   misplaced, or dangling **else**.

3.   "Red" will be written when the value is greater than −50 and less than 50.

4.   "White" will be written when the value is less than or equal to −50.

5.   "Blue" will be written when the value is greater than or equal to 50.

6.   The equivalent **if-else-if-else** logic is

```
If Value >= 50
    Write ("Blue")
else
    If Value <= −50
        Write ("White")
    else
        Write ("Red")
```

SECTION 6-5

1. matching

2. If you have *n* cases in a **switch** statement and there are no **break** statements in any of the cases, all of the cases will be executed sequentially when a match is made on the first case.

3. False, because there may be times when several subsequent cases need to be executed as the result of a match to a given case.

4. **default**

5. for menu-driven programs.

CHAPTER 7

SECTION 7-1

1. False, because a **while** loop repeats until the test expression is false.

2. False, because a **while** loop is a pretest loop not a posttest loop.

3. The **while** loop statements need to be framed, because without the framing, the value of *x* is never changed and you will have an infinite loop.

4. The correct code is:

```
x = 10;
while (x > 0)
{
    System.out.println( "This is a while loop");
    --x;
} //END WHILE
```

5. The loop will never execute, because the loop test is false the first time it is tested. Notice that *x* is initialized to 1 and is never < = 0.

6. This is an infinite loop. Notice that *x* is initialized to 1 and is incremented with each loop iteration. Thus, the **while** test of *x* > = *0* is always true.

SECTION 7-2

1. False, because a **do/while** loop repeats until the test expression is false.

2. True

3. The value of *x* is never changed within the loop, thereby creating an infinite loop.

4. The correct code is:

```
x = 10;
do
{
    System.out.println("This is a do/while loop");
    --x;
} //END DO/WHILE
while (x > 0);
```

5. The loop will execute once, because a **do/while** loop is a posttest loop.

6. Without the limitations of the computer, the loop will execute infinitely, because *x* starts out greater than 0 and is incremented inside of the loop. But, considering the physical limitations of the computer, it will execute about 2 billion times before wrapping around to a negative value and causing the test to be false.

SECTION 7-3

1. The three things that must appear in the first line of a **for** loop structure are:
    *   The loop counter initialization.
    *   The loop test expression.
    *   The changing of the counter value.

2. True

3. True

4. The loop will execute zero times, because the test condition false on the first test.

5. The loop will execute 11 times.

6. The **for** loop statements must be framed when there is more than one statement to be executed within the loop.

7. The inner loop will execute 5 times for every outer loop iteration. Thus, there are 5×10, or 50, total iterations.

8. decremented

SECTION 7-4

1. **continue**

2. **if**

3. The loop will execute twice. When *x* is incremented to 1 at the end of the first iteration, the **if** (x > 0) statement will be true in the second iteration, causing the **break** statement to execute to terminate the loop.

CHAPTER 8

SECTION 8-1

1. Methods eliminate the need for duplicate statements in a program.

    Methods make the program easier to design.

    Methods make the program easier to code and test.

    Methods allow for software reusability.

    Methods make the program more clear and readable.

    Methods provide the basis for classes in OOP.

2. nonvoid, void

3. signature, body

4. **return**

5. What the method accepts and what the method returns to the calling program.

6. The method signature provides the data interface for the method.

7. Optional modifiers, return type, method name, and parameter listing.

8. parameter

9. To return both a value and control to the calling program.

10. An argument is used in the method call, whereas a parameter is used in the method signature and receives the value of the corresponding argument when the method is called.

11. double loanPayment(double amount, double interestRate, double term)

SECTION 8-2

1. **void**

2. What the method accepts and what the method returns to the calling program.

3. By listing the method name and any required arguments as a statement with the calling program.

4.   False, a nonvoid method can be called with an assignment operator, not a void method.

5.   To return control to the calling program.

6.   void displayEmployee(String name, String ssn, int years, double salary)

SECTION 8-3

1.   Below the closing brace of *main( )*, and prior to the closing brace of the class that contains *main( )*.

2.   Just after the opening brace of *main( )*, or any place prior to their use within *main( )*.

3.   Just after the opening brace of the method, or any place prior to their use within the method.

4.   Global to the class in which it is defined.

SECTION 8-4

1.   The number or types of arguments provided in the method call.

2.   So that the same operation, such as printing, can behave differently depending on what it is provided.

3.   False, the compiler can only distinguish between parameter listings of overloaded methods.

4.   polymorphism

CHAPTER 9

SECTION 9-1

1.   By a class defining the behavior of its objects, we mean that the class defines how its objects act and react when they are accessed via the class methods.

2.   False, because encapsulation dictates only that the data and/or methods are packaged together in a well-defined unit.

3.   True

4.   encapsulation with information, or data, hiding

5.   True

6.   **private**

7.   implementation

8.  ```java
    public class CheckingAccount
    {
      //DATA MEMBERS
      private double balance = 0.0;            //ACCOUNT BALANCE
      private double minimum = 500.00;         //MINIMUM BALANCE TO
                                               //AVOID CHECK CHARGE
      private double charge = 0.5;             //PER-CHECK CHARGE

      //METHOD MEMBERS
      //INITIALIZE DATA MEMBERS
      public initialize(double bal, double min, double chg)
      {
        balance = bal;
        minimum = min;
        charge = chg;
      }//END CheckingAccount(double,double,double)

      //ADD DEPOSIT
      public void addDeposit(double amount)
      {
        balance = balance + amount;
      } //END addDeposit()

      //CASH A CHECK
      public void cashCheck(double amt)
      {
        //TEST FOR OVERDRAW
        if (amt > balance)
          System.out.println("Cannot cash check, account overdrawn.");

        //CASH CHECK
        else
          //CHECK FOR MINIMUM BALANCE
          if (balance < minimum)
            balance = balance - (amt + charge);   //DEBIT BALANCE WITH
                                                  //CHECK AMOUNT
                                                  //AND CHARGE

          else                                    //DEBIT BALANCE WITH
            balance = balance - amt;              //CHECK AMOUNT
      } //END cashCheck()

      //RETURN BALANCE
      public double currentBalance()
      {
        return balance;
      }//END currentBalance()
    } //END CheckingAccount
    ```
    ```

9.   CheckingAccount myAccount = new CheckingAccount();

10.   Truck pickUp = new Truck();

11.   Automobile convertible = new Automobile();

SECTION 9-2

1.   int Wheels();

2.   constructor

3.   The constructor has the same name as the class and has no return value.

4.   False, because constructors must not have a return type, not even **void**.

5.   A class constructor is called automatically when an object is defined for that class.

6.   False, because any method can be overloaded, including a constructor.

7.   You call a nonconstructor public method of a class by listing the class object name, a dot, and the method name with any required arguments.

8.   access, or get

9.   The term "message" is used for a call to a member method because when an object method is called, we are often sending information to the object.

10.   public MyClass(int value1, int value2)

11.   MyClass myObject = new MyClass(5,6);

CHAPTER 10

SECTION 10-1

1.   parent, base, or superclass

2.   child, derived, or subclass

3.   family of classes

4.   Two reasons for using inheritance are
      • Inheritance allows you to reuse code without having to start from scratch.
      • Inheritance allows you to build a family hierarchy among classes.

5.   IS-A

6.   False, because a line IS NOT A point.

7.   True, because a pixel IS-A point.

8.   True, because a pickup truck IS-A truck.

SECTION 10-2

1. True

2. **super**

3. False, because a **protected** member is inherited by any subclasses of the class in which it resides.

4. A **private** member is only visible within the class in which it is defined.

   A **protected** member is visible in any subclasses of the class in which it is defined.

   A **public** member is visible anywhere the class object is visible.

5. The reason that *Saving* class should not be derived from the *SuperNow* class is that a saving account is *not* form of checking account. Such a derivation would violate the IS-A principle.

6. *AndrewStaugaard:*   *accountNumber* = 0000
                             balance = 0.0
       MichaelJordon: *accountNumber* = 0010
                             balance = 10000
       BillGates: *accountNumber* = 0020
                             balance = 100000
                             minimum = 100
                             chg = 0.25

SECTION 10-3

1. True

2. False, because overloaded methods are statically bound at compile time..

3. True

4. statically

5. dynamically

6. run, or execution, time

7. An abstract class is a superclass for which no objects will ever be defined. A concrete class is a subclass for which objects will always be defined.

8. True

9. In the subclasses of the class in which the abstract signature is specified.

CHAPTER 11

SECTION 11-1

1. *java.awt*

2. frame

3. Frame myFrame = new Frame("This is my first frame");

4. myFrame.setSize(450,250);

5. myFrame.setVisible(true);

6. Create a GUI component object, register the object as a listener, and implement the corresponding event method to process an event generated by the object.

7. *windowClosing()*

8. addWindowListener(this);

9. *java.awt.event*

SECTION 11-2

1. Button myButton = new Button("Store");

2. add(myButton);

3. myButton.addActionListener(this);

4. *actionPerformed()*

5. if(event.getSource instanceof Button)

SECTION 11-3

1. *FlowLayout*

2. *GridLayout*

3. setLayout(new FlowLayout(FlowLayout.LEFT,20,10);

4. North, South, East, West, Center

5. setLayout(null);

6. At the top-left-hand corner of the window.

7. myButton.setLocation(20,30);

8. myButton.setSize(50,25);

9.   *getActionCommand()*

10.   setLayout(new BorderLayout(20,20));

11.   add(panel,"Center");

SECTION 11-4

1.   Label myLabel = new Label("This is my label");
      myPanel.add(myLabel);

2.   TextField myTextField = new TextField(20);

3.   TextArea myTextArea = new TextArea(10,50);

4.   myPanel.add(myTextField);
      myPanel.add(myTextArea);

5.   A choice box only allows for one item selection, while a list box allows for multiple item selection, when enabled.

6.   *getState()*

7.   To act as a container for menu components.

8.   MenuBar myMenuBar = new MenuBar();

9.   Menu myMenu = new Menu("My Menu",true);

10.   myMenuBar.add(myMenu);

11.   setMenuBar(myMenuBar);

12.   The font type, or name, the font style, and the font size.

13.   Approximately 1/72 inch.

14.   Font myFont = new Font("Arial", Font.BOLD, 16);

15.   myTextArea.setFont(myFont);

CHAPTER 12

SECTION 12-1

1.   False, because a file is a sequential access data structure.

2.   A communication path is established between the logical program object and the physical disk file

3.   stream

4.   *out* stream

5. *FileInputStream*

6. *DataOutputStream*

7. The standard *System* class and the standard *out* stream.

8. myFile = new DataOutputStream(new FileOutputStream("myFile.txt"));

9. yourFile = new DataInputStream(new FileInputStream(yourFileName));

10. *java.io*

SECTION 12-2

1. exception handling

2. Exception handling is required when opening files to catch a file-not-found or general I/O error.

3. checked

4. True

5. False, because exceptions that are not caught do not cause GUI programs to terminate prematurely.

6. **try**

7. True

8. *ArithmeticException*

9. False, because a **finally** block always executes regardless of whether or not an exception is thrown or caught.

10. True

SECTION 12-3

1. False, because the *DataInputStream* method provides methods to read primitive data types from files.

2. *Exception*

3. *writeUTF()*

4. myOutputFile.writeUTF(myName.getText));

5. displayText.append(myInputFile. readUTF));

6. myOutputFile.writeInt((new Integer(myAge.getText().trim())).intValue());

7. displayText.append(String.valueOf(myInputFile.readInt()));

8. close

9.   The *flush()* method flushes the output stream, causing any internally buffered data
      to be written to the file.

CHAPTER *13*

SECTION 13-1

1.   index and elements
2.   False, because the elements within a given array must all be of the same data type.
3. 1×11

SECTION 13-2

1.   double[] testScores = new double[15];
2. 1×15
3.   [0]
4.   [14]
5.   26, because the first element index is [0]

SECTION 13-3

1.   for (int index = 0; index < 15; ++ index)
          characters [index] = in.readChar();
      (Assumes that *in* has been defined as an object of the *KeyboardInput* class.)
2.   for (int index = 0; index < 15; ++ index)
          System.out.print(characters[index]) + "\t");

SECTION 13-4

1.   False, because the array name represents the address of index [0] of the array.
2.   void sample(char[] array)
3.   sample(characters);
3.   void test (char arrayElement)
4.   test (characters [5]);

SECTION 13-5

1. int[] values = { –3,–2,–1,0,1,2,3 };
2. 1×7
3. String[] family = {"Andy","Janet","Ron","David","Zane","Andrew"};
4. zeros
5. blanks

CHAPTER 14

SECTION 14-1

1. False, because Java supports recursion, which allows a method to call itself.
2. We can describe recursion as a "winding" and "unwinding" process, because recursion "winds up" when it places information onto a stack, and "unwinds" when the terminating condition is reached by removing information from the stack to calculate the final result.
3. A terminating condition.
4. If *n* is 0

   factorial(n) = 1.

   Else

   factorial(n) = *n* ∗ *factorial(n* – 1*)*
5. False, because recursion uses large amounts of memory to keep track of each recursive call.
6. True
7. stack
8. last-in, first-out, or LIFO

SECTION 14-2

1. The term *abstract* is used to indicate that data and its related operations are being viewed without considering any of the details of how the data or operations are implemented in the computer system.
2. *String*, *Graphics*, *Frame*, *Button*, as well as any of the other standard Java classes are examples of ADTs that we have been working with in the Java language.
3. modular

4. False, because a data structure provides a way of structuring or organizing data and an ADT defines the data to be operated on as well as the operations that can be performed on the data.

5. encapsulation with information hiding

6. method interfaces

7. You gain modularity through the use of ADTs, because ADTs are building blocks for use in software development.

8. You gain generality through the use of ADTs, because algorithms can be developed that depend only on the ADT method interface without concern for the implementation details of the ADT.

SECTION 14-3

1. The *fullStack()* method would return a value of **true** and the message "The stack is full!" would be displayed on the screen.

2. You can't randomly access the array holding the stack, because the array is a private member of the *Stack* class and can be accessed only via the methods defined for the class.

3. preincremented

4. False, because the array begins at index [0]. Thus, *Top* must equal *SIZE* − 1 when the stack is full.

5. −1

6. The functional difference between the *pop()* method and the *topElement()* method is that the value of *top* is not changed with the *topElement()* method and it is with the *pop()* method.

7. We had to include a *fullStack()* method in our implementation of a stack because of the finite storage capacity of an array.

SECTION 14-4

1. The *fullQ()* method would return a value of **true** and the message "The queue is full!" would be displayed on the screen.

2. False, because *rear* must be advanced not *front*.

3. If *front* is *MAX* − 1
       Set *front* = 0.
    Else
       Set *front* = *front* + 1.

4.   False, because the value of *front* can be greater than the value of *rear* due to the circular nature of the queue.

5.   When *front* == *rear*, there is only one element in the queue.

6.   We had to include a *fullQ()* method in our implementation of a queue because of the finite storage capacity of the array used to hold the queue.

7.   By using our *array* implementation of a queue, the element counter is equal to 0 when the queue is empty, and the element counter is equal to *MAXQ* when the queue is full.

APPENDIX B

UNICODE CHARACTER TABLE

Dec	Char	Dec	Char	Dec	Char	Dec	Char
0	^@ NUL	32	SPC	64	@	96	`
1	^A SOH	33	!	65	A	97	a
2	^B STX	34	"	66	B	98	b
3	^C ETX	35	#	67	C	99	c
4	^D EOT	36	$	68	D	100	d
5	^E ENQ	37	%	69	E	101	e
6	^F ACK	38	&	70	F	102	f
7	^G BEL	39	'	71	G	103	g
8	^H BS	40	(	72	H	104	h
9	^I HT	41	)	73	I	105	i
10	^J LF	42	*	74	J	106	j
11	^K VT	43	+	75	K	107	k
12	^L FF	44	,	76	L	108	l
13	^M CR	45	-	77	M	109	m
14	^N SO	46	.	78	N	110	n
15	^O SI	47	/	79	O	111	o
16	^P DLE	48	0	80	P	112	p
17	^Q DC1	49	1	81	Q	113	q
18	^R DC2	50	2	82	R	114	r
19	^S DC3	51	3	83	S	115	s
20	^T DC4	52	4	84	T	116	t
21	^U NAK	53	5	85	U	117	u
22	^V SYN	54	6	86	V	118	v

Dec	Char	Dec	Char	Dec	Char	Dec	Char
23	^W ETB	55	7	87	W	119	w
24	^X CAN	56	8	88	X	120	x
25	^Y EM	57	9	89	Y	121	y
26	^Z SUB	58	:	90	Z	122	z
27	^[ESC	59	;	91	[	123	{
28	^\ FS	60	<	92	\	124		
29	^] GS	61	=	93	]	125	}
30	^^ RS	62	>	94	^	126	~
31	^-- US	63	?	95	--	127	DEL

APPENDIX C

JAVA QUICK REFERENCE

Keywords

abstract	do	implements	private	throw
boolean	double	import	protected	throws
break	else	instanceof	public	transient
byte	extends	int	return	true
case	false	interface	short	try
catch	final	long	static	void
char	finally	native	super	volatile
class	float	new	switch	while
continue	for	null	synchronized	
default	if	package	this	

String Class Methods

Method	Description
compareTo(s2)	Returns 0 if the calling string object equals *s2*, else returns a negative value if the calling string object is less than *s2* and a positive value if the calling string object is greater than *s2*.
equals(s2)	Returns **true** if the calling string object equals *s2*, else returns **false**.
equalsIgnoreCase(s2)	Returns **true** if the calling string object equals *s2*, else returns **false**. Ignores case.
length()	Returns the length of the calling string object.
toLowerCase()	Returns calling string object with all characters converted to lowercase.
toUpperCase()	Returns calling string object with all characters converted to uppercase.
trim()	Returns calling string object with leading and trailing whitespace removed.

Font Methods

Method	Description
getFont()	Returns a font object representing the current font of the calling object..
getName()	Returns a string which is the current font name.
getSize()	Returns an integer which is the current font size.
getStyle()	Returns an integer which represents the current font style.
isBold()	Returns **true** if the font is bold.
isItalic()	Returns **true** if the font is italic.
isPlain()	Returns **true** if the font is plain.
setFont()	Sets the font of the calling component object.

Frame-Related Methods

Method	Description
*addWindowListener(**this**)*	Registers a listener for this frame object.
Frame()	Constructs a new frame without title.
Frame(String)	Constructs a new frame with *String* title.
Panel()	Constructs a new panel.
Panel(Layout Manager)	Constructs a new panel with this layout manager.
setSize(int, int)	Sets frame size to width by height in pixels.
setVisible(boolean)	Makes frame visible or invisible (true/false).
setForeground(Color)	Sets foreground color to *Color.c*.
setBackground(Color)	Sets background color to *Color.c*.

Layout Manager Methods

Method	Description
BorderLayout()	Constructs new border layout with no gaps.
BorderLayout(int,int)	Constructs new border layout with hGap, vGap.
FlowLayout()	Constructs new flow layout, center, 5 pt. gap.
FlowLayout(int)	Constructs new flow layout with alignment.
FlowLayout(int,int,int)	Constructs new flow layout with alignment, hGap, and vGap.
GridLayout(int,int)	Constructs new grid layout with rows and cols.
GridLayout(int,int,int,int)	Constructs new grid layout with rows, cols., hGap, and vGap.
setLayout(Layout Manager)	Sets layout for this layout manager.

GUI Component-Related Methods

Method	Description
add(Component)	Adds specified component to container.
*addActionListener(**this**)*	Registers a listener for calling action object and ***this*** frame.
addItem(String)	Adds *String* item to calling choice or list object.
*addItemListener(**this**)*	Registers a listener for calling item object.
append(String)	Appends *String* to text of calling text object.
Button()	Constructs a new button without label.
Button(String)	Constructs a new button with *String* label.
Checkbox()	Constructs a new checkbox without a label.
Checkbox(String)	Constructs a new checkbox with *String* label.
Checkbox(String, boolean)	Constructs a new checkbox with *String* label, set to a given boolean state.
Checkbox(String,CheckBoxGroup, boolean)	Constructs new checkbox with *String* label, in the specified checkbox group, to specified boolean state.
Choice()	Constructs a new empty choice box.
getSelectedItem()	Returns selected choice item of calling choice object.
getSelectedItems()	Returns selected list items of calling list object in an array of strings.
getState()	Returns boolean state of the calling checkbox object.
getText()	Returns text contained in calling text object.
Label()	Constructs a new empty label.
Label(String)	Constructs a new label with *String* text.
Label(String, int)	Constructs a new label with *String* text and specified alignment.
List()	Constructs a new empty list box.
List(int)	Constructs a new empty list box with specified number of items visible.
List(int, boolean)	Constructs a new empty list box with specified number of items visible, and true/false enabling multiple item selection or not.
Menu()	Creates a new menu without a label.

GUI Component-Related Methods (CONTINUED)

Method	Description
Menu(String)	Creates a new menu with *String* label.
Menu(String, boolean)	Creates a new menu with *String* label and tear-off enabled/disabled (true/false).
MenuItem(String)	Creates a new menu item with *String* label.
MenuBar()	Creates a new menu bar.
processItemEvent()	Processes an item event.
setLocation(int,int)	Sets component upper-left-corner location to (x, y).
setMenuBar(MenuBar)	Sets *MenuBar* object to frame.
setSize(int,int)	Sets component size to width, height.
setText(String)	Sets text of calling text object to *String*.
TextField()	Constructs a new empty text field.
TextField(String)	Constructs a new text field initialized with *String*.
TextField(int)	Constructs a new empty text field with specified number of columns.
TextField(String, int)	Constructs a new text field initialized with *String* with specified number of columns.
TextArea()	Constructs a new empty text area.
TextArea(String)	Constructs a new text area initialized with *String*.
TextArea(int, int)	Constructs a new empty text area with specified number of rows and columns.
TextArea(String, int, int)	Constructs a new text area initialized with *String* with specified number of rows and columns.

Event Methods

Method	Description
actionPerfomed()	Processes an action event.
getActionCommand()	Returns command name associated with this event.

Event Methods (CONTINUED)

Method	Description
getSource()	Returns object source of an event.
itemStateChanged()	Processes an item event.
windowClosing(WindowEvent)	Handles a window closing event.

Listener Classes and Methods

Class	Method(s)
WindowListener	*windowClosing(WindowEvent e)* *windowOpened(WindowEvent e)* *windowClosed(WindowEvent e)* *windowIconified(WindowEvent e)* *windowDeiconified(WindowEvent e)* *windowActivated(WindowEvent e)* *windowDeactivated(WindowEvent e)*
ActionListener	*actionPerformed(ActionEvent e)*
ItemListener	*itemStateChanged(ItemEvent e)*
TextListener	*textValueChanged(TextEvent e)*
AdjustmentListener	*adjustmentValueChanged(AdjustmentEvent e)*
KeyListener	*keyPressed(KeyEvent e)* *keyReleased(KeyEvent e)* *keyTyped(KeyEvent e)*
MouseListener	*mouseClicked(MouseEvent e)* *mousePressed(MouseEvent e)* *mouseReleased(MouseEvent e)* *mouseEntered(MouseEvent e)* *mouseExited(MouseEvent e)*

Graphics Methods

Method	Description

fillArc(int x,
    int y,
    int width,
    int height
    int start,
    int arcAngle)
	Draws and fills an arc with the calling graphics object color.

drawArc(int x,
    int y,
    int width,
    int height
    int start,
    int arcAngle)
	Draws a nonfilled arc with the calling graphics object color.

drawLine(int x1,
    int y1,
    int x2,
    int y2)
	Draws a line with the calling graphics object color.

fillOval(int x,
    int y,
    int width,
    int height)
	Draws and fills an oval with the calling graphics object color.

drawOval(int x,
    int y,
    int width,
    int height)
	Draws a nonfilled oval with the calling graphics object color.

fillRoundRect(int x,
    int y,
    int width,
    int height,
    int arcWidth
    int arcHeight)
	Draws and fills a rounded rectangle with the calling graphics object color.

fill3DRect(int x,
    int y,
    int width,
    int height,
    boolean raised)
	Draws and fills a 3D rectangle with the calling graphics object color.

Graphics Methods (CONTINUED)

Method	Description

*drawString(String text,
    int x,
    int y)*
	Draws a string with the calling graphics object color and font.

Math Class Methods

Method	Description
abs(x)	Returns the absolute value of *x*.
acos(x)	Returns the arc cosine of *x* (radians).
asin(x)	Returns the arc sine of *x* (radians).
atan(x)	Returns the arc tangent of *x* (radians).
ceil(x)	Rounds *x* up to the next highest integer.
cos(x)	Returns the cosine of *x* (radians).
exp(x)	Returns e^x.
floor(x)	Rounds down to the next lowest integer.
log(x)	Returns the natural log of *x*.
min(x,y)	Returns the smallest of *x* and *y*.
max(x,y)	Returns the largest of *x* and *y*.
pow(x,y)	Returns *x* raised to the power of *y*.
random()	Generates a random number between 0 and 1.
round(x)	Rounds *x* to the nearest integer value.
sin(x)	Returns the sine of *x* (radians).
sqrt(x)	Returns the square root of *x*.
tan(x)	Returns the tangent of *x* (radians).
E	Value of *e* (2.718281828459045)
PI	Value of π (3.141592653589793)

GLOSSARY

Abstract class A superclass for which objects will never be created.

Abstract data type (ADT) A collection of data and related operations.

Abstract method A polymorphic method in a superclass whose behavior will be defined in the subclasses.

Abstraction Looking at things in general terms, ignoring detail.

Access method A get method used to return the value(s) of a private class member(s).

Actual argument A value passed to a method during a method call.

Address A value that designates the memory location of a data element.

Algorithm A series of step-by-step instructions that produce a solution to a problem.

Applet A Java program designed only to be run over the Internet using a Web browser.

Application A Java program designed to be run on a computer just like any other computer program written in any other language.

Arc angle The amount of traversal, in degrees, from the start angle of an arc method of the *Graphics* class. A positive angle forces a counterclockwise traversal, while a negative angle forces a clockwise traversal.

Argument A value used within a method call.

Arithmetic and logic unit (ALU) That part of the CPU that performs all arithmetic and logic operations.

Array

An indexed data structure that is used to store data elements of the same data type or class.

Assembler

A program that translates assembly language into machine language for a given CPU.

Assembly language

A language that employs alphabetic abbreviations called mnemonics that are easily remembered by you, the programmer.

Attribute of a class

The data members that make up a class provide the class attributes, or characteristics.

Base class

A class from which one or more other classes are derived. Also called a *superclass.*

Baseline

The bottom of a string drawn by the *drawString()* method of the *Graphics* class.

Behavior

Used to describe how an ADT, or class object, will act and react for a given operation.

Block scope

The accessibility, or visibility, of a local variable defined in a given block of code, such as a method.

Bus

A signal path within a computer system.

Button

A GUI component that, when clicked, generates an event.

Byte code

A binary code generated by the Java compiler that is a low-level program similar to machine language but generic and not specific to any particular CPU. Any given computer will have its own Java interpreter that translates the generic byte code into machine language for that CPU.

Cache

High-speed RAM that is usually contained within the same chip as the CPU. Instructions waiting to be processed are fetched from primary memory and placed in the cache so that they are ready for execution when the CPU needs them.

Calling program	The program that calls, or invokes, a method.
Casting	Temporarily converting one type of data to another, as in type casting.
Checkbox	A GUI component that allows the user to select one of two possible states: checked or unchecked.
Checked exception	A predefined exception class in Java.
Choice box	A GUI component that allows the user to chose one of several items in a pop-up menu listing.
Circular array	An array that wraps around such that the first element of the array follows the last element of the array.
Class (abstract level)	An interface that defines the behavior of its objects.
Class (implementation level)	A syntactical unit that describes a set of data and related operations that are common to its objects.
Class method	A method that is not called with an object reference. A **static** modifier declares a method as a class method.
Compiler	A program that translates an entire program into machine code all at one time, before it is executed by the CPU.
Compiling	The process of translating source code to machine, or object, code.
Component	An item of meaningful data within a file. A graphical object within a GUI such as a button, text field, rectangle, oval, and so on.
Compound statement	Several statements framed by curly braces.
Concrete class	A subclass for which objects will always be created.
Constructor	A special class method that is used to initialize the data members of an object automatically when the object is defined.

Container	A window object, such as a frame or applet, that is used to hold GUI components.
Control structure	A pattern for controlling the flow of a program module.
Control unit	That part of the CPU that directs and coordinates the activities of the entire system.
Dangling else	An **else** that is not associated with a corresponding **if**. A dangling, or misplaced, **else** problem often occurs when improper framing is used within nested **if/else** logic.
Data abstraction	That property of an ADT that allows you to work with the data elements without concern for how the data elements are stored inside the computer or how the data operations are performed inside the computer.
Database	A collection of related files.
Data hiding	That property of a programming entity, such as a class object, that shields private data from operations that are not predefined to operate on the data.
Data type	A particular class, or category, of data elements.
Declaration	Specifies the name and attributes of a value but does not reserve storage.
Definition	Specifies the name and attributes of a variable or object and also reserves storage.
Derived class	An inherited, or subclass, class that will include its own members and also include members inherited from its superclass.
Dimension	The size of an array, such as $m \times n$, where m is the number of rows and n is the number of columns in the array.

Dynamic binding	Dynamic binding occurs when a polymorphic method is defined for several classes in a family, but the actual code for the method is not attached, or bound, until execution time.
Editor	A program that allows you to enter, save, and edit a source code program.
Element	A data value, in particular, a data value stored within an array.
Encapsulation	To package data and/or operations into a single well-defined programming unit.
Escape sequence	A special formatting character for text output.
Event	An action generated by a program user activating a GUI component, such as clicking button.
Event handler	A method used to process a GUI event.
Event listener	An object that has been registered to generate an event within a GUI.
Exception	An error generated within a Java program.
Exception handler	A Java program segment that is used to catch and handle errors as they occur during the execution of a Java program.
Exception handling	The process of handling an exception.
Family	A group of classes related through inheritance.
Fetch/execute cycle	The basic cycle that takes place when a program is executed by a CPU. The four basic operations of the cycle are *fetch*, *decode*, *execute*, and *store*.
Fibonacci sequence	A sequence of numbers such that the first two numbers in the sequence are 0 and 1. Then, each additional number is the sum of the two previous numbers in the sequence.

Field   An area used to store a meaningful collection of characters, such as your name.

FIFO   First-in, first-out; FIFO is associated with queues.

File   A data structure that consists of a sequence of components usually associated with program I/O. A means by which the program communicates with the "outside world"; a sequence of components stored in secondary memory; a collection of related records.

File stream   A channel for data to flow between the program and the outside world.

Firmware   Software stored in ROM.

Fixed repetition loop   A loop that will be executed a predetermined number of times.

Font   The name, style, and size of text as in `Courier`, ***bold/italic***, 10 point.

Formal parameter   A variable used in a method header that receives the value of the respective actual argument in the method call.

Frame   A graphical container used to hold GUI components in a Java application program.

Get method   An access method used to return the value(s) of a private class member(s).

Global identifier   A constant, variable, object, or data structure that is visible to the entire program.

Graphical component   A graphical object within a graphical user interface, such as a button, text field, choice box, and so on. Also, a graphical image such as a rectangle, oval, arc, line, string, or polygon.

Graphical user interface, GUI	A window-based program whereby input and output are handled via graphical components and program control is event driven via the components.
High-level language	A language consisting of instructions, or statements, that are similar to English and common mathematical notation
Identifier	A symbolic name associated with a constant, variable, method, data structure, class, object, and so on.
Implementation	The body of a method.
Index	An integer that locates an element within an array.
Information hiding	Accomplished when there exists a binding relationship between the information, or data, and its related operations so that operations outside an encapsulated unit cannot affect the information inside the unit.
Inheritance	That property of object-oriented programming that allows one class, called a subclass, or derived class, to share the structure and behavior of another class, called a superclass, or base class.
Instance	In object-oriented programming, an example, or specimen, of a class. We say that an object is an *instance* of a class.
Instance method	A nonstatic method which must be called with an object reference.
Instance variable	A private data member of a class. A variable that will be created for any given object of the class.
Instruction set	The set of machine instructions designed for a given CPU.
Interface	Something that forms a common boundary, or barrier, between two systems.

Interface of a class	The set of all **public** method signatures that forms a boundary to a class.
Interface of a method	The signature of a method that forms a common boundary between the method and its calling program.
Internal registers	That part of the CPU that provides temporary storage areas for program instructions and data
Interpreter	A program that translates and executes one high-level statement at a time. Once a given statement has been executed, the interpreter then translates and executes the next statement, and so on, until the entire program has been executed.
IS-A	The link between a derived class and its base class.
Iteration	A control structure, also called looping, that causes the program flow to repeat a finite number of times.
Keyword	A word that is predefined and recognized by a programming language.
Label	A line of noneditable text used to identify GUI components.
Layout chart	A graphical aid in laying out text output for a display screen or the components within a GUI window.
Layout manager	Standard classes in Java that lay out GUI components within a frame or applet so that they can be easily managed within the GUI.
LIFO	Last-in, first-out; LIFO is associated with stacks.
Linking	The process of combining object files needed for a program execution to form an executable file.
List	Another name for a one-dimensional array.
List box	A GUI component that allows the user to chose one or more items within a scrolled item listing.

Listener	An object that has been registered to generate an event within a GUI.
Local variable	A variable that is defined within a given block of code, such as a method. Local variables have block scope.
Logic error	An error created when the computer does what you tell it to do but is not doing what you meant it to do. Such an error is usually an error in thinking of the programmers part.
Loop control variable	A variable that is tested with each loop iteration to determine whether or not the loop will continue.
Machine language	A binary code, called machine code, that forms the instruction set for a given CPU.
Main memory	*See* primary memory.
Member	Any item declared in a class.
Menu	A set of user-selectable options.
Menu bar	A container on the top of a frame for holding menus.
Menu item	A selectable item within a menu.
Menu separator	A line between two menu items.
Message	A call to an object method.
Method	A subprogram designed to perform specific tasks, such as those performed by an algorithm.
Method body	The statement section, or implementation, of a method.
Method header	The method signature that forms a common boundary, or interface, between the method and its calling program.

Microprocessor	A single integrated-circuit (IC) chip that contains the entire central processing unit (CPU).
Misplaced else	An **else** that is not associated with a corresponding **if**. The misplaced, or dangling, **else** problem often occurs when improper framing is used within nested **if/else** logic.
Mnemonic	An assembly language instruction abbreviation.
Multidimensional array	An array with more than one dimension.
Nested looping	Looping structures that are located within other looping structures.
Nonvoid method	A method that returns a single value to the calling program.
Object	An instance, or specimen, of a given class. An object of a given class has the attributes and behavior described by the class that is common to all objects of the same class.
Object program	The binary machine-language program generated by a compiler; usually has a file extension of *.obj*.
Object-oriented programming	A form of programming whereby data and related operations are specified as classes whose instances are objects. The data and related operations are so tightly bound so that only those operations defined for a class can affect the class data. This idea of encapsulation and information hiding allows the easy formation of ADTs.
One-dimensional array	An array with one row and n columns that has a dimension of $1 \times n$.
Operating system, OS	A collection of software programs dedicated to managing the resources of the system.
Overflow error	An error that occurs when a numeric data type value exceeds its predefined range.

Overloaded method　A method that has different behavior depending on the number and/or class of arguments that it receives. An overloaded method is statically bound at compile time.

Package　A set, or family, of related classes contained within a unique directory.

Panel　A GUI component container that, when added to a frame or applet, allows you to achieve presentable layouts.

Parameter　A variable or object appearing in a method signature that receives an argument value when the method is called.

Parameterless constructor　A constructor that does not contain any parameters.

Pixel　A picture element which is a point of illumination on a display screen.

Point　A unit of font measurement, approximately 1/72 inch.

Pointer　A direct program reference to an actual physical address in memory. Java uses pointers extensively to implement programs but does not allow you, the programmer, to use pointers.

Polymorphism　Occurs when a method has the same name but different behavior within a program. Both overloaded and polymorphic methods exhibit polymorphism in Java.

Polymorphic method　A method that has the same name but different behavior for different classes within the same family. Polymorphic methods are dynamically bound at run time.

Portability　That feature of a language that allows programs written for one type of computer to be used on another type of computer with few or no changes to the program source code.

Posttest loops   A loop that tests a condition *after* each loop iteration as in the **do/while** loop structure.

Pretest loops   A loop that tests a condition each time *before* a loop is executed, as in the **while** and **for** loop structures.

Primary memory   Used to store programs and data while they are being "worked," or executed, by the CPU.

Private member   A member of a class that is accessible only to the public methods of the same class. Private members of a base class are *not* inherited by a derived class.

Problem abstraction   Provides for generalization in problem solving by allowing you to view a problem in general terms, without worrying about the details of the problem solution.

Program   A set of software instructions that tells the computer what to do.

Project file   A file that identifies the files that need to be compiled and linked to create a workable Java program.

Project manager   A program development tool which links several packages and classes together to build a complete workable program.

Programmer-defined method   A block of statements, or a subprogram, that is written to perform a specific task required by you, the programmer.

Protected member   A member that is accessible to both a superclass and any subclasses of the superclass in which it is declared. Thus, a protected member of a superclass is accessible to any descendent subclass within the family, but not accessible to things outside the class family.

Pseudocode

An informal set of Englishlike statements that is generally accepted within the computer industry to denote common computer programming operations. Pseudocode statements are used to describe the steps in a computer algorithm.

Public member

A member of a class that is accessible outside the class within the scope of the class. A public member of a superclass is inherited by any derived classes of the superclass.

Queue

A primary memory storage structure that consists of a list, or sequence, of data elements. All insertions of elements into the queue are made at one end of the queue, called the *rear* of the queue, and all deletions of elements from the queue are made at the other end of the queue, called the *front* of the queue. A queue operates on the *first-in*, *first-out*, or *FIFO*, principle.

Radio button

A state (on/off) button within a group of buttons that can be selected or deselected. Only one button within the group can be selected at any given time.

Random-access memory (RAM)

Volatile, read/write memory.

Reading

The process of obtaining data from something such as an input device or a data structure; a copy operation. A read operation is usually a nondestructive operation.

Read-only memory (ROM)

Nonvolatile system memory that contains firmware.

Record

A collection of related fields.

Recursion

A process whereby an operation calls, or clones, itself until a terminating condition is reached.

Recursive method

A method that calls itself.

Reference parameter

A method parameter that provides two-way communication between the calling program and the method. An array name is a reference parameter.

Return value   A value returned by a nonvoid method. The value replaces the method name in the calling program.

Root class   The class at the top of a class hierarchy. The root class in Java is the *Object* class.

Run-time error   An error that occurs during the execution of a program.

Scope   The largest block in which a given constant, variable, object, data structure, or method is accessible, or visible within a program.

Search   The process of finding a given data element. In particular, searching for a given element within an array.

Secondary memory   Nonvolatile memory, such as disk memory, used to store programs and data between program runs.

Selection   A control structure where the program selects, or decides, between one of several routes depending on the conditions that are tested.

Sentinel controlled loop A loop that terminates when a given sentinel value is entered by the user.

Sentinel value   A value that terminates a sentinel controlled loop.

Sequence   A control structure where statements are executed sequentially, one after another, in a straight-line fashion.

Set method   A method used to set the value(s) of a private class member(s).

Side effect   The process of altering the value of a global variable.

Signature   A header of a method that forms a common boundary between the method and its calling program.

Sort

The process of placing data elements in order. In particular, sorting the elements within an array.

Source code program

The program that you write in the Java language that normally has a file extension of *.java*.

Source object

In GUI event handling, the object responsible for an event.

Stack

A primary memory storage structure that consists of a list, or sequence, of data elements where all the insertions and deletions of elements to and from the stack are made at one end of the stack called the *top*. A stack operates on the *last-in*, *first-out*, or *LIFO* principle.

Standard method

A predefined operation that the Java compiler will recognize and evaluate to return a result or perform a given task.

Start angle

The angle of beginning for an arc method of the *Graphics* class, where 0 degrees is the 3:00 position.

State button

A GUI component, such as a checkbox or radio button, that has two possible states, on or off.

Static binding

Occurs when a method is defined with the same name, but with different signatures and implementations. The actual code for the method is attached, or bound, at compile time. Overloaded methods are statically bound.

Static method

A method that is not called with an object reference.

Stepwise refinement

The process of gradually adding detail to a general problem solution until it easily can be coded in a computer language.

Stream

A channel for data to flow between your program and the outside world.

String

A collection of characters.

Structured design	A methodology that requires software to be designed using a top/down modular approach.
Structured programming	Structured programming allows programs to be written using well-defined control structures and independent program modules.
Subclass	An inherited, or derived, class that will include its own members and also include members inherited from its superclass.
Submenu	A menu within a menu.
Superclass	A class from which one or more other classes are derived. Also called a *base class*.
Syntax	The grammar of a programming language.
Syntax error	An error created by violating the required syntax, or grammar, of a programming language.
System memory	ROM firmware that stores system-related programs and data.
Terminating condition	A known condition that terminates a recursive method call.
Text area	Several lines of editable or noneditable text.
Text field	A single line of editable text on a GUI.
Truth table	A table that shows the results of a logic operation on Boolean values.
Type cast	Converts data of one type to a different type, temporarily.
Utility method	A private method.
Value parameter	A parameter that allows for one-way communication of data from the calling program to the method.

Venn diagram A class family diagram that illustrates the common members within the family.

Void method A method that performs some procedural task or operates directly on class data, rather than returning a single value to the calling program.

Virtual memory Hard-disk memory that is being used by the CPU as RAM when no more actual RAM is available.

Visibility That part of the program code in which a constant, variable, object, data structure, or method is accessible.

Whitespace Blanks, tabs, new lines, form feeds, and so on, are all forms of whitespace.

Wrapper class A class that encapsulates a primitive data type along with methods that allow for conversion of the data type to/from strings as well as other methods useful in dealing with the primitive data type.

Wrapper object An object of a wrapper class.

Writing The process of generating data to a display monitor, printer, or file. In addition, data can be written to data structures such as arrays. A write operation is usually a destructive operation.

INDEX

!, NOT operator, 217
!=, not equal operator, 214
− −, decrement operator, 178
*, multiplication operator, 171
−, subtraction operator, 171
%, modulus operator, 171, 172
&&, AND operator, 217
/, division operator, 171, 172, 174
//, comment, 96, 100
\\, backslash escape sequence, 134
\?, question mark escape sequence, 134
\', single quote escape sequence, 134
\'', double quote escape sequence, 134
~~\a, bell escape sequence, 134~~
\b, backspace escape sequence, 134
\f, formfeed escape sequence, 134
\n, CRLF escape sequence, 131
\r, CR escape sequence, 134
\t, horizontal tab escape sequence, 134
\v, vertical tab escape sequence, 134
^, XOR operator, 260
{, begin block, 98
||, OR operator, 217
}, end block, 98
+, addition operator, 171
+, concatenation operator, 92
++, increment operator, 178
<, less than operator, 214
<=, less than or equal operator, 214
=, assignment operator, 87
==, equal operator, 214
>, greater than operator, 214
>=, greater than or equal operator, 214

A

abs( ), absolute value method, 176, 808
Abstract
level of a class, 811
Abstract class, 491, 500, 809
Abstract data type (ADT), 68–70, 69, 736–39,
    809
  data, 737
  encapsulation, 737
  information hiding, 737
  interface, 738
  method interface, 739
  operations, 737
  queue, 756–71, 821
    implementation, 775
    operations, 758–65
  stack, 742–56, 823
    implementation, 742–56
    operations, 741–42
Abstract method, 494, 809
abstract modifier, 347, 491, 494
Abstract windowing toolkit (AWT), 63, 70,
    515
Abstraction, 411, 809
  data, 69, 736, 812
  problem, 44, 55, 820
Access method, 435, 809
acos( ), arc cosine method, 176, 808
Actual argument, 809
Ada, 418
Address, 809
ADT. *See* Abstract data type
Algorithm, 33, 809
  effective, 42
  elegance, 735
  pseudocode operations, 43
  well-defined, 42
Alignment
  GUI component, 123
Amplitude modulation, 191
AND, && operator
  use of to control loops, 298, 302

C

C++, 418
Cache memory, 8, 810
Calling program, 342, 811
case statement
  as part of **switch**, 241, 243, 245
Casting, 446, 811
catch block, 618
ceil( ), rounding method, 808
Central processing unit (CPU), 3–6
  ALU, 4, 809
  control unit, 6, 812
  internal registers, 6, 816
Chaining
  of objects, 615
Character
  Unicode character table, 79, 799
Character data type, 78–90
Chart
  text layout, 135
  window layout, 577
Checkbox, 29, 333–38, 558–62, 811
Checked exception, 619, 621, 811
Checking account class, 472
Child class. *See* Subclass
Choice box, 267–71, 553–55, 811
Circular array, 811
Class, 66, 67, 68, 70, 71, 408, 410, 411, 412,
  462
  abstract, 491, 500, 809
  abstract level, 412–13, 811
  abstraction, 411
  as a syntactical unit, 413
  attribute, 66, 411, 810
  bank account, 471
  base, 810
  behavior, 66, 411, 412
  checking account, 472
  Color, 404
  composition diagram, 416
  concrete, 491, 811
  constructor, 428–33, 811
    format of signature, 429
  data member, 414
  DataInputStream, 612–23
  DataOutputStream, 612–23
  declaration format, 414

derived, 812
event, 517
family, 468, 813
file hierarchy, 613
FileInputStream, 612–23
FileOutputStream, 612–23
Font, 802
Frame, 803
Graphics, 509, 713–17, 807
hierarchy, 469–70
  IS-A relationship, 470
implementation level, 413–14, 811
inheritance, 467–503
InputStream, 612–23
inside view of, 413–14
interface, 412, 413, 462
KeyboardInput, 138–49
listener, 518
listener summary, 806
Math, 78, 176, 808
member, 817
method, 414, 427–39, 811
  access, 435
  naming of, 424
naming, 98
OutputStream, 612–23
outside view of, 412–13
packages, 450
private member, 475, 820
programmer defined, 70
protected member, 478–80, 475, 820, 821
public, 454, 475, 478
public member, 475
queue, 765
root, 822
savings account, 473
stack, 749
standard, 70
String, 90–95, 802
subclass, 468, 824
  declaration format, 471
superclass, 468, 810, 824
super-now checking account, 472
System, 612
wrapper, 582
Class method. *See* **static** method
Classpath, 451
clearStack( ) method, 711

Prentice Hall

YOU SHOULD CAREFULLY READ THE FOLLOWING TERMS AND CONDITIONS BEFORE OPENING THIS CD-ROM. OPENING THIS CD-ROM INDICATES YOUR ACCEPTANCE OF THESE TERMS AND CONDITIONS. IF YOU DO NOT AGREE WITH THEM, YOU SHOULD PROMPTLY RETURN THE CD-ROM UNOPENED, AND YOUR MONEY WILL BE REFUNDED.

IT IS A VIOLATION OF COPYRIGHT LAWS TO MAKE A COPY OF THE ACCOMPANYING SOFTWARE EXCEPT FOR BACKUP PURPOSES TO GUARD AGAINST ACCIDENTAL LOSS OR DAMAGE.

Prentice-Hall, Inc. provides this program and licenses its use. You assume responsibility for the selection of the program to achieve your intended results, and for the installation, use, and results obtained from the program. This license extends only to use of the program in the United States or countries in which the program is marketed by duly authorized distributors.

LICENSE
You may:
a. use the program;
b. copy the program into any machine-readable form without limit;
c. modify the program and/or merge it into another program in support of your use of the program.

LIMITED WARRANTY
THE PROGRAM IS PROVIDED "AS IS" WITHOUT WARRANTY OF ANY KIND, EITHER EXPRESSED OR IMPLIED, INCLUDING, BUT NOT LIMITED TO, THE IMPLIED WARRANTIES OF MERCHANTABILITY AND FITNESS FOR A PARTICULAR PURPOSE. THE ENTIRE RISK AS TO THE QUALITY AND PERFORMANCE OF THE PROGRAM IS WITH YOU. SHOULD THE PROGRAM PROVE DEFECTIVE, YOU (AND NOT PRENTICE-HALL, INC. OR ANY AUTHORIZED DISTRIBUTOR) ASSUME THE ENTIRE COST OF ALL NECESSARY SERVICING, REPAIR, OR CORRECTION.

SOME STATES DO NOT ALLOW THE EXCLUSION OF IMPLIED WARRANTIES, SO THE ABOVE EXCLUSION MAY NOT APPLY TO YOU. THIS WARRANTY GIVES YOU SPECIFIC LEGAL RIGHTS AND YOU MAY ALSO HAVE OTHER RIGHTS THAT VARY FROM STATE TO STATE.

Prentice-Hall, Inc. does not warrant that the functions contained in the program will meet your requirements or that the operation of the program will be uninterrupted or error free.

However, Prentice-Hall, Inc., warrants the CD-ROM(s) on which the program is furnished to be free from defects in materials and workmanship under normal use for a period of ninety (90) days from the date of delivery to you evidenced by a copy of your receipt.

LIMITATIONS OF REMEDIES
Prentice-Hall's entire liability and your exclusive remedy shall be:
1. the replacement of any CD-ROM not meeting Prentice-Hall's "Limited Warranty" and that is returned to Prentice-Hall with a copy of your purchase order, or
2. if Prentice-Hall is unable to deliver a replacement CD-ROM that is free of defects in materials or workmanship, you may terminate this Agreement by returning the program, and your money will be refunded.

IN NO EVENT WILL PRENTICE-HALL BE LIABLE TO YOU FOR ANY DAMAGES, INCLUDING ANY LOST PROFITS, LOST SAVINGS, OR OTHER INCIDENTAL OR CONSEQUENTIAL DAMAGES ARISING OUT OF THE USE OR INABILITY TO USE SUCH PROGRAM EVEN IF PRENTICE-HALL, OR AN AUTHORIZED DISTRIBUTOR HAS BEEN ADVISED OF THE POSSIBILITY OF SUCH DAMAGES, OR FOR ANY CLAIM BY ANY OTHER PARTY.

SOME STATES DO NOT ALLOW THE LIMITATION OR EXCLUSION OF LIABILITY FOR INCIDENTAL OR CONSEQUENTIAL DAMAGES, SO THE ABOVE LIMITATION OR EXCLUSION MAY NOT APPLY TO YOU.

GENERAL

You may not sublicense, assign, or transfer the license or the program except as expressly provided in this Agreement. Any attempt otherwise to sublicense, assign, or transfer any of the rights, duties, or obligations hereunder is void.

This Agreement will be governed by the laws of the State of New York.

Should you have any questions concerning this Agreement, you may contact Prentice-Hall, Inc., by writing to:

> Prentice Hall
> College Division
> Upper Saddle River, NJ 07458

Should you have any questions concerning technical support you may write to:

YOU ACKNOWLEDGE THAT YOU HAVE READ THIS AGREEMENT, UNDERSTAND IT, AND AGREE TO BE BOUND BY ITS TERMS AND CONDITIONS. YOU FURTHER AGREE THAT IT IS THE COMPLETE AND EXCLUSIVE STATEMENT OF THE AGREEMENT BETWEEN US THAT SUPERSEDES ANY PROPOSAL OR PRIOR AGREEMENT, ORAL OR WRITTEN, AND ANY OTHER COMMUNICATIONS BETWEEN US RELATING TO THE SUBJECT MATTER OF THIS AGREEMENT.

ISBN: 0-13-010806-5

INPRISE Corporation License Statement
JBUILDER UNIVERSITY EDITION

YOUR USE OF THE SOFTWARE DISTRIBUTED WITH THIS LICENSE IS SUBJECT TO ALL OF THE TERMS AND CONDITIONS OF THIS LICENSE STATEMENT. IF YOU DO NOT AGREE TO ALL OF THE TERMS AND CONDITIONS OF THIS STATEMENT, DO NOT USE THE SOFTWARE.

1. This Software is protected by copyright law and international copyright treaty. Therefore, you must treat this Software just like a book, except that you may copy it onto a computer to be used and you may make archive copies of the Software for the sole purpose of backing up our Software and protecting your investment from loss. Your use of this software is limited to education, evaluation and trial use purposes only.

2. INPRISE grants you a revocable, non-exclusive license to use the Software free of charge if you are a student, faculty member or staff member of an educational institution (K-12, junior college, college or library) ("Educational User"), or if your use of the Software is for the purpose of evaluating whether to purchase an ongoing license to the Software ("Evaluation User"). Government agencies (other than public schools and libraries) do not qualify as Educational Users under this License Statement. The "Evaluation Period" for use by or on behalf of Evaluation Users is limited to 90 days.

3. You may reproduce exact copies of the Software as provided by INPRISE and distribute such copies to Educational Users and Evaluation Users, so long as you do not charge or receive any compensation for such reproduction or distribution, and provided that the use of all such copies shall be subject to the terms of this License Statement.

4. If the Software is a INPRISE development tool, you can write and compile applications for your own personal use on the computer on which you have installed the Software, but you do not have a right to distribute or otherwise share those applications or any files of the Software which may be required to support those applications. APPLICATIONS THAT YOU CREATE MAY REQUIRE THE SOFTWARE IN ORDER TO RUN. UPON EXPIRATION OF THE EVALUATION PERIOD, THOSE APPLICATIONS MAY NO LONGER RUN. You should therefore take precautions to avoid any loss of data that might result.

5. INPRISE MAKES NO REPRESENTATIONS ABOUT THE SUITABILITY OF THIS SOFTWARE OR ABOUT ANY CONTENT OR INFORMATION MADE ACCESSIBLE BY THE SOFTWARE, FOR ANY PURPOSE. THE SOFTWARE IS PROVIDED 'AS IS' WITHOUT EXPRESS OR IMPLIED WARRANTIES, INCLUDING WARRANTIES OF MERCHANTABILITY AND FITNESS FOR A PARTICULAR PURPOSE OR NONINFRINGEMENT. THIS SOFTWARE IS PROVIDED GRATUITOUSLY AND, ACCORDINGLY, INPRISE SHALL NOT BE LIABLE UNDER ANY THEORY FOR ANY DAMAGES SUFFERED BY YOU OR ANY USER OF THE SOFTWARE. INPRISE WILL NOT SUPPORT THIS SOFTWARE AND IS UNDER NO OBLIGATION TO ISSUE UPDATES TO THIS SOFTWARE. INPRISE RESERVES THE RIGHT TO REVOKE THE LICENSE GRANTED HEREIN AT ANY TIME.

6. While INPRISE intends to distribute (or may have already distributed) a commercial release of the Software, INPRISE reserves the right at any time to not release a commercial release of the Software or, if released, to alter prices, features, specifications, capabilities, functions, licensing terms, release dates, general availability or other characteristics of the commercial release.

7. Title, ownership rights, and intellectual property rights in and to the Software shall remain in INPRISE and/or its suppliers. You agree to abide by the copyright law and all other applicable laws of the United States including, but not limited to, export control laws. You acknowledge that the

Software in source code form remains a confidential trade secret of INPRISE and/or its suppliers and therefore you agree not to modify the Software or attempt to decipher, decompile, disassemble or reverse engineer the Software, except to the extent applicable laws specifically prohibit such restriction.

8. Upon expiration of the Evaluation Period, you agree to destroy or erase the Software, and to not re-install a new copy of the Software. This statement shall be governed by and construed in accordance with the laws of the State of California and, as to matters affecting copyrights, trademarks and patents, by U.S. federal law. This statement sets forth the entire agreement between you and INPRISE.

9. Use, duplication or disclosure by the Government is subject to restrictions set forth in subparagraphs (a) through (d) of the Commercial Computer-Restricted Rights clause at FAR 52.227-19 when applicable, or in subparagraph (c) (1) (ii) of the Rights in Technical Data and Computer Software clause at DFARS 252.227-7013, and in similar clauses in the NASA AR Supplement. Contractor/manufacturer is INPRISE Corporation, Inc., 100 INPRISE Way, Scotts Valley, CA 95066.

10. You may not download or otherwise export or reexport the Software or any underlying information or technology except in full compliance with all United States and other applicable laws and regulations. In particular, but without limitation, none of the Software or underlying information or technology may be downloaded or otherwise exported or reexported (i) into (or to a national or resident of) Cuba, Haiti, Iraq, Libya, Yugoslavia, North Korea, Iran, or Syria or (ii) to anyone on the US Treasury Department's list of Specially Designated Nationals or the US Commerce Department's Table of Deny Orders. By downloading the Software, you are agreeing to the foregoing and you are representing and warranting that you are not located in, under control of, or a national or resident of any such country or on any such list.

11. INPRISE OR ITS SUPPLIERS SHALL NOT BE LIABLE FOR (a) INCIDENTAL, CONSEQUENTIAL, SPECIAL OR INDIRECT DAMAGES OF ANY SORT, WHETHER ARISING IN TORT, CONTRACT OR OTHERWISE, EVEN IF INPRISE HAS BEEN INFORMED OF THE POSSIBILITY OF SUCH DAMAGES, OR (b) FOR ANY CLAIM BY ANY OTHER PARTY. THIS LIMITATION OF LIABILITY SHALL NOT APPLY TO LIABILITY FOR DEATH OR PERSONAL INJURY TO THE EXTENT APPLICABLE LAW PROHIBITS SUCH LIMITATION. FURTHERMORE, SOME STATES DO NOT ALLOW THE EXCLUSION OR LIMITATION OF INCIDENTAL OR CONSEQUENTIAL DAMAGES, SO THIS LIMITATION AND EXCLUSION MAY NOT APPLY TO YOU.

12. HIGH RISK ACTIVITIES. The Software is not fault-tolerant and is not designed, manufactured or intended for use or resale as on-line control equipment in hazardous environments requiring fail-safe performance, such as in the operation of nuclear facilities, aircraft navigation or communication systems, air traffic control, direct life support machines, or weapons systems, in which the failure of the Software could lead directly to death, personal injury, or severe physical or environmental damage ("High Risk Activities"). INPRISE and its suppliers specifically disclaim any express or implied warranty of fitness for High Risk Activities.